W9-AMV-665

ARTICLES ON ______

COLONIALISM AND NATIONALISM IN AFRICA

A Four-Volume Anthology of Scholarly Articles

Series Editors

GREGORY MADDOX
Texas Southern University

TIMOTHY K. WELLIVER
Bellarmine College

A GARLAND SERIES

Series Contents

1. CONQUEST AND RESISTANCE TO COLONIALISM IN AFRICA

2. THE COLONIAL EPOCH IN AFRICA

3. AFRICAN NATIONALISM AND INDEPENDENCE

4. AFRICAN NATIONALISM AND REVOLUTION

VOLUME

2

THE COLONIAL EPOCH IN AFRICA

Edited with introduction by

GREGORY MADDOX

GARLAND PUBLISHING, INC.
New York & London
1993

Library of Congress Cataloging-in-Publication Data

The colonial epoch in Africa / edited with an introduction by
Gregory Maddox.
p. cm. — (Colonialism and nationalism in Africa ; v. 2)
Includes bibliographical references.
ISBN 0-8153-1389-6
1. Africa—History—1884–1960. 2. Colonies—Africa.
I. Maddox, Gregory. II. Series.
DT29.C575 1993
960.3—dc20 93–17822
CIP

Printed on acid-free, 250-year-life paper
Manufactured in the United States of America

Contents

Series Introduction vii

Volume Introduction xi

Colonial Policies and Administrations in Africa: The Myths of the Contrasts
M. Semakula Kiwanuka 1

Indirect Rule: The Establishment of "Chiefs" and "Tribes" in Cameron's Tanganyika
James D. Graham 23

Colonialism and Social Structure
Iheanyi J. Samuel-Mbaekwe 33

The Growth of the Pan-African Movement, 1893–1927
P. Olisanwuche Esedebe 48

Archbishop Daniel William Alexander and the African Orthodox Church
Richard Newman 65

Race, Science, and the Legitimization of White Supremacy in South Africa, 1902–1940
Paul Rich 81

Peasants, Capitalists and Historians: A Review Article
Frederick Cooper 104

The Emergence and Decline of a South African Peasantry
Colin Bundy 135

The Madman and the Migrant: Work and Labor in the Historical Consciousness of a South African People
John L. Comaroff and Jean Comaroff 155

Mtunya: Famine in Central Tanzania, 1917–20
Gregory Maddox 175

Kenya's Primitive Colonial Capitalism: The Economic Weakness of Kenya's Settlers Up to 1940
Paul Van Zwanenberg 193

Depression, Dust Bowl, Demography, and Drought: The Colonial State and Soil Conservation in East Africa During the 1930s
David Anderson 209

Colonialism and the Legal Status of Women in Francophonic Africa
Marlene Dobkin 232

"Cotton Is the Mother of Poverty": Peasant Resistance to Forced Cotton Production in Mozambique, 1938–1961
Allen Isaacman, Michael Stephen, Yussuf Adam, Maria João Homen, Eugenio Macamo, Augustinho Pililão 249

Colonial Chiefs and the Making of Class: A Case Study from Teso, Eastern Uganda
Joan Vincent 284

Colonialism in Angola: Kinyama's Experience
David Birmingham 305

Some Origins of Nationalism in East Africa
J.M. Lonsdale 317

The Origins of Nationalism in East and Central Africa: The Zambian Case
Ian Henderson 345

The Sources of Collective Rebellion: Nationalism in Buganda and Kikuyuland
Meddi Mugyenyi 358

Missionaries, Colonial Government and Secret Societies in South-Eastern Igboland, 1920–1950
Ogbu U. Kalu 369

Acknowledgments 385

Series Introduction

The study of African history as an academic discipline is a rather new field and one that still has its detractors both within and outside academics. The eminent British historian Hugh Trevor-Roper, now Lord Dacre, is once reputed to have said that African history consisted of nothing but "the murderous gyrations of barbarous tribes," while more recently the Czech novelist Milan Kundera has written to the effect that even if it could be proved that hundreds of thousands of Africans died horrendous deaths in the Middle Ages it would all count for nothing. At the very least, such views are a matter of perspective; for the 400 million or so people living in the nations of sub-Saharan Africa today history still shapes the rhythm of their destiny.

This collection of articles highlights for students and scholars the modern era in African history. It brings together published research on the colonial era in Africa, an era relatively brief but one that saw dramatic change in African societies. It highlights the ongoing research into the struggles for independence and social transformation that continue to the present. The authors of these articles eloquently rebut the Euro-centric bias of critics like Trevor-Roper and Kundera and claim for African societies and Africans their rightful place as agents of history.

The articles collected here cover the period between the "Scramble for Africa" in the late nineteenth century, when all but two nations in Africa became colonies of European powers, and the struggles to define the meaning of independence in Africa and throw off the last vestiges of white rule in the southern part of the continent. Such a concentration by no means implies that African societies before the late nineteenth century were tradition-bound or unchanging. They developed according to their own pace and played significant roles in world affairs from the days when West Africa provided a major proportion of the Old World's gold before 1500 through the era of the Atlantic slave trade. However, the colonial era created the modern map of Africa, and Africans transformed their societies politically, economically, and socially in the face of their forced integration into the world economy as producers of raw materials.

The articles in this collection chart the development of African historical studies. As the field emerged in the late 1950s and early 1960s, many historians sought to place the struggle by African peoples to liberate themselves from colonialism and racial domination within a historical tradition. Some scholars, inspired by T. O. Ranger's work, sought to link modern nationalist movements to resistance to colonial rule in the late nineteenth century. They also focused on the development of what they saw as a national consciousness that overlaid existing economic, ethnic, and religious communities.

The reaction to this approach was not long in coming within both African politics and historical scholarship. The ongoing struggles within African nations, often defined in ethnic terms, find their image reflected in early critical works such as those of Steinhart and Denoon and Kuper included here that question the development of national consciousness. More generally, as I. N. Kimambo of Tanzania has argued, there was a turn towards economic and social history that concentrated on the transformation and relative impoverishment of African societies under colonialism. Some scholars have gone so far in the search for the origins and meanings of community in Africa as to reject the modern nation state as of much use as a unit of analysis. Basil Davidson, one of the most influential pioneers in African historical research and a long time supporter of African liberation, has recently produced a volume that calls for a reconfiguration of African political life to fit the reality of African communities (*The Black Man's Burden: Africa and the Curse of the Nation State)*. This collection demonstrates the competition between these views and the shifts that have occurred over the last three decades.

This collection intends to make available to students and scholars a sample of the historical scholarship on twentieth century Africa. The articles come mainly from Africanist scholarly journals, many of which had and have limited circulations. It includes some seminal works heretofore extremely difficult to locate and many works from journals published in Africa. It also includes some works collected elsewhere but shown here in the context of other scholarship.

The articles collected here represent a growing and distinguished tradition of scholarship. Some are foundation works upon which the field has built. Many pioneer methodological innovations as historians have sought ways of understanding the past. All go beyond the often abstract generalities common to basic texts. Taken together they reveal the diversity and the continuity of the African experience.

Several people have contributed greatly to this project. Leo Balk and Carole Puccino of Garland Publishing have guided it through all its stages. Cary Wintz was the catalyst for the project. I. N. Kimambo critiqued the project and made many suggestions. The library staffs of the Ralph J. Terry Library at Texas Southern University, the Fondren Library at Rice University, and the University Library of Northwestern University, and especially Dan Britz of the Africana Collection at Northwestern, provided critical help. Bernadette Pruitt did some of the leg work. Pamela Maack was always supportive, and Katie provided the diversions.

INTRODUCTION

The hyperbole of this volume's title belies an extremely important debate. How can a relatively brief period be called an epoch? For much of sub-Saharan Africa colonial rule by Europeans lasted roughly two generations, from the 1880s to the 1960s. Within the British colonies colonial rule was "indirect rule" in theory, with African states and societies governed by their own laws administered by their own hereditary leaders. Although the terms differed, in practice, Portugal, Belgium, and even France followed the same general policy of administering African communities using local law and African intermediaries. Yet a sharp debate rages as to how much African societies changed under colonial rule.[1]

The articles collected here concentrate on the transformations and continuities in African societies during the height of the colonial era. Although they vary chronologically, most cover events between about 1900 and 1940. All deal in some way with the struggles by Africans to find space—socially, politically, or economically—within the confines of colonial rule.

One of the greatest debates surrounding the colonial era in Africa is over the degree and quality of change that occurred within African societies. The Nigerian historian J. F. A. Ajayi has long held that at their base African societies changed very little during the colonial era. The structure of colonies and then independent states remains a gloss over the fundamental units of African social organization that developed during the centuries preceding colonial rule. For Ajayi colonialism was not "a complete departure from the African past, but . . . one episode in the continuous flow of African history."[2]

Scholars from a variety of perspectives challenge this view in one way or another. In his imaginative reconstruction of the social history of peoples speaking western Bantu languages, Jan Vansina painstakingly lays out what he sees as a two-millennia-old political and social tradition shared by those who live in the central African rain forest. This region includes the hinterland to the Angola coast, the region most intensively mined for labor during the entire four hundred years of the Atlantic slave trade. Yet Vansina argues, based on linguistic evidence and oral traditions, that social and political change developed within a continuous tradition until the twentieth century. He entitles his chapter on the twentieth century "Death of Tradition."[3]

More prosaically, many scholars have seen the forced integration of African communities into a world economy as primary-product producers or sources of labor as bringing profound social and political changes to African societies. Walter Rodney developed this thesis arguing that colonialism culminated a process begun during the era of the slave trade.[4] Of course, this economic leveling accompanied a political leveling; the imposition of colonial rule destroyed African states and empires and made all subjects of foreign rulers.

Accompanying this integration came what John Iliffe has called an enlargement of scale for Africans. Colonies often linked together regions and states more intensively than had been the case up to the nineteenth century. The demand for export production from colonial governments forced millions of Africans to migrate from their homes as workers or agricultural immigrants into new territories. This movement presented the possibility for political mobilization along class or national lines that transcended pre-colonial political divisions.[5]

For many Africans part of this enlargement of scale was conversion to either Islam or Christianity. Both grew rapidly in adherents during the colonial era. Christianity brought access to western education necessary for employment above the level of unskilled laborer. It also brought a creed of spiritual equality, which, despite the best efforts of some European missionaries, many African believers translated into a call for full equality. Perhaps the fastest growing churches in Africa in this era, however, were African-led churches. Sometimes founders of these movements came out of missionary churches and even at times maintained loose ties with some denominations. Islam also grew rapidly during this era, gaining adherents as a counterweight to colonial domination.[6]

Ironically, this leveling effect of colonialism accompanied the growth of "tribalism" in much of Africa. Europeans equated ethnic and linguistic differences in Africa with the current ideas about the essential nature of national identity in Europe. They spent a great deal of time trying to identify tribes and tribal customs as the basis of administration and native law. Such attempts reified what had been much more flexible identities in pre-colonial Africa. In many cases, states in pre-colonial Africa had promoted a sense of common identity that carried over into the colonial period. In others, ethnic or tribal divisions recognized by colonial rulers reflected not so much linguistic or cultural divisions but functional divisions within broader regional African societies. In some cases, religion played a pivotal role in determining identity. This is not to say that there were no commonalities in between the kinship group or local community on the one hand and large states on the other in pre-colonial Africa. Such commonalities often operated on a much larger scale than the tribes recognized by colonial governments.[7]

What colonial rulers helped create as a means to divide and rule, Africans manipulated as a way to mediate the demands of colonialism. With the encouragement of colonial officials, ethnicity became the language of politics in much of Africa. Ethnic associations provided social services to migrants in cities or work places that colonial governments neglected. Anti-colonial politics sometimes became more a matter of ethnic alliance building than nation building.[8]

Even before the full consolidation of colonial rule, however, some Africans began to promote a critique of European rule based on a broader conception of African identity. African nationalist and pan-Africanist ideologies were not merely a reaction to European racism, they attempted to identify positive commonalities among Africans. They helped build an ideological basis for common action against colonial rule. While the struggle against colonial rule usually occurred within the context of specific colonies, many movements arising out of such ideologies argued for a pan-African conception of the struggle.

As the articles in Volumes III and IV of this collection show, nationalist politics in Africa required a leadership able both to argue the case for the rights of Africans in terms that the colonizers would recognize and to mobilize significant numbers of the population at large. Nationalist and pan-Africanist ideologies that began to develop before World War II provided the bridge. The creators of these ideologies were in many ways products of colonialism. They often were among the few in African colonies to obtain Western-style education. In many cases, Christian missions proved critical both in providing access to education and in presenting alternative visions of the world to adherents.

Elites still had to face the racially-justified opposition of colonial regimes and reach out for mass support. During the first four decades of the twentieth century, colonialism presented opportunities for some Africans and new, often crippling demands for most. For European governments, African colonies existed to benefit the metropolis. They had to pay their own way and compliment the metropolitan economy. Colonial powers exploited colonies, or different regions within the same colony, in one of two basic ways. For much of West, Central, and parts of Eastern and Southern Africa, Africans produced agricultural commodities for export on African owned farms. In most of Southern Africa and parts of East Africa and the Belgian Congo, Africans had to work on settler plantations, or in foreign owned mines. While there remain important elements of the colonial experience in common, peasant and settler colonies and regions developed distinctive differences also.

In either case, the infrastructure necessary for export production fell to foreign hands. In many regions of Africa this policy meant the destruction of African marketing systems that had proved quite capable of mobilizing surpluses for international trade. European-owned firms, European settlers, and Asian settlers from the Middle East or Indian sub-continent all received preferential treatment from colonial regimes determined to prevent "detribalized," commercially-oriented Africans from becoming a threat politically. The infrastructure itself, of course, met imperial needs, not African ones. Railroads, roads, and harbors all served export producing areas and links between regions within colonies, or between colonies, were neglected.

In peasant colonies the demand that African farmers produce a cash crop for export, usually a non-food crop, sometimes strained farming systems. Lethal famines came often to many regions of Africa during the early decades of colonial rule, probably more often than before. Even as transportation networks developed to the point where food imports to deprived regions became possible, a more generalized poverty often replaced the threat of periodic famine.[9]

Of course, some regions and some classes took advantage of the opportunities colonialism represented. In particular regions that could produce high value exports, such as coffee, often saw the emergence of a class of well off peasants. The key to these successes was the ability to raise productivity through a combination of environmental endowment and investment. For some this investment came from earnings in positions requiring skills or education.[10]

In settler colonies, this dynamic was very different. In South Africa, the demand for labor in diamond and gold mines, as well as Afrikaner farms, led to a policy of strangling potential peasant production in order to keep labor costs down.[11] Other settler colonies followed similar policies to a greater or lesser extent. In Kenya, for example, the colonial government forbade Africans from growing coffee.

Many Africans in settler colonies became migrant workers. Men had to leave families in increasingly overcrowded reserves and work for most of the year at mines or on plantations. Women and children left behind often had inadequate land or resources to grow enough food to survive and wages generally never supported more than a single worker. Sometimes, African families worked the same land their ancestors had but now as squatters on white-owned farms both with an uncertain tenure and subject to heavy labor demands.

The articles collected in this volume can be seen as an evaluation of the changes during the colonial era in Africa. They highlight the costs borne by Africans for whatever benefits "progress" brought. Perhaps most importantly they show the scale of the edifice against which Africans had to struggle.

NOTES

1. Iheanyi J. Samuel-Mbaekwe lays out much of this debate in his "Colonialism and Social Structure," *Transafrican Journal of History* 15 (1986), pp. 81–95 collected in this volume.

2. J. F. A. Ajayi, "The Continuity of African Institutions under Colonialism" in T. O. Ranger, *Emerging Themes in African History* (Nairobi, 1968), pp. 189–200; see also A. Adu Boahen, "Colonialism in Africa: Its Impact and Significance," in A. Adu Boahen, ed., *General History of Africa VII: Africa under Colonial Domination 1880–1935,* (Berkeley, 1990), pp. 327–339.

3. Jan Vansina, *Paths in the Rainforest: Toward a History of Political Tradition in Equatorial Africa* (Madison, 1990).

4. Walter Rodney, *How Europe Underdeveloped Africa* (Washington, 1982).

5. John Iliffe, A *Modern History of Tanganyika* (Cambridge, 1979), pp. 1–5.

6. C. C. Stewart, "Islam," and Richard Gray, "Christianity," in A. D. Roberts, ed., *The Colonial Moment in Africa: Essays on the Movement of Minds and Materials 1900–1940* (Cambridge, 1990) pp. 191–222, and pp. 140–190.

7. See Charles Ambler, *Kenyan Communities in the Age of Imperialism: The Central Region in the Late Nineteenth Century* (New Haven, 1988) for a discussion of these factors.

8. See the essays in Leroy Vail, ed., *The Creation of Tribalism in Southern Africa* (Berkeley, 1989) for examples.
9. John Iliffe, *The African Poor: A History* (Cambridge, 1987).
10. Gavin Kitching, *Class and Economic Change in Kenya: The Making of an African Petite Bourgeoisie, 1905–1970* (New Haven, 1980).
11. See Colin Bundy, "The Emergence and Decline of a South African Peasantry," *African Affairs*, 71, (1972), pp. 369–388 collected in this volume and Colin Bundy, *The Rise and Fall of the South African Peasantry* (Berkeley, 1979).

COLONIAL POLICIES AND ADMINISTRATIONS IN AFRICA: THE MYTHS OF THE CONTRASTS

M. Semakula Kiwanuka

Whereas there are few canons of English or American history that have escaped challenge in recent years, the same claim cannot be made for African colonial history. The tendency in recent years has been to seek and to exaggerate differences rather than similarities between colonial policies. As a result of this preoccupation, even what appears at first sight to be intensive research in the field of history or political science has sometimes produced results which are peripheral and superficial. While dissenting voices have been raised here and there pointing out the common characteristics of the colonial regimes,[1] the current fashion of stressing differences has prevailed. Partly because of decolonization and partly because of the Congo crisis, the 1960's resulted in an overproduction of literature of varying qualities. In the process the political scientist has excelled the historian in overproduction.

I

The intention of this essay is to reappraise European colonial policies in Africa, assessing the presumed virtues as well as the presumed illiberal policies. The discussion will focus on the methods of the imposition of colonial rule upon the African peoples and on the nature of colonial administrations. We shall also examine policies regarding "native chiefs," direct and indirect rule, and the policies of assimilation. We shall further examine the educational policies, the constitutional practices, and the highly publicized methods of training and preparing Africans for self-government and the connection between this and the peaceful and smooth transfer of power at the time of independence. To begin with, the view which has dominated African colonial historiography is the belief expounded by Rupert Emerson that "nations like individuals are products of heredity and environment . . . The environment enters into the heritage to change the direction of the national stream to enrich or diminish it."[2] An

1. See Hubert Deschamps, "Et Maintenant Lord Lugard?" Africa, XXXIII, 4 (1963), 296-306. Prominent among those who have stressed the differences is Michael Crowder, West Africa under European Rule (Evanston, Ill., 1968). See also L. Gann and P. Duignan, Burden of Empire: An Appraisal of Western Colonialism in Africa South of the Sahara (New York, 1959), especially 217-225.
2. From Empire to Nation. The Rise of Self Assertion of Asian and African Peoples (Cambridge, Mass., 1960), 60.

illustration of this view is the legendary stereotype of national characteristics, such as the brutality of the Germans. Consequently "German brutality and violence" toward her colonial subjects was widely publicized in the 1920's and 1930's. Prolonged or recurrent African resistance in German territories, for instance, was quoted as an example resulting from brutality and violence.[3] The purpose of the publicity was of course largely politically inspired, designed to justify the takeover of the former German colonies by the victors of World War One.

Unfortunately this politically motivated propaganda left behind one of the persistent ideas that other colonial powers used more gentle and civilized methods toward their African subjects. This concept is of course a myth, because the response of each colonial power was conditioned by the extent of the challenge or the degree of collaboration by the Africans. Throughout colonial Africa the so-called consent to agreements or treaties from African chiefs was generally obtained either under duress or by duplicity. It was not only the German Dr. Carl Peters who was notorious for such practices but other colonial agents as well. In his brilliant book on Southern Rhodesia, Philip Mason has shown how King Lo-Bengula was duped and later coerced by armed force.[4] The trading company involved in the Lo-Bengula case was neither German nor French, but British. The example of Lo-Bengula is not an isolated case.

To single out examples in Tanzania, therefore, while remaining silent about the resistance movements in neighboring Kenya and Uganda, creates a deliberately false impression, for a cursory glance at the history of the latter two countries, let alone of the former Rhodesias and South and West Africa, should dispel such an impression. Present evidence from Kenya for example has revealed the extraordinary degree of British violence, from the east coast to Mount Elgon. The British in Kenya, like the Germans in Tanzania and like all other colonial powers, were not ready to suffer defeat or humiliation from their new subjects. For this reason they were determined to use any amount of violence necessary. The case was summed up by a British official as follows:

> These people [the Ogadens] must learn submission by the bullets -- it's the only school; after that you may begin more modern and humane methods of education . . . . In Africa to have peace you must first teach obedience and the only tutor who impresses the lesson properly is the sword.[5]

II

When we turn to Uganda, we find that there was far more resistance to, and consequently more violence from, the British than has hitherto been admitted. Kabarega, King of Bunyoro-Kitara, a kingdom that traced its beginning to

3. See G. Gwasa and J. Iliffe, eds., Records of the Maji Maji Rising, Historical Association of Tanzania Publication No. 4 (Nairobi, 1968).
4. The Birth of a Dilemma. The Conquest and Settlement of Rhodesia (London and New York, 1958), especially 105-145.
5. G. Mungeam, British Rule in Kenya 1895-1912 (London, 1966), 30.

about 1200 A.D., fought first against Anglo-Egyptian imperialism in the 1870's and 1880's and then in the 1890's against the British. For nearly ten years, 1891-1899, Kabarega resisted British rule, hounded from one part of his kingdom to another, until he was overcome by armed violence in 1899 and deported to the Indian Ocean islands. Mwanga II, the King of Buganda, an equally ancient kingdom and the most powerful in East Africa during the nineteenth century, had at first collaborated with the British as a result of threats of deposition and deportation. But in 1896 he too decided to fight, and, like Kabarega, he was overcome in 1899, deposed, and deported. Both rulers died in exile.[6]

Evidence also suggests that the British had a far longer list of depositions and deportations of African rulers than historians would make us believe. In Uganda alone, where we have already mentioned the cases of Mwanga and Kabarega, Prince Mbogo, the Moslem leader, was deported in 1893.[7] In eastern Uganda, sumission of African chiefs was secured by threats of deposition. On the west coast of Africa the catalogue of depositions and deportations is equally long. In Central Africa Chief Kazambe of Zambia was driven out of his kingdom into the Congo by a British trading company.[8] All these examples help to explain one thing: that no colonial power with all its advantages of military superiority would accept defeat at African hands, but would go to any length to assert its authority. Invariably such authority could only be asserted by military coercion and violence. Consequently colonial brutality had no bounds.

By 1914 colonial regimes had crushed all resistance. The African resisters had underestimated the might and determination of those with whom they had chosen to do battle. Little did they realized that for the colonial power there could be no retreat. Dr. Roberts has summed up in the case of Zambia what was equally true for the rest of Africa: "Once the two great powers, the Bemba and the Lunda, had submitted, no other African in the area was rash enough to challenge the white man's firearms."[9]

The aftermath of the imposition of colonial rule led to the emergence of two types of Africans: first were the defeated, who resigned themselves to the rule of the imperial conquerors; second, the collaborators. The latter form an important and interesting group in our study of colonial history, for they were the men who read the signs of the times correctly and willingly jumped on the colonial bandwagon, thereby reaping the fruits of collaboration.

6. For Bunyoro, see R. A. Dunbar, "The British and Bunyoro Kitara 1891-1899," Uganda Journal, XXIV, 2 (1960), 229-241. For the rest of Uganda, see A. D. Low, "Uganda: The Establishment of the Protectorate, 1894-1919," in V. Harlow and E. M. Chilver, eds., History of East Africa, II (Oxford, 1965), 54-122. See also M.S.M. Kiwanuka, A History of Buganda from Earliest Times to 1900 (forthcoming).
7. James K. Miti, "A Short History of Buganda" (unpublished manuscript available from Makerere and London University libraries).
8. A. Roberts, "The Nineteenth Century in Zambia," in T. Ranger, ed., Aspects of Central African History (London, 1968), 71-96.
9. Ibid., 96.

With the defeat of the resisters, the colonial governments began to formulate philosophies and policies, such as "native" policies, land policies, and labor policies. In his An African Survey Lord Hailey noticed three main characteristics of land policies in Africa: the differences between the Franco-Belgian policies of the concessionaire system to companies or monopolies and those of alienating land to individuals as applied by the British.[10] But the important question is what effect these policies had on the African, and it appears that there was little difference in their overall effects. Whether in Kenya, Rhodesia, or the Belgian Congo, the least productive part of the land was left to the African. Nothing is more misleading than the presentation of statistics about acres or square miles of delineated land. Kenya, for instance, has a total area of 224,960 square miles. By 1926 only 16,000 of these were alienated to European settlers and 13,500 square miles were gazetted for African use. Although Lord Hailey claimed that the Northern Frontier Province had an average population density of less than one per square mile, it should be remembered that the Northern Frontier Province is a semiarid area, and that cultivable land in Kenya is centered along a narrow strip, much of which formed the so-called White Highlands.[11] Moreover, since the British as a colonial power had comparatively more colonies settled by Europeans -- South Africa, Southern Rhodesia, Zambia, Malawi, and Kenya -- than did the French, we can fairly argue that on balance the Africans in British colonies suffered far more than anywhere else on the continent from the sad effect of land expropriation during the colonial period, as was abundantly dramatized by the Mau Mau uprising in Kenya between 1952 and 1960.

A study of the colonial labor policies has produce the same stereotypes, and the same tendency to exaggerate the differences between the policies pursued by the different colonial regimes has persisted. French and Belgian regimes are said to have resorted more to forced labor than the British, and Lord Hailey wrote:

> Railway construction in the French Congo, and in early times in the Belgian Congo, presented painful evidence of the abuses which may attend the resort to forced recruitment in order to supply the deficiency of voluntary labor.[12]

According to Professors L. Gann and P. Duignan, French officials played an active part in mobilizing labor and in enforcing the cultivation of economic crops -- they relied on order more than on persuasion.[13] These views are exaggerated and give a false picture of distinctions which did not amount to a great deal in actual practice.

Labor policies, like methods of occupation, had far more in common than is often realized, and on balance the British regimes do not emerge with a very

10. An African Survey: A Study of Problems Arising in Africa South of the Sahara (London and New York, 1938), 717-718, 748.
11. See Kenya Land Commission Report 1934, Cmnd 4580 (London, 1934). See also Elspeth Huxley, White Man's Country: Lord Delamere and the Making of Kenya (2 vols.: New York, 1967); B. A. Ogot, "Kenya under the British, 1895 to 1963," in B. A. Ogot and J. A. Kieran, eds., Zamani. A Survey of East African History (Nairobi, 1968), 255-289.
12. An African Survey, 603.
13. Burden of Empire, 217-218.

bright image. Practically everywhere in Africa colonial regimes based their compulsory labor laws on the convenient pretext that native societies in Africa had always recognized the value of "supplying" (forcing) labor for common purposes. In Kenya forced labor prevailed as a system until it provoked an outcry from the churches.[14] But it was not only in the settler-dominated colonies where forced labor prevailed. Even in colonies described as "primarily African," like Uganda, forced labor prevailed as a system until 1917. Since Britain possessed more colonies similar to South Africa than had her colonial partners, it can be argued that on balance she had harsher and far more labor laws.

III

The greatest degree of difference in colonial regimes has been presumed to exist in the system of administration and in constitutional practices, especially insofar as they treated "traditional" authorities. Professor Emerson has asserted:

> The nature of the colonial setting and the contrasting colonial policies of the powers have played a significant role not only in the shaping of nations, but also in the development of nationalism, influencing the speed with which nationalist movements have swung into action, their membership and structure, the demands they pose and their tactics and strategy. . . . Such matters as the type of economy the imperial power encourages, the goals it sets, the colonial institutions it establishes, the civil and political privileges it extends to the people, the centralization of direct or indirect rule are all of major consequences in determining the character of the political mores which arise to challenge the colonial overlords.[15]

In their Burden of Empire, Drs. Gann and Duignan have argued that:

> The British were on the whole pragmatic and more respectful of established chieftain authority while the French were more legally minded, bound to the continental tradition of centralized administration. The French thus based their government on centralized rule from Paris and on the same administrative concepts that dominated their outlook on government at home. They generally saw themselves as the new chiefs, and the French service produced a whole generation of rois de la brousse who governed their districts with an iron hand. French Governor Generals exercised a much tighter control over local Governors than the British Governors over their local Residents or British Residents over their district commissioners. African chiefs were generally treated as subalterns rather than as partners in government. . . . Many tribal heads were deposed, titles were discontinued: some titles disappeared altogether and tribal areas were regrouped into larger units. This policy occasioned a great deal of friction, and the French system thus helped to undermine the power of the traditional chiefs and

14. See footnote 11.
15. Empire to Nation, 61.

> thereby had the unintended effect of facilitating the ultimate abolition of chiefly rule under African governments. The British desired legitimate chiefs and, unlike the French or the Portuguese, rarely deposed the dignitaries they appointed. They accepted a great variety of chiefly rule; they attempted to retain traditional legal institutions. They delegated both judicial and executive powers, such as the right to raise local taxes, maintain police forces and issue administrative order. The Chiefs were treated with much respect in public, and the British tried to gain their way through persuasion rather than command. The British saw the native state as a basis for the political future of their African empire.

Turning to the Belgians, the authors conclude:

> The Belgians like the French believed in extreme centralization. Leopold ruled the Provinces and Brussels ruled Leopoldville. The inhabitants of the Congo both white and black remained strictly excluded from all influence in government. Under the French Chiefs, however remained nothing but the agents of the administration without independent judicial or executive powers. Former soldiers or clerks with a knowledge of French were put into office only to be dismissed if they did not carry out their duties in a manner acceptable to the French.[16]

IV

The philosophy of indirect rule has distinguished ancestry among administrators such as Lugard and Cameron and among academics such as Margery Perham and Lucy Mair. The views of this school were excellently summed up by Sir Philip Mitchell, a former governor of Uganda and Kenya. According to Sir Philip,

> Indirect rule is founded on the conception that the most important duty of the government is to train and develop the African inhabitants of the country, so that their ancient tribal colonizations may be modernised and adapted by them in such a manner as to serve the present and the future as they have served the past. That our duty is not to facilitate the Europeanisation of exceptional individuals but the civilization of the mass.[17]

High sounding statements such as these are the source of most of the myths and legends regarding indirect rule and its supposed virtues. Few scholars have addressed themselves to the difference between what was said and what actually happened. Fewer yet have recognized the fact that the British colonial system came to be associated with the philosophy not so much because the British applied more indirect rule but because they talked more about it than others.[18]

16. Burden of Empire, 217-218, 221-222.
17. "Indirect Rule," Uganda Journal, IV (1936).
18. Similarly the French were associated more with the policy of assimilation largely because they talked more about it than, say, the British. But in actual practice the British Educational System with its indoctrination in things

The section quoted (pp. 299-300) from Gann and Duignan reflects all the stereotypes by making generalized statements which are difficult to support. But the most assertive claims for British Indirect Rule have been made more recently by Michael Crowder in an article published in Africa:

> There were such fundamental differences between the French and the British system that, it is not possible to place the French system of native administration in the same category as British Indirect Rule. Many historians of British colonial administration have looked upon Northern Nigeria, Uganda and Tanganyika as models of indirect rule. What is important is the very different way in which these [native] authorities were used. The nature and position of the power of the chief in the two systems was totally different and, as a corollary, so were the relations between the chief and the political officer, who was inspired by very different ideals . . . . The relations between the British political officer and the chief was in general that of an adviser.[19]

There are further examples of widespread practices in African which it is said were nonexistent in British colonies. We are thus told that the French flouted native authority, whereas the British systems depended on the advisory relationship between the political office and the native authority. We are further told that the French system placed the chief in an entirely subordinate role to the European officer and that the French and Belgians preferred appointed officers with no traditional authority, who would not head a local government unit nor administer an area which corresponded to a precolonial political unit. The French, like the Belgians, divided the country administratively into districts which frequently cut across precolonial boundaries, and in certain cases the French deliberately broke up the old political units.[20] Unfortunately the assumption that these administrative practices did not exist in British colonies cannot stand the test of critical examination even within the boundaries of a single territory. Any scholar who cares to look will find that all these practices existed throughout Africa and in great abundance.

Again, a brief examination of chieftainship under the colonial administrations shows that the differences upon which so much ink has been poured are largely mythical. Whether a chief was hereditary or appointed, whether he was under a British or a French regime, he owed his position to the approval of the colonial power, and he retained that position only as long as the colonial regime believed he was playing the role assigned to him. For this reason, the British, like other colonial regimes and contrary to the assertions of Gann and Duignan, deposed many African kings and chiefs. For instance in Buganda in 1926 a young District Commissioner forced the resignation of Sir Apollo Kaggwa, a man who

British produced the same type of elite as the French system. "British Europeanizers hoped to turn their African subjects into Black Englishmen, complete with middle class standards and morality." Gann and Duignan, Burden of Empire, 216. See also Emerson, Empire to Nation, 69.

19. "Indirect Rule: British and French Style," Africa, XXXIV, 3 (1964), 197-205.
20. Ibid. See also Crowder, West Africa.

had earlier been knighted by the British.[21] Semei Kakungulu, a veteran chief of the 1890's who did much to extend British rule in eastern and northeastern Uganda was promised a royal crown by Sir Harry Johnston but was summarily dismissed within a few years of that promise;[22] the British had all along regarded him merely as a functionary, and as soon as they gained a position of responsibility for the area of which he was chief, they dismissed him.

That certain chiefs under the French colonial regime ruled over more extensive territorial units than had their precolonial predecessors is not an indication of differences between British Indirect and French Direct rule. In western Uganda, King Kasagama of Toro was guaranteed a territorial unit which was larger than his predecessor's, as was King Ntare V of Ankole, whom the British helped to absorb the neighboring kingdoms of Mpororo and Buhweju.

In order to emphasize differences between British Indirect Rule and French Direct Rule, M. Crowder has asserted that the British, unlike the French, were not interested in administrative efficiency, because their main concern was chiefly legitimacy.[23] Many examples show, however, that the British were interested in efficiency as much as other colonial powers if it served their interests. Their record in Uganda, as demonstrated by the widespread use of Baganda agents, is perhaps the best example.[24] The Paramountcy (Kyabazingaship) of Busoga was founded by a Muganda appointed chief, Semei Kakungulu, despite the fact that there were legitimate chiefs in Busoga.[25] James Miti, a Muganda administrator, was appointed highest county chief in Bunyoro for many years,[26] and King Duhaga II of Bunyoro was deposed in the 1900's, allegedly because of inefficiency. The question was not one of "preference," as Crowder states, but one of convenience. If an appointed chief could do a job more efficiently and more quickly, he was put in the place of the legitimate chief.

It is also true that the French deliberately broke up the old territorial units in the Futa Jallon region. But such examples of territorial fragmentation were not confined to French rule. In Uganda the kingdom of Bunyoro was broken up for British military purposes.[27] In order to satisfy the European settler claims for land, Uganda's eastern province was transferred to Kenya in 1905 with the result of further fragmentation of the African peoples along the border.

21. See A. D. Low and R. C. Pratt, Buganda and British Overrule, 1900-1955 (London, 1960).
22. The life and career of Semei Kakungulu are well documented. See especially H. B. Thomas, "Capax Imperi: The Story of Kakungulu," Uganda Journal, V, 1 (1937), 125-136.
23. "Indirect Rule," 197-205.
24. A. D. Roberts, "The Sub-Imperialism of the Baganda," Journal of African History, III, 3 (1962), 435-450.
25. W. F. Nabwiso-Bulima, "The Evolution of the Kyabazingaship of Busoga," Uganda Journal, 31, 1 (1967), 89-99.
26. Dunbar, "Bunyoro Kitara," especially 104-112.
27. Ibid. See also Colonel Colville, Land of the Nile Springs (London and New York, 1895), 312.

Territorial reconstruction and fragmentation, like the establishment of colonial rule throughout Africa, marked the end of any independent rule by African chiefs. A traditional chief may have appeared more powerful under indirect rule, but his power and his position were no different from the appointed chief's, whether under a British or another colonial regime. In either case he was a mere instrument of colonial rule, his tenure secured only by unswerving collaboration, and any deviation from expected behavior exposing him to dismissal or deposition. It was not only under the French regime, as Lucy Mair has asserted, that the functions of African chiefs "were reduced to that of the mouthpiece for orders emanating from outside."[28] In Buganda, a presumed model of indirect rule, the Kabaka (king) was required under the Agreement of 1900 to be a mouthpiece for orders emanating from the British. As late as the 1950's, and even under the very progressive Governor, Sir Andrew Cohen, the King of Buganda was supposed to continue to be a mouthpiece of the colonial administration. When he refused, he was deposed and deported to England in 1953.[29]

V

The growth of African nationalism created a widening political gap between the traditional chiefs and the rising generation of nationalists, who, contrary to Gann and Duignan, resented the chiefs in most parts of Africa, even where they represented legitimate traditional authority. Nationalist opposition stemmed from the belief that these chiefs were the mouthpieces of the colonial regime which the nationalists were challenging, that these chiefs were the agents who carried out unpopular measures such as tax collection, recruitment of forced labor, and law enforcement.

David Apter has singled out Buganda as one place where the traditional chiefs enjoyed respect. A glance at the newspapers between 1920 and 1950 indicates clearly, however, that Apter overemphasized this popularity. The very serious riots of 1945 and 1949 in Buganda were directed primarily against chiefs and only indirectly against the British, with the chiefs' homes and properties subjected to systematic destruction. Moreover, the unpopularity of the chiefs was inevitable, whether in British Africa or in French Africa, because, rightly or wrongly, they were believed to represent a status quo. Kwame Nkrumah's hostility to Ashanti, like Ben Kiwanuka's conflicts with the Kabaka, were motivated by this belief. Not only Sekou Toure of Guinea but also Milton Obote of Uganda considered the chief a stumbling block.

It is thus clear that the search for differences rather than similarities has rendered much of the existing discussion on this subject unsatisfactory. If we are to understand what European colonialism was really about, we cannot

28. Lucy Mair, Native Policies in Africa (London, 1936), 210.
29. Colin Legum, Must We Lose Africa? (London, 1954); Low and Pratt, Buganda.
30. D. A. Apter, A Political Kingdom in Uganda: A Study in Bureaucratic Nationalism (Princeton, 1960).

ignore the factors which dictated colonial policies throughout Africa. Colonial regimes suppressed all independent centers of local resistance and some colonial officials became tyrants, though this may well have been due to individual character rather than to political philosophy. Furthermore, any balanced discussion of colonial policies should recognize that there was no consistent policy throughout the British or French African empires. Actions differed not only from one colony to another but from one district to another within a single colony, and the emphasis of certain policies differed from period to period. And sometimes the personalities of the colonial administrators were more important than the theories of direct or indirect rule, especially before the 1920's, when the machinery of colonial government, whether Belgian, German, or British, was still simple and depended primarily on the governor.

Under this simple state machinery tremendous responsibilities rested on the shoulders of a few isolated administrators. The realities of administration, whether Belgian, French, or British, generally differed from the elaborate theories of indirect or direct rule or of assimilation enunciated at home. Colonial portfolios changed hands with increasing rapidity. Thus Uganda's governor in the mid-1930's doubted whether Buganda was indirectly ruled, whereas in the 1940's Sir Charles Dundas had no doubt in his mind that indirect rule was the order of the day. Only when it suited their policies did the colonial regimes retain the traditional systems of government and support the chiefs. The British did so in certain parts of Uganda, but in Kenya almost no attention was paid to highsounding philosophies of indirect rule. In Tanganyika, before their overthrow, the Germans retained the kingdoms of Burundi and Rwanda but abolished those of Karagwah, Busubi, and Ruma.[31] The French retained the kings of Mossi in Upper Volta, and the Fulani emirs of the northern Cameroon provinces as well as in the Niger.[32]

One of the basic weaknesses of the existing discussions about British rule stems from a preoccupation with northern Nigeria and a temptation to ignore what took place in the rest of the British territories. But in fact, all the colonial governments encountered similar problems. Men and money were short and therefore all administrations required African agents: in Senegal L. Faidherbe based his rule on indigenous chiefs; H. Lyautey followed a similar policy in Morocco; in the French Congo, Governor General F. Eboué set up a system which strengthened indigenous institutions; and in 1917 J. Van Vollenhoven, the French Governor General of West Africa, decreed that traditional chiefs should be appointed.[33] During this period theories about indirect rule were also current throughout British Africa. But even in Nigeria no one can claim that indirect rule was practiced in the east, and in Central Africa indirect rule was not practiced throughout Zambia and Southern Rhodesia, not because of any difference in philosophy but simply because it was not in the interests of the British to rule indirectly in these areas.

31. See J. Iliffe, German Rule in Tanganyika, 1905-1912 (London, 1968).
32. Lord Hailey, African Survey, 185-225, 484-490; Gann and Duignan, Burden of Empire, 209-226.
33. See Hubert Deschamps, Les Méthodes et les doctrines coloniales de la France du XVIe siècle à nos jours (Paris, 1953), quoted in Gann and Duignan, Burden of Empire, 218. See also Deschamps, "Lord Lugard," 297-306.

VI

Supposedly striking differences have been observed between the educational policies of the various colonial powers, but an examination of the historiography on this subject reveals the same stereotypes with little relation to the facts. The literature particularly increased in volume as a result of the 1960 Congo crisis. As in the case of administrative policies, the British have received the more favorable publicity among historians and political scientists, who provide examples from Nigeria, Ghana, and Uganda. On the other hand, writers have maintained a discreet silence about British colonies like Tanganyika, Malawi, Zambia, and Southern Rhodesia. And, when writing about Nigeria and Ghana, few have made distinctions between the north and the south.

In order to understand the presumed differences in colonial policies regarding African education we shall examine what these educational systems produced. Attention will be focused on secondary and post-secondary education, because its products are believed to have determined the course of events at the time of independence. Education in English-speaking Africa has been fairly well documented. The classic Phelps Stokes Commission Reports of the 1920's and Lord Hailey's An African Survey have left for us a wealth of information on which to base balanced conclusions. It is clear from Lord Hailey's Survey that by 1939 in most of Africa there was little variation, whether in the philosophy of education or in its actual achievements, though many writers have been amazed at the extent to which the missionaries dominated the Belgian system of education. Thus René Lemarchand has commented: "Even on a continent where the association of education with religious missionaries is a commonplace, the reliance of the Congo on this type of educational colonisation is striking."[34] But anyone acquainted with educational systems in Africa knows very well that there was the same reliance on missionaries throughout the continent because of the general absence of state schools except in the French colonies. This predominance of mission education seems to have been taken for granted; neither the British governments nor the missionaries themselves saw anything odd in it.

A careful study of secondary education may reveal important similarities in the kind of higher education given to the Africa. For students in Uganda, Kenya, Tanganyika, Zanzibar, Malawi, and Zambia post-secondary education was supposed to be obtained at Makerere College in Uganda; in Nigeria it was provided at Yaba Higher College, Lagos; in the Gold Coast at Achimota; and in Sierra Leone at Fourah Bay. All these institutions were "founded with the intention that students should ultimately be able to meet the standards required for an English university degree."[35]

What is important to this discussion is not the existence of the colleges but the number of Africans who attended them and the standards of the qualifications they obtained. Makerere, for example, was founded in 1924 as a

34. See René Lemarchand, Political Awakening in the Belgian Congo (Berkeley, 1964), especially 122-142. J. Okum, a Kenyan educated in mission schools, found Belgian reliance on missionaries for education startling. See Washington Okum, Lumumba's Congo: Roots of Conflict (New York, 1963), passim.
35. Lord Hailey, African Survey, 1182-1183.

technical school and grew in academic status over the years. Yet by 1936 only a handful of its students had obtained the Cambridge School Certificate, and only a few of these qualified for exemption from London matriculation. The rest of the Makerere students pursued what Lord Hailey described as vocational courses.

A medical school was also founded at Makerere in the mid-1920's, and its products were referred to as doctors, although they were more specifically medical aids. A Colonial Office report on higher education in East Africa defined these Makerere doctors as "aids capable under some supervision, of running small district stations and hospitals by themselves."[36] The graduates of the Makerere medical school, who had been called doctors all along, were not awarded a degree in medicine until 1963, nor was their qualification academically recognized until 1957, when it was termed a licentiate in medicine and its holders described "as qualified to practice medicine in East Africa"; it was also in 1957 that the Makerere medical qualification was recognized by the British Medical Council. Yaba College at Lagos, Nigeria, had a similar history to Makerere's, though it was founded nearly ten years later in 1932. Another view of what were called Makerere and Yaba doctors in the 1930's and 1940's can be drawn from Lord Hailey's observation.

> There does not exist in Africa any institution designated to afford the African an opportunity of gaining full medical qualification in the sense in which that is understood in Great Britain or in countries which the British Medical Council has concluded agreements for reciprocal recognition of qualification . . . Both Yaba [Lagos] and Mulago [Makerere] would appear to contemplate that at some future date, they will be equipped to train fully qualified African practitioners. Though at the present they have more limited aims.

Justifying this attitude, Lord Hailey concluded:

> That the British Territories do not at present contemplate making a provision for Africans to take full medical degrees is largely due to acknowledged lack of necessary facilities for pre-vocational education.[37]

The actual number of medical graduates for East and Central Africa was pitifully small. In 1937 there were 31 students, 25 of whom were from Uganda, one from Kenya, 3 from Tanganyika, and 2 from Zanzibar. There were none from Malawi or Zambia. By 1939 it was still contemplated that "in some 10 years time the numbers will reach 100."[38] But even by the late 1950's the medical school population at Makerere in the academic year 1957-1958 was still only 89 students for the whole of Uganda, Tanganyika, Kenya, Zanzibar, Malawi, and Zambia; the number in the graduating class was seven.[39]

36. Ibid.
37. Ibid.
38. Ibid.
39. See Higher Education in East Africa (Report) (Entebbe, 1958). See also Report of the Working Party on Higher Education in East Africa (Nairobi, 1959).

After the second world war a fresh look was taken at African education in British Africa and new plans led to the foundation of university colleges which were in a special relationship with the University of London. Makerere University in Uganda was created by royal charter in 1949. At first only two-year general degree courses in the arts and sciences were offered, and even by the late 1950's the number of graduates about whom so much has been written was still extremely meager. Statistics supplied by the two reports on higher education in East Africa between 1958 and 1959 showed 29 in the first year degree and 25 in the final (second) year. Five of the finalists were Ugandans, 14 were Kenyans, 4 Tanganyikans, one Zanzibari, and one Zambian. The first year's bachelor of science general degree class totaled 16, who included neither Zanzibaris, Zambians, nor Malawians. The final year class totaled 15, of whom 2 were Ugandans, 5 Kenyans, and 8 Tanganyikans. No Zanzibaris, Malawians, or Zambians graduated in science at Makerere in 1957-1958. The same small figures are shown for the diploma courses in agriculture and veterinary science.[40]

For the west coast of Africa the picture was slightly better because of the higher secondary school output, and because many more people paid to go to college in Britian and America. For British Central Africa, The Central African Council Report on Higher Education for Africans in Central Africa clearly shows that little had been achieved there even by the mid-1950's. The evidence from this report also suggests that the Makerere figures included possibly more than nine-tenths of non-degree students especially in Uganda.[41] It should be clear, therefore, that the highly trained manpower which the British are believed to have left throughout their colonies did not exist except in the minds of the writers.

Let us now focus attention on the secondary school training and on graduates and medics in French Africa and the Belgian Congo.[42] According to available statistics there were 20,000 pupils in Congolese secondary schools by the late 1950's.[43] Considering the size of the Congo this does not compare badly with any regional grouping of French or British territories. A medical center, very similar to that at Makerere, was created in the lower Congo in 1925 by a number of medical professors of the Louvain University. In 1932 another group of Louvain professors created an intermediate agricultural college for training agricultural assistants, again similar to that at Makerere. In 1936 a school was opened for medical assistants, which offered a two-year preparatory course, four years of medical instruction, and a two-year probational period. In 1947 the Congolese University Center was created to coordinate the different schools and, on 21 February 1949 the project was granted a royal charter. This was followed by a grant of 675 acres to start building the Louvain University. The first pre-university students were admitted in 1954, and the first university courses began in 1956.

40. Ibid.
41. The Central African Council Report on Higher Education for Africans in Central Africa (London, 1953), 1-94.
42. Lord Hailey, African Survey, 1182-1290.
43. Georges Brausch, Belgian Administration in the Congo (London and New York, 1961), 1-94. See also Universities of Belgian Congo and Ruandwa-Urundi (Brussels, n.d.).

From this account it seems that the growth of university education in the Congo is not significantly different from that in East Africa, because until 1958 the majority of the Makerere students were not pursuing courses leading to degrees; the agriculturalists, the veterinarians, and the teachers were not awarded degrees until the 1960's -- if a Makerere agricultural student wanted a degree he had to go abroad. The Belgians were perhaps more honest, though less diplomatic, in not calling their medical trainees doctors, as did the British. All told, the number of degree students at Louvain in 1956 and later compares favorably with the numbers for British East and Central Africa.[44]

It is true that fewer Congolese trained abroad before 1960, but the gap becomes enormous only when compared with countries like southern Nigeria and Ghana, since the Tanzanian figures are small; and the Congolese situation was in some respects better than that of Malawi, Zambia, and Southern Rhodesia. By 1960 the Congo had many secondary school graduates and many people with post-secondary training, though they were not university graduates. Uganda, Kenya, and Tanzania also had many such people -- preachers, agricultural assistants, veterinary assistants, and people with technical training in civil engineering.[45]

When looking at French West and French Central Africa, the situation again compared favorably with the majority of the British colonies and was in certain cases even better. Probably because of their assimilationist philosophies, the French permitted a substantial number of Africans to receive advanced education quite early. Their Ecole de Medicine de l'Afrique Occidentale Française at Dakar was founded before the British schools at Makerere or Yaba. The French achievement, though by no means spectacular, was summed up by Lord Hailey as follows: "It [the Ecole de Medicine] may be said to be the most successful and certainly the largest effort in Africa to provide a colonial medical education with an acknowledged standard of efficiency."[46] By 1940 it had produced over 400 practitioners, a figure which was still a far cry from Makerere. But the French, like their British counterparts, did not then confer full medical degrees, which could be obtained only abroad. African medical practitioners in French Africa practiced in the State Service and were not permitted to have private practices, though an exception could sometimes be made for those with exceptionally high qualifications. The pattern was thus similar to that in the Belgian Congo and in the British institutions.

The most remarkable thing about education and educational qualifications in Africa is the bewildering diversity of nomenclature, a factor which seems to have escaped the attention of scholars. A "medical assistant" in the Belgian Congo, in respect to his course, was no different from his counterpart at Makerere or Lagos, however much the graduates of the latter two schools may

44. Central African Council Report.
45. Ibid., 18. There were few African lawyers in Kenya and Uganda at the time of independence and not more than five in Tanganyika. The situation in Malawi, Zambia, and Southern Rhodesia was worse. In 1961 there were 520 physicians in Tanganyika, but only 14 were Africans. Julius Nyerere was one of the first Tanganyikans to attend a British University and returned with a University degree during the first half of the 1950's.
46. African Survey, 1185-1186.

resent this comparison. He spent six years in training, two of them in practical laboratory work. The British called their trainees doctors, but their qualifications could not be registered until 1940 and were not recognized by the British Medical Council until 1957. The French allowed their trainees to practice medicine but also made it clear that the qualification they held was not a full medical degree. The Belgians were more rigid and did not permit their trainees, with equivalent qualifications as their British and French counterparts, to practice. Similarly, whereas many Africans were college graduates by the American definition, since they had spent three or four years in post-secondary training in various fields, it was a widespread colonial technique to deny them full academic qualification. The advantages of this denial were obvious, because it permitted the colonial powers to claim, as indeed they often did, that a colony lacked the trained personnel to staff an independent state, and thus gave them a pretext for delaying independence.

VII

The two aspects of colonial policies which have been prominently linked with political training were higher education and indirect rule. A hypothetical link has been discovered between these policies and the peaceful transfer of political power at the time of independence; and the Congo crisis of the 1960's highlighted and accentuated this connection. Judgment on Belgian failure to prepare the Congolese for independence by methods of indirect rule and by providing higher education has been severe, as summed up by A. P. Merriam in his Congo: Background to the Conflict. "We have many lessons to learn from our look at the Congo," he wrote in the preface. "We see . . . that man does not indeed live by bread alone, and that economic security cannot be successfully substituted for ideas."[47]

Other writers have been amazed at the "tremendous degree to which the Congo had been controlled by outside forces, the triumvirate of government, Catholic Church, and business,"[48] and they conclude that such an arrangement represented a strong power system which contributed to the stifling of independence and independent thought on the part of the Congolese. Dr. Merriam stresses the shortcomings of such "paternalism" and points out:

> The philosophy of mass education was against the education of the elite . . . . The British programme of sending numbers of their subjects to universities in England and Europe and America was considered foolish by Belgians. Paternalism fed the body . . . but it did nothing for the intellect . . . The basic weakness of paternalism was that it failed to prepare the Congolese for independence. It failed to give them a sense of belonging to their country. It failed to instruct them in the western system of government which it was assured they would undertake once the fact of independence was established.

47. The Congo: Background to Conflict (Evanston, Ill., 1961).
48. See M. Crawford-Young, Politics in the Congo (Princeton, 1965), especially 10-32.

He concludes:

> Perhaps the most serious lack in Belgian preparation of her colony was the failure to build up a group of educated Congolese who could participate in government and give the country a mature and considered leadership in independence. There was none equipped to teach. The average level of the Congolese at the Round Table Conference in February was something less than high school. The cabinets of the first government, which included very few graduates, was not much higher. There were no engineers. There were Bishops, journalists, accountants, medical assistants, teachers, civil servants, pharmacists, but no attorneys or architects. There were no doctors. No people trained at university level in what we could call a liberal education. There were no social scientists, no humanists; there was simply no group of truly educated people who were prepared to give enlightened leadership . . . Thus it was to a group of uneducated people that the Congo was turned over to independence.[49]

René Lemarchand makes the same judgment when he links education to so-called mature and enlightened leadership.

> The university students were a tiny fraction of the whole population and by the time they became available for political action, the less well educated had already seized the initiative. . . . Clearly the educationaly system was responsible in a large measure for the delayed political awakening of the Congolese elite (paternalism) operated to divert the aspirations of the Africans from the sphere of revolutionary politics.[50]

George Martelli blames the Congo tragedy on Belgian failure to prepare the Congoles when he writes: "The grant of Independence to the Congo . . . was the unkindest thing any nation could have done to another . . . . The Belgians should have started sooner to prepare the way by training more Congolese as government officials and civil servants."[51] Another example is found in Crawford Young's account of how the Belgians undermined the traditional prestige of the chiefs when he draws the following comparison: "Here the contrast with British policy was even stronger. There was nothing in the Congo remotely resembling the material prosperity of Baganda chiefs."[52] He thus picks an isolated example and depicts it as representing British policy, while remaining discreetly silent about other parts of Uganda, about Kenya, about Malawi, and about the Congo's neighbor, Zambia.

If this myth is to be exploded, indirect rule, which is believed to have provided political training for Africans, must first be reappraised. A careful study will show that indirect rule had nothing to do with the so-called reservoir of experience which was needed at the time of independence, precisely because the men who took over at independence were generally not the chiefs who had sat on the tribal councils; if they were in Nigeria, they were certainly not in East Africa and Central Africa.

49. Merriam, Congo, 38, 41, 51.
50. Lemarchand, Awakening, 140.
51. Leopold to Lumumba: A History of the Belgian Congo (London, 1962), preface.
52. Politics in the Congo, 188-189.

But perhaps most extraordinary and unfounded is the idea of a connection between university education and enlightened and mature leadership. When Dr. Merriam castigates the Belgians for not sending Congolese to Europe and America as the British did, he does not tell us how many Tanganyikans, how many Malawians, or how many Zambians were sent to Europe and America, or how many of those that were sent took over the government administration at independence. Dr. Merriam sees an able and enlightened leader in every physician and engineer, but not in an accountant, teacher, pharmacist, or Congolese medical assistant who had had the same training as his counterpart "doctor" in East Africa or Nigeria. By his criteria, Milton Obote of Uganda, Jomo Kenyatta and Tom Mboya of Kenya, or Kenneth Kaunda of Zambia would be disqualified for enlightened and mature leadership, because they held no university degrees. A biographical study of the legislators in Kenya, Tanzania, Malawi, Zambia, and even in Ghana shows that they were not all university graduates.

In the comparisons of the preparation through education and practical training in the art of government provided for the African, the British have once again come off best, and it seems that many writers have reached these conclusions from prior conviction rather than impartial investigation. Besides their unsubstantiated views of the value of indirect rule, scholars have been further misled on this point by the existence of Legislative Councils. As long as these bodies existed, it has been taken for granted that they provided the Africans with the necessary experience. No one has paused to ask how many or what kind of Africans sat in those councils, or what their role was: were they the men who led Africa into independence? what was their legislative experience before independence? or how long was the constitutional transition between the period of internal self-government and independence?

Rupert Emerson has asserted that,

> With the possible exception of the United States, Britain has consistently gone further than any other colonial power in endowing its dependent peoples with political institutions which had the makings of self-government in them. . . . In consequence it is the British territories which have consistently produced the most vigorous and mature nationalist movements.[53]

Unfortunately, Professor Emerson did not state which nationalist movement in Black Africa he had in mind. If he meant Ghana and Tanzania, he was certainly correct. Yet, I do not think that Nkrumah's Convention Peoples Party was any more militant and vigorous than Sekou Toure's Parti Democratique de Guiné in French Guinea, which by any standards was one of the best organized parties on the continent. Even if Professor Emerson had Tanzania in mind, his statement needs modification, especially where it ignores the special and peculiar circumstances which made that country emerge as it did. Only in neighboring Uganda did the so-called vigorous and mature nationalist movement not emerge.

The example of Ghana has often been misleading, because the transitional period of internal rule was nearly the longest in the history of Africa. Nkrumah became Leader of Government Business in 1952 and five years later carried

53. Empire to Nation, 77.

Ghana into independence. Uganda on the other hand held its first national election in 1961, the party which took over at independence came into power only in April 1962, and in October 1962 the country received independence. The catalogue can be repeated for country after country. But perhaps the best method of exploding the myth that the existence of the Legislative Councils automatically provided the African with experience in executive government is to study the membership lists of the Legislative Councils. We shall find that for nearly fifty years East and Central Africans were spectators rather than participants in government affairs; that in Kenya, Uganda, Tanzania, Malawi, Zambia, and Southern Rhodesia, "African Affairs" were handled by a clergyman or by a colonial minister, neither of whom was an African.

This point can be illustrated by a detailed study of one colonial legislature, such as that in Uganda, which was considered by many experts on indirect rule to have been a model.[54] Although a Legislative Council was established in 1920, no African member was nominated until 1945. Membership increased during the governorship of Sir Andrew Cohen (1952-1957), but the proper assessment of the British preparation of the African for constitutional government must go beyond the mere counting of heads to the discovery of how many who led the government into independence had sat in the Legislature and whether they had held executive responsiblity and for how long.

A detailed examination of the National Assembly elected members of the first nationalist government in Uganda in 1961 shows that of the forty-five members of the majority party only six were university graduates. Only one of them, J. C. Kiwanuka, had trained in Britain on a British scholarship. B. K. Kiwanuka, the leader of the government, had financed his own education, first in South Africa and later in England, and two more were graduates of United States universities, where their studies had been financed by private organizations; such students were generally classified by the British as private students, and during the late 1950's and 1960's were often given financial assistance toward the end of their courses. The remaining graduates in the government party were British-trained lawyers whose education had also been arranged through private organizations. As for government experience, only two members of the government party had sat in the colonial legislature and only one had had executive responsibility in the colonial government. B. K. Kiwanuka, who became Prime Minister, and his leading ministers such as Stanley Bemba and two of the graduates, Balamu Mukasa and Lawrence Sebalu, had never had executive responsibility.

A look at the opposition side for the 1961 election shows that the leader, Milton Obote had spent only one year at Makerere after the twelfth grade. In the Uganda Peoples Congress eight members had sat in the colonial legislature for periods of between one and seven years, but none, including Obote, held executive office. Nevertheless both the Democratic Party and the UPC non-graduate members were men of experience in their fields as teachers, trade-union leaders, or cooperative officers; in other words, although their formal education was below university level, their experience compensated to a

54. Details of the composition of the Legislative Council of Uganda can be found in the relevant Colonial Reports (London, 1950-1960).

considerable extent for the absence of formal education.[55] When we look at the results of the elections of 1961 and 1962, we find that the chiefs and others who had been nominated to the colonial legislature were not elected; with the dawn of party politics and universal suffrage, the so-called experienced legislators were driven out of politics. The pattern of the Uganda legislature at the time of independence was similar to many others, though in terms of educational background it was below those in Ghana or Nigeria. The Congolese legislature was not inferior to those of Malawi and Zambia in that respect, and it probably ranked with that of Tanzania.

These results help to emphasize that the majority of the men who led Africa into independence were not only new to the legislative councils, but represented the new politics everywhere in Africa -- the politics of party and political machine. The supposedly experienced administrators, the products of the self-government system of indirect rule, were not represented. The reason is not, as Gann and Duignan assert, that French methods of direct rule undermined that traditional authority leading to their eventual abolition but that, as self-government and independence drew near, those who had been traditionally privileged and sustained by the colonial authorities either were, or were believed by the nationalists to be, fighting for an out-dated status quo because they feared to lose the privileged status conferred on them by the colonial regime and because some believed that the best political course for Africa was evolutionary and not revolutionary. After independence, the old suspicion that chiefs were against the nationalists lingered on, and, as African political regimes became increasingly totalitarian, they could not permit what seemed to be centers of division among the masses; since kings and chiefs were believed to be a source of such division, the nationalists everywhere attempted to abolish them.[56]

But when all is said and done, we must stress that the connection which many Africanists see between the Congo crisis, higher education, and "enlightened mature leadership" is mythical not only for Africa but other countries. Political ability and intelligence are not necessarily equivalent with university education. Moreover, in the colonial world, where educational opportunities were so severely limited, many of the most intelligent and competent people never had a chance to attend university. Indeed, in most instances, the very intelligent and very able were shunned by colonial administrators because those who refused to obey without question were regarded as actual or potential agitators. This reaction toward nationalists was universal in the colonial world, not peculiar to Belgian or French rule.

55. On the opposition side there were five graduates, one was a lawyer trained in the United Kingdom, one from Makerere, one from India, and two trained in the United States. Only two of these had obtained their qualifications with the financial support of the colonial government in Uganda.
56. Some chiefs were incorporated into the new regimes and in that position retained some of their old influence, power, and prestige.

An Anglo-American Interpretation of African Colonial History?

It is clear that the contrasts between the colonial politics regarding indirect or direct rule, preservation of an attitude toward traditional chieftainship amount to very little. So are the supposedly overwhelming contrasts regarding educational policies. Why then has this interpretation persisted despite the thinness of evidence? Why has there been so much generalization? Can we speak of an Anglo-American interpretation of African colonial history? Let us first look for the source of the confusion. This seems to begin with the assumption that colonial policies in Canada, Australia, and Africa were the same. Because legislative councils existed from an early date, no one has cared to ask who sat in them. Were they Africans? In the case of Canada and New Zealand the question did not arise. But failure to ask this question in the case of Africa has resulted in an interpretation which ignores what colonialism was really about in Africa.

There is no better illustration of this confusion between British policies in the white dominions and Africa than the following statement made by G. H. Nadel and Harry Curtis.

> The British Empire possessed an aura of liberty and constitutionalism that were largely missing in other Empires. In the 1830's and 1840's a group of British political reformers led by G. E. Wakefield, Lord Durham and Charles Buller, had urged the adoption of a systematic policy based on the principle of responsible government.[57]

Rupert Emerson draws the same conclusion and asserts:

> The British (in contrast to the French) leaned towards a large devolution of power to the colonies themselves . . . which we recorded as constituting distinct and unique entities, while the French system has been based on a far greater centralization.[58]

But Professor Emerson does not tell us in which colonies in Africa this large devolution of power occurred.

I believe this kind of interpretation represents an attitude of mind rather similar to what Herbert Butterfield described as the "Whig interpretation of History."[59] That is, conclusions are reached not as a result of empirical research but as a result of prior convictions. Consequently, that whole process of specialized research which has in so many other fields reversed the previously accepted interpretations and set our minds afresh, has not yet been extensively applied to African colonial history. And as a result colonial policies have not been studied as colonial policies but as references to a presumed ideal model. Unfortunately this approach to historical study has tended to obstruct historical understanding because of the tendency to classify colonial regimes as "bad" or "good."

While it is true that the historian's craft must necessarily involve an element of selectivity and rejection, many historians have by a handy rule of

57. Colonialism and Imperialism (London and New York, 1964), 20-21.
58. Empire to Nation, 69-70.
59. H. Butterfield, The Whig Interpretation of History (London, 1950).

thumb carefully looked only at material, and often not very critically, which supported their assumptions. The net result of this method has been to produce a scheme of general history which concentrates upon the select British colonies which were presented as models. An extension of this result is the popular view that only the British practised indirect rule; that only they respected traditional institutions; that indirect rule transferred self-government to the Africans and thereby indirectly prepared them for independence; that only the British, by introducing legislative councils and by introducing higher education, prepared their colonial subjects for independence. These stereotyped contrasts are to my mind mythical and a subterfuge to the real issues at stake as the colonial powers saw them.

The other aspect of colonial policies which is often overlooked is that, whatever they were purported to be, they fluctuated depending on the personalities of the governors. Throughout the colonial world, policies were as flexible as circumstances demanded. All colonial regimes advanced economic justification of empire and the common denominator was a concern for the economic utility of the colonies. African colonies were colonies of exploitation and the aim was to maximize their resources. When the district commissioners encouraged Ugandans to grow cotton it was to keep the cotton mills of England going, not to enrich the Africans. Labor policies also had a great deal in common since every colonial regime relied on cheap and often compulsory labor in the attempt to make the colonies pay their own way. It was not only in European-settled colonies like the Belgian Congo that compulsory labor was employed, but also in "primarily African" colonies like Uganda. Thus, generalizations and comparisons seem idle; no colonial power had a monopoly on virtue or wisdom.

INDIRECT RULE: THE ESTABLISHMENT OF "CHIEFS" AND "TRIBES" IN CAMERON'S TANGANYIKA

James D. Graham

"An analogy is perhaps apt in subsuming the British effort to implement indirect rule in Tanganyika: it was as if a 14-lane superhighway was constructed to nowhere. Considering the vast energies that were invested in the development of the system of native administration, the sheer quantity of man-hours on the part of British administrators, African chiefs and sub-chiefs, and others, the contribution which native administration made to political evolution in Tanganyika is almost negligible in modern times."[1]

Sir Donald Cameron, Governor of Tanganyika from 1925-31, has reflected on his policy of indirect rule as a practical way to "administer the people through the instrument of their own indigenous institutions."[2] Although he recognized it, in part, as "a measure of expediency," Cameron nevertheless affirmed indirect rule as "the most important reform for which I was responsible."[3] As the most outspoken and dynamic governor who served under the League of Nations Mandate in Tanganyika, Cameron articulated and rationalized British presence in East Africa primarily in terms of his administrative policies. This article illuminates some of the contrasts and contradictions within Cameron's theory of indirect rule and between that ideology and the way in which it was put into practice under his administration. In order to understand these dialectics, we shall focus on administrative praxis under Cameron as specifically reflected in (1) the establishment of Njombe District as an administrative entity (1926); and (2) the confirmation of "chiefs" as rulers of various "tribes" in that district.

After the Colonial Office in London assumed the League of Nations Mandate over Tanganyika in 1919, Governor Horace Byatt set forth the general outlines of British administrative policy in Tanganyika.

"The policy which is being followed is to develop the people, so far as is possible, on their own lines and in accordance with their own ideas and customs, purified where necessary. No sweeping measures have been taken to dispense with the *Akidas*, but though they remain their status has been radically altered. Their privileges have been curtailed; their powers of punishment have been taken away, and they are being closely supervised. When vacancies occur, the wishes of the people as to a successor ascertained, and, if possible, a local man of influence is selected in preference to an alien. Every endeavour is being made to restore the old tribal organizations, and it is hoped that in course of time the German conception of the *Akida* system will cease to exist, even though the name may remain."[4]

1. William Friedland, "The Evolution of Tanganyika's Political System," unpublished manuscript (1965), pp. 43-44.
2. Donald Cameron, "Native Administration in Nigeria and Tanganyika," *Journal of the Royal African Society* (supp.) XXXVI (November 30, 1937), 3-5.
3. Donald Cameron, *My Tanganyika Service and Some Nigeria* (London, 1939), p. 282.
4. H.M. Stationery Office, *Report on Tanganyika Territory for the Year 1920* (London, 1921), p. 37. Long quotations like this are sometimes necessary in order to reflect the flavor as well as the substance of what was said.

Although German-trained clerks and *akidas* were often quite competent at their work,[5] official policy was "to encourage the establishment of a native authority and the participation of the natives in the management of their own affairs."[6] At the same time, Byatt's administration sought to consolidate villages, communities, and extended families into "tribal units";[7] and they established local courts to enforce new territorial laws.[8] Throughout the early 1920s, when communications were poor, the central administration in Dar es Salaam laid down few general guidelines in matters of local government. The District Officers continued to work through that combination of local "chiefs," elders, *akidas*, *jumbes*, and *boma* clerks which seemed most suitable to their particular localities.[9] By the time Governor Byatt left Dar es Salaam in 1924, local administrators had made "considerable progress" in "substituting traditional chiefs, where they could be found, for the *akidas*, and in giving them recognized powers of local government, largely by recognition of native courts under their jurisdiction."[10]

The problems involved in trying to select "chiefs" in the Njombe area during the Byatt administration were manifold. District Officers recognized, as early as 1920, that the people living in Upangwa had "no paramount chief, nor have they ever had one,"[11] and they found that government-trained *akidas* and appointed *jumbes* functioned relatively efficiently.[12] But despite the training and experience which competent African civil servants could bring to bear on their administrative work, some District Officers seemed determined to rule through "traditional" leaders if at all possible. To this end, they supported those *jumbes* who were willing to assume broad administrative duties over areas they had not previously administered. "Opportunity has been taken, whenever possible without undue disturbance, of aggregating small jumbeates. . . . On the death, resignation or incapacity otherwise of a junior native official with a small following, the people and the Sultan were consulted and the following aggregated to a capable man with whom all were in accord. Eight such jumbeates were so created throughout the year."[13] Such "jumbeates" were grouped into "sub-tribes" which, in turn, could be amalgamated into "tribes." The final stages of this "tribal" amalgamation in the Njombe area occurred in 1926, a year after Byatt's successor, Governor Cameron, had toured the Southern Highlands and talked with his field staff about indirect rule.

Sir Donald Cameron, assuming the governorship in 1925, instituted "little change" in Byatt's administrative system,[14] although he accelerated the process

5. H.M. Stationery Office, *1920*, p. 41; J.P. Moffett, ed., *Handbook of Tanganyika* (Dar es Salaam, 1958), p. 92.
6. H.M. Stationery Office, *Report by His Britannic Majesty's Government to the Council of the League of Nations on the Administration of Tanganyika Territory for the Year 1923* (London, 1924), p. 6. Margaret Bates has suggested that this approach was made so explicit only after Governor Byatt had read Lord Lugard's *The Dual Mandate in Tropical Africa*, published in 1922. Margaret L. Bates, "Tanganyika under British Administration 1920-1955," Diss. Oxford, 1957, p. 66.
7. H.M. Stationery Office, *1921*, p. 5; H.M. Stationery Office, *1923*, pp. 6-7.
8. *1923*, p. 9.
9. Bates, "Tanganyika under British Administration," p. 58.
10. Moffett, *Tanganyika*, p. 318.
11. Sec. 1733/1, Songea District, "Annual Report, 1920."
12. Sec. 1733/22, Songea District, "Annual Report, 1933."
13. Sec. 1733/1; 1733/8; 1733/9; 1733/15; and 1733/22 (Annual Reports from Songea District). One officer lamented that "the fact must be faced that few things come to the knowledge of an Administrative Officer beyond those which the natives wish him to know."
14. Bates, "Tanganyika under British Administration," p. 143.

and considerably escalated the rhetoric of indirect rule. A typical example of Cameron's reflections about indirect rule in Tanganyika best illustrates his ideology and the sense of mission which he brought to bear on his work:

> "In accord with the spirit of the Mandate and accepted forms of British Colonial policy our object is to teach these people and train them so that eventually in the end, however far removed in time that date may be, they may be able to stand by themselves. Let us leave them their own past on which their own nationalism may eventually evolve by natural growth under our stimulation and guidance. . . For the present and for many years to come the only way in which we could prevent the Natives from going under and becoming a servile people; the only way of keeping his society together; the only way in which he could be trained in public affairs—however simply in the earlier stages—was by the system of Native Administration that we introduced. . . . Above all, we are using their own indigenous institutions in order to promote higher standards of civilisation amongst them. That is the most vital principle in my conception."[15]

These were Governor Cameron's paradoxical reflections: that Tanganyikans had to be trained in, yet protected from, the ways of the modern world through indirect rule.

Upon assuming office in 1925, Cameron initially urged his field officers to put into practice the theory of indirect rule by finding and constituting native authorities who could strengthen and maintain what he viewed as "tribal organisation."[16]

> "With the decay of the tribal organisation we shall get a numerous body of broken and disgruntled chiefs, disaffected, quite naturally, and hostile to the British Administration. The natives will have ceased to be tribesmen and, no longer attached to their tribal institutions, will have become mere flotsam on the political sea of Tanganyika. No native will have any share in the administration of the country, but a class of politically minded natives will have arisen in the meantime (this must come with the spread of education, guard it as we may) and the soil prepared for it by ourselves. . . . Why then destroy the instrument that we *must* use? An instrument that we temper and adjust and endeavour to perfect—it is necessary to think in centuries and not in mere decades—is surely a more efficient instrument than one which is thrown on one side to rust."[17]

Thus, his determination to bolster the positions of 'traditional' leaders and institutions arose from and reflected Cameron's commitment to maintaining a British presence in Tanganyika. Through indirect rule he hoped to create a class of parochial "tribal" rulers who could be manipulated by British administrators: "If we strengthen the Chiefs and build them up, securing their positions for them and paying them generously out of their own Native Treasuries so far as the means of their people allow, we shall have the great majority of them on the side of the Government and not on the side of the political agitator."[18]

In the process of delineating "tribes" and strengthening "chiefs," the Cameron administration reorganized Tanganyika's twenty-two existing districts into forty-four smaller ones, which were to be supervised from eleven new provincial offices. The first circular issued from one of these provincial offices—the one located at Iringa in the Southern Highlands—set forth the basic administrative principles which were to guide

15. Cameron, "Native Administration," pp. 7-9.
16. Secretariat File (Sec.) 7777, fols. 15-16, 74.
17. Ibid., fols. 17ff.
18. Ibid., fol. 26.

British field offices in Njombe District. In this circular, the Provincial Commissioner of the Southern Highlands, F.J. Bagshawe, directed his staff to reconstitute district boundaries to concide more closely with major ethnic oı "tribal" divisions. Concomitantly, field officers were to discover and establish "chiefs" in each "tribe," and inform them of their rights and obligations. This circular, quoted at some length below, illustrates how Cameron's general ideas about indirect rule were specifically interpreted and formulated by one of his provincial commissioners.

> "Each tribe must be considered as a distinct unit: it sometimes happens that neighbouring small tribes are found to be closely related, and that they wish to amalgamate: they should be allowed and encouraged to do so and can be considered as one tribe. Each tribe must be entirely within the borders of a district: I have instructions to alter district boundaries within the province to this end at once, and to discuss alterations of the Provincial boundaries as soon as possible. Tribal boundaries must be settled.
>
> Each tribe must be under a chief. In some cases there is already a recognised chief, but in others there will be rival claimants from whom the chief must be chosen. The wishes of the whole people must be taken into consideration, for it is useless to try to establish a chief who is not accepted by at all events a large majority of his people. The greatest care must be taken to establish the right man. Frequently rivals can be made to support a majority by making them sub-chiefs, if the numbers of the tribe permit. . . .
>
> Remember always that a chief is a native, with a native's partially developed sense of right and wrong, passions and temptations. Remember also that he is your principal weapon in your work and that if he breaks you will have to make another. . . . Chiefs must be made to understand that we are increasing their power and paying them salaries, and that in return we expect a great deal more from them. They must collect their own taxes and must be held responsible that every man in their areas is entered in their tax registers, whether he pays or not; they must provide us with labour required, and they must see that the burden is equitably distributed amongst their people. They must be our executive in every matter affecting their people and their country, from the treatment of yaws to the upkeep of roads. . . .
>
> Chiefs and their subordinates must be held responsible for law and order in their areas. They must be taught to act without the aid of the *Boma* or of the police. If it is necessary to effect the arrest of a native the local headman should do it, calling upon his people to assist him when necessaıy. It should be very seldom necessary to send native police into a tribal area: they are the power 'behind the throne' and should be kept there."[19]

Bagshawe's idea of the roles "chiefs" were to play in indirect rule seemed almost indistinguishable from the roles *akidas* and *jumbes* had played under earlier administrations, aside from the admonition that "the wishes of the whole people *must be taken into consideration*" (italics mine).

19. Southern Highlands Province, "Provincial Circular No . 1" (February 1926). Some Provincial Circulars from the Southern Highlands have been collected by George Park, together with other important local records; they are deposited in the National Archives of Tanzania under Acquisition No. 28 and 28/2 (Ac. 28 and Ac. 28/2)'

Opposition to Cameron's desire to establish "chiefs" who could administer "tribal units" was voiced by Charles Dundas, Secretary for Native Affairs. Based on long experience in East Africa, Dundas knew that "tribes," as such, did not exist in many parts of the territory. He felt that government should encourage the growth of village and regional polities, rather than distinct and divisive "tribes." 'The people have, apart from certain ethnological affinities, this much in common that they do not really represent tribes so much as infiltrations and migrations of sections of tribes; there is in actuality no Gogo, Nyamwezi or Sukuma tribe, these are but names given to the inhabitants of the country. One consequence of this tribal conglomeration is that having no very definite distinctions, there are no rigid divisions and they are the more capable of amalgamating into larger combinations."[20] There was, as Dundas implied, every reason to encourage the development of democratic or meritocratic systems of local government, through which people could begin to evolve toward broadly-based forms of territorial democracy. But Cameron, as we have seen, ordered his District Officers to establish "chiefs" and "tribes," even though the job of creating "tribes" was a formidable one. This was especially so in the Southern Highlands; for "it was often not clear what was a tribe, how many tribes there were, what was a chief, in what manner their subjects expected the chiefs to rule, or how indirect rule could be organized where there were no traditional chiefs."[21]

It was Philip E. Mitchell, Assistant Secretary of Native Affairs (under Dundas), who most strongly supported Cameron's policy of establishing "tribes" and "chiefs" under indirect rule. In the spring of 1926 Mitchell travelled through the Southern Highlands, in order to ascertain whether the "hill tribes of Ubena Plateau" should be incorporated with "Ukinga and Upangwa" in a "natural district" bearing the name of Njombe.[22] Mitchell was enthusiastic about building a new district headquarters at Njombe (which at that time was little more than a picturesque waterfall on a hill), although there was little objective justification for his enthusiasm. Alternative plans, advanced in various parts by field officers in the area and passingly endorsed by Governor Cameron, would have established two districts: one (including Ubena, Uwanji, and Usengu) looking northward, and another (including the peoples of the Livingstone Mountains) oriented toward Lake Malawi.[23] Mitchell's views prevailed, however; and in August 1926 Cameron charged two British officers with the responsibility of administering Njombe District, a diverse area approximately the size of Wales. The location of the new district headquarters left most of Ukinga and Upangwa as remote from immediate adminitrative supervision as before, for the natural flow of communications from the Njombe District Office was northward. District Officers working out of Njombe, in fact, were never able to establish adequate communication with people in the Livingstone Mountains. Since 1926, the people of the Livingstone Mountains have been regarded as the reserve labor pool of a remote southern district, instead of continuing to develop in consonance with their pre-colonial history as an important productive area in south-eastern Africa.*

20. Sec. 11200, fol. 7.
21. Allison H. Redmayne, "The Wahehe People of Tanganyika," Diss. Oxford, 1964, p. 260.
22. Sec. 7986, fols. 16ff.
23. Ibid., fols. 5, 6ff., 12, 16ff.

*This is an extremely important point, the full analysis of which lies beyond the scope of this article. It is difficult, and ultimately unrealistic, to speak of any twentieth-century political system as though it could be discussed apart from broader economic perspectives. Some of the economic implications of Cameron's emphasis on political administration, with special reference to Njombe District, have been pursued in James D. Graham, "Migrant Labor in Tanzahia," *African Studies Review*, (Winter 1971;) and "The Tanzania Railway," *Africa Today* (Summer 1974).

The two British officers assigned to implement indirect rule (as defined by Cameron and Bagshawe) in Njombe District (as delineated by Mitchell) faced a formidable task. They immediately had to choose between the conflicting claims of would-be "chiefs," and they had to draw boundaries between "tribes" and "sub-tribes."[24] Since the district office was located in Central Ubena, they first selected a Paramount Chief for the Bena "tribe" from among the five Bena "sub-chiefs" and *jumbe* previously functioning in three different districts. Pangamahuti Mbeyela, probably the most widely known local leader, had already been recognized by the Songea District Office as chief of Southern Ubena; but the District Officers in Njombe rejected his claim to paramountcy over the newly constituted Bena "tribe," in favour of Kiswaga (formerly of Tukuyu District). Pangamahuti remained sub-chief in Southern Ubena, while Mwachuma became sub-chief in Kiswaga's area of Western Ubena. Dumuluganga, who had earlier been appointed by the Germans as a *jumbe*, was reconfirmed as sub-chief in Eastern Ubena. In Central Ubena, the ancestral home of many families in the area, Bernard Mwanyensa Gadau (a boy of ten) was recognized as the legitimate sub-chief under his uncle's "regency";[25] while the early Mwangera assumed the role of sub-chief in Northern Ubena. Within two years, one of these Native Authorities was dismissed for corruption, and two others were reported to be senile.[26] As Paramount Chief of the Bena "tribe," Kiswaga initially made little effort to supervise his subordinates, although he eventually responded to the pressures exerted by his neighbours in the district office—appointing some of his friends and relatives as replacements for those reported to be delinquent.[27] In Ubena, where the Njombe District Officers lived, indirect rule did not turn out to be all that Cameron and Bagshawe had envisioned.

If Native Authorities in Ubena found themselves closely scrutinized by District Officers, the "chiefs" in mountainous Upangwa and Ukinga usually managed to avoid such close supervision—by virtue of their distance and inaccessibility from Njombe. Among Kidulile's earliest initiatives, after confirmation as Paramount Chief in Upangwa, were (1) to move his court southward, even farther away from district headquarters; and (2) to ask that his friend, Makamba, be recognized as sub-chief for Northern Upangwa.[28] Reporting on their semiannual tours, District Officers argued that "the idea of a chief in the whole of Upangwa is new to the people," the people of Upangwa had "traditionally" been very independent, and it was therefore "more difficult for Chief Kidulile to establish himself and his authority" in the area.[29] While the Paramount Chief clearly used his position to advance the interests of his friends and relatives,[30] official reports tended to emphasize the progress that was being made toward "tribal" amalgamation under Kidulile and his "loyal sub-chief," Makamba.[31] Meanwhile, Kidulile was described as "an old man who is getting decrepit"[32]—a role which allowed him to "misunderstand" some of the more onerous

24. Ac. 28, file 58.
25. Southern Highlands Province File 26/6, fol. 8.
26. Njombe District, *District Book;* Ac. 28, "Tour Reports," fol. 50; Ac. 28/2, Njombe District, "Annual Report, 1928." Both Mwachuma and Mwangera were reported on adversely in 1928.
27. Southern Highlands Province File 26/6, 14ff.; Sec. 12779, fol. 35; Southern Highlands Province File 1/4; Njombe District, *District Book.*
28. Ac. 28, File 59.
29. Ibid.
30. Ibid.; Ac. 28, "Tour Reports," fol. 51.
31. H.M. Stationery Office, 1930, p. 31; Sec. 11677, Vol II Southern Highlands Province, "Annual Report, 1929" and "Annual Report, 1930"; Ac. 28/2, Njombe District, "Annual Report, 1929" and "Annual Report, 1931."
32. Sec. 11677, Vol. I, Southern Highlands Province, "Annual Report, 1929"; Ac. 28/2, Njombe District, "Annual Report, 1931."

duties he was ordered to carry out. By the mid-thirties, District Officers freely admitted the failure of indirect rule to develop any efficient form of local government in Upangwa.[33]

In Ukinga, where the mountains are higher and the population denser than in Upangwa, the Native Authorities appeared to have legitimate ancestral claims to power within the dominant ("royal") family of the area. Njombe's District Officers confirmed Mwemusi, the Paramount Chief, and Mwalukisa and Chelelo, his sub-chiefs, in the positions which the Tukuyu District Office had previously recognized; and they designated Mwaliwali as sub-chief in Uwanji, under Mwemusi's jurisdiction. The anomaly of including Uwanji as a northern extension of the Kinga "tribal unit" was pointed out as early as 1928, when a District Officer reported that the people there "would prefer to be under Merere with the Wasangu than under Mwemusi with the Wakinga, with whom they have less in common, either in language or custom."[34] The similarly anomalous position of the Wamagoma and Wamahanzi, who were assigned to Chelelo's sub-chiefdom, finally led one of Njombe's District Officers, in 1945, to recognize that large communities in Western Ukinga were "in most respects more like the Nyakyusa than the Kinga under whose Native Authorities they have been placed."[35] As Paramount Chief over these diverse "sub-tribes," as well as those who recognized themselves as Wakinga, Mwemusi did not often exert himself administratively.[36] Perhaps because no such "royal family" existed elsewhere in Njombe, District Officers hoped to work with Mwemusi and to help him realize the advantages of cooperating more fully with them. One administrative officer described Mwemusi as holding "probably as strong a position by tribal tradition as any Chief in the Province," although he was reluctant to "use it" as directed.[37] Before too many years had passed, it seemed apparent to the British that Mwemusi's "interest in the administration of his area" was "limited to drawing his monthly salary"; and District Officers were complaining that his people were being deprived of any "guiding influence."[38]

The "tribal" system of indirect rule probably created more problems in Njombe District and throughout Tanganyika than it solved. There was, for instance, no clear understanding of the "chief's" role in indirect rule. In some case the Native Authorities "saw themselves not as the servants of the administration but as the administration itself."[39] In a sense, each "chief" created his own role, or recreated it in the context of colonial power.[40] "Tribal" or "traditional" societies were seldom as clearly defined as Bagshawe or Cameron would have liked; and attempts to construct abstract, static "chiefdoms" in a rapidly changing colonial economy were generally ill-conceived.[41] In many cases, those designated as "chiefs" were able to exploit their administrative positions in advancing and consolidating their family interests. In fact, it was often neither the "chiefs," the "sub-chiefs," nor even the *jumbes*, but rather the *lugalugas* (village headmen) who carried out most of the day-to-day administrative duties—and they worked without pay! The ideology of indirect rule notwithstanding, local Native Authorities were poorly paid, if at all; and many

33. Ac. 28/2, Njombe District, "Annual Report, 1936."
34. Ac. 28, File 29.
35. Njombe District File P4/6/1, Njombe District, "Annual Report, 1945."
36. R.C. Northcote, personal correspondence, August 1966.
37. Ac. 28, "Tour Reports, " fol. 10.
38. Ac. 28/2, Njombe District, "Annual Report, 1934," "Annual Report, 1935," and "Annual Report, 1936."
39. Bates, "Tanganyika under British Administration," p. 106.
40. G.G. Brown and A.M.B. Hutt, *Anthropology in Action* (London, 1935), p. 40.
41. Bates, "Tanganyika under British Administration," p. 103.

indulged in low-level graft or petty speculation, especially where African appointees felt little loyalty to their colonial supervisors.[42]

While the funds allocated to local Native Authorities under indirect rule proved inadequate to win their widespread, wholehearted support, most of Cameron's British civil servants developed a deep commitment to the administrative system they were building in Tanganyika. The number of Europeans employed on Tanganyika's civil lists, supervising the implementation of indirect rule, grew rapidly during the prosperous years of Cameron's regime—from 575 in 1925, to 950 in 1929. District Officers, like those in Njombe, often worked long and arduous hours to establish and legitimize Native Authorities; and Cameron, in retrospect, took great pride in the *esprit de corps* which existed among his European staff.[43]

One of Cameron's most loyal and diligent staff members was Phillip E. Mitchell, Assistant Secretary for Native Affairs, who recalls travelling two-thirds of his time in office and visiting every district yearly.[44] His example probably helped to inspire various District Officers to tour their areas more often, take more accurate census data, and supervise the collection of local taxes more closely; and Cameron, in turn, channelled much of these increasing tax revenues into the hiring of more British field officers. Mitchell has reflected on the "cult" of indirect rule which moved Cameron and his staff to work so diligently, observing that they "were in danger of becoming a sort of orgiastic order of monks—if there can be such a thing."[45] Admitting that they "made many mistakes and got many things wrong," Mitchell particularly regretted that they "were compelled to try to establish Councils of Chiefs or headmen where there had not been any since the dim past," and that they had thereby "become embroiled in a lot of inefficiency and some pretence."[46]

It was the inefficiency of indirect rule which Cameron's former Secretary for Native Affairs, Charles Dundas, has also critized;[47] while Cameron's successor as governor, Sir Stewart Symes, questioned why so many of his European staff exuded "an almost apostolic fervour" about Tanganyika's system of "local self-government."[48] Indeed, insofar as indirect rule became an official ideology during the Cameron administration, it proved to be singularly unadaptable to changing circumstances.

> "Although indirect rule has been described as 'the progressive adaptation of native institutions to modern conditions,' actually the system was not designed originally to foster progressive institutional adaptation, nor has it always furthered the cause of self-government. It was adopted in the first place for reasons of expediency—as a cheap and easy method of local administration (since it made use of already existing tribal institutions and lines of authority), and as a way of winning the loyalty of native chiefs (since it reinforced their claims for authority) and so avoiding native insurrections against the Government....
>
> Once this expedient became an ideology and an accepted institution of local native administration, it actually worked against the development of political institutions along representative and elective lines."[49]

42. Martin T. Kayamba, *African Problems* (London, 1948), pp. 17-18.
43. Cameron, *Tanganyika Service*, p. 25.
44. Phillip E. Mitchell, *African Afterthoughts* (London, 1954), p. 133.
45. Ibid., p. 127.
46. Ibid., pp. 133-134.
47. Charles C.F. Dundas, *African Crossroads*, (London, 1955), p. 106.
48. Bates, "Tanganyika under British Administration," pp. 147-148.
49. Bernard T.G. Chidzero, *Tanganyika and International Trusteeship* (London, 1961), pp. 16-17.

It was officially acknowledged by the 1950's that indirect rule had outlived its usefulness, especially in those numerous cases where "the concept of a chief was absent"[50] among people who had been organized into "tribes." Another critique based on the hindsight of the fifties, in a quasi-official article, pointed out that indirect rule was not actually indirect, that "the control exercised by central government through the district commissioners was much more direct than is normally found in local government practice."[51] Although British administrators belatedly tried to modernize local government, it was not until popular elections were held and community development projects were initiated—in the context of massive political mobilization around TANU—that the local and territorial foundations for democratic government were laid among Tanganyika's millions of rural villagers. In 1962, after *Uhuru*, the TANU government stripped "chiefs" of their official powers and did away with virtually all the remaining anachronisms of "tribal" administration; in Ubena, "all hereditary offices were replaced with appointive positions and the office of Paramount Chief was eliminated altogether."[52]

By illustrating a specific context in which Governor Cameron enunciated his intention to maintain "tribal organisation" through indirect rule, we have seen how that policy was translated—through Cameron's subordinates (especially Bagshawe and Mitchell)—into the creation of a new administrative district with its own indigenous Native Authorities. As soon as Njombe District was officially constituted, the District Officers immediately set about delineating three "tribes" and confirming three Paramount Chiefs, nine sub-chiefs, and ninety-three *jumbes*.[53] But these Native Authorities did not develop the loyalty to the system of indirect rule which imbued many of their British supervisors with incredible energy and commitment. Paramount Chiefs either evaded District Officers by making themselves inaccessible, as did Kidulile and Mwemusi, or they cooperated only minimally, as Kiswaga was forced to do. Few "chiefs" or "sub-chiefs" during Cameron's time made any significant attempt to understand or live up to British civil service standards, while most of Cameron's staff and field officers (except those like Dundas) did not seek to introduce administrative policies which might have hastened the development of local or territorial democracy. Working from vague and misleading conceptions about African "chiefs" and "tribes," the Cameron administration tried to impose abstract, alien notions of government on diverse local populations who were continuing to evolve complex political systems of their own.

But they failed. British officials like Cameron, Mitchell, and Bagshawe devoted inordinate efforts to translating the theory of indirect rule into practice. The theory was pretentious, based on static and often inaccurate assessments of African political history; and the attempt to put that theory into practice confused everyone from District Officers to *jumbes* and "chiefs." If Cameron's version of indirect rule achieved any tangible or intangible goal in districts like Njombe, it was to foster "tribal" consciousness. By institutionalizing "tribes" as units of local government, a tactic known more colloquially as "divide and rule," Cameron hoped to maintain British presence in Tanganyika; but even that hope eventually faded. Seen on his own terms, Cameron's administration failed to create viable "tribal" institutions. Seen from a contemporary historical perspective, indirect rule provided little, if any, effective training in modern forms of local government.

* * *

50. Tanganyika Territory, *Local Government Memoranda No. 1* (Dar es Salaam, 1954), p. 4.
51. I. Woodroffe, "The Relationship between Central and Local Government in Africa," *Journal of African Administration*, IX, No. 1 (January 1957), 5.
52. Marc J. Swartz, "Continuities in the Bena Political System," *Southwestern Journal of Anthropology*, XX (1964), 251.
53. Sec. 11677, Vol. II, fol. 4.

COLONIALISM AND SOCIAL STRUCTURE

Iheanyi J. Samuel-Mbaekwe
P.O. Box 742 221
Houston, Texas 77274 – 2221
U.S.A.

The title of my paper is happily brief, but I fear that "Colonialism and Social Structure" may mislead many to expect an elaborate review of the world history of European expansion through colonization, with the tag "social structure" as a social scientist's afterthought. In fact, however, my range of attention is smaller than that and "social structure" in the title is more than a social scientist's convenient addendum to my concerns. Barring the pre-modern forms of internal European expansion by the Greeks and the Romans, it may be said that outward imperial expansions in the West have led to two principal forms of colonization. The first, beginning in the seventeenth century, was the classic form of colonization in which, in this case, Europeans rendered surplus by social and economic crises in European nations sojourned overseas to conquer and settle new lands in the Americas and in Australasia. After a lull in the earlier decades of the nineteenth century, the second form of European colonization took place in which European expansion outwards resumed seriously into Africa and Asia in the late nineteenth and twentieth centuries. But the character of this later form of expansion was different from the colonization of the Americas and Australasia. The European expansion of the nineteenth and twentieth centuries consisted of the export of surplus capital, not of surplus persons. The awkward experiences in Algeria, Rhodesia, and Kenya and the bizarre developments in South Africa notwithstanding, the colonization of Africa and many parts of Asia, and of the Indian sub-continent before these, was intended to create new economic structures and opportunities receptive to the expansion of European capitalism.

In this paper my concern with colonialism is restricted to its African form as it emerged in the late nineteenth century, with all its consequences which continue unto the present time. As an area of intellectual discourse, colonialism in this form has received very little attention in the mainstream of any of the disciplines in the social sciences. It is therefore not surprising that its conceptualization remains diffuse and fragmented. As the term has been used over half a century in various sources, colonialism in Africa seems to connote three distinct aspects of the social reality in the areas of Africa (and Asia) that experienced European conquest and rule in the nineteenth and twentieth centuries. First, colonialism has been understood to refer to the activities of European colonizers in the process of the conquering and ruling Africa. This is what has been most commonly referred to as colonization. Secondly, and separately, colonialism has also been used to denote the reactions of those who were subjected to European conquest and rule i.e. to colonization.

In these two conceptions of colonialism, there is a distinct attempt to understand the motives for the actions of the ruler and the ruled. We must agree with Aime Cesaire[1] that the motives of the colonizers were

> neither evangelization, nor a philantropic enterprise, nor a desire to push back the frontiers of ignorance and tyranny, nor a project undertaken for the greater glory of God, nor an attempt to extend the rule of law.

I would even agree with Cesaire that greed and lucre were the real motives of the colonizers. But men's motives are frail and in the long run of little worth in the analysis of social movements. Indeed, in spite of the emotive power of these two stands on the conceptualization of colonialism, their limitations seem self-evident. It is as limiting to restrict our understanding of colonialism to colonization and reactions to colonization as it is to reduce the meaning of the Industrial Revolution to Industrialization and the Luddite reactions to it in England or of the meaning of the French Revolution to the bizarre excesses of Robespierre and the Jocobins.

The study of colonialism in Africa has suffered because, as George Balandier so fruitfully pointed out in the early fifties, the two aspects of colonization and reaction to colonization were falsely separated. Balandier was convinced that the two aspects of colonialism would gain a fuller meaning if they were studied as part of the same colonial situation. Thirdly, then, colonialism has also been conceptualized, although its use is thin in this tradition, as the complex of relationships between the colonizer and the colonized, between the elements of European culture and of the indigenous culture. In the distinct style of French collectivist thought, from which this definition emerges, colonialism is seen as 'a force acting in terms of its own totality'. As Balandier saw it then, any present-day study of colonial societies striving for an understanding of current realities and not a reconstitution of a purely historical nature, a study aiming at a comprehension of the conditions as they are, not sacrificing facts for the convenience of some dogmatic schematization, can only be accomplished by taking into account this complex we have called the *colonial situation.*[2]

The colonial situation, which Balandier rightly believes to be the proper sociological conception of colonialism, would thus encompass the activities and even the dispositions of both the colonizer and the colonized, especially in their interactions. Balandier's *'la situation coloniale'* is a handsome contribution, the tenets of which have been largely ignored in subsequent attempts to master the multi-faceted reality of colonialism in Africa and Asia.

But Balandier was writing in the early fifties at the height of European colonial rule. His emphasis on the current realities was understandable, because even these were not sufficiently presented then. However, a major limitation of the concept of the 'colonial situation' is that it does not make sufficient allowance for the supra-individual consequences that flow from the colonial situation and that transcend the space-and-time specifications of colonization and reactions to colonization. Now that we have lived beyond colonial rule itself, we must update our political and sociological conceptualization of colonialism over and above the colonial situation. We must search for the totality of colonialism as a reality *sui generis,* as a phenomenon in its own right. So, then, in addition to the disparate activities of the colonizers and the colonized, and in addition to the totality of colonial rule, that is, the colonial situation, colonialism may be considered a *social movement* of epochal dimensions whose enduring significance lies in the *social formations* of supra-individual entities and constructs. These supra-individual formations developed from the volcano-sized social change provoked into existence by the confrontations, contradictions, and incompatibilities in the colonial situation.

Our approach deliberately ignores date demarcations. Periodization is a virtue in historiography. But it could turn into a vice if the demarcation dates of historiography are treated with sacred respect as iron gates in the study of social movements. Such dates as 1884, marking the Berlin Conference at which Africa was partitioned among European imperial nations, or 1870 – 1960, dates chosen by the editors of the five-volume *Colonialism in Africa 1870 – 1960*[3] as bracketing the colonial period, must all be treated as only rough guides by the social scientist concerned with colonialism. The major developments in colonialism blur across the dates of historiography. Similarly, we question the conceptual relevance of such terms as colonization and neo-colonialism. They may be useful in various ways, but since they derive from the view that colonialism can be terminated by legal proclamations, they fall short of the meaning assigned to colonialism. Colonialism cannot be terminated abruptly in one day or one year. Our use of colonialism, therefore, implies that the social formations that a social scientist is interested in could be traced to issues and problems that span the colonial situation into post-Independence social structures in Africa and Asia.

We are inclined to represent the social formations in colonialism as social structures in the sense in which Jean Piaget in 1968 and, particularly, Claude Levi-Strauss in 1963 understand social structures, as supra-individual models or ideal typifications of social existence. By social formation in colonialism we mean elaborated social models which are compositions of distinguishable sociological elements called institutions.

The distinction of this approach is that the study of colonialism transcends the particular activities of individuals, be they Frederick Lugard, Pandit Nehru, or Kwame Nkurumah. The more inclusive sense in which we represent colonialism here means precisely that individuals count for little in the larger intellectual arena of colonialism. In the light of the principles of structuralism, on which we lean for our conceptualization of colonialism, individual actors can at most be regarded as the handmaidens of history. In the same breath, we must emphasize that we should distinguish between the acts of creation by individuals and social formations which emerge by the force of their own existence from *social situations* irrespective of, sometimes in spite of, the wishes of individual actors. *Social formations* are social structures that emerge from the internal logic and force of their existence and are not amenable to the volitional acts of creation by individuals. Colonialism is important because it is more than acts of creation it embraces social formations whose dimensions even the most imaginative actors in the colonial situation could not predict.

To study colonialism in this manner is to seek to upgrade the intellectual potentials of the phenomenon of colonialism. Our view of colonialism is that it constitutes an epochal era in Africa. It represents a congenial of events and consequences which can be equated in significance to an epoch, in its Toynbean fullness. Indeed, we believe it will help our intellectual mastery of colonialism if we denote the attributes of epochs which colonialism in Africa shares with such dominant world epochs as the Industrial Revolution and the French Revolution.

While social change continues to be registered, as ever before, an epoch gives change a predictable direction. As it were epochs at once discipline and tame social change. Or, to put the matter differently, epochs make the future developments of events possible to forecast and determine.

A second attribute of epochs is that they introduce massive and enduring social formations. The developments that constitute an epoch shake up the extant social structures, then, in their place, they institute more permanent social forms and processes. A corollary of this second attribute of epochs is also noteworthy. Just as they tame and domesticate social change, epochs also consolidate social structures. The lava and rumblings that are shaken off by epochal movements get consolidated into enduring social structures, the outlines and contents of which become the subject matter for the study of social science.

A third attribute of epochs is that the social structures and the social processes that are formed from epochal movement retain their significance in the arena of human action and thought long after the epochs have ebbed away. Consequently, it is false analysis to restrict one's notion of epochal movement to events and processes that occurred only in the time-and-space definitions of the period or to judge its significance by its duration in time. Fourthly, epochal movements touch the lives and conduct of all persons in the areas covered by them. Epochs leave no room for individuals to choose to participate or not to participate in them. They are entirely supra-individual. They shape and mould human conduct and behaviour, or rather human action and thought find their full meaning within the confines of epochs that cover them.

Lastly, in the modern world at least, epochs serve to integrate their regions of impact into a consolidated world system, by re-arranging their location in such a world system. Epochs serve as the mechanism for the introduction of national and supra-national regional entities into the world system in which they thereafter function.

It is my contention that colonialism shares these attributes of epochs. It has not only led to the domestication and predictability of social change in Africa, it has also resulted in the formation of defineable forms of social structures. Moreover, the consequences of colonialism transcend the space and time boundaries of colonialism. The epochal significance of colonialism can be seen even more glaringly in the fact that it has helped to integrate Africa into the modern world system.

We are aware that our specialized approach to the study of colonialism runs against influential and established traditions of scholarship in African studies. Above all, it questions the tenets of the most illustrious and consolidated body of scholarship in Africa, namely the Ibadan school of History. Perhaps a little excursus into the sociology of knowledge with respect to the study of colonialism will be rewarding for the specification of our position.

Our attribution of social formations to colonialism challenges the doctrines of the two most advanced disciplines in African social studies. Social anthropology and social history developed in many ways, and for different reasons, as specialist fields for the study of precolonial Africa. Anthropology emerged as a help mate to the study of public administration in an effort to understand the political and social organizations of those African communities which the European colonizers were administering. The emphasis in social anthropology was, therefore, directed away from the study of colonialism and the colonial impact on African societies was reduced to the 'clash of cultures'. Blandier blames this neglect of the central problems of colonialism on the greater attention given to cultures rather than to societies and attributes it to the more or less conscious desire on the part of these anthropologists to avoid questioning the very foundations (and ideology) of the society to which they belong, the society of the colonial power.[4]

Anthropologists dominated the African field for a while. Their achievement, if limited in the longer run, was powerful while it lasted. But the image of Africa suffered considerable damage in that achievement, with the barbarism of the slave trade just before colonial rule and the poor 'image of Africa'[5] in Europe in this period, social anthropology's preoccupation with historical, 'primitive' and 'tribal' social organizations did further injury to the battered conception of Africa and rendered all that was African antithetical to world civilization. In addition, European historians even denied that Africa had any past worth remembering. As Jacob Ajayi sees the matter, the colonial rulers employed 'as a weapon of domination the demoralization and frustration that came from denying basic humanity to peoples of African descent by denying that they had a history'.[6]

It was in order to counteract this imperialist-motivated unsavoury account of Africa that the first organized programme of social history arose in Africa. The Ibadan School of History blossomed in the fifties and sixties to prove that the African past was not without its glories or that even the slave trade or missionary activities were not without their own components of civilized African actors. Championed by Kenneth Dike[7] and Jacob Ajayi,[8] its achievements were decisive in establishing new confidence and new traditions in African academia.

The strategies of the triumphant new social history were two. First, the Ibadan scholars went into the past beyond the time the anthropologists had covered to study past civilizations and kingdoms which existed long, long before the Europeans established their rule over the Africans. Secondly, the Ibadan School of History consciously and deliberately decreased the significance of colonialism in Africa. This view received careful articulation from Ajayi:

> In any long-term view of African history, European rule became just another episode. In relation to wars and conflicts of people, the rise and fall of empires, linguistic, cultural and religious change and the cultivation of new ideas and new ways of life, new economic orientations . . . in relation to all these, colonialism must be seen not as a complete departure from the African past, but as one episode in the continuous flow of African history.[6]

It is this viewpoint that has dominated African social history which is by far the most influential and established intellectual movement in Africa.

Jacob Ajayi summarizes the preoccupation of the Ibadan School of History with colonialism very well. He sees colonialism as an episode and not as we argue, an epoch. But it is noteworthy that colonialism in the Ibadan School is limited to colonialization and reactions to colonialization. It does not consider George Balandier's 'colonial situation'. It certainly falls far short of our characterization of colonialism in terms of social formations. It could be feared that the self-doubts and self-criticisms and the dwindling confidence that recently gripped the Ibadan School may be taken as less than a show of resilience of a famous school. The School shows clear signs of exhaustion borne out of limited theoretical premises. At least its paradigm of colonialism has imposed on it severe limitations in its potential for further expansion and renewal.

We believe there is an undiscovered territory in the realm of social formations which social historians and social scientists alike can explore in the study of colonialism. With the benefit of hindsight and of time-distance from the colonial

* From now onwards, I shall use the word *"we"* to represent the whole community of social scientists.

situation, future social historians will clearly see that the colonial period is unmatched in our history in terms of the growth and development of institutions, constructs, and social processes. In their model forms, they constitute what we refer to as social structures.

Obviously such a huge assemblage of new phenomena calls for some ordered classification. The resulting social formations are here grouped into three types. First, there are those social structures that are the transformations of pre-colonial indigenous institutions which, in their transformed state, operate within the new meanings and symbols of colonialism and in a widened new sociocultural system and framework. The moral and social order which formerly encased the pre-colonial indigenous institutions is burst by the social forces of colonialism, and they seek anchors in the changed milieu of colonialism.

The second type of social formation in colonialism consists of what we have chosen to call migrated social structures and constructs which were almost literally transported from metropolitan centres of the imperial West to Asia and Africa and grafted onto the new colonial situation. Such constructs as democracy and the rule of law with its peculiar Western connotations; such institutions as universities and national statehood; such establishments as bureaucracy and elected Parliaments: these and many more were models imported into the colonial situation, and they form the core of the resultant migrated social structures. Brought wholesale from Europe they acquire their own "life-world", to borrow a loaded term from Habermas,[10] and establish their unique parameters of social existence.

Thirdly, and lastly, there are what a social scientist could call emergent social structures in colonialism. These were not indigenous to Africa, and they were not brought from the outside. They were generated from the space-and-time span of colonialism. Although they have analogies in the west and elsewhere, these emergent social structures have a logic all their own and their peculiar situation in colonialism marks them out as distinct political and sociological structures, sometimes of baffling complexity. Urbanism in Africa and the formation of ethnic groups and ethnicity in colonialism are examples of emergent social structures which can be understood only when their emergence in colonialism is examined.

We should elaborate on each of these models of social formation in colonialism. We could start with the transformed indigenous social structures. These are indigenous only because tradition forms the core of their new existence. It seems fair to say that, from the point of view of those who have undergone colonialism, roughly speaking, all pre-colonial social structures and institutions are regarded as traditional and all colonial and post-colonial social formations are defined by the ordinary man and scholar alike as modern. But such a neat separation falsifies the changes that traditional institutions and social structures have experienced and the fragments of modernity they have picked up along the path of social change in colonialism. We prefer to speak of indigenous social structures and institutions because this epithet indigenous does not carry with it any notion of purity. The social formations we refer to are indigenous primarily in the sense that tradition forms the core of the social structures and institutions of which they are made.

A major consequence of colonialism was the new opportunity offered for expansion of pre-colonial social structures. But this opportunity led to the growth of certain institutions, retardation of some, and the demise of others. The changes that developed in colonialism led to the unprecedented growth of institutions that could take advantage of the new presence. The penetration of new alien institutions into pre-colonial societies was possible because the managers of many institutions took advantage of the new opportunities to re-organize and to re-order their network of rights and obligations by bringing in new entities and thereby enhancing their own positions vis-a-vis those of other institutions. These developments led to unwonted distinctions between certain elements of the social structures. This was possible because the new order made the logic of inter-dependence between the elements of pre-colonial social structures redundant.

Secondly, relative to these advantaged institutions, other elements of the pre-colonial social structures were retarded in stature. In other words, they remained at the level of the pre-colonial social structures. In their linkages with the other elements of the social structures they lost their rights, either outright or in diminished proportions, while their duties remained stagnant or even enhanced.

Thirdly, some institutions withered away in the reorganization and re-ordering of indigenous social structures in colonialism. The shedding of these institutions was necessitated by the attenuation of the functions they performed in the new order. Such institutions as were in direct opposition to the triumphant indigenous institutions that rose to high distinction in colonialism were defined out of existence in the new order. Indeed, such institutions derived their traditional importance primarily from their capabilities to limit the power of those indigenous institutions that now attained distinction in colonialism. The disadvantaged institutions suffered and some were shed from the transformed indigenous social structure.

Tradition benefited enormously from colonialism. By tradition we mean those surviving elements of pre-colonial indigenous social structures that members of various primordial groupings in the post-colonial period claim to be central to their social organizations. Such traditions as are claimed to be characteristic of these groups were strengthened by generalization in colonialism.

In pre-colonial societies in Africa, certain symbols of culture were reserved for those managers of institutions whose responsibility it was to guard the tradition of these societies. These might have been elders or members of the royalty. It was possible, of course, especially with reference to the nobility, that such symbols of tradition were monopolized by certain classes in order to distinguish them from the rest of society. Any attempts to appropriate these symbols by other groups could be punished with sanctions.

Examples of such symbols were plentiful in pre-colonial African societies. Thus, the higher classes wore elaborate and distinctive dresses that commoners were either not allowed to wear or which they could not afford. The story of the umbrella is particularly revealing. When first introduced into many parts of Africa, it was reserved for the nobility, particularly Kings. Dudley reported that the use of the umbrella by commoners was banned in Kanuri in Northern Nigeria well into the fifties.[11] Similarly, certain facial marks were in many instances the exclusive prerogative of certain classes. Also, if not in principle, in practice, polygamy was the attribute of nobility and its incidence was greatly limited among commoners.

But with colonialism there was a dramatic change. These restricted symbols of culture became substantiated and were generalized to all members of the distinct groups that were fighting for their separate recognition in the new order. Where in pre-colonial Africa the use of these symbols could be punished, their use by the general public in the new colonial order was rewarded by group approval. Thus the modern forms of traditional dress in Nigeria were royal or chieftain in origin, but they have spread to all levels of society with the help of the generalization which colonialism promoted. To put the matter differently, the generalization of symbols in colonialism consisted of making the elements of traditional high culture available for popular or general use.

There is a second type of generalization that came with colonialism and that resulted also in the expansion of tradition in Africa. There were quite a few societies that lacked certain institutions in their social structure which were present in other pre-colonial societies. This is to say, some social structures were underdeveloped and lacked key institutions which were present in more developed social structures in other pre-colonial societies. But the requirements of social existence in a new social order called for the establishment of these institutions and their integration or, if need be, imposition on other institutions to which they bore no relationships in pre-colonial indigenous social structures. This is the truth about a large number of 'traditional' social structures.

We may note two points here. First, there was a process of generalization that involved the down grading of the great kings, with the symbolic reduction of their titles from "Majesty" to "Highness", and the rise of minor chiefs to about the same status. Audrey Richards put the case of British-ruled Africa well

> The different pre-colonial indigenous authorities vary in type. They include kings with long lines of descent, princes, local rulers appointed to special posts by their king . . . clan elders and district or village headmen. . . In British Africa all authorities, however diverse, are described as chiefs [12]

This levelling process led to the expansion and promotion of chieftaincy in colonialism. Secondly, chieftaincy was generalized to areas where chiefs were not in existence before the colonial era. The rise of a class of so-called "warrant chiefs" was added an important element to tradition in these regions.[13] Measured by the number and the political strength of this new class of chiefs that sprouted up in colonialism, the era of colonial rule represents boom years for chieftaincy institutions in Africa.

There is a second way in which colonialism marked a qualitative shift in the structure of indigenous rulership in Africa. Again the pre-colonial situation is summed up very well by Richards.

> In many of these systems authority is maintained by means of an elaborate balance of power between the heads of different lineages, those of the king and of his agnatic kinsmen and those of the clan heads and hereditary chief-holders at court.[14]

These checks and balances in the structure of rulership were especially pronounced in the kingdoms. Kings and Emirs rose and fell based on their management of these checks and balances. The councils of state in Benin, Oyo, Ashanti, and the emirates of the Sudan in West Africa, of Buganda, Bunyoro and Toro in East Africa, and in other parts of pre-colonial Africa, in one way or the other restrained the power of kings. The pre-colonial era, in the nineteenth century, was clearly not of royal absolutism in Africa.

All these delicate checks and balances in the structures of indigenous rulership in colonialism were brushed aside or else considerably weakened to symbolic representations only. With the former kings this development led to a curious advantage.

> Thus we have the paradox of kings losing their sovereignty but as 'chiefs' increasing their powers over subjects because the traditional checks and balances to the exercise of their authority were neutralized.[15]

A second type of social formation occurred in Africa — migrated social structures which developed around models of social-organization imported to colonial Africa and engrafted onto the colonial situation. While the European components of these social structures form their core, they have acquired textures and variations in form that make them peculiarly African. In a real sense, these migrated social structures represent the outward expansion of European institutions to Africa.

We may deepen our knowledge of this expansion by contrasting it with an earlier form of European expansion to the Americas and Australasia in the seventeenth and eighteenth centuries. This earlier European expansion was essentially cultural. It was in the culture, not the organization, of Europe that the American colonialists took pride. In colonial Africa, it was the organization of

Europe, not its culture, that dazzled the colonized African. In a large sense, there was considerable resistance to the acceptance of European culture, but the organizational fragments that came with colonization were absorbed without discrimination. It is important to note that the European organizational pieces that came to us were virtually disembodied of their moral contents, of their substratum of implicating ethics. And yet the imported models were never engrafted onto any existing indigenous morality.

These two forms of European expansion have led to debilitating consequences, but in different directions. Louis Hartz has pointed out that what he calls the European fragments in the U.S., Canada, Latin America, Australia and even South Africa have experienced cultural immobility. Europe is able to advance in matters of culture and ideology, but these European fragments remain morally fixed with the elements of European culture they took away with them at their point of departure. In the words of Louis Hartz:

> There is a problem of traditionalism and change common to the societies that are fragments of the larger whole of European struck off in the course of revolution which brought the West into the modern world. For when a part of a European nation is detached from the whole of it, and hurled outward onto new soil, it loses its stimulus towards change that the whole provides. It lapses into a kind of immobility . . . in the realm of values and ideology. . . .[10]

We term this cultural fixation. European expansion to Africa, in the form of what could be called migrated social structures, has led to a different form of fixation. In post-colonial Africa, the models of the migrated social structures in the universities, civil service, and hospitals suffer from organizational fixation. We treat with respect the organization that we inherited from colonization and we are stuck with it. There is an organizational immobility in Africa largely because the morality and ethics that provide the stimulus for homegrown organizations in Europe for self-sustained refinement and expansion are absent from our migrated social structures.

In many instances, the organizational pieces that were brought to Africa were ones that were about to be modified or even discarded in Europe. As Van den Berghe has so courageously reminded us, the Oxbridge model of University that was given to universities like the Foray Bay college in Freetown, Ibadan, and Makerere in Uganda has resulted in these universities being not the more democratic version which was evolving during Britain's post-world war II Labour Government days but the Edwardian stereotype which the founders of these universities remembered from their own student days. As usual, the were thus a relatively low-cost colonial adaptation of an academic model which in Britain itself was already obsolete.[17]

So, just as 'the French of Quebec resembles Norman of the seventeent century, but in Paris modern French is spoken',[18] these universities. founded

time when English universities were searching for a new future in the post-World War II period, retain a lingering "Edwardian" structure in organization and administration long after English universities have progressed beyond the forties.

We now turn to the third type of social formation in colonialism, namely, emergent social structures. The inner character of colonialism is revealed best by the social formations that were internally generated by the social forces of colonialism in Africa. They grew with colonialism and in colonialism. Emergent social structures are the self-generations of colonialism. They emerged to meet societal needs which indigenous social structures and the migrated social structures could not fulfill in the new colonial environment. Unlike the first two types of social formations in colonialism, emergent social structures are difficult to discern for two major reasons. First, while indigenous social structures and migrated social structures represent formal aspects of the colonial and post-colonial situations, the emergent social structures represent the informal elements of colonialism. Secondly, emergent social structures are very often consciously smeared with tradition or modernity to give them the appearance of ultra-tradition or modernity.

My experience in teaching Public Administration and colonialism is that emergent social structures yield greater room for controversies, largely because the examples of this phenonenon are not generally acceptable, especially among people who grew up in these structures. We could here give an example of ethnic groups as emergent social structures. In pre-colonial Africa, the dominant form of social organization consisted of tribal societies which were geographically defined and in which persons found their total existence. With colonialism the integrity of tribal societies was destroyed. Popular views to the contrary, these tribal societies were not replaced case by case with ethnic groups. In many instances what resulted were ethnic groups that are composites of several entities. In 1800 an Ekiti man would have been astonished if he were called a "Yoruba man" whom he understood, if he was so knowledgeable, as a man from Oyo. In any case, an Ekiti would probably need an interpreter in order to communicate effectively with a Yoruba man in 1800. Eluwa, the secretary of the Ibo state union, confessed that by the early 1950's he participated in persuading many "Ibo's" to accept that they were Ibos. Hausa is a composition of several tribal organizations that found their common relevance in modern Nigeria.

We will give another example of a construct that falls into our model of emergent social structure. Tribes, with geographical boundaries clearly defined and with an autonomy of existence in the realm of values and morality, were dislocated by the forces of colonialism because these tribes were incompatible with the new widened integrated existence in colonialism. And yet under the aegis of colonialism there has developed a new phenomenon of tribalism. In spite of their verbal affinities, there is only a negative relationship between the terms tribes and tribalism. Tribalism is a construct that defines a model of behaviour that is unacceptable in our new poly-ethnic relationships. Tribalism does have a linkage with tribes, not because tribes exist any more but because the acts that constitute tribalism have atavistic aura of behaviours which are considered appropriate for a past form of existence in the tribal setting, but which are regarded as destructive in poly-ethnic systems of social life. A tribalist is a non-tribesman who exhibits anti-social behaviour in a non-tribal setting in such a way as to threaten the new forms of existence with reversion to a past form of restricted tribal social organization. A tribalist is never a tribesman and a tribesman can never be a tribalist. Our overall point is that the phenomenon of tribalism is not only unique to modern post-colonial Africa and perhaps Asia, but it was in fact generated in the re-organizations and re-orderings that were provoked in colonialism.

Let us now touch on an area in the social formations in colonialism that helps to differentiate and define the three models of social structures that we have sought to distinguish. This concerns the development of the moral order in colonialism. The social structures, which social scientists study, even in the form of abstract models that we adopt here, are shot through by underlying notions of morality, usually in sublimated forms. Whether it is the economic system, the sociologist's social structure, the political scientist's public realm, or even the psychologist's personal conception of superego injunctions, in any of these concerns of the social scientist there is an underlying normative order, a modernized sociological representation of concern with the philosopher's morality. Such morality, or its sublime reference, has been tied to the concept of society, and the partial exception of the absence of morality in International Relations can be understood in terms of its extra-societal dimensions. The state of anomie, or normlessness, that Emile Durkheim (1893)[19] discussed and the amoral patterns of politics in Southern Italy that Edward Banfield (1958)[20] described are significant because they are regarded as abnormal in Western experience. The rule in the West is that behaviour can be classified as either moral or immoral.

An important distinction of colonialism is that it has bred a duality of moral perspectives. In the colonized world of Africa there are two broad spheres of behaviours. In addition to the broad sphere of moral and immoral behaviours, there is another deep area of behaviour that is governed by amorality or lack of morality. It is this institutionalization of amorality as a central principle of social existence in the colonial and, now, post-colonial situations that poses a special problem area in the study of colonialism.

Broadly speaking, it seems fair to say that there is moral presence in the working of the transformed indigenous social structures and of the emergent of social structures. But the sprawling migrated social structures of colonialism were originally and have largely remained disinvested of any moral definitions. This amorality is particularly pronounced in the various apparatuses of the state and in the conduct of those aspects of public life associated with the migrated social structures. Challenged about the "morality" in his style of politics which induced the destruction and burning of houses of political opponents outside his own ethnic group but within his domain of political control in pre-civil war Nigeria, a prominent Nigerian politician retorted, 'politics is not church'. It was his own way of saying, 'politics is amoral'.

Notes

1. Aime Cesaire, *Discourse on Colonialism* (New York: Monthly Review Press, 1955), pp. 10 – 11.
2. Balandier, G. "La Situation Coloniale Approache Theoretique," *Cahiers International de Socioloque,* 11:35. Reprinted in Immanuel Wallwerstern, ed., *Social Change: The Colonial Situation* (John Wiley and Sone, 1966), pp. 34 – 61.
3. Gann, L.H. and Duignan, P. *Colonialism in Africa,* 5 vols. (London: Cambridge University Press, 1969).
4. Balandier, p. 56.
5. Curtin, P.D. *The Image of Africa: British Ideas and Action, 1780 – 1850,* (Ile-Ife: University of Ife Press).
6. Ade Ajayi, J.F. "In Search of Relevance in the Humanities," Festac Colloquim, 1977.
7. Dike, K.O. *Trade and Politics in the Niger Delta* (London: Oxford University Press, 1956.
8. Ade Ajayi, J.K. *Christian Missions in Nigeria: the Making of a New Elite* (London: Longmans, 1965).
9. Ade Ajayi, J.K. "The Continuity of African Institutions Under Colonialism." in *Emerging Themes in African History,* ed. T.O. Ranger (Nairobi: 1968), (230 p.) at pp. 189 – 200 East African Publishing House.
10. Jurgen Habermas, *Legitimation Crisis* 1973 (London: Heinemann Education Books, 1976), p. 192.
11. Dudley, B.J. *Parties and Politics in Northern Nigeria* (London: Frank Cass (Co. Ltd., 1968), 352p. illus.
12. Audrey Richards, *East African Chiefs* (London: Faber and Faber, 1960), p. 13.
13. Afigbo, A.E. *The Warrant Chiefs: Indirect Rule in Southwestern Nigeria 1891 – 1929* (London: Longmans, 1972).
14. Richards, p. 15.
15. Crowder, M. and Obaro Ikeme, eds., *West African Chiefs: Their Changing Status under Colonial Rule and Independence* (Ile-Ife: University of Ife Press, 1970), 453p. illus.
16. Louis Hartz, *The Founding of New Societies* (New York: Harcourt and Brace, 1964), p. 336.
17. Pierre Louis Van den Berghe, *Power and Privilege in an African University* (London: Routledge and Kegan Paul, 1973).
18. Hartz, p. 12.
19. Durkheim, E. *The Division of Labour in Society* 1893 (New York: Free Press, 1933).
20. Banfield, E.C. The Moral Basis of a Backward Society (New York: The Free Press, 1958).

References

Afigbo, A.E. 1972). *The Warrant Chiefs: Indirect Rule in Southeastern Nigeria 1891 – 1929.* London: Longmans.

Ajayi, J.F. Ade. 1965. *Christian Missions in Nigeria: the Making of a New Elite.* London: Longmans.

______. 1968. "The Continuity of African Institutions Under Colonialism". In *Emerging Themes of African History.* Ed. T.O. Ranger, Nairobi:

______. 1977, "In Search of Relevance in the Humanities." Festac Colloquium.

Banfield, E.C. 1958. *The Moral Basis of a Backward Society*. New York: The Free Press.

Balandier, G. 1951. "La Situation Coloniale: Approache Theoretique." *Cahiers International de Socioloque,* 11: 44 – 79. Reprinted in Immanuel Wallwerstern, ed. *Social Change: The Colonial Situation.* John Wiley and Sons, 1966, pp. 34 – 61.

Cesaire, Aime. 1955. *Discourse on Colonialism*. New York: Monthly Review Press.

Crowder, M. and Obaro Ikeme, eds. 1970. *West African Chiefs: Their Changing Status under Colonial Rule and Independence.* Ile-Ife: University of Ife Press.

Curtin, P.D. 1964. *The image of Africa: British ideas and Action, 1780 – 1850.* Madison: The University of Wisconsin Press.

Dike, K.O. 1956. *Trade and Politics in the Niger Delta.* London: Oxford University Press.

Dudley, B.J. 1968. *Parties and Politics in Northern Nigeria.* London: Frank Cass & Co. Ltd.

Durkheim, E. 1893. *The Division of Labour in Society.* New York: Free Press, 1933.

Gann, L.H. and P. Duignan, 1969. *Colonialism in Africa.* 5 vols. London: Cambridge University Press.

Habermas, J. 1973. *Legitimate Crisis*. London: Heinemann Education Books, 1976.

Hartz, L. 1964 *The Founding of New Societies.* New York: Harcourt and Brace.

Richards, A. 1960. *East African Chiefs.* London: Faber and Faber.

Van den Berghe, Pierre Louis. 1973. *Power and Privilege in an African University.* London: Routledge and Kegan Paul

The Growth of the Pan-African Movement, 1893–1927

P. Olisanwuche Esedebe

Two broad periods of Pan-Africanism may be distinguished: the period when most of the major constituent concepts were worked out and the period when, with some simplification, talk gave way to action. From 1893 onwards politically conscious men of African blood began to summon Pan-African meetings and to organise themselves into pressure groups, thus transforming Pan-African notions into a movement.

W. E. B. DuBois' assertion that the London conference of 1900 put the word 'Pan-African' into the dictionaries for the first time is largely responsible for the orthodox but erroneous view that that gathering was the first Pan-African convocation ever held. The Chicago congress of 1893 has an earlier and better claim. Opened on 14 August 1893, it lasted a whole week. Among the participants were Africans and persons of African descent in the New World, notably Alexander Crummell, Bishop Henry M. Turner (founder of the African Methodist Episcopal Churches in Sierra Leone and Liberia), the Liberian Massaquoi, Bishop Alexander Walters of the African Methodist Episcopal Zion Church and the Afro-American Frederick Perry Noble, secretary to the conference. European scientists, explorers and missionaries were also present; most of them had come to Chicago primarily for the World Columbian Exhibition held there that summer.

Edward Blyden and Booker T. Washington had promised papers which either failed to arrive in time or were never sent. The Rev. James Johnson's address was read by proxy. Altogether a hundred papers were given, most of them by Blacks, and on topics which included the predicament of African descendants in the New World, the role of Liberia in the regeneration of the African race and the duty of Afro-Americans to their kith and kin in the homeland. Contributing to the discussion Turner urged African exiles to return to the fatherland without further delay. His visits to the continent made him keenly aware of the dangers posed by the great Scramble, in particular to Liberia's independence.

The *Advance*, a local newspaper, considered the congress to be as notable as the Pan-Presbyterian, Pan-Methodist, Pan-Anglican, Pan-Missionary and Pan-Congregational convocations held in recent years. But in the opinion of the journal, 'none signified more than this Pan-African conference'.

Resentment at increasing European interference in the fatherland also found expression at another congress, called this time in Atlanta, Georgia (USA) in December 1895 under the auspices of the Steward Missionary Foundation for Africa of the Gammon Theological Seminary. Among those in attendance were Orishatuke Faduma, a Sierra Leonean of Nigerian extraction educated at Fourah Bay College, Freetown, and the Afro-American John Henry Smyth (1844–1908) who had seen service in Liberia as the United States' resident minister and consul and had been honoured by President Richard W. Johnson of Liberia with the title 'Knight Commander of the Liberian Order of African Redemption'. Defending 'native Christianity' Faduma maintained that there was no necessary connection between spiritual salvation and the adoption of European usages. He discarded his foreign name (William James Davies) just as Mojola Agbebi (formerly D. B. Vincent) and the Ghanaian S. R. B. Attoh Ahuma (formerly S. R. B. Solomon) had done. Faduma demanded 'a Christian life and thought expressed in Africa, not after the manner of a Frenchman, an American, or an Englishman but assimilated to Africa'. In his address 'The African in Africa and the African in America' Smyth attributed what he considered 'the appalling conditions' in the fatherland to the activities of European adventurers. European contact, he lamented, had not only led to the enslavement of millions of Black men in the Western hemisphere but was now threatening to destroy indigenous political systems and cultural values.

It was partly against the background of this growing anti-colonial sentiment among the African diaspora that the African Association was launched in England on 24 September 1897 mainly through the initiative of the West Indian barrister Henry Sylvester Williams. As the centre of wide imperial and missionary interests Great Britain was a natural focus for a protest movement. The organisation aimed to encourage a feeling of unity among men of African blood and protect their interests by circulating accurate information on matters affecting their rights and direct appeals to the metropolitan government. The founders of the association were convinced that the time had arrived when the voice of Black men should be heard independently in their own affairs and that this could best be achieved by a pressure group with headquarters in London, the imperial capital. Three patrons served it: J. Otonba Payne, a former registrar of the Supreme Court of Lagos; Dr Mojola Agbebi, a pastor of the United African Church, Lagos, and D. Augustus Straker, a lawyer, probably from the West Indies. Sylvester Williams, Otonba Payne and the Rev. H. Mason Joseph, a Master of Arts from Antigua, were made honorary secretary, treasurer, and president respectively, while Moses da Rocha of Lagos became assistant secretary and the Sierra Leonean Bachelor of Arts, E. A. Gibson, vice-president.

In July 1900 the organisation convened a Pan-African meeting with Alexander Walters in the chair. It was attended by 32 delegates from various parts of the African world, including W. E. B. DuBois, Benito Sylvain, then *aide-de-camp* to Emperor Menelik II of Ethiopia*, the Trinidadian medical practitioner John Alcindor, J. R. Archer, a prominent West Indian resident in Battersea district of London, and H. Sylvester Williams. From Africa itself came F. R. S. Johnson, a former Liberian attorney-general, G. W. Dove, a Sierra Leonean councillor, and J. Otonba Payne. Though Blyden, surprisingly, was absent, some of his ideas on the African past and arguments in defence of race individuality were echoed in the discussions. The ravages caused by European colonialism, the suppression of men of

* Benito Sylvain (1868–1915) has been ignored as an early exponent of Pan-African ideas. A Haitian by birth, he was a delegate to the Brussels Anti-Slavery Convention of 1891, where he read a paper, 'L'évolution de la race noire', which was full of Pan-African sentiments.

3.1. J. Otonba Payne: patron of the African Association

African blood in America, Europe and southern Africa as well as the problems facing Haiti, Ethiopia and Liberia were also considered.

At the end of the deliberations a statement entitled 'To the Nations of the World' was despatched to sovereigns in whose territories persons of African extraction might be found. A separate memorial protesting against the many injustices suffered by Africans and their descendants in the British empire was sent to Queen Victoria. The conference then set up a permanent Pan-African Association with a secretariat presumably to replace the African Association with offices at 61–62 Chancery Lane, London. Officers were elected for a term of two years as follows: A. Walters (president), the Rev. H. B. Brown (vice-president) and H. S. Williams (secretary). An executive committee of four men and two women was elected to assist the central body. Emperor Menelik and the presidents of Haiti and Liberia were made honorary members of the Pan-African Association. Branches were to be started in Africa, the Caribbean and the United States. Branch officers elected included Benito Sylvain (Ethiopia), Bishop J. F. Holly (Haiti), Edwin Vin Loch (South Africa), J. Otonba Payne (Lagos) and DuBois (USA). A conference of the Pan-African Association was to be held every two years, so a second congress would meet in 1902 in the United States, a third in Haiti in 1904.

As an attempt to institutionalise Pan-Africanism the Pan-African Association had great symbolic value and was therefore of considerable historical significance. However, its achievements did not amount to much. *The Pan-African*, launched in October 1901 and edited by H. S. Williams, promised to feature the progress and culture of the African world in subsequent monthly issues. It did not survive the maiden issue.

In March of the same year Williams had travelled to the Caribbean to involve his own people in the association's work and a meeting was held in Kingston (Jamaica) with the aim of starting a local branch. But while he was away some of the officers dissolved the association, allegedly for lack of funds. Williams and Walters hurried to London to re-establish the organisation. New appointments were made to the executive committee to replace those considered to have resigned: Bishop Small from Pennsylvania, Henry Smyth, Otonba Payne, the South African Tengo Jabavu, Lieutenant Lazare of Trinidad and the medical doctor R. N. Love. Born in Nassau (Bahamas) and educated in England and on the Continent, Love had spent many years in Jamaica fighting for the uplift of the Black masses. Williams was re-elected secretary until the next congress met in 1902, but the proposed conference never took place. Williams went to South Africa to practise law and was the first Black man to be registered there as a lawyer. He returned to England and then to the West Indies where he died in 1911. With his death the Pan-African Association lapsed into obscurity.

After the collapse of the Pan-African Association the task of keeping Pan-African ideals alive and airing colonial grievances was left to individuals. For example, seizing the opportunity offered by the death of Mary Kingsley, Blyden further elaborated the concept of the African Personality in a series of articles written for the *Sierra Leone Weekly News*. Mojola Agbebi gave a sermon that won Blyden's admiration and that of prominent persons of African descent in the New World. The occasion was the celebration of the first anniversary of the African Church in 1902. Under the guise of exposing the defects of the version of Christianity being offered to Africans, Agbebi drew attention to the discrepancy between the words and deeds of the imperialists. The publication of Mojola Agbebi's sermon in *The Sierra Leone Weekly News* for 14 March 1903 provoked widespread comment. 'This is the first time', exclaimed Blyden, 'I have known of a native African, imbued with European culture, uttering views so radically different from the course of his training, but intrinsically African and so valuable for the guidance of his people'. The Afro-American journalist John Edward Bruce (1856–1923) was no less impressed. Considering the sermon worthy of wider notice than it was likely to receive in the West African press, he republished it in the United States. In a congratulatory letter to Agbebi he wrote:

> I thank you with all my heart, dear good sir, and wish it were possible for me to shake your hand and tell you how proud I am of one, who is unquestionably an honour to the African Church and the African race . . . I am black all over, and am proud of my beautiful black skin, and that of my forbears, as the *blackest* man in Africa.

The cult of the African Personality reached its zenith in Edward Blyden's series of articles on 'African Life and Customs' in *The Sierra Leone Weekly News*. In 1908 they were reprinted in London in book form under the same title.

3.2. J. Casely Hayford, seen here (second right, seated) as a member of the 1920 London deputation of the National Congress of British West Africa

In appreciation of the articles also published in *The Sierra Leone Weekly News* Casely Hayford seized the opportunity to castigate the Europeanised African. In his opinion such a man was useless for the task of directing African life and African idiosyncrasies along the line of natural and healthy development. 'The superfine African gentleman, who at the end of every second or third year, talks of a run to Europe, lest there should be a nervous break-down, may be serious or not, but is bound in time to be refined off the face of the African Continent.' Like Blyden and Africanus Horton, Hayford saw a university rooted in African soil as 'the means of revising current ideas regarding the African; or raising him in self-respect; and of making him an efficient co-worker in the uplifting of men to nobler efforts'. He considered professorships in African languages to be the safest road to self-preservation. Casely Hayford subsequently

3.3. King Lewanika of Barotseland

expanded these ideas into a book, *Ethiopia Unbound: Studies in Race Emancipation.*

This growing racial awakening and the sporadic excursions into the African past were canalised in the Negro Society for Historical Research. Launched in the United States in 1911 by John E. Bruce and Arthur A. Schomburg, a Puerto Rican of African origin, the society seems to have been inspired by the American Negro Academy started by Alexander Crummell on 5 March 1897. Both Bruce and Schomburg were associated with the American Negro Academy, the former as an executive member, the latter as sometime president. Among the New World members of the Negro Society for Historical Research may be mentioned W. E. B. DuBois and the philosopher Alain Locke, the first Black American Rhodes Scholar at Oxford and editor of the anthology *The New*

3.4. Booker T. Washington

Negro and a leading spirit of the Harlem Renaissance. The African members included King Lewanika of Baroteseland (now an integral part of Zambia) who was made honorary president, Edward Blyden, Casely Hayford, Mojola Agbebi, Moses de Rocha, the South African F. Z. S. Peregrino and Duse Mohamed Effendi (later Duse Mohamed Ali). Educated at King's College, University of London, where he read history, Duse Mohamed was the son of an Egyptian army officer and his Sudanese wife. Offended by a statement on Egypt by Theodore Roosevelt of America, Duse Mohamed wrote his only book, *In The Land Of The Pharaohs. A Short History of Egypt from the fall of Ismail to the Assassination of Boutros Pasha*, which was acclaimed by the English press as the first book on Egypt by an Egyptian. 'His new fame got him the job of organising the entertainment for the First Universal Races Congress, which apparently he did with great success'. This congress was held in London from 26 to 29 July 1911 to discuss the relations between the so-called White and Coloured peoples. Among the participants were John Tengo Jabavu, DuBois, Mojola Agbebi and Edward Blyden.

It was the Races Congress which inspired Duse Mohamed to launch a journal in collaboration with Casely Hayford. Called *The African Times and Orient*

3.5. Marcus Garvey

Review: politics, literature, art and commerce: a monthly journal devoted to the interests of the Coloured races of the World, it ran for six years beginning in July 1912 and enjoyed a wide circulation in the United States, the West Indies, Egypt, East and West Africa as well as Europe and a number of Asian countries including India and Japan. Its chief support, however, came from West Africa and Casely Hayford is believed to have made substantial financial contributions to keep it going. African exiles such as John Edward Bruce, Booker T. Washington and William H. Ferris (author of *The African Abroad*) contributed articles. Biographies of such prominent men of African origin as Mensah Sarbah of the Gold Coast, the Egyptian nationalist Mustapha Kamil. J. E. K. Aggrey and the Afro-American scholar William Scarborough, as well as the musician

Samuel Taylor Coleridge, were a feature of the magazine. Another was the day-to-day reports and speeches on Africa made in the British Parliament.

The year Duse Mohamed launched his magazine was also the year Edward Blyden died in Sierra Leone. The first leader of comparable stature to emerge after his death was Marcus Garvey. It was he more than any other person who introduced the ideas of an African Nationality and the African Personality, hitherto restricted to a handful of intellectuals, to the uninformed masses in the villages and streets of the African world.

After a sound elementary school education supplemented by a pupil-teachers' course in the coastal town of St. Ann's Bay, Jamaica, where he was born on 17 August 1887, he joined Benjamin's Printery in Kingston. He was so proficient that at twenty he became master printer and foreman of one of the largest local firms. This in itself constituted a spectacular achievement since printing was a first-class trade in Jamaica at that time and some of the foremen of the big plants were imported from England and Canada. To keep pace with the ever-rising cost of living the printers' union went on strike in 1909. Though Garvey was promised an increase in pay he led the strike. 'He did the job efficiently, organised public meetings and for the first time demonstrated those oratorical talents which were to magnetise the Negro people and stir the world.' The agitators received money from sympathetic American printers but the union treasurer absconded with it, thereby shattering the morale of the strikers. As a result Garvey went to work at the Government Printing Office.

Still dissatisfied with the plight of the Blacks around him, he gave up his new job to embark on an extensive tour that took him to about a dozen countries in South and Central America, where he was shocked by the miserable conditions under which the Black diaspora toiled. In Jamaica, to which he returned in 1911, he learnt of the equally dehumanising conditions in the fatherland itself, thanks to the revelations of Jamaican and Barbadian ex-service men. As members of the West Indies regiment, these soldiers had been used by the British to subdue Africans and take their lands. All this made an indelible impression on Garvey's mind so that he became determined to end what he now considered the White man's duplicity and callousness. In 1912 he went to England and joined the staff of *The African Times and Orient Review* run by Duse Mohamed.

Meanwhile Chief Alfred Sam, an Asante trader in the United States, held out the hope of a better life in his country to thousands of frustrated African descendants in Oklahoma and Kansas. In July 1911 he set up the Akim Trading Company in New York and bought a ship, the *Liberia*, to promote emigration and trade. With the active support of such other West Africans as Orishatuke Faduma and the Rev. James Johnson, the chief launched the 'African Movement' which among other things aimed to maintain the cultural integrity of the African world. To achieve the economic independence of the race, it sought to develop the continent industrially, to build and acquire ocean liners for transportation and to establish institutions of higher learning.

Whatever Garvey owed to Alfred Sam's back-to-Africa campaign and discussions with Duse Mohamed is clearly outweighed by the inspiration the Jamaican derived from his compatriot Dr R. N. Love, a former executive member of the defunct Pan-African Association. We have the testimony of Mrs Amy Jacques-Garvey (author of *Garvey and Garveyism*, London, 1970) that Dr Love was the first man of African blood to make a deep impression on her husband.

It was before his sojourn in England that Garvey conceived the idea, however vague, of liberating the African race on a permanent basis. He was conscious, as Blyden had been, that the members of the race were disorganised and unlike the Jews possessed no financial or economic power. What people, Garvey asked, could hold their own in these competitive days against groups and communities that owned vast accumulated reserves and therefore enjoyed immense sustaining power? His travels revealed that whether in the western hemisphere or Europe or even Africa the Black man was treated like a beast of burden without political and economic rights. Would not a 'Negro National State' (Blyden would have said an 'African nationality') controlled by men of African blood solve the problems of the members of the race wherever they might be? Would not such a state set up businesses to be managed by Africans and their descendants and run for the benefit and greater glory of the race? Would not the Black man then rise to any height his ability merited instead of by the grace of his oppressors and detractors? For Garvey a people without authority and power was a race without respect. Like Blyden, Garvey realised that authority and respect were impossible without the rehabilitation of African values. Hence both men urged the Black man to cultivate self-respect, race pride, love of his dark skin, woolly hair, broad nose and thick lips. Little wonder the Jamaican felt disgusted by the affectation of several Africans he encountered in London. To him these 'intellectual monkeys' (Ki-Zerbo's phrase) appeared to be apologetic Black Englishmen rather than Africans proud of their race and complexion.

After presenting his ideas to some English liberals who approved of them, Garvey returned to Jamaica in July 1914 and laid his plan of redeeming the African people before the public. In August Garvey formed the Universal Negro Improvement and Conservation Association and the African Communities' League which subsequently attracted world attention as the Universal Negro Improvement Association.

The UNIA sought to improve the conditions of the African peoples with a view to establishing a nation in Africa where Black men would be given the opportunity to develop by themselves without creating the hatred and animosity that then existed in countries of the White race through African exiles rivalling them for the highest and best positions in government, politics and industry. The organisation believed in the rights of all men: Yellow, White and Black. The White race had a right to peaceful possession and occupation of its own territory. In the same way the Yellow and Black peoples had their rights. Only an honest and a liberal consideration of such rights could bring blessing and peace to the world. Other aims of the UNIA included the establishment of educational institutions, including universities, a world-wide commercial and industrial intercourse and agencies in the principal countries of the world for the protection of Africans and their descendants.

Though Garvey met little enthusiasm in his native island and no further encouragement from his British friends who were now preoccupied with the Great War, he did not abandon his plans. He kept on agitating almost single-handed with his limited means.

Meanwhile Alfred Sam's venture, remarkable in that it was led not by an African descendant but by an African, had at last got off the ground. In 1914 the *Liberia* carried some 200 exiles for resettlement on the Gold Coast. When the vessel anchored in Freetown harbour the local Anti-Slavery and Aborigines' Protection Society seized the opportunity to accord the emigrants a formal welcome. As its spokesman, James Johnson declared that African descendants in the New World were destined to play a crucial role in 'the upbuilding of our desolated Aboriginal Homeland, the repeopling of it, the regenerating of West Africa religiously, intellectually, morally, socially and otherwise'. With steamships engaged in intercontinental commerce and the development of local industries, Black men would achieve a great measure of economic independence. The possession of liners would further facilitate 'the gradual return of many of our exiled brethren in America, with all the enlightenment they have acquired, to the great Fatherland, the ancestral home which they, we understand, are longing for, and which has on her own part been very long waiting for them'.

The *Liberia* finally reached its destination in mid-January 1915. But the enthusiasm with which the exiles were received was robbed of warmth by the inadequate provisions made for them. The result was that only about sixty of them settled permanently; the rest of them found their way back to America. The impact of the 'African Movement' proved ephemeral largely due to unfavourable war-time conditions, the increasing loss of confidence in the chief himself and above all the opposition of the British Government. Not only did the colonial regime in Sierra Leone force the *Liberia* to spend nearly seven weeks in Freetown harbour, it even demanded a special tax of £25 per head. The colonial administration based in Accra was equally hostile. All this combined to cripple the movement.

Undaunted by the collapse of Alfred Sam's venture and the lukewarm reception accorded to the UNIA by Jamaicans, Garvey moved to New York in 1916 to try his luck in Harlem. Exploiting the contemporary excitement over the doctrines of 'democracy' and 'self-determination' which war-aims propaganda, especially Woodrow Wilson's famous Fourteen Points, had precipitated, Garvey put forward his plans for freeing Africa.

Garvey's ideas won immediate approval among American Blacks partly because of his fearless personality and partly because the circumstances were propitious. The Great War, British and American leaders claimed, was being fought to make the world safe for democracy. But with the end of hostilities they appeared to be unaware of the oppressive conditions facing demobilised soldiers of African blood and their countries as well. Garvey only needed to open his mouth for the disillusioned masses to embrace him. Thus the UNIA of New York fame was born. In January 1918 its organ, the weekly *Negro World* appeared, remaining in circulation until 1933 when the *Blackman* succeeded it. In its first years the former was published in English, French and Spanish. A flag for the race—a horizontal tricolour of red, black and green—was adopted. An African national anthem set to martial music was produced.

Garvey struck African Redemption Medals and created orders of chivalry with such titles as: Duke of the Nile; Earl of the Congo; Viscount of the Niger; Baron of the Zambesi; Knights of the Distinguished Order of Ethiopia, Ashanti and Mozambique. Though born into a Catholic family, Garvey set up an African Orthodox Church with Archbishop Alexander McGuire, an Afro-West Indian theologian, as its head. He also created the Black Star Steamship Company to carry African merchandise to the United States.

'Africa for the Africans', 'Ethiopia Awake', 'Back to Africa', 'A Black Star Line'. These were the slogans Garvey used to capture the hearts of Africans and their descendants. Contrary to popular belief, his aim was not to transport the Blacks in America to Africa. As he himself explained 'We are not preaching any doctrines to ask all the Negroes . . . to leave for Africa. The majority of us may remain here, but we must send our scientists, our mechanics and our artisans, and let them build the railroads, let them build the great educational and other institutions necessary'. Garvey wanted to end the exploitation of Africa and to use Africa's riches for the benefit of men of African blood. In the Congo villagers described him as an African who had been lost in America but was about to return in order to save his brethren. The story is well-known of how the King of Swaziland told a friend that he knew the names of only two Black men in the western hemisphere: the boxer Jack Johnson, who defeated his White opponent, and Marcus Garvey. When the Governor of British Honduras banned *The Negro World*, Garveyites staged the July 1919 uprising at Belize.

By 1919 Garvey had formed branches of the UNIA in many parts of the world. These branches held themselves in readiness for what was commonly but wrongly believed would be the first international convention of the Negro peoples. Plans for the convention included the drafting of grievances and a Declaration of Rights, the election of international officers and the discussion of special reports on political and economic aspects of the African problem.

The convention eventually took place throughout the month of August 1920 in Madison Square Garden, the largest auditorium in New York City. Delegates came from different regions of Africa, Brazil, Colombia, Haiti, Panama, the West Indies as well as Canada, England and France. About 25 000 representatives were inside the auditorium and thousands who could not be seated overflowed the adjoining streets.

In a long speech punctuated with applause Garvey presented his case for Africa's Redemption. After five hundred years of oppression Negroes were determined to suffer no longer. Despite promises made to Africans and their descendants during the Great War, they were deprived of the democratic rights for which they had shed their blood. Black American soldiers returning from the battlefields of Europe were beaten up or lynched in their uniforms in many Southern States. Since the other races had countries of their own, it was time the four hundred million Negroes of the world claimed Africa for themselves. If Europe was for the Europeans, Africa should belong to Africans and their descendants. Concluding, he warned that the African exiles were poised to return to their fatherland. He gave notice to the tenants, the European imperialists and colonists, to quit or face forcible eviction.

3.6. Black Americans lynched by a White mob

Officers of the Supreme Executive Council were then elected. The position of potentate, titular head of all the Black people of the world, was earmarked for an African residing in the continent. The Mayor of Monrovia, Gabriel Johnson, was chosen in view of the plans of the UNIA to send the first batch of repatriates there. George O. Marke, a Sierra Leonean civil servant educated at Oxford, became deputy potentate. The office of provisional president went to Garvey.

Similar conventions took place between 1920 and 1925. During the quinquennium two major deputations were despatched. One went to Liberia to secure land for the settlement of the diaspora. The other delegation was sent in September 1922 with a five-page petition to the League of Nations, Geneva. Signed by the executive officers of the UNIA on behalf of the Third Annual Convention of the Negro Peoples of the World, the petition recalled that the service rendered by the Black race during the war of 1914–1918 had enabled the Allies 'to defeat Germany in German East Africa, in German South-West Africa, in Togoland, the Cameroons, and other parts of the continent, as well as to defeat the common foe in Europe'. As a reward for this 'splendid service' the UNIA prayed the League to surrender to them 'for the purpose of racial development the mandates now given to the Union of South Africa; namely, German East Africa, (excluding Tanganyika) and German South-West Africa'. The petitioners were confident that if the territories were ceded as requested the

UNIA would be able to bring them within two decades to a level of development that would 'prove to the world and to the League our ability to govern ourselves'.

Overcome by impatience and demonstrating the impact of Garvey on some of his African followers, a West African Garveyite, John H. Davies of Sierra Leone, unilaterally issued a circular dated 6 December 1922 to the European metropolitan governments affirming that 'The expression "Africa for the Africans" is not merely a statement of fact but one of truth' and deploring White supremacy as detrimental to the interest, peace and happiness of the subject races. In the interest of world peace there should be a turning point. On the assumption that this was happening he deemed

> it necessary to point out that the whole continent of Africa should come under a Monarchical Government having one 'Common flag['] a Union African Flag flying throughout the length and breadth of the Continent and replacing every other flag.

Having appointed himself King and Emperor of Africa, Davies ordered all foreigners, with the exception of those lawfully married to men or women of African blood, to leave. Colonial administrations were also ordered to hand over to 'African Natives and Afro-Americans (*sic*) equal to the various positions'. This circular was passed on to Sir A. R. Slater, the Governor of Sierra Leone, by the Governor-General of French West Africa asking the former to look into the matter. In a reply, Governor Slater dismissed John Davies as a deranged mind who was not responsible for his actions, adding that steps should be taken to prevent the repetition of the offence.

The fate of John Davies' circular foreshadowed the failure of the diplomatic initiative launched by the UNIA and the imminent decline of the movement itself. Despite its considerable following, Garveyism was bound to suffer a setback mainly because of the unfavourable international political situation of the time. Threats to expel the imperialists from Africa by force naturally gave the colonial powers cause for concern, even though the provisional president of the continent was unlikely to muster enough warships to make good his boast. French and British colonial authorities began to suppress *The Negro World*. To possess any Garveyite publication became a serious offence punishable by imprisonment. Yielding to pressure from the United States and the metropolitan powers, Liberia, which the UNIA had planned to use as a nucleus for the proposed Negro National State, suddenly dissociated itself from the Garvey movement. Marcus Garvey himself was arrested and imprisoned for allegedly misusing the United States mail. After serving a short sentence he was deported to his native Jamaica.

With the removal of the redeemer from the United States, Garveyism suffered a setback from which it took many decades to recover. In the words of Claude McKay, 'Marcus Garvey had dreamed of a vast model colony in Liberia. But it was Harvey Firestone who realised the dream with his extensive [rubber] plantations'. Nevertheless it would be a mistake to suppose that Marcus Garvey achieved nothing. Apart from rehabilitating the colour 'black' he shook the

Black masses of the diaspora into an awareness of their African origin. Without setting foot on African soil he created for the first time a real feeling of international solidarity among Africans and persons of African stock.

This feeling of solidarity had already begun to manifest itself as early as 1917 when West Indian and African students in London launched a Union for Students of African Descent primarily for literary and social activities. An organisation called the African Progress Union, also based in London, appeared the next year with the aim of promoting the social and economic welfare of the Africans of the world. Among the prominent members of the APU may be mentioned Duse Mohamed Ali, the Ghanaian Robert Broadhurst, J. R. Archer and Dr John Alcindor. As we have already noted, the last two were present at the London congress of 1900.

It was also partly under the impact of Garveyism, though he disapproved of its propaganda tactics, that DuBois convened a series of Pan-African meetings between 1919 and 1927 as follows:

The 1919 Conference (Paris)
The 1921 Conference (London, Brussels, Paris)
The 1923 Conference (London, Lisbon)
The 1927 Conference (New York)

These Pan-African congresses have perhaps received more attention by scholars than they deserve, given their real significance in the history of the Pan-African movement. Because they have been dealt with elsewhere* in detail it is intended to refer to them only briefly here. The 1919 congress was held in Paris at the end of the First World War, with the specific objective of making recommendations to the Peace Conference about the German colonial territories and in particular the position of Black Americans who had fought in the war. The most prestigious African to attend was Blaise Diagne, the Deputy for Senegal, who served as High Commissioner for Recruitment of Troops in Black Africa. It was through his good offices that permission was granted by the French Government for the congress to be held in spite of objections by the American President, Woodrow Wilson.

The temper of the congress was moderate and the delegates did not go further than to urge that the 'natives of Africa must have the right to participate in the Government as fast as their development permits'. There was no demand for independence.

The congresses in London and Brussels in 1921 and London and Lisbon in 1923 did not move in a sensibly more radical direction. They repeated the demand for the participation of Africans in their own governments but did not mention independence or even self-government. Indeed the London and Lisbon sessions of 1923 were little more than sight-seeing tours while the New York session of 1927, the last to be directed by DuBois, had to rely on various Ladies'

* See for instance Colin Legum, *Pan Africanism—A Short Practical Guide,* Praeger, New York, 1962, and Vincent Bakpetu Thompson, *Africa and Unity: The Evolution of Panafricanism*, Longman, 1969.

3.7. Blaise Diagne: lent his prestige to the 1919 Congress

3.8. W. E. B. DuBois: 'father of Pan-Africanism', seen here at the 1945 Congress

Auxiliaries of New York Negro Churches for support. In these latter congresses Africans who attended did so only because they happened to be in the city chosen as the venue at the time.

Looking at the fortunes of Pan-Africanism from the closing decades of the eighteenth century to the first third of the twentieth, we find that the tendency to portray DuBois as 'the father of Pan-Africanism' is misleading. DuBois himself seems to be the originator of this myth, probably unconsciously. In a letter of 23 June 1921 to Charles Hughes, the American Secretary of State, he referred to the 1919 gathering as 'the first Pan-African Congress'. He made the same claim in an earlier communication dated 16 June 1921 which he sent to Sir Auckland Geddes, then the British ambassador to Washington D.C.

Actually Paul Cuffee, Edward Blyden, Africanus Horton, Bishop Alexander Walters, Henry Sylvester Williams or even Benito Sylvain all have equally valid if not stronger claims to the title. As the West Indian historian Hollis R. Lynch has rightly argued, Paul Cuffee (1759–1817) was 'the first major American-born Pan-African figure'. However, Blyden appears to be the earliest classic and greatest exponent of Pan-African concepts. Furthermore the idea of institutionalising the phenomenon itself and holding meetings at regular intervals goes back to the 1900 congress. Though DuBois attended it, the limelight was focused on such men as Sylvester Williams, Walters and Sylvain.

To say this is not to deny the significant contributions of DuBois to the *growth* of the movement. During the period 1919–1927 he with Marcus Garvey was among the leading spirits, though he did not work unaided. For instance, the 1919 meeting was made possible by the co-operation of the Senegalese politician

Blaise Diagne who used his influence to obtain the approval of the French Government. In conclusion, if DuBois was not the father of Pan-Africanism either as the *idea* or the *movement*, he was certainly one of its notable leaders in the first third of the twentieth century.

For further reading

APTHEKER, H. (ed.), *The Correspondence of W. E. B. DuBois: Vol 1 Selections 1877–1934*, University of Massachusetts Press, 1973.

DUBOIS, W. E. B., *The Souls of Black Folk*, New York, 1973 (with a new introduction by Herbert Aptheker).

ESEDEBE, P. O., *Pan-Africanism: The Idea and Movement, 1776–1963*, in press.

HAYFORD, C., *Ethiopia Unbound: Studies in Race Emancipation*, London 1911.

HOOKER, JAMES, *Henry Sylvester Williams: Imperial Pan-Africanist*, London, 1975.

JACQUES-GARVEY, A. (ed.), *Philosophy and Opinions of Marcus Garvey* (vols. 1 and 2), New York, 1973, (with a new preface by Hollis R. Lynch).

LANGLEY, J. A., *Pan-Africanism and Nationalism in West Africa 1900–1945*; O.U.P., 1973.

VINCENT, T., *Black Power and the Garvey Movement*, Ramparts Press, Berkeley, 1971.

ARCHBISHOP DANIEL WILLIAM ALEXANDER AND THE AFRICAN ORTHODOX CHURCH*

Richard Newman

The African Orthodox Church (AOC) is one of several links between black separatism in America and independence movements in Africa which remain largely unexamined. The church originated in the United States as an aspect of the Black Renaissance of the 1920s, a period of positive Negro self-consciousness, artistic flowering, and prideful identification of Diaspora blacks with their African heritage. The AOC spread to Africa where it played a part in the emergence of independent churches, the rise of cultural and political nationalism, and the interrelationships between these movements. The central figure in the spread of the African Orthodox Church within Africa was Archbishop Daniel William Alexander.

Alexander was born 25 December 1883[1] in Port Elizabeth, Cape Province, South Africa, the second eldest child of Henry David and Elizabeth Alexander. His Roman Catholic father was a native of St. Pierre, Martinique, who emigrated to Port Elizabeth. His mother's maiden name was Garcia and she was the child of a Cuban father and Javanese mother.[2]

The Corfield Report, which excoriates Alexander for his role in the Mau Mau rising in Kenya, charges him with first claiming Mauritian ancestry[3] to prove his parentage to the French authorities.

*I am grateful to Robert Edgar, who invited me to read an earlier version of this paper at a conference on "Afro-American Interaction with Southern Africa" at Howard University on 28 May 1979.

[1] T. D. Mweli Skota, editor of *The African Yearly Register: Being an Illustrated National Biographical Dictionary (Who's Who) of Black Folks in Africa* (Johannesburg, 1932?), 129, says Alexander was born in 1880.

[2] Thereis an incomplete, unpublished, handwritten autobiography among Alexander's papers from which this information is taken. Alexander's papers are now on deposit in the Pitts Theological Library, Emory University, Atlanta, Georgia. I was able to examine them briefly in South Africa in July, 1971. Arthur C. Terry-Thompson, *The History of the African Orthodox Church* (New York, 1956), 82, says Alexander's mother was Isabella Martini and that he was the "second son" of his parents. The informant of Frank H. Hulme in *Blackwall to Bloemfontein: An Unconventional Autobiography* (Durban, 1950?), 328, claims Alexander was the child of "a coloured American father and a coloured mother from Durban." This is repeated by Peter F. Anson, *Bishops at Large* (London, 1964), 267.

For Javanese in South Africa, see Izak D. duPlessis, *The Cape Malays* (Cape Town, 1944?), *passim*.

[3] Mauritians were often legally categorized as Europeans in South Africa.

At this point, according to Corfield, he assumed British nationality.[4]

Alexander was educated at St. Peter's Primary and Secondary schools in Port Elizabeth and the school of the Roman Catholic Sisters of Mercy. He became a boatbuilder by trade. Joining the British in the Boer War, he was captured at Colenso and sent to Pretoria.[5] After the fall of Pretoria to the British in 1900, Alexander joined the Anglican Church and was appointed chaplain at the Old Prison. He studied for the ministry under Canon E. Farmer, the Revs. H. Mtobi and W. A. Goodwin, and, later, Fathers Herbert Bennett and Latimer Fuller of the Community of the Resurrection.[6] In 1901 in Pretoria he married Elizabeth Koster.

Involving himself in South Africa's major Coloured political association, Alexander was elected secretary of the A.P.O., Pretoria Branch. The African Political Organization - later the African People's Organization - had been founded in 1902 and was led from 1905 by the Cape Malay physician, A. E. Abdurahman. Although its membership was primarily Coloured (that is, people of mixed African and European blood), the A.P.O. sought to be a united movement of all non-Europeans. It advocated extending the franchise to Coloureds outside the Cape, it identified with the British as opposed to the Boers, and, politically, it supported the South African Party.[7] Alexander also was elected secretary of the committee for purchasing the Lady Selbourne Township, Pretoria. Under the Hercules municipality, Lady Selbourne Township became one of the few areas where Africans could obtain freehold tenure and build their own houses.[8]

[4]F. D. Corfield, *Historical Survey of the Origins and Growth of Mau Mau* (London, 1960), 173. Government references for this document are Cmd. 1030, 1960, and Kenya Sessional Paper No. 5, 1959/60 (Nairobi, 1960). At Alexander's visit to the United States in 1929 the British consul in New York informed his embassy that Alexander was travelling on a French passport, No. 16, issued by the French consul in Johannesburg on 14 March 1927. The report further states that Alexander "was unable to get a British passport, but has always looked upon himself as a British subject and claims to be loyal to the British government." I am indebted to Robert Hill for this reference: F.O. 115/ 3380 (1929).

Corfield further alleges that Alexander was convicted of theft in Johannesburg in 1912 and classified as an agitator in 1929. The Veiligheid (Security Branch) of the South African Police is unable to furnish information on the first allegation and categorically denies the second. Fred B. Welbourn, *East African Rebels: A Study of Some Independent Churches* (London, 1961), 252, rightly draws attention to the questionable factual value of Corfield's source material.

[5]The battle of Colenso on 15 December 1899 was a major British defeat.

[6]One of the first projects of the Community of the Resurrection in South Africa was the establishment of a college for training catechists at Doornfontein in Johannesburg. According to the Rev. K. U. Davie, C.R., "I think Daniel William Alexander was probably under training as a catechist in our college and may possibly have got to the permanent diaconate." Letter to the writer, 20 November 1974.

[7]Sheila Patterson, *Colour and Culture in South Africa* (London, 1953). 159. See also J.S. Marais, *The Cape Coloured People 1652-1937* (London, 1939), 274-280.

The Rev. John S. Likhing, Alexander's later colleague as general secretary of the African Orthodox Church, was also provisional president of the African National Congress in Bechuanaland and Griqualand West Province as well as assistant chaplain to the A.N.C. See Skota, *The African Yearly Register*, 172; see also Peter Walshe, *The Rise of African Nationalism in South Africa: The African National Congress 1912-1952* (Berkeley, 1971), 226-227.

[8]Ellen Hellman, ed., *Handbook on Race Relations in South Africa* (Cape Town, 1949), 252. See also "Land Tenure by Asiatics and South African Coloured in the Transvaal," *Race Relations*, II, 5 (November 1935), 42-46.

We do not know why, but Alexander resigned from the Anglican Church and moved from Pretoria to Johannesburg, where he became an agent in the industrial branch of the African Life Assurance Society. He subsequently left this position, however, to become Grand True Secretary of the Independent Order of True Templars, Northern Grand Lodge. Re-elected to that office in 1920-1921, he refused nomination in 1922. The I.O.T.T., although basically a temperance organization, fulfilled the additional welfare, recreational, and economic functions of a lodge. Lodges play a significant role in Coloured life, especially among skilled artisans and the commercial bourgeoisie. Unlike most Coloured fraternal groups, however, the I.O.T.T. included women, Africans, and even whites in its membership.[9]

For reasons we do not know, Alexander left these socially and politically liberal and racially inclusive organizations and returned to an ecclesiastical vocation. He became affiliated with an independent religious body known as the African Church. On 15 September 1924, a group of dissident clergy of this church, including Alexander, met and passed a resolution which viewed with alarm the "retrogression" of their denomination. Calling it the oldest separatist church in the Union,[10] they said it had become controlled by an "uneducated clique" under its founder Bishop J. M. Kanyane Napo, a former Anglican. Also, its finances were in difficulty and there were problems with legal permission to officiate at marriages. Napo had founded the African Church in 1889. He had been a colleague of Mangena M. Mokone who opposed racial segregation in the churches, sought African religious self-government, and founded the Ethiopian Church in 1892.[11] The dissidents determined to seek affiliation with the African Orthodox Church, a new Negro denomination in the United States related to the Garvey Movement.[12]

In a subsequent meeting in Beaconsfield on 6 October 1924, the group made a formal break with the African Church and elected Alexander its head.[13] Present at this meeting was Joseph Masoga, the local agent for Marcus Garvey's newspaper, *The Negro World* and

[9]Patterson, *Colour and Culture*, 157, 310. Olive Schreiner's brother, W.P. Schreiner, prime minister of Cape Colony, was one prominent white member. For Schreiner's views on temperance, see Eric A. Walker, *W.P. Schreiner: A South African* (London, 1969), 52-53.

[10]They said it had been founded thirty-six years previously. In fact, the oldest independent church is the Tembu, founded in 1884 by Nehemiah Tile, an ex-Wesleyan. See C. C. Saunders, "Tile and the Thembu Church: Politics and Independency on the Cape Eastern Frontier in the Late Nineteenth Century," *Journal of African History*, XI, 4 (1970), 553-570.

[11]Bengt G. M. Sundkler, *Bantu Prophets in South Africa* (London, 1961), 39. For Tile's influence on Mokone, see W. M. Cameron, "The Ethiopian Movement and the Order of Ethiopia," *The East and the West*, II (1904), 376. There are biographies of Tile and Mokone in Skota, *The African Yearly Register*. For a fascinating account by Alexander himself, see "The Separatist Church Movement in South Africa," *The Negro Churchman*, V, 11 (December 1927), 3-4; VI, 1 (January 1928), 7-8.

[12]See Richard Newman, "The Origins of the African Orthodox Church," *The Negro Churchman: The Official Organ of the African Orthodox Church* (Millwood, 1977), iii-xxii.

[13]The minutes of both these meetings, in Alexander's handwriting, are among his papers.

the organizer of the Afro-Construction Church of the House of Athlyi.[14] It is reasonable to assume that Alexander knew about the African Orthodox Church from Garvey's paper.[15] The Afro-Construction Church of the House of Athlyi is an example of unusually strong African nationalism. Like the Rastafari cult in Jamaica, it also illustrates religious veneration of Marcus Garvey. The church still exists in the Kimberley area. Its remarkable literature (*The Holy Piby, The Royal Parchment Scroll of Black Supremacy*, and *The Promised Key)* has recently been discovered by Robert A. Hill who is preparing it for re-publication. These extraordinary documents dramatically link American, Jamaican, and South African relgious nationalist movements.

The African Orthodox Church had been founded in New York City on 2 September 1921, by George Alexander McGuire, a native of Antigua, a sometime Anglican priest, and one of the leading Negro clergymen of the Protestant Episcopal Church.[16] Although it has always welcomed white participation, the purpose of the new denomination was "to cast off forever the yoke of white Ecclesiastical dominance" and to express "the spirit of racial leadership ... in harmony with the aroused racial consciousness of the Negro people,"[17] that is, the black nationalism of the Garvey Movement.

Constituted primarily by West Indians of Anglican background, the church was - and continues to be - deeply committed to formal liturgy, a hierarchical priesthood, and defending the validity of its episcopal orders. McGuire received consecration at the hands of Joseph Rene Vilatte, metropolitan of the American Catholic Church in the U.S.A.[18] Villate's own consecration was derived from the Syro-Jacobite Patriarch of Antioch via Archbishop Francisco F. X. Alvarez, Mar Julios I, Metropolitan of the Independent Catholic Church of Ceylon, Goa, and India.[19] The display of "valid" ecclesiastical pedigrees in order to justify the legitimacy of their

[14]Sundkler, *Bantu Prophets*, 58.

[15]Alexander confirmed this in his address to the seventh General Synod of the AOC. Garvey's impact on Africa has always been underestimated. For the influence of *The Negro World*, see George Shepperson and Thomas Price, *Independent African: John Chilembwe and the Origins, Setting and Significance of the Nyasaland Native Rising of 1915* (Edinburgh, 1958), 494; George Padmore, *Pan-Africanism or Communism?* (London, 1956), 349; Amy Jacques Garvey, *Garvey and Garveyism* (Kingston, 1963), 285; Robert H. Brisbane, Jr., "Some New Light on the Garvey Movement," *The Journal of Negro History*, XXXVI, 1, January, 1951, 59; in "His Excellency: The Provincial [*sic*] President of Africa," *Phylon*, X, 3, Third Quarter, 1949, 262. Brisbane says the newspaper was even translated into drumcode and sent into the interior.

[16]Gavin White, "Patriarch McGuire and the Episcopal Church," *Historical Magazine of the Protestant Episcopal Church*, 38, 2 (June 1969), 109-141.

[17]Terry-Thompson, *History*, 50, 53.

[18]Vilatte is generally considered an ecclesiastical adventurer whose orders may have been technically valid but were certainly irregular. See Anson, *Bishops at Large*, 91-129. For a discussion of validity and regularity, see H. R. T. Brandreth, *Episcopi Vagantes and the Anglican Church*, 2nd ed., (London 1961), 8-15.

[19]There is an account of Alvarez in E.M. Philip, *The Indian Church of St. Thomas* (Nagercoil, 1950), 420-428, 430-431. While schismatic, his church had suffered from Roman Catholic, particularly Jesuit, persecution. It is fashionable to regard Alvarez and Vilatte as mere *episcopi vagantes* (i.e., wandering bishops without responsibility to any particular jurisdiction), or worse, although their consecrations were expressly commanded by Ignatius Peter III, Syrian Orthodox patriarch of Antioch and All the East. Admittedly, the patriarchate has since repudiated the claims of the Vilatte succession.

ordinations assumed great importance to the AOC both in the United States and Africa. In part, this was the case because its clergy tended to define themselves in relation to the Church of England where this legitimacy is taken for granted. It can certainly be argued that their lack of preferment in established denominations led both Africans and American blacks to seek alternative avenues for advancement and self-rule. For churchmen brought up on the doctrine of apostolic succession, it was only natural to seek legitimacy from the Eastern and Oriental Orthodox churches whose historical authenticity is universally recognized and even more ancient than that of Anglicanism.

The African Orthodox Church was tied to the Garvey Movement particularly through the person of Archbishop McGuire, who served as chaplain-general of the Universal Negro Improvement Association and was one of Garvey's most able lieutenants.[20] McGuire was aligned with Garvey in advocating prideful black sef-consciousness, a rediscovery of the African cultural heritage and black control over black institutions. Despite strong ties to Garvey and Garveyism, however, McGuire was always a churchman before he was a Negro nationalist or political activist, and the AOC perceived itself as a church rather than as a vehicle for social protest. Even so, the very creation of the church as a separate Negro institution made it an expression and manifestation of the black nationalism of the period.

In a petition to McGuire dated 24 September 1924, Alexander on behalf of himself and four other priests and their congregations asked to affiliate with the AOC. The Rev. Edwin Urban Lewis reported to the British government that McGuire read a letter on 29 October 1924,[21] to a "secret conference" at U.N.I.A. headquarters from the "Archdeacon of Pretoria" requesting admission for himself and 500 parishioners. Lewis recalls McGuire's response to have been: "Yourself and congregation coming over to us will be welcome, and as Lord Primate of the African Orthodox Church, should you make it possible for Sir Marcus Garvey to get in to that country I am sure that the day will not be far off when by virtue of my high office, I will consecrate you as bishop for South Africa."[22]

Lewis believed the AOC to be a "gang of religious fanatics who were seditious against the government of Great Britain," and so kept the British consul general in New York informed of its activities. The fact that Lewis himself was a one-time AOC priest who had been expelled by the Fourth General Synod for laxity of duty may have outweighed his expressed concern "for the safety of the Church of England." H. G. Armstrong, the British consul, apparently took Lewis seriously, however, for he later reported to his embassy: "It is generally understood that the consecration of clergymen by McGuire is part of his scheme to cause dissension, together with the Marcus Garvey association, among negroes of the British Empire."

[20]Wilson Record, "The Negro Intellectual and Negro Nationalism," *Social Forces*, 33, 1 (October 1954), 17. For the case that Garvey himself was the theologian of a civil religion, see Randall K. Burkett, *Garveyism as a Religious Movement* (Metuchen, N.J., 1978).

[21]According to Alexander's *Die Kategismus vir die wat leer vir Doop en Aanneming van de Afrikaanse Ortodoks Kerk* (Kimberley, 1951), 15, the church was founded in South African on 6 October 1924.

[22]FO 371/9633, No. 213. See also FO 115/3380. I am indebted to Robert A. Hill for this reference.

McGuire proceeded to authorize Alexander to act as his vicar apostolic "for the purpose of organizing an independent and local branch" of the AOC. "The various groups of our people in Africa and elsewhere must be given when prepared, their own self-governing churches within the Communion of the Holy African Orthodox Church," McGuire stated. Presumably on the basis of McGuire's authorization Alexander was styled "the Venerable Daniel William Alexander, Archdeacon and Vicar-General of the Diocese and Vicariates of the Cape of Good Hope and Rector of the Church of St. Augustine of Hippo."[23]

A provisional synod was held in Beaconsfield on October 6, attended by 400 people, at which the AOC of South Africa was officially organized. Perhaps McGuire requested, or required, more formal proceedings than the September petition. On the motion of the Rev. Ezekiel Leagise, the Synod voted to elect Alexander bishop, to seek affiliation with the AOC in America, and to ask McGuire for credentials authorizing Alexander to administer the diocese and to deal with the South African government on behalf of the church. The expectation was that Alexander would be consecrated at the next (the fifth) AOC General Synod in New York in 1925. Alexander reported on the "disabilities confronting natives" in the Church of England in South Africa, including the low education standards for black clergy. It was clear that both McGuire and Alexander saw the new church's mission to be "to arouse people of African descent in the Anglican Communion to declare for freedom by declining the crumbs which fall from the tables of their religious overlords, and to maintain and control their own ecclesiastical institutions."[24]

Alexander suggested he had severed connections with the Church of England, although it was the African Church of Bishop J. M. Kanyane Napo where he had been dean and vicar general and from which he had resigned. McGuire was highly enthusiastic at the whole turn of events. "The East and the West have met each other in the African Orthodox Church," he said, and without any missionary activity except through the news column of *The Negro World*, to which he expressed his thanks. McGuire used the occasion to ask rhetorically when Negro Churchmen (that is, Anglicans in America and the West Indies) would follow the example of brethren in the motherland, declare themselves free and "have the scales fall from their eyes." And, not least, "The remarkable thing about it all is that there is no appeal for funds."[25]

Events in South Africa evoked a poem from Rev. Sister Angelina Theresa, an AOC deaconess:

<u>There's a Cry</u>

There's a Cry from Pretoria!
"Come over and help us
In our efforts as men to be free."
How it sounds in the ear,
'Tis glad tidings we hear
From our Brothers at Home o'er the sea.

[23] "The Very Latest," *The Negro Churchman*, II, 11 (November 1924), 1.

[24] "The African Orthodox Church Links East with West," *The Negro Churchman*, II, 12 (December 1924), 1-2.

[25] *Ibid.*

They have caught the bright Vision,
They have seen the new light
Which appeared to our Primate
As he gazed into night, -
"This change shalt thou keep,
Go gather thy sheep
From their Spiritual bondage and sleep."[26]

Alexander himself composed a poem:

Work and Wait

Up brothers! 'Tis a mighty deed
Angels would covet to begin,
Clapping their wings in eager speed
A Universe to win.

Toil on! It is your Master's will;
His own bright world in chaos stood
Waiting the labors of His skill,
Ere he pronounced it "good."

Union is Strength! A phalanx stand
Breasting the world's contempt and scorn,
E'en should not palm-branch weigh your hand,
No crown your brow adorn.

Truth, - holy truth, deathless, divine
Engraven on the immortal scroll;
With God's eternal throne for shrine,
Empire from pole to pole.

Does this demand your reverend care,
A martyrdom of faith and zeal?
Armed for the battle, boldly dare
The issue, woe or weal.

Duty is ours, and high-souled trust
In Him no mortal can defy:
Work! For His law is good and just;
Wait! Truth can never die.[27]

Alexander soon travelled to the Transvaal where he received two Anglican priests into the AOC, D. F. Brown and Fred Hugels. They joined his original clergy: Michael Moncho, Ezekiel Leagise and James Monare.[28] Both Alexander and McGuire saw their labors as part of the new black spirit of the times. McGuire pointed out that Alexander, whose parents came from Martinique, illustrated "an instance of African forbears brought to the West in slavery contributing to the spiritual emancipation of their people in supplying them with their first independent native bishop." In the South

[26] *The Negro Churchman*, II, 12 (December 1924).

[27] *Ibid.*, III, 1 (January 1925), 4.

[28] "Our Church in South Africa," *The Negro Churchman*, III, 1(January 1925), 4.

African context, it is interesting that the AOC under Alexander, a Coloured, attracted African, Coloured, and white clergy, although most of its membership was African. This cooperation is, again, probably due to the fact that the church offered legitimacy, autonomy, and personal opportunity. Alexander wrote: "If the Black Race could only digest what is now being taught for our upliftment we would make all nations respect us. We need Race pride, respect for each other, and the ambition to achieve for ourselves that which is constructive and substantial...."[29]

When the South African church's Deed of Election, dated 6 October 1924, and signed by the Provisional Synod, reached McGuire it announced that Alexander had been named not merely bishop, but archbishop and primate. McGuire explained to his own followers in America that the Africans, as former clergy and laity of the Church of England, had organized a Province of the AOC and thus required the office of primate and archbishop; these were, of course, the same titles McGuire had evolved for his own position.[30]

The African AOC first Provincial Synod was held 1 January 1925, in Alexander's Beaconsfield church. Alexander celebrated mass, omitting for the first time the filioque clause from the Nicene Creed in accordance with Orthodox usage. Three clerical and six lay deputies were present as well as members of the church and "friends of our cause" including P. Jampies, "an influential citizen of Kimberley." John Balston was elected secretary and Charles Sweetwater treasurer. The decisions of the Provisional Synod were ratified changing the title of the bishop-elect to archbishop-elect since the AOC in South Africa would be a full church in its own right but in communion with the AOC in America. Perhaps this change grew out of Alexander's visit to various governmental agencies when he went to the capital to register the denomination.[31]

Each congregation was requested to contribute £7 towards Alexander's proposed visit to the U.S. to receive the episcopate. This was described as a particular burden under "the new Hertzog Government whose policy is to oust the Black man from his job to make way for the poor White." It was expected that "the Negroes of America" would pay Alexander's return fare.

The Provincial Synod of the new church was to meet quadrennially, with annual Diocesan synods. The Rev. Ezekiel Leagise was commissioned as archdeacon of Barkly West, and the Rev. Michael Moncho, archdeacon of Douglas and Hope Town. The Synod expressed hope that the American church would establish a Pan-African Church Synod to meet every four years to be attended by delegates from both provinces and patterned after the Pan-Anglican Synod. The purposes would be to discuss world-wide expansion, promote missionary endeavor, stimulate racial welfare and uplift movements, liberate black men from the influence of white missionaries, establish a central seminary and college, and seek full communion with the "Ancient African Church of Abyssinia."[32]

[29] *Ibid.*

[30] "The South African Church," *The Negro Churchman*, III, 2 (February 1925), 6.

[31] "The First Provincial Synod of South Africa," *The Negro Churchman*, III, 3 (March 1925), 2.

[32] *Ibid.*, p. 3.

Alexander sent a message to his "Fellow Churchmen in America," announcing that his receiving a valid consecration would "prove the key to our ecclesiastical freedom here in Africa." He suggested putting away selfishness, pride, and petty jealousies - perhaps because he sensed these existed for McGuire at his request for an archbishopric and primacy - and urged making common cause for the AOC by quoting the late President Kruger's motto "Unity Makes Strength." "Pray for all Negro clergymen," he advised, "who are still in ecclesiastical bondage, hankering after the few dollars they receive. Pray that they may come out of Egypt, and following our Moses, enter with us the Promised Land of spiritual liberty."[33] He announced that he had celebrated sung masses on Christmas eve and Christmas day with procession and incense. His work was complicated, he pointed out, by the necessity of preaching in English, Dutch, Sixosa, Sesuto and Lechuana. He planned to translate *The Divine Liturgy* so "all may understand our Catholic worship."

With no explanation, McGuire soon announced that he had appointed Isaiah Palmerston Samuels of Cape Town his commissary in the Union of South Africa "to gather such information as may be required of him." Samuel was McGuire's half-brother who had gone to Africa as an educator specializing in music.[34]

The same issue of *The Negro Churchman* carried a strongly worded statement on the new situation for blacks in South Africa at the defeat of the Smuts government. Entitled "This is Africa!," the byline gave the source as "From a Lay Contributor" but was most probably Alexander. The article pointed out that the new Nationalist government was "absolutely anti-native" and cited: the requirement that native women carry passes, the fact that lands were being taken and the Africans driven to barren tracts of "locations" to die from thirst and starvation, the selling of kaffir beer and the lack of legislative representation, education, hospitals, and housing.

McGuire was now openly hesitant about giving Alexander the episcopate, undoubtedly because the South African Orthodox Church saw itself as independent of the American church; "except in the matter of communion," McGuire noted, "we would have no other relations with them." Also, Samuels advised caution. "We shall deal justly with our brethren in Africa," said McGuire, "but must think prayerfully, carefully and patiently before entrusting to these natives the precious gift they seek."[35]

When the Synod met in September, it countered the desire of Alexander and his church to be autonomous and autocephalous by offering to receive them on probation as a "Mission Territory" under the control of an American bishop, with Alexander confirmed only as vicar apostolic, and with a grant of financial aid, "should our terms be acceptable."[36] Alexander accepted the terms: "because we have left the white man's church, and if we have boasted of our connection with you, should we today be too proud to undergo a two year's probation...?" but he did hint at an alternative affiliation

[33]"A Message from Africa," *The Negro Churchman*, III, 3 (March 1925), 3.

[34]"Commissary in South Africa," *The Negro Churchman*, III, 4 (April 1925), 2.

[35]"The Fifth General Synod," *The Negro Churchman*, III, 7 (July 1925), 1-2.

[36]"The Fifth General Synod a Great Success," *The Negro Churchman*, III,9 (October 1925), 3.

- with the AME Church - if their request were not granted at the end of the period. Alexander also mentioned that he had already been consecrated "at the hands of certain native bishops (not of the Catholic episcopate)." With some annoyance, McGuire pointed out that Alexander was using an episcopal seal and mitre on his stationery and signing himself the "Right Reverend."[37]

Alexander then furnished the AOC with a copy of his report to the government on churches and membership which showed considerable progress after eighteen months of work:

S. Augustine, Beaconsfield, Very Rev. D.W. Alexander, 210 members
S. Barnabas, Greenpoint, Very Rev. D.W. Alexander
S. James, Waldecks Plant, Ven. M. Moncho, 80
S. Peter's, Good Hope, Rev. Fr. M.J. Dithebe, 30
Good Shepherd, Home Station, Rev. Fr. G. Daniels
Railway Mission, Dronfield, Rev. Fr. G. Daniels, 198
Home Station, Warrenton, Rev. Fr. G. Daniels
S. Monica's, Kimberley, Rev. Fr. J. Monare, 29
S. Paul's, Veryu, Rev. D.W. Alexander, 20
S. Monica's, Johannesburg, Ven. D.F. Brown, 50
S. Bartalomew's, Johannesburg, Rev. Fr. J. Mamane, 106
S. Peter's, South Johannesburg, Rev. Fr. D.P. Morgan, 25
S. Cyprian, Fustonburg, Reader K.P. Hagano, 400

"God is working mightily for us," said Alexander, "And all under black leadership." Four of the clergy were new: a Roman Catholic, a Swedenborgian, an Anglican and a Wesleyan.[38]

Whatever doubts McGuire held either about "these natives" or Alexander's claim to equal him in ecclesiastical title and rank seem to have been dispelled by the time of the AOC's seventh General Synod in 1927. The happy solution was to be two provinces of the same church, one African and headed by a bishop consecrated by "Bishops of his own Race, whose ancestors were forcibly removed from their Motherland," the other American headed by another archbishop and primate - but both presided over by McGuire with the new title of patriarch or head of the entire church, now defined as a Pan-African Orthodox Conclave.[39]

Alexander arrived in New York 23 August 1927. On Labor Day he was confirmed and received minor orders from Bishop William E. J. Robertson. The same day he was ordained by McGuire. On Sunday, 11 September 1927, in the Church of St. Michael and All Angels in Boston, he was consecrated archbishop and primate of the African Province by McGuire, assisted by Bishops Robertson and Arthur S. Trotman. He was also awarded the honorary degree Doctor of Divinity by McGuire, a prerogative of Orthodox hierarchs.

At the consecration of an African for an African church by men of African descent, the congregation was visibly moved by the Gospel for the day: "Blessed are the eyes that see the things that ye see; for I tell you, that many prophets and kings have desired to see them, and have not seen them; and to hear those things which ye

[37]"The South African Church," *The Negro Churchman*, IV, 1 (January 1926), 5. It was the Ethiopian Catholic Church where Alexander first received consecration.

[38]"The South African Work," *The Negro Churchman*, IV, 7 (July 1926), 5.

[39]"The Seventh General Synod," *The Negro Churchman*, V, 9 (October 1927), 3-4.

hear, and have not heard them."[40] Even more dramatic, at the very moment of consecration - the laying on of hands and the statement "Receive ye the Holy Ghost" - there was a peal of thunder followed by a copious shower which fell in direct vertical sheets to the earth.[41]

After his return to Africa, Alexander began to organize new churches throughout the southern part of the continent and to receive into the African Orthodox Church a number of Anglican priests and laymen. The secessions from Anglicanism apparently aroused considerable interest and discussion.[42] Apart from establishing a new denomination, Alexander's most significant work was his role in the founding of other independent churches. The beginnings of the African Orthodox Churches in Uganda and Kenya have been well documented by F. B. Welbourn's study and need be treated here only in outline.

In 1925 Reuben Mukasa Spartas, a Ugandan Anglican, read *The Negro World,* founded the African Progressive Association, and vowed "to go to hell, jail or die for the redemption of Africa."[44] He corresponded with McGuire who put him in touch with Alexander in 1928. Alexander appointed Spartas a lay-reader. In 1929 Spartas announced his break with Anglicanism and the formation of the African Orthodox Church in Uganda: "a church established for all right-thinking Africans, men who wish to be free in their own house, not always being thought of as boys."[45]

At Spartas's request, Alexander came to Uganda in 1931 and on Trinity Sunday, 1932, ordained as priests Spartas and his brother-in-law Obadiah Basajjakitalo. Later that same year Spartas was put in touch with Nicodemus Sarikas, the Greek Orthodox Archimandrite in Tanganyika. Suspicious of Alexander's Orthodoxy, Spartas severed the relationship in order to petition Meletios II, the Greek Patriarch of Alexandria, for admission. Despite the question of Alexander's orders, in 1946 the Patriarchate received Spartas and the re-named African Greek Orthodox Church into full membership under its jurisdiction. This branch of the AOC thus became the first independent African church to place itself under European authority, the first

[40]Luke 10:23-24.

[41]Terry-Thompason, *History*, 75. The service is described in "Consecration Service." *The Negro Churchman*, V, 9 (October 1927), 7.

[42]Hellman, *Handbook*, 567. Alexander later received the African United Church of some 1000 members along with its founder, the Rev. Joel Davids who had seceded from the Anglican Church after being the first African ordained to the priesthood in the Transvaal. See "The African United Church Affiliates with the African Orthodox Church," *The Negro Churchman*, VII, 8 (October 1929), 6-7.

[43]*East African Rebels*, 77-100, 135-162.

[44]Quoted by Welbourn, *East African Rebels*, 81. An early nationalist, Spartas continued to have an active and controversial political career as a leader of the Sons of Kintu and the Bataka Party which grew out of it. See David E. Apter, *The The Political Kingdom in Uganda* (Princeton, 1961), 248-254. It is interesting that the motto of the Sons of Kintu - "One God, one aim, one destiny" - was that of Garvey's U.N.I.A. Spartas also wanted the patriarchial see of the AOC located in Africa. See *The Negro Churchman* VI, 11 (December 1928), 3; VII, 1 (January 1929), 4; VII, 6 (July 1929), 3-4.

[45]Quoted by Welbourn, *East African Rebels*, 81. This and the following information was confirmed in a personal interview with Spartas in Kampala on 25 July 1971.

church in the Vilatte succession to be accepted by a historic communion, and the first major contemporary expression of Greek Orthodox missionary interest.

Returning to South Africa from Uganda in late 1932, Alexander met James Beauttah, the Kikuyu nationalist leader, in Mombasa. Kikuyu resentment over British land and labor policies had come to a crisis in 1929 when the Church of Scotland Missions forbade clitoridectomy - the practice of female circumcision which was both the central rite of passage whereby girls were inducted into Kikuyu culture and society and the unifying symbol of the whole tribal system.[46] The Kikuyu had withdrawn from the Scottish, Anglican and other missions in large numbers, taking their churches and schools with them and eventually forming two new bodies: the Kikuyu Independent Schools Association (K.I.S.A.) and the Kikuyu Karing'a ("Pure") Education Association.

Schools and churches were closely intertwined institutions. Separation from the missions brought educational independence, but the Kikuyu were bereft of clergy to baptize their children. They appealed to the Anglican bishop of Mombasa who insisted on the abandoning of clitoridectomy as a prerequisite to future baptisms. The Kikuyu argued eloquently, basing their case on Scripture, but to no avail. Hoping that political autonomy might also mean religious autonomy, they then appealed to the bishop of Liberia, but he would not intrude into the ecclesiastical territory of the bishop of Mombasa.

Alexander had kept in touch with Kikuyu spokesmen[47] and was invited to Kenya since he led a church "of the Africans, governed by the Africans and for the Africans to make daily supplications to Almight God led by priests who have the welfare of Africans at heart."[48] Arriving in Nairobi in November 1935, Alexander was contracted by the Kikuyu for a period of eighteen months, within which he was to ordain African priests and to baptize.[49] Provided with an automobile, Alexander travelled widely throughout the area baptizing large numbers, preaching, and teaching.

The Kikuyu then began to criticize him for profiting too much from baptismal fees, for not setting apart a native clergy, and for baptizing so many people that his clerical successors would have difficulties maintaining themselves economically. Alexander found the Kikuyu a proud people unshakably committed to their independence and so "a hard bone to chew."[50] He ordained four men[51] and was

[46] Jomo Kenyatta, *Facing Mt. Kenya: The Tribal Life of the Gikuyu* (New York, n.d.), 125-148.

[47] Parmenas Mukeri, the Kikuyu Central Association leader who accompanied Kenyatta to London in 1931, was publicly welcomed by Alexander in South Africa on Mukeri's journey back to Kenya.

[48] Kikuyu Independent Schools Association connected with the African Independent Pentecostal Church, *Report and Constitution, 1938* (Nyeri, 1938), 2.

[49] Negly Farson, *Last Chance in Africa* (London, 1949), 129, mistakenly divided Alexander in two: "To get their own priests, the Kikuyus brought up a black Bishop from South Africa - from the Orthodox Church, which is almost like the Greek Church - and a Negro pastor from the U.S.A. named William Alexander...."

[50] Bartolomeo Moriondo, "Come conobbi l'Arcivescovo Ortodosso," *Missioni Consolata*, 46, 8-9 (September-October 1944), 94.

[51] Harrison Gacokia, Arthur Gatung'u, Philip Kiandi, and Daudi Maina.

forced to give them his vestments and his automobile. Ordaining two "high priests" and two "low priests," Alexander created an immediate schism. Although all parties looked to him as their spiritual father, two churches emerged: the African Orthodox Church related to Karing'a and the African Independent Pentecostal Church[52] related to the K.I.S.A.

Although the subsequent relationships among men, churches, and schools became highly complex, the point is that when Alexander sailed from Kenya on 7 July 1937, he left behind him "an ordained African clergy functioning outside the auspices of any Kenyan mission."[53] The cultural nationalism expressed in the independent churches and schools, with their leadership legitimized by Alexander, developed into increasingly overt forms of political nationalism. The culmination was the Mau Mau movement and, ultimately, Kenyan independence.[54] Also, as in Uganda, Alexander's Orthodoxy added a unique direction to the independent church movement by introducing "high church" elements such as the sign of the cross, the crucifix, the mass, and sacraments celebrated in a mixture of Anglican and Roman rites.[55]

Alexander had relatively less invovlement with the small branch of the African Orthodox Church which developed in the Gold Coast in the 1930s. Unlike the churches in Kenya and Uganda, however, it was for some time under his episcopal jurisdiction. Six black American missionaries formerly associated with the Garvey Movement went to West Africa in 1931 under the auspices of the African Universal Church. When support from that body failed, the Rev. Carey Harold Jones - the one missionary who continued - returned to the United States in 1945 to visit Archbishop Robertson, Alexander's co-consecrator and McGuire's successor as patriarch of the AOC. Robertson referred Jones to Alexander who received him into the African Province in 1955. Financial difficulties kept Alexander from

[52]Pentecostal here means apostolic rather than any of the charismatic characteristics usually associated with "Pentecostalism."

[53]Carl G. Rosberg, Jr., and John Nottingham, *The Myth of "Mau Mau": Nationalism in Kenya* (Nairobi, 1966), 130.

[54]Corfield, *Historical Survey*, 174, takes a somewhat contradictory view of Alexander's political influence. On the one hand, he reports the opinion of the district commissioner at Fort Hall that Alexander's presence contributed to the peace of the area; on the other, he asserts that Alexander's choice of ministers sowed "the seeds of future dissention." Kikuyu Central Association leaders he links to Alexander include Arthur Gathuma, Jesse Kariuki, Daudi Maina, Wambugu Maina, Job Muchuchu, and George Ndegwa. See also *The International Review of Missions*, 26 (1937), 67.

[55]On the basis of his experiences in Kenya, Alexander served as the model for a character in Elspeth Huxley's novel *Red Strangers* (London, 1939), 400-402. The story deals with three generations of a Kikuyu family and tells how their traditional life is altered by the coming of Europeans. The independent church movement, as Huxley describes it, provided an alternative way to the missions for the Kikuyu to become Christians - a way without sacrificing all their customs, especially polygamy, and a way to construct "a true Kikuyu Church, unpolluted by European prejudices." Huxley sketches a fictional character based on Alexander who is perceived as "a dignitary second to no one in importance, unless it might be King George" and is enthusiastically received by the Kikuyu. She mentions the South African base of the church and accurately reproduces details, such as the famous automobile by which Alexander travelled from Nairobi, but she takes liberties with his appearance, mentioning his "big beard." She pictures a large baptismal ceremony at the conclusion of which she has the archbishop's attendants extract a ten shilling fee from each new Christian.

ever visiting the Gold Coast, but six mission stations there remained under his authority until 1960.

That year - 1960 - saw the end of the loose affiliation between Alexander's churches in South Africa and the African Orthodox Church in America. Alexander provided for proper succession to his episcopacy by selecting two South Africans, Surgeon Lionel Motsepe and Ice Walter Mbina, for consecration. In June Patriarch Robertson and Archbishop Richard Robinson travelled to South Africa and, assisted by Alexander, consecrated Motsepe and Mbina in the Anglican Church of All Saints, Kimberley. Although we do not know the issues, Alexander and the Americans quarreled, and the patriarch excommunicated him; Robertson put Mbina in Alexander's place as administrator of the South African church. Further, Robertson declared Jones in the Gold Coast independent of Alexander's authority and raised Jones to the bishopric of a newly-created Province of West Africa.

Of the two new bishops, Motsepe soon died and in Natal Mbina seceded to form the Holy Orthodox Church, taking a substantial number of members with him. Alexander proceeded to rename his group the African Orthodox Church in the Republic of South Africa and to elevate his church building in Kimberley - named for St. Augustine of Hippo - from pro-cathedral to cathedral status. Alexander died in Kimberley Hospital on 14 May 1970, leaving a South African church of 20 congregations, 50 ordained clergy, and 4 bishops-elect.

Independent churches serve as entrees into white European Christianity and culture and also as conservers of black African civilization and leadership. This amalgam is particularly true of the African Orthodox Church. A constitutional statement affiliating AOC groups in Kenya and Uganda in 1943 specifically declares that a primary purpose of the church is "to preserve African customs and traditions in relation with spiritual and educational matters."[56] Sociological studies make clear that the AOC has in fact been a bridge between the new religion and old values. In Larteh, Ghana, the African Orthodox Church is the only one of the twelve local churches where menstruating women sit in the back of the church and are not permittted to receive Holy Communion. With the Larteh Salvation Army from which it split off, the AOC - unlike the other churches - allows polygamy, allows converts to keep all their wives, and allows any chief who is a member to perform traditional rites.[57] In Tiriki, Kenya, the AOC, in contrast to the other local separatist churches, permits polygamy and social and ritual beer-drinking and encourages its youth to participate in the traditional circumcision and intitiation ceremonies.[58]

Archbishop Alexander, of course, was not directly responsible for these African characteristics in churches not under his jurisdiction. In fact, churches and church life under his control were consciously and intentionally Western. But by his very existence he personified for nearly fifty years Africanization in church leadership, and not only in the denomination he founded. He legitimized the authority of a large number of independent denominations by ordaining their clergy. Alexander's appeal was that he symbolized an

[56] Corfield, *Historical Survey*, 175.

[57] David Brokensha, *Social Change at Larteh, Ghana* (London, 1966), 26-31, 165-166.

[58] Walter H. Sangree, *Age, Prayer and Politics in Tiriki, Kenya* (London, 1966), 190, 211-215.

external power with apostolic claims combined with the racial and national identity of a native African.

It is of course this claim to valid apostolic succession which sets Alexander apart from the charismatic leadership of other independent churches and which places him and the African Orthodox Church in a unique position vis-a-vis the traditional churches.[59]

The most significant recent implication of Alexander's episcopacy has to do with recent divisions among the Orthodox of East Africa. A small Westernized group remained loyal to the Greek Patriarchate of Alexandria, but, dissatisfied with Greek rule and still striving for an autocephalous national church, Father Spartas returned to independency. He led a large,[60] loose confederation of bodies which identified itself with the Coptic Church of Egypt. There was no formal affiliation, but the Copts admitted students from Spartas's group into their seminary in Cairo and, if reasonable conditions were met, considered consecrating a bishop. In the meantime this loose confederation referred to itself as Coptic - and justified the identification by its descent from Alexander. The history is now unknown or forgotten. Alexander is remembered as "a Negro from U.S.A. who came to East Africa through Ethiopia," and it is believed that he was himself consecrated by the Syrian Jacobite patriarch who sent him to East Africa. This consecration by a non-Chalcedonian Oriental patriarch is therefore perceived as tieing to Coptic Orthodoxy those who derive their orders from Alexander: "so in this case we are Originated with the Coptic Patriarchate of Alexandria."[61] More recently, Spartas has been received back into the Greek Church and consecrated a bishop.

Alexander was undoubtedly honest in denying both direct links to the Garvey Movement[62] and any political motivation in his ecclesiastical work.[63] Yet by establishing African churches with African

[59]To my knowledge the only other African prelate with a similar kind of claim was His Beatitude Mar Kwamin I, Prince-Patriarch of Apam, also known as Kwamin Nsetse Bresi-Ando or Ebenezer Johnson Anderson. A comparison is unfair since Alexander was a serious churchman while Bresi-Ando appears to have been a fraud. At one time associated with Jones in the Gold Coast, Bresi-Ando set out for the United States to meet the directors of the African Universal Church. He stopped in London, however, and on 6 March 1935, was elevated to the episcopate by the Most Rev. John Churchill Sibley, metropolitan of the (virtually non-existent) Orthodox Catholic Church in England and chancellor of the Inter-collegiate University, a notorious degree mill. Sibley had been consecrated by Frederick Ebenezer Lloyd, Vilatte's successor as primate of the American Catholic Church. Unlike these *episcopi vagantes*, many of whom were little more than, in Anson's phrase, "religious confidence men," Alexander did not traffic in bogus ecclesiastical titles and academic degrees,; he actually had priests and congregations under his charge, and, most important, he never consecrated other bishops. Bresi-Ando's curious career is described by Anson, *Bishops at Large*, 278-279. Information on Bresi-Ando's relationship with Jones was furnished by the archbishop in an interview with the writer in Accra on 1 July 1971. See also David Kimble, *A Political History of Ghana: The Rise of Gold Coast Nationalism, 1850-1928* (Oxford, 1963), 544. Appreciation for Alexander's restraint in ordaining is noted by Hulme, *Blackwall to Bloemfontein*, 328.

[60]Perhaps of several million adherents, although accurate statistics are difficult to obtain and verify.

[61]Correspondence dated 18 March 1972, from Dr. Robert Makodawa, Secretary General, The United Orthodox Independent Churches of East Africa - Coptic Patriarchate of All Africa.

[62]Brandreth, *Episcopi Vagantes*, 57.

[63]Corfield, *Historical Survey*, 174.

characteristics, Alexander manifested the cultural nationalism of Garveyism and encouraged the realization among Africans - learned long before by Europeans - that if they could control their own churches they could control other institutions of their own as well. Alexander found inspiration for independence in Garvey's newpaper and a vehicle for independence in the denomination related to the Universal Negro Improvement Association. Independent churches were the first achievement in the long struggle towards the realization of Garvey's goal of self-determination, "Africa for the Africans." Of course this was a goal articulated and worked for by others as well, but Alexander's biography supports Hodgkin's claim that it was the Garvey Movement "in which the strands of Ethiopianism and Pan-Africanism were closely interwoven."[64]

While Alexander's debt to the African patriotism and nationalism of Garveyite ideology should not be neglected, Alexander - like McGuire - was a churchman before he was a social critic or political activist, despite the fact that the origin of the African Orthodox Church in both Africa and the United States was a reaction against societies built on racism. The accomplishment of political independence has not lessened the growth of independent churches, and David Barrett emphasizes the fact that for these churches "independency is basically a religious phenomenon arising out of a religious need and now that the anti-colonial struggle has been won in most territories, it is free to turn its attention to religious issues."[65] From this perspective Alexander's role as churchman comes into clearer focus and informs a better understanding of his life, his significance, and the need for independent black churches to have their own identity, integrity and authenticity. As that need is fulfilled, the ecumenical importance[66] of the African Orthodox Church, the place of Archbishop Alexander as its chief African founder, and the historical place of the church in the development of Pan-Africanism can only become more widely appreciated.

[64] Thomas Hodgkin, *Nationalism in Colonial Africa* (New York, 1957), 101.

[65] David B. Barrett, *Schism and Renewal in Africa: An Analysis of Six Thousand Contemporary Religious Movements* (Nairobi, 1968), 247.

[66] J. E. Goldthorpe, *Outlines of East African Society* (Kampala, 1958), 223, draws attention to the "important departure" of a separatist church united with a major world church and points to the "double advantage" of the AOC in Uganda after 1946 when Spartas was recognized by the Greek patriarch of Alexandria: "local independence from mission control, but at the same time the full status of membership of a recognized major division of Christianity."

RACE, SCIENCE, AND THE LEGITIMIZATION OF WHITE SUPREMACY IN SOUTH AFRICA, 1902–1940*

By Paul Rich

Ideas of race in South African history have usually been seen in the context of the rise of white nationalism and apartheid. This has led to a focus upon the internal dynamics of Afrikaner political mobilization organized by such bodies as the Dutch Reformed Churches, the Broederbond, and the National Party.[1] More recently scholars have begun to examine the role of British racial ideas in South African politics. Leonard Thompson has shown in a recent study of the role of historical mythology in the development of apartheid ideology that some British notions of social Darwinism and race fitness were taken up in South Africa by both English- and Afrikaans-speaking race ideologues in the early years of the twentieth century.[2] Thompson's study did not pursue in any detailed manner the influence of British and United States racial ideology on the emergence of white South African racism, which was mainly seen through the development of Afrikaner nationalist consciousness.

Radical scholars have also begun to stress the importance of ideas generated in the imperial metropolis seeping through into South African political debate before and after Union in 1910. In the 1970s Martin Legassick began a reassessment of the British ideological impact at the time of the reconstruction in the Transvaal after the Anglo-Boer War. Legassick emphasized the role of class rather than ethnic divisions in white politics as an ideology of segregation began to be mobilized in defense of white settler power. He saw racial ideas as important in transcending Afrikaner-British divisions, since they underpinned a segregationist ideology that was an instrument of white mining interests bent on mobilizing cheap black labor.[3] In a series of unpublished seminar papers, Legassick's work was significant for directing attention to the role of English race theorists in systematizing a doctrine of racial segregation in order to rationalize a policy of perpetuating pre-capitalist economies in the African reserves. The research was strongly influenced by the sociological model of Harold Wolpe that explained the transition from segregation to apartheid in South Africa as a result

---

*I am grateful to the Nuffield Foundation for providing funds that made possible part of the research for this article.

[1] See, for example, W.H. Vatcher, *White Laager: The Rise of Afrikaner Nationalism*, (London, 1965); T. Dunbar Moodie, *The Rise of Afrikanerdom: Power, Apartheid and the Afrikaner Civil Religion* (Berkeley, 1979); Dan O'Meara, *Volkskapitalisme: Class, Capital and Ideology in the Development of Afrikaner Nationalism, 1934-1948* (Johannesburg, 1983).

[2] Leonard Thompson, *The Political Mythology of Apartheid* (New Haven, 1986); see also Christopher Saunders, *The Making of the South African Past* (Cape Town, 1988).

[3] Martin Legassick, "The Making of South African 'Native Policy,' 1903-1923: The Origins of Segregation," London, Institute of Commonwealth Studies (mimeo), 1972; "British Hegemony and the Origins of Segregation, 1900-1914," London, Institute of Commonwealth Studies (mimeo), 1973.

of the collapse of the subsistence base of the reserves. Migrant labor was see as undermining the rural peasant economy that had, in its initial phases, artificially subsidized African wage rates in the urban areas.[4]

More recently, Saul Dubow has reassessed this explanation for segregation by the revisionist school, pointing out that some of the English-speaking apologists for segregation in the early years of this century were not so much concerned with cheap African labor migrating from the reserves but with more general issues of social discipline and social control over the African work force.[5] Segregation in this instance appears more as an extension of Victorian fears of the "dangerous classes." The ideology was constructed to maintain social order as well as social and moral hygiene, which became a powerful mataphorical image in the drive for urban segregation in South Africa in the early twentieth century.[6] It was also evident from an analysis of the role of the administrative class in the South African state, such as the Native Affairs Department, that there was an independent bureaucratic rationale for segregation in terms of a desire to consolidate the department's control through such legislation as the 1927 Native Administration Act.[7] It is thus clearly inadequate to see segregationist ideology as the mere rationalization of capitalist class interests in South Africa's industrializing society.

These efforts at refining historical knowledge on the nature and trajectory of South African segregationist ideology indicate that it has to be taken far more seriously in its impact on South African political economy than many historians of an earlier liberal generation have imagined. Segregation was not simply the atavistic product of a pre-industrial frontier but was part of a wider pattern of modernization of South African society. To this extent, segregation can be seen, as John Cell has pointed out, as an extremely adaptive and protean ideology that focused a drive towards the "highest stage of white supremacy."[8] As part of this drive, there was a clear desire to incorporate modern and "scientific" modes of discourse within the segregationist lexicon. The burden of this paper is to show how this was for a period an important part of the South African debate on race before the emergence of apartheid. It was superceded in the 1930s by a language that was influenced by an anthropology emphasizing cultural rather than racial differences.

---

[4]Harold Wolpe, "Capitalism and Cheap Labour Power in South Africa: From Segregation To Apartheid," *Economy and Society*, XIV (1972), 425-56.

[5]Saul Dubow, *Racial Segregation and the Origins of Apartheid in South Africa, 1919-36* (London, 1989), 24.

[6]M. Swanson, "The Sanitation Syndrome: Bubonic Plague and Urban Native Policy in the Cape Colony, 1900-1909," *Journal of African* History, XV111, 3 (1977).

[7]Dubow, *Racial Segregation*, 77-127; "Holding a Just Balance Between White and Black: The Native Affairs Department in South Africa, 1920-33," *Journal of Southern African Studies* X11, 2 (1986).

[8]John W. Cell, *The Highest Stage of White Supremacy: The Origins of Segregation in South Africa and the American South* (Cambridge, 1982).

Race and the Drive for "Scientific" Segregation

The theorists involved in the South African debate on segregation after the Anglo-Boer War were small inter-locking groups of political activists, racist doctrinaires, and amateur anthropologists, some of whom came from missionary backgrounds. Much of their reading was second-hand and, until the rise of anthropological research in the 1920s and 1930s, there was little attempt to back up propositions with systematic evidence. Argument often fell back upon well-worn stereotypes, though this did not preclude a strong determination among many of them to try and develop a "scientific" vocabulary to justify segregation.

The appeal of science lay in the rapidly growing connections in the international scientific community by the early twentieth century. Scientific discourses began rapidly penetrating such new subject areas as geography, anthropology, and psychology at this time. The prominent missionary role in the discussion of race issues was beginning to be undermined by a new secular interest from ostensibly neutral "experts" who appeared to be gaining allies from within a new professional intelligentsia in efforts to influence policy at the level of the state. The newer scientific discourse in many cases ended up perpetuating older conceptions of African society inherited from nineteenth-century travellers and missionaries in a new guise. The scientific popularizers of race looked for tendencies described by Philip Curtin as "diversificationism" that emphasized aspects of human difference rather than similarity. Behind much of their thinking was the assumption that there was some form of order and hierarchy in human races in which the white, Anglo-Saxon race occupied the topmost position.[9]

Political debate in South Africa raged as elsewhere on the possible future outcome of the relationship forged by colonial conquest between blacks and whites. C.T. Loram, a prominent educationalist from Natal, identified three schools of thought on the issue: "repressionists," "equalists," and "segregationists." The latter Loram saw as holding the middle ground between the other two.[10] "Scientific" evidence to buttress the arguments of the segregationists was open-ended, since it could be used to support a variety of predictions regarding the future. Few Social Darwinists in South Africa held that Africans would completely die out in the face of advancing white colonial settlement, in contrast to many exponents of this view in the U.S. at this time.[11] The demographic balance in South Africa in which whites numbered some one million in the 1904 census compared to three and a half million Africans ensured that even the most ardent of white racists had to accept the permanence of African occupation in a "white man's country." Territorial segregationist ideology, as in the popular novel of the Milner Kindergarten member John Buchan, *Prester John* (1910), tended to be perceived in the early twentieth century in terms of different geographical regions of white and black land settlement. Cities and urban areas and the temperate

---

[9]Philip Curtin, *The Image of Africa* (Madison, 1964), 429-31.

[10]C.T. Loram, *The Education of the South African Native*, (London, 1927), 17-25.

[11]John S. Haller, *Outcasts From Evolution: Scientific Attitudes to Racial Inferiority, 1859-1900* (New York 1975), 209. One South African theorist of race, though, continued to believe as late as the 1890s that the "aborigines" of the continent would die out in the face of "Caucasian" advance. See F. S. Tatham, *The Race Conflict in South Africa* (Pietermaritzburg, 1894).

high veld regions were considered the abodes of whites, while the low veld areas and regions of dense African peasant settlement such as Transkei and Zululand were the terrain of Africans.[12] It was hoped that in time the rural peasant economies would undergo an internal evolutionary adaptation toward the white model of agriculture.

From the middle 1880s, a progressive erosion occurred in the Cape liberal impulse based on a civilizing ideal of progressively accomodating educated Africans into a single colonial society. In 1897 the liberal scholar and politician from Britain, James Bryce, wrote pessimistically in *Impressions of South Africa* that the "two races" of white and black in South Africa were "separated by the repulsion of physical differences" and would have "no social intercourse, no mixture of blood, but will each form, a nation by itself for all purposes save those of industry and perhaps of politics."[13] Bryce's observations indicated that even in the metropolitan heartland of the Victorian liberal tradition, there were growing doubts on the capacity for white and blacks to mix in a common society.[14] They provided a fillip for the development of segregationism in South Africa over the following decades.

The attack on the Cape *mission civilisatrice* developed in the years after the Anglo-Boer War during a period of reconstruction in the Transvaal under the British colonial administration of Lord Milner. A number of scholars have pointed to the long-term importance of the South African Native Affairs Commission of 1903-1905 under the secretary of native affairs in the Transvaal, Sir Godfrey Lagden. Though the Commission never specifically referred to "segregation" as such, it certainly envisaged the separate holding of land by whites and Africans.[15] Legassick has argued that the Commission represented more a synthesis of local ideas current in South Africa rather than those from the British metropolis.[16] This was due in part to the fact that opinion in colonial circles in Whitehall was unclear over the long-term direction of "native policy." There was a general preference for preserving indigenous African institutions in the belief that Africans did not like being pressurized into accepting too hasty a pace of change. But what theorizing there was tended to be of an academic kind that had little direct relationship to the actual situation on the ground in Africa.[17]

Some of the representatives of the British official mind also reflected this political skepticism. Lagden began to doubt as early as 1903 whether the Commission's work would lead to clear policies and considered that "we can do little

---

[12]Paul B. Rich, "Milnerism and a Ripping Yarn: Transvaal Land Settlement and John Buchan's Novel *Prester John*, 1901-1910," in Belinda Bozzoli, ed.,, *Town and Countryside in the Transvaal* (Johannesburg, 1983), 412-33.

[13]James Bryce, *Impressions of South Africa* (London, 1899), 465.

[14]Paul B. Rich, *Race and Empire in British Politics*, (Cambridge, 1986), 15-26.

[15]Cell, *Highest Stage*, 210-13.

[16]Legassick "British Hegemony," 3.

[17]Ronald Hyam, *Elgin and Churchill at the Colonial Office* (London, 1968), 371-72.

more than generalise our conclusions."[18] Towards the end of his stay as secretary of native affairs he felt increasingly vulnerable to attacks from white racial extremists in the Johannesburg press at a time of "black peril" scares relating to the large black servant population in the city. He wanted the "native question" to be debated in as "non-political" a manner as possible.[19]

The South African Native Affairs Commission was in many respects part of a holding operation by the colonial establishment in the Transvaal against pressures for a more overtly racist interpretation of South African politics that frequently resorted to a pseudo-scientific Darwinism. The *Transvaal Leader*, for instance, urged in the wake of the "disgraceful scenes" in the 1904 Cape elections, where white candidates had been "begging and manoeuvring for the votes of black men" that:

> we can say with scientific certainty that the process of evolution must be so prolonged as to deprive any speculations based on it of present political interest or importance, even were the negro or negroid races on an ethnological equality with the people of Aryan or Caucasian descent. That, however, is a position that no one yet maintains. The very formation of the negro skull is so antagonistic to the theory, recalling as it does the Neanderthal head, which is admittedly a member of the European race which existed many thousands of years before the dawn of history.[20]

This racism was of an impressionistic variety which sought authoritative backing from fewer "scientific" experts compared to that of the United States during the same period. The colonial establishment was concerned to try and lead white political opinion and reduce the influence of the racial extremists, who threatened to stir up feelings at a time when there were mounting demands for self-government. Lagden saw the arrival of the British Association for the Advancement of Science in South Africa for its 1905 annual meeting as an important opportunity for expert backing for a moderate position on the "native question." He declined an invitation to give a paper to the gathering himself, but asked Howard Pim to address it. He assisted Pim in visiting Basutoland (Lesotho) as part of his research for the paper, as this appeared a working model of the

---

[18]Godfrey Lagden Papers, Rhodes House Library, Oxford, A951/A7 Diary entry for 16 March 1903. In a memorandum on the SANAC report, Lagden felt that it was "desirable to move steadily and quietly so as to avoid any unnecessary disturbance of the native mind." He opposed the multiplications of African land holdings "scattered throughout the white population and owning the land of the country equally with them," since this would "accentuate feelings of race prejudice and animosity with unhappy results," Archives of the Transvaal Secretary of Native Affairs, Transvaal Archives Depot, Pretoria, SNA 265, *Memorandum by the Commissioner for Native Affairs upon the Report of South African Native Affairs Commission in its Relation to the Transvaal, 1905*, 1-4.

[19]Diary entry for 30 January 1905.

[20]*The Transvaal Leader*, October 19, 1904.

self-sufficient peasant reserve in southern Africa that was so favored by the segregationists.[21]

Pim had made a favorable impression on Lagden by interpreting the race issue in South Africa through a benevolent humanitarianism. While the race issue might be an "academic one" for the rest of the British empire, Pim had pointed out in in a 1903 paper to the Transvaal Philosophical Society, in the South African context there was a need for an agreed policy on it. He warned against direct methods of forcing Africans out into the labor market and was interested in maintaining the reserve economies less as a means for promoting cheap migrant labor for the mines than as a mechanism of social control.[22] He shared the view of James Bryce that black and white would be unable to live side by side, though he was concerned to pursue a humanitarian ideal through the logic of the free market. This meant championing the ideals of De Tocqueville in his work *Democracy in America*, for "if the Natives in this country work voluntarily as free men in the open market, we need not fear the degradation of the white man."[23] In 1905 Pim also urged a closer comparison between the situation in South Africa and that of the U.S. South for the apparently similar tendencies in both societies "must be due to racial difference of a fundamental nature, and for this reason must receive the closest attention and be treated with the greatest respect."[24] During this period liberal humanitarians internationally were not averse to trying to link a code of humanitarian ethics with what appeared to be self-evident race differences. It was only by the late 1920s and 1930s that a rejection of the whole notion of race differences would emerge.[25]

There was already a feeling of despondency in some black political circles by the time that Lagden left South Africa at the end of 1905. The Cape paper *Izwi Labantu* complained that Lagden had "lost the sympathy of the intelligent native" for his opinions were "simply theories thrown out as capitalist kisses to bolster up a policy which as far as his conduct of Native Affairs goes has been discreditable to the country and the credit of the British government."[26] The black elite in the Cape felt increasingly betrayed by the British colonial administration in the Transvaal. They saw the Milner administration as failing to make a strong stand against the white settler interests on the Witwatersrand who

---

[21] J. Howard Pim Papers, Church of the Province Archives, University of the Witwatersrand, Johannesburg, G. Lagden to H. Pim 29 November 1903, 6 and 24 April 1905.

[22] Howard Pim, *The Native Question in South Africa* (Johannesburg, 1903).

[23] Howard Pim, *The Native Problem in South Africa*, (Johannesburg, 1905), 11. "To think that we can civilise the native is an idle dream," Pim wote, "He must civilise himself or die," 13. See also Howard Pim, *The Question of Race* (Johannesburg, 1906).

[24] *The Native Problem in South Africa.*

[25] John David Shingler, "Education and Political Order in South Africa, 1902-1961" (Ph.D thesis, Yale University, 1973), 17; in Britain, though, many aspects of the old racial typology survived well into the 1940s, Rich, *Race and Empire*, 117-19.

[26] *Izwi Labantu*, March 20 1906. Some black papers had felt doubtful over Lagden's chairmanship of SANAC from the very beginning. "I do not think that the country will benefit under his chairmanship," wrote "a native." "He has not the training of a judge - a man who has studied impartially to perfection," *Koranta ea Becoana*, October 21 1903.

opposed the extension of the qualified Cape African franchise to the rest of South Africa.

This despondency grew in the following few years as there was mounting pressure for a "native policy" in South Africa with an "element of finality in it."[27] The attainment of Responsible Government in the Transvaal following the victory of the Het Volk Party of General Botha and General Smuts in 1907 provided a political focus for an attack upon the cautious trusteeship of the previous Milner administration. As the question of "Closer Union" in South Africa began to loom on the horizon, the issue of a coherent native policy for the new state increasingly permeated political debate.

This became evident with the founding of the Transvaal Native Affairs Society in 1908 "for the study and discussion of the South African native question, with a view to enunciating and advocating a liberal, consistent and practical Native policy throughout South Africa."[28] The Society soon proved less than liberal in refusing to admit Africans as members. It tended to represent English-speaking commercial and professional interests on the Witwatersrand. In March 1908 Howard Pim was elected chairman, and David Pollock secretary; the Society met on the premises of one of its members, a baker J.W. Quinn.[29] The colonial establishment in the Transvaal tended to avoid the body; the High Anglican bishop of Pretoria, Michael Furse, dropped out of it while the governor of the Transvaal, Lord Selborne, refused to become honorary president. At Pim's inaugural address as president, only sixty people were present.[30]

Despite its tiny size, the Transvaal Native Affairs Society was a significant catalyst of ideas on racial segregation, which had up until that time been debated in more elite circles of missionaries or groups of colonial administrators such as the Fortnightly Club founded by members of the Milner Kindergarten.[31] The Society was notable for discussing ideas on industrial education strongly influenced by the experiments of Booker T. Washington at Tuskegee in Alabama.[32] In the course of 1909, however, a split emerged between moderates and hard-liners led by an insurance broker named F.W. Bell. The Bell faction secured the support of a British anthropologist visiting South Africa, A.H. Keane, author of a number of anthropological works and a former vice president of the Royal Anthropological Institute. Keane was drawn to the South African debate as a virulent racist who dismissed Africans as of low intellectual capacity. A figure from the Victorian anthropological tradition, he had become marginalized from British anthropology by the early twentieth century through his refusal to

---

[27] A. Colquhoun, *The Afrikaner Land* (London, 1906).

[28] J. Howard Pim Papers, Transvaal Native Affairs Society, *Constitution and Rules*, Johannesburg, 1908, para. 1.

[29] J. Howard Pim Papers, Transvaal Native Affairs Society, Minute Book.

[30] *Ibid.*

[31] Legassick, "British Hegemony."

[32] *Transvaal Leader*, November 4 1908 and July 8 1909

accept the general enthusiasm for anthropometric measurement of skulls in preference for discovering racial differences through the study of language.[33]

Keane addressed the Transvaal Native Affairs Society in September 1909 and declared that Africans had "ceased to evolve" and were "incapable of development." He cited the work of the U.S. racist R.W. Shufeld, a physician from Virginia, whose work *The Negro: A Menace to Civilization* had become popular among Southern segregationists.[34] Such "scientific" support was welcome to the Bell faction, who were dismissive of Pim's humanitarianism and support for a trusteeship role for whites in the sub-continent.[35] Bell succeeded Pim as president in 1909 and in a series of pamphlets urged a program of radical segregation that would make the Africans "like fish out of water" in the urban areas. He strongly attacked the evolutionary arguments of Lord Selborne on the grounds that they would lead to the disappearance of the white race in South Africa.[36]

This emergence of racial extremism on the Witwatersrand occurred at a time when there was little formal anthropological research in South Africa. In Britain, some "Africa experts" such as Harry Johnstone urged that there should be far more interest in investigating the nature of African societies in South Africa.[37] This was a view that was echoed by Howard Pim in his retiring address as president of the Transvaal Native Affairs Society when he claimed that the "most obvious want of data sufficiently well established" made it hard to "justify our founding upon them a rational policy towards the native races of this country."[38] By the time of Union in 1910 segregation was still viewed by a number of observers as a rather dangerous experiment that had little sound scientific or empirical base on which to ground rational government policies.

Segregation, furthermore, appeared to be a strategy that contained the implicit danger of cutting South Africa from the ethical basis of statecraft that was generally considered to underlie the government in Britain. To some of Bell's supporters such as H.J. Crocker, this was not considered an especially serious problem. Restating the Darwinian view that the "ascendancy" of Western peoples was "physical and intellectual" rather than "moral and spiritual," Crocker argued that white rule in South Africa depended upon "some important modification of the ethical system upon which it is founded."[39] Other writers and opinion-formers

---

[33] A.H. Haddon Papers, Cambridge University Library, 4071, A.H. Keane to A.C. Haddon 27 January 1903; A.H. Keane, *Ethnology* (Cambridge, 1896), 10.

[34] *Transvaal Leader*, September 29 1909.

[35] Howard Pim, *The Native Problem: Presidential Address Read at the Inaugural Meeting of the Native Affairs Society, April 21, 1908* (Johannesburg, 1908), 1.

[36] Fred W. Bell, *The South African Native Problem: The Solution of Segregation* (Johannesburg, 1909), 13. Bell later reflected that the Native Affairs Society had come close to "being captured by those who may, I think, with reason be claimed as 'negrophilists,'" F.W. Bell Papers, Church of the Province Archives, University of the Witwatersrand, handwritten ms, n.d.

[37] Harry Johnstone, "The Native Problem and Sane Imperialism," *The Nineteenth Century* (August 1909), 234-44.

[38] Howard Pim, *A Plea For The Scientific Study of the Races Inhabiting South Africa* (Johannesburg, 1910).

[39] H.J. Crocker, *The South African Race Problem* (Johannesburg, 1908).

at this time took a different view and were anxious for South African policy to rest upon a more universal ethical basis. "Self-preservation," wrote Edward Dallas in 1909, was "not a matter of mere military dominance," for "the preservation of our moral status is as important. We hold almost as clear as life itself the mode of civilisation which is the expression of our national development—the organisation of social and public life in which the ideals of the race have found embodiment."[40] This anxiety found expression in some political speeches at the time, and in 1909 General Smuts warned an audience at Troyeville in Johannesburg that "if they wanted to push the ideal of segregation further they must be prepared for the gravest trouble that South Africa had faced in the course of its whole history."[41]

In the period after Union there seemed to be an increasingly favorable climate for segregationists to impress their ideas on political decision-makers. "Instinctively I feel the native problem cannot be longer shelved," Bell wrote to General J.B.M. Hertzog, the Union minister of native affairs in 1911, "if you tackle the problem you will need all the help possible from those whose heart is fired."[42] Segregationist ideology began slowly to permeate the administrative echelons of government, though it is clear that sections of the Native Affairs Department, especially from the Cape and Transkei, remained hostile to it for a considerable number of years. The Cape Native Affairs Department was particularly suspicious of the extensive resettlement of the African population that would be required if segregation were to be successfully implemented. This was felt likely to lead to disruption and the erosion of the more paternalistic structures of control which the Department has been able to build up through its system of native magistrates.[43]

Hertzog's espousal of segregationist ideas also alarmed a number of Cape politicians, such as John X. Merriman, who considered that "if it means trying to bottle the Natives up body and soul then we may as well pack up our portmanteaux, for the European race will perish."[44] The appeal of segregation to many white opinion-formers and political leaders lay in its apparent ability to guarantee the whites a place in a future South Africa. Even though Bell was driven to confess that South Africa could never be a complete "white man's country," he still felt sure that "certain large areas may be preserved for each race once the desirability and the principle of segregation be recognised."[45]

---

[40]Edward Dallas, *Notes on the South African Race Problem* (Johannesburg, 1909), 1. See also Trevor Fletcher, "The Native Problem: A Transcendental View," *The African Monthly*, 4, 24 (November 1908), 585.

[41]*The Star*, July 15 1910.

[42]F.W. Bell Papers, F.W. Bell to J.B.M. Hertzog, 26 September 1911.

[43]See, for example, the evidence of Edward Dower, Secretary of Native Affairs, to the Beaumont Commission, *Report of the Natives Lands Commission, Vol. 11, UG22-1916*, 230; Dubow, *Racial Segregation*, 80.

[44]John X. Merriman to M.T. Steyn, October 18 1912 in Phyllis Lewsen, ed., *Selections from the Correspondence of John X. Merriman* (Cape Town, 1966), 225.

[45]F.W. Bell Papers, F.W. Bell, *Farewell Address to the Transvaal Native Affairs Society* (Johannesburg, 1910).

The problem lay in being able to demonstrate the scientific validity of the segregationist idea to an audience that remained doubtful about both its morality and practicability. To a section of the South African professional class that was emerging at this time, the best way to justify it lay in the area of scientific evidence proving the essential differences of whites and blacks. Attention began to turn to the sociological and psychological aspects in which Africans were adjusting to the challenges of urbanization and industrialization in South Africa.

The Measurement of African Personality

In the years after Union, segregation in South Africa gained a number of adherents among the small South African professional intelligentsia as it took on a form that appeared politically feasible and morally acceptable, despite the doubts of earlier critics. In Natal, Maurice Evans became a popular exponent of the segregationist ideal. Addressing the Durban Native Affairs Reform Club in 1912, for instance, he drew on parallels with the U.S. South following a visit there the previous year. Like Pim, he was concerned with maintaining the cohesion of African peasant society in the face of advancing industrialization and was skeptical on the long-term prospects of an African urban population being able to survive. The point was to "protect, advise, assist, control, study to give the black man in our midst, not an individual opportunity but a racial opportunity."[46] Racial differences were a basic reality of South African life for Evans. Despite his acknowledgment that "zoologically we are of the same species," he exhibited a strain of neo-Lamarckian thought when he emphasized that races were different through the inheritance of acquired characteristics:

> through countless generations we have diverged, and the physical differences which are so plain to us are the outward and visible signs of mental and spiritual differences, and . . . no change or treatment and environment will within any time available to us, make the black man's mind and spirit, any more than a black man's body that of a white man.[47]

It appeared increasingly necessary to undertake some form of scientific measurement of what these supposed inherited differences really were. Evans's books *Black and White in South East Africa* (1911) and *Black and White in the Southern States* (1913) indicated the growing importance of American ideas on industrial training and the rustication of black peasant communities on South African race thinking.[48] This was to be taken a step further when some analysts began to approach the question of intelligence testing. By the First World War there was a growing popularity of biological and psychological theories of heredity in the British and U.S. scientific communities. Craniological and anthropometric mea-

[46]Maurice Evans, *Studies in the Southern States from a South African point of view*, Address to the Durban Native Affairs Reform Committee (Durban, 1912?), 10.

[47]*Ibid.*

[48]Paul B. Rich, "The Appeals of Tuskegee: James Henderson, Lovedale and the Fortunes of South African Liberalism, 1906-1930," *The International Journal of African Historical Studies*, 20. 2 (1987), 271-92.

surements appeared increasingly unreliable indices of race differences, and analysts were drawn to intelligence tests as a more accurate way of assessing the educational potential of different racial and ethnic groups. The tests, as Stephen Jay Gould has pointed out, were generally based upon the fallacy that the percentage variation of individuals with each group could also explain differences between groups, especially whites and blacks.[49]

The scientific community in South Africa, though small, was quick to respond to these methodological developments. The South African Association for the Advancement of Science (S.A.A.A.S), which had been founded in 1903, exhibited a continuing interest in the ideas and approaches of the scientific communities in Britain and the U.S., from where a number of its members were recruited. The meetings of the S.A.A.A.S. also had a strong symbolic importance since they demonstrated in a tangible form the inclusion of the new Dominion of South Africa in the British Empire-Commonwealth. Membership of the Association grew from 547 in 1915 to 770 in 1939, indicating the slow professionalization of science teaching in schools and universities. The Association's meetings acted as an important forum for a variety of groups, which included a number of missionaries and educationalists as well as civil servants in the early years. The Association enjoyed a fairly close relationship with the South African state, aided by the personal interests during the inter-war years of a number of prominent politicians such as General Smuts and Jan H. Hofmeyr.[50]

The Association's proceedings from the First World War included a Section F on social and anthropological issues, and these became dominated by the capacity of Africans to "adapt" and "evolve" towards the standards of "western civilisation." The participants in these proceedings usually avoided the earlier forms of anthropometric measurement and moved rapidly towards intelligence tests modelled on those developed by Alfred Binet and Theodore Simon in France and Henry H. Goddard, Lewis A. Terman, and R.M. Yerkes in the United States. Stephen Gottheid Rich, though, confessed to severe doubts in 1917 as to the applicability of the tests to Africans following a test conducted on 170 African children and students between 6 and 22 years of age at the Amanzimtoti and Adams Primary Schools in Natal. The Binet-Simon tests seemed to "test as much cultural conditions as of mental ability" and there were problems in establishing what was "normal progress" among Africans. Mission-educated Africans were not necessarily "typical" either, and the problem remained of establishing a valid test to assess the kind of educational curriculum that would "fit" Africans.[51]

The same year as this presentation, there appeared a book by an educationalist from Natal, Charles Templeman Loram, entitled *The Education of the*

---

[49]Stephen Jay Gould, *The Mismeasure of Man* (Harmondsworth, 1984), 146-233.

[50]Jan H. Hofmeyr, for example, declared when opening the 1929 meeting of the Association that the emergence of South African science could serve as a "Southern gateway . . . effectively to permeate Africa," Jan H. Hofmeyr, *Africa and Science* (Cape Town, 1929), 11.

[51]Stephen Gottheid Rich, "Binet Simon Tests in Zululand," *Report of the S.A.A.A.S.*, Stellenbosch 1917 (Cape Town, 1918), 482. For the importance of the First World War on the U.S. tests, see Daniel J. Kevles, "Testing the Army's Intelligence: Psychologists and the Military in World War 1," *The Journal of American History*, LV (June 1968), 556-81; Franz Samuelson, "World War I Intelligence Testing and the Development of Psychology," *Journal of the History of Behavioural Science*, 13 (1977), 274-82.

South African Native. This work was to have a marked impacton the debate on African educability for a considerable number of years. Loram was interested in the subject of "racial psychology," and the book was originally a doctoral dissertation submitted to the Teachers' College at Columbia University where intelligence testing had been developed through the work of Edward Lee Thorndike.[52]

Loram was a strong advocate of segregation at the time of writing the book, for he felt that the education of Africans should be geared towards industrial and agricultural rather than "literary and bookish" training.[53] He attacked what he saw as the "assimilationist" principles of the Cape system and stressed the differential patterns of mental development of whites and blacks on the basis of comparative tests of schoolchildren. In the case of arithmetic, for instance, he reported that African children were 30 to 100 percent slower than white children and less accurate. The "slowness" of Africans was, he claimed, "proverbial" and "until we realise that our educational programme must be based upon the peculiar characteristics of the people we are doomed to disappointment."[54]

Loram doubted whether these "peculiar characteristics" were rooted in a firm pattern of "arrested development," since a eugenic program involving "the spread of civilisation, selective breeding, improved environment, and better teaching" would in time "lessen the mental differences between Europeans and Natives."[55] The work blurred the distinction between heredity and environment and urged that both biological and social engineering were needed in South African "race relations" as it was being increasingly termed.[56]

The discussions in the S.A.A.S. reflected this growing interest in the importance of both heredity and environment in the years after World War One. This was a period in which there was mounting anxiety in white political circles over the possible threat to white racial purity through sexual "miscegenation" with black Africans. Sarah Gertrude Millin's novels of this period such as *Dark Water* (1921) and *God's Stepchildren* (1924) exemplify this preoccupation with interracial sexual liaisons and the emergence of a supposedly degenerate "half-caste" progeny.[57] In 1927 the Immorality Act, outlawing sexual relationships across the color line, was passed by the South African Parliament.

---

[52]*The Education of the South African Native*, 127.

[53]For the significance of Thorndike's work at the Columbia Teacher's College see Hamilton Cravens, *The Triumph of Evolution: American Scientists and the Heredity-Environment Controversy, 1900-1941* (Philadelphia, 1978), 15-86.

[54]Loram, *Education*, 192.

[55]*Ibid.*, 224-25.

[56]*Ibid.*

[57]J.M. Coetzee, "Blood, Flaw, Taint, Degeneration: The Case of Sarah Gertrude Millin," *English Studies in Africa*, 23, 1 (1980), 41-59. The attack on "miscegenation" occurred in scientific circles at this time as well. At the 1917 meeting of the S.A.A.S Rev Noel Roberts argued that there was a distinct "native mentality," which missions had to train in the art of reasoning. This "mentality" was based upon the "arrested development" of African children, whose "early promise" was checked by a wave of "sexualism" which in many cases took "entire possession of their natures to the exclusion of every other desire." The 1913 *Report of the Commission To Inquire into Assaults on Women* was cited in support of this assertion. N. Roberts, "Native Education From an Economic Point of View," *Report To The S.A.A.S.* (Cape Town, 1918), 99.

In academic circles, there was a similar interest in issues of heredity. The same year as Loram's book was published, H.B. Fantham took up the post of the first professor of comparative anatomy at the newly established University of the Witwatersrand in Johannesburg. Fantham brought considerable prestige to the post, having graduated from Cambridge (Christ's College) and University College, London, where he had been a gold medalist in zoology and a Derby research scholar. A passionate eugenicist, Fantham established a school of research at Wits and served on the university's senate, as well as being dean of the science faculty. In a number of public lectures he urged the need for sociologists to become "thoroughly versed in biological science" and outlined the basic precepts of eugenics and race fitness in terms of a Darwinian pattern of evolutionary development.[58]

Fantham was dismissive of Lamarckian ideas on the inheritance of acquired characteristics. In contrast to the rather more open-ended approach of such figures as Evans and Loram, he emphasized the notion of an ineradicable heredity. This was based upon the germ plasm theory of the German scientist August Weismann, who claimed that human heredity was shaped by an ineradicable "germ plasm" inherited from the earliest beginnings of *homo sapiens.* The influence of heredity was, Fantham claimed, "ineradicable, certain and immediate." This meant that in the study of human sociology "sentiment must be curbed or kept in bounds in accordance with scientific knowledge," since the goal of human improvement could only work in the context of a more basic set of hereditarian limits. Fantham warned of a general rise in the black birth rate and supported the banning of inter-racial marriages and sexual contact. The mentally unfit should also be sterilized. Such policies were necessary as part of a campaign for what Fantham termed a "eugenic conscience" in South Africa and he became active in establishing a series of committees on genetics and eugenics in the S.A.A.A.S.[59]

Fantham's emphasis on the centrality of heredity did not go unchallenged in S.A.A.A.S. circles. In a paper at the 1926 meeting of the Association, the professor of zoology at Rhodes University in the Eastern Cape, J.E. Duerden, attacked the "force" of heredity and the idea that "the germ plasm contains within itself something which must necessarily express itself in a certain fashion in the completed body." Duerden accepted that there were limits on the extent to which heredity could be malleable. In the case of experiments on improving the quality of ostrich feathers in South Africa, for instance, it was found that "with all our selection of germ plasm in the ostrich, interacting with the best of feeding and management, we have never been able to produce a plume beyond a certain

---

[58]H.B. Fantham File, Church of the Province Archives, University of the Witwatersrand, H.B. Fantham, lecture "Evolution and Mankind" delivered to the School of Mines, Johannesburg, July 9 1918.

[59]H.B. Fantham, "Heredity in Man: Its Importance Both Biologically and Educationally," *South African Journal of Science*, XX1 (1924), 498-527; "Some Factors in Eugenics, Together With Notes on Some South African Cases," *South African Journal of Science*, XX11 (1925), 400-212; "Some Thoughts on the Social Aspects of Eugenics, with notes on some further cases of human inheritance observed in South Africa," *South African Journal of Science*, XX111 (1926), 624-43; "Some Thoughts on Biology and Race," *South African Journal of Science*, XX1V (1927), 1-20.

length, or a certain width, or a certain lustre and grace of form."[60] The critics of the extreme hereditarian argument tended to work within the basic assumptioms of the germ plasm theory, though Durden doubted the contemporary stress on the "rising tide of colour" as it had been described in the United States and Britain in the writings of Lothrop Stoddard and Putnam Weale. Durden emphasized the importance of "Bantu studies" in the training of "experts," for in South Africa the "problem" was "no longer racial in the strict sense, not between white and black, but industrial and economic, though with peculiar features compared with other countries."[61]

Duerden's attack on the hereditarians reflected a growing realization in some quarters of the S.A.A.A.S that if the organization were to have any impact politically, it had to be geared to current debate on policy, especially in the areas of rescue work for "poor whites" and African educability. The Association had been considerably marginalized during the 1920s by the emergence of rival bodies formed to discuss and formulate policy on "the native question." In particular the Native Affairs Commission was established in 1920 as a result of the Native Affairs Act, and during the early 1920s succeeded in creating a significant role for itself in debate on racial issues. Loram became a prominent member of the Commission and at the 1921 meeting of the S.A.A.A.S. urged greater support for "experts" on the "native question," including political scientists, economists, psychologists and sociologists.[62]

In the course of the 1920s a number of liberals began to question the hereditarian orthodoxies of the eugenicists. One work that was especially important in this counter-attack was the book written by a former Rhodesian magistrate, Peter Nielsen, entitled *The Black Man's Place in South Africa*, published in 1922. This was critical of the craniological classification of races and debunked the mythology of skull measurements that was still finding support in some S.A.A.A.S. papers at this time.[63] Nielsen also attacked the notion of "arrested development" at puberty among Africans as being "another popular notion for which a sort of pseudo scientific authority may be quoted from encyclopaedias and old books of travel."[64] The work went on to dismiss the idea that there was a distinct "native mind" intrinsically different from that of whites and the Lamarckian concept that there could be inheritance of acquired characteristics.[65] Nielsen was in many respects one of the most important early South African

---

[60] J.E. Duerden, "Genetics and Eugenics in South Africa: Heredity and Environment," *South African Journal of Science*, XX11 (1925), 63.

[61] *Ibid.*, 69.

[62] C.T. Loram, "The Claims of the Native Question Upon Scientists," Presidential Address to Section E, S.A.A.A.S., 1921, *Proceedings of the S.A.A.A.S* (Cape Town, 1921), 100.

[63] The Cape liberal and amateur astronomer Alex Roberts, for example, claimed in 1922 that with the spread of education African physical features were changing "and in this direction it is interesting to state that the shape of the head of the outstanding Native leaders is quite different from that of the ordinary kraal native." A.W. Roberts, "Certain Aspects of the Native Question," *Report of the 20th Meeting of the S.A.A.A.S.* (Maputo, 1922), 98; *The Star*, July 15 1922; *The Cape Argus*, June 30 1922.

[64] Peter Nielsen, *The Black Man's Place in South Africa* (Cape Town, 1922), 10.

[65] *Ibid.*, 20-35.

critics of the whole gamut of images and popular mythologies inherited from the phase of European colonization of the African continent. He rejected the Darwinian assumption that human ethics were subordinate to the imperatives of natural selection and emphasized the importance of human intelligence in transcending the laws of biological struggle. White "superiority" was not based upon longer exposure to education, for "now that Western civilisation is spreading over the land the difference in the moral outlook of the two peoples tends to decrease; . . . and soon there will be no difference at all."[66]

Nielsen's book can be seen as representing a landmark within the local South African debate over the nature and direction of supposed racial differences. While many of its arguments were already becoming familiar at this time in liberal circles in Britain and the U.S., it was a significant local rejection of many of the basic assumptions of "diversificationism" implicit within most race thinking in South Africa. The book had an appeal to some of predominantly English-speaking liberals organized around the Joint Council movement in South Africa in the 1920s, especially as it undermined the idea that there was a distinct African "mind," which could be explored through various forms of "scientific" intelligence testing. One of the organizers of the Joint Council movement, J.D. Rheinallt Jones, went on to reject the idea of an "primitive mentality" rooted in the theories of the French anthropologist Levy Bruhl in an S.A.A.A.S paper in 1926.[67]

This did not prevent some of the liberals from becoming involved in various efforts at intelligence testing, especially those concerning the attainments of "poor white" children. The professor of philosophy at the University of the Witwatersrand, R.F.A. Hoernle, conducted such a test in 1926 on behalf of the Transvaal Education Department, though his conclusions were bitterly attacked in the Afrikaner nationalist paper *Die Burger* for alleged bias.[68] Hoernle acknowledged that the results were "experimental and provisional" in nature, though he did some lecturing on the tests to the YMCA in Johannsburg as well as the East Rand Teachers Association.[69] There was a considerable fund of interest in intelligence testing at this time among both welfare and educational circles in South Africa as they were seen as representing a "scientific" approach to the question of tackling the "poor white" issue. Hoernle was keen to mobilize more extensive academic support from colleagues such as the educationalist E.G. Malherbe teaching in the Department of Education at the University of Cape Town.

Intelligence tests also began to be examined with some interest in government circles in the course of the 1920s as a means of gathering evidence to tackle the "poor white" issue. Differences between different groups of white children were usually interpreted in terms of environmental differences, while those between whites and blacks were perceived in terms of heredity. In 1923 the

---

66*Ibid.*, 57.

67J.D. Rheinallt Jones, "The Need for a Scientific Basis for South African Native Policy," *South African Journal of Science*, XX111 (1923).

68*E.G. Malherbe Papers*, Killie Campbell Library, Durban, 425/1, R.F.A. Hoernle to E.G.M. 20 and 24 March 1926.

69*Ibid.*, R.F.A.H. to E.G.M. 25 March 1926.

commisioner for mental disorders, J.T. Dunstan, delivered the presidential address to Section F of the S.A.A.A.S. and made a comparison between "retarded" and "defective" white children. In comparison to the good prospects of educating the "retarded" white children, there was, Dunstan claimed, "such a deficiency of brain cells" among Africans that "neither education, nor environment, nor any other factor except a mutation, can lead to their rising to the level of advancement of the higher races."[70] This interest in intelligence testing continued throughout the 1920s, and in 1928 the psychologist I.D. MacCrone published some early research in social psychology (which he later disclaimed) examining the comparative scores of African girls in Rosettenville, Johannesburg, and those of London school children collected by the educationalist Cyril Burt. He concluded that there was an apparent peak in the average level of performance around 11-12 years for the African children and 13-14 years for the white children. This appeared to demonstrate the phenomenon of "arrested development."[71]

By the late 1920s, there were pressures to put this kind of research onto a more organized footing, especially with the onset of the Depression and the growing political importance of "poor white" issues in South African politics. In 1929, E.G. Malherbe was appointed director of the newly established National Bureau for Education and Social Research. Malherbe had been strongly influenced in his early approach to educational issues by C.T. Loram, who pressed him to go into a similar field as himself on "race relations."[72] Like Loram, Malherbe had studied at Columbia Teachers' College, where he kept close links with its academic teaching staff. However, a period of teaching in the newly formed Department of Education under the British educationalist Fred Clark at the University of Cape Town in the early 1920s had impressed on him the need to avoid areas of too great political controversy.[73] Loram himself had fallen out of favor with the Union minister of native affairs E.G. Jansen in the late 1920s and was forced to resign from the Native Affairs Commission in 1929. The following year he opted out of South African issues in a state of some bitterness and took a post as professor of race relations at Yale University.

Malherbe was determined not to fall into the same trap as Loram. In a paper to the S.A.A.A.S. he focussed upon the economic dimensions of the "poor white" issue, which he saw, on the basis of W.M. Macmillan's 1919 study, *The South African Agrarian Problem*, as one of transition from an agrarian to an industrial society. He condemned the "colour bar" as a barrier that checked the "natural growth of the native." Malherbe broadly supported the aims of industrial educa-

---

[70] J.T. Dunstan, "Retarded and Defective Children: Native Mentality: Mental Testing," *Report of the S.A.A.S* (Bloemfontein, 1923), 155.

[71] I.D. MacCrone, "Preliminary Results from the Porteus Maize Tests Applied to Native School Children," *South African Journal of Science*, XXV (1928), 481-84.

[72] E.G. Malherbe Papers, Killie Campbell Library, Durban, 619, C.T. Loram to E.G. Malherbe, 3 and 29 November 1928. By the folowing year Loram wrote despondently that there did not appear to be anyone else for the N.A.C."brought up in our traditions," 4 March 1929

[73] E.G. Malherbe Papers, MSS 606, Fred Clarke to E.G.M., February 26 1925. "Sometimes silence is the only possible form of support," Clarke wrote to Malherbe, "once you have given a clear statement of your own position."

tion for Africans.[74] During the following decade he began to direct the research of the National Bureau towards what he perceived to be the policy needs of the government and tried to influence official thinking towards alleviating the hardship of poor white families and breaking a cycle of pathology that was believed, on the pattern of the Jukes and Kallikak families in the United States, to run through several generations.[75] Malherbe was also keen to establish links with the mainstream white liberal establishment organized after 1929 around the South African Institute of Race Relations.[76]

The National Bureau tried to act as a forum for debate on African educability and provided the base for further intelligence testing by the psychologist of the Department of the Interior, M.L. Fick. This had involved the testing of individuals through the model of the Simon-Binet Tests and group tests modelled on the Army Beta Test devised by R.M. Yerkes in the U.S. during the First World War. The findings of Fick's study were based on 10,000 white, 817 Coloured, 762 Indian, and 293 African children. Fick challenged Loram's findings in his 1915-16 study by arguing that the scores showed significantly different levels of ability between white and African children. Even the mission-educated African children, he declared, did not grow up with pictures or diagrams and he suggested that African children "may have a different type of intelligence." In general there appeared to be "a complete lack of power of working as a group" among the African children, though the school teaching methods were found to be based on learning by rote, such that "when the child is faced with a novel situation that requires some initiative or independent activity, as in the intelligence test, it is confused and at a loss."[77] The "poor white" children, on the other hand, were tested on government-funded "indigent settlements." Two farms were tested before and after the introduction of a feeding scheme lasting a period of eighteen months. Though there were no significant increase in intelligence levels, "greater alertness and application" were noted in the school children and it was suggested that if the results were "corroborated by a longer period of feeding and stricter control, they hold out great possibilities for overcoming the apathy, lack of application and of initiative–qualities which appear to be the greatest obstacles in rehabilitating the majority of the poor whites."[78]

The impact of the research on intelligence testing on government educational policy in the 1930s appears, however, to have been limited. The research that Fick initially reported on at the 1929 meeting of the S.A.A.A.S. became

---

[74]E.G. Malherbe, "Education and the Poor White," *South African Journal of Science*, XXV1 (1929), 883-903.

[75]The Kallikak and Jukes family studies in the United States were recognized by a number of prominent South African psychologists at this time. See, for example, R.W. Wilcocks, "Intelligence, Environment and Heredity," *South African Journal of Science*, XXV111 (November 1931), 63-76. For the nature of the studies and their eventual rebuttal see Cravens, *The Triumph of Evolution*.

[76]E.G. Malherbe, *Never a Dull Moment* (Cape Town, 1981), 181. For the work of the S.A.I.R.R., see Paul B. Rich, *White Power and the Liberal Conscience* (Manchester, 1986).

[77]M.L. Fick, "Intelligence Test Results of Poor White, Native (Zulu), Coloured and Indian School Children and the Educational and Social Implications," *South African Journal of Science*, XXV1 (1929), 910.

[78]*Ibid.*, 913.

rather marginalized by the debate surrounding the report of the Native Economic Commission in 1932, which advocated the "adaptation" of African societies in the reserves towards those of white settler society in South Africa. This was represented as a middle course between the Cape ideal of assimilationism on the one hand and "repression" on the other. While segregationist in its acceptance of the idea of separate African land ownership in South Africa, it was nevertheless concerned with seeking to persuade and convince African political leadership of the just nature of the segregationist program.[79] It would be difficult to do this if it were seen as resting upon the premise that Africans were permanently inferior in their capacity for education compared to whites.

The role of black opinion in the issue of African educability became an additional important element in debate in the 1930s. An informed class of black opinion leaders had emerged in South Africa by the 1920s, whose political views became sharpened by the trajectory of segregation policy. In the Cape, for instance, D.D.T. Jabavu at the University College of Fort Hare was a strong exponent of Cape liberal ideals and a passionate defender of the color-blind franchise threatened by the legislation proposed by the Pact Government of J.B.M. Hertzog. In 1929 he challenged Fick's assertions concerning African mental inferiority at the S.A.A.A.S. meeting, maintaining that the differences were culturally induced. Jabavu backed up this assertion by pointing out that over the previous twenty years some 60 black South Africans had obtained higher degrees outside the country, while at the University College of Fort Hare a further 77 had passed the university matriculation, and 10 had graduated in the University of South Africa.[80]

The development of an articulate black intellectual opposition to the claims of the hereditarians helped buttress the opposition of the white liberal establishment to the continuing trajectory of segregation in South Africa. Jabavu became a member of the Committee of the South African Institute of Race Relations and during the 1930s many white liberals established much closer connections with members of the black political and educational elite. This black liberal opposition represented a generation of what Shingler has termed African educational modernizers who avoided nationalist ideals in favor of remodelling African society around norms of Christianity and industry and the creation of a black assimilationist elite.[81] Not all black leadership in South Africa accepted such goals, and the members of the Gamma Sigma Club, organized on the Witwatersrand by the American Board missionary Ray Phillips in the early 1930s, enthusiastically supported ideals of racial segregation.[82] The black input into the education debate proved important for the emerging group of white liberal critics of segregation in the early 1930s anxious to shift the debate away from race towards cultural attributes. Black leaders and intellectuals, however, remained

---

[79]The black newspaper *Ilanga Lase Natal*, though, wondered whether the concept of "adaptation" was not simply "repression" in another guise. *Ilanga Lase Natal* September 9 1932.

[80]D.D.T. Jabavu, "Higher Education and the Professional Training of the Bantu," *South African Journal of Science*, XXV1 (1929), 934-5.

[81]Shingler, "Education and Political Order," 29.

[82]Minute Book of the Gamma Sigma Club, African Studies Institute, University of the Witwatersrand, 20 March 1931; *The Star*, 18 April 1931. R.F.A. Hoernle was in the chair.

junior partners of the white liberals in this enterprise in the 1930s. Z.K. Matthews, a colleague of Jabavu's who taught anthropology at Fort Hare, hoped to establish discussion groups of black leaders which could debate such issues in a manner similar to the S.A.A.A.S. But such a scheme failed to get off the ground in the pre-war period and black leadership generally remained beholden to the white liberal establishment.[83]

New Departures

By 1930 a number of white South African liberals such as Edgar Brooks, James Henderson, and R.F.A. Hoernle had visited the United States and observed the progress of U.S. blacks in comparison to black South Africans.[84] To some of this group, the older ideals of segregation were found increasingly wanting in that they failed to allow for the creation of a Westernized urban black elite that could be incorporated into a common industrial society. Many liberals saw themselves as cultural intermediaries between what they termed "western civilisation" and a proletarianizing black African society.[85] They had a significant influence in the evolving political debate on black education in South Africa in the 1930s. The Report of the Inter-Departmental Committee on Native Education in 1935, for example, was notable for avoiding any supposedly "scientific" evidence of inferior African educability. It opposed the idea that education should be aimed at keeping Africans in segregated reserves.[86] It was impressed by the evidence of a number of witnesses, including Edgar Brookes, that there was no difference philosophically in the ultimate aim of education but only of "method" since "the education of the White child prepares him for life in a dominant society and the education of a Black child for a subordinate society."[87] Official ideology in South Africa by the 1930s was thus prepared to fall back on justifying the present social order through the previous historical legacy of colonial conquest than resorting to an argument for permanent black racial inferiority. This also related to its interest in gearing education to a changing economic pattern in which growing numbers of Africans were envisaged as leaving the reserve economies and coming into "contact with European economic life."[88]

Such a policy entailed the emergence of a more skilled or semi-skilled African work force, though there was also a continuing emphasis upon the need to maintain social cohesion. A number of new theoretical approaches began to be developed from both psychology and social anthropology to reinforce this shift away from race towards a cultural analysis of South African political and economic divisions. The ideas of the social anthropology school of Malinowski in Britain as well as U. S. anthropologists such as Franz Boas began to permeate the

---

[83] Z.K. Matthews Papers, microfilm, University of the Witwatersrand, Z.K. Matthews to Tennyson Makiwane, 18 September 1936.

[84] See for example Rich, "The Appeals of Tuskegee."

[85] Edgar Brookes, *Native Education in South Africa* (Pretoria, 1930), 15.

[86] *Report of the Interdepartmental Committee on Native Education, 1935-36*, U.G.29-1936, 86.

[87] *Ibid.*, 87.

[88] *Ibid.*, 89.

thinking of South African liberal discourse in the wake of the 1932 Native Economic Commission Report. The school of social anthropology rejected supposedly "scientific" determinants of racial difference in favor of a social model rooted in concepts of cultural change. Winifred Hoernle, the wife of R.F.A. Hoernle, and who taught anthropology at the University of the Witwatersrand, ardently defended this view in a presidential address to Section E of the S.A.A.A.S. in its 1933 meeting. In the process, she shifted the emphasis away from the historical study of African cultures towards an inductive study of their functioning components. She described social anthropology as emerging as a discipline that was no longer simply concerned with "lower cultures" but with more general issues of "culture contact," as African societies began a process of social transition towards a Western-style industrial order. This approach was to have a considerable impact on anthropological research in both South Africa and Britain in the course of the 1930s.[89]

In the case of psychology too there was a shift away from intelligence testing per se towards a wider study of inter-group relations. I.D. MacCrone stressed the need in 1932 for social psychologists to reach agreement on the criteria for measuring both personality traits and social attitudes and to begin tackling the question of "inter-racial attitudes."[90] By the middle 1930s this approach began to have some impact on liberal attitudes towards "race relations" in South Africa. MacCrone felt that race differences as such were a "pseudo problem" and that what was far more important was a study of the group psychology that underlay racial cleavages of a perceptual kind. MacCrone drew upon North American studies that showed that supposed differences between school children in northern and southern states were due to selective migration. He felt compelled to agree with the American scholar Otto Klineberg that these differences would disappear as the black "environment" more nearly approximated that of whites. What was far more significant than any supposedly innate racial differences were group contacts and the way that group psychology was formed.[91] MacCrone's ideas had an immediate impact on J.D. Rheinallt Jones, the director of the South African Institute of Race Relations, who reported to the annual S.A.I.R.R. meeting in Durban a series of tests on English and Afrikaner perceptions of each other in the South African context.[92] MacCrone's work was vital for adding a psychological dimension to the "frontier thesis" in South African historical debate. His *Race Attitudes in South Africa* (1938) advanced the idea that contemporary racial aversion in South Africa was a product of racial attitudes generated in the pre-industrial frontier setting and which had survived into the era of industrialization.[93]

---

[89] A.W. Hoernle, "New Aims and Methods in Social Anthropology," *South African Journal of Science*, XXX (October 1933), 74-92.

[90] I.D. MacCrone, "Psychology in Perspective" in *Our Changing World View* (Johannesburg, 1932), 16.

[91] I.D. MacCrone, "The Problem of Race Differences," *South African Journal of Science*, XXXIII (1936), 92-107.

[92] *The Natal Mercury*, 27 July 1936.

[93] I.D. MacCrone, *Race Attitudes in South Africa* (Johannesburg, 1938).

This shift away from hereditary explanations for intelligence differences also became evident in the important 1934 conference organized by E.G. Malherbe entitled "Educational Adaptations in a Changing Society." Here R.F.A. Hoernle attacked Fick's conclusions on African educability on the grounds that there was no clear scientific evidence for a distinct African "race psychology" and that any differences were culturally induced. This might still nevertheless lead, Hoernle acknowledged, to conclusions similar to the segregationists in that "Europeanisation" of Africans might be opposed on the grounds that it threatened their cultural unity but it could not be based on any hereditarian evidence. Citing the work of Nielsen, Hoernle argued that it "would be a gain for the discussion to be switched from attempts to demonstrate the inherent congenital inferiority of the Bantu to an examination of their disabilities under White rule or of the positive values inherent in traditional Bantu culture."[94]

The advocates of the unity of the human species ended up winning a limited victory in South African political debate in the 1930s. They were able to shift the intellectual ground towards a discussion of cultural rather than racial attributes in African educability. This shift was not immediately apparent in all areas of debate. The office of the psychologist of the South African government, Oswald Black, was keen in 1935 to initiate an investigation on mental development in children under the impression that both Loram and Fick's research showed that African intelligence was "arrested" at the age of 12 or 13.[95]

The debate also proved to be open-ended on the question of whether or not segregation was justifiable in order to maintain the social cohesion of African society. Hoernle argued in 1935 that there were at least two different meanings attached to the notion of one's "own" culture: the sense in which that which was the Africans' own was intrinsically different from that of whites, and the sense in which "own" was what they could make their own. This implied that there would not necessarily be a simple "adaptation" to "European" cultural norms and that Africans would preserve a number of features of their "traditional" culture and folkways.[96] This provided some intellectual support for a variant of segregation, and Hoernle was specially notable for leaving open in his 1939 Phelps-Stokes lectures the question of whether "total segregation" was a desirable way to preserve the "liberal spirit" in South African politics.[97]

The Afrikaner nationalist advocates of Christian national education also tended to avoid overtly "scientific" arguments of African inferior educability. In 1939, Dr. W.W.M. Eiselen, professor of volkekunde at the University of Stellenbosch and later secretary of native affairs under Dr. Verwoerd in the 1950s, wrote a non-commital forward to Fick's study *The Educability of the South African Native.* Grading based on intelligence tests could "hardly be accepted as reliable," Eiselen wrote, "unless it shows a distinct superiority in comparison with that based on

---

[94]E.G. Malherbe, ed., *Educational Adaptations in a Changing Society* (Cape Town, 1937), 448.

[95]J.D. Rheinallt Jones Papers, Church of the Province Archives, University of the Witwatersrand, AD843.B.93.4. O. Black to J.D. R-J, 26 March 1935.

[96]R.F.A. Hoernle, "Can SA Natives Develop Along Their Own Lines?," *Journal of Secondary Education*, XIV, 69 (November 1935), 25.

[97]R.F.A. Hoernle, *South African Native Policy and the Liberal Spirit* (Cape Town, 1939); *White Power and the Liberal Conscience*, 66-69.

Class achievment." Nevertheless, Fick's data did confirm for Eiselen that "the Native" was not "educable in precisely the same way as the European," though there was still a need for more data on the subject.[98]

Concluding Comments

In the period up to the outbreak of World War Two there was an emerging consensus among both liberals and Afrikaner nationalist intellectuals on the centrality of culture rather than race in South African debate. There was a continuing difference of emphasis upon the degree of this cultural difference and the nature that state policy in South Africa should take to promote greater cultural uniformity between different racial groups. "Scientific" arguments of race difference had a diminishing impact on the nature of this debate and were to become further marginalized once the war itself had begun. The bogus claims of national socialism in Germany made scientific racism increasingly unacceptable intellectually. Malherbe wrote acerbically in his private notebook some time during World War Two of the embarrassing memory of some of the claims made at S.A.A.S. meetings. It was an "amazing spectacle," he felt, "that men of science will come together annually in solemn conclave and pass upon [condone] results of measurement inaccurate the like of which they wd never have tolerated in their own scientific work."[99] Such comments hinted at a more aggressive mood among many liberally inclined scholars and educationalists in the post-war years against the abuse of science in the name of racial ideology. This increasing disrespect amongt Afrikaner intellectuals like Malherbe for such "scientific" measuring contributed to the growing importance placed by the advocates of volkekunde on the cultural differences of "peoples" in the formulation of the apartheid doctrine by 1948.[100]

---

[98] W. Eiselen, "Foreword," in M. Laurence Fick, *The Education of the South African Native* (Pretoria, 1939).

[99] E.G. Malherbe Papers, 565, E.G.M. Notebook entry during World War II.

[100] For the impact of Volkekunde on apartheid ideology see John Sharp, "The Roots and Development of Volkekunde in South Africa," *Journal of Southern African Studies*, 8 (1981), 16-36; Adam Kuper, "Anthropology and Apartheid," in John Lonsdale, ed., *South Africa in Question* (London, 1988), 33-51.

*Peasants, Capitalists, and Historians: A Review Article**

FREDERICK COOPER

Barely were Africanists given time to absorb the fact that African cultivators were not too caught up in the stagnation of 'tribal' economies to be deemed peasants, than they were confronted with the fact that in vast parts of Africa peasants had already been made into proletarians. However brief their moment in history, peasants continue to arrive at the bookstore; they have their own journal, and even a newsletter. What is being said in all those books and articles, however, does not neatly fall into place. Some scholars consider the peasant response to expanding markets for produce since the nineteenth century to be the great success story of African economic history. To others, peasantry means poverty. To some, peasant society is hopelessly backward-looking and politically fragmented; to others, peasants represent the one real hope for revolution. An occasional scholar is bold enough to generalize about the economic wellbeing or political values of peasants all across Africa, while a few writers have recently wondered if peasantry is a very useful category after all.

The tendency of writers on peasants – compared to writers on practically anything else – to devote pages and pages to discussions of definitions is revealing, as is the fact that none of these discussions has come any closer to resolution than the simple and sensible definition of Theodor Shanin published in 1966.[1] The partial nature of peasants' involvement in markets and the partial nature of their subordination to the state or to ruling classes – inherent in most definitions – suggest why this apparently specific economic category gives rise to so many contradictory viewpoints. Scholars, like anyone else, would like their words to suggest the character of the experience to which they refer. 'Peasantry' does not do so; it embraces the

* Review of Colin Bundy, *The Rise and Fall of the South African Peasantry* (London: Heinemann, 1979); W. G. Clarence-Smith, *Slaves, Peasants and Capitalists in Southern Angola 1840-1926* (Cambridge: Cambridge University Press, 1979); and William Justin Beinart, 'Production, Labour Migrancy and the Chieftancy: Aspects of the Political Economy of Pondoland, ca. 1860-1930,' Ph.D. Dissertation, University of London, to be published by Cambridge University Press. I want to thank Sara Berry, Naomi Chazan, William Freund, and Jane Guyer for comments on an earlier draft.

wretchedly poor and the moderately prosperous, the progressive and the reactionary. Its only specificity is its ambiguity.

Capitalist and lineage production are of course complex and diverse phenomena, but both concepts begin to explain how work is controlled, how surplus is appropriated, and how a system reproduces itself. The concept of a peasantry does not; it is not – as several scholars have argued convincingly – a mode of production.[2] The identification of the household as the key unit of peasant production does not tell us how a household head can actually maintain control over family labour, and the very forces that turned relatively subsistence-oriented households into peasantries – access to markets – sometimes undermined elders' control of young men and sometimes strengthened the family unit.[3] The concept lumps together a cultivator who faces a state that wants its taxes and its large share of marketing board receipts and a sharecropper facing a landlord whose power of eviction and control of credit allows him to intervene in every significant decision throughout the production process. Focusing on the peasant household will not bring us to an understanding of the class structure of the wider society or the dynamics of an economic system, nor does it sharpen the focus inward on a specific set of relations of production.[4]

[1] Theodor Shanin writes, 'The peasantry consists of small agricultural producers who, with the help of simple equipment and the labour of their families, produce mainly for their own consumption and for the fulfilment of obligations to the holders of political and economic power.' 'Peasantry as a Political Factor,' 1966, reprinted in Shanin, ed., *Peasants and Peasant Societies* (Harmondsworth, 1971), p.240. For a sampling of definitional exercises, see L. A. Fallers, 'Are African Cultivators to be Called "Peasants"'? *Current Anthropology*, 2 (1961), pp.108-10; John S. Saul and Roger Woods, 'African Peasantries,' in Shanin, pp.103-14; Bundy, pp.4-13; Martin A. Klein, 'Introduction,' *Peasants in Africa: Historical and Contemporary Perspectives* (Beverly Hills, Calif., 1980), pp.9-13; Terence Ranger, 'Growing from the Roots: Reflections on Peasant Research in Central and Southern Africa,' *Journal of Southern African Studies*, 5 (1978), pp.101-7; Theodor Shanin, 'Defining Peasants: Conceptualizations and De-conceptualizations Old and New in a Marxist Debate,' *Peasant Studies*, 8 (1979), pp.38-60. Clarence-Smith uses the term 'peasant' loosely, and Beinart not at all: both alternatives are quite reasonable.

[2] Judith Ennew, Paul Hirst and Keith Tribe, '"Peasantry" as an Economic Category,' *Journal of Peasant Studies*, 4 (1977), pp.295-322, Mark Harrison, 'The Peasant Mode of Production in the Work of A. V. Chayanov,' *ibid.*, pp.323-36; Henry Bernstein, 'African Peasantries: A Theoretical Framework,' *ibid.*, 6 (1979), pp.421-43; Harriet Friedmann, 'Household Production and the National Economy: Concepts for the Analysis of Agrarian Formations,' *ibid.*, 7 (1980), pp.158-84; Shanin, 'Defining Peasants,' pp.48-51.

[3] On a theoretical level, one can explain the economic basis for the exercise of authority by elders or household heads within a lineage mode of production. But as soon as one introduces the possibility of marketing produce, it is possible to show how existing relations of control can be strengthened, reinforcing the kinship structure, or undermined as younger men obtain direct access to cash and thus to the means of setting up independent households. The seminal article on control of labour in lineage systems is Claude Meillassoux, 'Essai d'interpretation du phenomène économique dans les sociétés traditionelles d'auto-subsistence,' *Cahiers d'Etudes Africaines*, 4 (1960), pp.38-67. In specific cases, Beinart explains the undermining of household heads' control through marketed production, while Sara Berry discusses the mobilization of resources through kinship and the strengthening of such ties: *Cocoa, Custom and Socio-Economic Change in Rural Western Nigeria* (Oxford, 1975).

[4] This point is argued with particular effectiveness by Friedmann, pp.159, 160.

But the ambiguity of the concept of a peasantry is itself its most valuable feature. The partial nature of capitalist penetration into the realm of production helps to explain both the joy of commercial capital at the ease with which profits could be made without the costs of subduing and supervising recalcitrant workers and the dismay which often ensued when peasants proved they could resist new demands or withdraw from cash crop production. The hard part is to move from static categories to processes: is peasant production a first step toward the creation of a class of wealthy producers who may use their command of local resources to control labour in new ways, becoming the embryo of a capitalist system, or is it a dead end, a way of generating produce that leads to nothing but still more produce and profits for non-producers? There is a strong logic to the first possibility, which Lenin stressed, but the forms of capital accumulation and labour control are complex, each can generate new contradictions, and none can be understood without looking beyond the agrarian community itself. The latter process – the 'underdevelopment of the peasantry' – has lately become a focus of attention, but current analyses have found its logic at the level of the world market and thus leave a major question: can the dynamics or the blockages of agricultural production be understood without penetrating into the logic and contradictions of the productive systems themselves?[5] Neither view of the direction of agricultural change gives sufficient attention to the tenacity with which cultivators have clung to land: the first view underestimates resistance within the rural community itself, while the second mistakes the barriers to the transformation of production for the smooth functioning of a world system that profits from the very lack of transformation. Another currently fashionable point of view at least specifies how one might take a more complex perspective: the capitalist mode of production 'articulates' with precapitalist modes of production, reshaping but not eliminating them. In practice, however, many writers have left the modes of production with which capitalism has articulated vague and overgeneralized, while the process of articulation itself is often conceived in functionalist terms, as a way in which precapitalist forms of agriculture paid the costs of reproduction for the capitalist mode.

Writing about different parts of southern Africa and in different terms, Colin Bundy, Gervase Clarence-Smith, and William Beinart confront the

[5] Robert Brenner brilliantly argues the case for centering the analysis on productive processes and class struggles in 'The Origins of Capitalist Development: A Critique of Neo-Smithian Marxism,' New Left Review, 104 (1977), pp.25-92. In the case of Africa in the colonial era, Colin Leys argues, the alternative directions of change were actual possibilities, and distinct processes of accumulation and class formation – each of which may generate its own blockages as well as dynamics – must be analyzed. 'Capital Accumulation, Class Formation and Dependency – The Significance of the Kenyan Case,' in Ralph Miliband and John Saville, eds., *The Socialist Register 1978* (London, 1978), pp.241-66.

problems of how agricultural systems change, the relationship of trade and production, the connection of local structures to world systems, and the importance of class and the state to economic change. By what they do and what they leave out, they force readers to look more closely at the most basic determinants of change: the control of labour, capital accumulation, and reproduction. No-one has done more than Bundy to stimulate this field of study, and if his new book appears somewhat anticlimactic, it is only because of the widespread and well-deserved impact which his similarly entitled article, published seven years before the book, has had. Seeking to refute the view that the dreadful condition of African cultivators in South Africa was largely the fault of their poor husbandry and unresponsiveness to the demands of a modern economy, Bundy showed that Africans had in fact responded with alacrity to the growth of a market in foodstuffs in the nineteenth century, a response which included technical innovation – adaptation of household production to the use of the plough – and crop diversification as well as expansion of output. This trend was reversed after the gold mining industry developed its voracious appetite for cheap labour and the produce market finally made capitalist forms of production on white-owned farms economically viable, and its reversal required not only the grabbing of immense quantities of land, but the determined intervention of the state to keep land from the hands of the most successful African farmers and to drive smaller-scale tenant farmers into wage labour. The rise-and-fall thesis has since been extended to most of southern and central Africa.[6]

The book is to a large extent the article writ large, and even in those terms it is well worth having: the wealth of evidence that Bundy provides makes his important thesis more compelling, and his ability to show that variations on the sequence of a rising and falling peasantry fit into a single pattern across all arable areas of South Africa is similarly valuable. But there is more to the book than that, and it is in Bundy's search for a still more general framework that one senses a subtle historian chafing at the bits of a crude theory.

Bundy originally emphasized a basic discontinuity in the history of a peasantry. Peasants rose in response to the market and fell before the onslaught of the state, which in turn was pushed by the forces of industrial and agricultural capital. While Bundy now piles the evidence for discontinuity even higher, he wants to subsume both phases of the process under a single theoretical position that emphasizes both continuity and the

[6] Colin Bundy, 'The Emergence and Decline of a South African Peasantry,' *African Affairs*, 71 (1972), pp.369-88; Robin Palmer and Neil Parsons, eds., *The Roots of Rural Poverty in Central and Southern Africa* (London, 1977). See the penetrating critique of this approach in Ranger, many of whose points apply to the books under review here, particularly Bundy's.

market. The entire process of 'peasantization' and 'proletarianization' are both part of 'peripheralization,' the incorporation of independent producers into the world system and the consequent 'development of underdevelopment.'

This is certainly an appealing framework for peasant studies, for the peasant is the centerpiece of the periphery, his partial incorporation into the market a reflection of the distinct position of peripheral economies in the world system. If one is going to make the peasant into a universal yet specific category, this approach may be the way. Unfortunately, the conceptual connections of peasant studies and underdevelopment studies are echoed in their conceptual inadequacies, an attempt to derive economic and social structures as well as a direction of change directly from a relationship of household to market without a specific analysis of relations of production. The theoretical weaknesses of underdevelopment theory – from the earlier formulations of Frank to those of Wallerstein – are by now familiar: it substitutes a grand teleology for analysis of causation and process; it gives the market a deterministic role in the world economy and either ignores production processes or treats them as mechanical derivatives of world market structures; it fails to consider the distinctive class structures of non-European societies and the various means by which upper classes restructured themselves to meet the demands of world markets; and it leaves the struggles of cultivators, peasants, and workers against capital as little more than transitory and futile gestures in the face of the inevitable course of the world economy.[7] Wallerstein's own writings on Africa have trumpeted the fact of incorporation into a world economy so loudly that they have obscured distinctive forms of that incorporation and the contradictions between them.[8] But how does a more knowledgeable

[7] Brenner's critique is particularly devastating. It is worth noting that Leys – whom Bundy cites — has moved (in his 1978 article) from a position close to Bundy's to one similar to Brenner's. See also William Freund's review of Wallerstein's *The Capitalist World Economy* in *Race and Class*, 21 (1979), pp.173-78.

[8] In a 1976 article, Wallerstein's focus on the world economy's increasing demand for commodities in the late nineteenth century led him to posit the dominance of peasant production in colonial policy: it was the 'path of least resistance.' South Africa's different path reflected the political influence of white settlers. Faced with the embarrassing situation of leaving Africa's most dramatic example of transformation as a political exception to an economic model, Wallerstein quickly reformulated his proposition. By 1979, the split household – partly engaged in labour, partly in agriculture – emerged as the universal feature of 'peripheral' economies, where he had once placed commodity production. Peasant production is just one form of labour in the periphery; the emergence of a mass labour force under managerial discipline but another; and we are even further away from being able to distinguish the history of South Africa from that of Nigeria. Indeed, there is nothing to distinguish: 'The process of incorporation may be thought of as a transformation that normally takes at least fifty years to complete.' Normally is a curious word and it embodies a curious conception of history. 'The three stages of African involvement in the world-economy,' in Peter C. W. Gutkind and Immanuel Wallerstein, eds., *The Political Economy of Contemporary Africa* (Beverly Hills, Calif., 1976), pp.30-57 (p.38 quoted), and Immanuel Wallerstein and William G. Martin, 'Peripheralization of Southern Africa, II: changes in household structure and labour force formation,' *Review*, 3 (1979), pp.193-207 (p.193 quoted).

historian, writing in more detail, fare with such a framework on the soil of South Africa?

Bundy finds the origins of the poverty of South African peasants in their initial prosperity, in their successful response to developing markets. He needs to show that the initial fact of incorporation caused people to become locked into the market and therefore vulnerable to any attempt by capital to change the form in which their contribution to the world economy was to be made, more vulnerable than relatively self-sustaining cultivators. On the level of the market, Bundy makes his case explicitly: peasants developed new wants, not only for consumption but for goods (ploughs) that had become necessary to farming. Cash became a necessity and wage labour the only alternative if cash crop production were subsequently hampered. Bundy ably shows how the marketing system narrowed the possibilities for accumulation within peasant production and made peasants vulnerable to indebtedness. Yet he also suggests that when market conditions were bad, peasants sometimes withdrew from growing grain for sale, and more recently, the cocoa-farmers of Ghana and the ground-nut growers of Senegal have reminded us that peasants can indeed secede from the world economy if the marketplace remains the primary means through which capital and the state exercise power over them.[9] Most important, Bundy points out again and again how peasants used the cash which their produce brought them to avoid the pressures of the state and white farmers to work for wages. Others combined peasant production with a variety of activities at the fringes of the capitalist economy – such as transport riding – to meet demands that 'subsistence' cultivators could only have faced through wage labour.

Although Bundy at one point (p.124) suggests that the parts of South Africa most fully incorporated into the market economy were the most vulnerable to wage labour, the bulk of his evidence indicates that Africans with the least ability to produce for the market were often the first to become dependent on wages, and the most successful peasants among the last. Sidney Mintz has argued that peasant cultivation and small-scale marketing in the Caribbean should be seen as a form of resistance to wage labour on plantations.[10] The dichotomy of inescapable incorporation and its absence does not do justice to the possibilities of economic activities and struggle.

Bundy also tries to make a direct connection between 'peasantization'

[9] If 'peasantization' is a meaningful concept, more attention is going to have to be given to 'depeasantization.' Donal B. Cruise O'Brien analyzes the 'broad move from commercial to subsistence agriculture' in Senegal as a response to low prices and government machinations in marketing. 'Co-operators and Bureaucrats: Class Formation in a Senegalese Peasant Society,' *Africa*, 41 (1971), p.275. See also Björn Beckman, *Organising the Farmers: Cocoa Politics and National Development in Ghana* (Uppsala, 1976), p.219, and Jon Kraus, 'The Political Economy of Conflict in Ghana,' *Africa Report*, 25, 2 (March-April 1980), p.16.

and 'proletarianization' through an argument about the 're-organization of their class structure.' (p.59). His evidence points to the emergence of differentiation among peasants: some had privileged access to land and markets, produced more than others, and acquired better capital resources. Some began to use wage labour. But to argue that such farmers formed a distinct class requires asking how they maintained and reproduced their privileged access to resources, how they controlled and utilized labour, and how these processes shaped the emergence of distinct collective interests and identity. This Bundy does not do: indeed, he barely discusses the peasant household – big or small – and gives no more than hints about the impact of the market on relations of production.

Even more revealing than the gap in Bundy's extensive research is the leap he makes across it. This missing step in his logic has much to do with underdevelopment theory, which suggests that one can derive a class structure directly from the nature of a region's connection with world markets, and such shortcuts are abetted by the tendency to consider 'peasant' a sufficient description of a form of production. William Beinart – who does not wear these blindfolds – has provided an especially rich and valuable analysis of the connection between production and class.

Even without knowing whether class structure was actually reorganized, it would be possible to argue that the simple fact that some people accumulated more land and cattle than others – in a situation where all were constrained by the land-grabbing of whites – hastened the alienation of the less successful from the means of production. Bundy would like us to see this phenomenon as 'a predictable feature of the underdevelopment of a peasant community as a whole.' (p.133). It is also a predictable feature of capitalist development. Indeed, some scholars are suggesting that a movement toward capital accumulation by Africans began in colonial central Kenya – despite land alienation and state policies which, as Bundy points out, were often modelled on those of South Africa – and blossomed into a rapid trend toward African capitalist agriculture once the class the earlier trends had spawned obtained control of the state.[11] The Kenyan case remains controversial, but it is clear that the development of African cash

[10] Sidney Mintz, *Caribbean Transformations* (Chicago, 1974), pp.180-224. The central issue is the extent to which peasants were able to open up alternative means of access to cash, and this requires specific analyses of the means by which they were opened or narrowed. Bundy and several of the contributors to Palmer and Parsons have begun to explain the techniques colonial states used to constrict markets, but the other side of the story needs to be explored.

[11] This argument is summarized in Leys, who draws heavily on unpublished studies of Kenyan agriculture by Michael Cowen and Apollo Njonjo. John Lonsdale and Bruce Berman have persuasively argued that the roots of African capital accumulation lie early in colonial rule. 'Coping with the Contradictions: The Development of the Colonial State in Kenya,' *Journal of African History*, 20 (1979), pp.487-506; Berman and Lonsdale, 'Crises of Accumulation, Coercion and the Colonial State: The Development of the Labour Control System in Kenya, 1919-1929,' *Canadian Journal of African Studies*, 14 (1980), pp.37-54.

crop agriculture has led to the crystallization of quite distinct class structures in different parts of the continent, distinct relationships between locally dominant agrarian classes and the state and commercial capital, a variety of forms of interaction and conflict between those classes and workers, tenants, and poorer peasants, and distinct patterns of capital accumulation.[12] We are back to the direction question: can we understand the dynamics of economic systems and the blockages they themselves create without penetrating into the organization of production and the nature of class structures?

The same question affects Bundy's analysis of the dramatic 'fall' of South African peasants. If anyone is Bundy's model peasant, it is the squatter – an African living on white-owned land, but with direct access to that land in exchange for some form of rent or labour service. These squatters were the key to the flourishing of peasant agriculture and were the prime targets – along with the smaller number of landowners – of the state's assault on the peasantry. Although Bundy tells us what the relationship of landowner to squatter resembled ('quasi-feudal'), he does not tell us what it was. While he rightly stresses that the attack on the squatters did not result in immediate and total victory, he tells us little of the evolution of the landlord-tenant relationship. For Bundy, the crucial point is that marketed agricultural produce came from the peasant in the late nineteenth century and from the capitalist in the twentieth. That only begins to get at the nature of the transformation in relations of production, and Stanley Trapido has suggested both what that entailed within the farm – reducing the number of squatters, cutting back their grazing and cultivation rights, and increasing the direct supervision of agricultural tasks – and the connection between labour control and the changing class structure in South Africa. M. L. Morris – in a sweeping and penetrating survey of agrarian labour that suggests a number of areas for further thought and research – stresses the specific and evolving forms that agricultural capitalism took. Labour tenancy dominated until the 1920s, and the predominance of remuneration in cash wages developed through 'imperceptible' changes, and persisted even longer in some regions. Morris argues that the refusal of Africans to accept agricultural employment unless some access to land, however minimal, was offered prolonged the labour system. The efforts of workers did seem to have lasting effects on the organization of labour. If tenancy was fully eclipsed, it was by the combination of mechanization and migrant labour together with the help of

[12] Joel Samoff cites examples of the distinct class structures that evolved from connections with world markets, but makes more of the connection than the diversity of its impact. 'Underdevelopment and Its Grass Roots in Africa,' *Canadian Journal of African Studies*, 14 (1980), pp.5-36. See also Lionel Cliffe, 'Rural Class Formation in East Africa,' *Journal of Peasant Studies*, 4 (1977), pp.195-224, and *idem*, 'Labour Migration and Peasant Differentiation: Zambian Experiences,' *ibid.*, 5 (1978), pp.326-46.

the Nationalist Government after 1948 which brought about this eclipse. While far from an antiquated labour system distinct from capitalism, the various forms of labour tenancy represent a particular type of solution to the problems of control and supervision of farm labour, made essential by the resistance of cultivators to their total cut-off from the land and to capitalist work-discipline. Its abandonment went along with an escalation of the ever-present coercion.[13]

If the capitalist-peasant dichotomy is too simple to get at the changing forms of agricultural production in South Africa, it also oversimplifies — in common with much current writing on capitalism in Africa – the relationship of production and reproduction. Bundy posits a sequence which, while essential to understand, underplays the on-going process of change within the white-owned land that formed his prime focus: peasant production developing, then being stunted, so that production becomes the sphere of capitalism, reproduction that of the atrophied peasant community pushed into Reserves. Yet even when remuneration in wages came to dominate on white farms, the continued residence of labour tenant families kept the sphere of reproduction within the capitalist farmers's estate, out of the wage-labour nexus but still under his eyes and subject to the very immediate threat of eviction. At times, the pattern of labour obligations within the estate allowed it to serve as the sphere of reproduction for some migrant labourers in cities, and it was the growth of urban labour that eventually threatened capitalist farmers' control of tenant labour. The demise of labour tenancy occurred at the very time when the contradictions of migrant labour in industry and mining were coming to the fore, when some opinion close to the seats of power thought of abandoning the separation of reproduction from urban production, and the migratory system was only preserved and extended in agriculture through the most coercive and deeply-

[13] Bundy refers to the delay before the full impact of anti-squatter legislation of 1913 was felt as 'lag' (p.215). Struggle might be a more apt term, and Bundy, in an article written with Beinart, has in fact sketched the persistence of resistance to capitalist domination in the countryside. 'State Intervention and Rural Resistance: The Transkei, 1900-1965,' in Klein, pp.271-315. On changes in labour and tenancy, see Stanley Trapido, 'Landlord and Tenant in a Colonial Economy: the Transvaal 1880-1910,' *Journal of Southern African Studies*, 5 (1978), pp.26-58; Tim Keegan, 'The Restructuring of Agrarian Class Relations in a Colonial Economy: the Orange River Colony, 1902-1910,' *ibid.*, 1979, pp.234-54; M. L. Morris, 'The Development of Capitalism in South African Agriculture: Class Struggle in the Countryside,' *Economy and Society*, 5 (1976), pp.292-343. As Alan Richards argues in an excellent comparative essay, forms of labour tenancy should not be regarded as archaic – as terms like quasi-feudal would suggest – but as efforts of landowners to come to grips with the problems of supervision where market incentives are high but control incomplete. 'The Political Economy of *Gutwirtschaft*: A Comparative Analysis of East Elbian Germany, Egypt, and Chile,* *Comparative Studies in Society and History*, 21 (1979), pp.483-513. For another case of tenancy as struggle – in which the tenants constrained the landowners more than they could in South Africa and shaped a vastly different system of agrarian relations irrespective of land and labour law — see Frederick Cooper, *From Slaves to Squatters: Plantation Labor and Agriculture in Zanzibar and Coastal Kenya, 1890-1925* (New Haven, 1980).

penetrating exercise of labour control that the African continent has known.[14]

Bundy's book contains a wealth of material that points to a fuller understanding of the complexities of agricultural change, and his rhetorical flourishes around the concept of underdevelopment only serve to obscure a much more powerful contribution. Whether or not the peasant is doomed to die a 'natural' death through the inevitable course of the world economy, Bundy has shown that the South African peasant was murdered. He has documented thoroughly the impact of mining and the realignment of class forces – away from the interests of merchant capital in peasant agriculture – that lay behind the shift in state policy from doing what was simplest – acquiescing to the growth of peasant farming and collecting its commercial fruits while avoiding the expense and resistance any other approach would have provoked – to doing what was necessary to bring about a decisive transformation in agriculture. This is not to deny that there were continuities – the increasing powerlessness of African societies, the continued narrowness of marketing mechanisms – yet the particular result which ensued cannot be explained in such terms. To explain how and why white landowners and the state finally came to contest head on the determined efforts of Africans to shape, however they could, the conditions under which they farmed, one must penetrate into the production process itself and reassess the changing class forces in South African society.

Instead of entering his analysis on the relationship of the peasant to the market, W. G. Clarence-Smith locates the crux of change in the 'articulation of modes of production.' Distinct relations of production existed in the 'colonial nucleus' of Southern Angola, which was moving, as slowly as property-owners could make it, from slave to wage labour, and in the peasant societies around it, where relations of production were influenced by the nucleus without being made over in its image. These distinct and changing modes of production in turn provide clues to understanding the forms of social behaviour, racial categories, and political action that developed and the efforts of particular classes to shape economic and social change in often-opposed ways. Clarence-Smith's approach promises analysis of those areas where Bundy touched but chose not to dwell – the production process and the class struggle.[15]

[14] Morris, *op. cit.* The re-alignment of class forces in South Africa in the 1940s is being studied by Dan O'Meara, and some aspects of the contradictions in migratory labour that arose at that time are analyzed in 'The 1946 African Mine Workers' Strike and the Political Economy of South Africa,' *Journal of Commonwealth and Comparative Politics*, 13 (1975), pp.146-73. See also Stanley Greenberg, *Race and State in Capitalist Development* (New Haven, 1980).

[15] Much has been written lately on the articulation of modes of production, and an unusually clear and sensible introduction to the issue is Aidan Foster-Carter, 'The Modes of Production Controversy,' *New Left Review*, 107 (1978), pp. 47-73.

It is a promise that is only partially fulfilled. With 104 pages of text (including cryptic notes) – only 76 of which are given over to the heart of the analysis of Southern Angola from 1840 to 1926 – there is hardly space to probe complex changes in a large and varied territory. Although the slave mode of production is a point of departure for Clarence-Smith, he tells us all we get to know about slave labour in, literally, a few sentences.[16] Later, he tells us that the transition to wage labour was relatively smooth, partly because limited wage payments were gradually introduced as the slavery issue was haltingly addressed, but mainly because enslavement had separated people from their lands and had 'instilled certain skills and work rhythms which were easily carried over into wage-labour' (p.32). But without telling us what those rhythms were, the nature of supervision and control, the notions of time involved in labour, how slaves were prevented from finding new land to cultivate, and so on, he leaves us with an intriguing suggestion rather than an analysis of a transition in modes of production. Clarence-Smith's chapter on 'The Peasant Economy' is a whirlwind tour of different crops and products and the people that grew them, barely pausing to mention the implications that the new patterns of production had. He concludes with a two-paragraph discussion of the relations of production that sounds more like a definition of the lineage mode of production than an analysis of Angola. We are told that 'these relations of production remained broadly predominant throughout the period under consideration [but were] progressively eroded and modified by the effects of increasing articulation with the capitalist mode of production,' but all we learn of *how* the relations of production themselves were changed by the new demand for commodities (without diminishing subsistence production) is that 'leisure time was being converted into labour time' while firearms increased productivity (in hunting and slave catching presumably), (p.69). That sounds awfully close to the tired, old vent-for-surplus model, which is not what one expects from a Marxist.[17]

It is not that detail is desirable for its own sake, but that certain kinds of detail are called for by Clarence-Smith's own theoretical perspective. In Marxist theory, a social formation is an historically specific construct. A lineage, slave, or capitalist mode of production is an abstract concept, but it is the specific 'articulation' of modes of production that shapes and changes social formations, and which Clarence-Smith seeks to describe. The point

[16] Clarence-Smith is only a little more detailed in his article, 'Slavery in Coastal Southern Angola, 1875-1913,' *Journal of Southern African Studies*, 2 (1976), pp.214-23.

[17] For a critique of the vent-for-surplus model, stressing its ideological implications, see W. M. Freund and R. W. Shenton, '"Vent-for-Surplus" Theory And the Economic History of West Africa,' *Savanna*, 6 (1977), pp. 191-96. Even from a less radical viewpoint, the inadequacies of this kind of argument are considerable. See Berry, pp.1-6, 87-88 and John Tosh, 'The Cash-Crop Revolution in Tropical Africa: An Agricultural Reappraisal,' *African Affairs*, 79 (1980), pp.79-94.

of materialist analysis, as Marx himself stressed, is to discover the hidden, underlying structures and processes. Unfortunately, Clarence-Smith compresses so much that labelling structures sometimes substitutes for analyzing their basic nature.

The best section of his book suggest how much beyond a labelling exercise one can go. By controlling trade in parts of Angola, chiefs monopolized horses and firearms and built up a following of young men known as *lenga*. The lenga proved to be a basis for accumulation through raids and the forcible collection and sale of slaves, cattle, and rubber. For the first time, significant differences in style of living emerged within societies outside the colonial nucleus. It was precisely this group that was jeopardized by the beginnings of more effective Portuguese control. They began to rely more on the extortion of tribute and met with more resistance. Faced with the erosion of their means of accumulation and control, chiefs and lenga tried to manipulate the early system of labour migration as a source of revenue – extorting fees from migrants – but for many Angolans, an incentive toward labour migration was to avoid the predations of the lenga.[18] Labour migration became part of the terrain of struggle of partially formed classes.

This takes Clarence-Smith to the verge of a potentially important analysis of the dead-ends of certain kinds of economic change, of the creation of groups committed to transitory forms of production, yet shaping the character of subsequent changes as they cling to power. Even in the colonial nucleus, the class which Clarence-Smith labels 'capitalist' was not very capitalistic: it had little capital, no great reliance on wage labour, and little dynamism. Yet Clarence-Smith's discussion is far too cryptic to be extended to the generalizations he would like to make about the era: the extension of colonial rule in the 1900s 'largely erased the differences between the reactions of specific peasant societies'; 'feudal nobles, social bandits, mission theocrats and independent peasants were all swept away to make room for a relatively uniform subject peasantry which was obliged to provide commodities or labour power on the terms dictated by colonial officials' (p.74). Clarence-Smith, however, shows that peasants provided commodities very inconsistently; that the relations of production within the various peasant societies changed little; and that the state had only modest control over the flow of migrant labour, and hardly any ability to exploit it within Portuguese territory. When we are told about local patterns of change, they seem more complex than his conclusions, and studies in parts of Africa where commodity production was more intense suggest that such

[18] See also the article Clarence-Smith wrote with R. Moorsom, 'Underdevelopment and Class Formation in Ovamboland, 1845-1915,' *Journal of African History*, 16 (1975), pp. 365-81.

peasantries were far from uniform and only partially subjected.[19] Clarence Smith's epilogue on the rapid development of plantation agriculture and mining in the 1960s only serves to emphasize the dead ends of the earlie period and the stagnation of the intervening years. The stunted capitalism of the early twentieth century – the harshness without the accumulation – needs more specific examination to explain situations where notions of an ever-growing ability to extract commodities and labour tell us little.[20]

Many of Clarence-Smith's peasants, like Bundy's, eventually had to see jobs as migratory labourers. While Bundy thinks that the effectiveness o the ties which linked peasants to a world market was a step toward thei becoming workers, Clarence-Smith's evidence suggests that the weaknes and impermanence of such mechanisms, exacerbated by the mountin predations of the Portuguese state and its disruption of hunting and othe economic activities (plus natural disasters), could also foster the exodus c wage labourers. While in South Africa, the disruption of rural economie was part of a process of accumulation and transformation of relations c production, in southern Angola extraction, repression, and patches c wage-labour agriculture did not lead to any such systematic transformatio Mining interests in Namibia gladly soaked up the migrant labour that can forth, but whether this was anything near an optimal structure for capitalis as a system to extract surplus from this vast region and substanti population is less clear. While Bundy has demonstrated how a dynam economic system can be built on the impoverishment of the majority of i people, Clarence-Smith has shown that it is easier to destroy econom structures than to exploit a population effectively. Although Clarenc Smith might have given us a more detailed picture and a more caref analysis, he has nonetheless contributed to understanding the complexiti of southern Africa.

William Beinart has taken a much smaller area, and he has actually do what Clarence-Smith has claimed to be doing and what Bundy has le largely unexamined, analyze the changing nature of agricultural producti and the two-way relationship of the organization of production inside local area with the wider structures of South Africa. It would be a mistak however, to exaggerate the differences in approach, especially betwe Bundy and Beinart, who have collaborated together as well as influenc

[19] Even within Tanganyika, the distinct patterns of peasant production were important were the forms of social and political change which they engendered. These complexities brought out especially well in John Iliffe, *A Modern History of Tanganyika* (Cambric 1979).

[20] Hopefully, such an analysis will come from the forthcoming book on Mozambique Leroy Vail and Landeg White. Meanwhile, see their 'The Struggle for Mozambique: Capit Rivalries, 1900-40,' *Review*, 3 (1979), pp.243-75, and Vail's 'Mozambique's Chart Companies: The Rule of the Feeble,' *Journal of African History*, 17 (1976), pp.389-416.

each other's work. Beinart's study would make much less sense without Bundy's overview. Both are engaged in a parallel effort: to analyze the connection between the prosperous capitalist economy of South Africa and the poverty of African agriculture. Beinart's peasants in Pondoland rise and fall, although not quite on Bundy's schedule. But on several questions, important differences in approach to agrarian history emerge. Beinart not only shies away from two of the most basic words in Bundy's vocabulary – peasantry and underdevelopment – but states explicitly why he is doing so. The use of the term 'peasantry,' he writes, 'tends to obscure the very real differences in the relations of production in various parts of the subcontinent' (p.14).

Class formation looks different when viewed from inside. Rather than equating differentiation with class formation and reducing it to a universal characteristic of underdevelopment, Beinart looks at the specific bases of chiefly power in the early period: the concentration of settlements and the need for defence in the aftermath of the Mfecane increased the power of chiefs, especially the paramount, and this power was extended into the realm of production by the concentration of cattle collected in tribute, fines, and raids, and the demand for labour service for works of collective importance, although the accumulation of capital in cattle was modified – and the political position of the paramount reinforced – by the extensive provision of cattle loans. Then, the arrival of traders in Pondoland brought direct access to market to the individual household and – along with the passing of the devastation of the Mfecane – contributed to economic decentralization. As maize grew in importance relative to cattle, the household became more important still as a productive unit and the importance of the chief to production diminished. Chiefs remained major cattle owners, and they acquired a vested interest in the trading system by collecting license and other fees from the traders, but their ability to exercise power in the production process – the essence of class power – weakened. So production for the market went along with a diffusion of economic power, and only after the erosion of local agriculture and the consolidation of the power of the South African state did the chiefs and the educated men who served them (both of whom used their salaries and their privileged access to agricultural resources to reinforce their position) reverse the trend yet again, leading to the gradual emergence of a dominant rural class, now dependent on the state.

The inside view gives a different view of the relationship of local agriculture and labour migration as well. The origins of migrations lie in the efforts of Pondo to incorporate the gold mines into a broader pattern of economic life, which they tried to integrate as best they could. Neither the argument that labour migration followed the decay of rural production nor the dichotomy of capitalist production and Reserve reproduction is sufficient to dissect patterns of change in Pondoland. Labour migration and crop production expanded together in the early decades of this century. After the epidemics of cattle disease in 1897 and 1912-13, a period of wage labour was a means of restocking, restoring the ability to use the plough in maize production as well as to exploit cattle directly. Pondo migrants to the gold mines often sought advances in the form of cattle which their families would raise while the migrant worked for little or no cash, an arrangement which the mines only tolerated, never encouraged, and eventually stopped. Apart from the use of wage labour as a new means to cope with the old problem of periodic natural disasters, wage labour came to be part of the household's economic cycle, playing a complex part in a wider division of labour. Ploughs and draft animals reduced the demand for male labour; they also increased the need for capital. Most important, Beinart analyzes the relationship of migrant labour to conflicts and contradictions within the household. Heads of household wanted to control the labour of younger men within the rural economy and to be sure that what was earned abroad would be brought back to contribute to rural production. The elders were, it seems, the architects of the cattle advance system, a way of insuring that the migrant would return. But the migrant system itself – especially given the mines' dislike of the advance system – had within it the potential for individual economic action, for withdrawal from the large household, and – slowly – for a degree of accumulation by new households. Such processes were of even greater and more lasting importance in parts of colonial Kenya, and this should make scholars wary of a monolithic view of the relationship of agriculture and migrant labour as a slide from the former to the latter.[21] Even in situations where the development of local agriculture was severely constrained, the combination within a social group of migration and local production could constitute an important means of resistance to total immersion in the wage economy.

The arguments of Beinart and Bundy begin to converge in the 1930s. Crop producers in Pondoland did not die a natural death; but they took a long time to roll over and die, perhaps for the reasons suggested above. Hemmed in by a labour-tenancy-wage-labour frontier, a barrier in organization of production as well as in landownership, faced with the deliberate undermining of markets in grain and cattle, forced to meet the

[21] David Webster also stresses the connections of migration to gold mines and generational conflict in southern Mozambique, only elders seem to have done better than their Pondo counterparts in controlling earnings, perhaps because Pondo had fuller access to the market. 'Migrant Labour, Social Formations and the Proletarianization of the Chopi of Southern Mozambique,' *African Perspective*, 1978/1, pp.157-76. See also Colin Murray, 'Migration, Differentiation and the Developmental Cycle in Lesotho,' *ibid.*, pp.127-44, and Lionel Cliffe and Richard Moorsom, 'Rural Class Formation and Ecological Collapse in Botswana,' *Review of African Political Economy*, 15/16 (1979), pp.35-52. On Kenya and Zanzibar, see Berman and Lonsdale; Lonsdale and Berman; and Cooper.

exactions of chiefs – now acting as agents of the state – agriculturalists could not maintain their productivity. Beinart has examined Pondoland with admirable attention to the specifics of locale and history, but with equal sensitivity to its place in South Africa and to the essential questions of agrarian history. His excellent thesis should focus attention on the dynamics of agricultural production, on the mechanisms by which it was fostered, hindered, and channelled, and on the contradictions and struggles that went on within small places in a big world.

These works as a whole suggest just how difficult it was to develop capitalist agriculture in Africa. The brutal success of South African landowners and the state in engineering such a transformation is likely to make the process seem somehow natural and inevitable. An East Africanist is especially likely to be struck by the differences between that experience and the singular lack of success of efforts to create wage-labour plantations on the Kenyan coast, with both white and Arab planters, while the famous attempt to build the White Highlands is beginning to look to historians less like a small South Africa than an unsuccessful one, crimped by a failure to subdue the independence of African cultivators or even to pull the state out of its ambivalence into a decisive assault on the peasantry. The failures of French planters in the Ivory Coast and of Belgians in the Congo are familiar, and the presence of wage-labour plantations scattered over various parts of Africa hardly ever led to the pervasive development of capitalist relations of production that took place in South Africa and Rhodesia.

The problem with capitalist agriculture was that it depended on two of the most coercive and difficult acts possible in agricultural societies: the once-and-for-all alienation of land and the daily struggle to make workers obey. The kind of authority which a landowner's ability to evict a tenant gave him over such questions as what kind and how much of crops to plant constituted an altogether different level of control than that exercised by colonial states through local rulers and police forces as a consequence of military conquest.[22] Landowners had to exercise not only legal ownership but actual control over people on their estates: in coastal Kenya in the early twentieth century, the concentration of land in a limited number of hands – reinforced by the social distinctiveness of the landowners – led to little control over production and even a limited ability to extract rent, for the landowners – indifferently supported by the state that had sanctioned their titles – failed to act as a class to check the mobility of squatters and evict tenants who failed to provide rent or labour.[23]

Still, transforming control of land to control of labour on that land was

[22] Beinart notes how chiefs' power over production diminished during the period when they were becoming agents of the state.

[23] Cooper, Chapter 5.

such a large departure that Stanley Trapido refers to it as the 'second alienation'. For the landowner to take direct control over all aspects of farming, directing workers to perform specific tasks under his supervision, relegating the independent cultivation by tenants to increasingly insignificant portions of the estate and fractions of the labour tenant's time, was an immense and ill-understood task. Even in South Africa the problems of supervising and keeping workers in a pure wage system engendered decades of uneasy compromise.[24] This transformation required not merely changes within the estate, but systematic action by a class: the anti-squatter laws of South Africa were needed to make sure that some landowners would not attract tenants from others by making less rigid labour demands, and even so the stuttering implementation of even the most draconian legislation owed much to the efforts of African tenants to play off different landlords, and different sources of income – however small – against each other. Capitalist accumulation implied this double alienation – from land and from time – and it had to be applied systematically and generally. The mere amassing of capital – for example the islands of Portuguese plantations built up in southern Angola – did not produce a rural proletariat.[25]

Accumulation remains an elusive concept and a process – in its different manifestations – that remains largely unexamined. Despite the pioneering work of Trapido, Morris, and others the connection between labour control within the estate and the exercise of class power within the wider society is still one of the most neglected – and the most essential – aspects of agrarian history in South Africa and elsewhere. For all that is unique in South Africa's history, there is something of the classic pattern of capitalist development there. Still, capitalist development itself, as Barrington Moore, Jr., has emphasized, followed distinct paths, and Moore's Prussian Road, or labour-repressive capitalism, has been a very useful starting point for analyses of South Africa. The prior establishment of a distinct landowning class is thus crucial to understanding both the potential for transforming the system of production and the continued reliance on coercion – rather than an evolution toward a market in labour – to shape the nature of the labour system. The transformation of that class into agricultural capitalists helps to explain how it could find common ground with mining interests and – for all the conflicts that ensued – develop an increasingly sophisticated system of labour control and a powerful ideology

[24] Trapido, p.56. See also Morris and Keegan, and for an explanation why so many classes who already controlled access to land did not take the next step or did so very cautiously, see Richards.

[25] The elusive subject of primitive accumulation is discussed in Karl Marx, *Capital*, trans. by S. Moore and E. Aveling (New York, 1967), Vol. 1, pp.713-74; Brenner, pp.66-67; and in reference to some Kenyan situations, Leys and Cooper, pp.173-76.

of domination. And one can better understand the conjuncture out of which the economy and society of South Africa developed if one also understands the quite different histories that unfolded where repressors were not so capitalist (as in Southern Angola) or where capitalists could not convince the state to carry out enough repression (Kenya).[26]

But is the accumulation of nondivisible rights in land, the reliance on state authority to enforce those rights, the division of society into owners and workers, and the tight control of workers' time and movements the only form which accumulation can take in an agricultural economy? In fact, studies of rural Africa are suggesting that commodity production often leads to the concentration of wealth and the formation of distinct groups of accumulators, but that the process of accumulation takes different forms and shapes society in different ways. The expansion of cocoa production in parts of the West African forest belt involved a sharing of property rights between local people with a prior claim to land and immigrants who planted trees, the mobilization of ties of clientage and kinship to provide labour and other resources, and a persistent pattern of investment through which labour for a tree-owner was often a step toward becoming a tree-owner oneself. Instead of relying on state-enforced titles to ensure possession of the coconut trees they were planting, Giriama 'accumulators' near the Kenyan coast needed the testimony of 'witnesses' to their possession, and this fostered different attitudes toward community than systems of ownership based on outside sanctions and rigid property rights. Significantly, this pattern led to substantial accumulation, while the nearby, more fertile coastal belt – where the state enforced titles – stagnated through conflict between landowners and squatters. Would the wealthiest peasants in certain circumstances evolve into a capitalist class – exploiting wage labourers – when access to land became narrowed?; would the wealthiest peasants seek to convert farm income into access to power at the national level rather than reinvest in agriculture and augment both exploitation and production?;[27] would rich peasants act as political brokers

[26] Barrington Moore, Jr., *The Social Origins of Dictatorship and Democracy: Lord and Peasant in the Making of the Modern World* (Boston, 1966). For applications to South Africa, see Stanley Trapido, 'South Africa in a Comparative Study of Industrialization,' *Journal of Development Studies*, 7 (1971), pp.309-20; Martin Legassick, 'South Africa: Capital Accumulation and Violence,' *Economy and Society*, 3 (1974), pp.253-91; Morris, and Greenberg. The colonial state's attempt to build capitalist agriculture on the coast of Kenya and in Zanzibar might be considered a 'washout' on the Prussian Road (Cooper, p.275). Another variant on this pattern is dissected in Jonathan M. Wiener, 'Class Structure and Economic Development in the American South, 1865-1955,' *American Historical Review*, 84 (1979), pp.970-92, and idem., *The Social Origins of the New South: Alabama 1860-1885* (Baton Rouge, La., 1978).

[27] In cocoa producing areas of the Ivory Coast, both the labour system and the relationship of agriculture to the national economy limited the extent of agrarian class formation. It was possible for 'peasant-workers' to become 'peasant-planters,' as labour was both cheap and had the possibility of acquiring cocoa holdings, without becoming bourgeois planters, completely

to poorer peasants, masking their own privileges and exploitation? or would rich peasants use their access to central authority to end their reciprocal ties with the local community and accelerate accumulation?; would subordinate rural strata become increasingly distinct and increasingly hostile toward the rich?[28] All these possibilities, to some extent at least, have occurred, and the Leninist paradigm – a transition from peasants to kulaks to capitalists – appears to be one of several possibilities. The study of class formation in Africa is going to have to be more subtle than the search for the elusive kulak or the efforts to identify the petit-bourgeoisie; pre-capitalist class structures must be understood more fully, and so must the precise manner in which colonial rule and the extension of capitalism reshaped them. But unless we see that forms of production were shaped by specific classes – and by the ongoing struggles of competing classes – it will be impossible to understand the directions and blockages of economic change.[29] The most basic questions are still unanswered and are only avoided by the widespread stress on the progressive underdevelopment of peasantries: what makes some agricultural systems stagnate and some evolve, while others are destroyed or replaced?

Besides the impoverished peasant and the accumulating peasant, historians have to consider the ornery peasant. This was the figure that especially bothered colonial officials and still frustrates their successors. Although officials often learned that capitalist agriculture's requirements of systematic expropriation, close supervision, and eternal vigilance were beyond the capabilities of colonial bureaucracies, while African accumulators (of various sorts) could likewise enmesh a state in the consequences of their exploitativeness or make demands of their own on the state, they also found that peasants could be a much less dependable source of commodities and revenue than some theories suggest. Central to such analyses is the way peasants become 'locked in' to a world market. Ironically, the emphasis on *the* market has been so strong that specific marketing mechanisms have scarcely been studied. Yet when one looks at how colonial – and post colonial – powers behaved, there is such consistency in their

caught up in the circuit of capital; at the same time, the decisive breakthrough into the bourgeoisie occurred at the national level, so successful planters invested in education or politics. Jean-Pierre Chauveau and Jacques Richard, 'Une "péripherie recentrée": à propos d'un systémé local d'économie de plantation en Côte d'Ivoire,' *Cahiers d'Etudes Africaines*, 17 (1977), pp.485-523. Iliffe also notes (p.462) that in areas of Tanganyika where production was high and population dense, the tendency to develop wage labour was limited by the high availability of family labour, which strengthened labour control through kinship mechanisms.

[28] For some particularly illuminating case studies, see Berry; Cruise O'Brien; David Parkin, *Palms, Wine and Witnesses* (London, 1972); Chauveau and Richard; Cliffe and Moorsom; Iliffe; P. M. van Hekken and H. U. E. Thoden van Velzen, *Land Scarcity and Rural Inequality in Tanzania* (The Hague, 1972); Beckman. See also Samoff and Clife, 'Rural Class Formation.'

[29] Leys, esp. pp.245-46.

ambivalence that one might doubt how dependably peasants filled their role in the world economy, and states devoted such attention to controlling both marketing and production that the locks in *the* market must have been weak. And far from a dose of coercion being necessary mainly in the early phases of incorporation into the world economy, compulsion seem to have grown when peasantries should have been tied into their dependence.[30]

Although nothing an agricultural officer of a colonial state or a development economist of the World Bank says should ever be taken at face value, the enduring laments about African backwardness, obsession with subsistence cultivation, lack of interest in what the British sometimes called 'economic crops,' and the supposed modesty of their wants may actually reveal something about a system of economic domination that did not penetrate to the point of production. For all the Yoruba cocoa-growers who leapt into the world market, there were Lango farmers who resisted pressures to grow cotton for decades and eventually did so not only because old crops declined, but because they began to get a better deal for cotton.[31] And as all the failed food production projects of recent years, as well as the declining production of some of Africa's most faithful cash crop growers, suggest, official skepticism about peasants may not have been so foolish after all.

Capitalist farmers could survive only by extracting surplus labour; they could adjust what they did, but their existence as a class was incompatible with withdrawal from either produce markets or labour markets, and they had no protection, from having labour tied down within the individual estate, from the forces within the wider economy that shaped wages and profits. The proletarian had to work, and his work patterns had to adjust to the shifting demands of capital. Peasants might provide commodities, but they were partially shielded by their direct access to land and family labour, outside of the circuit of commodities, from the forces that lay behind the unavoidable impetus for steady production and improved productivity intrinsic to capitalist relations of production.[32] Peasants often responded vigorously to market incentives; the problem for colonial states was that peasants were not predictable. They could not be counted on to stay in the market when it was rigged against them or simply bad, nor was it sure how they would respond to demands to intensify production. The cultivator's continued ability to grow food, whether he was also growing crops for sale

[30] The dose of force argument is made, for example, in Wallerstein and Martin, p.195. However, see some of material on market manipulations in Palmer and Parsons as well as a modest number of studies like Roger J. Southall, 'Farmers, Traders and Brokers in the Gold Coast Cocoa Economy,' *Canadian Journal of African Studies*, 12 (1978), pp.185-211.'

[31] John Tosh, 'Lango Agriculture During the Early Colonial Period: Land and Labour in a Cash-Crop Economy,' *Journal of African History* 19 (1978), pp.415-39.

[32] Brenner.

or working for wages, is often regarded as a subsidy to capitalism, lowering wages or commodity prices needed to insure the reproduction of a labour force; but the cheapness was difficult to separate from the automony.

Predictability – in the face of both bust and boom – was intrinsic to imperialism. The need to remove obstacles to the smooth flow of marketed goods in West Africa is well understood; the need to establish sufficiently strong and regularized institutions throughout South Africa to meet the challenges of controlling a mass labour force in the mines has more recently been connected with the imperial thrust in South Africa.[33] But for all the tendencies – in many cases decisive tendencies – to do what was cheap or to grab what was to be grabbed, there is much evidence that imperialism involved a rethinking of production processes as industrial capitalism demanded access to commodities and labour that was both more regular and more intense.[34] Trapido has noted Milner's advocacy of a fully capitalist form of production in South African agriculture, but his most interesting comments concern the increasingly uneasy coexistence of South African liberals' attitudes toward peasant production with the imperialist ethic in the age of industrial capitalism. Closely linked with merchant capital, Cape liberals at first saw trade and peasant production as progressive. But then the pressures toward creating a mass labour force first led the liberal message to become less relevant, and then led its contents to change: 'the belief in private land ownership as a civilising agency [turned into] the belief in the dignity of wage labour.' And the dignity of the mass labour force, unlike that of independent producers, did not require Africans being incorporated into the polity. Precisely because the period between mineral discoveries and Union involved fundamental changes in the organization of production and a realignment of class forces – which

[33] A. G. Hopkins, *An Economic History of West Africa* (London, 1973), pp. 124-66; Norman A. Etherington, 'Labour supply and the Genesis of South African Confederation in the 1870s,' *Journal of African History*, 20 (1979), pp.235-53; A. Atmore and S. Marks, 'The Imperial Factor in South Africa in the Nineteenth Century: Towards a Reassessment,' *Journal of Imperial and Commonwealth History*, 3 (1974), pp. 105-39; S. Marks and S. Trapido, 'Lord Milner and the South African State,' *History Workshop Journal*, 8 (1979), pp.50-81.'

[34] Catherine Coquery-Vidrovitch writes of a phase of predatory colonialism, 1890-1930, that faded into a highly coercive trading economy. Predatory colonialism was every bit as brutal as she suggests, but much more ephemeral. Timothy Weiskel, for example, has shown that the French had exhausted the potential for rubber collection in Baule areas of the Ivory Coast by 1907 and had to think about mobilizing a rural labour force by different means, leading to a more intrusive form of intervention and escalating resistance. But even then getting the commodities remained an elusive problem. Coquery-Vidrovitch, 'La mise en dépendance de l'Afrique noire: essai de periodisation, 1800-1970,' *Cahiers d'Etudes Africaines*, 16 (1976), pp.23-35; Weiskel, *French Colonial Rule and the Baule Peoples: Resistance and Collaboration, 1889-1911* (Oxford, 1980), p.237.

could endanger previously dominant rural classes – the impetus toward segregationist policies became acute.[35]

The transformation of relations of production was equally at stake as British policy makers in London pondered the kind of agricultural organization and class structure that they should foster in Zanzibar as they tried to remake a slave economy. Recognizing that planters' class identity depended on continued production, they sought to maintain plantations and transform the violence of slave labour into the orderliness of wage labour, vainly struggling to instill a sense of work discipline into ex-slaves. In this instance, the strong belief that the continuity of production required landlords and managers transcended the fact that these landlords were non-white and had minimal political influence. In Buganda and Northern Nigeria as well, the British thought they could transform the ruling class of authoritarian states into a landowning class, although such policies involved a rather fanciful conception of what such a class was capable of doing.[36]

In Zanzibar by the 1920s – unlike South Africa – officials had stopped talking about the need for regular work as they had in the 1900s: they had grudgingly come to accept, and to manipulate, a system that combined squatting, part time labour, and migrant labour on plantations, as well as substantial peasant production of cloves. On the coast of Kenya, the final attempt of authorities to suppress squatting by the Giriama people and to pressure them into the labour market provoked a rebellion in 1914, which was put down, but in the end the defeated rebels returned to their spread-out settlements and to squatting arrangements even more lax than those which the South African state regarded as anathema: it was easier to burn huts than to maintain work discipline. Coastal squatters – Giriama and ex-slaves – grew grain, but did not sell as much as slaveowners had been able to in the nineteenth century, would not grow sesame, which slaves had once been forced to grow and which was being produced in other parts of Kenya, and refused to grow cotton, which the administration was pushing. The defense of subsistence cultivation remained an essential part of cultivators'

[35] Trapido, 'Landlord and Tenant,' p.32, idem., '"The Friends of the Natives"; Merchants, Peasants and the Political and Ideological Structure of Liberalism in the Cape, 1854-1910,' in A. Atmore and S. Marks, *Economy and Society in Pre-Industrial South Africa* (London, 1980), pp. 247-74 (p. 258 quoted); Shula Marks, 'Natal, the Zulu Royal Family and the Ideology of Segregation,' *Journal of Southern African Studies*, 4 (1978), pp.172-94; P. Rich, 'The Agrarian Counter-Revolution in the Transvaal and the Origins of Segregation: 1902-1913,' in P. L. Bonner, ed., *Working Papers in Southern African Studies* (Johannesburg, 1977), pp.55-122.

[36] Cooper, Chapters 2 and 3; Mahmood Mamdani, *Politics and Class Formation in Uganda* (New York, 1976), pp.41-49; Bob Shenton and Bill Freund, 'The Incorporation of Northern Nigeria into the World Capitalist Economy,' *Review of African Political Economy*, 13 (1978), p.14.

efforts to limit the power of old oppressors and new ones over them.[37] The British were learning that Africa was not India, that the power of precolonial aristocracies was very difficult to transform into control of land and labour. While the economic power of the Arab planters of Zanzibar, the emirs of northern Nigeria, or the Mourides of Senegal was fundamental to the colonial economy, and colonial states often assisted chiefs – whether 'traditional' or the creation of colonial rule itself – in exploiting labour to produce cash crops, the production process itself proved very difficult – if not dangerous – to reshape and control.[38]

Colonial states were certainly not going to turn away anyone who presented them with cocoa, ground nuts, or palm oil, and the kind of merchant-state connection that was transcended by the capitalist-state link in South Africa was more enduring in West Africa, even as it led to productive systems of varying degrees of predictability. In much of East Africa, the emergence of small-scale production stemmed less from colonial officials' wise recognition of peasant virtue than from their ability to call failure success. They had failed to extend plantation agriculture, shape suitable planter classes – white, brown, or black – or create a disciplined work force. They could still obtain commodities, but not always the ones or the quantities they wanted. If the encounter with African cultivators had revealed the difficulties of extending capitalist production to Africa, it demonstrated the need for other kinds of control to do what mere incorporation into a world market would not.

Taxation – the most basic technique of compelling a minimum contribution to the cash economy – often frustrated the taxers themselves because it gave so little control over how the contribution was to be made, and in its more exacting forms, taxation provoked large-scale emigration and resistance.[39]

Even cruder were schemes of compulsory cultivation which all the

[37] Cooper, Chapters 5 and 6. The continued production of food by cash croppers is also stressed by Tosh, 'Cash-Crop Revolution', p.91. The most important exception which he notes – the Senegambia – has recently become less of an exception.

[38] Two examples of attempts (at different stages of colonial rule) by colonial states to use different kinds of precolonial elites to intensify production, one leading to mass flight, the other to peasant disorders, are discussed in Richard Roberts and Martin Klein, 'The Banamba Slave Exodus of 1905 and the Decline of Slavery in the Western Sudan,' *Journal of African History*, 21 (1980), pp.315-94 and M. Catherine Newbury, '*Ubureetwa* and *Thangata*: Catalysts to Peasant Political Consciousness in Rwanda and Malawi,' *Canadian Journal of African Studies*, 14 (1980), pp.97-111.

[39] The escalation of taxation in Kenya in the 1920s produced serious unrest in Nairobi and efforts at total avoidance of the state – and with it labour and produce markets – on the coast. The state retreated part way. High taxation was a major reason for extensive emigration from French to British West Africa before 1945. Cooper, pp.265-66; Berman and Lonsdale; A. I. Asiwaju, 'Migrations as Revolt: The Example of the Ivory Coast and the Upper Volta before 1945,' *Journal of African History*, 17 (1976), pp.577-94.

colonial powers tried at one time or another. All were quite distinct from market production: prices were fixed and production quotas set, to be filled either on communal patches or individual farms under official supervision. The Germans in Tanganyika tried forced cotton cultivation, with disastrous results; the Belgians considered encouraging Belgian, then African farmers to set up capitalist food producing enterprises in Shaba, then turned to compulsory cultivation when that failed; the Portuguese in Mozambique tried forced cultivation of cotton and rice; the French used forced labour on European-run estates and later requisitions of specified quantities of food from farming communities; the British in Zanzibar used compulsory food cultivation during World War II. Most such efforts were successful only as long as an official kept his eyes on the fields, and they were as likely to produce unrest or a mass exodus as crops.[40]

Where neither capitalist farmers nor state officials controlled directly what and how much was to be grown, the question of how peasant production could be manipulated was central. Studies of sharecropping in the Southern United States and of a great variety of forms of tenancy in Latin America emphasize that even without a predominance of wage labour, the exercise of class power in ways that varied from thuggery to debt bondage was essential to expanding production.[41] This was the kind of control that proved so difficult to exercise in most of Africa. Instead, great emphasis was placed by the state and merchant capital on monopolistic control of commodity purchasing and a host of marketing regulations that shaped the decisions peasants made. An expanding range of administrative regulations focused on conditions of production: rules about close settlement, cattle dipping, cattle culling, use of improved seeds, and so on strongly affected production, and often provoked resistance in forms that varied from refusal to change techniques to movement away from controlled settlements to smuggling to produce hold-ups to withdrawal

[40] Iliffe, pp.168-69; Bogumil Jewsiewicki, 'Unequal Development: Capitalism and the Katanga Economy, 1919-40,' in Palmer and Parsons, pp.317-45; Leroy Vail and Landeg White, 'Tawani, Machambero!: Forced Cotton and Rice Growing on the Zambezi,' *Journal of African History*, 19 (1978), pp.239-63; Jane Guyer, 'The Food Economy and French Colonial Rule in Central Cameroun,' *ibid.*, pp.577-97; F. B. Wilson, 'Emergency Food Production in Zanzibar,' *East Africa Agricultural Journal*, 10 (1944), pp.93-100; Asiwaju.

[41] Wiener, 'Class Structure and Economic Development in the American South'; Roger Ransom and Richard Sutch, *One Kind of Freedom: The Economic Consequences of Emancipation* (Cambridge, 1977); Arnold Bauer, 'Rural Workers in Spanish America: Problems of Peonage and Oppression,' *Hispanic American Historical Review*, 59 (1979), pp.34-63; Friedrich Katz, 'Labour Conditions on Haciendas in Porfirian Mexico; Some Trends and Tendencies,' *ibid.*, 54 (1974), pp.1-47; Kenneth Duncan and Ian Rutledge, eds., *Land and Labor in Latin America: Essays in the Development of Agrarian Capitalism in the Nineteenth and Twentieth Centuries* (Cambridge, 1977); Juan Martinez-Alier, *Haciendas, Plantations and Collective Farms* (London, 1977).

from cash-crop production and to political action.[42] Restrictions on hunting, cutting trees, and gathering forest products limited sources of income or subsistence and made the important general point that useful resources in the environment were not goods to which all people had 'rights' – but were part of a property-oriented world.[43]

Most striking is the escalation of such regulation over much of Africa in the period after the Depression; Low and Lonsdale aptly term this era the 'second colonial occupation'. As the importance of growing more cash crops has increased, the agricultural extension agent has sought to penetrate where colonial states had found few direct means to enter. Rather than the apparently increased dependence of African peasants on the market leading to a more self-regulating system, controls have escalated along with the stakes and independent nations have used marketing boards, 'cooperative' societies, and regulations in the same 'quest for control' that preoccupied colonial states. Even socialist Tanzania has tried to assert control over peasants and foster productivity: the effort led to much coercion and little success. Other nations tried to create a rural bourgeoisie without a rural proletariat – relying on mechanization – while others tried to create a rural proletariat without a rural bourgeoisie, employing workers on state farms. None of these schemes has been effective.[44]

Nevertheless, the predominance of the world market and international capital in shaping the economic choices of peasants and the extent of the state's control are so important that Henry Bernstein has gone so far as to argue that peasant labour should be regarded as a wage-labour equivalent, with the real power over what and how much is produced lying within the capitalist mode of production.[45] He is correct to stress the entire range of

[42] The importance of rural reactions to such pressures in early resistance movements and later manifestations of mass politics emerges in, for example, Terence Ranger, 'The People in African Resistance: A Review,' *Journal of Southern African Studies*, 4 (1977), pp.125-46; Allen Isaacman, *The Tradition of Resistance in Mozambique* (Berkeley, 1976); Iliffe; and J. Forbes Munro, *Colonial Rule and the Kamba: Social Change in the Kenya Highlands 1889-1929* (Oxford, 1975).

[43] Several historians of eighteenth century England have noted the connection between the gradual development of capitalist agriculture and the transformation of various rights which tenants once had – such as hunting and foraging – into crimes. But in some African cases that have been studied, the disjuncture stands out: the restrictions on cultivators' use of nature led not to a transformation in agricultural systems, but to the decay of an ecosystem. Douglas Hay, et al., *Albion's Fatal Tree* (New York, 1975); E. P. Thompson, *Whigs and Hunters: The Origins of the Black Act* (London, 1975); Leroy Vail, 'Ecology and History: The Example of Eastern Zambia,' *Journal of Southern African Studies*, 3 (1976), pp. 129-55; Iliffe.

[44] D. A. Low and John Lonsdale, 'Introduction,' *The Oxford History of East Africa* (Oxford, 1976), Vol. 3, p.12; Frances Hill, 'Experiments with a Public Sector Peasantry: Agricultural Schemes and Class Formation in Africa,' *African Studies Review*, 20, 3 (1977), pp.25-42. Iliffe; Bernstein; Michaella von Freyhold, *Ujamaa Villages in Tanzania* (London, 1979); Goran Hyden, *Beyond Ujamaa in Tanzania: Underdevelopment and an Uncaptured Peasantry* (London, 1980); Cruise O'Brien.

[45] Bernstein, *op. cit.*

controls that affect peasants' autonomy, but he blurs the implications of the fact that the controls he discusses circle around the point of production rather than enter it directly. The issue of whether someone actually tells the cultivators, 'Hoe that row,' remains critical. One cannot understand the nature of social structures and social movements in rural areas if one forgets the difficulties of establishing direct control over production, the consequences of allowing cultivators to have access to land, or the different ways in which production can be organized and controlled.

It is thus misleading to take an overly linear view of African agricultural history. Change has proceeded more by jerks – at which the basic nature of class power and labour control was contested – than by progressive incorporation. Although the cumulative effect of the lurches has often made it extremely painful for small-scale producers to withdraw from the market, it has not necessarily insured that such producers would make the desired contributions to the world market. Even the threat of withdrawal can make the state back down before peasants, as Senegal's marketing boards did in doubling the price paid to producers for ground nuts in 1974. There is evidence that food production and even long-dormant craft production can be revived as cash-crop production drops, and it would not be surprising if these trends deepened in parts of Africa, while in others a basic transformation of relations of production took place.[46] So the myth of a lazy peasantry frequently persists among African leaders as it did among colonial officials and conceals from themselves the more threatening fact that, to a significant extent, there remains what Goren Hyden calls an 'uncaptured peasantry'.[47]

It is also questionable to see 'proletarianization' as the last stage of a direct sequence: independent cultivator to peasant to impoverished cultivator to worker. Some peasants did not become workers; some cultivators became workers because they could not become peasants; some workers became peasants. Some areas that were the least connected to export markets before the colonial era became the leading suppliers of workers, while some of the most incorporated were the least 'proletarianized'.[48]

[46] Donal B. Cruise O'Brien, 'Ruling Class and Peasantry in Senegal, 1960-1976: The Politics of a Monocrop Economy,' in Rita Cruise O'Brien, ed., *The Political Economy of Underdevelopment: Dependence in Senegal* (Beverly Hills, Calif., 1979), p. 223; Merrick Posnansky, 'Necessity Is the Mother of Invention in Ghana,' paper presented to the African Studies Association Convention, Philadelphia, 1980. This is not to minimize the extent to which peasants became involved in the circuit of commodities or that worsening conditions in produce markets could drive them into wage labour, but only to suggest that a more specific and less teleological analysis than underdevelopment theory has given us is needed.

[47] Hill, p. 37; Hyden. Hyden's argument that peasants in Tanzania retain considerable autonomy despite the best efforts of the colonial and post-colonial state is an important corrective to much current scholarship, but his comments on peasant production itself are overgeneralized and not as convincing.

The migration routes of southern Africa, like the fields, were a terrain of struggle. The contract systems, the pass laws, and the compounds with which states attempted to curtail labour mobility and channel labour where it was in demand not only point to the importance of the interventionist state in Africa, but also to the weakness of an economic system that – except in certain areas – had largely failed to gain control over rural production. Workers used desertion, movement between farming, 'formal' work, and illegal or irregular endeavors, and collective action to evade, manipulate, or alter, as best they could, the harsh forms of labour control imposed on them. How much they could shape the conditions of wage labour was affected by, and in turn affected, the conditions of agriculture. Beinart's argument that labour migration could be part of conflict between young men and household heads, and that the setting up of independent, producing, households could result from labour migration points to a set of questions that need to be explored. This is not the place to examine labour history, only to say that labour and agriculture must be studied together, and both must be understood in terms of household structure, class power, and changing forms of production, domination, and resistance in small farms and big industries.[49]

Even if the sequence of transformation is not a simple one, the apparently symbiotic relationship of capitalist production to reproduction in preserved and atrophied precapitalist modes of production remains a powerful and

[48] In Kenya, for example, coastal people were the most fully involved in the nineteenth century export economy, but were able not only to minimize the extent of labour participation in the twentieth century, but also to have some say over the form it took. The Luo were passed by in the nineteenth century, but quickly came to be the mainstay of the contract work force in the twentieth.

[49] Giovanni Arrighi's seminal article on the creation of a proletariat in Rhodesia has had a great influence on African labour history, and deservedly so. Yet it shares with many studies of agriculture an overly linear view of change. Arrighi argues that 'political' means had first to be used to force labour out of rural areas, but with the decline of land and the raising of the costs, through state action, of marketing crops, a permanent change took place, so that 'economic' factors alone could bring forth workers year in year out. The dichotomy of the political and the economic is most un-Marxist; it ignores the coercive nature inherent in capitalist production, the ways in which the actions of the state and capital continuously and consciously reshape the parameters of choice for workers, and the ways workers strive to alter those options. Charles van Onselen has a much better sense of how workers tried to subvert or use the migratory system, and has brilliantly analyzed labour control within compounds, but the rural side remains much sketchier. Arrighi, 'Labour Supplies in Historical Perspective: A Study of the Proletarianization of the African Peasantry in Rhodesia,' in Arrighi and John Saul, *Essays on the Political Economy of Africa* (New York, 1973), pp.180-234; van Onselen, *Chibaro: African Mine Labour in Southern Rhodesia 1900-1933* (London, 1976).

influential argument.[50] At the very least, this 'articulation' explains why it was possible for capitalists to pay wages below the cost of reproducing their labour force. But the argument does not suggest how difficult it was for capital and the state to mount a more direct attack on independent cultivation, the struggles of workers and peasants to shape patterns of labour, or the instability of migratory labour systems. The idea of physical movement between capitalist production and precapitalist reproduction is too neat to account for the long persistence of labour tenancy in capitalist agriculture in South Africa, Rhodesia, or Kenya – where reproduction and production were combined within the capitalist estate – or the simultaneous growth of crop production and labour migration in Pondoland before the 1930s or in central and western Kenya over a longer period, all in areas that were supposed to be the region of reproduction.[51]

Some copper mines in Northern Rhodesia – seeking labour from an area where peasants had been given poor access to markets and where ecosystems had been disrupted, but where substantial land was still available – quickly moved to bring reproduction under their wing by getting miners' wives to settle next to mine towns and grow food; only they found that the women asserted more independence of both mines and husbands than they were supposed to. When the contradictions and costs of migratory labour mounted in the late 1940s, mining capital in Zambia moved toward 'stabilization' of labour; in South Africa, after some consideration of a similar direction of change, the state escalated coercion

[50] Claude Meillassoux, *Femmes, greniers, capitaux* (Paris, 1975); Michael Burrawoy, 'The Functions and Reproduction of Migrant Labour: Comparative Material from Southern Africa and the United States,' *American Journal of Sociology*, 81 (1976), pp. 1050-87; Pierre-Phillipe Rey, *Les alliances de classes* (Paris, 1973). This necessarily brief comment on certain tendencies in this argument is not meant to diminish the importance or the complexity particular authors have given it, especially in reference to South Africa. Harold Wolpe, 'Capitalism and Cheap Labour-Power in South Africa: from Segregation to Apartheid,' *Economy and Society*, 1 (1972), pp.425-56, and Frederick Johnstone, *Class, Race and Gold* (London, 1976). But see the criticisms of Meillassoux in Martinez-Alier.

[51] J. K. Rennie rightly stresses the instability of tenancy in Rhodesia, and argues that the basic tension was between poorly capitalized white farmers, who wanted tenants to be both preserved and restricted to labour tenancy, and more mature capital, which tended to create landless proletarians. The pressures of the tenants themselves also need to be considered. In coastal Kenya, squatter resistance to both restrictive tenancy legislation and labour recruitment was to a significant extent successful, and even in the White Highlands, legislation passed in 1918 against squatters modelled on South Africa's did not break the squatters on the farms of both white settlers and leading Kikuyu chiefs, so that renewed attempts to make squatters into workers after World War II led to violent squatter resistance. J. K. Rennie, 'White Farmers, Black Tenants and Landlord Legislation: Southern Rhodesia 1890-1930,' *Journal of Southern African Studies*, 5 (1978), pp.86-98; Cooper, Chapters 5 and 6; Frank Furedi, 'The Kikuyu Squatters in the Rift Valley, 1918-29,' in B. A. Ogot, ed., *Hadith 5* (Nairobi, 1975), pp.177-94; idem., 'The Social Composition of the Mau Mau Movement in the White Highlands,' *Journal of Peasant Studies*, 1 (1974), pp.486-505; Berman and Lonsdale.

to maintain the system in the face of its instability.[52] Reproduction and production could thus be combined within the capitalist estate or the mining town – or within the African commodity-producers community – as well as divided geographically; and each combination might favor the interests of particular factions of capital, foster different strategies on the part of capital and different forms of struggle by workers, shape social formations in distinct ways, and lead to conflicts and contradictions as well as profits.[53] The problem that South Africa and colonial states faced was not just how to undermine, then preserve, a peasantry, but how to exercise control over each facet of a complex and changing field of struggle. The widespread crises in labour systems in many parts of Africa from the late 1930s to the early 1950s coincided with the escalation of the state's intervention in peasant agriculture: both upheavals reflected in different ways the contradictions of the drive for cheap labour and cheap produce and the quest for control over production processes in an era of intensified production.[54]

Since most discussions of peasants begin with terminology, mine shall end with that subject. Marxist scholarship would be greatly furthered by a long moratorium on the use of the words 'peasantization' and 'proletarianization', although 'peripheralization' deserves a permanent place in a museum of gobbledygook. Not only is the use of such words an act of violence against language, but they pose a danger to thought processes as well. Like 'urbanization' and at least some of the other process-nouns which non-Marxist sociologists prefer, such terms bear some relationship to processes which do take place. But the terms favored by Marxists and non-Marxists alike share a tendency toward teleology; they carry an implication that these things simply happen. The attachment of a label can delude us into thinking that we understand the nature and causes

[52] The intended and actual role of women in linking the production and reproduction processes in the Zambian mining industry is brought out in the illuminating article by George Chauncey in this issue. See also Charles Perrings, *Black Mineworkers in Central Africa: Industrial Strategies and the Evolution of an African Proletariat in the Copperbelt 1911-41* (New York, 1979); Michael Burawoy, *The Colour of Class on the Copper Mines; From African Advancement to Zambianization* (Lusaka, 1972); Helmuth Heisler, *Urbanisation and the Government of Migration: The Inter-relation of Urban and Rural Life in Zambia* (London, 1974); Jane Parpart, 'Labour and Capital on the Copperbelt: African Labour Strategy and Corporate Labour Strategy in the Northern Rhodesian Copper Mines 1924-1964,' Ph.D. Dissertation, Boston University, 1981; O'Mara.

[53] Michael Cowen has emphasized in the case of Kenya the distinctive positions and conflict among international capital, estate (settler) capital, indigenous capital (African landowners using wage labour), and small-scale commodity producers. 'Capital and Peasant Households,' unpublished paper, Nairobi, 1976. For a different view, see Leys.

[54] The crisis had much to do with the rising cost of reproducing urban labour in an era of expanding commodity production and rising prices, which both preceded and followed the special burdens of World War II. This era is being studied by, among others, William Freund, Lester Lee, and myself.

of a process when we are only beginning to see what is going on. The uniformity which such terms suggest makes a valid, if unoriginal, point that remote parts of Africa are part of a world system, but blur the more elusive question of what the dynamics of that relationship are. Perhaps all Africans, however much they have resisted and however much they have bent the nature of agriculture and work in particular directions, are all headed into a unitary category. But the experiences of Angola, Mozambique, and Zimbabwe suggest that it is stunted forms of capitalism, regimes that intensify production without transforming the structures through which that production takes place, that are the most vulnerable to revolutionary change. We must be careful about seeing change as a roadway when the most important changes are occurring in cul-de-sacs.

A final word must be queried – peasantry. The recent focus on peasantries has been far more instructive than most of the fads Africanists have followed: it has given us a sense that African agriculture has not been static and at least some idea of the fundamental division – in work rhythms, in the way labour is motivated and controlled, in the social structures that different forms of production engender – between the small-scale farm using family labour and the large-scale capitalist enterprise, using wage labour and authoritarian direction. The word 'peasant' will remain useful as a descriptive term. Certainly, European, Latin American, and Asian history – as well as African – has been made much richer by studies that took off from this loosely defined category and transcended its imprecision by the detail with which they analyzed particular social and economic structures. But it is harder to say – after a couple of decades in which peasant studies have been very much in vogue – that generalizations have become any sharper. Indeed, some of the most important analytical articles which the *Journal of Peasant Studies* has recently published – much to the credit of its editors – have questioned the very concept contained in the journal's title.[55] But the dangers of putting too much weight on the concept of a peasantry is evident in the willingness of the editor of a new collection of articles on 'Peasants in Africa' to generalize, 'Most peasants have difficulty feeding themselves,' and to suggest that one of our future tasks should be 'to examine the emergence of a distinctive peasant consciousness'.[56] Even if they were less inaccurate,

[55] Ennew et al.; Bernstein; Harrison; Friedmann.

[56] Klein, pp.25, 32. Klein is one of several Africanists who have searched for a peasant consciousness under the influence of James Scott. In a thought-provoking book, Scott argues that revolutionary movements in Southeast Asia can be understood in terms of a distinct 'moral economy' characteristic of a peasant economy: peasants would willingly pay landlords and states, so long as the terms of payment were sufficiently flexible that they did not risk pushing peasants below a subsistence minimum. The rigidity and intensification of demands under colonial states pushed peasants, in bad years at least, below that point and violated the moral economy. It is a very good idea to examine the political values and forms of collective

such generalizations would have little relation to the category of peasant; and there is little point in pursuing people's consciousness in a social formation that has not been specified. We will do better to examine the responses of ruling classes and ordinary cultivators to the expansion of world markets and the ways in which their struggles have shaped different systems of production, class structures, and political conflicts. And the study of the way rural cultivators, rural workers, and urban workers overlapped and interracted is a more fruitful way of examining class formation and political movements than the isolation of the culture and politics of supposedly unitary categories. Beinart, looking at a small piece of Africa, has suggested what one might see by peering into the realm which the concept of peasantry leaves obscure, and Trapido and Morris have similarly begun to peer into the capitalist estate to examine the shaping and the transformation of labour processes. It is hard to see, however, how any of this work could have been done without the efforts of Colin Bundy to strip away the mythologies of the backward African cultivators and to raise the most basic questions about the structures and dynamics of African agricultural history. Most academics seem to think that the highest accomplishment of scholarly work is for it to spawn a host of similar studies. But it would be a better compliment to the achievements of the scholars who have looked deeply at African peasants if their successors did not so much follow their footsteps as pioneer still newer pathways.

action that arise out of particular economic structures, but Scott's argument loses force by equating the structure that can foster such concepts with a peasantry. E. P. Thompson, in his original formulation of the concept of moral economy, saw it as the outgrowth of a particular class structure, not as an attribute of a specific group, artificially isolated, and that is a much more precise way to use the concept. Scott has been criticized for not considering the nature of class structures or the dynamics of agriculture; struggles could take place over subsistence minima or over a surplus. Scott, *The Moral Economy of the Peasant: Rebellion and Subsistence in Southeast Asia* (New Haven, 1976); E. P. Thompson; 'The Moral Economy of the English Crowd in the Eighteenth Century,' *Past and Present*, 50 (1971), pp.76-136; Michael Adas, 'Moral Economy' or 'Contest State'?: Elite Demands and the Origins of Peasant Protest in Southeast Asia,' *Journal of Social History*, 13 (1980), pp.521-46.

THE EMERGENCE AND DECLINE OF A SOUTH AFRICAN PEASANTRY

by Colin Bundy
St Antony's College, Oxford

Much of South Africa's history revolves about the transition of a majority of her people—the rural African population—from their pre-colonial existence as pastoralist-cultivators to their contemporary status: that of sub-subsistence rural dwellers, manifestly unable to support themselves by agriculture, and dependent for survival upon wages earned in 'white' industrial regions or on 'white' farms. The transition is an obvious one, and its external aspects have been described often enough: the diminution of Africans' lands by conquest and annexation, the creation of 'reserves', the deterioration of these into eroded, overstocked and overcrowded rural ghettoes, and their function as the supply source of migratory labour.

The most widely accepted explanation of the 'failure' of African agriculture in South Africa to provide a living for people who were once herders and farmers is found in the works of de Kiewiet, Marais, Macmillan and others, who stress the destructive impact of white rule, the dislocation of the traditional economy and social order, and, especially, the hammer-blow of sudden land shortage. They were consciously writing corrective history, replacing the pro-settler complacency and misrepresentation of Theal and Cory; de Kiewiet was at pains to dispel the comfortable fiction that Africans continued even after the Frontier Wars to enjoy an agreeable *dolce far niente*, stressing that rural Africans underwent hardships 'of a much greater degree than is normally conceded'. Without available land for all, 'one of the corner-stones of tribal life had been wrenched away;' the cash nexus dissolved the old self-sufficient economic order, while rising consumption needs 'threw upon the tribes a burden their subsistence economy could not bear.'[1] The frailty of the subsistence economy was in large measure due to the 'unscientific and wasteful' agriculture and the 'ignorance and neglect' of 'native life'.[2]

A rather different emphasis is met in the works of D. Hobart Houghton, who has written widely on the economic history of the reserves. His explanation derives even more explicitly from a theoretical insistence upon the dual

Colin Bundy, who was a student at universities in Natal and the Transvaal, is now working on South African history for a doctorate at Oxford University.

1. C. W. de Kiewiet, 'Social and Economic Developments in Native Tribal Life', *Cambridge History of the British Empire*, Vol. VIII (Cambridge, 1936), pp. 811, 812, 819.
2. C. W. de Kiewiet, *The Imperial Factor in South Africa* (Cambridge, 1937), p. 150 et passim; *A History of South Africa* (London, 1941), p. 197 et passim.

nature of the South African economy, the parallel existence of 'self-subsistence' and 'market' sectors of the economy. He argues that, for a variety of reasons, Africans failed to adapt the tribal economy to the novel condition of relative land scarcity, or to learn from their white neighbours more modern methods of farming. The 'failure to adapt their economy' is the 'root cause of their distress', and the failure is accounted for in terms of the shortcomings of the traditional or subsistence sphere of the dual economy: lack of technical knowledge, the inhibiting forces of social custom and a hostility to innovation, and a lack of response to market incentives. The thesis is underscored that these flaws stem from the nature of African society, that they are so deeply rooted there as to resist the enlightenment and economic rationality of

> 'far sighted administrators . . . missionaries . . . [and] agricultural demonstrators . . .. Failure to effect significant change in agricultural methods should not be attributed to lack of zeal on the part of a noble band of dedicated workers, but must be explained in other ways.'[3]

These approaches—and the liberal tradition of South African historiography—posit the fundamental, inherent weakness of the traditional economy, and the inability of Africans either to adapt that economy or to forsake it for participation in the market economy. This explanation overlooks or underestimates a phenomenon to which Monica Wilson has recently drawn attention: an initial period of 'early prosperity' in the reserve areas of South Africa (and in the territories that today are Botswana, Lesotho, and Swaziland), followed only later by the symptoms of underdevelopment and sub-subsistence (i.e. a level below that of normal subsistence).[4]

This paper makes some preliminary suggestions about the history of African agriculture in South Africa, and particularly about the response by African peasants to economic changes in the late nineteenth century. It argues that there was a substantially more positive response by African agriculturists to market opportunities than has usually been indicated; that an adapted form of the traditional subsistence methods provided for hundreds of thousands of Africans a preferable alternative to wage labour on white colonists' terms; that a smaller group of African farmers made considerable adaptations, departing entirely from the traditional agricultural economy, and competed most effectively

3. For Houghton's writings generally on reserves and dual economy, see his *Some Economic Problems of the Bantu in South Africa* (Johannesburg, 1938) S.A.I.R.R. Monograph Series, No. 1; *The Economy of a Native Reserve*, Vol. 2 of *Keiskammahoek Rural Survey* (Pietermaritzburg, 1952); (ed.), *Economic Development in a Plural Society* (Cape Town, 1960), esp. p. 11; *The South African Economy*, (2nd edition, Cape Town, 1967) pp. 70–71 et passim; 'Economic Development in the Reserves', *Race Relations Journal*, **29**, (Jan. 1962). The quotations here are from 'The Economy of a Native Reserve', pp. 2–3, and 'Economic Development in the Reserves', pp. 10–11.
4. M. Wilson and L. Thompson (Eds), *The Oxford History of South Africa*, Vol. 2 (Oxford, 1971), p. 55. Apart from her most useful treatment (*ibid.*, pp. 49–71), earlier treatments of this phenomenon include H. M. Robertson, '150 Years of Economic Contact between Black and White', *S. A. Jnl Econ.*, **2**, 4 & **3**, 1; S. T. van der Horst, *Native Labour in South Africa* (London, 1942), esp. pp. 103–5.

with white farmers. In explaining the subsequent failure of this response and these adaptations, it is suggested that the crucial post-mineral period was one in which non-market forces predominated; in which discriminatory and coercive means were utilized by the wielders of economic and political power to disadvantage the African peasantry; and that an economy was created whose structure was such as to render 'market forces' highly favourable to the white, capitalist sector. The decline in productivity and profitability of African agriculture—and the corollary of greater dependence by Africans on wage labour—is in an important sense the outcome of the nature of capitalist development in South Africa.

In short, I maintain that it is tenable to speak of the creation of an African peasantry in South Africa during the nineteenth century: a peasant I take to be a rural cultivator enjoying access to a specific portion of land, the fruits of which he can dispose of as if he owned the land; and who, by the use of family labour, seeks to satisfy the consumption needs of his family and to meet the demands rising from his involvement in a wider economic system.[5] This definition focuses attention both upon the relationship between the cultivator and the land he farms, his crops, cattle, ploughs, and pastures, and upon the relationship between the cultivator and the holders of economic and political power outside his own social stratum, the transfer of surplus in rents, taxes, exchange, and labour. A feature of the transition of rural Africans from farmer-pastoralists to a reservoir of cheap, rightless, and largely migrant workers is that a portion of the peasantry was proletarianized almost as soon as it emerged as an identifiable element in the political economy.

Obviously, the transition varied in chronology and detail from area to area, but its broad features have a general applicability. Highly schematically:

(i) After the initial shock of collision between colonists and farmer-pastoralists, the latter adapted considerably, and in areas of greatest contact a peasantry emerged which sought in part to meet its requirements through participation in the produce market.

(ii) At first, such participation was favoured by imperial and colonial authorities, by missionaries and settlers: the peasants provided a buffer against hostile tribes, and economic activity was profitably advanced.

(iii) African peasants displayed a tenacious preference for a life that drew subsistence from a family plot rather than from wage labour at low levels of remuneration. White farmers, in the period before mineral discoveries, sought for their part to ensure an increased labour supply; they did so either by levying taxes and fees and enacting laws to compel and control a labour flow, or by establishing quasi-feudal relations. This latter recourse best fulfilled the needs of white farmers who themselves were only shallowly involved in market production; in many instances, it gave absentee landlords a rent income;

5. This definition is derived from E. R. Wolf, *Peasants* (New Jersey, 1966), pp. 2, 11–13; and from J. S. Saul & R. Woods, 'African Peasantries', in T. Shanin, (Ed.) *Peasants and Peasant Societies* (London, 1971), pp. 103–15.

and it proffered to African squatters a *de facto* peasant existence, and blunted the severity of laws and taxes.

(iv) Mineral discoveries and economic growth evoked a rapid spread of peasant production, and increased peasant participation in the new market and entrepeneurial opportunities; innovation and diversification took place, and a group of relatively well-off African peasants and small commercial farmers emerged. Simultaneously, however, the competing needs of old and new employers of African labour, the gradual commercialization of agriculture, and the intensification of white political authority, greatly increased the pressures on the peasantry: an assault was launched upon the peasant's participation in the cash economy on his own terms—i.e., as a seller of produce rather than as a seller of labour. Real wages were kept permanently low in mines and on farms, and as their increase was no longer to be an equilibrating factor on the labour market, 'political mechanisms became of crucial importance in closing gaps between supply and demand.'[6] There ensued not only an attempt to coerce more labour, but also an attempt to decrease the level of African competition in the produce and land markets. The early twentieth century saw a substantial rise in the social cost of peasant participation in the produce market, and a correlatively increasing reliance by peasants upon migrant labour for a cash income.

(v) One must ask why the transition process halted where it did; why the peasantry was not completely proletarianized; why South Africa's capitalist development proceeded (and proceeds) with the retention of certain pre-capitalist features. The answer lies largely in the comprehensively disadvantaged state of the peasantry by the second decade of this century: so reliant was the peasant sector upon migrant labour, so patently incapable of local development, that an adequate labour supply was assured. Moreover, the embedding of migrant labour in the economic structure conferred benefits on all the major interests which had a political voice in the state. For urban employers, it meant that labour was kept cheap, unorganized, and rightless, that overhead costs were kept to a minimum, and the formation of an urban proletariat was restricted. For white workers, it provided the security of membership in a labour elite: the protection of white labouring interests meant a partial solution to the Poor White problem—Afrikaner squatters were more fortunate than their black counterparts. For white farmers, it meant that low wages and the impermanence of compound life kept the labour force closer at hand, once the threat of black agricultural competition had been avoided.

c. 1830–1870: the emergence of a peasantry

At the beginning of the nineteenth century, most African peoples who were beginning to encounter white missionaries, hunters, traders, soldiers and settlers

6. G. Arrighi, 'Labour Supplies in Historical Perspective: a study of the proletarianization of the African peasantry in Rhodesia', *Journal of Development Studies*, **6**, 3, (April 1970), pp. 197–235.

were still pre-colonial cultivators. In the first third of the century, small communities of peasants lived either on or around mission stations, or in the vicinity of markets like that at Grahamstown. Somerset and other imperial officials favoured the 'civilizing' influence of the missions as an aid to peaceful rule; and looked to the creation of 'quiet and useful neighbours'. The missionaries themselves were conscious of the creation of a peasant class: as early as 1820, Philip wrote:

> 'By locating them on a particular place, getting them to build houses, enclose gardens, cultivate Corn land, accumulate property, and by increasing their artificial wants, you increase their dependency on the Colony, and multiply the bonds of union and number of securities for the preservation of peace.'[7]

The *mfecane* (the dispersal of Africans westwards occasioned by the rise of the Zulu state) provided the Cape with its first significant numbers of African farm labourers, who in turn were able to use skills and stock thus accumulated to become peasants. The migration of the Mfengu into the Ciskei in 1835 marks the creation of the first sizeable peasant community in South Africa. Some 17,000 Mfengu entered the colony comparatively rich in cattle, and without strong chiefly authority; they proved willing to enter service in order to accumulate cash and stock, they adopted the plough, tilled more extensively, and transported their produce to nearby markets for sale or barter. They 'soon became the chief economic power' among the Cape African tribes,[8] and were to serve as an agency of change, especially as numbers of them settled in most districts of the Colony.

The frontier wars of the 1830s, 1840s and 1850s were the violent expression of the pattern of those decades, in which mission and trade activity, and the extension of imperial authority, made corrosive contact with the political and economic organization of the tribes. Under the first sweeping expropriations of grazing lands, the mission station offered an alternative mode of access to the means of agricultural production, access that was not the less prized by the enterprising tribesman who thereby escaped the social sanctions upon accumulation exercised by his chief. By 1848, missions in the Cape held almost 450,000 acres either by deed or by 'ticket of occupation'.[9] In their replies to a questionnaire of 1848, Ciskei missionaries attested to the prevalence of agricultural innovation and diversification amongst mission-oriented peasants. They raised vegetables, wheat, barley, maize, and millet, they bought 'spades, ploughs, waggons, and other useful articles'; they reared and purchased draught animals expressly for tillage and transport, and saved 'considerable sums' of money.[10]

7. cf. D. Williams, *When Races Meet* (Johannesburg, 1967), esp. quotations from Somerset, Cuyler and Philip on pp. 16, 18, 31 respectively.
8. Robertson, '150 Years of Economic Contact', *loc. cit.*
9. B. Hutchinson, 'Some Social Consequences of Nineteenth Century Missionary Activity among the South African Bantu', *Africa*, **28,** 2 (April 1957).
10. A. E. du Toit, *The Earliest South African Documents on the Education and Civilization of the Bantu* (Pretoria, 1963), pp. 40, 57, 64, 73 et passim.

The Xhosa and Thembu cattle-killing of 1857 saw an acceleration of the integration of the colonial and traditional societies, on terms largely of the former's choosing. Tens of thousands of Africans, in response to the messianic exhortation of prophets among them, sacrificed their means of subsistence in an ill-fated attempt to reverse at a stroke the process of their domination. They sped it instead. Perhaps 20,000 died, and 30,000 survivors sought sustenance as labourers in white employ. Sir George Grey, then Governor, vigorously promoted a dual policy of land expropriation and civilization, by which he intended the rapid creation of a distinct small-holding class and of a wage-earning class: 'useful servants, consumers of our goods, contributors to our revenue, in short, a source of wealth and strength to this colony'.[11]

From the mid-50s to 1870, the annexation of the Ciskei and the extension of control over large areas of the Transkei brought increasing numbers into inescapable relations with traders, magistrates, and employers. But the tribesmen did not succumb *en masse* to these forces: the same forces which pressed some into bondage enabled others to escape; land expropriation during the wars was accompanied by grants to Mfengu and other loyalists; the large influx of traders into the Ciskei and Transkei is also an index of the increased sales of animal and agricultural products by Africans. Mfengu, Thembu, Gcalekas, Ngqikas and others demonstrated in the 1860s how effectively peasants could adjust to their new circumstances: crucial in the dispersal of new methods were the Mfengu and Thembu migrations into the Fingoland and Emigrant Tembuland areas of the Transkei in 1864–66. Throughout the Ciskei, North-Eastern Cape and western Transkei, peasants gained a foothold as land-holders and cultivators, selling grains, forage, stock, and animal products. They won prizes at agricultural shows in competition with white farmers, and a statistician noted in 1870 that 'taking everything into consideration, the native district of Peddie surpasses the European district of Albany in its productive powers.'[12] The Wittebergen reserve raised such quantities of wheat, maize and millet that the area served as 'the granary of both the Northern Districts and the Free State too'. Hundreds of Mfengu, Thembu and others—especially in the districts of Peddie, Victoria East, Queenstown and Kingwilliamstown—bought land, and many more leased land from white proprietors. From these districts, and from Stutterheim, Bedford, Somerset, Glen Grey and Keiskama Hoek came reports of sale of large quantities of agricultural surplus.[13] An extremely significant development was the adoption by African peasants of sheep-raising and wool production: 17,000 lbs of wool was sold from the district of Peddie alone in 1864; and it was estimated in 1870 that Africans in the Eastern Cape sold produce worth £150,000—white produce in the same area was worth £582,000.[14]

11. Cited in Hobart Houghton, (Ed.) *Economic Development in a Plural Society*, p. 3.
12. W. L. Blore, *Statistics of the Cape Colony* (Cape Town, 1871), p. 137.
13. Wesleyan Missionary Society archives, Box XV, South African, H. H. Dugmore to W. Boyce, 1/11/1869; Cape Commission on Native Affairs, 1865.
14. Cape Commission on Native Affairs, 1865; Blore, *Statistics of the Cape*, p. 109.

In general terms, the adoption of the plough and other implements, of new crops and methods, had provided a superior mode of production to precolonial agriculture, and many Africans responded to the imposition of taxes and the desirability of traders' wares by participating in the produce market. White farmers complained in this period of an acute labour shortage. The 'little' labour forthcoming is often attributed to the lack of responsiveness by tribesmen to the opportunities opened up by cash wages. Part, at the very least, of this shortage was due to the preference of the land-based African for meeting the new wants by selling his produce, a preference reinforced by a resistance to a qualitative change in his social relations. Even the drastic effects of large-scale land expropriation were cushioned, as the Cape possessed neither the coercive instruments, nor its economy the need, to clear all white-owned land of African occupiers. Land speculators and farmers alike, in the absence of a developed commercial agriculture, found it more profitable to have African tenants (who might be cash tenants, tenants paying in kind, tenants performing labour dues, or a combination) on their lands. The leasing of land to Africans for cash or kind was known as 'kaffir-farming', an inelegant phrase that nevertheless conveys accurately the source of non-productive white land-owners' profits. The establishment of these quasi-feudal relations on extensive lands of low cash value provided a short-term answer to white labour needs; afforded a rent income to absentee proprietors; and permitted the development of a numerically significant sector of the African peasantry (hereafter referred to as 'squatter-peasants'.)

In Natal, too, by 1870 the basic patterns of land usage were established, and the transition from precolonial cultivator to peasant was well under way, with numbers of mission-based and peri-urban peasants or small farmers. A prominent feature in this British colony was the prevalence of the quasi-feudal relations described above. Land speculators, particularly land companies, had secured vast holdings since annexation in 1843: a single company held nearly 1,000,000 acres of superior farming country. Falling land values during the depression of the mid-1860s saw land ownership concentrated in still fewer hands—to such an extent that immigration schemes aimed at swelling Natal's meagre white population (less than 20,000 in 1870) were crippled by the dearth of available arable land for settlers. The circumstances which frustrated the Immigration Board spelt to African cultivators an opportunity of pursuing an agricultural life not radically different from that of their precolonial existence. They resided in huge numbers upon nominally 'white' lands: quite apart from the 2,000,000 acres of government reserves, Africans could, and did, choose between occupation of unalienated crown lands, of unoccupied land owned by individuals or companies, of mission lands, or of land provided in exchange for labour-service or rent by white farmers and graziers; the greater freedom attainable on unoccupied lands might be offset by the prospects of accumulation when in service.[15]

15. For note 15, see next page.

Under these conditions, Natal's peasants were 'rapidly becoming rich and independent', complained the 1852-53 Native Affairs Commission; they 'preferred the most independent state, and hence has arisen the uniformly insufficient supply of labour.' The major proprietors in the colony found that their easiest source of revenue lay in renting land to Africans; prior to 1870 these latter were 'able to withstand pressures on them to work for the white man and had been able to pay their taxes by selling off their surplus grain or cattle.'[16] It was estimated in 1874 that 5,000,000 acres of land belonging to whites were occupied by Africans, and with a good proportion of the peasantry capable of ignoring the blandishments and bullying of prospective employers, the Natal government was forced to import labour in the form of indentured Indian workers and various immigration schemes.

1870–1886: new opportunities, successful—and unsuccessful—peasants

The discovery in 1867 of diamonds in the soil of Griqualand West wrenched the Cape, and South Africa, out of the slough of depression of the 1860s. Men flocked to the diamond fields to seek their fortunes, and others followed to provide goods and services. Roads and railways etched their simple economic geometry across the land: from the ports to the mines. The Cape's Governor exulted in the commercial resurgence:

> 'Probably no more prosperous year is noted in its annals . . . the prices of produce ruled high in both the Colonial and the European markets; and trade, thus rendered brisk, attained an extraordinary development. . .'[17]

For African peasants, this quickened pace had a dual impact. It suddenly raised demands for labour, on mines, roads, and railways, and also on white-owned farms whose owners increased their food production. The Cape Assembly, elevated to 'responsible government' in 1872, did its best to accelerate supply to meet these demands: new taxes, pass laws, location laws, and vagrancy laws reflected the industry of the legislators and the interests of their constituents. At the same time, however, new markets and opportunities presented many peasants with an enhanced cash income to meet new taxes and growing consumption wants, and the early 1870s saw a virtual explosion of peasant economic activity. Five hundred waggons of corn were sold by Fingoland's peasants in 1873, as well as a wool crop worth £60,000; and in 1875 the trade of Fingoland 'at lowest computation' was adjudged to be worth £150,000. From Gaikaland, Gcalekaland, Tembuland and East Griqualand came similar reports: peasants were selling cattle in order to invest in sheep; the number of traders across the Kei trebled; African produce in 1875 was estimated

15. For a fuller discussion, see H. Slater, 'The Changing Patterns of Economic Relations in Rural Natal, 1838–1914', unpublished seminar paper, Institute of Commonwealth Studies, London University, January 1972.
16. S. Marks, *Reluctant Rebellion: the 1906–8 disturbances in Natal* (Oxford, 1970), p. 119.
17. Public Record Office, CO 48/460, Desp. 54, Barkly to Kimberley, 27/5/1872.

to be worth £750,000. A single firm bought £58,000 worth of African produce, while a merchant's house in Port Elizabeth boasted an annual turnover of goods for the African trade of £200,000.[18] New methods and resources rippled from tribe to tribe, and even amongst the most 'backward' tribes crop diversification and wider cultivation were common by the 1880s.

Agricultural success was hard won. Despite the colonial stereotype of the 'indolent savage', the converse was occasionally acknowledged. In Glen Grey, commented a traveller,

> 'man for man the Kafirs of these parts are better farmers than the Europeans, more careful of their stock, cultivating a larger area of land, and working themselves more assiduously.'

A magistrate from a neighbouring district concurred: 'Taking man for man, and acre for acre, the native produces more . . . than the European . . .' While an official in a district of 7,000 people argued, cogently enough, that it should

> 'be conceded that the people in this neighbourhood who have in one year raised 250,820 lbs of wool of a superior quality and excellent get up, besides 7,484 muids of corn, who attend to 77 waggons, which are mostly employed in the transport business, to say nothing of the labour they undertake . . . cannot fairly be charged en masse with indolence.'[19]

The reaction by Natal's Africans to changed economic circumstances also took the form of a rise in production in response to opportunities. Magistrates from a dozen districts reported in the late 1870s and early 1880s that

> 'the high wages the natives now obtain, together with the profitable sale of their superfluous crops, and also the increase amongst their flocks and herds, tend rapidly to enrich them;'

that Africans were 'a race who are eminently fitted for taking advantage of any favourable opportunity for sale or barter'; and that

> 'the natives become richer and yearly cultivate a larger acreage with the plough, besides engaging in transport riding on their own account.'[20]

Africans accumulated enough capital by transport-riding or other services to settle as farmers; peasants competed with white settlers at sales of Crown land. Such enterprise continued to reduce the flow of labour, and a report by the Ixopo magistrate differs from several others only in its stylistic individuality:

18. Cape Parl. Papers G.21-'75, G.16-'76, G.12-'77, G.17-'78; J. Noble, *Descriptive Handbook of the Cape Colony* (Cape Town, 1875), pp. 230–1; Br. Parl. Papers, C.2000, Frere to Carnavon, 13/11/1877.
19. V. Sampson, 'A Letter on Frontier and Natal Travelling', *Cape Monthly*, 3rd Ser., v. II, June 1880; de Kiewiet, *Imperial Factor*, p. 150, fn. 3. Cape Parl. Papers, G.16-'76, p. 74.
20. Natal Blue Book, Native Affairs (NBBNA) 1877, magistrate of Umlazi; NBBNA 1878, magistrates Weenen & Umkomaas, NBBNA 1880, magistrate Umgeni.

'It has been seldom that Natives here have been at all dependent on wages, earned by entering the service of the whiteman [sic]. Nay! All, or nearly so, have ploughs . . . enabling them to dispose of produce on a much larger scale than formerly . . .'[21]

But—and the *caveat* is crucial—progress and prosperity were not bestowed freely or equally. The danger in sketching the impressive advances made by peasants in the post-diamond years is that an overly roseate picture of conditions in the peasant areas may emerge. Room must be found in the painting for the less fortunate and less able, the poor, the hungry, and the resourceless. Particularly after 1876, when the diamond boom tailed off and recession set in, to be cruelly compounded by the droughts of 1876–78, certain peasant communities evinced want and distress. It was in Ciskei districts—Kingwilliamstown, East London, Victoria East, Peddie—the areas where peasants had been established for the longest time—that impoverishment and proletarianization of a proportion of the peasantry were most evident. The recurrent symptoms were that the young men in the area could not obtain land; that overcrowding of people and stock was increasing; and that more and more men left the land each year in search of work. Some comments will be made later on why and how proletarianization took place: for the moment it need merely be noted that falling production and overcrowding in the Ciskei was greatly exacerbated by the confiscation of the Ngqika lands, as well as the destruction of their crops and herds, during the war of 1877–78.

A further aspect of the 1870s and 1880s, closely related to the foregoing, is the degree of differentiation and social stratification taking place amongst the peasantry. This process was sedulously fostered by magistrates, missionaries and mercantile interests, who held that the tribes would be rendered more peaceful, more tractable, and more profitable. It was given further impetus by the ambitions and enterprise of individual peasants, who appreciated not merely the material benefits of being a successful farmer, but also that mission lands or individually-owned land afforded an escape from the political and social obligations to chief and tribe. At one end of the spectrum was the class of landless young men in the Ciskei, who had no other resource to dispose of than their labour. One can identify various other strata—peasant migrants, marginally self-sufficient small peasants, better-off 'middle' peasants using family labour—all the way up to the group of farmers who consolidated early peasant successes, and became small commercial farmers. These last-named bought and/or hired land; they were conspicuously loyal to the government; their farms were distinctive for the amount of improvement and re-investment of capital in the shape of fencing, irrigation, improved stock breeds, and for the adoption of mixed farming. Their transition from the peasant to the capitalist mode of production involved greater material differences and more fundamental changes in their social relations than did the transition from pre-colonial cultivator

21. NBBNA, 1879, p. JJ18.

to peasant. Traditional responsibilities to one's kinship group, and the re-distributive norms of the tribe, were replaced by profit-seeking and exploitative relations; African farmers of this class had tenants and wage labourers on their lands—and they used the Cape's Masters and Servants Act to punish defaulters. Their life-style, in material and ideological aspects, closely resembled that of small, solvent farmers of other races in South Africa.

In the Boer republics, on the eve of the Witwatersrand gold strikes in 1886, the tempo of economic life lagged considerably behind that of the British colonies. The Dutch farmers, on the spacious farms granted them by the state, practised extensive stock-farming, usually growing only enough crops to meet their own requirements. Currency was scarce—particularly in the South African Republic (Transvaal)—and the itinerant pedlars who were the chief contact outlying farmers had with the exchange economy were content to take stock or farm produce. State expenditure and revenue were minimal, and the South African Republic's precarious solvency had slithered into bankruptcy when that country was annexed by Shepstone and his two dozen policemen in 1877. It was in the republics that the territorial rights of the tribes had been most brusquely ignored; after a combination of conquest and concessions—aided where post-*mfecane* conflict and migrations had weakened resistance—the incoming trekkers announced ownership over virtually all land within the new states' boundaries. In the Transvaal, the burgher councils set aside 280,000 morgen (the treaty areas) plus 580,000 morgen (government locations) for African occupation—out of a total of 71,000,000 morgen!

On the face of it, a land-allocation so lop-sidedly in favour of the dispossessors made impossible the creation of a peasantry. In fact, the republics' coercive equipment was so lacking, their rule so tenuous, and the value of land so low for so long, that Africans occupied, tilled, and grazed nominally white lands in enormous numbers; their ability to subsist not drastically altered, and their involvement in the exchange economy almost entirely discretionary. In the South African Republic, only £3,000 in taxes was collected from three quarters of a million Africans in the 1870s, and, sniffed a British official after Shepstone's annexation,

> 'I can come to no other conclusion but that the late government did not attempt to collect from any of the strong and powerful tribes.'[22]

In the Transvaal, two main types of peasant response are evident. Firstly, where possible, Africans occupied state or private lands, paying rent where they had to, and evading it where they could. The imperatives of the exchange economy were so low that little transformation of the traditional methods seems to have taken place. Secondly, where land expropriation had been more

22. P.R.O. CO 879/13, Conf. Print African No. 156, 'Report on Province of Transvaal', by W. C. Sargeaunt, p. 15.

effective, African peasants stepped up production, disposed of their surplus, and 'adopted the only method open to them, and proceeded to buy back when possible the land of which they had been deprived.'[23] Although this happened more frequently after the discovery of gold, there were reports in the late 1870s that 'not only the chiefs but individual kaffirs in the district of Rustenburg are anxious to acquire landed property;' and that 'in several instances the blacks are paying high rents to acquire irrigated lands.'[24]

Ruses were adopted to foil the ban on land purchase by Africans, the most common of which was the use of a missionary as a 'dummy' purchaser; 'leases' which were *de facto* sales were also resorted to. On mission stations and near those town markets which existed, Transvaal peasants raised and sold quantities of grains, fruits, and animal products.

The commercial economy was far more firmly established by 1886 in the Orange Free State than in its northern neighbour. The Free State had already begun to claw its way out of an abyss of depression in the late 1860s, in part by its conquest of the rich grain lands of the Southern Sotho, and in part by increased production of merino wool. Next door to the diamond fields, the republic was well situated to prosper further, and a considerable amount of early agricultural commercialization and economic recovery occurred between 1870 and 1875. The persistent litany of farmers for labour was answered by a thicket of proclamations and laws, notable for their unambiguous determination to force Africans on to the labour market. The statutes undoubtedly made life difficult for their targets, especially those who were effectively denied access to land. But for a majority of the Africans, quasi-feudal relations were secured, and squatter-peasants on fertile state and private lands were probably less subject to the pressures of the market and the tax collector than their counterpart in Natal. Angry farmers denounced the 'idle existence' of squatters, protesting that '*de Kaffers te rijk zijn, om zich eenig zints met werken te vermoijen*' (the Kafirs are too rich to trouble themselves with anything to do with labour); that they congregated on unoccupied farms while white farmers were deprived of servants.[25] Absentee landlords were content to receive rent in cash or kind; a Mr Green in the Harrismith district held 50,000 morgen (or 106,000 acres) on which there were over 100 'kraals', more than 800 squatters. Too much pressure on squatter-peasants bore the twin dangers of provoking resistance, or of their departure to more amenable areas. Peasants in the Free State exchanged or sold grain and stock; the republic imported a major part of its grain from Basutoland, and in its early history, the Barolong within the Free State acted as middlemen.

23. F. J. Newnham, 'Transvaal Native Locations History', Unpublished typescript, 1908; Royal Comm. Soc. Lib., Mss55V.
24. P.R.O. CO 879/16, Conf. Print African No. 204.
25. Cited in H. J. van Aswegen, 'Die Verhouding tussen Blank en nie-Blank in die Oranje-Vrystaat, 1854–1902' (Unpublished D.Phil. thesis, Univ. of OFS, 1968), p. 492. cf. also pp. 493–500.

1886–1913: peasant self-sufficiency under attack

The discovery of gold in 1886 reproduced with greater intensity the commercial quickening that had attended the diamond boom. Between 1886 and 1899, opportunities for gain and expansion were again seized by some peasants, and notable advances recorded, but the pressure on the peasantry was also increased on a number of fronts. The 1890s saw the emergence of gold-mine owners as a powerful interest group in South Africa. The cost structure of the mines demanded that an increase in the labour supply be achieved by means other than higher wages: baldly summarized, the mine-owners' demands were for cheap labour and cheap foodstuffs. By the turn of the century, the mines had agreed upon a maximum wages average, and the real wages for African miners were dragged down from the 'heights' of the early 1890s (when African miners could earn £4 a month and more) to a level which was not to alter substantially until World War II. The demand for foodstuffs began in earnest the commercialization of South African agriculture, and raised further the value of land. It was now less profitable, twice over, for white farmers to have African squatters—or white *bywoners* (squatters)—on their lands. The subsequent pressures on African squatters had a counterpart in the process that pushed thousands of indigent Afrikaners out of the countryside into the towns in the early twentieth century. A natural disaster that added significantly to the man-made difficulties of the peasantry was the rinderpest epidemic of 1896–97 that killed off Africans' cattle in numbers exceeding 80 per cent in some districts.

By entering the labour market, the mines had the effect of making farmers' demands for labour more shrill and remedies more drastic. The laggard nature of agricultural commercialization afforded the peasantry an important degree of protection, however; there remained in colonies and republics some access to land on the relatively easy quasi-feudal terms. As a general rule, where peasants retained relatively undisturbed control of their agriculture—that is, where the coercive powers of the relevant state authority were insufficient to enforce its will—it still remained possible, and certainly more attractive, to extract from their plots sufficient surplus to meet the demands of landlord and government as well as consumption needs. Two accounts, from either side of the employment line, illustrate this: the 1893–94 Cape Labour Commission explained that labour was in short supply because Africans could meet the necessities of life 'with little effort' and, because many of them were lease-holders or land-owners, could not be attracted to white employment: 'These [Transkeian] territories' observed the commissioners,

> 'appear to produce labour for work outside them somewhat in proportion to the length of time their inhabitants have enjoyed good government. . .'

Or, as Pondo peasants told recruiting officials,

> 'Why should we work, is not the country ours, and have we not lots of land

and many women and children to cultivate it? We prefer to remain as we are.'[26]

Between 1886 and 1899, the pattern noted in the Ciskei in the 1870s became apparent in certain areas of the Transkei: Fingoland, Tembuland, and East Griqualand. That is, agriculture in these areas displayed the seemingly contradictory signs of advancement and of degeneration. There were still peasants who had sufficient capital, or enterprise, to adapt and succeed, but others succumbed to economic pressures, either to cling on desperately at the lower strata of the peasantry, or to be extruded as migrant workers. It was no longer profitable in the 1890s to export grain to the large towns, and there were many reports of peasant underproduction for want of markets. Wool was increasingly resorted to as a source of cash income—and sheep wrought a heavy toll on deteriorating grazing land. Several officials, recounting rising indebtedness, falling production, and pressures on land, said specifically that their districts were not as prosperous as they had been ten or twenty years earlier.[27]

In Natal, the 1890s saw peasant subsistence slide even faster towards disintegration. The Achilles heel of the squatter-peasant was his insecurity of tenure; commercial agriculture began to take advantage of this weakness. Whereas less than 2,000,000 acres were under European cultivation in 1875, 5,800,000 acres in 1893 (and over 7,000,000 by 1904) were being farmed by white Natalians. In almost every case, this meant a reduction *in pari passu* of land used by squatters; in addition, farmers and other landlords began to raise rents and other fees payable by squatters.

In the northern republics, as has been suggested, squatters were harder to dislodge, and peasants also demonstrated other means of defending their chosen way of life. In the South African Republic, as mentioned, Africans purchased and hired a considerable amount of land: one tribe leased no less than 22 farms for grazing; others bought 18 and 11 farms respectively. Just over a quarter million acres of land were bought in the Transvaal—and population pressure on this land was only half that on government locations.[28] In the Free State, a new form of peasant-squatting became widespread, a form of sharecropping or 'farming-on-the-halves', in which white proprietors supplied seed and land, African peasants farmed the grain, and the returns were shared. There crystallized around this practice a growing class of relatively well-off peasants in the Orange Free State, and share-cropping was also a prominent feature of the Eastern Cape.

The Anglo-Boer war had galvanic effects upon certain sections of the peasantry, bestowing quick profits on those who were in a position to supply produce or draught animals at inflated prices to the troops. Many availed themselves of the wages, considerably in excess of those normally paid in South Africa,

26. Labour Commission, G.3-'94, p. 5; Native Affairs Bluebook, G.42-'98, p. 111.
27. See Cape Parl. Papers, G.3-'94, pp. 71, 76, 110; G.9-'94, pp. 55, 63.
28. Newnham, 'Transvaal Native Locations', p. 19.

offered by the British Army, and translated their savings into land purchases or improvements. Other peasants were disrupted, harried, looted, and dispersed by the exigencies of war. In broad terms, the decade after the war was one in which a sustained, several-pronged offensive was launched by white legislators and administrators in all the regions joined by the Act of Union in 1910, against the self-reliance and independence of the peasantry. A determination by would-be employers of cheap labour to make untenable those quasi-feudal relations permitting a peasant existence outside the labour market was reinforced by fears of African competition, both in the produce market and in the land market.

In the Transvaal, where peasants remained less fully integrated into the capitalist economy than elsewhere, Africans withheld the greater proportion of their labour from mines and farms for five or six years after the war.[29] They were afforded the necessary 'bargaining basis' to be able to do so partly by higher wages in construction activity, and in part by that level of subsistence still available from peasant agriculture. This latter was enhanced by the continuing high incidence of absentee landlordism in the Transvaal, where most of the 1,300 farms held by land companies, as well as much privately owned land, were leased to Africans. African peasants, Horwitz has indicated, 'showed a keener insight into the functions of capital and the market . . . than did the whites'—and the land company agents certainly held the same view. They would not rent land to white *bywoners* who were 'uninterested in farming for profit and paid no rent', but found African small-holders profitable tenants.[30] Further, the Milner administration, solicitous as it was of the needs of mining capital, was less sensitive to the demands of Dutch farmers in the Transvaal. By allowing squatters on crown land, the Commissioner for Native Affairs, Godfrey Lagden, presented Africans with a preferable alternative to renting white-owned land, and the tax discriminating in favour of farm labourers was abolished. Lagden's expressed reason for refusing to apply existing anti-squatter provisions is an interesting commentary upon the role of the peasantry within the Transvaal economy: apart from the risk of driving Africans out of the territory, wrote Lagden,

> 'it would tend to place a good deal of land out of cultivation which is now of benefit to the country . . . moreover, they [the peasants] produce a considerable amount of cereals, especially mealies, used for consumption in this country.'[31]

29. See D. J. N. Denoon, 'The Transvaal Labour Crisis, 1901–6', *Jnl African History*, **7**, 3 (1967), pp. 481–94 for a discussion of this.
30. R. Horwitz, *The Political Economy of South Africa* (London, 1967), p. 34; D. J. N. Denoon, 'Reconstruction in the Transvaal, 1903–5', (Unpublished PhD. thesis, Cambridge, 1965), p. 71.
31. Denoon, *Ibid.*, 'Reconstruction', pp. 104–5, 109; Lagden in 'Report by the Commissioner for Native Affairs relative to acquisition and tenure of land by Natives in the Transvaal' (Pretoria, 1904), p. 4, and 'Report of Native Affairs Department', Transvaal, 1903–4, p. B18.

It seems that a proportion of these cereals was used as cheap food for the labour force being recruited with unremitting vigour by the mines.

The 1907 electoral victory for Botha and *Het Volk* in the Transvaal was also a victory for Afrikaner farmers, and they now moved against the economic independence of the squatter-peasant. The 1908 Natives Tax Act imposed a levy of £2 on squatters, while labour tenants were wooed with a tax of £1. In the northern regions, rent squatters were moved from some farms by direct government action; rents rose sharply in all areas. This sniping was succeeded by the heavy artillery of the 1913 Natives Land Act.

Despite the concentration by most historians on the prohibition of land purchase by Africans in 'white' areas, and the demarcation of 13 per cent of the surface area of the country as Reserves, a more important function of the act was that squatters and share-croppers were to be reduced to the level of labour tenants. The pressure for the act, argues Francis Wilson, came almost entirely 'from those who wished to ensure a cheap supply of labour by eliminating squatters and by doing away with the system of farming-on-the-half.'[32] The closing of the free market in land not only soothed white fears—expressed throughout the previous decade—about the amount of land purchased by Africans, but also effectively put the brake on the process of class differentiation in African rural areas, thus inhibiting the growing group of small commercial farmers, potential competitors with white farmers. This slowing down of stratification (or 'class suppression') also meant avoiding the creation of a permanently landless majority of Africans, whose urbanization would have further drained the supply of rural labour, as well as posing a potential political threat.[33]

In the Orange River Colony, farming-on-the-halves spread even more widely after the war, producing at the upper reaches extremely comfortably-situated peasants and small farmers; they used 'up to date machinery', sold a lot of grain directly to merchants, on equal terms with whites, and ran large herds of sheep, goats, and cattle.[34] Even before the war a member of the Volksraad was

> '*bevreesd dat Kleurlingen de boeren langzamerhand zullen uitboeren. Kleurlingen worden nu al langzamerhand rijker dan blanken. Wij moeten onze burgers te hulp komen*' (. . . worried that Coloureds [Africans] would outfarm the [white] farmers. Coloureds were gradually becoming richer than whites. We must come to the aid of our citizens.)

A separate chapter of the 1913 Lands Act specifically outlawed farming-on-the-halves in the Orange Free State: said an economic historian fifteen years later,

32. F. Wilson, 'Farming, 1866–1966' in *Ox. Hist. S. Africa*, vol. 2, p. 129.
33. cf. M. Legassick, 'Forced Labour and Racial Differentiation in South Africa', (Unpublished paper, 1972).
34. Department of Native Affairs Bluebook, U.G.17–1911, esp. pp. 52–3, 127–9, 153–4.
35. Cited in van Aswegen, 'Verhouding tussen Blank en nie-Blank', p. 581.

'"To put it quite bluntly", as was said at the time, "The Natives have become too rich."'[36]

In Natal, where the ravages of rinderpest had been most severe, the peasantry came under greater pressures, and possessed less resources effectively to counter them. The peasant's income and his access to land were attacked from half a dozen angles. Firstly, the government tightened the labour-coercive screws as tightly as it dared: the Identification of Native Servants Act (1901), its amendment (1904), the amended Masters and Servants Act (1901), the amended Squatters' Rent Act (1903), and the imposition of a Poll Tax on all male adults (1905) graced the statute books. The direct contribution by Africans to the revenue rose after poll tax by £76,490 to a total of £306,484. At the same time, rents rose sharply all over Natal, while the profits available from dairy-farming and wattle-planting led to the purchase by farmers of much land from the companies. A wave of evictions of peasants in occupation of such lands took place in 1905–6, especially in the Natal Midlands.[37] Peasants who could afford it sought security of tenure through the purchase or hire of land, but were blocked here too: further sale of crown land to Africans was suspended in 1904, while white farmers unwilling to perpetuate old or permit new rent-paying squatters sought to change the relations to those of labour-tenancy.

The Bambatha rebellion of 1906–7 bears a close family resemblance to the Ngqika rebellion of 1877–78—an unavailing effort to throw off by force the burdens of economic under-development. A Natal peasant, although he had fought for the government against Bambatha, was only too keenly aware of all these pressures:

> 'The government had them [Africans] by the head and the farmers by the legs . . . They were extremely poor. How much remained of their earnings after they had paid their taxes and their rents and bought food for their children? . . . the Europeans had taken up every available bit of good ground. Natives, generally speaking, were poverty-stricken and had no means of making wealth.'[38]

In the Cape, the employers' anthem of labour-shortage was still being sung, and a new verse had been added: that of opposition to more productive African peasants, and an awareness of the threat of African competition. As elsewhere, share-croppers and wealthy squatters were a particular target.[39] A 1908 Committee examined the status of squatter-peasants in the Eastern Province, and found that they were 'forming a distinct and very numerous class', that they were displacing Europeans from the land, and 'considerably enhancing' the labour shortage.[40] Control over squatters was stepped up assiduously in

36. D. M. Goodfellow, *A Modern Economic History of South Africa* (London, 1931), p. 232.
37. Natal Native Affairs Commission 1905–6, pp. 27, 259, 363, 398, 436, 723, et passim.
38. *Ibid.*, evidence of Nkantolo, p. 711.
39. Cf. Cape Parl. Papers, G.12*–1904, pp. 5, 23, 43, G.46–1906, pp. 18–19, G.24–1908, pp. 12–13, and esp. G.46–1908, passim.
40. G.46–1908, *Report . . . on the Occupation of Land by Natives in Unreserved Areas.*

successive Location Acts of 1892, 1899, and 1909. In the 1890s, many squatters were driven off farms in the Eastern Province, causing stock loss and much land 'to be thrown out of cultivation'. In 1905, the Cape Mounted Police took over the enforcement of the widely-evaded anti-squatting measures. Landlords passed the higher fees directly on to their tenants, and in 1909–10, many squatter-peasants were driven off their plots for refusing to pay the higher licence fees of the 1909 Act. Much is usually made of the fact that the 1913 Lands Act was constitutionally inapplicable in the Cape, but less often is it appreciated how effectively the Cape had undermined the position of the peasantry without the aid of the 1913 Act. A squatting population of at least 40,000 (and probably much more) was reduced by the 1909 Act to 7,000 by 1931; a 1930 Report indicated that of 1,990 farms owned but not occupied by whites in South Africa, only 74 were in the Cape.[41]

By 1913, the peasant sector showed serious signs of agrarian degeneration, and the transformation of the once fertile reserve areas into teeming rural slums was well under way. Yields per capita were falling, and after the 1920s, the absolute yield dropped. Areas which had been food exporting, then grimly self-reliant, now needed to import grain, and peasant families could only subsist with the remittance of wages by migrant labourers. There is a vast and depressing body of evidence as to the nature and extent of underdevelopment in the Reserves: malnutrition, infant mortality, desiccation, erosion, social evils, indebtedness, and hopeless poverty are its recurrent themes.[42]

Conclusions: the peasantry and underdevelopment

With this skeletal history serving as a background, it may be useful to isolate some of the economic factors which affected the development of, and the decay of, peasant agriculture, in addition to those measures already described, aimed directly at reducing peasant independence or competition.

The most obvious and the most far-reaching single factor is the shortage of land available to the peasantry; it is

> 'the key to the status of inferiority, exploitation, poverty, lack of culture, in a word the status of underdevelopment . . . of [peasants] who participate all too fully in the social process of capitalist development.'[43]

The disequilibrium between the peasant population and its basic means of production was brought into being by the sweeping expropriations of the first

41. J. S. Marais, 'African Squatting on European Farms in South Africa, with Particular Reference to the Cape Colony (1892–1913)', Unpublished seminar paper, ICS, University of London, 1967.
42. See especially the following: *Report of the Native Economic Commission, 1930–2*, U.G.22–1932; Social and Economic Planning Council, *Report No. 9*, U.G.32–1946; *Keiskammahoek Rural Survey* (4 vols, Pietermaritzburg, 1952); 'Fagan Report', U.G.28–1948; 'Tomlinson Commission Report', U.G.61–'55. Reports of the Native Affairs Departments and Native Affairs Commission since 1910; Transkeian Territories General Council, Proceedings and Reports.
43. A. G. Frank, *Capitalism and Underdevelopment in Latin America*, (New York, 1969), p. 136.

half of the nineteenth century, but its effects were greatly increased after the 1890s, when the quasi-feudal system of squatter-peasants on white lands came under pressure. Politically, too, by the end of the nineteenth century it was no longer held necessary in the Cape to have a 'buffer' class of African smallholders, and the policy of fostering such a class gradually gave way to one in favour of creating a uniformly small-peasant rural population.[44]

Another long-term factor was the changing character of African involvement in the money economy: a change that can be summed up as the movement from 'discretionary' spending to 'necessary' cash requirements. The spread of traders into every corner of the peasant areas saw a sharply rising index of purchases of agricultural implements, clothes, blankets, tin and iron ware, fuel, and new foodstuffs, which gradually became necessary to subsistence. There are many forces at work here: the psychological ones of habit and reliance; state insistence on certain purchases, such as European clothing; the decline in the face of competition from manufactured goods of peasant crafts; and the importance and expense of education as a new requirement.

A further aspect of peasant-trader relations which diminished the peasant's access to his own surplus was his contractual inferiority. In the trader's hands were concentrated the several economic functions of purchaser of agricultural produce, purveyor of manufactured goods, and supplier of credit. Trader and peasant enacted in microcosm the adverse terms of trade of a colonial relationship.

Perhaps the most important variable introduced into structural relations after the mineral discoveries was the relative ease of access of capitalist white farmers and peasant farmers to markets. W. M. Macmillan has pointed out that 'to locate the native reserves, it is no bad rule . . . to look for the areas circumvented or entirely missed by even branch railway lines.'[45] The costs of ox-waggon borne produce made competition (especially in grain) prohibitive; late nineteenth and early twentieth century documents are replete with reports of peasant underproduction for want of market access. As the Chief Magistrate of the Transkei put it,

> 'The easy access to the labour market . . . contrasts with the difficulty or absolute lack of transport for agricultural produce. . .'[46]

The peasant sector also suffered an almost total dearth of public or private investment. In addition, one must bear in mind the drain of human capital from the area in the form of migrant labour, and the lack of social investment in terms of health, welfare, and education. This—as well as outright discrimination against African-raised produce at some points—is starkly contrasted by the responsiveness of the South African state to the needs of white farmers.

44. The Glen Grey Act of 1894, with its insistence upon the principle of 'one man one lot' and equal-sized lots was a major step in this direction; see also van der Horst, *Native Labour*, p. 309, and *Keiskammahoek Rural Survey*, vol. 4, pp. 129–30.
45. W. M. Macmillan, *Complex South Africa* (London, 1930), p. 212.
46. Cape Parl. Papers, G.24–1908, p. 24.

All these factors are mutually reinforcing and self-perpetuating in their effects. They all contributed to the diminution of the surplus-generating capacity of the peasant, and to a lessened control by the peasant over the disposal of his surplus: at the same time that the possibilities for accumulation were thus restricted, the capitalist penetration raised the demand for a cash income. The peasant's increasing involvement in migrant labour depleted the intensity of economic activity in the peasant areas, thereby reproducing the necessity for more migrant labour.

I suggested at the outset that the creation of an African peasantry in South Africa was also the process of transition from a rural population of pastoral-cultivators to a rural population of land-based, sub-subsistence migrant workers, and that the emergence and decline of the peasantry was a necessary component of, and not separate from, the process of capitalist development in South Africa —that the structural underdevelopment of the peasant sector was the other side of the coin of capitalist development in South Africa. If I have adequately demonstrated that which I set out to, then the dualist model of the South African economy is a misleading one: the distance between the races in economic, cultural, and political spheres was not an original state lessened by capitalist development, but rather the outcome of that development;[47] and explanations of the underdevelopment of the peasant sector which rest upon the inherited backwardness and inadequacy of that sector are incorrectly premised. The conventional wisdom of South African economic historiography—already questioned in these pages[48]—stands in need of a continuing re-examination.

47. Arrighi, 'Labour Supplies', *loc. cit.*
48. F. R. Johnstone, 'White Prosperity and White Supremacy in South Africa', *African Affairs*, **275**, 69, (April 1970).

the madman and the migrant: work and labor in the historical consciousness of a South African people

JOHN L. and JEAN COMAROFF—*University of Chicago*

I

It is perhaps ironic that we learnt our most profound lesson about consciousness in rural South Africa from a madman. The lesson was all the more remarkable because it came in a wordless encounter, a meeting in 1973 at a mental hospital for Tswana outside Mafeking. Famous for an ingenious costume that he would never remove, the man was, literally, a prophet in polythene robes. His crazy clothes spoke the language of his obsession. His boots, standard issue for mineworkers, were topped by intricately knitted leggings, the painstaking product of many unravelled orange sacks. He wore a cloak and a bishop's mitre, fashioned from black plastic garbage bags. Across his chest was stretched a brilliantly striped sash, on which were stitched three letters: SAR. For his white attendants, these were the most obvious signs of his delusion, although they noted that he also "heard" things. The other patients, however, regarded him as an inspired healer, sent to them in their affliction. SAR was his church, and he its sole embodiment. The letters stood for South African Railways, alongside whose track the hospital lay. In fact, at the very moment we encountered him, the night train for Johannesburg rattled by with its daily cargo of migrants. Later, as we puzzled to decipher his message, we kept returning, as he did, to SAR. It was a message that spoke directly to his fellow inmates—and also to the black paramedical staff. For, in this world of peasant-proletarians, the railway forged a tangible link between rural and urban life, hitching together the dissonant worlds of the country and the city.

We had long been aware of the importance of the distinction between these worlds for the Tshidi-Barolong, the Tswana people among whom we worked. One of our earliest conversations in Mafikeng, their capital, had been with a man who, while respected, was neither rich

This essay explores the nature of historical consciousness, and its relation to culture, among the Tshidi-Barolong, a South African Tswana people. On the basis of the imagery of two informants—a "madman" and a former migrant laborer—it examines not merely the content of Tshidi consciousness, but also its expressive forms. These differ from the narrative modes of representation associated with "history" in Western contexts, and build on various poetic devices—most strikingly, on the rhetoric of contrast. Thus the opposed concepts of work and labor, one associated with setswana *(Tswana ways) and the other with* sekgoa *(European ways), are major tropes through which Tshidi construct their past and present. Such rhetorical forms appear, on examination, to occur widely in situations of rapid change. As a result, this excursion into the poetics of history illuminates very general questions concerning the connection between consciousness, culture, and representation.* [South Africa, Tswana, culture, consciousness, history, poetics, representation]

nor high-born. This "everyman" epitomized the older generation of peasant-worker, having spent his young adult life laboring in the gold mines in Johannesburg. Now he surveyed his parched corn field, and said laconically:

> Here I struggle, but I work for myself (*iterela;* the reflexive of *direla,* "work [do] for"). The soil is stony and there is no rain. I struggle, but I call no one "boss." Out there, where we labor *(bereka)* for the whites, they pay us money. But the mine, like the grave; has use only for your body. When it has done with you it spits you out, and you are finished! Useless!

Despite its poignancy, this commentary on the experience of alienation was in some ways unremarkable. Oppressed workers elsewhere have been apt to see the mine as a predator, the industrial workplace as a tomb (see, for example, Van Onselin 1976; Gordon 1977; Nash 1979; Taussig 1980; cf. also D. H. Lawrence 1922; Eliade 1962). What is more, our attempt to pursue the exegesis further proved fruitless. We were simply unable to elicit statements that tied exploitation to a coherent notion of class antagonism or even racial conflict. This, it seemed, had been one of those rare moments when otherwise mute experience found voice in a fortuitous clutch of images.

But longer familiarity with the Tshidi taught us that these images were not fortuitous, and that the meaning of the old migrant's message was widely shared. The clue lay in the form of his utterance: by a subtle choice of words, the vernacular term for work (or, more precisely here, "work for myself") was nicely distinguished from that used for labor done for whites. The first, *itirela,* implies "making oneself." It is the reflexive form of the Setswana *go dira,* "to do" or "to make." *Bereka,* on the other hand, comes from the Afrikaans *werk,* and connotes wage labor (apparently for all Sotho-Tswana speakers; Ziervogel and Mokgokong 1985). As we shall see, these terms form a significant opposition, carrying with them a fan of associations interlaced in the Tshidi imagination: work contrasts with labor as does self-construction with self-destruction; as time logged "out there" with the creative processes of production and reproduction "at home" *(mo gae);* as the enduring value of cattle with the capricious flow of money. But these contrasts are neither frozen in a timeless cultural scheme nor played out in a narrative vision of history. Rather, they provide a versatile and poetic language, one capable of giving voice to both the musings of the migrant and the creations of the crazy prophet. In them, as in the polythene robes, lay a key to the Tshidi sense of themselves, of the making of their present world.

II

It has become almost commonplace to ask why social classes seem so seldom to act for themselves *(für sich);* why class consciousness, the assertion of collective identity and interest, arises so infrequently—even under apparently favorable conditions (for example, Wallerstein 1979[1972]:173; Marks and Rathbone 1982:26–27). The question itself raises a prior issue, however: What exactly do we take as expressions of collective consciousness? Is it possible that, for a long time, Western social scientists, in both the Weberian and Marxian traditions, sought them in the wrong place? Social and political historians, especially those studying the collective consciousness of the dominated, have increasingly had to look beyond formal institutions or statements, and into the texture of the everyday (see, for example, Thompson 1963; Genovese 1972). This has also been the case in the African context. Van Onselin (1973, 1976), for instance, argues that the consciousness of Southern Rhodesian miners (1900–20) cannot be measured "by the presence or absence of associations and organizations which manifestly articulate worker interests" (1973:237). It was expressed, instead, in everyday acts of resistance to the labor discipline of particular mines; in such tacit and taciturn forms of defiance as foot-dragging and absenteeism. Here, then, consciousness is not found in explicit statements of common predicament on the part of a social group, but in the implicit language of symbolic activity. Yet this only underscores the problem. In what sense does a set of inarticulate practices amount to *consciousness*? If we accept that the latter is more than just explicit social reflection—that, like "ideology," it may hide itself in everyday activity—is it any different from the anthropological conception of culture? And, if so, does this not leave unanalyzed the relationship between conventional meaning and the processes of thought and action through which history is made?

This is the general problem which informs our analysis here, although we confine ourselves to a single social context. It is, however, a context in which issues of historical consciousness at large, and class consciousness in particular, arise in acute form: that of a black South African people drawn into the labor market and made to eke out an existence from a combination of small farming and wage work. Like others, Tshidi have been steadily impoverished by the rise of the regional political economy and have become yet another division in its reserve army of labor. In this respect, they are in no doubt that they are "oppressed" (*patikega;* "pressed down"), although they do not have a straightforward sense of themselves as members of either a class or a community of workers. Being peasant-proletarians, they have long migrated between a rural "homeland" and the town, their journey articulating the worlds of agricultural production and wage labor, idealized past and discordant present.[1]

The Tshidi understanding of their modern situation is, quite explicitly, a consciousness of history; that is, it evokes the *making* of the social world, past and present. But this history is seldom spontaneously told in narrative style; that is, as a linear account of events.[2] Nor can it be readily distilled, from its various expressive forms, into an "objective" chronicle. It is captured, as the migrant implied—and we shall show in more detail below—in the dynamic interplay of a series of distinctions, contrasts which describe two radically different epochs that have come to coexist in time. These contrasts are sometimes acted out, sometimes spoken of, and always anchored in everyday activities.[3] Together they compose a meaningful account of a changing world and the place of the Tshidi within it.

Of course, this kind of historical reckoning is at odds with the conventional Western view of history as an account of "real" events and processes. At the heart of that view lies a distinction between reality, the actual making of history, and representation, the terms in which its story is told and acted on. Mitchell (1986), a literary critic, has recently argued that this distinction is basic to modern Western thought; it certainly underlies the familiar contrast between text and context, the concept and the concrete. But, as Mitchell goes on to suggest, representation itself is also believed to have two distinct modes: realism, where images aim to be faithful reflections of the world; and rhetoric, where those images, by their very form, evaluate the world as they portray it. The first tends to be seen as the medium of factual historical narrative, the second, of interpretive poetics. Philosophers, semioticians, and historians have disputed the soundness of this distinction as an analytic principle; few, perhaps, would defend it any longer. Yet its effects on our ways of seeing have been profound (cf. Friedrich 1979:442). Above all else, it leads directly to the assumption that poetic modes of representation are less true, more ideological, than are realistic narratives of the past. Poetic forms belong, at best, to the separate realm of aesthetics or mythology; at worst, to the dirty tricks of ideology. Either way, however, rhetoric is usually held to distort the collective imagination, breathing false life into sober social facts. In the final analysis, then, there can be no poetics of history.

But where does this leave the madman and the migrant? Neither speak in the genre of narrative realism. The madman may present the more dramatic picture; like many of his kind, he is dismissed, by those unfamiliar with his language, as a false prophet, a psychotic whose costume reflects no more than the workings of his own tortured mind. Yet even if he is defined as psychotic, he may nonetheless be the voice of history. Foucault (1967), for one, insists that the insane speak eloquently of their social world. Our madman, of course, uses visual imagery, while the migrant relies on verbal metaphor. But both use poetic expression to offer an authentic commentary on the Tshidi past and present. Friedrich (1979:441ff.) has argued that the poetic is a pervasive aspect of all kinds of language; characterized by "figures and tropes . . . intensification of form . . . [and] association by analogy," it is the language "that most significantly interacts with the imagination" (1979:491–492). In constructing their distinctions and contrasts, the madman and the migrant certainly use such instruments, although they do not limit themselves to words alone. Indeed, together they remind us that historical consciousness is not confined to one expressive mode. It may be created and conveyed—with great subtlety and no less "truth"—in a variety of genres.

The point is not limited to non-Western peoples, or to those at the peripheries of the modern world system. The Tshidi fondness for viewing history in terms of a set of contrasts recalls an observation made by Raymond Williams. In his study of *The Country and the City* in modern English literature (1973), he notes that the rural/urban opposition served as a very general model for interpreting a radically changing social order. Inasmuch as this opposition lent itself to the expression of differing visions of English life, it evoked a complex discourse about society, production, class, and gender—a discourse, that is, about history. Just as, among the Tshidi, the madman and the migrant spoke in contrasting ways of the same theme, so it was with different English writers. Some appeared to take the gulf between city and country as a self-evident fact of life, and proceeded to explore its social and symbolic associations. Others stressed the interdependence of the rural and urban worlds, and insisted on tracing the contradictory relations that united them in a single order. It is not only in Africa that those caught up in processes of radical change come to terms with their history by means of suggestive oppositions.

III

It is hardly surprising, in a context like South Africa, that modern Tshidi consciousness should hinge on the contrast of work and labor. For the past 135 years, after all, others have sought to induce them into the market economy and, more often than not, to transform them into laborers. In fact, one of their earliest recollections of the Boer presence in their midst goes back to 1851–52, when their chief refused the settlers military support for a punitive raid against another "recalcitrant" Tswana chiefdom (Molema 1966:41f.). Southern Tswana had always showed deep suspicion of anyone who threatened their autonomy; so much so that, as early as 1820, some royals of the neighboring Tlhaping fled their capital after warning the ruler that "the missionaries will make you their servant" (Campbell 1822(1):77). And there is no question that the Tshidi believed the call for military aid to be a pretext (Molema 1966): "The Boers only wanted to make us work *(bereka)* for them, to make us pay taxes," we were told in 1969 by a 90-year-old woman. The Tshidi were correct. Abused and attacked for their refusal, they were forced into a lengthy exile—from which they returned to find themselves being drawn ever more tightly into the colonial arena and its market for manpower and goods. Inasmuch as the past century in South Africa has "entailed the making of an African working class" (Marks and Rathbone 1982:2), its history, from the perspective of the victims, is above all else a labor history (Molema 1920:253–258)—although that is by no means all it is.

The colonial process introduced Tshidi not merely to wage work, but also to other features of commodity production—most notably, money, the supreme standard of value, and the clock, the measure of human labor time. In South Africa, as elsewhere, the experience of "time, work-discipline and industrial capitalism" (Thompson 1967) went together. But the forms of European capitalism were not implanted into a vacuum. The way in which Tshidi set about making sense of the whole process was mediated, as it always is, by an existing set of cultural categories. Indeed, the experience of wage labor was of needs to be filtered through indigenous notions of human activity and the nature of work, just as money had to be understood in relation to local concepts of value, embodied, especially, in cattle (Comaroff and Comaroff n.d.[a]).

This, however, was not a confrontation between a primordial folk tradition and the modern world. Quite the contrary, Tswana "tradition" *(setswana)* was to be fashioned during the course of the 19th century. If not wholly invented (Ranger and Hobsbawm 1984), it was at least to be objectified; to be made into a heritage with imagined reference to the past but with its signs oriented toward the present. Moreover, *setswana* emerged in complementary opposition to *sekgoa* ("the ways of the European"), itself also a product of the encounter between Protestant imperialism and Africa. As this suggests, the discourse of contrast—of work and labor, cattle and money, and so on—had its roots deep in the colonial process itself. That process, of course, was to shape the political geography of South Africa, dividing yet binding the city and the countryside, white and black, the industrial workplace and the scheduled "native" reserve. And it was to bring the Tshidi face-to-face with the three interlocking agencies that were most active in remaking their social predicament and their historical consciousness: the mission, the market economy, and the colonial and postcolonial state.

It was the encounter with the first of these agencies, the Methodist mission, that laid the basis for the distinction between *setswana* and *sekgoa*. This encounter, in fact, paved the way for the dualistic vision of the world—and its expression in the concepts of work, time, and value—through which the political economy of apartheid was later to be understood. We have considered the role of the mission and its relationship to the other agencies of the colonial process elsewhere (Comaroff and Comaroff 1986; also J. Comaroff 1985). It is enough here to repeat a few well-established points about that process.

By the 1820s, when the Tshidi first made contact with the Methodists, their world was in the grip of forces let loose by the rise of the Zulu state. The waves of fugitives put to flight by Tshaka's regiments preyed on the settled agrarian peoples of central southern Africa (Lye 1969). In so doing, they opened the way for the missionary effort that, along with other forces, was to transform these peoples into a peasantry. The evangelists entered this theater of war with technical skills capable of making a decisive difference—guns, plows, irrigation methods, and the means of long-distance communication. Like other Tswana, the Tshidi actively sought them out. Almost from the start they became mediators among the displaced populations of the interior. Later that role was extended to relations between the chiefdoms and the Boers, whose trek from the Cape brought them into this same historical arena in 1837.

The role of the church in this chapter of southern African colonial history was at once ironic and contradictory. For its intervention, in the name of protecting the natives, was to prepare them for their eventual subordination—though not always in obvious ways (J. Comaroff 1985:123f.). Insofar as the evangelists engaged in secular politics, they saw such activity as part of their larger "civilizing" mission. It helped in the task of enlightening the savage and bringing him into the social and cultural universe of Christian Europe. In the same vein, the Protestants quickly learned that, while the Tswana appreciated the "practical" benefits of their presence, they did not show the same enthusiasm for their "spiritual" message. This was blamed on the African's "carnal view of spiritual things" (Broadbent 1865:178). As a result, the mission emphasized practical reconstruction, seeking to lay the basis for conversion by transforming the person through mundane activities of everyday life.[4]

Methodism was itself a product of the industrial revolution in Britain, having been directed, in particular, to the emerging working class of the northern river valleys (Troeltsch 1949; Warner 1930; cf. Weber 1958). Drawing on metaphors from the factory and the foundry, it spoke of individual salvation through arduous self-construction. And its emissaries to the slothful heathen—the "lazy Kafir," as Molema (1920:254) bluntly puts it—tried to make their stations living examples of productive enterprise. Here they demonstrated the utility of the plow and the pump, preached the virtues of sober discipline, and installed the clock and bell to mark out routines and ensure that time was well spent (Moffat 1842:339; cf. Wilson 1971:72; Oliver 1952:42). Here too, as the other side of their spiritual coin, they taught the value of the "varied treasures of commerce" (Mackenzie in Dachs [ed.] 1975:72) and the supreme enabling power of money (Warner 1930:125).

Needless to say, the British evangelists held very different concepts of personhood, production, and value from those they found among Tswana. In the interplay of the two cultures each came to define itself in relation to the other, each reaching a new awareness of its distinctiveness at the very moment that it was being transformed by the encounter itself. From the Tshidi perspective, mission Methodism was presented to them both as a narrative—a story of the "Good News" of Christ's coming—and as a "faith" *(tumelo)* in His "word" *(lehoko),* a coherent body of beliefs and practices offered to them as an alternative to the taken-for-granted world they inhabited. This, in turn, encouraged them to contrast the Christian message to their own mode of doing and being—and to speak of *setswana,* "Tswana ways." Even the act of naming it had the effect of making the latter appear as a systematic tradition. Of course, Christianity was itself part of an embracing colonial presence, the mission being merely its most visible face. It was this European presence that came to be described as *sekgoa,* the ways of *makgoa,* white people.

The impact of the mission was at once symbolic and material. Its faith in the moral worth of commerce ensured that evangelists would foster the production and sale of agricultural surpluses. They also nurtured a desire for "civilized" goods. Yet, while the nonconformists cherished the ideal of a rural Christian peasantry, they actually prepared the Tswana for wage labor. For they instilled in them "wants" that could only be satisfied through entry into the colonial economy, and made them thoroughly familiar with the signs and values of the industrial workplace. In the early years of the "mineral revolution;" in fact, many southern Tswana men (especially Batlhaping) spontaneously sought employment at the diamondfields (Shillington 1982; Holub 1881(1):294). The mission had begun to convert them into colonial subjects.

But this source of "voluntary" labor was quite inadequate to the growing demand as South Africa entered an era of accelerated industrial development in the late 19th century. It was during this period that the Tshidi experienced firsthand the conditions of the colonial workplace. Control over the labor supply increasingly became the object of struggle among colonial capital, white farmers, the Imperial government, and the Tswana populations (sometimes championed by evangelists). It is instructive, for example, that Molema, a Tshidi historian, describes the founding of the Union of South Africa as the result of Rhodes' sustained battle to force black labor into the market (1966:180f.). Despite the strenuous efforts of such missionaries as Mackenzie to "save" the Tswana peasantry from destruction at the hands of "the capitalists" (Comaroff and Comaroff 1986), the Tshidi, like other native populations in the region, were progressively undermined by ecological disaster and politico-economic domination. The advent of the South African state formalized this process of dispossession by extending taxation, limiting access to land, and progressively confining blacks to the lowest and most insecure reaches of the labor market. A far cry, alas, from the liberating image of free trade and dignified labor!

IV

Let us return, then, to the signs and categories of modern Tshidi consciousness. We begin with the root contrast between work and labor.[5]

In *setswana, go dira* means "to make," "do" or "cause to happen." It includes a wide range of activities, from cultivation, cooking, and creating a family to pastoralism, politics, and the performance of ritual. As in the past (Brown 1931:308), *tiro* is generally translated as "[a] work" and stresses the *act* of fabrication. It yields value in the form of persons, things, and relations, although it may be undone by sorcery and other malign forces. But *tiro* is not an abstract quality or a commodity to be exchanged. It cannot exist as alienable "labor power." We were told more than once that, in the remote past *(bogologolo),* even the energies of a serf were only available to his master as part of a total bond of interdependence. They could not be given over to another person unless the relationship itself was transferred. Work, in short, is a positive aspect of human activity, and is expressed in the making of self and others in the course of everyday life.

As this implies, two interrelated features of work are foregrounded here: (1), that the self-construction of the person occurs in relation to others, and (2), that it is a creative *process*. Not only are social beings made and remade by *tiro,* but the "product" is inseparable from the process of production itself. As Alverson (1978:132) has noted, "an individual not only produces for himself, but actually produces his entitlement to be a social person."[6] This is captured in the various inflections of *go dira*. Its simple reflexive form, *go itira,* means "to make oneself" or "to pose as," a notion with ambiguous moral implications. It suggests a form of self-enhancement that is egocentric and antisocial; hence the common usage *go itira motho* (lit., to make oneself a distinct person) connotes "to be proud" or "haughty." Furthermore, *go itira* may be contrasted with *go itirela*—the reflexive extension of *direla* ("to work for")—which translates as "to make (work, do) for oneself" in a positive sense. Alverson (1978:134) confirms that this term also embodies a critical set of values for Tswana in Botswana: the building of wealth in family and social relations, in cattle and clients, in position and possessions. The creation of these forms of wealth is dubbed "great work." Value, in other words, lies in extending the self through ties of interdependence. Thus the significance of wealth objects, most notably cattle, is that they signal rights in people. By extension, power is a matter of personal autonomy, but this entails a position of control *within* a field of material and social exchange, not merely a state of individual self-sufficiency.

We have explained elsewhere[7] that the stress on the making of persons, relations, and identities was a feature of the precolonial Tshidi chiefdom. Although this polity underwent complex changes during colonial and postcolonial times, its internal organization was dominated by two principles that shaped social and material life. The first was agnation, which laid down the terms for the allocation of rank and, with it, control over people, position, and property. The second was a form of endogamy that encouraged close kin marriage, and so wove a dense fabric of overlapping relations, which linked people in multiple, often contradictory ways. As a result, while free citizens were integrated into a nesting pyramid of political units—households, agnatic segments, wards, and sections—their status, the definition of social ties, and the composition of groups were always open to contention. In fact, in this system, where bonds were inherently ambiguous, individuals *had* to negotiate their social connections with one another. And so the world was always in flux, shifting with the ebb and flow of everyday social exchange—a process that placed the onus on household heads to "build themselves up" by making alliances and accumulating "greatness" and "wealth."

This process of social creativity was continuous. As elsewhere in Africa, the making of relations and statuses was typically a process rather than an event. It has long been noted, for instance, that a Tswana marriage is defined in both everyday and legal contexts by a drawn out series of acts and exchanges that gradually bring it to maturity (Comaroff and Roberts 1977). A union is built up over time, the final transactions that complete it sometimes being made after the death of one or both parties (J. L. Comaroff 1980). This and other interpersonal bonds are best described as states of "becoming," not "being"; they exist (or, more accurately, mature) in the continuous present. As a result, Tshidi are reluctant ever to define social ties in such a manner as would close them off from the possibility of growth or transformation. Such enquiries as "Are you married?" or "Do you have children?" are often answered with a curt "Not yet!" *(ga e se)*—even by elderly women. For the Tshidi, relations and identities are potentialities to be realized and remade in the unceasing work of daily life.

The creation of social value, however, was threatened by countervailing forces, driven by the conflicts generated within the social system itself. Thus, close agnatic rivals, for example, sought to "eat" one another, to erode each other's autonomy by politico-economic and ritual means. A man who had been eaten—a metaphor, as we shall see, that suggested feminization—became not only a junior in agnatic rank, but also a client, and eventually lost all self-determination. He was, as Willoughby notes, "absorbed by another personality" (1932:227). Such a man and his family might be called upon to supply labor to his patron during the agricultural season. Like a woman, he had relatively little control over his own movement in space and time. Sorcery also played an important part in these processes of destruction, its malevolent influence undermining all positive social action. Not surprisingly, "great work" involved the protection of one's efforts, and those of one's dependents, from the ever-present danger of being undone (*dirologa;* reversive extension of *dira*). Men took great pains to fortify their homesteads and fields against attack.

The concept of *itirela,* then, implied the work of social life. It expressed a vision of the world in which the construction of the person, the accumulation of wealth and rank, and the protection of an autonomous identity were indivisible aspects of social practice. The converse of self-construction was the eclipse of personal viability, an overshadowing caused by the invasion of malign human or spiritual forces. In extreme form, such an invasion led to the death of the self. As an early observer put it

> When a man's relatives notice that his whole nature is changed, that the light of the mind is darkened and character has deteriorated so that it may be said that the real manhood is dead, though the body still lives; when they realize that to all intents and purposes the human is alienated from fellowship with his kith and kin, they apply to him a name *(sebibi* or *sehihi),* which signifies that though the body lives and moves it is only a grave, a place where something has died or been killed. The essential manhood is dead. It is no uncommon thing to hear a person spoken of as being dead when he stands before you visibly alive. When this takes place it always means that there has been an overshadowing of the true relationships of life [Brown 1926:137–138].

As this suggests, the self lived only in its interaction with others. The object of *tiro* was to avoid social death; to continue producing oneself by producing people and things.

Of course, not all human beings were equally capable of such activity: chiefs and ritual experts, for example, had unusual creative power. Above all, though, male work differed fundamentally from that of females. Before the introduction of the plow, women were associated primarily with agriculture and reproduction. They were the source of the most basic social value, human life itself. But their very fertility generated a polluting heat *(bothitho)* that could "spoil" *(go senya)* the ritual, political, and economic projects of men (among them, rainmaking and initiation, ancestral veneration and animal husbandry). Thus they were held to need physical confinement and were denied an active role in the transactions that shaped the public world—especially cattle exchanges and politico-legal debate. By contrast, males were regarded as "cool" *(tshididi);* they had the qualities necessary for effective social production and, in particular, for the management of stock. As public actors, men represented themselves and their families through the medium of cattle, the currency against which they exchanged rights in women and dependents. With beasts they made clients of other men, and entered into alliances with both the living and the dead, extending themselves as they built and rebuilt a centralized political community.

But male and female production were not merely opposed and complementary, just as women and men were not simply opposed and complementary social beings. While wives did hold fields in their own right, had their own granaries, and exercized some control over the use of their harvest, they were not independent producers. Their "works"—the fruits of their reproductive and agricultural labor—were appropriated by men in one or another capacity. The general point was made repeatedly in Tswana poetics: thus the origin myth of the male initiation, the most comprehensive of their creative rites, told how the social world was born when the raw fertility of females was domesticated by men. The ritual itself went on to dramatize the seizure, by males, of the process of childbirth, which was then put to the purposes of social rebirth—just as, in the context of everyday life, women were harnessed to the reproduction of the polity, providing the material base that subsidized male politics and ritual.

Female "work" was controlled through communal politico-ritual processes. Crucial here was the regulation, by the chief, of the agricultural cycle and the conversion of the space-time of female activity to the rhythms of the male social calendar. Only a ruler could begin the cycle of cultivation by "giving out the seed time." Time, for Tshidi, was not an abstract entity, a resource that could be separated from the flow of human action and events. If there was no action, there was no time either to be spent or wasted; this was implicit in the processual nature of *tiro,* and in the Tswana stress on relations and identities as "states of becoming" (above, p. 197). In fact, the vernacular *lobaka,* a "period of time" (or "duration") also connotes "space." In dispensing the "time for beginning to sow," a chief, who also "owned" the land and could bring the rain, *created* the time and space within which women might produce the crop. Their work, ordered by the tempo of the growth cycle, culminated in the ritualized return of the harvest to the chiefly court at a first fruits ceremony (*go loma thôtse;* J. Comaroff 1985:66). This rite of renewal, in which households participated in their recognized order of seniority, also spelled out the hierarchical structure of the political community. The place of female labor in the recreation of the polity could not have been more vividly enacted.

The Tshidi conception of *tiro,* then, was part and parcel of a distinct world of meaning and action. It contrasts sharply with the notion of labor in the culture of 19th-century European colonialism.

We have noted that the Protestant missions among the southern Tswana opened the way for British colonialism; that their impact was more in the practical sphere of production and exchange than in the realm of the sacred; and that they spoke of a free market of the spirit, a moral economy that required the Africans to be cut loose from their "communistic relations . . . letting in the fresh, stimulating breath of healthy competition" (Mackenzie in Dachs 1975:652). This entailed a conception of person, property, and labor cast in the fervent images of 19th-century industrial capitalism (Comaroff and Comaroff 1986). It celebrated the private estate, commerce, and the ideal of material and spiritual accumulation; each mortal was exhorted to lay up treasures for him or herself by dint of sheer effort. All this, of course, demanded participation in a monetized system of exchange. Quite explicitly, the black convert was to be recreated as he was drawn into the colonial economy and, through it, into "the body of corporate nations" (Livingstone 1858:34). Money was the vital medium of this transformation, alike the means and the measure of self-improvement.

The nonconformist mission projected this ideology most tangibly in its discourse about labor. Methodist rhetoric, in particular, drew on the symbols of the industrial workplace, teaching the Tshidi that wage-labor was the divine instrument of redemption (J. Comaroff 1985:132). They spoke of labor as a commodity to be measured against other commodities, to be bought and sold in the market (cf. Marx 1967[1867](1):167ff.). Counted in hours and valued in coins, it was the price of life eternal, to be husbanded wisely on individual account. Labor power was an alienable part of each human being and should be spent in pursuit of a solitary salvation. The labor relation, moreover, was assumed to be an ethical one. Worker and master each had a function, performing their role as a divine calling (Warner 1930:146f.). Industrious self-discipline went along with an acceptance of the given "design" of the social world. Like Wesley before them, the Protestant missionaries in South Africa encouraged docility in the workplace. Its trials and sufferings were to be bravely borne, for they were the means of moral advancement.

Labor, in sum, was the key to salvation, and the missions sought to impress this on the natives of South Africa by both word and deed. Their efforts were to play into other forces of imperialism and colonialism in complex ways that we cannot pursue here. Suffice it to say that the Protestants were instrumental in instilling the signs and conventions, the values and wants, of the colonial marketplace, a fact that was exploited by the more cynical agencies of proletarianization that were to follow. With the rapid development of mining and industry in the late 19th century, and the rise of the South African state in the early 20th, the southern Tswana found themselves being steadily impoverished (Shillington 1985). Coerced into the insatiable urban labor market, they were drawn ever more tightly into the industrial capitalist economy. Cattle gave way to cash as the primary currency. Yet, because income was kept below a level sufficient to support workers and their dependents, much of the population was trapped into an uneasy combination of wage-labor and subsistence farming.

Compelled to move between the urban workplace and the arid "homeland," Tshidi migrants soon produced a sardonic commentary on the lesson of free labor. This, as we might expect, was less a narrative of dispossession than a symbolic elaboration of the contrast between work and labor. For, as Alverson was to observe in Botswana, "wage-labor violates the very definition of 'doing' " (1978:136). From the earliest years of this century, Tshidi have spoken, in their everyday practices and poetic forms, of the experience of alienation. They talked of the impact of labor that depletes rather than enhances the self; labor that denies a worker control over the products in which he invests himself and so vitiates a world of meaningful relations. The testimony of Tshidi migrants dwelt particularly on the theme of dehumanization. Drawing on brute physical images born in the racist workplace, these men characterized themselves as yoked beasts with no understanding of the situation into which they were drawn. Having lost control over their personal time and space, they were overshadowed, eclipsed. As Tswana have long said, migrant workers are "outside" *(kaha ntlè);* in forced exile to the realm of the whites, they are external to the creative life of the community.

Bereka, the construct that captured this process in Tshidi thought, was inextricably bound up with their conception of money. As our migrant made clear, *bereka* is "work-for-money," a necessity brought upon them by the inescapable need for cash. The term *madi,* derived from English, is a homonym for "blood," a fact which, to Tshidi themselves, seemed tragically appropriate. Where working conditions were often dangerous and destructive, the equation of the wage with the worker's substance was especially direct. But the Tshidi also spoke of money in the way they did of spilled human blood, as "hot"—that is, as a negation of life. It burns those who try to hold on to it, they would assert, and "runs through your pockets, leaving you hungry." In contrast, "cattle always return to make you fat." Here the heat of money earned by *bereka* was set against the cool stability of livestock produced by *tiro.* Its destructive flow ran counter to the enriching exchanges of bovine currency. As this suggests, the beast had become the symbol of a lost world of economic self-sufficiency, representing the freedom from the labor market of which all Tswana migrants dream (cf. Alverson 1978:123; Peters 1983). But money tended to "eat" cattle, for people were often forced to convert their wealth into cash, or to concentrate all their energies into *bereka.* As workers, Tshidi men saw themselves as less than fully social beings; they were "women" or "children," "draught oxen," "donkeys," or even "tinned fish" (cf. Alverson 1978:225f.). In the world of *bereka,* they were socially dead, the vehicles of someone else's profit.

It will be patent, now, why the contrast of work and labor carried with it such a wealth of associations: why *tiro* connoted socially contextualized production that "built up" persons, generated value, and was realized in such stable media as cattle—while *bereka* occurred "outside," destroyed and emasculated, and was paid in the capricious coin, which has "no real owner." Let us be clear about the status of these oppositions, however. We hold that, far from being neutral signs, they were ideological forms produced by the Tshidi engagement in a continuous history. Specifically, they emerged out of the colonial encounter, a process that incorporated the Tswana peoples into a contradictory social order, and gave rise to a discourse of contrast. *Tiro* and *bereka,* it turns out, are *setswana* and *sekgoa* in the active voice, the practices that made a difference in a world of cultural distinction and social inequality. As such, we repeat, these terms have not been static—just as the relationship of black South Africans to their rulers has not gone unchanged. Indeed, it may be that the contrast itself is yielding in some contexts: for example, amongst younger wage earners oriented primarily toward the city, and those in Botswana less caught up in the radical divisions of the South African political economy

(Patrick Molutsi, personal communication). But, well into the 1970s, the rhetoric of contrast provided most older Tshidi men, in the rural area at least, with an imaginative trope for organizing their experience and for wrestling with its conflicts. It is to this process, especially as personified in the madman and the migrant, that we now return.

V

The contrast between work and labor, with its rich texture of associations, is called on constantly by Tshidi in their everyday lives. It is as pervasive in the implicit statements of their architecture and argot as it is in the explicit debates of their "customary" courts. Here we can offer only a few highly selective illustrations to show that the madman and the migrant draw on a shared vocabulary; that their home-made images have echoes elsewhere on the cultural landscape, and capture familiar nuances of Tshidi experience.

Perhaps the most implicit use of the rhetoric of contrast by the Tshidi was to be found in their conceptual map of the rural domain. This domain hinged on their former capital, Mafikeng, which now lies just a half mile from the white town of Mafeking. These two towns are separated by a century of colonial history,[8] and by the madman's railway line. The very name "Mafeking," a corruption of the vernacular for "the place of rocks," made a subtle comment on that history, marking the distinction between the local white politico-economic center and the seat of the chiefship, which remained the anchor of the Tshidi sense of *setswana*. Mafeking was the most immediate citadel of *sekgoa*, and from it emanated demands for taxes, and for labor both domestic and distant. Its rectangular ground plan, broad streets, and neatly fenced bungalows contrasted sharply with the sinuous paths and circular compounds of its black counterpart. The terms on which Tshidi engaged with the wryly named "White City" were quite explicit. The only blacks allowed on its curfewed streets at night were those who carried letters of permission from their employers. In Mafikeng, the statement *"ke ya mmerekong"* ("I'm going to work"; from *bereka*) implied a journey over the railway bridge beside the offices of the watchful Bantu Affairs Commissioner, who articulated all movement between the domains of work and labor.

There was a bitter historical irony in this. In the precolonial past, Tswana controlled the labor of serfs, usually Sarwa ("bushmen") and Kgalagadi. Compelled to reside in the bush *(naga)* outside the town, these subject peoples were thought of as subhuman creatures of the wild. Now the Tshidi themselves lived "outside" Mafeking, coming in to deliver their labor to masters who regulated their time and space. The pageantry of power and dehumanization could hardly have been more obvious; the center of their world had become the unmarked periphery, the wild almost, beyond the boundaries of the white town. And with every crossing of the bridge—itself a colonial metaphor of very general application, as Paul Scott has driven home[9]—the structure of their life world was physically traced out.

But, as we have stressed, the contrasts of Tshidi consciousness are not fixed or unchanging. With shifts in the line of distinction—the "border" (Williams 1973:264)—between work and labor, *setswana and sekgoa,* the imaginative weight of these categories has changed. Again the symbolism of space provides an apt instance. As a consequence of the policy of separate development and the creation of ethnic "homelands" for black South Africans, the government designated Mafeking as the first headquarters of Bophuthatswana ("the United Tswana People"). To this end, they laid the foundations, in the 1960s, of a large residential area, equidistant from Mafeking and Mafikeng. Built to accommodate the "new" citizens of the putative homeland, the township in fact recreated the familiar structure of the urban "location" for black workers. This was the architecture of wage-labor: the two-roomed, rented units stood in relentless monotony along well-lit and eminently policeable thoroughfares. No livestock could be held in its fenced yards, which were also too small for cultivation.

The Tshidi reacted immediately to this unwelcome addition to their divided landscape. They had long contested the imposition of the homeland, of which this was the most recent expression (J. L. Comaroff 1974:*passim;* J. Comaroff 1985:38f.), and they now resisted all attempts to fit them into the new residential mould. They flatly refused to move into the completed houses, which were left to the mixed population—the "sell-outs," as they dubbed them—that began to move in from elsewhere to work for the administration. The government had called its creation Montshiwa Township, named—provocatively, Tshidi assumed—after their once independent ruling dynasty. They themselves tended instead to refer to the place as the "Government Compound," evoking the restrictive enclosures of the mine. The population of the township was said to be "naked" *(ba apogile);* it had been divested of the physical and social relations of a proper *setswana* life. Thus entrapped in the habitations of *bereka,* the world of rents and wages, there was no space for self-creation, no time to generate wealth in people. Montshiwa Township might have been nearby, but, by a rhetorical leap of the imagination, it had been placed over the border. Those who lived in it might reside in the rural area, but they were unmistakably citizens of the realm of *sekgoa.*

An altogether more explicit rhetoric of contrast was to be heard in the Tshidi courts. These courts *(makgotla;* sing. *kgotla),* and especially that of the chief, had always occupied a position of great importance in Tshidi life. Often described in the ethnographic literature as something akin to a Western law court, the *kgotla* was much more. An arena for political debate, dispute, communal ritual, and other collective processes, it was the forum in which most public discourse took place—the context in which Tshidi spoke among themselves in the language of *mekgwa le melao ya setswana,* the conventions of *setswana.*[10] But colonial overrule transformed the *kgotla* into a cog in the administrative machine; it became a "customary" tribunal. As such, it could only try minor matters formally defined as *setswana,* applying *mekgwa le melao* to arrive at its decisions. On the other hand, anything *sekgoa*—that is, anything involving relations between Tshidi and whites, or too serious for the chief—had to be handled by the colonial (and later the postcolonial) judicial system. *Sekgoa* law focused on contracts, constitutions, and individual culpability; not only did it enforce the ideas of personhood, property, and status for which the mission had prepared the Tshidi, but it seemed to underpin the entire system of wage-labor. Moreover, the chief's *kgotla,* the final court of appeal in indigenous dispute processes, now became a court of first instance, from which cases went to the Bantu Commissioner's Office. Just as Mafeking had come to encompass Mafikeng, so the *kgotla* was encompassed by the courts of *sekgoa.*

The procedures and aesthetic styles of these courts differed greatly. For Tshidi, who had a rich tradition of public oratory—they even nicknamed men by their known rhetorical gifts and idiosyncrasies—the *sekgoa* courts were marked by their impoverished discourse. "A magistrate only wants to know what happened," an irritated old man told us, echoing the perception of many Tshidi. " 'Quickly! Was this law or that law broken?' He is not interested in people's lives!" In the *kgotla,* time was not an issue, and "facts" were debated as part of the construction and negotiation of biographies (Comaroff and Roberts 1981); in *setswana,* by contrast to English, "fact" and "deed" are indistinguishable. A case *(tsheko)* was itself an aspect of *tiro,* a moment in the constant process of social engagement. The magistrate or the Bantu Commissioner, whose courts were invested by tangible signs of state power, belonged firmly in the domain of *bereka.* Not only were they situated in Mafeking, but, more often than not, defendants appeared before them because of an offense allegedly committed at work, because they had violated the property of whites, or because they had defaulted on the obligations of some or other *sekgoa* contract. And usually they had to pay for their crimes by "serving time" or by forfeiting their cash wages.

Not surprisingly, Tshidi complained bitterly about the South African legal system, and sometimes gave their protest a visible, if unsubtle, touch of poetic justice. In 1969, some young men named a tree behind the chief's *kgotla,* "the Bantu Commissioner's Office," and delighted in relieving themselves against it after public assemblies. More constructively, Tshidi tried, where possible, to have their disputes heard in the *kgotla,* even if the social consequences were potentially more grievous. Dealing with *sekgoa* law had itself become a part of the *setswana* dispute process; quite overtly, Tshidi used their creative powers to the full in eluding its control.

However, it was not just in respect of the structure of the legal system that Tshidi reflected on *setswana* and *sekgoa, tiro* and *bereka,* or used the categories to capture the transformations of their world. These terms also ordered the content of public discourse. An especially notable instance involved the construction of marriage. As we said earlier (p. 197), a union here was held to be a "state of becoming," a relationship which matured over many years and through many social exchanges. Tshidi were quick to note that migrant labor disrupted this process, and that migrants often took partners while away. As a result, the *kgotla* was presented with innumerable cases of neglect by females and frequently had to establish the status of unions. Most commonly, it had to decide whether the woman was really "a wife" of the male defendant, or had just been a casual partner with little further claim on him. The ambiguities surrounding the marriage process had always allowed for such arguments, but the impact of wage-labor was to increase their incidence to epidemic proportions.

In order to deal with these difficulties, the Tshidi, like other Tswana, made ingenious use of loan words to extend the opposition of *setswana* and *sekgoa* to heterosexual bonding. The vernacular term for the marriage process, *nyalo* (*go nyala,* masc.; *go nyalwa,* fem.), which had formerly covered all potential conjugal ties, became restricted in its reference: it was now used only for properly constructed (that is, *setswana*) relations. Casual liaisons, especially those created in the realm of *bereka* (or between visits to that realm) were called, in Afrikaans, *donkie trou,* "donkey marriage." These liaisons, in contrast to the drawn out exchanges of *nyalo,* were established by *vat en sit* ("grab and settle"). The allusion, clearly, was to the undignified coupling of animals, an emphatically nonsocial event brought about by reducing human beings to beasts of burden. Furthermore, the use of Afrikaans, the language of domination, was not coincidental. Like the term *bereka* itself, it assigned blame to those who had unravelled the Tshidi social world. Over time, the *kgotla* felt it necessary to address the issues raised by these unions, and chiefs developed a policy in respect of them. They began to award some rights of support to the women concerned but, significantly, made such awards in terms of cash or consumer goods rather than cattle, the currency of *setswana* marriage. Although these settlements clearly distinguished *donkie trou* from other unions, they were explicitly intended to recognise that new forms of relationships were being produced in the wake of wage-labor, relationships that had to be situated within the Tshidi world.

But it is perhaps the madman and the migrant themselves who best illustrate how Tshidi invoke the contrast of *tiro* and *bereka* to act upon their world. As we have noted, the madman suffered "delusion" only by Western definition. To Tshidi he was a *moporofeta* (a prophet), a term borrowed, like the polythene robes, and put to work in the particular historical conditions of postcolonial South Africa. A visionary in popular terms, he was seen to make visible, in his idiosyncratic concoctions, something implicit in the experience of many Tshidi. There was a quality of bemused recognition in the way they responded to him, though few could explain this in words. In one sense, of course, he was a token of a type, a "Zionist"; that is, a member of a Christian cult that seeks to merge elements "traditional" and "European" (J. Comaroff 1985:Ch. 7; Fogelqvist 1986). Yet in another sense he was unique, for he had executed the Zionist collage in a highly original manner—revealing once again the unpredictability of the human imagination, even while on a short cultural rein.

The madman, then, is one of those who "insists on the connections" (Williams 1973:264) between the elements of a contradictory world; one who bears the insignia of continuity quite literally on his chest. South African Railways had carried him to the gold mines as a young migrant, and it had brought him back again when the Spirit called him to return once more and "work" *(dira)* among his own people. We never learned why he had been committed to the asylum. It may have been his fondness for standing as mute witness near the railway depot in the white town where returning laborers alighted. Like madmen and witches everywhere, he offered genteel society an image of itself that it would rather forget. For, to all who looked at him, one thing was clear: he had worked on himself with laborious care to bring together in startling anomaly things that, "normally," were kept well apart.

In contrast to the migrant, who tried to cut himself off from the signs and memories of mine work, the prophet, despite having freed himself from wage-labor, would not give up his old miner's boots, and was said to receive spiritual inspiration from his "headquarters" in Gauteng (Johannesburg; lit. "the place of gold"). The letters "SAR," too, were a constant reminder of the relationship of center and periphery. And his habit evoked both the vestments of the high church and the gaiters of the colonial military, each reproduced through the remaking of waste commodities, a characteristic activity of the peasantariat. But around his knees, neck and wrists he also wore the strips of cowhide that Tswana have long used to bind the body in healing and protection. Indeed, he was every inch an exemplar of the interdependence of rural and urban, work and labor, *setswana* and *sekgoa*. What is more, his regalia expressed an effort to reconcile these discordant categories, recalling Foucault's claim that we label as psychotic those who confront contradictions that the rest of us suppress (1967).

Although he expressed himself in a rather different manner, the migrant relied on the same categories, his words and actions mapping out the tension between "here" and "there," "inside" and "out," "work" and "labor." Yet his rhetoric used these distinctions to highlight discontinuities, not connections. Thus he portrayed his past as a set of contrasting moments: those of self-creation were opposed to those of alienation as life is opposed to death, *setswana* to *sekgoa*. Imagery, here, was all of a piece with biography. The migrant's response to the contradictions of his world was to unhitch the country from the city, to escape from the domain of *bereka*, and to return to Mafikeng ("here," "inside") to a future of *tiro*.

This attempt to reverse the signs of incorporation and domination animated much of contemporary Tshidi practice, from their pursuit of cattle wealth to their energetic healing cults. Intimate experience had convinced the migrant that the opposition of *setswana* and *sekgoa* permitted no resolution. While a young generation of Tswana might seek, and even realize, some form of satisfaction at the workplace (cf. Guy and Thabane n.d.), their elders harbored few such hopes. The latter were also unversed in, or unmoved by, a universalist discourse that spoke of democracy, liberation, or labor politics. They were keenly aware that the inroads made into their universe by wage work had reduced them to bondage; the invocation of stark rhetorical distinctions enabled them to ponder a solution, not by synthesis or reconciliation but by separation and withdrawal. Thrust back into the realities of a rural subsistence, they asserted the authority of a male-oriented "tradition" in which the fruits of *bereka* were devalued. What is more, until the 1970s, these men seldom confronted the conflicts of neocolonialism in direct political struggle, seeking instead to remake a recognizable world beyond the predators' grasp. In so doing, however, they also turned their backs on a consciousness of social class—and of class relations and antagonisms—as an organizing principle of South African society. Similarly, their historical imagination, with its stress on inescapable contrasts, did not fit well with a vision of revolution; a revolution that promised to remove those very contrasts and the forces underlying them. Indeed, the revolutionary process now spreading through Southern Africa challenges this generation of Tshidi ever more insistently to reconsider their dualistic worldview.

VI

We have been concerned, in this essay, with the poetics of history. Specifically, we have tried to trace out the way in which Tshidi create a sense of themselves by imaginative play with the categories of their culture. We have shown how the opposition between *sekgoa* and *setswana* took form in the colonial process; how it came to mediate that process, with work and labor as its primary tropes. It is not of direct significance to us here whether or not oppositions are universal features of the human mind, the deep structural bases of culture; this, in any case, would tell us little about the way in which human consciousness takes its form in time and space. Our focus, rather, is upon the way in which the poetics of contrast enter into historical processes.

As we have noted, the rhetorical use of contrast is widespread, especially in situations of radical social change. It appears, with similar force, in English literature (Williams 1973), in the semantic categories of changing coastal Kenya (Parkin 1979), and in the values of modern Shetland Islanders (Cohen 1979). But perhaps there is something unusually acute about the contradictions of a racially coded colonial society, a society in which the distinction between ruler and ruled is made to seem prescriptive and unyielding. Whether or not this is true, the poetic use of contrast and opposition in the Tshidi context makes two general points about the very nature of culture and consciousness.

The first is that culture always intervenes directly in consciousness and its expression. Thus the Tshidi contrast between *tiro* and *bereka,* for instance, was not just a function of the impact of industrial capitalism; it was a product of the dynamic interplay between its cultural forms and those of the precolonial order. Many anthropologists will see the point as self-evident, but it has often been overlooked in even the most sensitive of historical analyses. To return to a celebrated case (above, p. 192), Van Onselin treats worker consciousness as a matter of reaction and resistance to the conditions of wage labor. The behavior of miners is seen to have been shaped largely by what they were protesting against, not by the cultural categories which they carried with them into the mine. This introduces the second point, namely, that culture and consciousness are not the same thing, and cannot be reduced to one another. There is a complex set of issues tied up in this statement, for it evokes the uneasy encounter between the anthropological concept of culture and the Marxian concepts of ideology and consciousness.

The anthropological concept of culture has long been criticized for overstressing the implicit and categorical, for treating signs and symbols as if they were neutral and above history, and for ignoring their empowering and authoritative dimensions.[11] On the other hand, Marxist theory has been taken to task for neglecting both the meaningful bases of consciousness and the expressive forms of ideology. The effort to draw together the two perspectives, and so to address the shortcomings of both, lies at the core of much theoretical debate. We have sought to make a modest point in the context of that debate. It is that consciousness is best understood as the active process—sometimes implicit, sometimes explicit—in which human actors deploy historically salient cultural categories to construct their self-awareness. Its modes, we have shown, may be subtle and diverse; and it is as crucial to explore the forms in which a people choose to speak and act as it is to examine the content of their messages.

Indeed, as we have seen, a people may not express their historical consciousness as conventional history at all. Hence, if we seek a narrative of events, or an account of past relations, we may be led to conclude that they lack all such consciousness; we may even be tempted to speak of theirs as a "cold" society. But the conclusion would be false. There is every reason to expect people caught up in processes of change to use the poetics of contrast to impose meaning on their world. Tshidi, like many others, often talk of their past and present in rhetorical terms, playing on the capacity of verbal and nonverbal images to connect and separate, attract and repel, transform or reinforce. Among them, to return to Mitchell's point (above, p. 193), history and its representation are not nicely distinguishable. History lies *in* its representation; for representation is as much the making of history as it is consciousness speaking out. Moreover, realism and rhetoric do not stand opposed. The poetry of representation, in short, is not an aesthetic embellishment of a "truth" that lies elsewhere. Its puns and metaphors, jokes and irreverencies, are the stuff of everyday thought and action—of the human consciousness through which culture and history construct each other.

notes

Acknowledgments: This paper was read at a conference on *Culture and Consciousness in Southern Africa* at the University of Manchester (September 1986) and at a workshop in African history and anthropology at Harvard University (May 1986). We should like to thank participants at both meetings for their helpful comments. We are especially grateful to Paul Friedrich and William Hanks, of the University of Chicago, for their thoughtful criticisms.

[1]We do not suggest that, from a structural perspective, black South Africans live in two distinct worlds (or are caught up in a "dual" economy). It is now widely recognized that the colonial process drew them into a single, overarching political economy. We shall argue that the dualistic imagery in Tshidi consciousness arises from contradictions in their experience of that process.

[2]This is not to say that Tswana cannot produce narrative histories—or historians. Among the Tshidi, Molema (1966) and Matthews (1945), both mission school alumni, are notable examples. But, here as elsewhere, there is a great difference in style between formal historical scholarship and the everyday historical discourses of a people.

[3]As this implies, consciousness is not merely the sum of stated attitudes found amongst a population. The point is worth stressing, as this reduction is often made in the Western social sciences—a notable instance in the recent anthropological literature being Godoy's (1985:210) critique of Taussig (1980).

[4]There is a second, more subtle level of irony here too. The spiritual message contained in the Christian narrative—the story of God and his son, Jesus Christ—was widely rejected by the Tshidi. But the practical innovations of the mission (its nonnarrative discourse) were quickly accepted. It was through them that the implicit ethos of Protestantism was impressed upon the natives. Christianity, in other words, required a nonnarrative medium—practical innovation—to serve as the vehicle of its ideological "story."

[5]By translating *dira (itira)* and *bereka* as "work" and "labor," we are arbitrarily specifying the use of these English terms. However, this seems the best way of capturing the contrast. There is a theoretical precedent, of course: Marx's analyses of the special character of labor under capitalism (see, for example, Firth 1979:179f.; Wolf 1982:74f.; cf. Schwimmer 1979). Another point of clarification is in order here. It is difficult, in the Western context, to discuss the meaning of "work" without taking into account its opposition to "leisure"; this opposition being part of the ideological apparatus of industrial capitalism. (For a summary statement from an anthropological perspective, see Parkin 1979:317f.) The mission sought to introduce the same set of ideas to the Tshidi. Indeed, a dictionary compiled by an evangelist in c.1895 (Brown, revised edition, 1931) translates *boiketlo* as "leisure." This is misleading, however. *Boiketlo* (from *iketla,* "peace") connotes "ease, comfort, convenience, and taking one's time"; it is not reducible to an antonym of *tiro.* Nor, as we shall see, is it the opposite of *bereka,* which also refers to a state of being rather than a mode of activity. The converse of *bereka* is a return to the world of *tiro.*

[6]Alverson found much the same in Botswana as we did in South Africa on Tswana consciousness. He also notes the contrast of *dira/itirela* and *bereka* (1978:118). While there are theoretical differences in our analyses, we take this as confirmation of the ethnographic findings.

[7]See, for example, Comaroff and Roberts (1981), J. L. Comaroff (1982; n.d.), J. Comaroff (1985), and Comaroff and Comaroff (n.d.[b]) for analyses of Tswana social systems and over both the short and the long run. We rely on those studies as background to the present account.

[8]Mafeking, later famous for its Anglo-Boer war siege, was established as the headquarters of the Crown Colony of British Bechuanaland in the late 19th century (see J. L. Comaroff [ed] 1973). It also served as the administrative center of the Bechuanaland Protectorate until the latter became the Republic of Botswana in 1966.

[9]See Paul Scott's *The Jewel in the Crown,* the first volume of *The Raj Quartet.* In the ethnographic literature, Gluckman's (1968) use of the metaphor of the bridge—to capture a dramatic moment in the contradictory relationship of colonizer and colonized—is especially well-known.

[10]*Mekgwa le melao ya setswana* is typically glossed as "Tswana law and custom," although the dictionary translations of *mekga* and *melao* are usually given as "customs" and "laws," respectively (see, for example, Schapera 1938). For reasons discussed elsewhere (Comaroff and Roberts 1981:Ch.3), however, we resist such legalistic translations, and prefer to view *mekgwa le melao* as an undifferentiated set of signs and conventions.

[11]There have, of course, been several recent efforts to address and redress at least some of these criticisms (see, for example, Bourdieu 1977; Sahlins 1981, 1985).

references cited

Alverson, Hoyt
1978 Mind in the Heart of Darkness. New Haven, CT: Yale University Press.
Bourdieu, Pierre
1977 Outline of a Theory of Practice. Richard Nice, transl. Cambridge: Cambridge University Press.

Broadbent, Samuel
1865 A Narrative of the First Introduction of Christianity Amongst the Barolong Tribe of Bechuanas, South Africa. London: Wesleyan Mission House.
Brown, J. Tom
1926 Among the Bantu Nomads. London: Seeley Service.
1931 Secwana-English Dictionary. Tiger Kloof: London Missionary Society.
Campbell, John
1822 Travels in South Africa . . . Being a Narrative of a Second Journey. 2 Vols. London: Westley.
Cohen, Anthony P.
1979 The Whalsey Croft: Traditional Work and Customary Identity in Modern Times. *In* Social Anthropology of Work. Sandra Wallman, ed. pp. 249–268. London: Academic Press.
Comaroff, Jean
1985 Body of Power, Spirit of Resistance. Chicago: University of Chicago Press.
Comaroff, Jean, and John L. Comaroff
1986 Christianity and Colonialism in South Africa. American Ethnologist 13:1–19.
Comaroff, John L.
1974 Chiefship in a South African Homeland: A Case Study of the Tshidi Chiefdom of Bophuthatswana. Journal of Southern African Studies 1:36–51.
1980 Bridewealth and the Control of Ambiguity in a Tswana Chiefdom. *In* The Meaning of Marriage Payments. John L. Comaroff, ed. pp. 161–196. New York: Academic Press.
1982 Dialectical Systems, History and Anthropology. Journal of Southern African Studies 8:143–172.
n.d. Sui Genderis: Feminism, Kinship Theory, and Structural Domains. *In* Feminism and Kinship Theory. Jane Collier and Sylvia Yanagisako, eds. Stanford: Stanford University Press. Forthcoming.
Comaroff, John L., ed.
1973 The Boer War Diary of Sol T. Plaatje: An African at Mafeking. London: Macmillan.
Comaroff, John L., and Jean Comaroff
n.d.[a] Goodly Beasts and Beastly Goods: Cattle in Tswana Economy and Society. *In* Herders, Warriors and Traders. John G. Galaty and Pierre Bonte, eds. Boulder, CO: Westview Press. Forthcoming.
n.d.[b] The Long and the Short of it: An Essay in Historical Anthropology. *In* Time and Social Structure: An Old Anthropological Problem Revisited. Jane Guyer, ed. Forthcoming.
Comaroff, John L., and Simon A. Roberts
1977 Marriage and Extra-Marital Sexuality: The Dialectics of Legal Change among the Kgatla. Journal of African Law 21:97–123.
1981 Rules and Processes: The Cultural Logic of Dispute in an African Context. Chicago: University of Chicago Press.
Dachs, Anthony J., ed.
1975 Papers of John Mackenzie. Johannesburg: Witwatersrand University Press.
Eliade, Mircea
1962 The Forge and the Crucible. Stephen Corrin, transl. London: Rider.
Firth, Raymond
1979 Work and Value: Reflections on the Ideas of Karl Marx. *In* Social Anthropology of Work. Sandra Wallman, ed. pp. 177–206. London: Academic Press.
Fogelqvist, Anders
1986 The Red-dressed Zionists: Symbols of Power in a Swazi Independent Church. Uppsala: Uppsala Research Reports in Cultural Anthropology.
Foucault, Michel
1967 Madness and Civilization: A History of Insanity in the Age of Reason. Richard Howard, transl. London: Tavistock.
Friedrich, Paul
1979 Language, Context, and the Imagination. Anwar Dil, ed. Stanford: Stanford University Press.
Genovese, Eugene D.
1972 Roll, Jordan, Roll: The World the Slaves Made. New York: Pantheon Books.
Gluckman, Max
1968 Analysis of a Social Situation in Modern Zululand. (2nd impression.) Rhodes-Livingstone Institute Paper No. 28. Manchester: Manchester University Press for the Rhodes-Livingstone Institute.
Godoy, Ricardo
1985 Mining: Anthropological Perspectives. Annual Review of Anthropology 14:199–217.
Gordon, Robert
1977 Mines, Masters and Migrants. Johannesburg: Ravan Press.
Guy, Jeff, and Motlatsi Thabane
n.d. Perceptions of Mining: Labour, Mechanization and Shaft Sinking on the South African Gold Mines. Paper Read to a Conference on Culture and Consciousness in Southern Africa, University of Manchester, September 1986.
Holub, Emil
1881 Seven Years in South Africa. 2 Vols. E. E. Frewer, transl. Boston: Houghton Mifflin.
Lawrence, D. H.
1922 Sons and Lovers. New York: Modern Library.

Livingstone, David
1858 Missionary Travels and Researches in South Africa. New York: Harper & Brothers.
Lye, William F.
1969 The Distribution of the Sotho Peoples after the Difaqane. *In* African Societies in Southern Africa. Leonard Thompson, ed. pp. 191–229. London: Heinemann.
Marks, Shula, and Richard Rathbone
1982 Introduction. *In* Industrialization and Social Change in South Africa. Shula Marks and Richard Rathbone, eds. pp. 1–43. London: Longman.
Marx, Karl
1967[1867] Capital: a Critique of Political Economy. 3 Vols. New York: International Publishers.
Matthews, Z. K.
1945 A Short History of the Tshidi Barolong. Fort Hare Papers 1:9–28.
Mitchell, W. J. T.
1986 Iconology: Image, Text, Ideology. Chicago: University of Chicago Press.
Moffat, Robert
1842 Missionary Labours and Scenes in Southern Africa. London: Snow.
Molema, Silas Modiri
1920 The Bantu Past and Present. London: W. Green & Son.
1966 Montshiwa, Barolong Chief and Patriot, 1815–96. Cape Town: Struik.
Nash, June
1979 We Eat the Mines and the Mines Eat Us. New York: Columbia University Press.
Oliver, Roland
1952 The Missionary Factor in East Africa. London: Longmans, Green.
Parkin, David
1979 The Categorization of Work: Cases from Coastal Kenya. *In* Social Anthropology of Work. Sandra Wallman, ed. pp. 317–336. London: Academic Press.
Peters, Pauline
1983 Cattlemen, Borehole Syndicates, and Privatization in the Kgatleng District of Botswana: An Anthropological History of the Transformation of the Commons. Ph.D. thesis. Boston University.
Ranger, Terence O., and Eric Hobsbawm
1984 The Invention of Tradition. New York: Cambridge University Press.
Sahlins, Marshall
1981 Historical Metaphors and Mythical Realities: Structure in the Early History of the Sandwich Islands Kingdom. Ann Arbor: University of Michigan Press.
1985 Islands of History. Chicago: University of Chicago Press.
Schapera, Isaac
1938 A Handbook of Tswana Law and Custom. London: Oxford University Press for the International African Institute.
Schwimmer, Erik
1979 The Self and the Product: Concepts of Work in Comparative Perspective. *In* Social Anthropology of Work. Sandra Wallman, ed. pp. 287–315. London: Academic Press.
Scott, Paul
1978 The Jewel in the Crown. The Raj Quartet, Vol. 1. London: Heinemann.
Shillington, Kevin
1982 The Impact of Diamond Discoveries on the Kimberley Hinterland: Class Formation, Colonialism and Resistance among the Tlhaping of Griqualand West in the 1870s. *In* Industrialization and Social Change in South Africa. Shula Marks and Richard Rathbone, eds. pp. 99–118. New York: Longman.
1985 The Colonisation of the Southern Tswana 1870–1900. Johannesburg: Ravan Press.
Taussig, Michael
1980 The Devil and Commodity Fetishism in South America. Chapel Hill: University of North Carolina Press.
Thompson, Edward P.
1963 The Making of the English Working Class. London: Gollancz.
1967 Time, Work-discipline and Industrial Capitalism. Past and Present 38:56–97.
Troeltsch, Ernst
1949 The Social Teaching of the Christian Churches. Vol. 2. Olive Wyon, transl. London: George Allen and Unwin.
Van Onselin, Charles
1973 Worker Consciousness in Black Miners: Southern Rhodesia, 1900–1920. Journal of African History 14:237–255.
1976 Chibaro. London: Pluto Press.
Wallerstein, Immanuel
1972 Social Conflict in Post-independence Black Africa: The Concepts of Race and Status Group Reconsidered. *In* Racial Tensions in National Identity. Ernest Q. Campbell, ed. pp. 206–226. Nashville: Vanderbilt University Press. [Reprinted in The Capitalist World Economy, Immanuel Wallerstein. Cambridge: Cambridge University Press, 1979, pp. 165–183.]
Warner, Wellman J.
1930 The Wesleyan Movement in the Industrial Revolution. London: Longmans, Green.

Weber, Max
1958 The Protestant Ethic and the Spirit of Capitalism. Talcott Parsons, transl. New York: Scribner's.
Williams, Raymond
1973 The Country and the City. New York: Oxford University Press.
Willoughby, W. C.
1932 Nature-worship and Taboo. Hartford: Hartford Seminary Press.
Wilson, Monica
1971 The Growth of Peasant Communities. *In* The Oxford History of South Africa. Vol. 2. Monica Wilson and Leonard Thompson, eds. pp. 49–103. Oxford: Oxford University Press.
Wolf, Eric
1982 Europe and the People without History. Berkeley: University of California Press.
Ziervogel, D., and P. C. Mokgokong
1985 Groot Noord-Sotho Woordeboek/Comprehensive Northern Sotho Dictionary. 2nd edition. Pretoria: J. L. Van Schaik Ltd/UNISA.

submitted 23 September 1986
revised version submitted 26 January 1987
accepted 27 January 1987

Journal of African History, 31 (1990), pp. 181–197
Printed in Great Britain

MTUNYA: FAMINE IN CENTRAL TANZANIA, 1917–20*

BY GREGORY MADDOX
Texas Southern University

FAMINE, the acute lack of food for a population which leads to starvation, can be caused both by a failure in production and by structural inequalities in entitlements to that food which is available. A famine, however, can be more than just a conjunction of disaster and vulnerability; it can result in changes in the relationships between groups within a society and between that society and the rest of the world.[1] For the Gogo people of Ugogo in central Tanzania,[2] the famine between 1917 and 1920 which they call the *Mtunya* ('The Scramble') is remembered not only as the worst famine in their famine-ridden history, but as the one event which locked them into a subordinate position within the colonial economy and eventually reduced those without cattle to a state of chronic vulnerability to famine. The *Mtunya* began during World War I when a drought followed hard upon both German and British war-time requisitions that had drained the arid region of men, cattle and food. During that famine one British official estimated that 30,000 of the region's 150,000 people died and tens of thousands more fled their homes.[3]

The *Mtunya* was the most deadly of the many famines that have visited Ugogo. Peter Rigby,[4] John Iliffe[5] and Clarke Brooke[6] have all stressed the

* Research for this paper was carried out in Tanzania with the permission of the Tanzanian National Scientific Research Council, at the Tanzania National Archives, Dar es Salaam, at the Public Record Office, London, and at Rhodes House Library, Oxford University. An earlier version of this paper was presented at the Canadian African Studies Association meeting in May 1988 at Kingston, Ontario. I would like to thank the participants in that conference and Pamela Maack, M. W. Akalou and Howard Beeth for their comments on earlier drafts of the paper.

[1] John Iliffe, *The African Poor: A History* (Cambridge, 1988), 156–7.

[2] Ugogo, the land of the Gogo, occupies what are now the Dodoma and Mpwapwa Districts of Dodoma Region and much of the Manyoni District of Singida Region. Under German rule, and British adminstration until 1925, Ugogo was combined with what is now Singida District into an enlarged Dodoma District. There were substations at Singida, Mpwapwa and Kilimatinde (which was replaced by Manyoni as a station in the mid-1920s) that reported directly to the District Office in Dodoma. District reports from Dodoma contain information from all parts of the District while subdistrict reports concentrate on either Kilimatinde or Mpwapwa.

[3] Tanzania National Archives (hereafter TNA) 967.828, Dodoma District Reports, H. Hignell, Annual Report for 1925.

[4] Peter Rigby, *Cattle and Kinship among the Gogo: A Semi-Pastoral Society of Central Tanzania* (Ithaca, N.Y., 1969), 20–1, and 'Politics and modern leadership roles in Ugogo', in Victor Turner (ed.), *Colonialism in Africa 1870–1960*: III, *Profiles of Change: African Society and Colonial Rule* (Cambridge, 1971), 401–2, where he calls the colonial accounts of the *Mtunya* 'slightly exaggerated'; my own research supports the view that the *Mtunya* caused major dislocations among the societies of the region.

[5] John Iliffe, *A Modern History of Tanganyika* (Cambridge, 1979), 269.

[6] Clarke Brooke 'The heritage of famine in Central Tanzania', *Tanzania Notes and Records*, no. 66 (1967), 20.

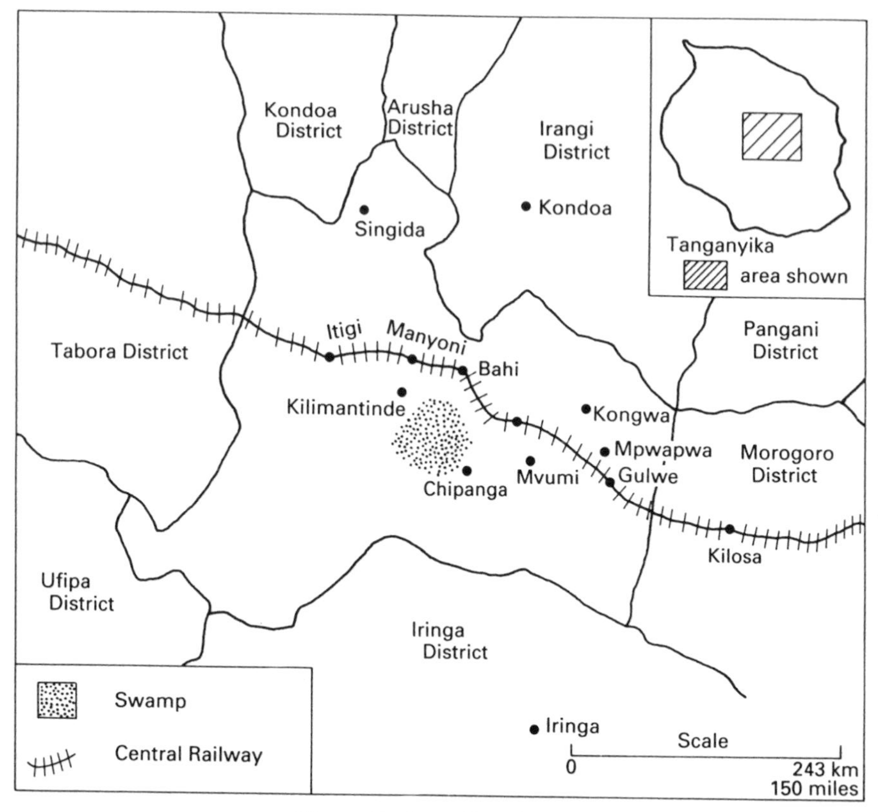

Fig. 1. Dodoma District, 1921

chronic nature of famine in central Tanzania before and after World War I.[7] In particular, as Iliffe and Brooke have noted, Ugogo held no immunity from the devastating spread of rinderpest and associated environmental degradation that struck all of East Africa in the last two decades of the nineteenth century. In a sense, though, the Gogo present a variation on the general course of economic and ecological change in eastern Africa during the early colonial period. In much of the rest of the region, the 1880s and 1890s are recalled as the time when natural disaster coincided with the advent of colonial rule to destroy the autonomy of local societies.[8] In Ugogo the

[7] See also C. J. Sissons, 'Economic prosperity in Ugogo, East Africa, 1860–1890' (Ph.D. thesis, University of Toronto, 1984); and G. H. Maddox, 'Leave Wagogo, you have no food: Famine and survival in Ugogo, Tanzania, 1916–1961' (Ph.D. thesis, Northwestern University, 1988), chs. 2 and 3.

[8] See Helge Kjekshus, *Ecology Control and Economic Development in East African History: The Case of Tanganyika 1840–1940* (London and Berkeley, 1977); Charles Ambler, *Kenyan Communities in the Age of Imperialism: The Central Region in the Late Nineteenth Century* (New Haven, 1988); Douglas H. Johnson and David M. Anderson (eds.), *The Ecology of Survival: Case Studies from Northeast African History* (London and Boulder, 1988), especially the Introduction, 1–24, and chapters by Richard Pankhurst and Douglas H. Johnson (47–70), Richard Waller (73–112), and David M. Anderson (241–

memory of the disasters of the late nineteenth century has been overlaid by the *Mtunya*, and for the Gogo that greater and more recent disaster has come to serve as a metaphor for changes that began before the Great War and the drought that followed hard upon it and continued to develop long after the rains returned.

I

The hardships that culminated in the *Mtunya* began with the war. For the people of Ugogo the first sign of the war came when the German District commander of the region, remembered locally as 'Dondwa',[9] ordered the *akida* (African government officials) and *jumbe* (government-appointed village headmen) to have their people grind grain to be given to the government. The administration had the food brought to depots set up at stations along the central railway, including Gulwe near Mpwapwa, Kikombo, Dodoma and Bahi.[10] At first, when the fighting remained concentrated in the north, requisitions of supplies remained limited to grain; however, as the Allied forces began to take territory in late 1915, the Germans also began to demand livestock for their troops.[11] By 1916 the Germans had taken 26,000 of the estimated 300,000 cattle in the region.[12]

Throughout the remaining period of German rule the administration also conscripted men both for training as *askari* (African soldiers) and as porters. Most of the campaign was fought on foot, and as a result, demand for porters was even greater than the demand for *askari*. Before the Germans left, one British official estimated that they had conscripted approximately 35,000 men in Ugogo.[13]

These requisitions caused people to take their cattle and small stock, and young men, as far away as they could. Mzee (elder) Petro Gazo of Mbabala, south of Dodoma, recalled that, after his father had been conscripted, the rest of his family, led by one of his uncles, spent the remainder of the war hiding in the forest south of their home around Mvumi.[14] In Sagara, north of Mpwapwa, Mzee Mwakala stated:

> The Germans took a lot of food for their soldiers. They took it by force... Who could pay you? What good was money then? Enough!... We had to run away. We went to the mountains with our families, and our cattle, and our food. In Sagara, the Germans took not only millet, but they took the cattle and goats. The people were running here and there, trying to hide. Sometimes the cows and goats had to go to water by themselves. The people ran up the mountains because of the war.

60); and James L. Giblin, 'Famine, authority and the impact of foreign capital in Handeni District, Tanzania, 1840–1940' (Ph.D. thesis, University of Wisconsin, 1986).

[9] Interviews were conducted in the Dodoma Region of Tanzania in 1986 and 1987. Full transcripts of all interviews are available in Maddox, 'Leave Wagogo', appendix. Interviews are referred to by accession numbers. I/48/122A, 123A Chamwilo, etc.

[10] I/49/124A–129A Nyaulingo, etc.; I/48/122A, 123A Chamwilo, etc.; I/45/114A–117A Kaloli, etc.; I/3/3A Kongola; I/17/14A–26A Chidoza, etc.; and I/38/87A–95A Magagi, etc.

[11] Brian Gardner, *German East* (London, 1963), 87.

[12] TNA 967.828, Dodoma District Reports, District Political Officer to Chief Secretary of German East Africa, 5 December 1916.

[13] *Ibid.*

[14] I/27/38A Gazo.

It was safer there. Then, the mountains were covered by thick forest, and there were many caves a man could put his family and food in. Sometimes, though, the Germans found the caves and made the people in them give all their things or go and fight for the Germans.[15]

The only change in the situation after the British occupied the region was the language in which the demands were made. During the war the British in German East Africa faced many of the same problems as had their German adversaries. Due to lack of transport, Allied forces had to live off the land as much as possible and rely on portage for the movement of most of their supplies away from the railway. Adding to the problems of the Allied forces, their European, South African and Indian troops suffered heavily from disease during the campaign. The British administration therefore had only slightly more reservations than the Germans about how to get the supplies and labour it thought necessary to win the war. If people in the colony thought they had better uses for their supplies, the military stood ready to take what they wanted by force.[16]

Military officials systematically confiscated food and impressed labour. When the area was handed over to the civilian administration at the end of 1916, one of the first reports stated that 'Owing to demands made of them for food supplies for the troops some shortages are expected along the Central Railroad.'[17] Although the British made much of paying on the spot for whatever they took, a fact noted by some older informants,[18] force nevertheless underlay their efforts. In July 1917 the District Political Officer (D.P.O.) reported, 'The system employed is as follows: each certain number of families are asked to grind a certain quantity of grain which is subsequently collected and paid for', leaving unstated but apparently understood by his audience the fate of any family unwise enough to refuse the request.[19] The D.P.O. also continued to recruit labour extensively. By April 1917, 24,146 men had been conscripted into the Carrier Corps from the area under the control of the *boma* (Government Office) at Dodoma. However, labour was becoming increasingly hard to find. C. W. Duff, the D.P.O., reported:

The District is now thoroughly depleted and it is becoming increasing difficult to find labour for the numerous calls made by me... In spite of the very large number of men absent from their homes there will be a sufficiency of food for the people.[20]

The officer's assessment of the food situation, made just before the main harvest, proved wildly optimistic. The D.P.O. himself admitted in March 1917 that shortages due to confiscation were occurring throughout the region.[21] However, local officers were still collecting cattle and labour as fast

[15] I/52/159A–164A Kalunju, etc.

[16] For a summary of the impact of the war on the colony as a whole, see Iliffe, *Modern History*, 246.

[17] Public Record Office, London: Colonial Office Files (hereafter CO) 691, vol. III, 'Administration of occupied area up to 1 December 1916', Col. W. J. Monson.

[18] I/38/87A–95A Magagi, etc.

[19] TNA 967.828, Dodoma District Reports, D.P.O. to Administrator Occupied Territory, 29 July 1917.

[20] TNA 967.828, Dodoma District Reports, Periodic Report, 15 April 1917.

[21] CO 691, vol. III, C. W. Duff to Administrator in Charge Occupied Territory, 19 March 1917.

as possible from Africans at the same time that the European staff were having to eat imported food. By December, 35,000 tons of maize had been sent to German East Africa to feed military personnel and civilians, yet the administration was still collecting 4,300 head of cattle a month throughout occupied territory.[22]

Despite the knowledge that the harvest in 1918 would be inadequate, both for the colony as a whole and for Ugogo, requisitioning of food continued along with labour conscription. In Ugogo the D.P.O. hired local agents, including educated Africans and a Greek merchant remembered locally as 'John Supiru', to collect food after the harvest.[23] Governor Horace Byatt, in Dar es Salaam, received an anonymous letter charging that the agents were taking all the food they could find and leaving the people of the area at risk of famine. Duff responded by saying that an unsuccessful applicant as a food-collection agent had written the 'malicious' letter. He claimed that people had surplus crops but were not bringing them in for sale because they had no need for money. Duff concluded:

> In a district as large as this it is a matter of extreme difficulty for me to know exactly what can be sold without causing a famine say eight or nine months hence. My position here is one of extreme delicacy. On the one hand I have the Military Authorities asking for as much food as I can give them and on the other hand the future provisioning of the native population to think of. In conclusion I can only state that the situation is not one for alarm and is being handled as tactfully as possible and is under my direct control.[24]

Duff's words echo across the next three years.

In addition to the general food shortage, the influenza pandemic of 1917–18 also made itself felt locally. By November 1918, Byatt had reported its presence in German East Africa.[25] The disease killed many people already weakened by hunger. The Gogo called this disease *Kapatula*, 'Shorts', after the short pants that the British wore and the short interval between infection and death. Many informants referred to the time of famine before the end of the war as the *Kapatula*, reserving the name *Mtunya* for the period of famine after the war.[26] This conclusion comes both from the association of the famine with the British take-over of Ugogo and from the extension of the famine well into 1920. Although rainfall for 1918 was around the average (26·35 inches in Dodoma[27]) the timing was disastrous. Rain usually falls in Ugogo only between November and April. The 1918–19 rains did not begin until well into 1919, and no rain at all fell in March, a critical time for the ripening crops.[28] Only in 1919 did the colonial government finally begin to be concerned about the deaths occurring in the region, and the pitifully small

[22] CO 691, vol. III, minutes of a meeting in Sir Ernest Moirs' Office, Ministry of Munitions, 17 December 1917.

[23] I/31/46A–51A Musa, etc.

[24] TNA 967.828, Dodoma District Reports, D.P.O. to Byatt, 29 July 1917.

[25] CO 691, vol. XV, H. Byatt to Secretary of State, 4 November 1918.

[26] I/35/54A–60A Lepichiu, etc.; I/32/52A Biringi; I/51/143A–158A Mpilini, etc.; and I/49/124A–129A Nyaulingo, etc.

[27] L. E. Y. Mbogoni, 'Ecological crisis and food production in Dodoma 1920–1960: Colonial efforts in developing the productive forces' (M.A. thesis, University of Dar es Salaam, 1981), 54.

[28] CO 691, vol. XXI, P. J. Sillitoe to H. Byatt, 24 March 1919.

amounts of relief imports then provided came too late for thousands of starving Gogo.

For the people in Ugogo it was a time to utilize all the strategies they knew to survive food shortages. These strategies were complicated by the need to conceal grain, cattle and men from the government. Mzee Kaka of Nala, a young boy during this famine, recalled:

> My family got food from the bush during the [*Mtunya*]. We would dig roots and collect fruit in the bush. My parents also went to work for other people and would be paid with husks from grain. My family owned a few head of cattle, only two or three. During the war, everyday we would take our cattle and hide them in the bush so that the soldiers could not get them.[29]

Mzee Msadu of Handali said that he spent several months sleeping in the bush with his family's cattle.[30] Whole villages were abandoned; the elders of Zoissa, north of Mpwapwa, said they took all their food and cattle into the hills and left the village behind.[31]

Hiding the cattle became difficult as grass and water became scarce during the dry season. Mzee Msaka of Bihawana, south of Dodoma, went with his father when they clandestinely took their cattle almost 100 miles to the Bahi Swamp, in the Rift Valley, to find water. Many of the cattle died along the way. When they got to the swamp they found water and grass, but the water there proved poisonous. By the time they had returned home with the rains, most of their cattle had died.[32]

Once the stored grain and then the husks had run out, people began to search the bush for food. It was at this stage that deaths from famine began to occur. Often the children would be sent to the forest for food.[33] They collected a range of fruit, roots, grass seed and nuts, but some people became so hungry that they began to boil and eat the leather from their sandals.[34] Others went to the bush and never returned. Mzee Gazo remembered:

> Very many died [during the *Mtunya*]. And in my family we had deaths two times. Our father did not survive with us. He died coming back from the forest. Then there were many people coming and going to the city where they begged for food and tried to get something to use. They looked for a way to survive wherever they could. They went from place to place. They had to wander because this was a great famine. Then in March they returned home. They were not able to get a harvest. Many more died.[35]

People also began to seek out others who had grain to exchange. Cattle owners could both trade their stock for grain and sell cattle for cash. Cash prices for cattle, however, dropped sharply. They fell from a maximum price of 40 rupees in 1916 to 8 rupees in 1918.[36] During 1919 the British officer stationed in Kilimatinde claimed that cattle sales were non-existent due to

[29] I/29/42A Kaka. Saving and using the hulls from sorghum and millet was a common famine-prevention practice.

[30] I/35/61A–73A Mzena, etc.

[31] I/51/143A–158A Mpilini, etc.

[32] I/28/39A–41A Msaka, etc.

[33] I/30/42B, 43A–45A Kaka, etc.

[34] I/38/87A–95A Magagi, etc.

[35] I/27/38A Gazo.

[36] TNA 967.828, Dodoma District Reports, 6 Dec. 1916, and Report for the Year Ending 31 March 1919, P. J. Sillitoe. For the early years of British rule, the German East African rupee remained the currency of the colony. It was divided into 100 hellers. 15 rupees equalled 20 East African shillings. Iliffe, *Modern History*, xviii.

deaths from starvation,[37] and, writing in 1925, the D.P.O. in Dodoma recalled that cattle had been sold for as little as a single rupee per head.[38] Even if people had money it was almost impossible to buy grain in any of the shops before 1919.[39] As a result, stock owners preferred to trade with grain holders rather than sell for money. Livestock were often taken long distances but many herders failed to find anyone willing to take cattle for grain.[40] Mzee Cheliga, who later worked in the Ministry of Agriculture in Dodoma, both before and after Independence, recalled his father telling him that one cow would bring only 5–10 kg of millet during the famine. As Mzee Cheliga wrote:

> What was most useful in those bad days was food – millet etc. Cattle were useless because they were dying in their hundreds due to lack of pasture which resulted from poor rainfall, and therefore general aridity.[41]

Cattle lost value compared to grain despite the sharp decline in the total cattle population.

Those without cattle searched desperately for work. Normally, people short of food could find supplies by helping in the fields of their neighbours who were better off. The amount of food paid in return for a day's labour would be determined by the closeness of the neighbours and the relative status of the households. As with the price of stock, the 'wage' paid by households with surplus grain also declined during this time to what is remembered as an unprecedented low. Mzee Kaka recalled his parents being away for a long period working for others and returning with only husks of grain.[42] Father Steven Mlundi and Mzee Lyacho of Dodoma both said that a person could only get enough food for one day by working during the famine, much less than had been usual in the past.[43]

People could also seek work in the larger settlements of the region along the railway or, until the end of the war, for the military. As we have already noted, the government hired thousands of porters and labourers on public works. Indeed, as the famine worsened, desertions from labour units in the region dropped from 10 per cent a month to zero.[44] Wages for work for the government remained constant throughout the period at 25 to 30 hellers a day. However, despite continuing demands for porters to transport food from the railway to the villages, during 1919 the supply of labour came to far outstrip the demand for it.[45]

If people could find no food locally they had to go outside Ugogo in search

[37] TNA 967.825, Manyoni District Reports, F. C. Buckley, Kilimatinde Sub-District Report for the year 4 Jan. 1919 to 31 March 1920.

[38] TNA 967.828, Dodoma District Reports, H. Hignell, Annual Report for 1925.

[39] I/35/61A–73A Mzena, etc.; TNA 967.825, Manyoni District Reports, F. C. Buckley, Kilimatinde Annual Report, 20 March 1920; and I/27/38A Gazo.

[40] I/28/39A–41A Msaka, etc.; and I/3/3A Kongola.

[41] I/43/113A Cheliga. Mzee Cheliga provided written responses to questions, from which this quote comes.

[42] I/29/42A Kaka.

[43] I/6/6A–7A Sikana and Lyacho; and I/5/5A Father Steven Mlundi.

[44] TNA 967.828, Dodoma District Reports, Periodical Report for Dodoma District, D. W. Duff, 15 April 1917.

[45] TNA 967.828, Dodoma District Reports, Annual Report for 1919–1920, H. Hignell, 23 April 1920; and Ambler, *Kenyan Communities*, 138–41.

of subsistence. Many took cattle to trade, but others went with nothing at all. Bibi Fundi of Veulla who lived in Tabora at the time recalled:

I saw the *Mtunya* because many Gogo came to Tabora then, carrying their things on their heads... We would give them husks, potatoes, cassava and yams. We would give the food free. First we would give them food so they could regain their strength. Then, after they were strong, the host and his guests would go together to work in the fields. Then they would return home and cook food again. The whole family, men, women, and children, would go together to work.[46]

Mzee Sahali of Hombolo, who lived in Handeni as a child, said that among the Zigua of that region the Gogo were put to work cultivating cassava for food.[47] Many informants remembered members of their families or friends going east to Kilosa, south to Iringa, or north to Kondoa and Arusha in search of food.[48] Father Steven Mlundi described the situation:

So as a boy, I could see people coming from these parts and trying to go eastwards. In the east, they thought, there was better farming. There was food. It was always green there, they thought. And then many died.[49]

When the strategies that maintained the independence of households proved inadequate, many had to resort to pawning children or becoming dependants of those few people with food. Within Ugogo, a few areas seem to have been better off than others. In those areas the *Watemi* (chiefs) and other wealthy cattle-owners and those who had extra grain were able to increase their followings.[50] With the loss of stock in the region to confiscation and drought, the remaining cattle-owners in areas with relatively more grain could control more labour and food. These fortunate individuals were able to take advantage of their control over labour in the years after the famine to greatly increase their wealth through agricultural production for the market.

II

The way in which the Gogo remember these events not only recalls the hardship of the *Mtunya*; they have developed a collective explanation for both the causes and the effects of the famine. The Gogo place the blame for the suffering squarely on the Europeans who forced them to give up their food, cattle and young men, and on the shopkeepers who symbolized their growing dependence on outside markets for their produce.

One well-known Gogo story about the *Mtunya* successfully captures the

[46] I/34/54A–60A Lepichiu, etc.

[47] I/33/53A Sahali.

[48] I/36/74A–81A Mapalasha, etc.; I/39/96A–101A Luangi, etc.; I/30/42B, 43A–46A Kaka, etc.; and I/17/14A–26A Chidoza, etc.

[49] I/5/5A Father Steven Mlundi.

[50] Hugh Hignell, Provincial Commissioner, to Chief Secretary, 'Report on the Wagogo', 19 June 1927, Dodoma District Book. The District Books for Tanzania are available on microfilm from the Co-operative Africana Microfilm Project of the Centre for Research Libraries in Chicago, Illinois. In particular, some informants recalled people moving to Mvumi, and as a result the *Mtemi*, Mazengo, seems to have strengthened his position as the strongest *Mtemi* in Ugogo (I/17/14A–26A Chidoza, etc.; and I/36/74A–81A Mapalasha, etc.). The surplus food may, however, have come from the mission station at Mvumi rather than from local production.

main thrust of their interpretation. During the *Mtunya* a group of hungry people heard that there was food in Dodoma town. They made their way there and went to the *boma* to ask for food. The British officer sent them away saying, 'We have no food. You must find it for yourselves.' These people then crossed the railway into town. They went to the shops owned by Indian traders and begged for food. The shop-owners took sticks and beat the people and drove them away, saying '*Ondokeni*, *Wagogo*! *Ondokeni*! *Hamna chakula*!' ('Leave, Gogo! Leave! There is no food!'). While they continued desperately to search for food, it began to rain. When they finally understood they would get no food that day, the people went to the railway bridge that crossed a stream near the *boma*. There, sheltering under the railway bridge out of the rain, they went to sleep. During the night, the rain turned into a thunderstorm. The stream-bed quickly filled as the trickle of water turned into a flood. Most of the people, too weak from hunger to save themselves, were swept away and drowned.[51]

This story has been widely told and associated with the *Mtunya*, because in a number of important ways it sums up the relationship between the people of Ugogo and the colonial government and its economy as well as their continuing relationship to their marginal environment. The Gogo were ignored by the government, exploited by the colonial economy, and alienated from the forces that controlled their physical world. For the Gogo, then, this story is their interpretation of a terrifying loss of autonomy, a loss of the ability to control the reproduction of their own society. Many different versions of the story are told throughout Ugogo. Indeed, the event upon which the story is based may not even have occurred during the *Mtunya*. Two particularly knowledgable informants, one of them Hasan Biringi, the scion of the *Watemi* of Dodoma, date this flood to a famine in the 1920s.[52] There is no record of such an incident in either the regional or central government archives. This lack of written confirmation by no means implies that this incident did not occur; it may only reflect the colonial attitude that the death of a few more 'natives' during a famine was unworthy of comment. This story, although quite possibly 'untrue' in one sense, to most people 'truly' reflects the state of affairs during the *Mtunya*.

The Gogo also have an interpretation of the effects on their society of this famine. The *Mtunya* disrupted regular social relationships. The Gogo therefore use this famine in a negative way to define their social norms. All that was forbidden, all that was 'uncivilized,' took place during this famine. When the famine ended they had to reconfigure their society in the light of the new strains caused by the famine and colonial rule. This interpretation perhaps stresses the extent of social disorganization because it also explains why the people of Ugogo are now dependent on the outside world for survival.[53]

[51] I/28/39A–41A Msaka, etc. Other versions are found in: I/40/102A–106A Chipanga, etc.; I/25/31A–36A Baja, etc.; I/17/14A–26A Chidoza, etc. For the two versions dating it later see I/32/52A Biringi; and I/34/54A–60A Lepichiu, etc.

[52] See I/32/52A Biringi; and I/34/54A–60A Lepichiu, etc.

[53] See Ambler, *Kenyan Communities*, 1–4; Richard Waller, '*Emutai*: crisis and response in Maasailand, 1883–92', in Johnson and Anderson (eds.), *Ecology of Survival*, 74–5; and J. L. Giblin, 'Explaining the death of Mzee Mtunte: the decline of authority

The collective metaphors to which the *Mtunya* has given life, and especially the images of social disorder and dislocation, flow from individual memories of the famine. Death touches the memory of those who survived this time, and almost everyone remaining alive who remembers the *Mtunya* has their own story of death. Ernest Kongola wrote that his father recalled of the time: '*Hivyo walikuwa wakifa kama wanyama tu*'[54] ('Then the people died like mere animals'). Many reported seeing people dead along the paths. Bibi Salima of Bahi remembered:

> During the *Mtunya* I was travelling from Itigi to Bahi. Along the path I saw a great many dying. The people's skulls littered the ground like coconuts. I became so afraid that I refused to go any further, and my parents had to take me back to Itigi.[55]

Mzee Msaka told of going with his half-brothers from Bihawana to Dodoma to sell cattle for food. They came upon a man carrying a large child. The child could not walk from hunger. The man was coming along very slowly because the child was heavy. Later in town, they saw the man again but without the child. On the way home, they found the child lying by the side of the road with a large rock on his chest. His father had just left him there.[56] According to other accounts, people died in such numbers that there was no time to bury them; instead they were simply stuffed in baobab trees.[57]

With the further disintegration of society as the Gogo knew it, hungry people increasingly resorted to violence to obtain food. Several informants recalled that it became dangerous to travel around by yourself with either food or cattle. People had to travel at night. People 'scrambling' for survival were sure to attack you.[58] Mzee Luangi said:

> During this famine also, people would get together and go to the *tembe* [homestead] of a wealthy person. They would surround it and say, 'We have come to eat your cattle; join our feast.' The wealthy man could do nothing but eat.[59]

The more usual ties which bound those with food to those without had broken down under the stress of the famine. Those with food felt less obligation to help those without, quite possibly because they themselves had very little surplus. Increasingly, if a man had food or cattle to lend, he would demand a pawn in return. Households with dependants which could not be fed often looked upon 'selling' a child as preferable to having it starve. The pawning of children became quite widespread. Sergeant Brian O'Kelly of the Military Labour Corps, stationed in German East Africa, witnessed some of these transactions during 1918 in the context of continued requisitions of food. He wrote a letter on this subject that eventually came to the attention of the War Department in London. As a result the D.P.O. in Dodoma, Captain P. J. Sillitoe, was called upon to explain. Sillitoe replied that 'No instances of Wagogo [Gogo] desiring to sell their children came to my knowledge, and special inquiry on the point has failed to elicit any

---

and environmental control in Northeastern Tanzania under German colonial rule', paper presented at the Canadian African Studies Association meeting (Kingston, Ontario, 1988), for similar accounts of the way communities interpret disasters.

[54] *Historia Fupi wa Mbeyu ya Wjenvuliza Toka 1666 Mpaka 1986 : 'Mbukwa Muhindi wa Cinambi'* (Dodoma, 1986), 14.

[55] I/39/96A–101A Luangi, etc.

[56] I/28/39A–41A Msaka, etc.

[57] I/35/61A–73A Mzena, etc.

[58] I/31/46A–51A Musa, etc.

[59] I/39/96A–101A Luangi, etc.

information to that effect'.[60] Sillitoe's conclusion was belied both by informants and later colonial reports on the famine.[61] The practice of pawning dependants for food was certainly a common response to famine; however, as with other ways of obtaining food, the advantage during this famine shifted to the supplier of food.[62] Less food was required to gain control of a child, and preferences for females became more marked. Several informants mentioned that a boy could be had for as little as one cow while a girl close to marriageable age would go for two. The girls would usually marry into the family that bought them.[63] Mzee Mkotia of Handali claimed that his father obtained a potential wife for him during the *Mtunya* for only one cow. He, however, refused to marry her, and she was married to another member of the family.[64] The boys could either be redeemed or remained as dependants in the household of their purchaser. One informant claimed that if the parents could not repay the debt, a boy would have to work for seven years and then he could return to his family.[65] Others said that during this famine the household giving a child received no food or cattle for it. The child stayed with the household which had food during the famine, and worked. Then the parents would bring part of their harvest to the wealthy household to pay for the child's upkeep.[66] According to Mzee Mnyambwa of Chipanga, children were even taken to Dodoma and 'sold' to the shopkeepers there. He remembered:

> Parents would take their children to the rich people in Dodoma, especially those who owned shops. When the parents got food from the rich people they would tell the children, 'I am going someplace to prepare the food.' The parents then returned home. The children would stay and be given a broom and have to work.[67]

These differing accounts of the process of pawning children reflect the lack of rules regarding such transactions. In each case, parents and benefactors negotiated the terms of the transaction.

According to some informants, children were also abandoned if their families had no food for them. Bibi Mtemi of Bahi described the fate of one child:

> When families went to the forest to search for food, if they did not have enough for their children, they might leave them in the forest. One woman was left in the forest and found by another family. The other family took her home and raised her. When the time came for her to marry, she became engaged to a very wealthy man. Her real parents came and claimed the bridewealth. The woman said, 'No, you are not my parents. These are my parents.' Her parents went to the office of the European government to get her to give them the bridewealth. She refused. She

[60] CO 691, vol. XXI, P. J. Sillitoe to H. Byatt, 24 March 1919. I could find no copy of O'Kelly's letter in either the Colonial Office archives or the War Office archives in London, nor in the Tanzania National Archives.

[61] For example, Dodoma District Book, H. Hignell to Chief Secretary, 'Report on the Wagogo', 19 June 1927.

[62] Ambler, *Kenyan Communities*, 60–2.

[63] I/37/82A–86A Ali, etc.; I/51/143A–158A Mpilini, etc.; I/38/87A–95A Magagi, etc.; I/39/96A–101A Luangi, etc.; I/40/102A–106A Chipanga, etc.; and I/41/107A–112A Mnyambwa, etc.

[64] I/35/61A–73A Mzena, etc.

[65] I/47/119A–121A Mapuga, etc.

[66] I/38/87A–95A Magagi, etc.; and I/36/74A–81A Mapalasha, etc.

[67] I/41/107A–112A Mnyambwa, etc.

said to the *Bwana Shauri* [District Officer], 'These are my parents. These others I do not know.' So the bridewealth went to the parents who raised her.[68]

Memories like this indicate not only how famine corroded family relationships but also a decline in the value of labour. Combined with the reduction in bridewealth payments, they marked a significant shift in wealth in the region. Those people fortunate enough to have some surplus food or to retain herds of cattle increased their control over labour in the years after the famine, while those who had lost labour and cattle found it increasingly difficult to meet their subsistence needs from their own production.

Not only do people recall losing family members; many informants claimed that cannibalism became common.[69] The stories of abandoned children and cannibalism are quite possibly apocryphal. European accounts do not mention any cases of people driven to the final resort of eating others in order to stay alive. These memories, however, do indicate that the people of Ugogo recall the *Mtunya* as a time when all the bonds of normal society were broken. Survival is remembered as the only concern, and any means that promoted it were evidently legitimate. The normal rules of social behaviour were remembered as suspended; they returned only when the rains came again.

As the famine continued after the end of the war, the British colonial government began to try to bring some order to the disorganized central region of their new territory. While some of the individual officers sent to Dodoma District were acutely aware of the suffering caused by the famine, preventing deaths from starvation was only a means to an end – the pacification and eventually exploitation of the region as a part of the colonial economy. Thus the methods used to combat the famine forced the people of the region to pay, in some form or another, for whatever assistance they received. Both the famine and the means used by colonial officials to combat it are an example of what Iliffe has called 'conjunctural' impoverishment.[70] However, the loss of cattle by households turned out in many cases to be permanent in the years following the famine; the *Mtunya* led to an increase in the proportion of the population of Ugogo in the structurally impoverished position of lacking cattle, and hence, within the context of Gogo society, lacking control over even their own labour.

In Ugogo the new administration under Sillitoe was slow to begin supplying relief. Writing in March 1919, Sillitoe noted:

The famine began to get serious towards the end of January last. Until then anxiety was kept in check by the hope for rain. From the beginning of January energetic steps were taken to assist the Wagogo [Gogo]. The town-dwelling natives and those in regular employment received no assistance whatever but had to purchase in the open market from traders.[71]

The administration's definition of relief operations, in this case, was to sell food to shopkeepers at reduced prices. Apparently, no free issues were made. Prices varied according to the source of the food. The first shipments were sold at a price of eleven hellers per pound, which included a profit margin for

[68] I/45/114A–117A Kaloli, etc.

[69] I/37/82A–86A Ali, etc., I/45/114A–117A Kaloli, etc., and I/40/102A–106A Chipanga, etc.

[70] Iliffe, *African Poor*, 4–7.

[71] CO 691, vol. XXI, P. J. Sillitoe to H. Byatt, 24 March 1919.

the government. By March 1919 grain was being sold at four hellers per pound, a 50 per cent discount on the cost.[72] Money had become the single most important determinant of who survived and who died. Not only was money required to buy relief; the administration made an effort to collect taxes. For the year ending 31 March 1919, 74,184 rupees were collected in Dodoma, 39,024 in Kilimatinde, and 37,791 in Mpwapwa. Mzee Mwalaka of Sagara, near Mpwapwa, said:

> It was during the *Malali* [meaning "many died", as the *Mtunya* is called in Mpwapwa] that the English came to rule the country after the war. What did they do? They demanded that the people pay tax.[73]

While cattle prices dropped below 25 rupees a head and wages were as low as 25 hellers a day, only the most fortunate could hope to survive.[74] H. G. Hallis, Chief Secretary to the government, reported in May 1919 on an inspection visit made to the district:

> The famine had undoubtedly been severe, and as a result there have been several deaths amongst the very young and the very old. A large number of cattle have also died of starvation, and the famine-stricken natives have in many cases been obliged to sell their herds at low prices... This food will tide over the period till the next harvest in June, but although good rains have fallen, so much of the seed grain has been eaten that the crops will be very scanty, and it will be necessary to make provision against the scarcity that will be felt towards the end of the year.[75]

Later colonial administrators did not take so sanguine a view of the effectiveness of early relief efforts. They recognized the disastrous results of not bringing food in quickly enough and of trying to keep costs to a minimum. In 1920, F. C. Buckley, the assistant D.P.O. at Kilimatinde, commented in a report to the D.P.O. in Dodoma:

> The food shortage 1918/1919 had been acute, and the famine extended right through 1919/1920 only slightly easing during June, July, and August 1919, the harvest months. The famine of 1918/1919 cost many lives, the number may be placed at several thousands, and it enforced emigration on a large scale.[76]

These deaths had occurred despite Sillitoe's earlier assertions that anyone in the district who needed food could get it.

During 1919 the colonial administration began to realize that more extensive relief measures would have to be carried out if Ugogo was to become governable. More food was imported as shipping opened up after the war, and officers in the region now began to issue food, either free or directly to labourers in return for work. Transport difficulties still limited most issues to stations along the railway line; as a result, relatively few people have memories of that relief.

When, in 1919, Hugh Hignell took over from Sillitoe as D.P.O., he found the district ungovernable due to the famine. In 1925 he remembered the situation:

[72] *Ibid.* [73] I/52/159A–164A Kalunju, etc.

[74] TNA 967.828, Dodoma District Reports, P. J. Sillitoe, Annual Report for the Year Ending 31 March 1919.

[75] CO 691, vol. XXI, H. Hallis to Secretary of State, 1 May 1919.

[76] TNA 967.825, Manyoni District Reports, F. C. Buckley, Annual Report for the Year Ending 20 March 1920.

Thirty thousand natives are said to have died of famine and they sold their cattle by the hundred for a rupee a piece on Dodoma market... amongst those remaining great numbers had pawned their children – husbands had left their wives, mothers their children and, in fact, family life had disintegrated. With the war, Spanish influenza, and famine following closely on their heels, no wonder that the Wagogo [Gogo] believed that a malign fate was pursuing them. Out in the country you might see a tribesman in the distance but you could seldom approach him. Sir Horace Byatt had to leave ducks he shot on the water at Mtango's because every tembe was promptly deserted at the approach of Capt. Sillitoe's messenger. It was an appalling state of affairs.[77]

Given the exactions imposed by the British in the name of winning the war, it is no surprise that few people waited around to become the Governor's bird dogs. The fear of requisitions of food and conscription had driven people into the bush, and made them extremely wary of contact with Europeans. The alien *akida* and *jumbe* who had not been killed by their former subjects had congregated in Dodoma and Mpwapwa. Likewise, the 'scramble' for food had so unsettled the population that even the links between people and their *watemi* had broken down. Hignell later described the situation:

Looking around [in 1920] it was found that it [the district] had no system of administration at all. The Gogo chiefdoms gone – the German system had gone – and the famine had so churned up the population that some chiefs had no people at all and others had masses of men living in their country who refused to acknowledge them as chief....[78]

The first order of business for the administration under Hignell was to ensure that there would actually be people to administer. Food was sent to stations along the central railway and then carried by porters, when they could be found, to other stations. However, the shortage of labour meant that many areas never received food, and starving people often had to try to walk miles to the nearest depot. At these depots, food continued to be sold or issued for work, with only the old receiving it free. In some cases, food was loaned to people on promise of repayment after harvest.[79]

In addition to government relief efforts, the Church Missionary Society (C.M.S.) missions also brought some food to distribute to those in need. People living near Buigiri (near Dodoma), Mvumi, Kilimatinde, Kongwa and Mpwapwa all recalled getting food from the mission.[80] Mzee Hanatizo Chamwilo distributed food for the mission seminary school. Mzee Chamwilo, who taught at the C.M.S. seminary at Kongwa, remembered:

I was in charge of distribution of food at the mission so I always had food. When I gave the people a kilogram each, I would get a *debe* [a petrol tin of grain, about 20 kilograms]... I would give it out to everyone who asked for it, not just the people of the mission... I would go myself to Gulwe to collect it at the [railway] station.

[77] TNA 967.828, Dodoma District Reports, H. Hignell, Annual Report for 1925.

[78] H. Hignell to Chief Secretary, 'Report on the Wagogo', 19 June 1927, Dodoma District Book.

[79] TNA 967.828, Dodoma District Reports, H. Hignell, Annual Report for 1919–1920.

[80] I/48/122A, 123A Chamwilo, etc.; I/47/119A–121A Mapuga, etc.; I/45/114A–117A Kaloli, etc.; I/35/61A–73A Mzena, etc.; and I/36/74A–81A Mapalasha, etc.

I had to go there three times during the famine to get food. I went with a group of men who carried it on their heads back to Kongwa. We would walk on the road from Kongwa to Gulwe until Chambule and spend the night there. But on the way back, they could not stop – we walked the whole way with sacks of food on their heads. We would start from Chambule in the morning, get the food at Gulwe, then walk back to Kongwa in one day. We knew we would never return if we stopped with the food. Thieves, or just hungry people, would attack us and kill us and take the food... I would usually take between twenty and twenty-four men... I was the only one in charge. No European would go with us... One day, we were carrying maize back to Kongwa. One of the porters made a little hole in his sack and began to eat some of the maize kernels that came out. He died before we reached Kongwa. What happened was that he took some water and his stomach swelled up. It gave off a sound like a drum. Then he died.[81]

Despite the attempts by the government to distribute grain and the efforts of the C.M.S., the people of Ugogo rarely recall the relief brought by the British. Many say that the British did not know the Gogo yet.[82] Others claim that the British brought food, but that this benefitted only those with money as it was sold in the shops.[83]

Although relief efforts did not directly reach a large proportion of the population of Ugogo, the injection of food did help. Along with the end of the war and the end of large-scale confiscation of food, people were able to settle down long enough to plant and harvest a crop. The rains in 1919–20 were above average, despite a long break in January. As a result the harvest proved sufficient for most people to last the entire year for the first time in three years.[84] Hignell reported the improving situation:

Now thanks to a wonderful harvest and the wise prohibition of the slaughter of female stock throughout the country, which effectively prevented the dissipation of the Wagogo's [Gogo] wealth in cattle, the former prosperity of this District can be restored... From now on it should be a case of reaping where we have sown... This District should not be famine stricken again for many years. Never in any previous year the natives say have they planted such large shambas [fields] and this in face of greatly reduced population should mean plenty in the land for two years at least, from this crop alone.[85]

The harvest came to a population much reduced from that at the beginning of the war. The actual number of deaths from famine between 1917 and 1920 is, of course, unknowable. The estimate of 30,000 made by Hignell in 1925, and repeated by Rigby[86] and Iliffe,[87] seems based on the population estimates of 1913 and 1921, which show a drop in population of about 30,000 for all of Dodoma District (including the Singida subdistrict, which is not a part of

[81] I/48/122A–123A Chamwilo, etc.

[82] I/41/107A–112A Mnyambwa, etc.; I/52/159A–164A Kalunju, etc.; I/39/96A–101A Luangi, etc.; I/27/38A Gazo; and I/17/14A–26A Chidoza, etc.

[83] I/30/42B, 43A–46A Kaka, etc.; I/35/61A–73A Mzena, etc.; I/36/74A–81A Mapalasha, etc.; and I/6/6A–7A Sikana and Lyacho.

[84] TNA 967.828, Dodoma District Reports, H. Hignell, Annual Report 1919–1920; and TNA 967.825, Manyoni District Reports, F. C. Buckley, Kilimatinde Annual Report 1919–1920.

[85] TNA 967.828, Dodoma District Reports, H. Hignell, Annual Report 1919–1920.

[86] Rigby, *Cattle and Kinship*, 21–22.

[87] Iliffe, *Modern History*, 269.

Ugogo) from 299,400 to 270,900.[88] Hignell's estimate, which applied to Ugogo only, apparently assumed that most of the thousands of refugees from Ugogo during the famine had returned or been replaced by immigrants seeking land free from the tsetse fly by 1921.[89] Hignell's estimate of 30,000, made by the one colonial official who had the most direct knowledge both of the famine and of the people of Ugogo, remains the best guide to the scale of the disaster.

III

The people of Dodoma have a prosaic description of the end of the *Mtunya*. According to a story repeated throughout the area, and even in other areas struck by famine at the same time, the people planted their crops in December of 1919.[90] Mzee Msaka remembered:

> Many did not cultivate, but there came very heavy rains. Then, after the time for the new crops, the millet began to grow. Now the grass also grew, and when they returned, the millet was growing. Although they did not cultivate, all the cattle had died. They could not eat the grass because many had eaten the cattle as food. Many people had been going around searching for a living. When they returned home, they had fields stuffed with millet.[91]

The contrast of this legend with the story of the people and the flood, recounted earlier, is instructive. The story of the bridge and the flood indicates the results of the destruction of the social relationships that promoted survival in the arid region. It also clearly identifies who the destroyers were. For the people of Ugogo, this story has become a metaphor for their relationship both to the colonial state and the outside world in general. The story of the 'miracle harvest' marks the return to a secure and normal life in Ugogo. The famine ended when people were able to return to their homes. They attempted to recreate the social relationships that made orderly society, and survival, possible in the harsh lands of Ugogo.

Reconstruction after the famine did not restore, in its entirety, society as it had been. Individuals such as the *Mtemi* of Mvumi, Mazengo, came out of the famine able to control more labour than previously. Such men were able to use this labour in the years after the war to greatly expand production of grain and groundnuts. In contrast, those households left without cattle after the famine became increasingly dependent upon working for their wealthier neighbours to earn the access to cattle needed in order to fulfil a variety of social obligations, including bridewealth, and to ensure survival during dry

[88] 'Population', Dodoma District Book.

[89] Maddox, 'Leave Wagogo', 182–84.

[90] I/28/39A–41A Msaka, etc., where Father Damus claims the story is also common in Usandawe.

[91] I/28/39A–41A Msaka, etc.; I/41/107A–112A Mnyambwa, etc.; I/29/42A Kaka; I/35/61A–73A Mzena, etc.; I/40/102A–106A Chipanga, etc.; and I/36/74A–81A Mapalasha, etc. Others said the harvest came from the plantings in 1919 which had not sprouted, and that people got a harvest despite not planting; see I/30/42B, 43A–45A Kaka, etc.; and I/37/82A–86A Ali, etc.

years. Hignell promoted these arrangements, as opposed to either migrant labour or increased market production for poorer families, arguing that any lost income to the colony from people working for their neighbours would be made up in reduced expenditures on famine relief. Although his policies were not always appreciated in Dar es Salaam, food shortages never approached the severity of the *Mtunya* between 1920 and 1941. However, a change of policy in the mid-1930s, after the departure of Hignell, stressing the direct exploitation of each household, produced a decade and a half of killing famines starting in 1941.[92] This effectively completed the process of the structural impoverishment of most of the people in Ugogo begun during the *Mtunya*.[93]

The *Mtunya* was a man-made famine. It was caused by the theft of food, cattle, and men from local communities by Europeans and their agents. The Gogo of today recall with horror the results on their society of these pressures. They emphasize the extent of the lawlessness and social disorganization of the time because they see the *Mtunya* as the one event that marks the end of their ability to reproduce their own society from their own resources. After the years of scrambling, it was money, not cattle or social relationships, that allowed people to survive.

SUMMARY

In the Dodoma Region of central Tanzania the people called Wagogo name a famine that struck between 1917 and 1920 the *Mtunya* – 'The Scramble'. This famine came after both German and British miliary requisitions had drained the arid region of men, cattle and food. The famine, which killed 30,000 of the region's 150,000 people, is more than just a good example of what John Iliffe has called 'conjunctural poverty'. The *Mtunya* and the response to it by both the people of the region and the new colonial government also shaped the form of the interaction between local economy and society and the political economy of colonial Tanganyika. The Gogo, in their own interpretation of the famine, stress the ways in which this famine made them dependent on the colonial economy. For them, this famine represented a terrible loss of autonomy, a loss of the ability to control the reproduction of their own society.

[92] D. M. Anderson. 'Depression, dust bowl, demography, and drought: the colonial state and soil conservation in East Africa during the 1930s', *African Affairs*, LXXXIII (1984), 321–42.

[93] Maddox, 'Leave Wagogo', chs. 6 and 7.

Revue canadienne des études africaines / Canadian Journal of African Studies
Volume IX, nº 2, 1975, 277–292

Kenya's Primitive Colonial Capitalism The Economic Weakness of Kenya's Settlers Up to 1940

Paul Van ZWANENBERG *

Oh ! I'd love to be a farmer
Yes ! It must be sheer delight
To leave the farm and come to town
And talk through half the night
To run the farm on overdraft
And mortgages and debts,
And dodge the undeveloped tax
By taxing cigarettes.

Oh ! I'd love to be a farmer !
Not the kind who ploughs the land
And sweats from morn to dewy eve,
With rough and horny hands :
But one who plays at politics
And grinds his axe all day
It really is a topping game
And somehow seems to pay !
Oh ! I'd love to be a farmer
Yes there's really such a charm
In being *called* a farmer though
One doesn't need to farm. [1]

Primitive Colonial Capitalism is a concept of similar nature to Marx's "so called Primitive Capitalism." [2] Primitive capitalism was a shorthand notion which referred to the violent methods used to accumulate capital in the preindustrial phase of the British experience. It was a period in which the incipient capitalist classes struggled against the multifarious elements of the old society. It was a period characterized by violence and brutality between the various groups involved. It is in these two senses of violence and struggle in a preindustrial period in

* University of Dar es Salaam, Tanzania.

1. *The Kenya Critic*, 3 June 1922, under "Dogged Doggerel," (second and fifth) verse. *The Kenya Critic* was a newspaper which published weekly in 1922 and 1923. Copies can be found in the Kenya National Archives.

Britain that we draw parallels with the much shorter period of colonial pre-industrial Kenya. The comparisons between the two societies goes no further than this as the processes of economic growth were historically of a different character. Primitive colonial capitalism refers to the period of relative domestic violence and brutality with the local community. It was a period when the settlers were struggling to establish large scale capitalist farming against a peasant alternative, at a time when they were short of finance and agricultural skill. Until 1940 the local people were continuously being pressured and coerced to become short term migrant labourers. The system as it affected the local people was one of growing repression similar in character to the one found further south in Rhodesia or South Africa. Flogging without trial on settler farms was part of the accepted order, while racial bigotry was widely institutionalized in all legal enactments. Less visible, but an essential part of the order, was the system of regressive taxation. The taxes paid by the peasantry were utilized to provide the infrastructure for the European farms. These elements did not occur by chance, they occurred because the settlers were desperately short of finance to deal with the many exigencies of large scale farming. To exist and prosper the settlers needed to capture the State and to organize the entire society in such a way that they would be able to exploit every element in it to provide the financial accumulation necessary for their activities. The fact that they failed to capture the State was in the end the reason why they failed to dominate as in the South. Up to the end of the 1930s, the politically involved settlers were becoming deeply entrenched in the critical committees of the political machine and were able to influence affairs through such means. The violence and brutality of the State was directly related to the needs of the settlers. In this paper we shall attempt to outline and to document the economic poverty and the technical inadequacy of the settler majority.

I – THE CLASSIFICATION OF SETTLERS

The European sector of the economy can usefully be classified into three groups, two of which may be seen as incipient classes. At the top was a small coterie of very wealthy farmers, some of whom had titles indicating their aristocratic British origins, and all of whom had considerable private incomes from sources outside Kenya. Grogan and Delamere are perhaps the best known of these individuals, but there were a number of others. Not only were they characterized by their wealth but also by their access to political power. In this sense therefore they represented an incipient settler ruling class. This group was unusually aware of its ruling class potential, and was able to set the social tone and ethos of the entire white community.

Secondly there were the company farms ; which were often branches of larger concerns such as the tea plantations owned by Brooke Bond in the Kericho District. Some of these firms, like Brooke Bond, were branches of international joint stock companies, able to mobilize finance through their parent company.

---

2. Karl Marx, *Capital*, vol. 1, Part 8.

Such companies had no problem of a shortage of finance or lack of skill. These agricultural branch companies had their counterpart in the branches of the international trading and finance companies which today dominate the Kenya economy. But up to the period of the 1940 war these companies played a minor rôle in the economy as a whole.

The third group were by far in the majority numerically ; these were the relatively small scale settler farmers. Unlike the other two groups they were always short of finance up to 1939 and as a consequence the area of land which they farmed was severely limited. At no time before 1940 was more than 10% of the total area owned and alienated land under cultivation, while another 20% was used for cattle ranching. This group represented an actual agricultural settler petty bourgeoisie class, permanently insecure during the 1920 and 1930s, both in a political and economic sense, and in fear of being thrown into the ranks of "poor whites." This class was dominant in the sense that they were numerically by far the largest group in the active political arena ; they were dominant in the sense that their racist sentiments against the African and Asian populations were acted upon. It was the interests of this group therefore which were behind the characteristic growth which we outlined above. These small white farmers had every reason to fear the superior competitive power of Asian commerce, and African peasant cash crops. It was probable that the only way these settlers could defend themselves was to create such a strict political, social and economic divide that competition was reduced to a minimum.

There are unfortunately no known statistics to elucidate the economics of this agricultural structure. There appears to have been a tendency from the beginning of settlement for a concentration in the pattern of ownership. By 1912 five individuals or syndicates owned a fifth of the total of the alienated land. [3] What had occurred was described by T. O. O'Shea, an old settler when writing a reminiscing article in 1958 :

> The market in land went up and up. Kiambu farms of 600 acres freehold that only a few years ago had been given away for a case of whisky or the cost of a passage out of the country, sold freely at £2, then £4 and even £8 an acre. Every man in Nairobi was mixed up in selling in one way or another. Buying and selling options became as popular a form of gambling as football pools today. [4]

In the pre-1914 period, O'Shea had been an employee of Newland Tarlton and Company, a land agent ; and he was also concerned with the Colonial land department. O'Shea was therefore in the position to have inside information concerning land matters. It seems most probable that a small number of the wealthy group of settlers were concerned to own large parts of the Highlands,

3. M. P. K. Sorrenson, *Origins of European Settlement in Kenya*, (Oxford, 1968), 145. C. Speller, "European Agriculture in Kenya," 30 June 1931, sent from Lord Cranworth to Lord Passfield and to be found in the Passfield private papers East African Collection, misc. 156, vol. 6, pp. 54–84. This article can also be found in Colonial Office 533/415/17308 and at Rhodes House Library (hereafter RH), MacGregor Ross papers Mss. Afr 1178, vol. 4, (2).

4. *Kenya Weekly News*, (hereafter *KWN*), 4 July 1958, "Booms and Slumps in Kenya." I am indebted to Mr. Matson for pointing out this article to me.

which they could then sell off to incoming settlers as land prices rose. The majority of settlers came after 1914, many of whom had to purchase land which had already been bought up but which had remained undeveloped. It is the economic situation of the majority to which we now turn.

As already asserted the majority of the settler farmers were characteristically short of cash. Part of the explanation for this shortage was possibly to be found in the practice among the minority of the large landowners of withholding wide areas of the land they had obtained from the market until its price had risen. There were persistent complaints of land speculation in the daily newspapers, but no evidence was ever produced which could prove that land prices were being kept artificially high, at a level which led to the impoverishment of incoming settlers.[5]

A second factor of considerable importance was that most of the incoming settlers did not have large private fortunes which they could expend establishing their new farms. The policy of the Colonial authorities was to encourage men of "standing", i.e. men of financial means. But in practice this policy seems to have been concerned more with a man's "social rank" rather than with his bank account.

It is of course impossible to weigh up the exact importance of the above two factors on the basis of hearsay evidence. But that both factors were important there can be little doubt as the level of indebtedness will show. A third factor of importance which was conducive to the chronic cash shortage was the commercial bank policy of the 1920s. The banks lent cash to settlers on the supposed value of the land they owned rather than on the expected value of the crops. As a consequence, as many of the small scale settlers had more land than they were using productively, they found themselves paying interest on credits which were not being used for crops. The burden of small scale settler debt hampered capital accumulation on the farms during the period of rising prices during the 1920s and absolutely empoverished them in the period of falling prices during the 1930s. These settlers were therefore dependent for their financial survival on being able to pay "low" wages to their labour. Those groups who gained in the short term from this exploitative situation were the commercial banks and the larger land-owners ; these two groups were able to make considerable gains from land sales and from credit. The most critical problem faced by the petty bourgeoisie settlers up to 1940 was to find an appropriate means of credit ; easily available, at low rates of interest.

II – THE INSOLVENT ECONOMY

Whether rates of interest are high or low is of course relative. Here I speak of interest rates only in terms of the small scale settler inability to pay them *and* accumulate finance at the same time. On the whole, only short term, high interest

---

5. Paice private letters held at Royal Commonwealth Society Library, letter of 20 May 1932 ; *The Kenya Critic*, 10 June 1922 ; 16 June 1922 ; 19 August 1922 ; etc. *East African Standard*, 25 July 1931, p. 37 ; also see, "Robertson" in *Kenya Biographies*, E.A.P.H., 1971.

finance was available so far as these farmers were concerned. Some of the important evidence on this question of rates of interest to the white farmers had come from V. Liversage who was employed as Kenya's government economist during the 1930s. In 1945 Liversage published a short book, *Land Tenure in the Colonies* which he devoted a fifth of to the discussion of agricultural debt. Liversage pointed out that a high level of debt was contracted during the periods of prosperity, i.e. during the 1920s when the high prices of export commodities provided the means to repay interest on credits obtained on non-productive resources. But during the period of low prices during the 1930s, the returns to the farmer were reduced while the debt repayment remained rigid so that farmers were forced to make their repayments out of capital. He argued that farming was an unusually unfavourable industry within which to contract fixed debt due to the many uncertainties of prices and vagaries of the weather, and to the long period between investment and receipts. [6]

The Colonial Administration became concerned with the farmers' credit problems during the period of the slump in 1921 and 1930s as the impoverished situation of the small scale settlers threatened the economic viability of the colony. In 1921 Northey pointed out that most of the settlers were "working on borrowed capital." He feared that many could not carry on as the banks were "no longer prepared to make advances." The banks had a habit of reducing credit on the smallest down turn of prices ; such credits were the life blood of farming. The 1921 crisis was shortlived. [7] The question was mentioned by members of the Ormsby Gore Commission of 1925, when they noted that complaints had been received concerning credit restrictions and the high rates of interest charged on advances. Also, banks charged eight per cent on good security on monthly balances and that ten per cent or even more was often charged, which resulted in the resort to private money lenders. [8]

The weakness of the petty bourgeoise colonial farmers financial welfare was hidden behind the high commodity prices during the 1920s. The Director of Agriculture had understood that "the margin between the cost of production and prices realized is great enough to yield a profitable return on farming pursuits generally in the Colony," but that "in the absence of these favourable conditions the farming community could not bear the comparatively high interest charges required by banks and mortgages." However, the weakness of the credit structure was not just the interest rate demands but the lack of adequate forms of credit required.

The available credit – providing agencies were firstly branches of British commercial banks – Barclays D.C.O., the Standard Bank of South Africa and the National Bank of India ; then there were the branches of British merchant banks, Arbuthnot Latham, Dalgety's Mitchell Cotts, John Gillatts, J. W. Milligan,

---

6. W. Liversage, *Land Tenure in the Colonies*, (Cambridge, 1945). Although the book is couched in general terms, Liversage's experience had been mainly confined to Kenya.

7. General Northey, the Governor to Secretary of State, 31 January 1921, Public Record Office (P.R.O.), C.O. 533/255.

8. July 1925, P.R.O., C.O 533/333/33909.

Jardine Matheson and Joseph Travers, who would advance loans in order to handle the producer's crop ; and finally there were the private money lenders, of which Shah Vershi Dershi, an Indian trader, was one of the largest, but there were many others.

This credit structure was not institutionally directed toward long term loans, as was pointed out by the Hall Commission of 1929. While short-term loans were available, long-term credit was not, yet it was this latter type of credit that was necessary for fencing, mechanical equipment and farm buildings, i.e. for fixed capital assets. The short-term loan was easily available from the commercial and merchant banks. Longer term loans were usually provided through mortgages, raised on commercial banks. The Hall Report emphasized the importance of adequate credit facilities.

> There is a pressing need for further credit facilities and we recommend the Government to institute a specific enquiry into the means whereby such facilities may be most safely and economically provided. [9]

By 1934, when the gravity of this problem had by this time been brought to the attention of everyone in the Administration, a report by the Board of Agriculture to the Carter Commission suggested ; (a) long-term credits of five years or more for permanent improvements, land purchase, etc., (b) intermediary credit of between nine months and five years to purchase livestock, implements and to maintain coffee until bearing, and (c) a short-term credit in the form of bills, overdrafts, etc., to even out seasonal variations in outgoings and receipts and to carry produce over the marketing period. [10] Up to 1929, the credit structure of the colony had developed without any government support beyond the protection of the banks as institutions ; the high level of debt had only been paid by the settlers in the 1920s due to the prevailing high produce prices.

III – THE FAILURE OF PRIVATE CREDIT AND THE DEPRESSION

The economic depression radically changed the credit worthiness of the European farmers. The first report of the Land and Agricultural Bank, in 1931, pointed to the problem. Referring to the previous decade they said :

> A justifiable optimism had led to a much ill-timed enthusiasm and even recklessness in putting capital into the land. The natural result was an inflated value placed upon land. [11]

The "ill-timed enthusiasm" had affected the Administration, the creditors and the white farmers alike. It took the *Kenya Weekly News* in February 1933 to spell out what the enthusiasm had entailed.

---

9. *Report of the Agricultural Commission*, (Government Printer, 1929), pp. 19 and 20.
10. "Report of the Board of Agriculture" in the *Kenya Land Commission Evidence and Memoranda, III*, London, 1934, 3082.
11. *Annual Report of the Land and Agricultural Bank of Kenya for 1931*, (Government Printer), p. 5.

> credit was on too lavish a scale... it was not discriminatory and... in a considerable degree it became related rather to the value of the land than to current production. [12]

The article blamed the government for the atmosphere of over-optimism, which they had fostered with protective duties and favourable railway rates. What had occurred and what no writer stated, was that land speculation during the 1920s had raised land prices beyond their productive capacity, in a groundswell of optimism and high produce prices. Credit had been assessed on the basis of land prices and not on its productive capacity, with the result that, when land prices fell, the debtors were left with debts which had become impossible for them to repay. As the *Weekly News* pointed out :

> The banks progressively curtailed the credit facilities previously granted and in some cases discontinued them. Private loans on mortgage became difficult to obtain. Those merchants who continued to extend advances on the security of crops did so on a restricted basis. [13]

The exact quantity of debt is hard to assess accurately. The coffee board suggested after careful investigation in 1933 that three quarters of the country's coffee growing settlers had a total debt of £1.4 million. Another committee in 1936 estimated that the total figure of debt for all the small settlers was over £3.0 million, which was roughly equal to the total value of domestic exports at the time. [14] The total figure of debt was probably much higher if we had the statistics for the "bourgeoise aristocratic settlers." Lord Delamere himself had a debt of £230 518 in 1931. [15] During the 1930s the price of land had collapsed and had left behind a level of debt among all the white farmers which threatened the future of white settlement in Kenya. All the facts pointed in the direction of the collapse of the export based economy of Kenya as a viable entity. But there was no collapse, settlerdom was assisted and supported by the Colonial and Imperial governments through a number of Ordinances which provided immediate financial aid, long-term capital loans and a stay order on creditors. [16]

IV – THE LAND BANK

The Land Bank saw the light of day in 1930 – just in time. It was such an obvious requirement for a rudimentary plantation economy that it is surprising at first that it took the onslaught of the Depression to bring it onto the scene. It was not a bank in the sense that it "manufactured money," nor was its function to mobilize local savings. The capital of the bank was raised from the London money

12. *KWN*, 17 February 1933, p. 14. See also *The Interim Report of the Agricultural Indebtedness Committee*, (Government Printer, 1936), p. 11.

13. *KWN*, 17 February 1933, under "Report of Committee appointed by Board of Agriculture to enquiry into the credit structure of farming."

14. For coffee indebtedness see R.H., Mss. Afr.s.596, File no. 4, and C.O. 533/461/38216, and "Coffee Board of Kenya Monthly Bulletin," February 1936, vol. 11, no. 14.

15. Ministry of Finance and Development 1/3755/39/465 ; K.N.A.

16. The bills to these laws can be found in the *Official Gazette*, 24 April 1928, pp. 361–388.

market on a Government guarantee, and the capital was lent out to local farmers at lower rates of interest and under different criteria than the Commercial houses and banks would lend in Kenya to farmers. [17]

Governor Northey had asked for a Land Bank in 1919 to assist the Soldier Settlement Scheme. Then in March 1921 he wrote to London :

> The world-wide depression in trade has hit the producers in this colony so hard during the last six months that the necessity for a Land Bank had become acute and I fear that, unless such a Bank can be established, many of them will be faced with bankruptcy.

In 1921 the *Leader,* a settler-based daily paper reported that the Convention of Associations had been given the full proposals for a Land Bank by Mr. Holm, the Director of Agriculture. These proposals had been worked out by the Treasury Department. The aim of the proposed Bank was "to assist the man who was in need of financial assistance." Mr. Holm pointed out that "there was no doubt that the establishment of the Bank was one of the chief factors in the Agricultural progress of South Africa," where he had previously worked in the Agricultural Department. [18]

Northey had asked the Colonial Office to raise £1 000 000. He continuously pressed them on this matter but the Crown Agents and the Treasury in England refused to raise £50 000, even to save the flax industry from dying, as they felt that the Colony's credit was overstrained. Hence the project was dropped.

The question of the Land Bank was brough up again in 1928 by the Administration. Meetings were held with officials of Barclay's and the Standard Bank of India, who were invited to cooperate in the venture. Both refused on the grounds that they did not want to be mixed up with local political controversy. [19] This viewpoint was held by most of the commercial interests operating in Kenya at this time. [20] The interests of the commercial houses and the small farmers were at variance ; the one arguing that the risks were considerable and so demanding high interest rates, and the other short of capital and needing low interest rates in order to be able to accumulate to sustain further growth. As long, therefore, as Sir E. Grigg, the Governor (1925 to 1930), did not want to drive out the existing private mortage companies as he had told the Crown Agents, the problem of accommodating the commercial companies to the Land Bank was

---

17. For a discussion on colonial banking, see W. T. Newlyn and D. C. Rowen, *Money and Banking in British Colonial Africa, A Study of the Monetary Systems of Eight British African Territories,* (Oxford Press, 1954), pp. 80–133.

18. *The Leader,* 11 January 1921, p. 21 ; Northey to Secretary of State commenting on the final draft of the Economic Commission, C.O. 533/214, and Northey to Secretary of State, 1921, C.O. 533/259, Northey to Secretary of State, 12 June 1921, over flax, C.O. 533/261.

19. Loc. cit.

20. E. A. Brett, "Development Policy in East Africa Between the Wars. A Study of the Political Influence Involved in the making of British Policy, 1919 to 1939," London, Ph. D., 1966.

insurmountable.[21] The problem was that the members of the Colonial Office did not understand these incompatible interests. They had been to immense pains to investigate the whole problem ; the settler representatives had been asked what they wanted, the question had been discussed with each commercial bank in turn,[22] and they had investigated the legal problem.[23] The Colonial Office had been dilatory in their whole approach to the problem of setting up a Land Bank in Kenya, their sensitivity to the interests and concern with minutiae had left the main recipients, the small settlers, out of consideration altogether, so that the *East African Standard* had some justification for commenting that :

> the history of the Land Bank movement is one of the most disappointing incidents in the history of Kenya during the last three or four years... Kenya is not equipped to finance its agricultural industry on a sound basis. The credits are either supported by London banks who admit that they do not want the business, or by merchant houses in London who restrict their facilities as soon as their position is affected by world wide factors.[24]

In 1930 the commercial banks' opposition to the Land Bank suddenly ended. The slump in prices left the banks with a large number of unprofitable creditors. The banks stopped loans and encouraged the formation of the Land Bank, which would ensure repayment of their outstanding debts.

The cautious pace of advance by the Colonial Office to provide finance had left the Administration in Kenya with no institutional means to provide aid to the small white farmer. Finance was found immediately from Government surpluses through the Agricultural Advances Ordinance of 1930. Government surpluses had been £707 976 in 1929, fell to £205 496 by 1933, and at this rate would have been quickly exhausted. The purpose of the measure was to give help to those who had "exhausted existing sources of credit."[25] The monies were to be used for "the payment of interest on mortgages and overdrafts" that is "where necessary to retain deserving farmers on their land to prevent foreclosure," which pleased the commercial banks. Only the most heavily in debt were to be left to the hands of their creditors.[26]

The rules of the Board were issued by Grigg, the Governor. These instructions were at variance with those originally approved by the Colonial Office. Under Grigg's rules the Board could provide up to 50% of the bills of creditors, so long as the other 50% should lie in abeyance for another three years ; applicants were to take no further credit ; the advances could pay off the mortgage or hire

21. Crown Agents to A.C.C. Parkinson, 28 October 1929, C.O. 532/388.

22. Loc. cit. ; this a large file concerned with the problem of setting up the bank and includes minutes of discussions with the interested parties.

23. C.O. 533/394/16000. This file is mainly concerned with the legal aspects of the Land Bank.

24. *EAS*, 11 October 1930, leading article.

25. The Central Agricultural Advances Board was appointed on 4 June 1930. The Board had £ 100 000 to lend. The Attorney General's statement of purpose to the legislative council is included in this file. C.O. 533/399/16164.

26. Ibid. : "Report by the Chairman of the Central Agricultural Advance Board."

purchase agreement ; and that repayment of advances or loans should wait two or three years until the farmers had recovered.[27] Grigg had tacitly accepted that there were conflicting interests between the small farmers and their creditors by protecting the one from the other, yet the issue was avoided and the creditor was guaranteed that he would eventually be paid by government. The point was that "foreclosure by the mortgage was an over present threat" and that the Board's security provided for the continuation of farming by the participants.[28]

After 1934 the Board stopped giving out new credit, and it was decided to wind up its operations. The Land Bank took over the administration of the scheme ; £119 000 was owing at this time ,and by 1937 this figure had only been reduced to £93 319. The Bank therefore, recommended that the interest charges should be waived in order that the outstanding debt could be collected.[29] The Agricultural Advances Amendment Ordinance of 1938 put this into effect. The reasons put forward were that some of the participants of the scheme had become more depressed after 1930 "owing to the long duration of the recession in prices of primary products, aggravated by droughts and locust infestations, and many participants are now faced with unduly large arrears of interest."[30] The Board had originally been a temporary measure, had become semi-permanent offering outdoor relief to indigent white settlers.

It is of interest to note the change of tactics of Sir Edward Grigg when he gave confidential evidence to the Hilton Young Commission in 1931, in relation to the rôle of private banks. He said :

> The end of private enterprise... is for many reasons now in sight, and the State must definitely step in if not only farming is to prosper, but the financial stability of both the Colonial Government and the Railway is to be assured. The economic position of the colony as a whole now turns on this necessity.

Grigg, perhaps more than any other governor since Northey, was an outright supporter of the small European settler. Unlike Northey he had a more profound grasp of their needs, and although he tried to defend all the various European interests, when pushed, the interests of the small farmers came first. He went on to define what he meant above : "In Kenya hitherto settlement has been entirely haphazard" as the settlers used their own capital and that of the Banks. But the,

> Banking system of Kenya has been carried far beyond the normal range of operations of a Commercial Bank... the banks take the view that further financing of farming on the present basis is not within their proper duties.[31]

27. Loc. cit.
28. *Annual Report of the Land and Agricultural Bank*, (Government Printer, 1934), p. 22.
29. Ibid., 1937, p. 4. The report showed the outstanding capital charges annually.
30. Agricultural Advances Amendment Bill, the *Official Gazette*, 22 Mars 1930, p. 169.
31. Evidence given by Sir E. Grigg to the Hilton Young Commission on the 17 March 1931. As the evidence was confidential it was not printed with the report, but can be found among the Passfield Papers held at the Library of the London School of Economics, vol. II, folio 407466.

Grigg was advocating state provision of credit as he recognized that the commercial houses had ceased to find the Kenya farmers a profitable enterprise.

It was, then, under these pressures that the Land Bank saw the light of day in 1930. The government of Kenya was authorized under the Ordinance to raise £240 000 from the City of London. The cash was raised at an interest of 4.7% and the bank was able to charge the farmers 6.5%. Within the first year of its operations 256 applications had been received requesting £417 000. Only 56 of these could offer a property as security unencumbered by a mortgage or other charges. In 1933 the capital of the bank was raised by £260 000 from another loan and in 1936 permission to raise another £500 000 was obtained.

By 1936, 542 mortgages had been registered with the banks ; this meant that the Bank had taken over the liability for the mortage deed. Prior to the establishment of the Land Bank "the amount which had been lent to the farmers is, in the opinion of the Board, in excess of 60% of today's value of the property." Thus the Bank's rôle, according to the 1932 report was "to persuade the mortgagee to accept a lesser sum for the release of the title deeds and be content with a second mortgage security for payment of any outstanding balance." [32]

A large proportion of the Bank's finances were used to buy out creditors, by 1938 the Bank had lent £834 489 to the small white farmers, and on its own accounting, £328 148 had been lent for the purpose of discharging existing mortgages. [33] The original purpose of the Bank had been subverted by the needs of the depression, and instead of being used as cheap credit for development purposes it was used to maintain the white settlers on their farms. The Land Bank does appear to have been successful in reducing rates of interest. The Bank Manager of the Bank of South Africa was staying with Paice in 1935 and told him that the rate of interest of overdrafts was being reduced from 8% to 6%. [34]

V – THE INEFFICIENT ECONOMY

The major failure in establishing the petty bourgeoise white settlers in Kenya before 1940 was the lack of suitable financial agencies. The gross insecurity which was behind the growth of racial bigotry, and which seems to have characterized all white settler colonies in Africa and elsewhere, was at heart based upon a grossly inadequate financial base. Let me add so that we can avoid oversimplicities, that racialism has cultural roots in the imperial nation, that the colony only provides the conditions in which it can flower and that once given these conditions racial ideology and racial structures become deeply imbedded into heart of the community. Here I am concerned with the "conditions" in Kenya which allowed racialism to flower.

32. *Land Bank Report, op. cit.*, 1932, p. 7.
33. Ibid ; these figures have been aggregated from the nine Annual Reports of the Bank.
34. The Paice Letters, citation 5, to his mother, 17 February 1935.

The financial insecurities of the small scale settlers were compounded by their lack of farming skills. The lack of finance and the lack of skill led directly to small scale single crop and mainly maize farming in the period up to 1940.

This lack of settler farming skills was mentioned by *the Leader* in February, 1922 in a farmer's supplement.[35] *The Leader* was a newspaper that supported the existence of the small white farmer, so that when they argued that farmers in Kenya were not using crop rotation methods of any kind and that yields on many farms were dropping drastically, it can be assumed that the newspaper was not being unnecessarily critical. The article in question pointed out that maize farmers should not be taking two crops off the same piece of land without a fallow period.

The Director of Agriculture expressed his serious reservations concerning one-crop farmers in his Annual Report of 1927 and 1928. He doubted the efficiency on "too large a proportion of holdings." "There are many," he pointed out, "who are not likely to succeed under any circumstances." But the high prices and the preferential railway rates for maize allowed one-crop farmers to survive. However the depression years hit these farmers very hard and leaders of European opinion began to recommend a movement towards mixed farming. In 1931 the *Kenya Weekly News*, a newspaper designed specifically for farmers, tried to institute essays on "The Practicability of Mixed Farming."

The Leader also argued at this time :

> It has now become a generally recognized fact that the greater part of the farming area of the Colony is not only pre-eminently suited for mixed farming but in a great many districts the turnover to mixed as opposed to single crop farming is the only feasible alternative to the recurrence of the present slump.[36]

Yet despite such protestations neither the settlers nor the administration had the necessary resources to initiate the change to mixed farming. By 1938 the administration was still asserting that the "future of agriculture in Kenya will be mixed crops and livestock farming. The bulk of the Highlands is suited to the system."[37]

The single cash crops was the major form of farming in Kenya up to 1940. It was a short-term method of land use as it left the grower open to all the hazards of crop failure due to climate or to the vagaries of the market. The single crop was mainly maize and as a method of farming it could not survive without consistent external supports.

Despite a number of allegations concerning the widespread nature of single crop farming among the Europeans, there was little statistical corroboration to support the assertions until 1929. In 1929 there were just over 1 000 maize

35. *The Leader*, 11 February 1922.

36. *KWN*, 13 February 1931, and *The Leader*, 12 June 1931 : see also the *Annual Agricultural Report*, 1927, 3–4, 1928, p. 5.

37. Agricultural Ministry Library ; "Memorandum of Agricultural Development in Kenya," January 1938.

growers which had dropped to 816 five years later, while the 931 coffee growers had increased to 993 by 1937. But it is difficult to know whether these figures illustrate the problem. All the circumstantial evidence points in this direction. There was, for instance, a schedule sent in to the Colonial Office concerning 73 farmers who had been given financial aid through central Agricultural Advances Board. Each farmer's crop was named, and only 22 farmers were producing up to two crops, maize and coffee, or maize and wheat, and then it was pointed out that most of these were producing 90% maize. [38]

Perhaps the most convincing evidence was produced by V. Liversage, the Government Agricultural Economist. Liversage was employed by the administration throughout the 1930s. Agricultural departments in England has begun to employ economists at about this time in order to increase efficiency, and Kenya was emulating the mother country. In 1936 Liversage undertook the first serious attempt to analyse the efficiency of the European economy.

Classification of the Production on European farms, 1936 (nos. of farms)

	Crops only	**Livestock only**	**Mixed crops & livestock**	**No development**	**Total**
Small farms	264	116	125	85	590
Others	687	135	395		1,217
Total	951	251	520	85	1,807
% of Total	52%	14%	29%	5%	100%

This table summarizes Liversage's findings. He classified 264 holdings as small on the grounds that the value of their output was unlikely to exceed £500 per annum and "would not support the kind of settlement in which occasional home leave, education of children abroad, an annual holiday at the coast, club membership and bar bills and a motor car of recent model is visualised." He argued that these farmers would benefit by extended credit facilities. The holdings devoted to stock or crops alone were more open to the fluctuations of market prices than were the mixed farms. Not included in the above table were 179 farms which had been abandoned, which together with the 85 which were virtually unused, give a total by 1936 of 264 farms which had been taken up but not been brought into production. The figure is illustrative of the poor use to which most of the Highlands had been put. [39]

Liversage also wrote an unpublished manuscript after he left the administration's service. This work is primarily concerned with the methods of marketing controls in Kenya in 1930s and early 1940s, but in it Liversage took his analysis of the European economy in 1936 a step further ; pointing to the gross inefficiency

38. C.O. 533/23047 *passim.*

39. Memorandum, "The State of European Agriculture in Kenya," 1936, *African Affairs,* 10/7/1427/1, KNA, Liversage, "What is Wrong with European Agriculture in Kenya," in *The East African Agricultural Journal,* October 1945, pp. 80 and 82.

and lack of everyday knowledge of many of the farmers, to the competition of the European products with the products of farmers in Europe and, as in the 1936 article, to the poor output of the European farmers in Kenya.

He pointed out that a stranger to the country would find "dairy farmers who did not know how to milk, arable farmers who depended on native headmen to organize their work and get it done." Liversage describes these men not so much as "amateur farmers" but as "amateur capitalists." He was pointing towards one of the important characteristics of Kenya settler farmers. Few settlers would undertake any manual work. One settler for instance, noted that ninety-nine per cent of the settlers "do not work." He wondered if this fact was due to the sun's rays, which was the commonly held belief! Living at 6 000 feet was said to impose "a great strain on the organism of people" (white people) and the "effects of the vertical rays of the sun and of certain radiations" were thought to preclude all physical exertion in case of dire consequences. Such beliefs were a suitable rationalization to avoid physical effort and were the background to the low standard of farming knowledge.

Liversage gave the impression that, while some plantations and general farms were well managed, the majority of private farms were grossly inefficient. There were dairy farms without hand-reared calves, wheat growers without rotations and small tea, flax and pyrethrum growers who had failed to maintain their soil fertility.[40] He argued that many of the farm products, such as wheat, maize, potatoes, livestock, dairy produce and wool were competing with the products of temperate climates, while also dealing with transport costs. Australia and New Zealand produced wheat and butter, but using family labour with a high level of skill. Kenyan farmers, on the other hand, used labour which was both poorly paid and unskilled. He concluded "the important factor was undoubtedly the low level of knowledge, skill and industry on the part of the majority of the farmers and the high standard of living expected." This should have led to farming on a large scale, yet his own analysis of farm size against output had shown that half of the general farms were not self-supporting.[41]

In quite another context, Leggett had argued along similar lines. He had shown that the average coffee planter was producing between fourteen and twenty tons a year. But, he pointed out,

> it it impossible for a twenty ton crop to pay for skilled management and leave a profit. It seems that a large proportion of the total planting has been in small patches and some of it on doubtful soil. Quite half the total crop is of very poor quality... and is produced at a working loss.

Leggett wanted the industry "nationalized" in order to reduce its overheads by this he meant that it should be organized through joint stock companies.[42]

40. "Trusteeship in Africa," (n.d.) written in 1945, pp. 147–150, R.H., Mss. Afr.s. 5102, pp. 147–150.

41. Ibid., pp. 150–160.

42. Leggett, Memorandum presented to the *Joint Select Committee on Closer Union*, (HMSO, 1931), vol. 3, Appendices 10 and 57.

While Leggett's argument was definitely slanted to make his point, there is a Board of Agriculture report to the Colonial Office to the effect that "the acreage of the typical coffee plantation may be taken to be 160 acres of bearing coffee with an output of forty tons." It continues,

> The coffee industry has been largely built up by the small man with a small capital, who, as soon as his plantation has reached the producing stage, has found it necessary to borrow capital to meet incalculable expenses. [43]

CONCLUSION

The depression in Kenya had thrown into sharp relief the problem of introducing plantation farming into Kenya. Between 1936 and 1940 many of the smaller white farmers abandoned their farms due to lack of any means and under pressure from mortgages. When C. E. Mortimer, the Agricultural Commissioner for Land and Settlement visited the Uasin Gishu and Trans Nzoia in 1937 (the areas of settlement immediately after the 1914–1918 war), he was "impressed by the large area of undeveloped and unoccupied farms." In some instances he noted, "the farms appeared to be partially developed and abandoned ; in others no sign of development could be discovered." Mortimer thought that in some cases commercial banks and large companies in England had taken them over and were "merely holding out for a rise in land prices." This was the old situation of "land speculation" which had apparently been so common in the 1920s, reasserting itself. The Delamere estates in Laikipia were a particularly bad example of a completely undeveloped farm ; another was the estate of Lord Howard of Walden who owned 24 241 acres, "as a sort of private game reserve" which was completely undeveloped. [44] These two examples were not representative as they were people of the richer settlers. Mortimer's survey in 1937 showed that 348 estates had failed, of which over 200 came from the Uasin Gishu and Trans Nzoia areas. Of the 348 estates, 191 were smaller than 1 000 acres and only 57 were larger than 2 500 acres. [45] It was the smaller estates which had collapsed during the depression despite all the efforts to revive them.

It would appear from this account that white settlement in Kenya had all but failed and in fact this was the case. But the war from 1939, the introduction of Lend-Lease, and even more direct settler participation in the Administration provided the necessary political conditions for a massive injection of cash and

43. *Report from the Kenya Board of Agriculture, 1931*, C.O. 533/411/17182.

44. In Land Office Archives Nairobi (L.O.), 11093. "Outspans and Stock Routes," Stockowners conference 10–11th March, 1936. L.O. 31530 *passim* ; Mortimer to PC Rift Valley, L.O. 22420, 19 April 1937 and subsequent letters especially D.C. Laikipia to P.C. Nakuru, 4 October 1939, regarding Delamere, L.O. 22420. A note on Lord Howard of Walden's land (L.O. 31530, II, 59). See also in these three files, 31530, I, II, IV, "Precis for Executive Council re revision of Underdeveloped lands," 1st August 1929, and Minutes of 71st meeting of the Advisory Land Board, 1st March, 1937. These are just a few of the documents dealing with the undeveloped farms at the end of the 1930s.

45. The results of the 1937 have been compiled by the author from the individual schedules of each farm to be found in L.O. 31530, I, II, III.

technology. Since 1941 the large farm sector in Kenya has prospered to the extent that the big farms have simply not survived to this day, but despite all the changes which have occurred over the last 30 years are still considered essential to the export led farming sector.

The full story of settlement in Kenya is more complex and more subtle than I have accounted for here. The settlers in Kenya were tough and brutal, as settlers everywhere tend to be, due to the marginal social and physical conditions under which thew have to exist. It is not at all surprising that they chose a form of social Darwinism as their creed. The years of settlement up to 1940 in Kenya have the same feel of economic violence and brutality as one sometimes has about the 17th and 18th centuries in British history. In a somewhat crude sense both represent a period of primitive pre-industrial capitalism where the potential bourgeoise and the petty bourgeoise struggled to exploit the local people to the utmost of their ability. The comparison is limited of course, as the people of the 20th century have had the financial and technical means available to avoid this initial period altogether ; in fact the initial period of struggle to provide the base for capital accumulation lasted a mere 40 years in Kenya, and if European ideas had not been so rigid it might have been avoided altogether.

But such thoughts do not aid the process of understanding the recent past. The stresses and strains of the colonial settler societies further south in Rhodesia and South Africa seem to have had a similar quality to them. Doris Lessing's rightly famous works have the same feel of poverty and brutality. The precondition for the firm establishment of a settler petty bourgeoise landed class was massive government support, and it needed a war of the dimensions of the 1939–45 period to bring in the rationalization of colonial settler production. The war created the conditions for the convergence of the interests of the Imperial power, the Colonial authority and the settler producers. The post 1945 era for the settlers was to provide an entirely new experience, of new prosperity and new conflicts.

DEPRESSION, DUST BOWL, DEMOGRAPHY, AND DROUGHT: THE COLONIAL STATE AND SOIL CONSERVATION IN EAST AFRICA DURING THE 1930s

DAVID ANDERSON

THE STRONG INFLUENCE of colonial agrarian policies on the process of decolonization in Eastern Africa has been recognized by historians for some time. Most recently, David Throup has emphasized the role of the anti-terracing campaigns in Kikuyuland during the 1940s in furthering the cause of the Mau Mau movement, while almost twenty years ago Lionel Cliffe stressed the close correlation between the enforcement of agricultural change in Tanganyika and the growth of organized nationalism.[1] Similarly in Uganda, rural protest, significant between the wars in the Bataka movement, played a part in the campaign for political independence.[2] The 'second colonial occupation', as it has been called, with its 'do good' justification for meddling in African agriculture, heightened political consciousness by giving African farmers something to complain about.

The colonial state may have been correct in its policies, and wise to resort to compulsion, but it failed to show the farmer what tangible benefits the conservation effort would bring on the land, and rarely could it provide an adequate incentive for this effort. While this view of the failure of colonial agrarian reform is now well understood, much less attention has been given to the process by which these new policies emerged. Before the outbreak of the Second World War a number of factors had already acted to persuade administrators in London, and in the colonies, that the agrarian condition of East Africa demanded drastic action. This article examines why these new policies evolved during the 1930s, and investigates the complex manner in which each of the various levels of the colonial administration came to play a part in their formulation.

The author is a Research Fellow in History at New Hall, Cambridge. Earlier versions of this article were discussed at a workshop on 'Conservation Policy in Africa' at Queen Elizabeth House, Oxford, and by the East African Studies seminar at the African Studies Centre, Cambridge, whose comments are all gratefully acknowledged.

1. D. W. Throup, 'The Governorship of Sir Philip Mitchell in Kenya, 1944–1952', unpub. Ph.D. thesis, Cambridge 1983, esp. chapters 3, 6 and 8; L. Cliffe, 'Nationalism and the Reaction to Enforced Agricultural Change in Tanganyika during the Colonial Period', in L. Cliffe and J. Saul (eds), *Socialism in Tanzania: An Interdisciplinary Reader* (EAPH, Nairobi, 1972), pp. 17–24. See also D. A. Low and J. M. Lonsdale, 'Introduction: Towards the New Order 1945–1963', in D. A. Low and Alison Smith (eds), *The Oxford History of East Africa*, iii (Oxford, 1976), pp 45–46
2. C. C. Wrigley, *Crops and Wealth in Uganda* (East African Institute of Social Research, Kampala 1959), pp. 52–55 and 80–81. Also his 'Changes in the East African Society', pp. 515–516, and C. Gertzel, 'Kingdoms, Districts and the Unitary State: Uganda 1945–1962', pp. 67–69, both in D. A. Low and Alison Smith (eds) *History of East Africa, iii*.

It was during the 1930s that the British administration in the East African territories first began to take an active interest in the patterns and methods of African agrarian production. This interest was initially prompted by the desire to increase African agricultural production, as a way of meeting some of the difficulties of the Depression, but rapidly became preoccupied with the apparent threat posed to the productive capacity of African lands by overcrowding, overproduction, and soil erosion. As the decade moved on, the question of the conservation of the natural resources of the colonies became a more important subject of concern, and attention to it contributed to a very fundamental shift in colonial policy, towards the development of rural East Africa. By 1938, both the Colonial Office in London and the administrators in East Africa were committed to a policy of direct intervention in the husbandry practices of African farmers and herders, in any circumstance where it was feared that these practices might be detrimental to the long-term productivity of the land. The period 1930 to 1938, when the passive principles of 'indirect rule' began to give way in colonial thinking to a more active and interventionist strategy of administration, is therefore crucial to any explanation of African response to colonial rule in the years leading up to Independence.[3] In particular, if we are to understand the role of rural protest in the process of decolonisation, we must first come to grips with the changes in colonial attitudes towards African agrarian production during the 1930s. The first tinkerings with the mechanism of agrarian production before 1939 formed the embryo of what were to become the large-scale development projects of the post-war years. The Betterment Campaigns, Land Utilization Schemes, and Rehabilitation Projects which absorbed the energies and funds of the local administration and the metropolitan resources provided under the Colonial Development and Welfare Act during the 1940s and 1950s, should be seen as a direct consequence of those policies devised before the war.

Four major factors worked to encourage the move towards policies of intervention in African agriculture: the economic reassessments brought about in the colonies, as elsewhere, by the Depression of the early 1930s; the international alarm generated by the catastrophic experience of the southern plains of America in the Dust Bowl, at its height in 1935; the recognition during the 1930s that rapid increase in the human and stock populations of the African Reserves was creating serious pressure on the land; and, finally, the fear that

3. On the moves towards colonial reforms during the 1930s, see R. D. Pearce, *Turning Point in Africa: British Colonial Policy, 1938–1948* (Cass, London, 1982); P. Hetherington, *British Paternalism and Africa, 1920–1940* (Càss, London, 1978); D. J. Morgan, *The Official History of Colonial Development*, vol 1 (Macmillan, London 1980), pp. 14–63; R. Robinson, 'The Moral Disarmament of African Empire, 1919–1947', *Journal of Imperial and Commonwealth History*, **8** (1979/80), pp. 86–104. Recent debate in this journal has examined the connections between pre-war reforms and post-war decolonization; see J. Flint, 'Planned Decolonization and its Failure in British Africa', *African Affairs*, **82**, no. 328 (July 1983), pp. 389–411, and the reply by R. D. Pearce, 'The Colonial Office and Planned Decolonization in Africa', *African Affairs*, **83**, no. 330 (January 1984), pp. 77–94.

the apparently increasing incidence of drought conditions in many parts of East Africa over the period 1926 to 1935 indicated that the region was becoming progressively more arid. The relative influence of each of these factors naturally varied between the three British East African territories, depending upon differences in political, economic and environmental circumstances, but they combined to shape an essential backcloth to the agrarian reforms worked out by the eve of the Second World War.

The Depression

The Depression struck savagely at the economies of all the African colonies from 1929 until 1935, affecting both European settler agriculture and African production. Many European settlers in Kenya and Tanganyika came near to bankruptcy as their export markets collapsed, and only the resilience of the sisal planters and the slow but steady recovery of coffee prices offered hope for the survival of the settler farming sector.[4] The vast majority of white settlers lacked the reserves of capital necessary to withstand the slump, and so met their crisis politically, rather than economically, by pressuring the government to prop up their production with subsidies and forms of protection. By exposing the weakness of the settler economy, the years of the Depression generated a wider debate that questioned the very validity of the settler position in East Africa. Not surprisingly, in responding to the Depression the settler communities adopted a defensive posture, and especially in the case of Kenya, they actively campaigned to establish greater security for their status and long-term position in the colony.[5] The focus of white settler anxiety during the Depression was therefore the legitimacy of European land ownership, the very keystone of white settlement. The appointment of the Kenya Land Commission in 1933 presented a direct challenge to the settler community to justify their position, while also offering the opportunity to entrench their claim to unalienable rights to land ownership. It was in the arena of the Kenya Land Commission that the first skirmishes over African land use were fought.

Although the Commission was intended to establish that adequate provision had been made in Kenya for the land needs of the African population, criticism of indigenous patterns of land use and African farming practices became prominent in the enquiry. These issues were brought to the fore as the settlers

4. E. A. Brett, *Colonialism and Underdevelopment in East Africa: The Politics of Economic Change 1919–1939* (Heinemann, London 1973), pp. 184–185; C. C. Wrigley, 'Kenya: The Patterns of Economic Life, 1902–1945', in V. Harlow and E. M. Chilver (eds), *The Oxford History of East Africa*, ii (Oxford 1965), pp. 247–250; N. Westcott, 'The East African Sisal Industry, 1929–1949: The Marketing of a Colonial Commodity during Depression and War', mimeo, (London, September 1983); M. F. Hill, *Planters Progress* (Coffee Board of Kenya, Nairobi 1956).
5. On the Kenya settlers and the depression, see, C. C. Wrigley, 'Kenya: The Patterns of Ecomonic Life', pp. 247–260; G. Bennett, 'Settlers and Politics in Kenya, up to 1945', in V. Harlow and E. M. Chilver (eds), *Oxford History of East Africa*, ii pp. 318–328; M. G. Redley, 'The Politics of a Predicament: The White Community in Kenya 1918–1932', unpub. Ph.D. thesis, Cambridge 1976, chs 10 and 11; P. Mosley, *The Settler Economies: Studies in the Economic History of Kenya and Southern Rhodesia 1900–1963* (Cambridge 1983), pp. 178–180.

fought a political battle to prevent the African Reserves being extended at the expense of the White Highlands.[6] African husbandry was typically stigmatized as wasteful and deleterious to the soil, and settler witnesses before the Commission commonly expressed concern that soil erosion might spread from African lands, where they could already identify it as a potentially serious problem, to the white-owned farm lands. In fact, many parts of the White Highlands were already experiencing soil exhaustion and declining fertility as a result of overproduction through cereal monoculture.[7] But in the settler view this was not where the problem lay. Instead, they drew attention to the large numbers of African 'squatters' occupying European-owned farms, and particularly the illegal and uncontrolled movement of Africans onto farms left unoccupied as a result of the Depression.[8] The actual cause of land degradation was less important to the settlers than was the politicization of the whole question of African land use; the point was, quite simply, that if the African could not manage the land he had, where was the sense in giving him more land to abuse? Having put forward their view that African husbandry placed the fertility of the Kenyan soil under threat, the settler community further argued that, in the stringent days of the Depression, they lacked the finance to cope with the problem themselves, and therefore that government should accept the burden of responsibility. The Kenya Arbor Society, formed in 1934, joined the many settler Farming Associations in bombarding the administration with pleas for action against the evils of African husbandry. Conservation of the soil became the overt issue after 1933, but behind this lay the emotive question of the sanctity of the White Highlands. Settler concern was not purely environmental, and was only given expression because of the need to meet the economic crisis of the Depression.[9]

6. The findings of the Commission are presented in the *Kenya Land Commission (Carter) Report*, Cmd. 4556 (1934), but the *Kenya Land Commission: Evidence and Memoranda*. 3 volumes (Nairobi 1934), is a more useful account of the proceedings. For a clear example of the settler view, see pp. 3295–3300: evidence of Capt. The Hon. H. F. Ward, 're: Additional Land for Natives'. For a study of the Land Commission see R. M. Breen, 'The Politics of Land: the Kenya Land Commission, 1932–1933, and its effects on land policy in Kenya', unpub. Ph.D. thesis, Michigan State University 1976.

7. *Kenya Land Commission: Evidence*, pp. 1803–1805, evidence of the Solai Farmers Association: pp 1815–1818, evidence of Maj. F. D. Boyce, representing the Sabukia Farmers Association; pp. 1876–1878, evidence of the Eldama Ravine Farmers Association; pp. 1789–1790, Secretary's Precis, commenting on European cereal farming. On maize monoculture, see V. Liversage, 'Official Economic Management in Kenya 1930–1945', typescript 1945, Rhodes House Mss. Afr. s. 510; and Liversage to Director of Agriculture, January 1936, Kenya National Archives (KNA) CNC/10/4.

8. *Kenya Land Commission: Evidence,* pp. 2072–2074, evidence of E. G. Whittall; pp. 2410–2415, evidence of Maj. R. M. Dunbar; pp. 3313–3322, evidence of H. D. Hill. On squatters see, R. M. van Zwanenberg, *Colonial Capitalism and Labour in Kenya, 1919–1939* (EALB, Nairobi 1975), pp. 215–221. R. M. van Zwanenberg and A. King, *An Economic History of Kenya and Uganda, 1800–1970* (Macmillan, London 1975), p. 39, estimate that 20 per cent of European farms were left unoccupied during the depression.

9. *Kenya Land Commission: Evidence*, p. 1786, Secretary's Precis, clearly stated what the settlers saw as the most crucial principle in the issue of African land use. Although acknowledging that only 'barren, rocky, waterless land was left for the natives' in the Baringo District, the Commissioners were advised that: 'There is one principle which should be here affirmed before

The slump in commodity prices also hit hard at African producers. The steady trend of the 1920s, which had seen the prices for most African crops improve significantly, notably maize in Kenya and cotton in Uganda, came to an abrupt end. This much Africans and European settlers shared, yet whereas the settler response to this crisis was defensive, the response of many African producers was essentially aggressive. With only limited margins of profit to be gained even from most cash crop production, and influenced by many factors other than price, African farmers continued to increase their cultivated acreages throughout the years of the Depression. Sometimes this expansion of production was stimulated by government encouragement, in other cases it was a more independent response to local economic conditions.[10] Kitching and Mosley have each illustrated the point that the 1930s was a decade during which African cultivation in Kenya increased significantly, with producers able to ride out depression, often by enlarging their activities in local markets.[11] This parallels the experience of Uganda, where cotton and coffee acreages continued to increase slowly through the early 1930s, rising more dramatically after 1934, and also the case of Tanganyika, where the government encouraged regional self-sufficiency in food crops with its 'Plant-More-Crops' campaign. In their response to the Depression the governments of Uganda and Tanganyika had fewer alternatives than their Kenya counterparts. Cotton cultivation was already expanding dramatically in Uganda, and as Wrigley has shown, it was not easy for the African producer to respond quickly to fluctuations in the price received for his crops. By maintaining the expansion of cotton through the early 1930s the Ugandan economy recovered reasonably speedily as the Depression lifted.[12] The Tanganyika administration, lacking an economically important African grown export crop, attempted to avoid the need for imports of foodstuffs by encouraging greater local production.[13]

considering what solutions may be sought: It is that Government has been responsible for the mistake and that the cost, whatever it may be, of providing sufficient land and water for the natives concerned ought and must be provided by Government'. On the strong conservation lobby in Kenya during the 1930s, see the *Annual Report of the Kenya Arbor Society, 1936 and 1937,* in KNA PC/RVP.6A/11/26, and R. Ward, *Deserts in the Making: A Study of the Causes and Effects of Soil Erosion* (Kenya Arbor Society, Nairobi 1937), in PRO CO 533/483/6.

10. R. M. van Zwanenberg and A. King, *Ecomonic History of Kenya and Uganda*, pp. 208–213; K. Ingram, 'Tanganyika: Slump and Short-term Governors, 1932–1945', in V. Harlow and E. M. Chilver (eds) *Oxford History of East Africa*, ii, pp. 596–598; 'Greater Production in Kenya: Government Campaign in the Native Reserves', *East African Weekly*, 26 November 1931.

11. G. Kitching, *Class and Economic Change in Kenya: The Making of an African Petite-Bourgeoisie* (Yale UP, London 1980), ch. 4; P. Mosley, *The Settler Economies*, ch. 3 and Conclusion. See also I. D. Talbott, 'Agricultural Innovation and Policy Changes in Kenya in the 1930's', unpub. Ph.D. West Virginia 1976.

12. C. C. Wrigley, *Crops and Wealth*, pp. 59–61; J. Vincent, *Teso in Transformation* (Univ. of California, Berkeley 1982), pp. 210–211; V. Jamal, 'The Role of Cotton and Coffee in Uganda's Economic Development', unpub. Ph.D. thesis, Stanford 1976, p. 31, for cotton prices through the colonial period; and for a broader view, C. Ehrlich, 'The Uganda Economy, 1903–1945', in V. Harlow and E. M. Chilver (eds), *Oxford History of East Africa*, ii, pp. 455–469.

13. J. Iliffe, *A Modern History of Tanganyika* (Cambridge 1979), pp. 301–305, 342–345, and 349; N. J. Westcott, 'The Impact of the Second World War on Tanganyika, 1939–1949', unpub. Ph.D. thesis, Cambridge 1982, ch. 2; K. Ingram, 'Tanganyika: Slump and Short-term Governors', pp. 596–597.

The years of the Depression therefore worked to emphasize the potential, and often very real antagonism between the settler farming economy and African agrarian production. In the settler perception, the African economy continued to press in on him, at a time when his own economy was under threat. This antagonism became manifest in many ways, but the issue of land use and conservation took on greater importance as settlers tried to stake claim to the land in the face of an expanding African agrarian frontier. The cause of the European settler in East Africa was not helped by the realization that, in many respects, African agrarian production in Uganda and Tanganyika withstood the rigours of the Depression better than did the settler dominated economy of Kenya. This did not escape the notice of the Colonial Office, and was a matter that troubled the Kenya settlers, who came to fear that their security as a community was under greater threat than ever, and that their control over the utilization of land in Kenya needed to be further bolstered if the fragile resources of the soil were to be preserved.[14]

Images of the Dust Bowl

The devastation that could be brought about by erosion of the soil was forcefully demonstrated by the experience of North America in the 'Dust Bowl' of the 1930s. Through the reports of newspapers and magazines the images of the agricultural wasteland of the southern plains of America, an area that had previously been rich farmland, reached East Africa. Pamphlets and books alerting people to the dangers of erosion and instructing them on methods of soil conservation began to arrive in East Africa before 1930. This copious literature, much of it emanating directly from the United States Department of Agriculture's Soil Conservation Service, under the guidance of Hugh Bennett,[15] seemed to have particular relevance to the overcrowded African Reserves of Kenya, to heavily populated parts of upland Tanganyika, and to many intensively cropped areas of Uganda. Several of these publications were produced in the late 1920s, the most famous being Bennett and Chapline's popular study, *Soil Erosion, a National Menace.*[16] Such studies warned

14. For a full discussion of the sharp differences between Kenya and her two neighbours over the inter-war period, see E. A. Brett, *Colonialism and Underdevelopment in East Africa,* chs. 6 and 7.

15. The impact of this American literature is clear in the early Kenyan pamphlets on soil erosion; V. A. Beckley, *Soil Deterioration in Kenya* (Kenya Department of Agriculture Bulletin, no. 4 of 1930), and by the same author, *Soil Erosion* (Kenya Department of Agriculture Bulletin, no. 1 of 1935). For the impact on Central and Southern Africa, see J. McCracken, 'Experts and Expertise in Colonial Malawi', *African Affairs,* **81,** no. 322, pp. 110–114; and W. Beinart, 'Soil Erosion, Conservationism, and Ideas About Development in Southern Africa', paper presented at the workshop on 'Conservation Policy in Africa' at Queen Elizabeth House, Oxford, October 1983. For a biography of Bennett, see W. Brink, *Big Hugh* (Macmillan, New York 1951).

16. H. H. Bennett and W. R. Chapline, *Soil Erosion, a National Menace* (United States Department of Agriculture, Civ. 33. 1928). Later publications by Bennett were equally influential, see *Soil Conservation* (New York 1939), *Our American Land. The Story of its Abuse and its Conservation* (United States Department of Agriculture, Misc. Pub. No. 596, 1946), and (with W. C. Pryor) *This Land We Defend* (New York 1942).

against the possible dangers of over-taxing the soil, and as the story of the Dust Bowl unfolded between 1930 and 1936, the horrific prophecy of these writings came surging home to observers everywhere. Because of the Dust Bowl soil erosion was not only viewed as a serious national problem, but became the first global environmental problem. The grand scale of the issue was portrayed in articles appearing in learned journals and farming periodicals throughout the 1930s, under such evocative titles as *Erosion and the Empire* and *Soil Erosion in Tropical Africa*, and most vividly of all in Jacks and Whyte's book *Rape of the Earth.*[17]

These images compounded the concern of the Kenya settler over the land issue, and caused Agricultural Officers all over British Africa to examine their own localities for signs of this menace. In a sense, it became fashionable to be aware of soil erosion, and the zeal with which many young officers pursued the problem is testimony to the fact that the acquisition of a Diploma in Agriculture came to have a knowledge of this aspect of agricultural science as one of its essential requirements. Armed with their new perceptions, this small cadre of Agricultural Officers quickly identified the danger areas of East Africa—Kondoa and Sukumaland in Tanganyika, Kitui and Baringo in Kenya, and Teso and Kigezi in Uganda.[18] Others would be added to this list later, and in each case the prevention of soil erosion was to be a prime justification for interfering in customary patterns of African land use. In the case of Kenya, the cause was given the active and vociferous support of the settler community, while in Uganda and Tanganyika, as we shall see, the issue was taken up with rather more caution.

As well as the American influence, the conservation lobby in Southern Africa encouraged the East African administrations to tackle the problem of land degradation. Links of kinship and camaraderie drew the settler colonies of Eastern and Southern Africa together, and Kenya's settlers were never reluctant to draw upon the example of South Africa. Recommendations made by the South African Drought Commission of 1922 for legislation to control many aspects of African husbandry were reiterated to the Kenya Land Commission in 1933, and in particular the 'firm hand' advocated by the South African Com-

17. G. C. Watson, 'Erosion and the Empire', *East African Agricultural Journal*, (1936), pp. 305–308; H. C. Sampson, 'Soil Erosion in Tropical Africa', *Rhodesian Agricultural Journal*, **33**, (1936), pp. 197–205; G. V. Jacks and R. O. Whyte, *The Rape of the Earth: A World Survey of Soil Erosion* (Faber and Faber, London 1939); and many others. The best study of the Dust Bowl is D. Worster, *Dust Bowl: The Southern Plains in the 1930s* (Oxford UP, 1979).

18. *Tanganyika Territory Annual Report, 1934*, Appendix VI, 'Measures taken in various Provinces, 1933 and 1934, in connexion with soil erosion', pp. 171–176; 'Soil Erosion in Tanganyika Territory: A Brief Account of the Problem, the Prime Causal Factors, and some suggested lines of cure and prevention', from the Informal Conference at Dodoma, 16 May 1929, CO 822/26/9; C. Maher, '*Soil Erosion and Land Utilisation in the Ukamba (Kitui) Reserve*' (Nairobi 1937), and '*Soil Erosion and Land Utilisation in the Kamasia, Njemps, and East Suk Reserves*', (Nairobi 1937); *Report of the Teso Informal Committee* (Department of Agriculture, Entebbe 1937); C. C. Wrigley, *Crops and Wealth*, pp. 65–66; For a brief general survey of early conservation measures in East Africa, see Lord Hailey, *An African Survey* (HMSO, London, revised 1956), pp. 1036–1048.

mission was applauded by Kenya's settlers.[19] The South African Soil Erosion Conference of 1929, and the creation of a Soil Erosion Council in the Union, resulted in the implementation of anti-erosion schemes by 1933. These schemes were under taken on European farm land, with heavy subsidy from the State, in precisely the manner which the Kenya settlers wished their own government to adopt. South African influence was therefore important, but practices and policies in South Africa were themselves guided to a large extent by the American experience.[20] The crucial aspect of both the South African and the American examples lay in the willingness of the State to enforce better husbandry through legislation.

Demographic Pressure

The need to enforce conservation measures was given greater urgency during the 1930s by the realization that the population of East Africa was increasing rapidly. Demographic statistics for the region are notoriously unreliable, but it is clear that after a period of stagnation (or even decline), the populations of all three East African territories began to increase in the mid-1920s, growing more dramatically in the 1930s.[21] The population of Uganda would seem to have begun a slow increase after 1923, with the period 1927 to 1933 marking a very alarming climb from estimates of 3·1 million to 3·6 million. A slower, but steady rate of increase continued until the end of the 1930s.[22] Broader estimates suggest a 25 per cent increase between 1918 and 1936, while Hailey puts forward a less conservative figure of 60 per cent for the years 1921 to 1948.[23] These figures take on a gloomier significance when linked to the greater areas of land being placed under cultivation. Reports from the Uganda Department of Agriculture indicate that land pressure was most severe in

19. *Interim Report of the South African Drought Investigation Committee, April 1922* (Govt. Printer, Cape Town 1922), reprinted in M. Glantz (ed), *Desertification: Environmental Degradation in and around Arid Lands* (Westview Press, Boulder, Colorado 1977), pp. 233–274. Also *The Report of the Native Economic Commission, Union of South Africa, 1930–1932* (Govt. Printer, Pretoria 1932); *Kenya Land Commission: Evidence,* pp. 3295–3300: evidence of Capt. The Hon. H. F. Ward.

20. W. Beinart, 'Soil Erosion, Conservationism, and Ideas About Development', pp. 11–16; Lord Hailey, *An African Survey,* pp. 1016–1017; J. C. Ross, *Land Utilization and Soil Conservation in the Union of South Africa* (Pretoria 1947), passim; 'National Fight Against Soil Erosion in South Africa', *East African Standard,* 8 March 1930.

21. Much of the following discussion is based on the data assembled in R. R. Kuczynski, *Demographic Survey of the British Colonial Empire, ii* (Institute of International Affairs, Oxford 1949), chs 7–10; C. J. Martin, 'Some Estimates of the General Age, Distribution, Fertility and Rate of Natural Increase of the African Population of British East Africa', *Population Studies,* 7, (1953/54), pp. 181–199; and J. E. Goldthorpe, 'The African Population of East Africa: A Summary of its Past and Present Trends', Appendix 7, *Report of East African Royal Commission, 1953–1955,* Cmd. 9475 (HMSO, London 1955), pp. 462–473.

22. R. R. Kuczynski, *Demographic Survey,* ii, pp. 239–240. C. J. Martin, 'Some Estimates of the General Age ... ', calculates that the annual rate of natural increase over the period 1931 to 1948 was 1·4 per cent. This is quoted in the *Report of the East African Royal Commission,* p. 31.

23. J. D. Tothill, *A Report on 19 Surveys done in small Agricultural Areas in Uganda, with a view to ascertaining the position with regard to Soil Deterioration* (Department of Agriculture, Entebbe 1938), pp. 5–6; Lord Hailey, *An African Survey,* p. 1046.

areas where population increase could be correlated with an expansion of the cultivated acreage.[24] This was true of Teso, where cotton cultivation had been expanded while livestock holdings had also become greater, and in Kigezi, where local migration contributed to an estimated population increase of 75 per cent between 1931 and 1948.[25] These calculations are, of course, imprecise, and few sources agree as to the exact rate of growth or the actual levels of population, yet the upward trend of the decade is unmistakable.

A similar, though less spectacular pattern, has been presented for Tanganyika, where population increase was identified from 1928. An estimated population of 4·1 million in 1921, gradually climbed to 5·2 million by the eve of the Second World War.[26] The effect of this trend on land use was perhaps more localized than in Uganda, and with more land available for expansion the 'Plant-More-Crops' campaign went ahead. The frontiers of cultivation were being pushed forward at the same time by the tsetse reclamation schemes. In Sukumaland alone some 8,000 square kilometers were opened up to human settlement between 1924 and 1947.[27] However, the campaigns to encourage African production did eventually spark a revival of interest in the problem of soil erosion, with Agricultural Officers becoming 'concerned about the long-term effects on the soil of this non-voluntary effort'.[28]

The pattern of European settlement having been clearly established in Kenya in the mid-1920s, with the final demarcation of the African Reserves, it had become apparent within only a few years that these Reserves were too small to house their rapidly growing populations. From an estimated figure of 2·5 million in 1925, Kenya's African population had risen to 3 million by 1935, and to 3·5 million by 1940. Densities of population stood at over 140 persons per square mile in the Kikuyu districts of Fort Hall and Kiambu by 1938, and over 220 persons per square mile in the Luo area of Central Kavirondo, where land pressure was as serious as in parts of the Eastern Province of Uganda.[29] European settlers farming lands adjacent to the African Reserves were most acutely aware of this overcrowding, as they witnessed degradation setting in across the farm boundary. For these farmers the spectre of erosion galloping

24. J. D. Tothill, *A Report on 19 Surveys in Small Agricultural Areas*, passim; W. S. Martin, 'Soil Erosion Problems in Uganda', in J. D. Tothill (ed) *Agriculture in Uganda* (Oxford 1940), pp. 73–87.
25. *Report of the Teso Informal Committee*, pp. 13–19; D. J. Vail, *A History of Agricultural Innovation and Development in Teso District, Uganda* (East African Studies Program, Syracuse 1972), pp. 127–135; Lord Hailey, *An African Survey*, pp. 1046–1047.
26. R. R. Kuczynski, *Demographic Survey*, vol 2, pp. 339–343.
27. J. Illife, *A Modern History of Tanganyika*, p. 316. See also D. W. Malcolm, *Sukumaland: an African People and their country* (OUP, London 1953), passim.
28. A. Coulson, *Tanzania: A Political Economy* (Oxford UP, 1982), pp. 48. E. Harrison, *Soil Erosion: Tanganyika Territory* (Govt. Printer, Dar-es-Salaam, 1938), passim.
29. R. R. Kuczynski, *Demographic Survey*, vol. 2, pp. 145–150; *Kenya Land Commission: Evidence*, pp. 971–1039, 'Memo: An Ecomonic Survey of the Kikuyu Reserves', by S. H. Fazan, suggests a rate of growth in the Kikuyu districts of 1·6 per cent per annum over the inter-war period. The *Report of the East Africa Royal Commission* accepts C. J. Martin's estimate of 1·9 per cent per annum, p. 31.

out of the Reserves and into the White Highlands seemed all too real.[30] Government recognition of population pressure was implicit in the terms of reference of the Kenya Land Commission, but, as we have seen, any suggestion that more land should be freed for African use met with stiff opposition from the settler community. Their influence lay behind the final decision of the Commission to freeze the apportionment of lands once and for all. While this satisfied settler opinion it was a controversial decision, taken in clear recognition that the pressure on African lands was becoming more severe. It was the opinion of the Commission that the problem was not primarily one of land shortage, but of land use.[31]

Land pressure created by population increase and by expanding cultivation was further exacerbated by the accumulation of larger numbers of livestock by groups of sedentary cultivators. These purchases were often financed by the surpluses gained from greater agricultural production, but because the arable acreage was normally expanded at the expense of grazing land, this resulted in more livestock having less land to graze. In these circumstances the problem of overcrowding could emerge with alarming rapidity. Kitching has demonstrated that this occurred in the Kikuyu Reserve of Kenya during the 1930s, and both Vincent and Vail have shown that it formed a substantial part of the land problem in the Teso District of Uganda, while the development of cotton cultivation coupled with the increased purchase of livestock—financed by the earnings from cotton—clearly contributed to the pressure on land in Sukumaland.[32] Even in the drier rangelands where human population was more sparsely settled, there were visible signs of land pressure by the late 1920s. In districts such as Machakos and Baringo, in Kenya, the imposition of quarantine regulations had restricted the marketing of African livestock while the alienation of important dry season grazing lands for European settlement had seriously undermined the viability of local herding systems.[33] The reduction of livestock numbers was seen to be the simplest solution to the overgrazing and degradation of these rangelands, but the unwillingness of African herders to sell low-quality scrub stock at the prices offered by European buyers gave support to the view that African cattle should be culled through the direct

30. The trespass of African cattle on European farmlands, in search of water and grazing, did much to intensify settler awareness of land degradation and land shortage. See my doctoral thesis, 'Herder, Settler, and Colonial Rule: A History of the Peoples of the Baringo Plains, Kenya, c. 1890–1940', unpub. Ph.D thesis, Cambridge 1982, esp. chs 4 and 5.

31. The whole tone of the Report of the Commission makes this evident, but for specific examples; *Kenya Land Commission: Report,* sections 536, and 1980–2558. For a critique of the Report, see R. M. Breen, 'The Politics of Land', ch. 5.

32. G. Kitching, *Class and Economic Change in Kenya,* pp. 106–107 and 217–224; J. Vincent, *Teso in Transformation,* pp. 194–197; D. J. Vail, *A History of Agricultural Innovation . . . in Teso,* pp. 127–135; P. F. M. McLoughlin, 'Tanzania: agricultural development in Sukumaland', in J. C. de Wilde, et al, *Experiences with Agricultural Development in Tropical. Africa,* vol. 2, (Johns Hopkins UP, Baltimore 1967), pp. 415–450.

33. J. Forbes Munro, *Colonial Rule and the Kamba: Social Change in the Kenya Highlands, 1889–1939* (OUP, Oxford 1975), pp. 77–80; D. M. Anderson, 'Herder, Settler, and Colonial Rule', pp. 72–85.

action of the government, either by some form of cattle tax, or by compulsory purchases.[34] Calculations of the 'carrying capacities' of grazing lands were accordingly made, and these were set as targets for the reduction of African livestock. Events in Machakos in 1938, and later in Sukumaland, were to show that enforced culling was not easy to implement, but the idea of limiting human and stock populations within well defined zones, based on the estimates of the lands' 'carrying capacity', remained a guiding principle as land use planning became the concern of colonial government in Africa.[35]

Drought

From the mid-1920s through to the mid-1930s rainfall levels in much of East Africa were significantly below average. Drought was most pronounced in the low-lying semi-arid areas of Northern Uganda, Northern Kenya, and the plains of the Rift Valley, but also affected the agricultural areas in the Highlands of Kenya, and around the shores of Lake Victoria.[36] Drought heightened perceptions of environmental crisis, providing ammunition to those who would fire warning shots over the question of soil conservation, but also raising fears of food shortages in the affected areas; it was only when drought became famine that the colonial administration generally concerned itself with the consequences. Concern was greatest in Tanganyika, where drought was more widespread and famine more common. The dry areas of Ugogo and Uzigua experienced drought and famine in 1926, 1928–30, and from 1932–35; but in such unproductive areas this was not unusual, and so raised little anxiety. Localized, isolated droughts in areas where they were not expected had more impact. In 1925 and 1933 the Tanga hinterland experienced serious droughts, and the same occured in Bugufi in 1929, and in Tunduru from 1930 to 1932.[37] Droughts such as these seemed to indicate that East Africa was 'drying up', calling into question the long-term future of agriculture and animal

34. *Interim Report of a Committee appointed to Advise as to the steps to be taken to Deal with the Problem of Overstocking in order to Preserve the Future Welfare of the Native Pastoral Areas* (East Africa Pamphlet no. 293, Nairobi 1941), and the papers connected with this Committee, KNA ARC(MAWR)-3Vet-1/8 to 16. Stock marketing was more successful in Tanganyika, see P. L. Raikes, *Livestock Development and Policy in East Africa* (Scandanavian Institute of African Studies, Uppsala 1981), passim. See also, *Kenya Land Commission: Evidence*, pp. 3103–3114, evidence of Maj. H. H. Brassey-Edwards, pp. 3290–3295, evidence of a Delegation of Elected Members.

35. R. L. Tignor, 'Kamba Political Protest: The Destocking Controversy of 1938', *International Journal of African Historical Studies*, **4**, 2 (1971) pp. 237–251; P. F. M. McLoughlin, 'Tanzania: Agricultural development in Sukumaland', passim. The work of Allan and Trapnell, in Northern Rhodesia, was particularly influential in this, see W. Allan, *Studies in African Land Usage in Northern Rhodesia* (Rhodes-Livingstone Papers, no. 15, Oxford 1949, though carried out much earlier), and C. G. Trapnell and J. M. Clothier, *The Soils, Vegetation and Agricultural Systems of North-West Rhodesia* (Govt. Printer, Lusaka 1937).

36. *Meteorological Department Annual Report, 1921–1928* (Govt. Printer, Nairobi); J. C. Bille and H. H. Heemstra, *An Illustrated Introduction to the Rainfall Pattern of Kenya* (ILCA Working Document no. 12, Nairobi 1979); *Uganda Protectorate Annual Reports, 1925–1936* (HMSO London); *Tanganyika Territory Annual Reports, 1926–1936* (HMSO London). Of course, there were exceptions to the general pattern: see for example J. Forbes Munro, *Colonial Rule and the Kamba*, pp. 192–193.

37. J. Iliffe, *A Modern History of Tanganyika*, pp. 315–316.

husbandry in the affected areas. The main thrust of policy in Tanganyika was to eradicate famine by increasing food production, but by over-taxing the soil this policy could be seen as accentuating the damage caused by drought. Leading members of the Tanganyika Department of Agriculture began to suggest that, while the eradication of famine was a positive aim, the permanent loss of soil fertility was too high a price to pay, drought being a major indicator that the processes of degradation were advancing.[38]

With the notable exception of Karamoja, drought had less effect in Uganda. In many parts of the protectorate the cultivation of drought resistant cassava had been actively encouraged since the last serious famine at the end of the First World War. In Teso each farmer was 'persuaded' to cultivate at least one quarter of an acre of manioc, and local schemes were devised to collect seed for the next years planting immediately after the harvest in order to provide a reserve against drought.[39] Food shortage was never serious, but from 1927 to 1930 the erratic nature of the rainfall and a period of drought combined to hamper the cotton crop.[40] Shortage of rains in Karamoja over the same period, and again in 1933 and 1934, led to anxiety lest the arid north might be extending its dusty tentacles into the fertile lands adjacent to the south. This was reflected in government surveys of Karamoja conducted during the mid-1930s, focusing upon the dual problems of water supply and desert encroachment, themes then also receiving attention in West Africa in regard to the southward drift of the Sahara into the savannah lands.[41]

In Kenya droughts were most dramatic in the pastoral areas of the Rift Valley and the North-East. The droughts of 1927–29 and 1933–34 took a heavy toll of African livestock, but to the alarm of observers this did little to relieve the pressure on the parched grasslands. These periods of drought did much to further agitation for direct action to control stock numbers as, far from restoring the equilibrium between land and livestock, it demonstrated the formidable powers of recovery of African cattle herds.[42] The privations of the

38. 'Memo. on Soil Erosion in Tanganyika Territory', prepared for the Conference of Governors of British East Africa, June 1938, CO 822/88/6; 'A Review of the Position in Regard to Soil Conservation in Tanganyika Territory in 1938', CO 852/249/15.

39. D. J. Vail, *A History of Agricultural Innovation . . . in Teso*, pp. 106–108; *Report of the Teso Informal Committee*, passim.

40. Uganda Protectorate Annual Reports, 1927–1930. J. D. Tothill (ed), *Agriculture in Uganda*, pp. 189–190.

41. Wayland to Bottomley, 22nd April, 1937, enclosing E. J. Wayland and N. V. Brasnett, *Interim Report on Soil Erosion and Water Supplies in Uganda* (Uganda Prot., 1937) and Minutes by Stockdale, 24 May 1937, and Flood, 9 August 1937, CO 822/82/6. On West Africa, see E. P. Stebbing, 'The Encroaching Sahara: the threat to the West African Colonies', *Geographical Journal*, **85** (1935), pp. 506–524; B. Jones, 'Dessication and the West African Colonies', *Geographic Journal*, **91** (1938) pp. 401–423; and L. D. Stamp, 'The Southern Margin of the Sahara: Comments on some recent studies on the Question of Dessication in West Africa', *Geographical Review*, **30** (1940), pp. 297–300.

42. *Kenya Land Commission: Evidence*, pp. 3103–3119: evidence of Maj. Brassey-Edwards and Capt. E. J. Mulligan; pp. 3142–3147: evidence of H. E. Welby; C. Maher, *Soil Erosion and Land Utilisation in the Kamasia . . . Reserves*, passim; 'The Native Stock Problem', *East African Standard*, 9 April 1930.

migratory locust denuded pasture and croplands still further in a major invasion during 1928. Locust swarms recurred annually in East Africa throughout the next decade.[43] Although the agricultural areas of Nyanza and the Central Province escaped the worst effects of drought and locusts, in 1929 the combination of two consecutive failed harvests led to food shortages in Kitui, Embu, and Meru Districts, and in parts of Nyanza. This famine was serious enough to warrant the setting up of a Food Control Board, and the prohibition of the export of foodstuffs from the affected areas.[44] Government awareness of these environmental problems was undoubtedly sharpened in 1929 by an expenditure of over £60,000 on famine relief and £55,000 on the anti-locust campaign, and by further sums expended for these purposes in Nyanza from 1931 to 1933, and in the Rift Valley from 1931 to 1934 and again in 1938–39.[45] Drought had a cost that could be measured in financial as well as environmental terms.

The Evolution of Policy

The issue of soil conservation had emerged as a central concern of government in East Africa by 1938. While the responses devised were broadly similar across all three territories, the factors we have noted so far influenced the formulation of policy within each territory to varying degrees. Most significantly, differences appear in the extent to which political factors played a role in the evolution of the new conservationist ideology. In Kenya, where white settler pressure acted on the administration, and where the images of the Dust Bowl were most vividly and frequently reiterated as warnings of the threat posed, government action was better co-ordinated and quickly adopted a colony-wide perspective. Steps toward direct intervention in African farming practices can be plotted through the strategy for native agriculture in 1931, the Report of the Kenya Land Commission, the Department of Agriculture pamphlets circulated in the early 1930s, the visit to the colony by the Colonial Office Agricultural Advisor Frank Stockdale, and the visits of Kenyan officials to South Africa and America to observe conservation methods.[46] Particularly important in giving continuity to this gradually evolving policy was the work

43. E. Harrison, *History and Activities of Locusts in Kenya and Relative costs of Destruction*, (Department of Agriculture, Nairobi, Bulletin no. 9 of 1929); D. L. Blunt, *Report of the Locust Invasion of Kenya*, (Department of Agriculture, Nairobi, Bulletin no. 21 of 1931); *Kenya Colony Annual Reports, 1928–1939*. For Uganda, see J. D. Tothill, *Agriculture in Uganda*, pp. 518–521, and for Tanganyika, *Tanganyika Territory Annual Reports, 1927–1939*.
44. *Kenya Colony Annual Report, 1929*, pp. 17–19 and 28.
45. *Kenya Colony Annual Report, 1929*, pp. 17–21; See various correspondence and accounts in KNA PC/RVP.6A/11/5 to 7, on famine relief, and KNA PC/RVP.6A/11/9 to 11, on anti-locust measures.
46. G. Kitching, *Class and Economic Change in Kenya*, pp. 61–62; *Kenya Land Commission Evidence*, pp. 3065–3072, evidence of Mr Alex Holm (Director of Agriculture); V. A. Beckley, *Soil Deterioration in Kenya* and *Soil Erosion*, both passim; F. A. Stockdale, *Report on His Visit to South and East Africa, Seychelles, The Sudan, Egypt, and Cyprus, 1930–1931*, (Colonial Office, London 1931), passim; C. Maher, *A Visit to the United States to Study Soil Conservation*, (Department of Agriculture, Nairobi 1940), passim.

of an Agricultural Officer named Colin Maher. Committed to the cause of soil conservation from an early stage, Maher fought what amounted to a fully-fledged campaign from 1932 to 1938 to publicise the potential dangers of soil erosion in Kenya. A prolific writer, he contributed a multitude of newspaper and magazine articles on the subject, while also compiling many length reports and memoranda for circulation among his colleagues.[47] The setting up of a Soil Conservation Service in 1938, under his dynamic leadership, was something of a personal triumph, but it also stood as testimony to the power of the many settler pressure groups who had actively supported this cause; after all, the new Soil Conservation Service would work for the benefit of white farmers.[48] Lacking these strong unofficial accomplices, those Agricultural Officers in Uganda and Tanganyika who advocated similar developments had to adapt their ideas to fit in with the prevailing policies of the Agricultural Department.

In Uganda the determining factor was the commitment towards African cash crop production, attention being drawn to soil conservation by falling crop yields through declining fertility. The first detailed report on soil deterioration in Uganda, a collection of surveys compiled and analysed by the Director of Agriculture, Tothill, was prompted by the fears of the Empire Cotton Growers Association.[49] It was the Teso District that absorbed much of Uganda's conservation effort, where cotton yields had declined most sharply during the late 1920s and early 1930s, despite a rapid acreage expansion stimulated by the introduction of oxen ploughing.[50] A committee set up to look into the problem in 1935 made several suggestions for far reaching changes in farming methods. Among these were the resettlement of people from overcrowded and exhausted areas of the District, the introduction of a cattle tax to discourage the accumulation of livestock, and the enforcement of mandatory contour ploughing. After discussion the measures actually implemented were more piecemeal; earthwork bunds were constructed on only about 4,000 acres; selected small areas were closed to livestock to rest the pasture; and strip cropping with grass barriers was enforced. Of these, and many other methods of conservation suggested in Teso, only the strip-cropping proved really successful in the long-term. Supported by a well administered Bye-law, 90 per cent of all cotton land in Teso had been strip-cropped by 1941. An important

47. For details of his career, see his personal file, KNA Min. of Agr./2/274, and also D. M. Anderson, 'Herder, Settler, and Colonial Rule', pp. 110–113 and 253–257. Several of his publications have already been cited, others of interest include *Peasantry or Prosperity?*, (East African Problems no. 3, East African Standard, Nairobi 1943), and 'The People and the Land: Some Problems', *East African Agricultural Journal*, 7 (1942/43) pp. 63–69.
48. Brooke-Popham to Ormsby-Gore, 18 September 1937, and minutes by Flood, 30 September 1937, and Stockdale, 13 October 1937, CO 533/483/7; 'Soil Conservation and Soil Erosion in Kenya Colony, 1937 and 1938', CO 852/249/16; MacDonald to Brooke-Popham, Despatch no. 810, 11 December 1939 KNA PC/RVP.6A/11/23.
49. J. D. Tothill, *A Report on 19 Surveys in small Agricultural Areas*, passim.
50. J. Vincent, *Teso in Transformation*, pp. 173–177; G.B. Masefield, *A History of the Colonial Agricultural Service* (Oxford 1972), pp. 103–104.

factor in this was the imposition of cash fines for failure to comply with the regulations. The shortening of the fallow period, as a result of increased population and greater cultivation, was recognised as the real cause of the decline in soil fertility in Teso, but this could not be so easily handled by legislation at a local level without a much greater commitment to enforcement.[51] Soil erosion was an important question in Uganda by 1938, but it was monitored and treated only in those areas where it seemed likely to threaten the cash crop economy.

A local approach was adopted in Tanganyika. Here the settler community was mainly involved in the plantation production of sisal, and in the growing of coffee. The uncertain political status of the territory during the 1930s absorbed much of the settlers political energies, the rest being taken up with belated attempts to control the spread of coffee production among Africans.[52] Therefore, the Tanganyika settlers did not make political currency out of the erosion question as their Kenya neighbours did. An initial flush of concern over soil erosion in 1930 saw the formation of a Standing Committee to monitor the problem in the Territory, but, in the words of John Iliffe, 'the urgency faded'.[53] In their need to increase revenue and curtail expenditure to meet the rigours of the Depression, the Administration adopted a more cautious attitude. The Plant-More-Crops campaign went ahead, but the question of soil erosion was never completely ignored.[54] The onus for implementing conservation regulations was handed down to the Native Authorities from 1930, and over the following seven years the majority of Tanganyika's Authorities passed local regulations making certain anti-erosion measures compulsory in their Districts. The results were, naturally, minimal and localized. The basic methods were similar to those advocated elsewhere in Africa at the time, and borrowed heavily from the experience of both Kenya and Nyasaland. They included the demonstration of terracing on the contour; the protection of forests; green manuring (in parts of the Central Province); the provision of better water resources by the construction of dams and wells; and the resting of areas of pasture. Often these measures were applied alongside the anti-tsetse campaign, new husbandry regulations being enforced on newly-cleared areas as the settlers arrived.[55] Policies in Tanganyika were determined firstly

51. *Report of the Teso Informal Committee*, passim; *Interim Report of the Agricultural Survey Committee*, (Department of Agriculture, Entebbe 1937), pp. 2–6; D. J. Vail, *A History of Agricultural Innovation . . . in Teso*, pp. 127–135; 'Memo: Soil Erosion in Uganda', May 1938, CO 822/88/6; Mitchell to MacDonald, 12 May 1939, CO 852/249/15.
52. N. J. Westcott, 'The Impact of the Second World War', ch.2; K. Ingram, 'Tanganyika: Slump and Short-term Governors', pp. 605–610.
53. J. Iliffe, *A Modern History of Tanganyika*, pp. 348–349.
54. For example, see *Tanganyika Territory Annual Report, 1934*, Appendix VI 'Measures taken in various Provinces, 1933 and 1934, in connexion with Soil Erosion', pp. 171–176.
55. 'Memo: Soil Erosion in Tanganyika Territory', 28 May 1938, CO 822/88/6; 'A Review of the position in Regard to Soil Conservation in Tanganyika in 1938', 27 March 1939, CO 852/249/15; Lord Hailey, *An African Survey*, pp. 1036–1038; J. Iliffe, *A Modern History of Tanganyika*, pp. 349–352, points out that the erosion 'crisis' predicted by some agriculturalists during the 1930s in Tanganyika never materialized.

by the need to expand production, both of cash crops and food crops, and secondly by the local circumstances of population pressure and drought.

Awareness of an environmental threat to the land, and of a consequent threat to the future viability and profitability of farming, prompted more thorough research into the methods of arable and pastoral production in Africa.[56] This was first initiated in the colonies themselves, with each Agricultural Department mounting its own set of investigations. In Tanganyika, the Agricultural Research Station at Amani, was reopened in the 1920s, and over the next decade its influential, though sometimes controversial research, was focussed increasingly on problems connected with soil erosion. During 1932 Amani hosted a conference of soil chemists from all over East and Central Africa. Two years earlier the Tanganyikan Standing Committee on Soil Erosion had solicited the co-operation of Amani, encouraging the Institute to carry out research on the causes and processes of land degradation.[57] This work ultimately sought to demonstrate the value of better husbandry under strictly controlled conditions of land management, and contributed substantially to the opinion that African land could be made more productive *if* appropriate techniques were employed.[58]

The research effort in Uganda took a rather different form, but also reached conclusions that encouraged those who wished to institute reforms in African agriculture. At Serere, in Teso District, experiments were undertaken to establish the cause of fertility loss, and by 1935 results clearly suggested that the breakdown of the soil structure was fundamental to the problem. Where the actual mechanics of the soil were breaking down, fertilizers and manures would do little to maintain the fertility of the earth. The alarming message here was that after a certain point in the breakdown of the soil the decline in fertility was irretrievable; modern methods of agriculture would be of little use. The implications of this were quickly appreciated by the Empire Cotton Growers Association, who supported much of the research; to be sure of maintaining soil fertility you not only had to gain a detailed knowledge of local soil

56. G. B. Masefield, *History of the Colonial Agriculture Service*, pp. 76–87; Lord Hailey, *An African Survey*, pp. 912–917.
57. H. H. Storey, *Basic Research in Agriculture: A Brief History of Research at Amani, 1928–1947*, (Govt. Printer, Nairobi n.d., but probably 1950); Papers concerning the Informal Conference of administrative officers, held at Dodoma May 1929, and Minutes by Passfield, 25 April 1930, and Stockdale, 29 January 1930, CO 822/26/9; *Technical Conferences of the East African Dependencies: Proceedings of a Conference of East African Soil Chemists held at the Agricultural Research Station, Amani*, (Govt. Printer, Nairobi 1932), and the connected papers in CO 822/47/3; *Tanganyika Territory Annual Report, 1934*, p. 39.
58. H. H. Storey, *Brief History of Research at Amani*, passim. And for specific examples H. E. Hornby, 'Overstocking in Tanganyika Territory', *East African Agricultural Journal*, **1** (1935/36) pp. 353–360; R. R. Staples, H. E. Hornby and R. M. Hornby, 'A Study of the Comparative effects of goats and cattle on a mixed grass-bush pasture', *East African Agriculture Journal*, **8** (1942) pp. 62–70. Work at Amani on soil classification and mapping was also very important, see G. Milne (ed), *A Provisional Soil Map of East Africa*, (Amani Institute, Tanganyika, 1936).

chemistry, but had to enforce cultivation methods that would not jeopardize the productive capacity of the land.[59]

Investigation of the erosion question in Kenya initially concentrated upon pastureland, with experimental schemes being set up to recondition overgrazed grasslands and then allow stock back on, in a controlled system of grazing management. In both Machakos and Baringo these experiments demonstrated that rested pasture would recover, and that recovery could be maintained if stocking levels could be kept low enough to prevent a further cycle of overgrazing. These minor successes were the basis for considerable faith in the process of reconditioning in Kenya, and led to the conviction, held by many administrative officers and many settlers, that the compulsory destocking of overgrazed pastures would end the threat of erosion, while also easing congestion in the African Reserves as a whole.

The cumulative result of this research effort in East Africa clearly indicated that action could be taken to prevent, and to ameliorate soil erosion, but that where African husbandry was left unchecked the consequences were likely to be dire. If something could be done, then most people believed something should be done.[60]

These uncoordinated local investigations were gradually given greater coherence and purpose as the Colonial Office became more concerned with the problem of soil conservation. The Colonial Office had first taken notice of the peculiar difficulties of tropical agriculture and at the end of the First World War, acknowledging the need for greater research when Viscount Milner established an Imperial College of Tropical Agriculture in Trinidad. Opened in 1922, and given its Royal Charter in 1926, the College quickly became recognized as an international centre for research, its post-graduate Diploma in Tropical Agriculture, involving a year spent at Cambridge followed by a year in Trinidad, recognized as a prestigious qualification. The problems of land management in the tropical environment, including the evils of soil erosion—which were well known in the West Indies—were the bread and butter of the Trinidad syllabus.[61] In the early 1930s graduates of the Trinidad College began to infiltrate the colonial administration, better qualified in their subject and more in touch with current trends in research and thinking than the previous generation of colonial agricultural officers could ever have hoped to have been. These men dominated the recruits to the Kenyan Department of Agriculture by 1935, a large proportion of them progressing quickly through the

59. 'Memo: Soil Erosion in Uganda', May 1938, CO 822/88/6; C. C. Wrigley, *Crops and Wealth*, pp. 64–66; J. D. Tothill, *Agriculture in Uganda*, pp. 101–110.
60. *Interim Report of a Committee to Deal with the Problem of Overstocking, passim;* 'Soil Erosion and Soil Conservation in Kenya, 1937 and 1938', CO 852/249/16; J. Forbes Munro, *Colonial Rule and the Kamba*, pp. 215–223. D. M. Anderson, 'Herder, Settler, and Colonial Rule', pp. 217–260.
61. G. B. Masefield, *History of the Colonial Agricultural Service*, pp. 37–43; 'Tropical Agriculture: Work of the Trinidad College', *East African Standard*, 5 April 1930.

ranks to hold senior posts by the 1940s.[62] The Colonial Office itself took more notice of this cadre of experts as it began to re-examine the administration of the colonies and overhaul its own bureaucracy. With the appointment of an Agricultural Advisor to the Colonial Office in 1929, and the creation of a separate Economic Department within the Colonial Office in 1935, and later through the establishment of numerous advisory committees connected with questions of colonial administration and development, such as the Advisory Council on Agriculture and Animal Health, the Colonial Development Advisory Committee and the Colonial Research Council, the Council Office sought to coordinate its policies over a wide range of topics throughout the colonies.[63]

As questions connected with land degradation become ever more prominent in the day to day business of the Colonial Office, soil erosion—or rather, the fear of it—was the common thread that bound together agricultural policies for the tropical colonies. From being a problem identified and handled at a local level in each colony in 1928, soil erosion had by 1938 come to assume an important position in general policy making for the colonies, demanding a coordinated response from Whitehall. As the problem transcended the various levels of administration, from the District Officer to the Permanent Secretary, its implications were given new meaning and the policies for its amelioration were framed more broadly. From the examples of the Districts of Kondoa in Tanganyika, Teso in Uganda, and Baringo in Kenya, we can identify four phases in this gradually expanding policy:

i. Initial expressions of concern about land degradation within the District.
ii. Official recognition of the problem by the District administration.
iii. Action at the District level, with the implementation of anti-erosion measures.
iv. Wider colonial concern, with the formulation of large-scale plans at Provincial, or even Colony level, and applications for central funding for ameliorative measures.

As the table below illustrates, by 1938 each of these three Districts, from widely diverging starting points and through divergent sets of agricultural policy aims, had arrived at the same basic approach to the question of land degradation.

The time delay of about ten years between recognition and action can perhaps be dismissed as the natural slow gestation of a conservative bureaucracy. To some extent this is true, but the passing of time also saw an accumulation of forces in favour of agrarian reforms in Africa, and allowed the facts and figures to be gathered and analysed. The Colonial Office began to examine the relationship of cause and effect in African husbandry, and as a result were

62. G. B. Masefield, *ibid*, pp. 43–48; *Colonial Office Lists, 1929–1948* (HMSO London), give the qualifications of Kenyan Agricultural Officers, though not for other colonies. By 1948 almost half the field staff and more than half the technical staff were Trinidad trained.

63. G. B. Masefield, *ibid*, pp. 41–42; Sir C. Jeffries, *The Colonial Office* (Allen & Unwin, London 1956), pp. 108–113.

TABLE

Phases in the evolution of Soil Conservation policies: Kondoa, Teso, and Baringo, 1928 to 1938

	Kondoa	Teso	Baringo
i.	1928—Kondoa described as being 'deeply eroded'.	Late 1920s—Falling yields noted by Empire Cotton Growers Assoc, and overstocking of area discussed.	1928—Drought causes first comments on land degradation.
ii.	1930—District administration comment on erosion, especially gullying.	1932—Teso officially acknowledged to have lowest cotton yield in Uganda.	1929—First official concern, connected to the issue of overstocking.
iii.	1932—Native Authority Bye-Laws begin to deal with conservation measures. 1933—Kondoa described as 'worst erosion' in Tanganyika. 1937—Secretariat in Dar-es-Salaam marks area as 'first priority' in anti-erosion work.	1935—Informal Committee formed by District administration to advise on conservation measures. 1937—General surveys of erosion throughout colony. Teso main area of concern. 1938—Strip cropping, and other conservation measures implemented.	1930—Reconditioning schemes begun in District, funded by Provincial administration. 1933/34—Kenya Land Commission highlights land use problems, identifying Baringo as an acute example. 1935/37—Surveys of erosion throughout colony declare Baringo to be 'among the worst'.
iv.	1938/39—Development plan drawn up for Kondoa, and requests made to central government for finance.[64]	1938/39—Uganda administration seeks CDF funding for resettlement and re-afforestation schemes, to prevent spread of erosion.[65]	1938/39—Detailed Rehabilitation Scheme drawn up for Baringo, supported by central government, and put forward for consideration by the CDF.[66]

prepared to reassess their own role as reformers. Mounting concern led to a gradually mounting commitment to act.[67]

An ideology of conservation, based upon soil erosion, had emerged within the Colonial Office before the Second World War. The Dust Bowl, at its height in 1935, and its cost spectacularly measured in pounds of soil lost per

64. I am grateful to John Iliffe for allowing me to use his notes on Kondoa District, mostly from the Tanzania National Archive (TNA). The following sources were used in compiling the table: Gillman Diaries, entry for 6 October 1928, Rhodes House Library; Kondoa-Irangi Annual Reports, 1920–1934; re. gully erosion in Kondoa, TNA 691/109/2; re. meeting on soil erosion, 1937, TNA Sec. 19685/2/279; re. plans for rehabilitation and development, TNA CP 26393/1/1 and CP 26393/2/1A.

65. Teso column compiled from: *Report of the Teso Informal Committee; Interim Report of the Agricultural Survey Committee; Report of the Uganda Cotton Commission, 1938,* (Govt. Printer, Entebbe 1939), pp. 15–27; J. D. Tothill, *A Report on 19 Surveys in small Agricultural Areas;* J. D. Vail, *A History of Agricultural Innovation . . . in Teso,* pp. 127–135; E. J. Wayland and N. V. Brasnett, *Interim Report on Soil Erosion in Uganda,* in CO 822/82/6; 'Memo: Soil Erosion in Uganda', May 1938, CO 822/88/6; Mitchell to MacDonald, 12 May 1939, CO 852/249/15.

66. Baringo column compiled from: *Kenya Land Commission: Evidence,* pp. 1773–1799, Secretary's Precis of the Rift Valley Province proposals and recommendations, and pp. 1800–1906, all evidence concerning Baringo; Governors Deputy to MacDonald, 13 August 1939, enclosing Memo. by E. M. Hyde-Clarke, 'Baringo District Rehabilitation Scheme', January 1939, and reply, 11 December 1939, KNA PC/RVP.6A/11/23; C. Maher, *Soil Erosion and Land Utilisation in the Kamasia Reserves,* passim.

67. 'Soil Conservation in the Tropics', by Sir F. Stockdale, prepared for the Netherlands Conference on Tropical Agriculture, 1939, CO 852/249/17.

person and square feet of topsoil blown hundreds of miles across country, had made conservation of the environment an international issue. This impact did much to push the Colonial Office to tackle the issue on an equally grand scale. Administrators from the colonies and bureaucrats from Whitehall travelled to America to see the devastation at first hand and, more importantly, to view the anti-erosion measures being applied by the United States Soil Conservation Service.[68] But the Americans, for all their efforts to deal with the problem, were barely worth their acknowledged status of 'experts' on soil conservation. Having created one of the most serious single environmental disasters known to man they simply had to set about trying to solve it.[69] In a sense, there were no 'experts'; only those who were doing something. More of necessity was being done in North America than elsewhere, and so it was primarily from this pool of experience that the Colonial Office drew its ideas. Even when the Colonial Office tried to draw upon more appropriate examples from Africa, they discovered that all roads led back to Hugh Bennett and the American Soil Conservation Service. Before establishing a Soil Conservation Service in Kenya, it was suggested that an Agricultural Officer be sent to Basutoland, where anti-erosion schemes were reportedly at a more advanced stage. The Basutoland administration responded enthusiastically to the request to entertain the Kenyan visitor, but asked that the trip be postponed until their own Soil Conservation Officer had returned from his fact-finding tour to the United States.[70]

It was during Malcolm MacDonald's second term at the Colonial Office that soil conservation was given priority as a matter of very real Imperial importance. Macdonald did much to crystallize the ideas on agrarian reform into harder policies, but even before his return the Colonial Office had already begun to throw its weight behind the push for a conservation-conscious agrarian strategy. The previous year, in June 1937, Ormsby-Gore had pledged the government to greater expenditure on anti-erosion measures in East Africa, acknowledging that direct action was now an urgent necessity.[71] This was followed in February 1938 by a circular to all colonies, demanding that they

68. D. Worster, *Dust Bowl: The Southern Plains in the 1930s*, pp. 10–25; 'Notes on Soil Conservation Work in America', by Sir F. Stockdale, 17 November 1937, following his visit to the United States, CO 533/483/7.
69. This was a common theme in the writings of Hugh Bennett. See also P. B. Sears, *Deserts on the March* (London edition, 1949), and V. G. Carter and T. Dale, *Topsoil and Civilisation*, (Univ. of Oklahoma Press, revised edition 1974, first edition 1955), a book dedicated to Bennett.
70. High Commissioner Basutoland to Brooke-Popham, 25 September 1937, CO 533/483/7. For the American influence in Southern Africa, see W. Beinart, 'Soil Erosion, Conservationism, and Ideas About Development', pp. 25–26.
71. On MacDonald, see J. Flint, 'The Failure of Planned Decolonization', pp. 398–402, but also R. D. Pearce, 'The Colonial Office and Planned Decolonization', pp. 78–80. Ormsby-Gore to Wade, 23 June 1937, and Minute by Stockdale, 9 June 1937, arguing strongly for increased expenditure, claiming present efforts against erosion to be 'about as affective as attempting to build a bridge across Sydney harbour with a Meccano set', in CO 533/483/6. For one of the earliest official references to the dangers of erosion in East Africa, see *Report of the East Africa (Ormsby-Gore) Commission*, Cmd. 2387, pp. 32 and 72.

submit an annual account of all the conservation work undertaken by their various departments each year. Some colonies were slow to respond to this circular—after all, erosion was not a pressing issue in *all* parts of the Empire—but the Colonial Office sent out regular reminders until all the reports were furnished. As the fat files containing colonial soil erosion reports from 1938 onwards testify, this was a subject about which every colonial administration was expected to be aware.[72] Soil erosion can be seen to have reached its place as a topic of 'High Policy' in East Africa when a special session of the 1938 Governors Conference was devoted to a discussion of conservation policies. The papers prepared for this meeting were later published in full and circulated to other colonies, a rare enough occurance in itself to signal that something of significance was taking place.[73] A similar indication was provided by the demand for a pamphlet on soil conservation in Tanganyika, prepared in 1937 by Harrison, the Director of Agriculture. The initial print-run of 600 copies was distributed in East Africa, and sent to other colonies for their information, but interest was so great that the Crown Agents were asked to arrange for the printing of a further 500 copies in 1938, these being sent, on request, as far afield as British Guiana, the Gold Coast, and Fiji.[74]

At the Colonial Office in London one man stands out as having been most influential in all of this: Sir Frank Stockdale. Looking at his career, one might be tempted to suggest that as Stockdale gained position, so did the question of soil erosion. Stockdale first became concerned with the problem of land degradation in the tropics as Director of Agriculture in Ceylon in 1920, where he was responsible for setting up anti-erosion work on the large tea estates. By the 1930s, as Agricultural Advisor to the Colonial Office, his particular experience of the problem made him more sensitive to the rumblings of concern in the colonies about the threat of erosion. As the issue of soil conservation became a recurrent theme in Colonial Office discussions on tropical agriculture, it was Stockdale who provided the 'expert' opinion and made policy recommendations; who advised which ideas should be supported and which dismissed; who drafted the minutes that alerted many of his junior, and less experienced officers, to the essential importance of the erosion question. Above all, it was Frank Stockdale who encouraged the Colonial Office to view conservation of the soil as an issue common to all the British colonies.[75] With his close contacts with Hugh Bennett and others involved in the American fight against bad

72. Lord Harlech's (Ormsby-Gore) despatch no. 74, 9 February 1938, CO 852/249/15. Annual Reports from the Colonies on soil erosion can be found in CO 852, beginning in 1938–39, CO 852/249/15 and 16.

73. 'Papers concerning the Conference of Governors of British East Africa, June 1938', CO 822/88/6, later published as *Soil Erosion, Memoranda by the Governments of Uganda, Kenya, and Tanganyika*, (Govt. Printer, Nairobi 1938).

74. Crown Agents to Under Sec. of State, Colonial Office, 25 August 1939, CO 852/250/1.

75. G. B. Masefield, *History of the Colonial Agricultural Service*, pp. 161–162; F. Stockdale, 'Soil Erosion in the Colonial Empire', *Empire Journal of Experimental Agriculture*, 5 (1937); Minute by Stockdale, 9 June 1937, CO 533/483/6; and, for an early example, Minute by Stockdale, 29 January 1930, CO 822/26/9.

farming, Stockdale was committed to direct action to enforce better husbandry on often reluctant and sometimes ignorant farmers.[76] But it would be wrong to see Frank Stockdale as the orchestrator of a campaign to draw attention to the erosion issue. He did not create the problem, it landed on his desk in the form of reports and memoranda from the various colonies and, as the official with overall responsibility for colonial agricultural policy, he set about trying to make sense of it and devising policies that would tackle it.

It is interesting to note that by 1938 Stockdale was already suggesting that the methods of constructing anti-erosion works then being advocated in the colonies were, in many cases, counter-productive. Following the American experience once again, Stockdale calculated that the overall productive capacity of most African lands could not sustain the current costs of maintaining anti-erosion works, particularly where heavy mechanization was involved. It was uneconomic to rehabilitate, or even protect, African lands by such capital-intensive means. Instead, the natural landscape should be used as the basis for conservation planning, and where larger works of construction were deemed necessary these should be undertaken without the use of heavy machinery.[77] By this time the Colonial Office was already considering proposals for the amelioration of land degradation involving mechanization and its attendant high costs. These were accepted as the large-scale solutions to what were viewed as large-scale problems, and after 1945 mechanization played a significant part in the implementation of development schemes throughout British Africa. Indeed, although the costs of such action were high, the implications of solving the landuse problem by labour intensive means went far beyond the advantages apparent in simply applying methods of good husbandry. Voluntary labour cost the colonial administration nothing, but was a heavy burden to the farmer, who objected to this interventionist policy, however well meaning it may have been.[78]

Conclusion

The rise of soil erosion as a subject of 'Imperial importance' was not an isolated development, but was part of a much wider and historically more significant transition in British colonial thinking that took place during the 1930s. However real or imaginary the economic and environmental crises were, the 1930s became a decade of reassessment in British colonies and in the Colonial Office itself. It cannot simply be argued that events in the

76. Minute by Stockdale, 9 June 1937, CO 533/483/6; Stockdale to Dr J. H. Reisner, United States Soil Conservation Service, 26 October 1937, and reply 9 November 1937; and, 'Notes on Soil Conservation Work in America', by Stockdale, 17 November 1937, all in CO 533/483/7; Bennett to Reisner, 6 December 1937 CO 533/483/8.
77. Notes on Soil Conservation Work in America', by Stockdale, 17 November 1937, CO 533/483/7.
78. D. W. Throup, 'The Governorship of Sir Philip Mitchell', pp. 212–261; L. Cliffe, 'Nationalism and Reaction to Enforced Agricultural Change', passim; C. C. Wrigley, *Crops and Wealth*, pp. 76–79.

colonies forced a shift in policies, or that an awakening of concern for African development in London prompted a new set of policies 'from above'. Both explanations are unsophisticated, and ignore the movements of ideas that went from colony to London and back again, that were modified by experience both within and outside the Empire, and that often resulted in reforms that went far beyond what was initially intended. The cumulative effect was important, and by the late 1930s administrators in East Africa and senior members of the Colonial Service in London were well aware that the reforms they contemplated were certain to be profound and pervasive.[79] How far they connected the beginnings of 'development' in East Africa with ultimately accelerating the process to decolonisation, is a much broader question; what is clear is that the changes of the 1930s established a framework within which the policies of the late 1940s could be implemented. The Second World War was, of course, to add important parts to this structure, but to fully understand the effect of the War, and the reasoning behind the agrarian reforms of the post-war years, we must recognise the significance of the shifts in policy accomplished during the 1930s. The policies that had evolved by 1938 were the product of a combination of local and international circumstances, of a complex interaction between the various levels of the colonial administration each with their own perceptions of the nature of the problems that confronted them. Soil conservation became a fundamental issue because it lay at the very heart of the strategies that emerged for African development.

79. Wade to Ormsby-Gore, 17 March 1937, and reply 23 June 1937; Minute by Stockdale, 9 June 1937, all in CO 533/483/6; Brooke-Popham to Ormsby-Gore, 18 September 1937, and related papers, in CO 533/483/7; 'Soil Conservation in the Tropics', by Stockdale, June 1939, CO 852/249/17.

MARLENE DOBKIN
University of Massachusetts at Boston.

Colonialism and the Legal Status of Women in Francophonic Africa*

The effects of European colonialism upon peoples of the world have been multifold, but little can compare with the zeal and fervor with which the French attempted to legislate dignity and status to African women. In her mission to civilize West and Equatorial Africa, France attempted to graft a system of jurisprudence onto societies whose social and juridical systems differed markedly from that of the metropolitan government.

This paper is a brief analysis of French colonial legislation in West and Equatorial Africa and its effect upon the status of women under French control until the early 1960's. The expressed purpose of this legislation was to alter the traditional rôle of women in French Africa to meet the standards of French society. Far too often, however, the French lacked knowledge of indigenous customs and ignored traditional patterns of behavior. They promulgated legislation which resulted in conflict, upheaval and disorientation in many of those same societies who were to benefit from these laws.

The focus of this study will be limited primarily to the rural patrilineal societies of francophonic Africa. Substantive data culled from the literature will be drawn upon to point up the conflicts that arose from the inadequate understanding by the French of traditional values and norms. Moreover, such important factors as economic changes, urbanization and industrialization, very much a part of the French colonial heritage, will be neglected in a concern with legislation. In effect, disparate value systems as represented in the legislative

* This paper was originally submitted in different form in 1963 as a Master's Thesis at New York University. My deep thanks go to Dr. Elliott Skinner for his guidance in the earlier version of this article. Drs. Martin and Marion Kilson have been kind enough to read a first draft, but responsibility for the ideas presented here is of course my own.

manipulation of African society by the French will receive the full attention of this study and as such will reveal only part of the total situation.

African women were a source of dismay to French administrators who had their own conception of 'natural law', *e.g.*, a universal morality and truth which seemed lacking to African women, at least in comparison with their own society's norms.[1] An early statement in 1920 by Lieutenant Governor Hesling of the Upper Volta is illustrative:

> "From the standpoint of the present situation, the condition of indigenous women is entirely abnormal and contrary to the fundamental principles of human rights [. . .] which necessitates the enactment of profound reforms [on our part]. [. . .] the condition of indigenous women appears [. . .] outrageously contrary to the essential principle of human rights and civilization."[2]

Hesling, among others, believed that few if any of the traditional indigenous customs concerning women were worth saving. African women were seen to be objects or chattels—creatures who could be inherited by men in the same way that land might pass from a man to his brother.[3] What appeared to be the abject status and lack of individuation of the indigenous female—lacking a juridical personality and unable to protect herself from what was viewed as cruel, endless toils and inhuman indecencies fostered upon her by her society—horrified French administrators. The Mandel Decree of 1939 and the Jacquinot Decree of 1951 were promulgated to intercede in those areas believed to be of gravest concern: the right of consent to marriage, regulation of bridewealth, and minimal age at marriage.[4] The validity of African customs in these areas as the natural outgrowth of the felt needs of a society, what Rheinstein has called "the formalized outward expression of [. . .] a society's life and values"[5] was not recognized by the French who attempted rather to adapt African traditional systems of law to Western industrial society. Western conceptions of contract as the mechanism regulating the life of an individual contrasted markedly to African conceptions of social relations predominantly based on ascribed status. As the Kupers point out, a meeting

1. See D. PAULME's excellent discussion of European condemnation of African marriage customs in *Women of Tropical Africa*, Berkeley, 1963, p. 4. R. MAUNIER's article, "La femme noire en Afrique française", *Le Monde Colonial Illustré*, 1939, gives a good presentation of the so-called abject status of African women to the French public.

2. Quoted in Sister MARIE-ANDRÉ DU SACRÉ-CŒUR, *La femme noire en Afrique Occidentale*, Paris, 1939, Appendix 1, p. 259.

3. Abbé J. SASTRE, "La mission de la femme africaine", in M. DU ROSTU, *Femmes africaines*, Paris, 1959, p. 13 ff.

4. See Appendices I and II.

5. M. RHEINSTEIN, "Problems of Law in the New Nations of Africa", in C. GEERTZ, *Old Societies and New States*, Glencoe, 1963, p. 221.

of two such philosophies hardly resulted in a harmonious blend.[1]

The French, as the heirs of the great Roman tradition, extended their institutions and laws wherever they established themselves. Certainly West and Equatorial Africa were to be no exception. An inherent ethnocentricity—a belief that their own laws which worked well enough for them were superior to those of any pagan society—blinded them to the realities of the African situation.

Women in Traditional African Society

Just what aspects of women's traditional behavior violated the norms of French culture? In the traditional patrilineal societies of West and Equatorial Africa[2] the direct well-being of the society rather than that of the individual was of utmost importance. The institution of marriage, essential to the continuity of the society, pointed to woman's real worth—namely her presumed fertility. Marriage was not a contract between two individuals, but as in many non-European parts of the world, an alliance between two sets of kin groups in which the potential source of fecundity was transmitted.[3] As Lucy Mair points out in a general discussion of African marriage, freedom of choice for a woman in such circumstances is limited.[4]

A woman who may have lacked certain European 'rights' such as consent to marriage, did have safeguards in that she could not be treated like a slave, she could not be beaten without reason and her spouse could not refuse to support her. A marriage contract primarily concerned with the fecundity of a woman provided redress in case of the woman's sterility or for the unbearable personality of one of the partners.[5] The payment of bridewealth upon marriage in fact served to equalize the loss of this 'procreative potential' from one social group, who in effect were losing their right to filiate the children born to this woman. To quote Mair again, "the marriage payment [. . .] legalizes a marriage, determines the legal paternity of children and creates the relationship of affinity between the kin of the spouses."[6]

If a man died, his wife and children were considered attached to

1. H. and L. Kuper, *African Law: Adaptation and Development*, Berkeley, 1965, p. 6.
2. Such societies as the Ndiki, Fang, Mossi and Betammadibe, to be discussed below.
3. J. Bertho, "Le problème du mariage chrétien en Afrique Occidentale Française", *Africa*, 17 (4), 1947: 252. C. Lévi-Strauss' model of marriage (*Structural Anthropology*, New York, 1964) viewed as sociologically part of a series of reciprocal transactions between groups, would be relevant here.
4. L. Mair, *New Nations*, Chicago, 1963, p. 74.
5. Bertho, p. 254.
6. Mair, p. 75.

the husband's collectivity for the duration of their lives. In a patrilineal society, the custom of the levirate permitted the individual to inherit the wife of his brother. The potentiality of procreation which had been validated by the husband's kin group through the payment of bridewealth to the woman's kin at marriage did not have to be returned, often years later, if the woman remained within the group. These customs, which were shocking to the European mentality, were perfectly logical, cohesive and justifiable in those societies where they were practiced. Consent of the individual to either marriage or the levirate in these circumstances seemed to be an unacceptable luxury. The French, however, preferred to view this as a deprivation of the woman's legal rights. A particular value, what Balandier calls that of a 'capital creator' did exist, with sexual freedom often permitted the unmarried young woman even if betrothed at an early age. Legal rather than sexual possession at marriage changed a woman's status from girlhood to maturity.[1]

The unique status of women as it exists in contemporary Western industrial society has few parallels elsewhere in the world. What shocked the French seems to strike one investigator, Henri Labouret, as inconsistent with the history of Western civilization. His historical analogies, focusing on the status of women in ancient Greece and Rome indicated to this writer that the consent of a woman at marriage was of secondary importance within the history of European society where the personal convenience of the spouse was not considered in the over-all concern for an advantageous alliance. Nineteenth century marriages in France also reveal many instances of women being forced to marry against their will.[2] This lack of introspection did not hinder the French from believing that African women were subject to forced marriages, that they appeared to lack freedom of choice of their mate and that they could not dispose of their own person. Despite this convenient fiction, African marriages did provide an escape mechanism in the form of elopement which served to mitigate conflict, not at all a valid way-out in nineteenth century European society.

Labouret stressed the fact that gifts and payments so characteristic of marriage in West and Equatorial Africa were not paid 'to buy a woman' but to assure the father and his family of the legal sanctity and profit of the offspring of marriage.[3] In contrast to European societies in which marriage is the starting point for a new family

1. G. Balandier, *Sociologie actuelle de l'Afrique noire*, Paris, 2nd. ed., 1963 p. 12.

2. H. Labouret, "Situation matérielle, morale et coutumière de la femme dans l'Ouest-Africain", *Africa*, 13 (2), 1940: 97 (especially p. 105).

3. *Ibid.*

replete with its own autonomy and patrimony, African marriages can often be viewed as extensions of the patrilineal family. In this context, marriage "does not give birth to a new social organism [. . .], it is merely the necessary means to assure the continuity of the family group."[1] Marriage is basically the acquisition of rights *in uxorem* (sexual, domestic and economic rights on a woman) as well as rights *in genetricem* (rights to filiate a woman's children). The use of the term status with regard to women in francophonic Africa does not imply high or low ranking vis-à-vis men, but a status rather that conferred reciprocal obligations and benefits between men and women.[2] Missionaries as well as administrators could not focus upon the collective rather than the individual importance of the African woman under their tutelage. The individual, according to Christian conceptions, does not exist for the society—rather, society is organized for him. The French, influenced by European concepts of democracy and Church doctrine, sought to valorize the individual. Although writers like Delavignette strongly protested that one could not administer justice by transplanting European regulations to African soil,[3] the desire to end the uncivilized status of African women through legislation was a strong one, ultimately sanctioned in law.

The Legislation.

Despite the intermittent periods of toleration of the traditional laws and customs of subject peoples,[4] colonial policies of assimilation gained impetus. It was thought that indigenous people, as the result of French guidance, were to evolve to a point over the course of time where they would act in a French manner and renounce their traditional way of life, achieving the status of *gens de couleurs*.[5] Certainly, from 1848 onward, the French constitutions clearly showed that all peoples within the boundaries of French territory were to be envisaged as future Frenchmen. Betts, who has made an excellent summary of French colonial policy between 1890 and the First World War, has characterized three periods of colonial expansion as follows:

1. At first, the Europeans in their civilizing mission had to spread the Christian faith during the period of overseas expansion.
2. The belief in reason, which characterized much of the 18th century,

---

1. Sister Marie-André du Sacré-Cœur, p. 48.
2. T. O. Elias, *The Nature of African Customary Law*, Manchester, 1956, p. 95.
3. R. Delavignette, *Freedom and Authority in French West Africa*, London, 1950, p. 90.
4. This was generally known as the policy of association, which was prevalent during the early years after French control was established.
5. J. D. Fage, *Introduction to the History of West Africa*, London, 1955, p. 167.

replaced the proselytism of Christianity and gave the Europeans a feeling of moral superiority.

3. Social Darwinism led to a belief in racial superiority of the colonial power and ethnocentrism.[1]

However, much of colonial policy was in fact haphazard and poorly formulated, without a precise program in advance. The mode of enacting laws indicated some of the problems of the high degree of French centralization:

"According to the senatus consult of May 3, 1854, legislation for the French colonies [. . .] takes the form of a 'simple decree'. No imposition was made on the control of such decrees by Parliament of France or the Council of State. These decrees relating to the colonies are promulgated in the *Journal Officiel de la République Française* or in the *Bulletin des Lois* and do not become a force in the colonies until they are published in the official journal."[2]

Native courts were modified before the new laws were passed, and matters concerning marriage and divorce were deemed too important to be handled by native tribunals. In their place, courts presided over by an administrative official (most often European) assisted by interpreters and assessors whose function it was to help explain customary law[3] were set up. These courts lacked a clearly formulated course of sanction. While one administrator might have punished adultery with a fine of 100 Congolese francs, another might impose a prison sentence of one year.[4] In the absence of a native penal code, arbitrary judgments were the rule and not the exception.

Turning to the first of the French Decrees, the Mandel Decree promulgated in 1939, its provisions dealt with aspects of marriage and related custom considered unacceptable as follows:

1. Actual age of the parties to be married;
2. Child betrothal;
3. Consent of the parties to be married;
4. The problem of the widow;
5. The establishment of an age of maturity at which time an individual could freely marry.

The Mandel Decree defined the minimum age for contracting marriage in the A.O.F. and the A.E.F. as 14 years for women and 16 years

1. R. F. Betts, *Assimilation and Association in French Colonial Theory: 1890-1914*, New York, 1961, p. 70.
2. R. L. Buell, *The Native Problem in Africa*, New York, 1928, II, p. 923.
3. J. Vanderlinden, "The Recording of Customary Law in France during the 15th and 16th Centuries and the Recording of African Customary Law", *Journal of African Law*, 3 (3), 1959. The author points out that although as early as 1453 there was a desire to collect the customary law in written form, the actual implementation and resultant codification was insignificant.
4. Buell, pp. 1011-1012.

for men. It declared that the consent of the spouses was *indispensible*[1] for the validity of a marriage. It nullified the custom of the levirate if the woman involved refused to be party to such a custom. The Jacquinot Decree, passed in 1951, upheld the earlier Mandel Decree. It also affirmed that in countries where the institution of bridewealth was customary, a girl who reached the age of 21 years, or who had been legally divorced could freely marry without interference by anyone who might gain material advantage from her engagement period or marriage. Bridewealth was to be determined in a given area by the Chief of the Territory, and Tribunals of the First Degree were empowered to judge excessive demands on the part of the parents concerning these payments. These courts also functioned to permit the official registration of marriage on civil records without the consent of the parents of the spouses. In effect, women were freed from the control of their guardian or father. The French penal code was used to enforce both the Mandel and Jacquinot Decrees, with the severest penalty for impeding their provisions calling for imprisonment up to 5 years.

The French took the institution of marriage which had been regulated by tradition and made a statutory institution of it, hoping to endow the African woman in some way with a new status—to relieve her of the disabilities and obligations that were incompatible with the standards of 'civilized society'.

Despite Martin Lewis' conclusion in his analysis of the French colonial policy of assimilation that no serious effort to carry out this policy occurred,[2] an examination of the attempts of the French to modify African customary life through legislation is a refutation of this position. Conflict situations arose from the implementation of such legislation, which spread through all the reaches of the overseas African territories. Let us look now at the extent of the failure of the laws.

The Failure of the Laws.

Contrary to French expectations, the end result of the legislative acts was disequilibrium. With few exceptions, all the efforts made by French administrators and officials did not work in either raising the status of the African woman or in emancipating her.[3] This new social differentiation aroused strong reactions in many cases, and in

1. Emphasis mine.
2. M. D. LEWIS, "One Hundred Million Frenchmen: The Assimilation Theory in French Colonial Policy", *Comparative Studies in Society and History*, 4 (2), 1962: 153.
3. V. THOMPSON and R. ADLOFF, *The Emerging States of French Equatorial Africa*, Stanford, 1960, p. 328.

Gabon, Balandier reported the development of antifeminism, attributed to the fact that women had become 'wrongheaded'.[1] Many of the same writers who were influential in bringing about the passage of these laws were appalled and bewildered at their devastating effects. The institution of marriage was removed from the nexus of social relations in which it had previously functioned, and was isolated by judicial tampering. In this acculturative situation, the impact of disparate value systems, reflected in systems of jurisprudence, could only lead to unpleasant ends. The very nature of social groups changed as a result of the clash, with the individual loosing his psychological support in the extended family and more and more dependent upon himself.[2] Writers like Abbé Zoa spoke of the search for a new 'soul' and a means of identification.

One of the major concerns of the legislation was the question of consent as indispensible to the validity of marriage. Sister Marie-André du Sacré-Cœur, one of the law's staunchest proponents, in 1959 could not fathom the many conflicts that arose from its implantation. To cite one case:

> "In June 1958, in the Sudan and Upper Volta, several girls refused outright the husband proposed by their family. Everyone was against them and said they had to accept, because their family said so. 'If you don't marry this man, you will be chased out of the house.'"[3]

Although at first blush it would appear that the law could grant the woman protection in her choice of marriage partner, one must keep in mind as Sister Marie-André du Sacré-Cœur has, that the parents in the above case may in fact have already spent the bridewealth and gifts well in advance of the finalization of the marriage.

The Mandel Decree caused many disturbances among the considerable Moslem portions of societies under French control. The idea that consent of a betrothed couple was necessary for the validity of a marriage and the idea that young people were able to marry without anyone's consent but their own wrecked havoc upon basic Islamic customs.[4] The issue of consent also was prominent in Dugast's study of the Ndiki of the Cameroun. Consent which was previously unknown in this society as the French viewed it, underwent drastic reinterpretation. As a result of the legislation, women quickly decided that conjugal life was a heavy strain, husbands were not always

1. G. Balandier, "Social Changes and Problems in Negro Africa", in C. Stillman, ed., *Africa in the Modern World*, Chicago, 1955, p. 66.
2. Abbé J. Zoa, "Le problème de la dot", in Du Rostu, p. 63.
3. Sister Marie-André du Sacré-Cœur, "La jeune fille rurale", in Du Rostu, p. 31.
4. V. Thompson and R. Adloff, *French West Africa*, Stanford, 1958, p. 577.

supportable, maternities were one's own concern and the society be damned. Marriage and the procreation of children, formerly the bulwark of the society changed dramatically. The custom of women spending 3 to 4 years, first with one husband and then another, arose. Children seemed to suffer the most as they got left behind according to traditional custom as the woman moved on. Sudden emancipation of women without any adequate preparation resulted in new social mobility for women who could travel about easily leaving their small compounds for the excitement of Yaoundé, Douala, or other urban centers where they lived with little restraint or surveillance. They often returned home with some savings amassed from prostitution in the towns. Despite the introduction of free consent to marriage, stabilization of such unions was not what the French had foreseen. Men tended to remain faithful to the old system, but young girls found the responsibilities of marriage often a heavy burden to endure and protested against the familial organization.[1]

Mercier, in working with the Betammadibe of Dahomey,[2] reported that European contact not only modified the traditional forms of marriage but contributed to the weakening of family and parental authority. Three types of marriage were traditionally practiced in this society: the first arranged by families of the young people, replete with negociations and rituals, was finalized when the bride cohabitated with her husband. Up to this point, she was not only permitted to take a lover, but expected to do so. The second type of marriage was similar to an elopement, with the consent of the parents usually obtained after the fact. The third type was regularized abduction outside the local community itself.

As a result of the French decree requiring consent of the spouses, there was an increasing reluctance on the part of the women to cohabitate with the legal husband. In the place of this traditional pattern, an extension of the third type of marriage, abduction, not following the exogamous restrictions spread within the tribe itself. It became an acceptable idea that the abductor had to pay compensation, influenced by the cash value of labor brought to the Betammadibe from contact with the French economic system. Recourse to the courts severely affected the old order and a delicate equilibrium was thrown off balance. Sexual liberty before marriage had acquainted the girl with personal freedom and with the arrival of European legislation, elements of tension and instability of marriage due to the sudden curtailment of sexual freedom was further reinforced by the

1. I. Dugast, *Monographie de la tribu des N'Diki (Banen du Cameroun). II: Vie sociale et familiale*, Paris, 1960, p. 256 ff.

2. P. Mercier, "Le consentement au mariage et son évolution chez les Betammadibe", *Africa*, 20 (3), 1950: 219.

relatively new concept of individual consent to the marriage. The third form of marriage, that of an escape valve, became the normative mode. If the traditional forms of marriage were followed, the individual consent of the woman, far from a negligible factor, would have permitted her a way out through elopement. Mercier has described unpleasant situations resulting from the change in marriage patterns. Men who were engaged no longer wanted to render traditional services and gifts to their prospective father-in-law. The French idea of remuneration of labor gave the male population a monetary sense of their own worth. The fiancé less and less often allowed sexual liberty to his fiancée and tended to take the place of the official lover. The gifts he formerly gave to his mistress were now given to his intended bride, since her freedom of choice had suddenly loomed before him. As soon as a man's wife moved in with him, the husband often suspended the traditional gifts and services that he still owed to her family.[1]

The law did not envisage that elopement would also undergo a change. Its scope had been extended from a mere institutionalized escape valve to a more and more necessary means of resolving tensions and conflicts. Compensation for elopement which were formerly unknown emerged, with the Indigenous Tribunals bearing the brunt of the new notion of compensation. Originally set up to carry out the precepts of customary law, these bodies were now faced with a new phenomenon arising from the indirect influence of the French. The idea of remuneration for 'lost' women arose, with an almost cynical cosmopolitan agreement developing between the husband and the beloved to determine the exact worth of a particular woman. Compensation tended to become a game among families.[2]

The custom of the levirate also received special treatment in French legislation. This practice becomes meaningful only when viewed in terms of the traditional safeguards for women. Unable to inherit property from a deceased husband, a woman could become destitute upon being widowed. The bridewealth paid upon her marriage had long since been 'eaten up' and her return to her kinsmen would be rendered doubly difficult without recompense. Inheritance by a brother of her dead husband, however, would allow the woman to retain her place in the collectivity in which she had made her home over the years, as well as protect the future of her children. If, however, the woman followed the implications of the Mandel Decree and accepted the implicit assumption that there was something morally wrong in being 'inherited', she would be out in the cold, lacking traditional safeguards with no customary law to protect her.[3] Before

1. *Ibid.*, pp. 224-225.
2. *Ibid.*, p. 226.
3. J. OBOA, "Le rôle de l'épouse", in DU ROSTU, pp. 75-76.

French control, a woman could be integrated relatively easily into the lineage of her spouse despite the lack of consanguineal tie. The ideas of emancipation enforced by the Mandel Decree permitted women to believe that they were their own masters. A woman traditionally could avoid the levirate if she wanted, if repayment of the bride price were made. If she were young, she might contract another marriage, in which case her new husband was obliged to make repayment. If, however, a widow did not remarry, choosing not to follow traditional patterns, she had the task of raising her children without any anchor. The independence foisted upon her by the colonial administration was out of place in traditional society, since the woman belonged neither to the social grouping of her deceased husband nor did she fit very comfortably into the bosom of her family of orientation.[1]

Looking now at the provisions of the law which permitted any woman over 21 years of age or whose marriage had been previously dissolved to contract marriage, one can note Labouret's dismay at the transformation that occurred to the indigenous societies of the A.O.F. Marriage had become a very fragile thing, with young people able to overturn matrimonial compensation without recourse to the advice of their parents. Elopements or divorce prevailed, preventing the maintenance of familial solidarity. Women learned European principles of the disposition of their own person from the Indigenous Tribunals and scorned the advice given them by their families concerning their proposed marriages. They refused some marriages that were suitable and accepted others that were not. As they realized their errors, they divorced to contract other unions that were just as ephemeral as their previous ones.[2] Phillips saw the old edifice of the community tottering, with the societies of the A.O.F. breaking up into more and more independent *ménages*. Phillips' comment that "colonial statutory law is sometimes ill-adjusted to African customary law in relation to marriage and kindred matters [. . .] with great divergence in rules made by native authorities and the practice of native courts in respect to matrimonial issues"[3] is an apt one.

Another major area meriting attention is that of divorce. Kimble, in his study of Tropical Africa, points out that while in former time divorces were not as easy to obtain, the relative freeing of women from the control of their families brought about serious problems in this realm. Under the indigenous system, adultery was viewed only to a limited extent as grounds for divorce. With the new concept of

1. Mme HOUECHENOU, "La femme seule", in DU ROSTU, p. 84.
2. H. LABOURET, *Paysans d'Afrique Occidentale*, Paris, 1941, p. 286.
3. A. PHILLIPS, *Survey of African Marriage and Family Life*, London, 1953, p. iii.

'worth' brought to the woman, she began to exact Western conceptions of fidelity upon her spouse.

"The husband's relations with a woman other than his wife cannot ordinarily be challenged by the wife. In legal proceedings, the wife's adultery is commonly regarded as a ground for divorce. However, if there is persistence or else if it involves desertion, this is most often seen as the real grounds of divorce. In the case of customary marriage, it has not usually been thought that this state of law calls for any interference by way of legislation. However, nowadays [1960] with increasing formalization of the grounds of divorce, there are signs of a tendency for adultery to be recognized as a ground on which the wife will be entitled to divorce."[1]

Bridewealth also came within the scope of the new laws. A girl whose parents might try to prevent her marriage was no longer in a dependent position. Inflation and a money economy also introduced by the French had their influence on the marriage payment which reached fantastic proportions. As a woman became detached from her family group as a result of her new ability to choose her mate, inflation in bridewealth jumped completely out of bounds. It was not at all unusual for parents to prolong courtship in order to extort more gifts. Often a young man would be rejected for a wealthier suitor even after many of his gifts had been accepted. Robin, in his study of Moslems in Senegal, believed that the control of bridewealth by administrators was almost impossible to achieve and suggested rather that the French administrators be better served in investigating and codifying native marriage practice rather than changing marriage practices in the rural areas.[2] Excessive bridewealth demands were often the cause of appearances before the Tribunal. The following case quoted in Sister Marie-André du Sacré-Cœur is interesting to examine:

"A young Cameroonian Christian [. . .] was promised in marriage to a man of 55, who had three wives. The father of Bernadette had already spent an installment payment of 85,000 CFA francs against the total bridewealth and several gifts. The young girl reached the age of 15 and the husband-to-be claimed her. She refused to go live with him. He waited some months demanding that her father make her obey, but Bernadette obstinately refused this husband. The potential husband asked for reimbursement of what he had already paid out and Bernadette's father tried forcibly to carry her to the prospective bridegroom. The girl succeeded in running away and taking refuge at the Mission. Then she went to the Tribunal to demand her liberty. Thanks to the Mandel and Jacquinot Decrees, she was able to marry a wooer of her choice."[3]

1. G. Kimble, *Tropical Africa*, New York, 1960, II, p. 225.
2. J. Robin, "L'évolution du mariage coutumier chez les musulmans du Sénégal", *Africa*, 17 (3), 1947: 192 (especially p. 200).
3. Sister Marie-André du Sacré-Cœur, *La femme noire...*

Once again, Sister Marie-André du Sacré-Cœur is not concerned with the traditional nature of the involvement of the girl's family in accepting payment toward the bridewealth before the marriage was consummated, fully anticipating that their child would be duty-bound to obey. As a result of the law, many families refused to send their daughters to mission schools for fear they would not accept the husband chosen for them. Marriages had become a well-paying business as a result of the economic changes wrought by the French. In fact, a sort of legend of the young girl 'worth a million' emerged, indicating the extremes to which these abuses reached. Figures quoted by Dugast show that bridewealth in the Cameroon underwent a change from about 900 CFA francs in 1936 to 40,000 CFA francs in 1953, to 110,000 CFA francs in 1956.[1]

Balandier in his study of the Fang of Gabon[2] views the moral looseness of women linked inextricably to the concept of commodity introduced by the French. The movement of women is a logical outcome of the cycle of economic exchange the French introduced in the acculturative situation, with family disorganization second in importance to the needs of market demands. Abbé Zoa has also pointed up the commercial aspects of the bridewealth and in its wake, an increase in the amount of bachelors and spinsters because of the high cost of marriage. Prostitution, abortion, and sterility multiplied as a result of the 'Plan Individuel', which Abbé Zoa saw to be hardly efficacious in maintaining a stable, functioning social order.[3]

The last provision of the Mandel Decree dealt with the official sanctioning of monogamy. Closely associated with the high cost of the bridewealth clandestine polygamy developed. Men who were outwardly monogamous had permanent liaisons with women. The children of these unions were recognized but no bridewealth had been paid. Since according to the Mandel Decree, mutual consent was all that mattered, these women were able to leave their homes and lineages to take up residence as they pleased. As far as the legislators were concerned, these were legal unions. Nominal Christians living with these women escaped the reproaches of the Clergy, which they undoubtedly would have received had they installed two or three women in their household. As Tardits points out, there was no law to prevent an initially monogamous man from becoming polygamous as long as he did not make an official declaration on this subject at the time that his marriage was solemnized. These so-called monogamous marriages were brief in duration and often followed by others. Tardits sees this to be the brutal results of the devious efforts of the legislators to

1. Dugast, p. 257.
2. Balandier, *Sociologie actuelle...*, p. 189.
3. Zoa, p. 66.

enforce their conceptions of morality upon people whose customs in fact differ.[1]

Balandier also speaks of the high proportion of divorce in Gabon which can be tied in with inflation and the increase in bridewealth. In the canton of N'Dou-Libi, for example, during the course of one year 206 marriages out of 521 (approximately 39%) ended in divorce. The author has used the term 'restrained polygamy' to sum up quite aptly this situation due to the high cost of women.[2]

Conclusion

Although one could argue that the French in their civilizing mission in West and Equatorial Africa attempted to bring the benefit of their experience as a technological, industrialized nation to their colonies, the evidence seems to point rather markedly to their failure especially in the sphere of women's rights. As Atangana clearly points out, African societies to which the French legislated were judged by European values and not in terms of historical or social context.[3] Ultimate political control resting in the hands of the French determined the outcome of the clash between the two distinctive systems.

Certainly one can view rules and regulations with roots within one or another segment of a society in terms of their organic emergence to meet the requirements of maintaining social control. These sanctions and controls, whether or not they maintain equilibrium and whether or not they are dysfunctional to some degree, at least have the virtue of being an outgrowth of the inner conflicts of the particular culture. Having an inner evolutionary tendency, these rules attempt to cope with political, economic and social arrangements within the society. Rheinstein's comment that "law is not a body of rules that can be unified or modified at will by government fiat, it is part of a society's set of norms of behavior"[4] is pertinent here.

The colonial experience, in attempting to graft European-based legislation to African soil, produced monstrosities of misunderstanding and dislocation of fundamental institutions which had their *raison d'être* in the history and growth of a particular culture. The problem in francophonic Africa was that its rulers attempted to replace African legal norms with their own at too rapid a pace, and were unaware of those elements of customary law that had significance in regulating

1. C. Tardits, *Porto-Novo: Les nouvelles générations africaines entre leurs traditions et l'Occident*, Paris, 1958, p. 65 ff.
2. Balandier, *Sociologie actuelle...*, p. 192.
3. N. Atangana, "La femme africaine dans la société", *Présence Africaine*, 17, 1957: 133.
4. Rheinstein, p. 224.

social relations within the community. Delavignette believed that the educated elite should have been permitted a share in the administration of customary law and would have served admirably as innovators of social change, influencing local customs in the direction of European customs toward which many had identified.[1] Writers like Delavignette and Labouret saw all too clearly the weaknesses of the French system but were unable to do much to stem the tide of French legislation. It is clear that there was an inherent contradiction to the spectacle of one culture attempting to impose its philosophy of freedom on another. The head-on collision that occurred was inevitable.

APPENDIX I

Mandel Decree (15 June 1939)

ARTICLE PREMIER. — En Afrique Occidentale française et en Afrique Équatoriale française, la femme avant quatorze ans révolus, l'homme avant l'âge de seize ans, ne peuvent contracter mariage.

ARTICLE 2. — Le consentement des futurs époux est indispensable à la validité du mariage.

Seront nulles de plein droit, sans que la partie qui se dirait lésée par la prononciation de la nullité puisse, de ce fait, réclamer aucune indemnité :

1° Toute convention matrimoniale concernant la fillette impubère, qu'elle soit ou non accompagnée du consentement de la fille ;

2° Toute convention matrimoniale concernant la fille pubère, lorsque celle-ci refuse son consentement ;

3° Toute revendication de veuve ou de toute autre personne faisant partie d'une succession coutumière, lorsque cette personne refuse de se rendre chez l'héritier auquel elle est attribuée.

APPENDIX II

Jacquinot Decree (14 September 1951)

ARTICLE PREMIER. — En Afrique occidentale française, en Afrique équatoriale française, au Cameroun et au Togo, les citoyens ayant conservé leur statut personnel contractent mariage suivant la coutume qui leur est propre, sous réserve des dispositions du décret du 15 juin 1939 et de celles qui font l'objet des articles ci-après.

ARTICLE 2. — Même dans les pays où la dot est une institution coutumière, la fille majeure de vingt et un ans, et la femme dont le précédent mariage a été

1. DELAVIGNETTE, p. 90.

légalement dissous, peuvent librement se marier sans que quiconque puisse prétendre en retirer un avantage matériel, soit à l'occasion des fiançailles, soit pendant le mariage.

ARTICLE 3. — Dans ces mêmes pays, le défaut de consentement des parents, s'il est provoqué par des exigences excessives de leur part, ne peut avoir pour effet de faire obstacle au mariage d'une fille mineure de vingt et un ans.

Il y a exigence excessive chaque fois que le taux de la dot réclamée dépasse le chiffre déterminé, suivant les régions, par le chef de territoire.

ARTICLE 4. — Les tribunaux du premier degré sont habilités à juger des différends résultant de l'application de l'article 3, ils sont tenus, chaque fois qu'ils constatent qu'il y a eu exigence excessive de la part des parents, d'en donner acte gratuitement au requérant. Ce document lui permet de faire enregistrer son mariage par l'officier d'état civil sans le consentement des parents de la fiancée.

ARTICLE 5. — Tout citoyen ayant conservé son statut personnel peut, au moment de contracter mariage, faire inscrire par l'officier d'état civil, sur l'acte de mariage, sa déclaration expresse de ne pas prendre une autre épouse aussi longtemps que le mariage qu'il contracte ne sera pas régulièrement dissous.

Cette déclaration constitue l'acte spécial dont il est fait mention à l'article 339, alinéa 2, du Code pénal applicable en Afrique occidentale française, en Afrique équatoriale française, au Cameroun et au Togo.

"COTTON IS THE MOTHER OF POVERTY": PEASANT RESISTANCE TO FORCED COTTON PRODUCTION IN MOZAMBIQUE, 1938–1961

Allen Isaacman, Michael Stephen, Yussuf Adam, Maria João Homen, Eugenio Macamo, and Augustinho Pililão

During the past decade historians have increasingly come to recognize the dominant role that capitalism has played in shaping the twentieth-century history of Africa. They have given particular attention to the mechanisms of capital accumulation and the related process of underdevelopment. What has often been overlooked or understated has been the struggle of workers and especially peasants[1] against the appropriation of their labor. As Colin Leys has noted, "in one critical respect underdevelopment theory tends to resemble development theory—it concentrated on what happens *to* the underdeveloped countries at the hands of imperialism and colonialism, rather than on the total historical process involved, including the various forms of struggle against imperialism and

[1]We would like to thank the FRELIMO Party and the government structures in Gaza and Cape Delgado provinces for the assistance and guidance which they provided. The Rectoria of the Universidade Eduardo Mondlane and the coordinating commission for the July activities offered important financial and logistical aid which facilitated our research. Alpheus Manghezi and Salamão Zandamela played an important role in our brigades' fieldwork in Gaza province. Aquino de Braganca, Harry Boyte, Isabel Cassimiro, José Charzin, Anna Charzin, Sara Evan, Barbara Isaacman, Joseph Pampalk, Susan Rodgers,and June Stephen made perceptive criticisms of an early draft of this article. Finally, we want to thank all our informants from whom we learned a great deal. Obviously, without their assistance this study could not have been written.

For the purposes of this essay we have defined peasants as "rural cultivators, living in household units, who control the land they work as either tenants or smallholders and whose surpluses are appropriated by a dominant class which does not participate directly in production." The key issue is the transformation of communal cultivators into peasants which is linked to the broader process of class differentiation. In many parts of Mozambique, the creation of a peasantry antedated the cotton regime, while in other zones, where capital and state penetration had been minimal, such as Niassa and Cabo Delgado, preliminary data suggest that the imposition of forced cotton production precipitated this transformation. For an important new collection of essays on peasants see Martin Klein, ed., *Peasants in Africa* (Beverly Hills, 1980).

colonialism which grow out of the condition of underdevelopment."[2]

In its most extreme form this economistic tendency has had the effect of reducing the subordinate classes to mere producers of surplus value whose own history lacked any meaning or significance within the colonial-capitalist context. It denied them the dignity of historical agents who played a role in shaping their own destinies and instead cast them as either impotent or impassive victims.

This interpretation acquires a certain logic in the context of peasant resistance because of the weak competitive position of the peasantry vis-à-vis the union of the colonial state and capital. Peasants divided from each other by space, ethnicity, religion, primordial kinship affiliations, the tyranny of their work schedule and a host of other factors were relatively powerless and generally failed to mount large-scale opposition which lends itself to detailed historical analysis.[3] Instead peasant protests tended to be isolated, covert, and often passive, their limited aims and systemic importance hard to measure and easy to ignore.

The nature of the sources available to historians reinforces the tendency to neglect peasant resistance in the literature. Colonial officials and representatives of European capital were often unaware of the hidden forms of peasant protest which could only succeed if they remained clandestine. Moreover, when discovered, actions such as work slowdowns and boycotts were treated as yet one more indication of the "lazy and uneconomic nature of the African" rather than being carefully treated and documented as serious expressions of rural discontent. Oral data, on the other hand, is often replete with examples of peasant protest, but these accounts do not tend to be situated precisely in time or space and the motivation for a specific action is often blurred or overly generalized. Ex post facto explanations to satsify contemporary political realities pose an additional problem.[4]

Given these deficiencies in the data it becomes extremely difficult to reconstruct with any precision the frequency and geographic

[2]Colin Leys, *Underdevelopment in Kenya* (Berkeley, 1975), 20.

[3]Among these exceptions were the Maji-Maji rebellion, the Bambatha rebellion and a series of insurgent peasant actions in the Transkei and the Zambesi Valley. See John Iliffe, "The Organization of the Maji-Maji Rebellion," *Journal of African History*, VIII (1967), 495–512; Shula Marks, *Reluctant Rebellion* (Oxford, 1977); Allen Isaacman, *The Tradition of Resistance in Mozambique* (Berkeley, 1976); William Beinart and Colin Bundy, "State Intervention and Rural Resistance: The Transkei, 1900–1965," *Peasants in Africa*, 271–314.

[4]During our fieldwork we observed on several occasions that former cotton producers explained their opposition in the revolutionary language of FRELIMO.

scope of peasant resistance, or how it changed over time—questions of considerable importance to historians. Yet neither the data problem nor the dominance of capital is sufficient reason to ignore the struggle of peasants. Acting within the serious constraints imposed by the colonial-capitalist system, they were, to varying degrees, able to alter their living conditions and in some cases the outcome of their history. From this perspective, the example of peasant resistance to the cotton regime in Mozambique, an extremely controlled and repressive system, is particularly instructive.

The Cotton Regime—An Overview, 1938–1961

As in other parts of Africa, the Portuguese colonial regime sought to extract from its colonized people cash crops or other exchange value commodities which could be sold on the world market. The failure of the Republican government (1910–1926) to exploit effectively the colony's human and natural resources and thereby reduce Portugal's balance of payments deficit and national debt was one of the factors that precipitated the military coup in 1926 and two years later brought Salazar to power.[5] Under his regime Lisbon exercised close supervision over the colonies which, whenever possible,[6] were to be reserved for exploitation by Portuguese capital and in all cases were to provide significant economic benefits to the metropole. These principles were enshrined in the Colonial Act of 1930.[7]

The expansion of cotton production in the colonies figured prominently in the Salazar regime's economic plan. In 1927 only 5 percent of the ginned cotton used in the Portuguese textile industry came from Lisbon's possessions; the remainder was purchased on the world market.[8] Salazar's objective was to reverse this tendency and to make Portugal self-sufficient through her colonies. This, in turn, would reduce the balance of trade deficit and facilitate the expansion of the textile industry. Because of its fertile soils, good

[5]For a discussion of the ascension to power of the Salazar regime with specific reference to the importance of the colonies, see Alan K. Smith, "Antonio Salazar and the Reversal of Portuguese Colonial Policy," *Journal of African History*, XV (1974), 653–667.

[6]For varying interpretations on this point see *ibid.;* Louis de Brito, "Algumas notas a proposito de História Contemporanea de Moçambique" (unpublished ms., 1978); Leroy Vail and Landeg White, "The Struggle for Mozambique: Capitalist Rivalries, 1900–1940," *Review* III (1979), 243–275.

[7]Smith, "Antonio Salazar," 665–666.

[8]Arquivo do Instituto de Algodão (A.I.A.), Junta de Exportação de Algodão Colonial (J.E.A.C.), Propoganda Moçambique, "Elementos Para o Seculo," Gastã de Mello Furtado, June 15, 1954.

rainfall, accessible ports, and minimal contribution to the colonial economy, Portuguese officials designated Mozambique as the center of overseas cotton production with Angola assuming a subordinate position.

In 1926, the colonial regime opted for a labor-intensive system based on forced peasant production and requiring minimal investment.[9] The system was modeled on the Belgian Congo which, Portuguese officials noted enviously, "had achieved brilliant results, and raised cotton production within a ten-year period from 4 to 4,000 tons.[10] The Portuguese regime passed legislation establishing cotton zones and granting concessions to local commercial interests each of which received the exclusive right to purchase at fixed prices the cotton that peasants within the region were compelled to grow. The concessionary companies were then to sort and gin the cotton and sell it overseas, preferably to the Portuguese textile industry.

For more than a decade, this legislation was not vigorously implemented in Mozambique. The low fixed price paid both to the peasants and the concessionary holders, competition for local labor with higher paying sisal, tea, and sugar plantations within Mozambique, and the South African mines and Rhodesian farms, and the fact that much of the best land in northern Mozambique initially remained outside the concessionary system all combined to undercut Lisbon's plans. The inability or unwillingness of many local administrators to force peasants to grow cotton also affected output.[11] Thus in 1931, five years after the system had been introduced, production was down by 50 percent from the 1926 level, and most of the Mozambican cotton was sold on the higher-priced international

[9]Cotton production in Mozambique could have been organized in a number of different ways. One possibility would have been for Portuguese industrial capitalists to make large-scale inputs into cotton growing which would have given ita capital-intensive character. Alternatively, either the state or industrial capital might have created financial incentives to motivate European settlers to organize plantations. A third possibility would have been to stimulate "free" peasant production. The failure to adopt any of these strategies is linked, in part, to the weakness of Portuguese capital which lacked the resources and interest to finance the first, and to guarantee a reasonable return to either planters or peasants. Thus, in the period immediately after World War I European cotton plantations established in southern Mozambique all had failed miserably and those rural cultivators producing for the markets chose to cultivate peanuts, sesame seeds and food crops which were more profitable than cotton.

[10]Boletim Oficial de Moçambique (B.O.M.), Series 1, no. 37 (September 11, 1926), 221.

[11]Direção dos Servicos de Agricultura, *Algodão* (Lourenço Marques, 1934), 1–18; Leroy Vail and Landeg White, "Tawani Machambero: Forced Cotton and Rice Growing on the Zambezi," *Journal of African History*, XIX (1978), 245–246.

market, compelling the Portuguese textile industry to purchase 99 percent of its ginned cotton abroad.[12]

To help remedy this situation, Lisbon agreed the following year to pay a bonus to the concessionary companies on all cotton exported to the metropole on Portuguese ships.[13] This neomercantile policy narrowed the price differential and redirected most of Mozambique's cotton to the Portuguese market.[14] It had no impact, however, on the more fundamental problem of the relatively low level of colonial production vis-à-vis rapidly expanding metropolitan industrial requirements. In 1935, for example, 80 percent of the 2.5 million kilograms of cotton produced in Mozambique went to Portugal, which nevertheless had to purchase an additional 21 million kilograms at a cost of more than $10 million.[15] Although Mozambican output increased substantially in 1936 and 1937, the shortfall remained largely unchanged. As a result, the powerful textile industry, provoked by paying substantially more for foreign cotton, demanded vigorous state intervention. In 1938, the Salazar regime, itself concerned about the balance of trade deficits and continued dependency on external cotton sources, initiated a far-reaching program designed to put teeth in the earlier legislation and insure a basic shift in rural production.

At the heart of this policy was direct state control over all aspects of production and marketing. A State Cotton Board (Junta de Exportação de Algodão Colonial) was established to oversee the development of cotton production throughout the colonies.[16] The Board began a vigorous campaign to distribute additional concessions to local companies which had sufficient capital to construct and maintain ginning mills and markets and to pay the salaries of a small number of European field agents *(propagandistas)* and overseers *(capatazes)*.[17] Within a few years, agreements had been signed with twelve firms, each of which received substantial territory in which it enjoyed a buying monopoly (see Table I).

The Junta, working closely with the Portuguese textile industry

[12]A.I.A., J.E.A.C., Propoganda Moçambique, "Elementos Para o Seculos," Gastão de Mello Furtado, June 15, 1954.

[13]This decree (number 21, 226) was passed on April 22, 1932.

[14]A.I.A., J.E.A.C., Propoganda Moçambique, "Elementos Para o Seculo," Gastão de Mello Furtado, June 15, 1954.

[15]*Ibid.*

[16]B.O.M., Series 1, no. 27, July 6, 1938, 293–297; Nelson Saraiva Bravo, *A Cultura Algodoeira na Economia do Norte de Moçambique* (Lisbon, 1963), 105–117.

[17]*Ibid.*, B.O.M., Series 1, no. 45 (November 9, 1946), 459–466.

TABLE I
CONCESSIONARY COMPANIES

Name of Company	District	No. of Cotton Zones
Algodeira do Sul de Save, Lda.	Gaza and Inhambane	10
Companhia do Buzi, S.A.R.L.	Manica and Sofala	1
Companhia Nacional Algodeira	Manica and Sofala	6
Companhia da Zambézia, S.A.R.L.	Tete	1
Sociedade Algodeira de Tete, Lda.	Tete	
Companhia Agricola E Comercial Lopes e Irmaos	Zambézia	1
Sena Sugar Estates Ltd.	Zambézia and Manica and Sofala	2
Monteiro e Giro Lda.	Zambézia	3
Companhia dos Algodões de Mocambique	Mozambique; Cabo Delgado; Zambézia	23
Companhia Agricola e Comercial João Ferreira dos Santos	Mozambique	6
Sociedade Algodeira de Niassa	Niassa and Mozambique	5
Sociedade Agricola Algodeira	Cabo Delgado and Niassa	10

and the concessionary companies, both of which had representatives on the Board, fixed mandatory dates for planting the cotton, determined the type of seeds to be distributed, and defined the various qualities of cotton. It also recommended to the provincial governor-general the price per kilogram to be paid to the peasants by the concessionary companies and to the concessionary companies by the Portuguese textile industry. At the district level, local Board representatives suggested to state officials the minimum acreage that each peasant had to cultivate. Unlike the earlier system, the Cotton Board also prohibited export of Mozambican cotton to foreign countries.[18]

The revitalized cotton regime depended, in the final analysis, on the effective mobilization of peasant labor. Thus, the policy had four goals: (1) to increase the number of peasants compelled to grow

[18] *Ibid.*

cotton; (2) to insure that those cultivators legally required to produce cotton actually did so; (3) to expand the number of hours each day that rural producers devoted to cotton; and (4) to maintain downward pressure on the price structure.

Competing claims for labor of other capitalist interests complicated the ability of the cotton regime to mobilize the peasants. One of the central features of Mozambique's political economy was the large number of men from the rural areas who worked as migrant laborers in South Africa and Rhodesia. Although the number of legal migrants varied from year to year during the period 1936 to 1960, between 75,000 and 105,000 Mozambicans annually worked in the South African gold mines,[19] and a large number were also employed in agriculture. Figures for Rhodesia are not available, although, for a somewhat later period, U.N. reports estimated that about 100,000 Mozambicans, primarily men, were working on Rhodesian farms, mines and in service areas.[20] Most of the migrant laborers, especially those in South Africa, were recruited from the provinces of Inhambane, Gaza, Manica and Sofala (see map). In addition, a significant, although appreciably smaller, number of rural men worked on European sugar and tea plantations located primarily in Zambésia and on sisal plantations in Cabo Delgado. Sena Sugar, the largest of these, employed more than 30,000 Mozambicans in 1940.[21]

The principal way of increasing the number of cotton producers was to distribute additional territory to the concessionary companies. This policy had the effect of creating a dynamic cotton frontier with new areas rapidly incorporated into the system and the inhabitants registered and given cotton cards which specified how much land they farmed and the amount of cotton seeds they received.[22]. Initially, each of the zones was 50 kilometers, but in the 1940s was increased to 120 kilometers. Since there was no limit to the number of zones a concessionary company could accumulate, most firms tended to absorb as much territory as possible. They gave only limited consideration to the quality of the land, since their basic concern was total output and not individual productivity, and more territory meant more cultivators and greater production. Given this

[19]For statistics on the number of Mozambicans working in the mines, see Centro de Estudos Africanos. *The Mozambican Mines* (Maputo, 1977), 24c.

[20]For various estimates on the number of Mozambicans working in Rhodesia see United Nations Economic and Social Council, E/5812, 20, and United Nations General Assembly, A/AC/108/1.338/Add. 3.

[21]Vail and White, "Tawani Machambero," 247.

[22]Bravo, *A Cultura Algodoeira,* 109–111.

logic it is not surprising that the larger firms, such as the Companhia dos Algodões de Moçambique, controlled twenty-three zones covering half the area of the densely populated provinces of Zambésia and Moçambique, while the Sociedade Agricola Algodoeira had a monopoly over most of Cape Delgado.[23]

Although no precise figures are available on the number of peasant producers before 1938, it is possible to estimate this figure based on total annual output. If one assumed that productivity per peasant in the middle 1930s was equal to the 1940–1943 average of about 90 kilograms per producer, the number in 1935 would have been slightly more than 20,000, and in 1937 approximately 80,000.[24] By 1939 the number of cotton producers actually registered had skyrocketed to more than 534,000 and by 1944 to 791,000, three-fourths of whom were in the three northern provinces. Such an increase is particularly significant when one takes into account the large, though indeterminant, number of child laborers who, though not registered, aided their parents.[25]

To strengthen the position of the concessionary companies vis-à-vis other capitalist interests, the state passed legislation in 1946 (decree 38.844) which specifically prohibited other labor recruitment within the cotton zones. Theoretically, the companies were guaranteed a monopoly position for the concessionary companies and their industrial allies in Portugal.[26] Two years later the state introduced broad production guidelines in part to guarantee that all adults living within the concessionary holdings produced cotton, including widows and men up to sixty years of age who had previously not been compelled to participate.[27]

[23]The principal growing areas in the south were Muchopes and Zavala in Inhambane district and Bilene and Guija in Gaza district. In 1964 there were only slightly more than 94,000 cotton producers in these two districts—a small fraction of the 791,000 total. A.I.A., J.E.A.C., "Relatório da Inspecçao de J.E.A., 1940–1945," João Contrieras, O Inspector dos Servicos Algódoeiros Ultramarinos da J.E.A.C. to Presidente da J.E.A.C., May 1945.

[24]*Ibid.*

[25]It was common in most families for older children to be involved in production though legally not obligated until they reached their eighteenth birthday.

[26]B.O.M., Series 1, no. 45 (November 9, 1945), 466. This was not always the case, especially in southern and central Mozambique. In the former, large numbers of men were recruited to work in the South African mines which meant that in the district of Gaza, for example, 80 percent of the cotton cultivators were women (A.I.A., J.E.A.C., "Papeis Diversos, 1941," J. Anachoreta, Chefe da Sub-delegaçao do Sul de Save, September 1941). On the Sena Sugar estates and the holdings of the Companhia de Buzi all cotton production was done by women (A.I.A., J.E.A.C., 601/8, José Maria Marques da Cunha, Administrador de Cheringoma, December 7, 1945; A.I.A., J.E.A.C., "Confidencial 1947," Sub-Delgado J.E.A.C., December 20, 1947; Vail and White, "Tawani Machambero," 248).

[27]Bravo, *A Cultura Algodoeira,* 117.

From 1938, the concessionary companies could count on the colonal regime to mobilize and control labor. Under the law, the Cotton Board dictated when peasants had to begin planting and reseeding, the number of times the fields were to be weeded, and the final harvest dates, while African police known as *sipais*, state-approved chiefs and local administrators were instructed to use whatever coercive methods necessary to guarantee production. Together with the smaller number of company field agents and overseers, who received *de facto* legal status, they supervised all phases of production.

The mere presence of any state or concessionary company officials was sufficient to intimidate most peasants, as is evident from the memoirs of one Protestant missionary in Niassa Province. "Administrator Cunhal," he noted, "tyrannized the blacks. He was always accompanied by several *sipais* armed with truncheons and kept a *palmatório* (paddle) and a *chicote* (whip) in his car."[28] As one producer recalled, they had good reason to be afraid. "If we refused to grow cotton they arrested us, put us in chains, beat us and then sent us to a place from where we didn't come back."[29] Peasants who rejected the seeds which the chiefs distributed or who failed to produce the established minimum quantity were sent to work on forced labor gangs building railroad lines and other state projects, were compelled to work on sisal, tea and sugar plantations for little or no remuneration, or were deported to São Tome.[30] When *sipais*, who regularly patrolled the fields, noted that a particular cotton plot was not properly weeded or that only a portion of the demarcated area was under cultivation, they beat the guilty party and, if a woman was involved, sexually abused her as well.[31] Repeaters went to jail for a minimum of thirty days, depending on the whim of the company overseers and local administrators. Peasants covertly

[28]John Paul, *Memoirs of a Revolution* (London, 1975), 71.

[29]Quoted in Eduardo Mondlane, *The Struggle for Mozambique* (London, 1970), 85.

[30]José Alberto Gomes de Melo Branquinho, *Prospecção das Forcas Tradicionais Districto de Moçambique* (Lourenço Marques, 1965), 170; interview with Makwati Simba, Xavier Jossene, Mondwai Muene e Amelia Macuacua, February 13, 1979, in Chibuto; interview with Benjamin Mavunga, February 12, 1979, in Chibuto; interview with Nhacatala, July 28, 1979, in Chai; group interview, July 23, 1979, in Namuno.

[31]Interview with Rita Mulumbua of Niassa Provincia, quoted in Mondlane, *Struggle for Mozambique,* 80; interview with Makwati Simba; interview with Salomão Macamo, February 16, 1979, in Guija; A.I.A., J.E.A.C., 953, "Brigada Tecnica de Cabo Delgado," J. Costa Rosa, Regente Agricola, April 1949.

planting other crops or caught working in their family plots during restricted hours suffered similar fates.[32]

State and company authorities employed a variety of strategies to increase the percentage of the work day that the rural population allocated to cotton production. Given their monopoly of power, it was relatively easy for local administrators, many of whom were in the pay of the concessionary companies,[33] to impose a fixed work schedule. Cotton producers from such disparate area as Chibuto in Gaza district and Montepeuz in Cabo Delgado recounted how, although they were initially ordered to spend the morning on their cotton fields, the time period was subsequently extended through the early afternoon.[34] In some regions peasants could only work in their family gardens after 5:00 p.m., in the evening when there was a full moon, during the early hours of the morning before 7:00 a.m., and on those Sundays when they were not required to work on the large cotton fields of the chief.[35] In other areas the work day was elongated by increasing the size of the cotton plot,[36] or by establishing minimum production requirements. In Niassa district, local government officials declared in 1951 that any male who failed to produce 400 kilos of cotton would be sent to work without remuneration on European tea estates—a powerful incentive to spend longer hours in the cotton fields.[37]

[32]Branquinho, *Prospecção das Forcas Tradicionais Districto de Mocambique*, 170; interview with Makwati Simba, Xavier Jossene, Mondwai Muene e Amelia Macuacua, February 13, 1979, in Chibuto; interview with Benjamin Mavunga, February 12, 1979, in Chibuto; interview with Nhacatala, July 28, 1979, in Chai; group interview, July 23, 1979, in Namuno; interview with Rita Mulumbua of Niassa Provincia, quoted in Mondlane, *Struggle for Mozambique*, 80; interview with Makwati Simba; interview with Salomão Macamo, February 16, 1979, in Guija; A.I.A., J.E.A.C., 953, "Brigada Tecnica de Cabo Delgado," J. Costa Rosa, Regente Agricola, April 1949.

[33]Interview with Professor A. Quintanilha, March 7, 1979. Professor Quintanilha served as the director of the Centro de Investigação Cientifica Algodoeira throughout much of the period of the cotton regime and was a major spokesman for reforming the system.

[34]Group interview with Marco Chongo, Sideone Mabunda, Salomão Macamo, Ezequiel Mabasso, Stefano Filipe and Manuel Sitoi, February 16, 1979, in Guija; interview with Benjamin Mavunga; group interview, communal village, Luis Carols Prestes, February 2, 1979, in Gaza; joint interview with Chico Nhulialia and Costa Gaio Napire, May 2, 1979, in Nampula; interview with Eugenio Niquaria, July 24, 1979; in Montepuez; group interview with Daima Magaga Mbela, Kndaba Nchamada Otinga and Mangane Nkula Nquenia, July 30, 1979, in Macomia; interview with Pruan Hassan, July 20, 1979, in Montepuez.

[35]*Ibid.*

[36]*Ibid.*

[37]A.I.A., J.E.A.C., "Papeis Diversos, A Flegueira e Sousa to Governador de Niassa," February 21, 1952.

A variety of highly exploitative legal and extra-legal practices depressed the payments the peasants received and guaranteed a high rate of return both to the local Portuguese capitalists who controlled the concessionary companies and to the metropolitan textile interests. By lobbying on the State Cotton Board and by maintaining close relations with Mozambican colonial administration and the foreign ministry in Lisbon, concessionary officials were able to keep the price paid to Mozambican peasants artificially low. In 1938, for example, one kilogram of first quality cotton sold in southern Mozambique for six and a half cents and second quality for as little as four cents,[38] which represented a 15 percent reduction in price when compared with the period immediately before the revitalization of the cotton regime.[39] During the next twenty-five years the price paid for cotton increased at an appreciably lower rate than that for any other agricultural commodity produced in Mozambique except rice, which was also a forced culture.[40] By 1958 first quality cotton sold for approximately eleven and a half cents per kilogram—less than one-half the price paid in neighboring Southern Rhodesia and slightly more than two-thirds the price paid in Uganda and Kenya.[41]

Although concessionary companies benefitted from the low prices, the Portuguese textile industry benefitted even more. State pricing policies established rates for ginned cotton well below the world market price (see Table II). The metropolitan factories then

[38]A.I.A., J.E.A.C., "Papeis Diversos, 'Despacho'," J. Anachoreta, Chefe do Subdelegado do Sul de Save, June 12, 1940.

[39]*Ibid.*

[40]See *Estatisticas Agricolas, Provincia de Mocambique, 1941–1961.* The relative low value of cotton production is also reflected in the following table for 1945 whose figures were obviously rounded off by the author, João Gaspar Faria, "Produção Algodeira," *Seara Nova* 1083 (1948), 2:

Crop	Production/hectare (kgs.)	Income/hectare (dollars)
Algodao Caroco (cotton)	203	$ 51.09
Arroz (rice)	1.000	199.36
Feijao cafreal (beans)	1.000	199.36
Mandioca (manioc)	2.000	299.04
Mapira (sorghum)	1.300	299.04
Milho (corn)	2.500	488.40
Batata (potatoes)	2.500	623.00

[41]Bravo, *A Cultura Algodoeira,* 179–185.

produced low quality textiles which were exported to Mozambique under near monopoly conditions—since legislation stifled the development of a local textile industry and discriminatory tariffs effectively blocked non-Portuguese imports—and sold at inflated prices. In 1944 Lisbon established a ratio of fifteen and a half to one between the retail price of cotton cloth and the price peasants received for raw cotton. In reality the disparity was even greater. A 1945 study estimated the differential at thirty-one fold and a 1949 survey in the *Lourenço Marques Guardian* found that on average a peasant had to produce 115 kilograms of raw cotton to be able to purchase 1 kilogram of finished cotton.[42] Little wonder, the newspaper noted, that most Africans were forced to wear rags or go without any clothing at all.

TABLE II
COMPARATIVE PRICES FOR GINNED COTTON

Year	Mozambican Cotton Price (approximate)*	World Cotton Price (approximate)*
1947–48	$ .46	$ .77
1948–49	.47	.86
1949–50	.48	1.33
1950–51	.49	1.32
1951–52	.53	1.00
1952–53	.54	.83
1953–54	.53	.83
1954–55	.53	.90

SOURCE: Bravo, *A Cultura Algodoeira*, p. 186.

*Conversions from Portuguese escudos to dollars based on year figures published in *World Currency Charts* (San Francisco, 1969).

Their tattered clothing symbolized the impoverishment of the cotton producers who, forced to meet state-imposed work schedules, also found it difficult to satisfy their own food requirements. Although the colonial regime established different production calendars from one part of the country to another depending on the time of the first rains, these schedules universally created a serious production bottleneck. Peasants, compelled to attend first to their

[42]Faria, "Produção Algodoeira," 202; guardian (L.M.), April 8, 1949.

cotton fields, had insufficient time to clear and plant their family gardens. After the first cotton seeds were planted, it was often necessary to reseed large areas and almost immediately thereafter to begin to weed the fields. Weeding had to be done three or four times during the agricultural cycle, which reduced the possibility of planting supplementary food or cash crops and precluded having sufficient time to care for the crops already sown. Throughout most of the country peasants had to harvest the cotton in June or July and then spend two weeks on the several trips needed to carry it to the concessionary company markets. This created labor shortages at the critical moment when sorghum, corn, and other basic crops needed to be harvested.[43]

The results were both predictable and disastrous. Food shortages occurred with great regularity, and there was hardly a time, especially during the first fifteen years of forced cotton production, when famines were not noted by the colonial authorities and contemporary observers.[44] In 1951, for example, between 3,000 and 4,000 cotton producers were reported to have died of famine in Mogvolas in northern Mozambique.[45] As late as 1959 a confidential government report acknowledged that "the majority of the population is underfed" and warned that "it is absolutely necessary that

[43]Group interview with Makwati Simba; group interview, communal village, Magul, February 20, 1979; interview with Faria Lobo, May 4, 1979, in Nampula; interview with Pruan Hassan; interview with Amasse Niuta, communal village Nawana, July 20, 1979, in Montepuez; A.I.A., J.E.A.C., "Confidencial 1947, 'Relatório Especial Sobre Mercados'," António de Freitas Silva, 1947.

[44]*Ibid.*; A.I.A., J.E.A.C., 601/8 "Relatório," Administração de Mecona, October 23, 1946; A.I.A., J.E.A.C., 9494, "Rotacoes e Afolhamento," A. Flegueiras Sousa to Chefe da Delegacao da J.E.A.C., March 28, 1950; A.I.A., J.E.A.C., Gastão de Mello Furtado to Governador Geral, August 15, 1951; A.I.A., J.E.A.C., "Confidencias, 1947–59," Gastão de Mello Furtado to Presidente J.E.A.C., September 1, 1959; Armando Castro, *O Sistema Colonial Português em Africa* (Lisbon, 1978), 277; group interviews, communal village Magul and communal village Magude; joint interview, Chico Nhulialia and Costa Gaio Napire; interviews with Pruan Hassan and Faria Lobo.

The question of famines is related to the broader issue in Marxist literature of the articulation of capitalist and precapitalist modes of production. There is substantial debate on whether the earlier modes were destroyed, conserved or transformed as capital sought to insure a continued transfer of value from the periphery. In Mozambique, preliminary research suggests that the impact varied from one part of the country to another and that the "conservationist" theory needs to be reconsidered in light of the substantial transformations in technology and production patterns which occurred in many rural areas. For a discussion of this issue see C. Meillasoux, *Femmes, Greniers et Capitaux* (Paris, 1976); P. Rey, *Les Alliance de Classes* (Paris, 1976); P. Rey, *Capitalisme Negrier* (Paris, 1976); H. Wolpe, "Capitalism and Cheap Labor in South Africa," *Economy and Society*, I (1972). Bridget O'Laughlin has argued convincingly in her forthcoming study that the imposition of cotton in Chad resulted in a fundamental transformation of the precapitalist mode of production.

[45]Armando Castro, *O Sistema Colonial*, 277.

cotton producers have sufficient food supplies to enable them to work."[46] Many peasants supplemented their meagre diets by eating roots and tubers and planting manioc which, though of lower nutritional value than other food crops, required only a minimal amount of labor.[47] The deflated price structure and the low level of cotton production, moreover, prohibited the overwhelming majority of peasants from purchasing the food they had been unable to produce, let alone other basic commodities which many had been able to buy before the introduction of the cotton regime.[48] As one peasant recounted:

> My whole family produced cotton for the Companhia Agricola Algodeira. . . . They paid us very badly for it. It was extremely difficult to make a living because we were badly paid for it, and we didn't have time to look after our other crops. . . . The time of cotton growing was a time of great poverty, because we could only produce cotton; we got a poor price for it, and we did not have time to grow other crops. We were forced to produce cotton. The people did not want to; they knew cotton is the mother of poverty.[49]

This system of forced cotton cultivation operated until 1961. During its twenty-three-year history the cotton regime underwent a number of modifications in detail. In the late 1940s the state mandated that some of the more marginal land be dropped out of the system, and organized a number of planned cotton-growing communities *(concentrações)*. In 1954, concessionary holders received permission to export a portion of their crop to other markets but only after paying an additional 12 percent export tax which made their cotton appreciably less competitive.[50] Despite these changes, the basic objectives of the system, the alliance between industrial capital, commercial capital and the state, and the coercive character

[46]A.I.A., J.E.A.C., "Confidencias 1957–59," Gastão de Mello Furtado to Presidente de J.E.A., September 1, 1959.

[47]*Noticias,* July 19, 1941; Bravo, *A Cultura Algodoeira,* 97; A.I.A., J.E.A.C., 952, "Relatório da Brigada Technica de Nampula," J. Costa Rose, Regente Agricola, October 1949; A.I.A., J.E.A.C., "Confidencias 1957–59," Vasco de Sousa da Fonseca Lebre to Chefe da Delegacao de J.E.A.C., March 10, 1958; group interviews with Pruan Hassan, *et al.,* and Daima Magaga Mbela, *et al.*; joint interview with Chico Nhulialia and Costa Gaio Nampire.

[48]Group interview with Maulana Samate, *et al.,* July 29, 1979, in Balama; group interview with Adridhi Mahanda, *et al.,* July 23, 1979,in Balama.

[49]Quoted in Mondlane, *Struggle for Mozambique,* 87.

[50]B.O.M., Series 1, no. 46 (November 9, 1949), 461–465; *Diario de Moçambique,* February 18, 1954; Vail and White, "Tawani Machambero," 254.

of the cotton regime remained unaltered. Claims that "the authorities having squeezed the local Africans for fifteen years, began to relax their pressure,"[51] stand in stark contrast to the testimony of former cotton producers and contemporary Portuguese observers alike.[52]

Forms of Peasant Resistance

It was against this very powerful alliance that the peasants were pitted—an alliance whose continued success depended on its control over land, labor, and capital. Clearly the rural population had few possibilities to influence the supply and organization of capital and only slightly greater opportunity to affect the availability of land. They could and did, however, contest the amount of time they would put into the cotton system. Stated somewhat differently, the central arena of struggle focused on the appropriation of labor—there the peasants sought continually to minimize their involvement and, simultaneously, improve their working conditions.

Three possibilities existed for withholding labor. Peasants could attempt to withdraw from the cotton regime, to withhold regularly a portion of their labor, or to boycott the system at strategic moments. Although, for purposes of analysis, these possibilities are treated as distinct, in reality the second and third were sometimes linked, and cotton producers often engaged in either or both of the latter forms of protest before opting to flee. Similarly, some cotton producers who tried unsuccessfully to free themselves from the system subsequently participated in these alternative acts of defiance.

Permanently withholding labor, a common reaction, took a variety of forms. To avoid the tyranny of the cotton regime, many peasants deserted to neighboring countries, especially Tanganyika, Nyasaland, and South Africa, or fled to relatively uncontrolled areas in the backwater regions of the colony. In both cases they sought to regain their freedom and some measure of control over their economic destiny. Others who engaged in covert acts of sabotage, convinced state and concessionary company officials that their lands were unsuitable for cotton production and thereby gained

[51] Vail and White, "Tawani Machambero," 254.

[52] A.I.A., J.E.A.C., "Papeis Diversos," A Flegueira e Sousa to Governador de Niassa, February 21, 1952; A.I.A., J.E.A.C., 83 (1958/1959), Júlio Bossa to Chefe da Delegaçao de J.E.A.C., November 28, 1958; A.I.A., J.E.A.C., "Confidencias 1957–59," A Felgueiras e Sousa, March 26, 1957; A.I.A., J.E.A.C., "Armando Antunes de Almeida to Subdelegado de J.E.A.C.," September 29, 1959; interviews with Makwati Simba, Benjamin Mavunga, Pruan Hassan with Chico Nhulialia and Costa Gaio Napire.

exemption from the system. Whatever the concrete form, these acts of defiance represented the harshest blow an individual could strike against the cotton regime.

Throughout the twenty-five years of forced cotton production there were recurring reports of labor flight from all cotton zones of the country. Their clandestine nature precludes precise government statistics, but contemporary Portuguese observers noted the large-scale and debilitating effects. As early as 1940 one official in southern Mozambique complained that flight had already become a serious problem. "Africans fleeing the province of Sul de Save because of cotton is not something new. In 1938 it was reported that many natives abandoned their lands after setting fire to their huts."[53] Six years later his counterpart in Niassa district complained that, although he had registered 7,447 cotton producers in the administrations of Metangula and Unango, "the actual figure was appreciably smaller since just prior to the planting season many of the peasants fled to Niassaland."[54] A concessionary company field agent in the Mutarara region of Zambesia noted with disgust that between 1956 and 1957, some 500 of the 2,200 registered cotton producers had slipped across the border into Niassaland.[55] The recurring nature and cumulative effect of the clandestine migrations is reflected in the 1951 observation of the bishop of Beira: "The exodus of the indigenous population to the neighboring countries is an uncontestable fact and it is provoked exclusively by the rigorous demands of cotton."[56]

Individual flight was both arduous and dangerous. Peasants often had to walk several hundred kilometers through unfamiliar surroundings, sometimes with children on their backs. They faced a number of difficulties, including lack of food and shelter, attacks from marauding bandits and the ever-present threat of capture by police patrols. To overcome these dangers individual "fugitives" often linked up to form temporary bands in which they shared knowledge and food, and provided mutual protection.[57]

[53] A.I.A., J.E.A.C., Papeis Diversos, "Despacho," J. Anachoreta, Chefe do Sub-delegado do Sul de Save, June 12, 1940.

[54] A.I.A., J.E.A.C., 601/8, "Relatório," José Candido pereira Burugete Secretário da Administração de Maniamba, September 18, 1946.

[55] A.I.A., J.E.A.C., "Confidencias 1957–59," João Bello Practico Agricola da J.E.A., to Sub-delegado de J.E.A.C., February 13, 1957.

[56] See Sebastião Soares de Resende, *Ordem Anti-Communista* (Lourenço Marques, 1950), 140–142.

[57] Group interview, communal village Likangane, July 27, 1979, in Macomia; interview with Benjamin Jacob, July 27, 1979, in Macomia.

Smoldering resentment occasionally motivated entire communities to flee *en masse,* depriving the concessionary companies of critical cheap labor. Such large-scale migrations occurred less frequently than individual flight because of a general fear engendered by the colonialists' close surveillance, and harsh retribution for those caught. Nevertheless, a number of villages, especially those located near international borders, opted for such a strategy. In 1949 a State Cotton Board official noted the difficulty in maintaining cotton production in the northern frontier regions "because of the substantial migration of Makonde, Makua and Yao peasants who escaped to foreign territories."[58] Several cotton cultivators from the area recounted their long march to freedom. "On the prearranged night we brought out knives and clubs in order to protect our wives and children who were carrying food. We moved cautiously in the dark on forest tracks to avoid the *sipais* whom we had been informed were located at Nachidoro. We resolved to struggle to the last drop of blood to avoid capture." After a difficult journey they arrived at the River Rovuma and crossed safely into Tanganyika.[59] A contemporary of theirs in Gaza district recounted a similar story of many people fleeing from Chibuto to Swaziland and South Africa so that they would not have to cultivate cotton.[60]

Despite their suffering many cotton producers were initially reluctant to break all links with their families and traditional homelands. Instead of migrating to adjacent countries, numerous peasants fled to sparsely populated areas. Generally, this was a short-term solution to an immediate threat created by the anticipated arrival of *sipais* and cotton overseers. Men, and in some cases their families, hid in the forests or mountains in temporary makeshift shelters. They lived on hunting and gathering and the food brought clandestinely by their families. Life was extremely difficult, and most ultimately fled to neighboring countries. Some, however, returned reluctantly to their villages after a few months where they were severely punished.[61]

[58]A.I.A., J.E.A.C., 952, "Brigada Tecnica de Cabo Delgado," Vasconde Souse de Fonseca Lebre, September 30, 1949.

[59]Interview with Benjamin Jacob.

[60]Interview with Benjamin Mavunga.

[61]Group interview, communal village, Luis Carlos Prestes; group interview, communal village Magude, February 28, 1979, in Macia; group interview, communal village Nawawana, July 20, 1979, in Montepuez; interview with Benjamin Jacob; group interview, July 27, 1979, in Macomia.

Several documented cases exist of cotton producers who created permanent refugee communities in remote zones beyond the effective control of the colonial regime. Most were situated in rugged mountainous areas or in coastal swamps, where the difficult topography served as a natural barrier against Portuguese penetration. The harsh environment severely limited production potential, however, and the refugees had to survive on roots, tubers and wild game. Such autonomous communities were reported in the districts of Monapa, Mogincual, Mocamia, Balama, Mueda, and Montepuez, all located in northern Mozambique.[62]

Several of these refugee communities were able to maintain their independence for a number of years, surviving both the harsh environmental conditions and armed Portuguese incursions. Pruan Hassan recounted his experience in the mountains near Meloco in Balama:

> We managed to defend ourselves through extreme vigilance. As we were on the top of the mountain when the Portuguese came, we allowed them to climb half way before we rolled boulders down on them killing some. Some of our people hid themselves in caves. When the Portuguese arrived, they placed scrub and wood in the front and set it alight thinking that all those inside would suffocate to death with the smoke—then they left. But as our people were deep inside the cave, the smoke didn't reach them, no one died. So we continued to live there.[63]

A number of peasants duped state and concessionary company officials into believing that their lands would never yield cotton and thus should be dropped out of the system. They accomplished this by covertly cooking all or a substantial part of the cotton seeds before planting them. Such actions required collective agreement which, according to informants, only occurred after substantial and sometimes acrimonious debates over the viability of such a tactic. Suspected state informers and collaborators were either excluded from these secret evening meetings or intimidated into silence. One elderly woman who participated in clandestine meetings at Sierra Chanavane in Gaza district recounted that, "Chief Mailene called all the people together one evening where they agreed that they did

[62]Group interview with Pruan Hassan, Nemkuela Makorkuru, Masera Tahura, Materi Nhande and Rashide Rocha, July 20, 1979, in Montepuez; group interview, July 27, 1979, in Macomia, interview with Eugenio Niquaria.

[63]Interview with Pruan Hassan.

not want to continue cultivating cotton because they had no time for their food crops. After some discussion they all agreed to cook their seeds."[64] More often the initiative came from disenchanted peasants who compelled the chiefs to participate.[65]

Once this collective decision had been made, those involved went through all the motions of clearing, sowing, and weeding, but few or no plants germinated. Cotton officials and the colonial authorities were naturally surprised at the low yield, which they attributed to the poor quality of the soil or other natural deficiencies. By repeating the subterfuge over a two- or three-year period, many peasants freed themselves from the tyranny of the cotton regime.

Peasants successfully implemented this strategy in locations as diverse as Magude, Manjacaze, and Chibuto in Gaza district, and Montepuez, Pemba, and Mueda in Cape Delgado.[66] Testimony from colonial officials confirms that this type of sabotage occurred throughout the country.[67] While there is no clear evidence that this strategy was clandestinely transmitted from one area to another, the substantial interregional labor migrations and the fact that distant villages were aware of these acts of defiance, which often took on heroic proportions, suggest that such an informal network existed.[68]

As a result of the difficulties in identifying or detecting this practice, peasants were rarely caught. Those who were, however, suffered harsh retribution—destruction of food crops, systematic beating and long-term incarceration.[69] Moreover, this hard-won exemption did not necessarily guarantee freedom from forced cultivation, as events in Sierra Chanavane in Gaza illustrate. There

[64]Interview with Amelia Macuacua, February 10, 1979, in Chibuto.

[64]Interview with Amelia Macuacua, February 10, 1979, in Chibuto.

[65]*Ibid.*; interview with Marcos Chonga, *et al.*; group interview, communal village, Luis Carlos Prestes; group interview with Romeu Mataquenha, Tirani Ntuka and Mussa Vaquina, July 19, 1979, in Montepuez; group interview with Pruan Hassan, *et al.*; interview with Júlio Miambo, September 14, 1979, in Maputo.

[66]*Ibid.*; Sheri Young, "Changes in Diet and Production in Southern Mozambique, 1855–1960," 11–12.

[67]Interview with Engineer Ferreria de Castro, September 25, 1978, in Maputo; interview with Manuel Alves Salvador, February 12, 1979, in Xai-Xai.

[68]Group interview, communal village Likangane, July 27, 1979, in Macomia; interview with Benjamin Jacob, July 27, 1979, in Macomia; A.I.A., J.E.A.C., 952, "Brigada Tecnica de Cabo Delgado," Vasconde Souse de Fonseca Lebre, September 30, 1949.

[69]A.I.A., J.E.A.C., "Confidencias 1957–59," João Bello Practico Agricola da J.E.A., to Sub-delegado de J.E.A.C., February 13, 1957; interview with Marcos Chonga, *et al.*; group interview, communal village, Luis Carlos Prestes; group interview with Romeu Mataquenha, Tirani Ntuka and Mussa Vaquina, July 19, 1979, in Montepuez; group interview with Pruan Hassan, *et al.*; interview with Julio Miambo, September 14, 1979, in Maputo.

the peasants, who had effectively sabotaged cotton output, were told that they no longer had to cultivate cotton, but in the following year they were ordered to grow rice, an even more labor-intensive crop which yielded lower returns than cotton.[70]

Covertly withholding a portion of their daily labor represented the most widespread act of peasant defiance. This strategy was both less risky than most forms of permanent withdrawal and the most immediate way to minimize the production bottleneck which jeopardized food production. One way to achieve this objective was to avoid, whenever possible, the various production requirements that the state and concessionary company sought to impose. Although the European overseers carefully measured and demarcated the amount of land on which each peasant had to cultivate cotton, there were not sufficient numbers of *capatazes* to insure that all, or even most, of the land was actually cultivated. One Cotton Board official writing about the southern districts noted in 1941 that "the vast majority of the indigenous population is not cultivating the minimum specified area."[71] That this phenomenon was not limited to southern Mozambique is reflected in official statistics from the northern districts of Zambésia, Mozambique, Niassa and Cabo Delgado. In the period between 1940 and 1943, some 630,000 cultivators planted only 211,000 hectares. This figure represents a per capita average of only two-thirds of the general requirement per cultivator.[72] Seventeen years later an agricultural official reporting to the governor of Tete complained that "most of the cotton fields in the concessionary area of the Sociedade Algodiera in Tete are not being cultivated at the minimum required level."[73] And even within these reduced cotton areas many peasants clandestinely planted food crops.[74] "I have received recurring information that the peasants in Gaza are planting corn and manioc fields assigned for cotton production,"[75] a high Cotton Board official noted with anger.

An alternative strategy was to begin planting the cotton fields after the designated dates but before the *sipais* arrived, using the

[70]Group interview in Sierra Chanavane, February 17, 1979.

[71]A.I.A., J.E.A.C., Dossier VZ5 (1940–42), J. Anachoreta, Chefe de Sub-delegaçao do Sul de Save, April 23, 1941.

[72]Bravo, *A Cultura Algodoeira,* 127.

[73]A.I.A. J.E.A.C., 2201/8 (1958), O Regente da B.T. de Tete ao Governador do Distrito de Tete, July 20, 1958.

[74]Interview with Makwati Simba, *et al.*; group interview, communal village Nacate; group interview, communal village Imbou, July 31, 1979, in Mueda.

[75]A.I.A., J.E.A.C., Papeis Diversos 1941, J. Anachoreta, Chefe da Sub-delegaçao de Sul de Save, September 4, 1941.

initial part of the rainy season to work in the family garden. In 1947 the senior agricultural officer in Quelimane noted that "the preparation of the cotton fields is way behind schedule in a number of areas."[76] His counterpart to the north in António Enes described an alternative ploy that the peasants commonly used to gain additional time: "The Africans in this part continually fabricate excuses why they have not seeded any cotton yet. This year it is the lack of rain."[77] Reports from cotton company officials and colonial authorities in Makonde, Macomia, Marrupa, and Manganja during the second half of the 1940s testify to the regularity with which the rural population planted late.[78] This delaying tactic often went unnoticed or was explained as yet another indication of the "uneconomic nature of the Mozambican peasant." "You are no doubt familiar with the indolence of the blacks," wrote one local administrator. "They have the habit of waiting to the last moment which reflects their laziness and bad will . . . which in this case prejudices cotton production."[79] The failure of state officials to recognize these acts as conscious efforts to maximize food production makes it difficult to ascertain how widespread the practices were. Nevertheless, Saraiva Bravo, the leading colonial cotton analyst, stated that they occurred frequently.[80]

In addition, peasants almost invariably weeded their cotton plants fewer times and later than the Board required.[81] Similarly, official reports indicate widespread opposition to burning the plants after the harvest.[82] While the rural cultivators recognized that these steps would improve the quantity and quality of their cotton, they

[76]A.I.A., J.E.A.C., Confidencial 1947, José da Cunha Dias Mendes, Regente Agricola ao Chefe do Posto da J.E.A.C., December 9, 1947.

[77]A.I.A., J.E.A.C., Arquivo Technico, 9352, Boletims de Informação, C.A.M., 1946/47, Concelho de António Enes, Posto Administrativo do Namapondo, April 10, 1947.

[78]See, for example, A.I.A., J.E.A.C., 608/8, Mario Guimares Agente de Fiscalizacao 31, 1946; A.I.A., Arquivo Technico, 1352, Boletim de Informaçao, 1946/47; A.I.A., J.E.A.C., 952, "Brigada Technica de Cabo Delgado," Vasco Sousa de Fonsesca Leone, September 30, 1949.

[79]A.I.A., J.E.A.C., Papeis Diversos, F. Barbosa to Rafael Aqapito Guerreiro, October 28, 1939.

[80]Bravo, *A Cultura Algodoeira,* 120.

[81]Interview with A. Quintanilha; A.I.A., J.E.A.C., Confidencial 1947, Jose da Cunha Dias Mendes, Regente Agricola ao Chefe do Posto da J.E.A.C., December 9, 1947; A.I.A., J.E.A.C., Arquivo Technico, 9352, Boletim de Informaço, C.A.M., 1946/47, Concelho de António Enes, Posto Administrativo do Namapondo, April 10, 1947; see, for example, A.I.A., J.E.A.C., 608/8, Mario Guimares Agente de Fiscalização 31, 1946; A.I.A., Arquivo Technico, 1352, Boletim de Informação, 1946/47; A.I.A., J.E.A.C., 952, "Brigada Technica de Cabo Delgado," Vasco Sousa de Fonesca Leone, September 30, 1949.

[82]*Ibid.*

were also aware that the time spent could be more productively used growing food and cash crops.

Similar reasoning motivated a number of peasants to sell the minimum amount of their cotton necessary to avoid punishment, while scattering the rest along the roadside, rather than making the repeated two to four journeys to distant markets for modest returns. A confidential national report assessing the problems of rural marketing concluded in 1947 that "many peasants refuse to sell the cotton, preferring to burn it and scatter the ashes."[83] One former cotton producer recalled:

> It took us three days to carry the cotton to the market at Montepuez. Each evening we had to sleep in the forest. And when we arrived at the market the police were waiting for us with new sacks and without even letting us eat, ordered us home to bring more cotton. On the way home my father, exhausted from the journey, told us to bury the empty sacks in the forest. We subsequently burned the remaining cotton which was of second quality and scattered it in the forest. Others in our village did the same.[84]

Identical acts of sabotage were reported in Balama and Porta Amelia in northern Mozambique.[85]

In addition to covertly withholding a portion of their labor, cotton producers openly defied the state-concessionary company alliance by refusing to either accept or plant the cotton seeds. Despite the obvious danger, boycotts seem to have occurred with some regularity, especially in the years immediately after the introduction of forced cotton production. Official government reports indicate that such protests took place in such diverse parts of Mozambique as Guija in 1938, Manganja in 1939, Unango and Metangula in 1945, Nampula and Makonde in 1946, and Montepuez in 1948.[86]

[83]A.I.A., J.E.A.C., Confidencia 1947, "Relatório Especial sobre Mercados," António de Freitas Silva, 1947.

[84]Group interview, communal village Nacate; interview with Amasse Niuta, communal village Nawana, July 20, 1979, in Montepuez.

[85]Group interview, communal village Aldeia Comunal Nacate; A.I.A., J.E.A.C., 901, "Plano do Trabalho 1958," Julio Bossa, Sub-delegado ao Chefe da Delegação de J.E.A.C., May 13, 1958.

[86]See, for example, A.I.A., J.E.A.C., J. Anachoreta Chefe da Sub-delegaçao do Sul de Save to J.E.A.C., December 16, 1939; A.I.A., J.E.A.C., Diversos, 1939, José da Cunha Sousa Dias Mendes to Chefe da Delegação da J.E.A.C., January 13, 1940; A.I.A., J.E.A.C., "Copiador Geral de Notas 4° Trimestre 1947, Gestão de Mello Furtado to Director de C.I.C.A., October 4, 1947; A.I.A., J.E.A.C., 601/8, "Relatório," Abel A. Texeira Rebelo, Administrado do Conselho de Nampula, 27, 1946.

The most spectacular of the documented examples occurred at Buzi in 1948, where 7,000 women organized a strike and refused to accept the seeds that the administrator ordered to be distributed. They maintained that with their men absent, working on nearby sugar plantations, they had neither sufficient time nor labor to produce cotton and food. In a token compromise to the militancy of the women, the administrator offered to exempt pregnant women and mothers of more than four children from cotton production. The others, however, were compelled as before.[87]

A variant of this strategy was to withhold the product of their labor unless overall working conditions were improved. In 1958, in the area of Guija in southern Mozambique, for example, hundreds of peasants held a meeting to protest the abusive actions of the Companhia Algodoeira do Sul de Save. At this gathering, organized by Gabriel Mucave, Paulo Chongo, and Simone Sithoi, many people stood up and spoke angrily of the abuses and suffering they had endured. They resolved "not to sell the cotton until the authorities agreed to raise the prices." A *capataze* named Barboza who was present fetched a weapon and attempted to intimidate the protesters, a number of whom were arrested. Ultimately, the colonial administrator arrived armed and, after much heated debate, agreed that in the following year cotton prices would be increased to four escudos.[88] A few years earlier in the neighboring area of Magude a similar boycott had resulted in an increase to three escudos per kilo.[89]

Similar considerations motivated discontented peasants to rob company warehouses where cotton was stored and to resell their produce at interior markets. Often this involved collaboration with night watchmen and warehouse workers who themselves had, in the past, been forced to cultivate cotton. A substantial amount of cotton, for example, was stolen from the warehouse and experimental station at Mutuali in northern Mozambique in 1958.[90] Although authorities confiscated the identity cards of the nearby peasants and threatened reprisal, they failed to recover the cotton or to identify those responsible. There were three robberies reported in a ninety-day period at the principal SAGAL warehouses at Montepuez in

[87]A.I.A., J.E.A.C., "Confidencial 1947," Sub-delegado J.E.A.C., Beira, Antonio Mira Mendes to Chefe da Delegação da J.E.A.C. (L.M.), December 20, 1947.

[88]Interview with Simone Sitoi, February 26, 1979.

[89]*Ibid.*

[90]A.I.A., J.E.A.C., Papeis Diversos, C. Pedro Carvalho, Regente Agricola ao Director de C.I.C.A., January 9, 1958.

1963.[91] These robberies, defined by the colonial-capitalist state as criminal actions, nevertheless represent a legitimate expression of peasant protest and are clearly different from the predatory actions of criminals who preyed indiscriminately on all sections of society.[92]

This is also a relevant distinction when considering the numerous cases of peasants who adulterated the cotton they sold to combat the artificially depressed prices and the manipulation of weights and quality standards by concessionary company officials. The most common tactic was to place small pebbles in the center of the sacks of cotton. Other objects used to increase the weight included sand, particles of bricks and pumpkins. The peasants then pounded the cotton, increasing the volume in proportion to the weight and more effectively hiding the foreign objects. Despite the inspection of the cotton sacks at the market and the severe punishment meted out to those who were discovered, neither the colonial regime nor company officials were able to suppress this practice.[93]

The Significance of Peasant Resistance

Throughout this article we have examined the various forms of peasant resistance without specifying the ways in which they may have varied over time or space or among different segments of the peasantry. Before delineating temporal and regional variations, it is important to stress that resistance was not a knee-jerk reaction of all peasants. Instead, it was a carefully considered decision, which carried very serious consequences. Given the repressive environment, it is hardly surprising that many people were intimidated. "How could we resist," asked two former producers increduously, "the *sipais* and overseers were always on our backs."[94] Many other peasants could only think of the immediate survival of their families

[91] Arquivo de Corpo Policial de Moçambique, Montepuez.

[92] See E. J. Hobsbawm, *Social Bandits* (London, 1969). In terms of the Southern African context, see Charles van Onselen, "South Africa's Lumpen-proletarian Army 'Umkosi Wa Ntaba' the Regiment of the Hills, 1880 to 1920," World Employment Research Programme, International Labour Office (Geneva, 1976), 37–38; Allen Isaacman, "Social Banditry in Zimbabwe (Rhodesia) and Mozambique, 1894–1907: An Expression of Early Peasant Protest," *Journal of Southern African Studies*, IV (1977), 1–30.

[93] Interview with Manuel Alves Saldanha; interview with Marcos Chongo, *et al.*; group interview, communal village, Luis Carlos Prestes; interview with Makwati Simba, *et al.*; interview with Romeu Mataquenha, *et al.*; group interview, communal village Nacate; group interview, communal village Kikangane; group interview, Macomia.

[94] Joint interview with Chico Nhulialia and Costa Gaio Napire.

and channeled all their time and energy trying to eke out a living within the confines of the cotton regime.

Still others actively collaborated in order to improve their material conditions. Indeed, the cotton regime could not have been maintained without the participation of the chiefs and village headmen who admonished their followers to obey the colonial authorities, distributed the seeds, and revealed to company officials and colonial authorities the names of those peasants who failed to satisfy their legal obligations.[95] In return the chiefs and their coopted subordinates received the right to use forced peasant labor on their own cotton fields, which were appreciably larger than those of their subjects.[96] Moreover, in a number of regions chiefs and village headmen received the higher price for cotton reserved for white planters as well as prizes (including homes, bicycles, and radios) for "stimulating production."[97] In those areas not particularly suitable for cotton production, the chiefs and headmen were often allowed to cultivate whatever cash crops they desired.

Although often punished for the insubordination of their followers, most chiefs remained loyal to the system and were able to accumulate a relatively large amount of capital which they and their immediate relatives used to acquire agricultural implements, additional wives, and, in some cases, to employ small numbers of workers. In short, the cotton regime reinforced, and in some areas created, divisions within the peasantry, leading, especially in southern Mozambique, to the development of small capitalist farmers. These emerging class cleavages, in turn, were a critical factor in determining the rural reaction to the cotton regime.

To a lesser degree than the chiefs many *sipais* also benefitted from the cotton system. Drawn from the ranks of the peasantry, they and their families not only escaped the cotton system but were also exempt from forced labor as long as they rigorously enforced the dictates of the concessionary company officials and the local administrators. While it is true that they were subject to the capricious whims of their colonial master and often suffered from his excesses, they were able to use their position to appropriate small

[95]A.I.A., J.E.A.C., "Dossier Diversos, 1939–41," J. Furstenau Chefe de Delegação, September 12, 1941; A.I.A., J.E.A.C., 601/3, Antonio Mira Mendes, December 1945; A.I.A., J.E.A.C., 605/8, Luis Salema, February 1946; group interview, communal village Magul, February 20, 1979; group interview with Felippe Costa, *et al.*, February 19, 1979, in Gaza; group interview with Arrihdi Mahanda, *et al.*; group interview with Daima Magaga Mbela, *et al.*; interview with Pruan Hassan.

[96]*Ibid.*

[97]*Ibid.*

amounts of wealth and sometimes labor from the subject population and to extract sexual favors.[98]

Far more numerous than the collaborators were the thousands, or perhaps hundreds of thousands, of men and women who at one time or another defied the cotton regime. Unfortunately, all but a few remain anonymous, and, apart from the emerging class distinctions, there is no evidence that ethnicity, sex, or age were significant factors in determining who resisted. On the contrary, the available data suggest that insurgents were drawn from all sectors of the cotton-producing population.

Although opposition tended to be generalized, there are indications that age and sex criteria were important in determining participation in one specific form of resistance—flight. While there are numerous oral accounts and colonial reports of entire families fleeing, the most common phenomenon seems to have been for men to desert alone, and there are only a few indications of women fleeing without their families. In part, this reflects the fact that, once free and across international borders, men had greater employment possibilities. Moreover, they probably had, or thought they had, a better chance to survive the rigors and dangers of clandestine flight. On the other hand, women, with stronger ties to their children and greater responsibility for feeding their families, were undoubtedly more reluctant to abandon their homelands except as part of a larger group. A similar argument holds in the case of elders, leading us to hypothesize that, when all other things such as geographic proximity to the frontier were equal, the rate of defection was probably highest among younger men. Apart from the flight, however, there is no evidence that age, sex, or ethnicity *per se* were important factors in determining who resisted—witness the economic boycott of 7,000 women in Buzi or the fact that 50 percent of the female cotton producers on the Sena Sugar estate were "absent" in 1942.[99]

With regard to changes in the forms of resistance over time, two contradictory tendencies seem to have operated. On the one hand, virtually all the broad categories of resistance—permanently withholding all labor, regularly withholding a portion of the labor, and short-term boycotts—were reported throughout the entire period,

[98]Interview with Valente Yoti, February 19, 1979, in Xai-Xai; joint interview with Chico Nhulialia and Costa Gaio Napire; group interview with Aide Matupera, *et al.*, July 27, 1979, in Macomia.

[99]A.I.A., J.E.A.C., "Confidencial 1947," Sub-delegado J.E.A.C., Beira, António Mira Mendes to Chefe da Delegação da J.E.A.C. (L.M.), December 20, 1947; Vail and White, "Tawani Machambero," 251.

although it is impossible to determine quantitative changes from one year to another. On the other hand, conspicuously absent from the records of the 1950s are documented examples of open defiance by entire communities which either refused to accept or to plant the seeds as they had done previously. Moreover, virtually all of the examples of cooking the cotton seeds occurred shortly after the system had been imposed. Thus, it would appear that, as the state and companies began to consolidate their power through more careful surveillance and intensified intimidation, they were able to contain or eliminate those insurgent activities that explicitly challenged the system. Increased surveillance and border patrols in the 1950s may have also reduced the number of peasants deserting the cotton regime, and surely made it a more difficult prospect.

Given this shift in power, it seems likely that in the early years there was a greater tendency to engage in actions to either escape or reject the system. As these options diminished, however, alienated peasants placed greater emphasis on withholding a portion of their labor and improving their relative economic conditions. The sales boycotts in southern Mozambique and the formation of an African cotton cooperative in northern Mozambique—the only explicit collective actions in the 1950s—point in that direction.

As in the case of temporal variations, the evidence supporting regional differences is suggestive at best and is linked to the broader patterns of labor migrations and the political economy of each zone, issues falling outside the scope of this preliminary study.[100] At this point the data suggest that there were somewhat greater opportunities to resist in the northern districts of Cabo Delgado and Niassa than probably anywhere else, although in no part of the country did the state-concessionary company alliance have sufficient manpower to mount a campaign of constant surveillance. Because both districts, but especially Niassa, were considered marginal, backwater areas, the state apparatus was appreciably weaker than in other parts of the country. Moreover, the transportation and communications systems were largely undeveloped in Niassa and Cabo Delgado—further reducing the potential for state or company surveillance.

Several official reports from Cabo Delgado highlight the inability of colonial-capitalist forces to supervise the cotton regime effectively. The administrator of Mocimboa de Praia, explaining to his

[100]Isaacman is currently writing a history of forced cotton production which will situate forced cotton production within both Mozambique's political economy and the political economy of the larger region.

superiors in 1946 why the peasants were able to flaunt the system, noted that "the impact of the concessionary company overseer is minimal since he lives 50 kilometers from the closest cotton fields and lacks transport as I do."[101] Three years later a visiting representative of the Cotton Board observed that several posts in the region of Quissanga lacked administrators, permitting "the hostility to cotton production to be both open and extreme."[102] Moreover, in 1958 another Cotton Board member noted that concessionary company officials and state appointees in many parts of Cabo Delgado were unable to prevent "peasants from abandoning their cotton crops in the field rather than bringing them to the market."[103]

In addition, both Niassa and Cabo Delgado had vast unpopulated areas. This space facilitated the establishment of maroon communities, which to date have only been documented in these areas. The relatively sparce populations also reduced the possibility of detection both for those fleeing the country and those establishing refugee communities.

Spatial considerations are important in at least three other respects. Regardless of province, cotton producers living farther from the main centers of Portuguese colonial rule and concessionary company headquarters faced less serious constraints than did their counterparts located in closer proximity to the seats of power. Similarly, those peasants living near international borders enjoyed an obvious advantage in terms of flight. Moreover, even within the most controlled environment, free social space existed,[104] or could be created which enabled peasants to plan collective actions undetected. Evening meetings, family gatherings and religious festivals all provided such potential, as did separatist churches. Although further research is needed, documentation of recurring seed cooking, of the flight of entire villages, and of community-wide boycotts supports such a hypothesis.

Given the fact that most resistance was limited in scale and did

[101]A.I.A., J.E.A.C,. 601/8; João Tavares de Melo, Administrador de Macimboa de Praia, February 22, 1946.

[102]A.I.A., J.E.A.C., 952, "Brigada Technica de Cabo Delgado," J. Costa Rosa, March 13, 1949.

[103]A.I.A., J.E.A.C., 901, "Planos de Trabalho, 1958," Julio Bossa, Sub-delegado to Chefe de Delegaçåo de J.E.A.C., May 13, 1958.

[104]Sara Evans and Harry Boyte have recently defined the concept of "free social space" as "the terrain in class divided society that retains a measure of independence." It is in this uncontested zone that the subordinate classes have the opportunity to plan and organize collective action (Sara Evans and Harry Boyte, "Free Social Space," unpublished ms., 1978).

not explicitly challenge the cotton regime, one must ask whether such actions were merely futile gestures or whether they assumed an importance that transcended the individual protests. Clearly, they failed to paralyze the system, since cotton exports from Mozambique increased by 700 percent between 1938 and 1961. Nevertheless, peasant opposition was significant.

While it is impossible to calculate how much cotton might have been produced had the rural population acquiesced, there is no doubt that by withholding all or a portion of their labor, they substantially reduced output. The flight of thousands of peasants permanently deprived the cotton regime of critical labor, while the widespread planting of less than the minimum acreage further reduced potential output. Even after the 1948 legislation which established guidelines of one hectare for each adult male between eighteen and fifty-five, and a half-hectare per adult woman, the land under cultivation was appreciably less. In 1950, for example, 424,000 peasants in the north averaged only 0.47 hectare per producer.[105]

The tendency to circumvent the state-imposed agricultural schedule also limited total production. Peasants, aware that planting late and weeding fewer times and less carefully affected yield, were nevertheless prepared to assume the consequences in order to increase the amount of time they could spend in their gardens. Similar considerations motivated many cotton growers who refused to burn the plants after the harvest, thereby jeopardizing future production, because the unburnt plants provided an ideal host for diseases and parasites. Both factors contributed to Mozambique's low yield per acre[106] and frustrated the companies' plans to impose a more stringent production schedule and a system of two harvests per year.[107]

Thus, while production did increase substantially, it fell far short of its potential and failed to achieve the Salazar regime's objective of self-sufficiency for the Portuguese textile industry. As late as 1949 the minister of the colonies bemoaned "the stagnation in cotton production over the past years" which he attributed in great part "to

[105]Bravo, *A Cultura Algodoeira,* 135.

[106]Although yield per hectare is not an extremely precise indicator because it reflects the level of technology employed, rainfall, disease incidence as well as labor input, it is interesting to note that throughout virtually the entire period under examination, Mozambican output was appreciably lower than in neighboring colonies utilizing a similar system of peasant production. For comparative statistics during the final years of the system, when output had reached its high point, see Bravo, *A Cultura Algodoeira,* 129.

[107]Interview with A. Quintanilha.

the disinterest of the native population."[108] He had good reason to complain. Because cotton imports from Mozambique and Angola were not keeping pace with Portugal's industrial needs, the textile industry was required to purchase in 1949 more than 8 million kilograms, or 21 percent of its requirements, on the world market at double the fixed state price.[109] These cotton purchases, valued at approximately $55 million, added significantly to Portugal's balance of trade deficit and limited the capacity of the textile companies to accumulate capital. This shortfall continued throughout the 1950s. In 1959 the textile industry had to purchase 28 percent of its cotton abroad at a cost of $101 million.[110]

The abolition of the forced cotton concessionary regime in 1961 and the simultaneous shift to a settler-based plantation system testifies both to the ultimate failure of the cotton regime and to the tenacity and cumulative impact of peasant resistance. It also calls into question the general proposition that both the colonial state and capital, recognizing that forced labor was inefficient, were nevertheless prepared to accept flight, sabotage, and other forms of resistance as a necessary concomitant of the system. In the case of Mozambique they could not contain the localized, clandestine, and highly effective protests. Ultimately the powerful textile industry and the state decided that a new system of production had to be introduced and that the concessionary companies were both cumbersome and unnecessary. It is within this context that the abolition of the cotton regime must be seen, although other factors such as growing international criticism of forced labor in Mozambique were certainly significant.

Beyond the long-term impact on the system, the struggle of the peasants affected, to varying degrees, their own living and working conditions. For producers who fled or successfully burned their seeds, it meant freedom from physical abuse and greater control of their economic destiny. But even those who could not evade the cotton regime were often able to reduce the level of exploitation through their actions. In response to widespread peasant protest against food shortages and warnings from some administrators that the rural population was not able to reproduce itself, the colonial regime passed a number of laws after 1946 which required that peasants be allowed to allocate a specific amount of land and time

[108] *Noticias,* November 1, 1949.

[109] A.I.A., J.E.A.C., "Propoganda Mocambique," Elementos Para o Seculo, Gastao de Mello Furtado, June 15, 1954; Bravo, *A Cultura Algodoeira,* 70.

[110] Bravo, *A Cultura Algodoeira,* 70.

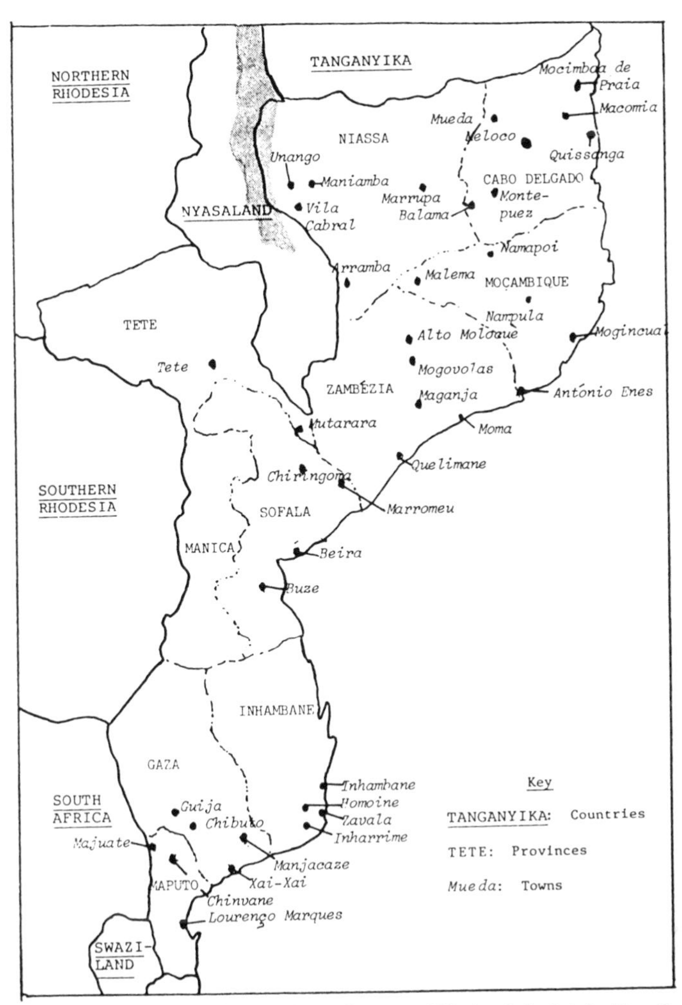

Mozambique: Principal Cotton Locations and Major Administrative Centers

for food production.[111] Although these laws were implemented slowly and only at the discretion of local administrators, by the 1950s the number and intensity of famines seems to have diminished. Nevertheless, food shortages remained a recurring problem. Similarly, in many marginal cotton areas peasant hostility precipitated by low yields and minimal returns ultimately convinced the Cotton Board, despite opposition from the concessionary companies, to exempt these regions from future production.[112] In the

[111]See, for example, B.O.M., Series 1, no. 45, November 9, 1956, 459–466; interview with Faria Lobo, May 4, 1979.

[112]*Ibid.*, interview with A. Quintanilha, March 7, 1979.

same way, frontier zones in Niassa district, which had been centers of discontent and desertions, were transformed into "free zones" in the late 1940s in which cotton production was optional.[113] Finally, in the Makonde highlands of Cabo Delgado, where both the state and concessionary officials had met constant resistance, peasants in 1949 obtained permission to organize a cotton cooperative in which there was no external supervision, coercion or minimum production requirements.[114]

In the final analysis, these protests did narrow the freedom of action of the concessionary companies. Their overriding objective of increasing the number of bonded peasants and the amount of time they had to devote to cotton production was clearly frustrated. While none of these gains altered the system as a whole, they had far-reaching implications for a large number of peasants. Genovese's discussion of similar slave protests in the American South is very much to the point.

> Their actions did not challenge slavery *per se,* nor were they often meant to, any more than striking workers means to challenge the capitalist system. Yet in an important sense the slowdowns and resistance to work contributed more to the slaves' struggle for survival then did many bolder individual acts that may have reflected a willingness to attack slavery itself. The slaves did make gains in their everyday living conditions, which some latter-day ideologues, in the comfort of their studies, dismiss as mere sops to keep people quiet but which often meant the difference between agony and a chance to live with at least a minimum of decency.[115]

While this article has focused on resistance at the level of production, peasants were more than mere producers of surplus value. They took a number of other actions to assert their own dignity and community strength and to validate their cultural identity. Acts of defiance, including attacks on chiefs and *sipais* who were the immediate symbol of oppression, occurred with regularity, despite the obvious danger.[116] Arson offered an opportunity to settle old scores in a manner that was relatively simple and could easily be

[113]A.I.A., J.E.A.C., Comp. Alq. Moc., February 13, 1945; A.I.A., J.E.A.C., Nampula, Gastão de Mello Furtado to Sub-delegado de J.E.A.C., December 6, 1947; A.I.A., J.E.A.C., 84 (1957–59), Elias Goncalves Valente to Chefe da Delegação da J.E.A.C., October 23, 1957.

[114]A.I.A., J.E.A.C., "Confidencias 1947," Eugenia Ferreira de Almeida to Chefe da Delegação da J.E.A.C., March 10, 1947; inerview with Cornelio Joao Mandando.

[115]Eugene Genovese, *Roll Jordan Roll* (New York, 1976), 621.

[116]Interview with Benjamin Mavunga and Pruan Hassan; group interviews with Aide Matupera, *et al.,* and with Anasse Muite, *et al.*

concealed, which probably explains the reason why a number of warehouses and smaller rural collection centers were burned to the ground. In two instances informants admitted that angry peasants had started the fires.[117] While the other fires may have been caused by carelessness or spontaneous combustion, the possibility of peasant involvement cannot be discounted.

In addition to these violent acts, there are also numerous examples of deeply rooted cultural expressions of resistance. Protest songs provided a safe medium through which cotton producers could articulate their opposition with little fear of detection. Examples are found throughout the country. Women in the Quelimane area sang "Tonje Nyankwira" as they worked in their fields:

Ay O Ay earthing up the coton! (Chorus)
I've been beaten, I've been beaten—cotton! (Chorus)
Gardening for the man, gardening for the man—cotton! (Chorus)
This year we cultivate cotton (Chorus)
Gardening for him, I see hardship—cotton (Chorus)
This year I'm cultivating the cotton (Chorus)
I've been beaten! I've been beaten!—cotton! (Chorus)
I've been tied up! I've been tied up!—cotton! (Chorus)[118]

As Vail and White emphasize, "to this day the word for cotton—tonje—evokes an almost automatic response: nyatwa—sufering."

Further to the south, the Gaza, peasants sang the following song as they carried the cotton to market:

We worked and were paid nothing
We were forced to work in the fields (Chorus)
Until Xinavane (Chorus)
We carried cotton on our head (Chorus)
We were beaten in this land (Chorus)
Lopes beat us (Chorus).[119]

Other songs sung in Cabo Delgado and Inhambane ridiculed the European *capatazes* and mocked the *sipais* and collaborating chiefs.[120] Most of these protest songs were sung during the work day within earshot of the European overseers, who, without

[117]Interview with Benjamin Mavunga; interview with Eugenio Niquaria, July 24, 1979, in Montepuez. To a very small degree the arson and seed burning affected the capital accumulation of the concessionary companies as well.

[118]Quoted in Vail and White, "Tawani Machambero," 253.

[119]Interview with Benjamin Mavunga.

[120]See, for example, Hugh Tracey, *A Musica Chope*, trans. M. H. Barradas (Lourenço Marques, 1949); group interview with Maulani Samati; interview with Makwati Simba.

understanding, remained content because the music signified peasants at work.

Sculpture in northern Mozambique also provided an effective medium through which to depict the dual themes of misery and ridicule. The despair engendered by the cotton regime is a common motif of Makonde art, as exemplified by the caricature of an anguished female cotton producer, head in hand. And skeletal figures obviously suffering from hunger are a variation on this theme. These sculptures, initially carved by cotton producers to supplement their meager earnings, reflected anger born of hunger.[121] The Makua M'pika mask and other Makonde figures, on the other hand, take the features of the *capatazes* and *sipais* and subject them to ridicule by distortion.[122] As in the case of song, the colonial consumers who purchased most of this art failed to grasp the significance of these cultural expressions.

Several "assimilated" poets combined the Portuguese language with their personal experiences to protest the suffering of the rural poor. Jose Craveirinha's *Poem* depicts the misery of a Shangaan who has lost her son to the South African mines and at the same time "scratched the maize from the ground and achieved the miracle of one hundred and fifty-five bales of cotton."[123] This theme is continued in *When Bullets Turn to Flowers,* an anthology of writing by FRELIMO (the Front for the Liberation of Mozambique) militants.[124]

The link between FRELIMO and the cotton resisters goes well beyond sculpture and poetry. Many of the peasants who fled to Tanzania and Niassaland became involved in the struggle for independence. Among them were such future militants as Alberto Chipande[125] and Raimando Pachinuapa,[126] both of whom helped to organize the first African cotton "cooperatives" in the early 1950s as an alternative to the system of forced production.[127] President Samora Machel emphasized that his own political education began,

[121]Group interview, communal village Nandimba, July 3, 1979, in Mueda, group interview, communal village Muila, August 1, 1979, in Mueda.

[122]The best examples of this art are found in the Museum at Nampula.

[123]For the English translation see Margaret Dickenson, ed., *When Bullets Begin to Flower: Poems of Resistance from Angola, Mozambique, and Guine* (Nairobi, 1972), 46–50.

[124]*Ibid.*

[125]Alberto Chipande is currently minister of national defense.

[126]Raimando Pachinuapa was formerly governor of Cape Delgado and he now oversees the functioning of all provincial governments.

[127]Interview with Cornelio João Mandando, July 30 and August 1, 1979, in Mueda.

"not from the writing in the book, not from reading Marx or Engels, but from seeing my father forced to grow cotton for the Portuguese and going with him to the market where he was forced to sell it at a low price—much lower than the white Portuguese growers."[128] Cocote Zimo, a member of the FRELIMO army from the beginning of the armed struggle, presented a similar account.

> My father was engaged in forced cultivation. . . . He had goats and sheep but the colonial troops took them without paying. . . . Our fathers carried the maxila, received whippings and beatings . . . it angered me to see the suffering of my parents . . . they supported me when I joined FRELIMO and went to other parents to persuade their sons to join to be able to rest from suffering.[129]

Thousands of cotton producers who did not initially flee to Tanzania actively organized FRELIMO cells in those areas of Cape Delgado and Niassa where opposition to cotton had been particularly strong, such as the Makonde highlands in Cape Delgado and the Maniamba region in Niassa. Other peasants covertly provided food, shelter and strategic information to the liberation forces. Their support proved critical. As their homelands were liberated, the existing vestiges of the cotton regime[130] and other colonial capitalist institutions were immediately dismantled. The central role of the cotton producers during this initial phase suggests that greater attention needs to be given to the peasant base of FRELIMO, which has been often overlooked.

[128]Quoted in George Houser and Herb Shore, *Mozambique: Dream the Size of Freedom* (New York, 1975), 11.

[129]Interview with Cocote Zimo, July 23, 1979, in Montepuez.

[130]In 1961 compulsory production was abolished, though a variety of extra-legal and illegal coercive practices persisted.

COLONIAL CHIEFS AND THE MAKING OF CLASS: A CASE STUDY FROM TESO, EASTERN UGANDA

JOAN VINCENT

THIS is a study of Teso District, eastern Uganda, during a period of colonial administration from 1896 to 1927.[1] A group of appointed chiefs was brought into being and maintained within a local political environment in which neither traditional rulers nor a principle of hereditary succession to political office were recognised. The growth of the bureaucratic and authoritarian aspects of client chiefship is traced, along with changes in the relations of the chiefs with the colonial regime and with the people they ruled. In time, their increasing powers of coercion and their accumulative control of patronage led to the emergence of a class interest among them. This became crystallised in the mid-1920s when, as a body, they maintained a conservative stance within a colonial administration geared to change.[2]

The 'confusion which bedevilled the official mind' confronted with stateless societies has been admirably discussed by the historian for Lango, John Tosh (1973: 473). In neighbouring Teso, too, the British administration was faced with chiefs who were 'bureaucratic creatures of the colonial government' (Tosh 1973: 474). Although anthropologists have contributed a great deal to the analysis of stateless societies—the work of Colson, Evans-Pritchard and Fortes providing classic examples—the tribe is not always the most useful unit for understanding political events after the introduction of colonial rule. Attempts to relate the acephelous/centralised dichotomy to colonial bureaucratic innovation and success proved invalid (Fallers 1956: 242; Apthorpe 1959). Moreover, in a wider context than that of administration, the uneven regional development of a colonial territory might outweigh any continued importance attached to cultural differences.[3]

This essay begins, therefore, with a brief historical overview of the establishment of colonial administration in Teso District where Baganda conquest and British consolidation effectively undermined the diffuse power structure of a localised Iteso gerontocracy. The administrative unit that became Teso District in 1912 contained other than Iteso within its boundaries but a process of homogenisation led to a hierarchy of Iteso client chiefs becoming firmly grounded within the newly created political arena. Two major cleavages subsequently developed within the society: one between chief and peasant, and another between the northern and southern parts of the district. The course of political events between 1896 and 1927 becomes comprehensible in terms of these two oppositions; their resolution did much to shape the character of local politics in Teso in the years that followed.

Administration of Teso from Kampala was inaugurated in 1899 by the British appointment of Semei Kakunguru, a Muganda general engaged in building up a small personal satrapy in the east, as Native Assistant in charge of Bukedi. The onslaught of Kakunguru's mercenaries was both forceful and destructive and its excesses apparently led to his recall by the British in 1902, whereupon the administration of the area was placed under the control of the Mbale Collector. In 1909 a separate collectorate was established around Kumi, which over the next few years extended its boundaries and consolidated an increasing number of Iteso, Lango and Kumam peoples. In 1912 this administrative unit was re-named Teso District.

For the first decade Baganda Agents were retained, initially to fill chiefly offices and then to act as advisers to Iteso chiefs. There was no pan-tribal organisation demanding its administration as a unified district and the five counties (see Fig. 1) were treated as separate compartments until 1918 when a district-wide system was established in which a hierarchy of county, sub-county, parish and village chiefs was set up along with councils of local notables at each level. Council members were at first appointed, later elected to office. Both chiefs and representative officials were responsible to the District Commissioner whose important inter-hierarchical position between the Central Government and the locality provided a lynch-pin in the political and economic development of the district.[4]

Fig. 1. Teso District

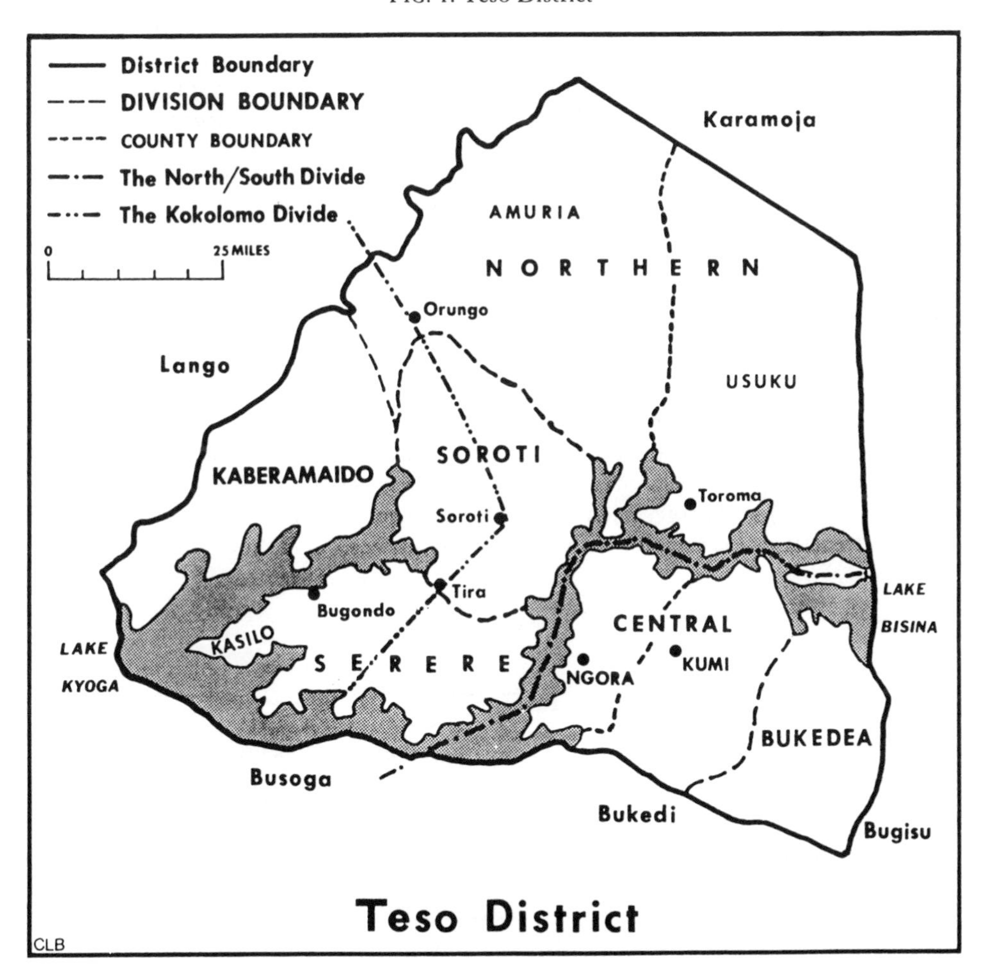

Between 1896 and 1934 the amorphous population of Teso was transformed into a closely administered, cash-crop growing, taxed and locally represented peasantry. Although the nature and course of events was shaped to some extent by the pattern of conquest, bureaucratic administration and representative politics, it was also a product of the patterning of conflict which emerged as different elements within Teso society jockeyed within the political arena. Thus, in order to perceive the political process by which Teso client chiefs became sufficiently established to affect the trend of social and economic development, we must inquire into the politicisation of the various groups within the district.

From the start, the definition of the Teso political community and the manner in which it was constructed shaped the forms that confrontation took. The initial actions of the British administrative secretariat and the departmental officers determined the very arena in which conflict took place. It was they who, to a great extent, not only held the ropes but also laid down the rules of the game. As a small, closely interacting group of individuals, these officers were distinguished first by their transient roles as individuals on the Teso political stage and, secondly, by their orientation towards a wider political arena than the district. These structural characteristics distinguished district officers from chiefs as bureaucrats. Client chiefs in Teso were bureaucrats and politicians both, and it was their skilful manipulation of office and role that led to the emergence of a privileged chiefly class.

Teso District: The Creation of a Local Political Arena

Descriptions of Teso prior to the advent of the Baganda suggest it was populated predominantly by Eastern Nilotes although communities of Bantu-speaking peoples were to be found in the south and west. These were largely Bakenyi and Banyoro, the former fishing off the shores of the Serere peninsular and throughout the inland waters of the region, the latter engaged in trade across Lake Kyoga. In the east, Swahili-speaking Arabs, Nubians and Asians engaged in trade and commerce along a well travelled route from Karamoja to the slopes of Mount Masaba. According to not wholly reliable censuses of the population, 3% of Teso's population in 1911 were non-Iteso, increasing to 6% by 1921 (see Fig. 2). Iteso relations with Bantu 'minority groups' were, by and large, friendly, almost symbiotic in nature, social intercourse and intermarriage making for fluid group boundaries. Their relations with fellow

Fig. 2. The African Population of Teso District, 1911–1931

	1911	1921	1931
Iteso	243,012	249,415	298,062
Bantu-speaking groups	7,651	9,495	15,942
Eastern Nilotes	—	17	172
Nilotes	—	5,691	1,235
Luhya (Kavirondo)	—	54	214
Nubi, Somali and Swahili	—	57	595
Others	—	—	287
Totals	250,663	264,729	316,507

Nilotes in the east and north—Lango, Kumam and Karamojong—were, by contrast, frequently hostile, dominated by cattle raiding.

Not until Baganda conquest in 1896 did any political authority extend over an area of more than a few square miles. Indigenous leadership was gerontocratic; there was no institutionalisation of hierarchical office or ranking of groups—apart from that to be found in all small-scale societies where elders, youths and womenfolk are set apart by the specialisation of their labour and their opportunities for social power. The Iteso age organisation that mobilised the young men of the communities was apparently locally coordinate like that of the Karamojong, linking only neighbouring homesteads (Dyson-Hudson 1967). It neither resisted the Baganda in 1896 nor mobilised labour in the years that followed.[5] Decision-making was in the hands of local Big Men, and only on the basis of kin and community could such men muster groups of any size in the face of external threats.[6]

Such horizontally articulated political organisation checked any deep or rapid military penetration by Kakunguru's forces and prevented the easy consolidation of administrative units in the years that followed. Garrisons could be established only within the homesteads of Iteso collaborators and only under such protection could aliens, Baganda and European officials, catechists and traders operate. Beyond these isolated strongholds, the countryside was passive or hostile according to the measures taken by the garrison to live off the land and the direction their forays took. Bishop Kitching, a contemporary, assessed Kakunguru's achievement in Teso thus: 'The way in which he handled the country is a good illustration of the rare capacity of the Baganda for organisation and government, and also of rapacity and over-bearing towards all whom they consider beneath them. Order was indeed established but rather after the method of making desolation and calling it peace' (1912: 31). Within a few years the Teso administrative system was regarded as a model for eastern and northern Uganda, where similar diffuse political authorities were encountered. Its significant historical contribution was, however, the creation of a cash economy which engendered rural inequalities greater than any known in the indigenous political system.

Various patterns of inequality emerged as Big Men in different regions responded differently to Baganda incursions. Those in the west tended to welcome Baganda support against Lango attacks; those who encountered the Baganda as they moved northwards and eastwards met them with armed resistance, bringing forth the scorched earth policy described by Kitching. Any advantage the Baganda gained by winning over or eliminating a local leader was measured by the extent of his influence over neighbouring areas. Such influence seems to have covered at most an *etem*, an area of between fifty and a hundred square miles roughly equivalent to a modern sub-county. The subsequent usefulness of a Big Man to the administration depended more upon the number of followers who considered it worth their while to come within his orbit than upon the number over whom he already had influence.

Before the introduction of a superior technology (guns against spears) and the conqueror's 'protection' of some individuals at the expense of others, mechanisms of subsistence technology and land use tended to distribute population fairly evenly in a diastolic patterning (Meggitt 1967) of group interaction. Since leadership depended upon an ability to attract followers, no one Big Man could build a base that perdured for any length of time. Kakunguru's conquest disturbed this form of ecological adaptation, destroying the concommitant egalitarian society. By force of arms an hierarchical administration was established in which Baganda chiefs and their hirelings dominated, along with a few favoured Iteso gerontocrats whose skill in the 'politics of survival' (Ajayi 1968) surpassed that of their fellows. In establishing some Big Men as chiefs at the expense of others, and by backing them with armed force so that their relations with their erstwhile followers changed markedly in calibre, Baganda overrule re-shaped group interaction within the society at large. Petty chiefs coerced people into caravan porterage and building forts and roads. Bantu-speakers were recruited to Baganda service, first as interpreters, intermediaries and scouts and later as clerks and catechists. The overall effect of Baganda penetration was to render Iteso communities more dependent upon political leaders unchecked in their abuse of power by traditional mechanisms and, moreover, backed by the armed force of aliens; to provide an hierarchical structure of administrative chiefs within which individuals of all groups (save women) might advance, provided they acquired Luganda and accepted Baganda patronage; and finally, to secure the entry of the British colonial power into the region. Baganda rule in Teso, although historically short, was thus radical in its impact.

Yet, the indigenous political institution of Big Manship survived the holocaust. With the institutionalisation of client chiefs its locus of operation shifted from control over men, women and cattle to privileged access to guns, labour and the money economy.[7] Moreover, the investment of the old set of political facilities in the domain of the new provided capital for the Teso client chief to rise to social, political and economic power. The networks of influence and patronage which engendered Iteso Big Manship provided the New Men of Teso politics with the makings of a political machine that went virtually unrecognised by the British until it was eventually used against them. Big Manship proved not only resilient, but extraordinarily adaptive to the exogenous changes brought about by colonial rule.

Phase 1: 'From Chaos to Law and Order'

The British took over the administration of the region in 1902, their first task the definition of the political community. Where the fabric of Teso society was most ruptured by Baganda mercenaries (the southeast), development proceeded most rapidly; where the incursions of the Baganda had been more conciliatory (as in the southwest) obstacles to change arose; where the Baganda failed to penetrate (the north) the involvement of the Iteso within the developing society was slowest and the economy least changed. If we choose to see in the years that followed, the British administration holding the ropes, as it were, around an arena in which local combatants struggled for local power, we become aware of the topological characteristics of the Teso political arena, pulled as it is first in one direction and then in another, first including, then excluding different localities, groups and sub-groups. During interregnums (such as 1902 or, for that matter, 1962 when an independent Uganda was established) such elasticity becomes politically significant.

A northern limit to the Uganda Protectorate had been established with a line of treaties obtained by McDonald in 1898. This area of some three and a half thousand square miles provided opportunities for a district officer posted to the east to carve out a colonial estate of some magnitude. Yet, although there was an element of individual empire-building by pioneer administrators, both British and Iteso,[8] in the final analysis the location of boundaries was largely a response to the forces encountered. For the first twelve years the shifting boundaries of Teso District ebbed and flowed as Big Men whose communities were being raided from the north tried to come within its orbit and rebel leaders in the east tried to avoid its jurisdiction.

Now, if government is taken to be the regulation of public affairs, and the critical element in government is seen to be its public character, the first goal of penetration is clearly the consolidation of 'an enduring, presumably perpetual group with determinate boundaries and membership, having an internal organisation and a unitary set of external relations, an exclusive body of common affairs, and autonomy and procedures adequate to regulate them' (Smith 1966: 115–16). The need to seek out and establish such a public in Teso was especially critical. Earlier experiences in Buganda and the western kingdoms in no way prepared the colonial power for an amorphous mass of peoples among whom no State had previously been consolidated. It was therefore necessary first to establish boundaries around a 'public', the nature of which must in some way be defined, and then to consolidate the shifting population contained within these boundaries. And this in the face of the differing interests of the groups encountered in the process.

Not until 1923 was Teso District consolidated in its first coherent form. When the question of boundaries arose in 1920, the District Commissioner reported that 'a distinction, although not very marked [must be recognised] between the population of the western and middle and eastern parts. There is practically a dividing line Orungo-Soroti-Tira-Serere, to the west of which are Kokolimo speaking people, who are apparently regarded as an inferior type of Kumam . . .'[9] (see Fig. 1). Although the cultural complexion of western Soroti and Serere was recognised, heavily populated as they were with clansmen of the Kaberamaido Kumam, the extent of their political involvement in Teso affairs between 1912 and 1927 passed almost unrecognised by the administration, unlike that of the Banyoro and Bakenyi. In 1925 Ateso was officially adopted as the language of the district administration, Luganda and Swahili having been used before that date. This not only reflected but helped determine the changing composition of the secretariat; more significantly, the difficulty of acquiring Ateso fostered the growth of an exclusive indigenous elite.

Realignments of Kumam, Lango and Iteso served three specific administrative purposes. First, they countered the growth of peripheral factionalism; secondly, they made possible the use of one indigenous language, Ateso; and, thirdly, they served to create a political identity on a district-wide basis which would legitimise both the administrative boundaries of the new political unit and the District Commissioner as representative of the 'people of Teso' in his relations with sub-groups within the society, with other districts and with provincial and central government.

In response to the administrative search for political identity, ethnic competition preempted the symbiosis which had previously existed between Iteso pastoralists and the Bantu-speakers. The introduction of an administrative bureaucracy and mission-fostered education, although not excluding the sons of Iteso Big Men from opportunities for political advancement, had nevertheless favoured Bantu-speakers. British efforts to create a culturally homogeneous district within the Protectorate led to the blocking of their upward mobility within the local structure and to denial of the legitimacy of minority 'tribal' groupings as such. Whereas the 1911 Uganda Census categorised the population in tribal terms, the local administration recognised civic statuses, a distinction being made between 'natives' and 'resident' and 'floating aliens'.[10] 'Resident aliens'—Bakenyi, Banyoro and Basoga—paid taxes to their own chiefs who were obliged to tour widely to collect them; Iteso 'natives' paid taxes to resident parish chiefs, while 'floating aliens' owed their taxes to other regions. All Baganda were included in the last category thus rendering their estates in Teso anomalous and paving the way for a complete 'Itesoisation' of the chiefly structure. In 1925 'minority' chiefs were abolished and every adult male resident was taxed in Teso regardless of his place of origin.

If the first problems of local administration involved defining the criteria on which membership in the political community rested and fixing its boundaries, the next task was the pinning down and control of its inhabitants. In the early days many opted out of the Teso system by choosing to reside beyond its borders where taxes were lower or non-existent. This was a matter of some moment for chiefs since not only were their chances of promotion advanced by good performance in mobilising labour, but a proportion of their income was derived from *per capita* taxation. Many in Teso society were, by virtue of their primary occupations, already extremely mobile. Pastoralism, trading, fishing and, to a lesser extent, bush cultivation all required a certain amount of individual and group mobility. Bakenyi fishermen, for example, maintained networks of kin and affinal ties that extended around the eastern shores of Lake Kyoga and crossed numerous administrative boundaries. Banyoro and Basoga similarly came and went between western Teso and their lacustrine homelands, while Iteso pastoralism and inheritance patterns called for the movement of cattle and personnel over wide areas. Movements to avoid taxation and enforced cash-crop cultivation were thus easily articulated with existing migratory patterns. For certain periods of the year or in localities where heavy labour demands were made, young men were prone to 'visit kin' elsewhere for extended periods, returning months later when the tax hue and cry was over, the work on roads or in the sudd completed. All this an administration had cause but not power to prevent. The county touring books of 1913 suggest the magnitude of the problem. Characteristic entries read:

A Musoga headman has been found in the district, collecting tax from Basoga removed from his country into this district. The removals are not of recent date and the practice is an objectionable one . . .[11]

Some of the removals to Busoga have been trace by DC Busoga. 97 removed, of whom 24 were Ganda and Soga. The County agent for Serere who is concerned with the collection of tax for non-natives of the district has been instructed to report and discourage immigration of Busoga.[12]

Provincial Commissioner on tour to District Commissioner, Teso and Lango: '(a) it is the duty of District Officers to discourage migrations . . . (d) A chief who encourages migrations is not fit for his post and will not retain it after such conduct has come to the notice of this office . . .'[13]

'May 1913. ADC Lango and DC Kumi agreed that chiefs should come to locate their men. The Kenyi emigrants in the Kelle region planted cotton so as not to be returned to Teso.'[14]

The Teso DC attributed his problems of control to the greater effectiveness of his administration compared with others. He observed that: 'Border-hovering continues to be a fairly popular pastime with the people and but little abatement can be looked for until administration on both sides of the boundary is approximately identical.'[15] Not until Lango, northern Busoga and eastern Bunyoro were as effectively administered as Teso could a concerted effort be made to prevent migrants from choosing to leave a Teso parish where high taxes accompanied directed economic and social change, for a neighbouring district where taxes were lower and intervention less. For the most part, such migrants were young men, whose labour the administration most valued, and the problem was aggravated by the fact that the neighbouring regions where they settled were largely areas of marginal administrative returns. No prompt action on the part of Lango and Busoga district officers could realistically be expected. Yet, by 1917, the stabilisation of Teso's tax paying population had been achieved, largely through the coercive powers of local chiefs and the heavy penalties they were able to inflict. Chiefly powers became grossly magnified at this time as the process of political development shifted into higher gear.

Phase 2: 'The More Dangerous Stage'

In 1917 the Provincial Commissioner (Eastern Province) suggested that: 'Instead of alluding to the general progress in Native Affairs as in former reports, it is now more correct to consider this matter from the point of view of two main stages of progress. The first stage being along the line from utter chaos to law and order and the second, and more dangerous stage, being along the line created by the counter currents related to economic development.'[16]

In the first stage of development, Teso chiefs were ascribed an important role in countering economic individualism among a people advancing much more rapidly than the administration could countenance. Their less conspicuous and self-chosen role among the counter currents was realised somewhat belatedly by the British administration. One Provincial directive read:

> The natives are but children and require for many years to come firm and sympathetic guidance. They are quite unfitted for a policy of individualism; feudal and communal systems should be supported in every way. The peasant must in no way be encouraged to break away from the restraining influence of his chief who, in turn, must be under the guiding influence of the District officers ... The premature introduction of a general system of individualism would be disastrous.[17]

This policy effectually established chiefs, however tyrannical, since peasants could no longer 'vote with their feet' as they had in earlier times. Political participation thus involved either submitting to chiefly demands or departing from the district altogether which, as we have seen, was no longer advantageous. Either way, the law and order stage had been achieved.

The 'second and more dangerous stage' of colonial rule brought into existence in Teso a peasantry whose productivity was geared to the demands of a centralising power. Yet, paradoxically, its development was contrary to the directives of both the Provincial Commissioner and the Director of Agriculture.[18] Those pioneer administrators who turned blind eyes to orders forbidding the extension of the district's boundaries northwards also sponsored the development of cotton growing, regardless of the fact that preferred cash-crops were under trial at Entebbe. Both innovations were 'adventures' of local officers in disregard of higher authority (Lawrance 1957: 36; Postlethwaite 1947: 44–5). Forces at work in the local situation and regional factors within Teso are again relevant. Just as it was necessary to consider the west, south and north separately with respect to penetration and consolidation, so now different patterns of economic development must be recognised.

FIG. 3. Measures of Development, by County, 1920

		Population	*Poll Tax (Shs.)*	*Cotton Production (Tons)*	*No. of Bicycles*
South	Kumi	79,534	19,701	1,400	118
	Bukedea	30,477	—	—	54
West	Serere	36,659	10,622	600	93
North	Soroti	50,726	12,561	450	62
	Usuku	45,674	9,316	350	35
Totals		243,070	52,200	2,800	362

Four 'measures' of development reveal the comparative prosperity of the south (Fig. 3). The population size of each county reflects, to some extent, its ability to support its locally born population and attract incomers (through town growth and expanding commercial and wage opportunities). The poll tax collected indicates not only population size but the efficiency of chiefs.[19] Cotton production figures and the number of bicycles (taxed) serve as indicators of the relative wealth of each county.[20] While the figures are not sufficiently reliable to make the calculation of ratios worthwhile, differences between the district's three regions are, nevertheless, apparent.

Cotton seed was apparently first introduced into Teso District by the Church Missionary Society and by 1907 cotton was being grown throughout southern and western Teso, its distributional climax lying between Kumi and Ngora, the administrative and missionary headquarters respectively. It was exported from Bugondo which was developed as a port at this time. Population density in the southern counties seems to have greatly increased; missionary endeavours became more intensive and schools, hospitals, cotton ginneries and trading posts became so concentrated in this area that when, in 1919, it was decided that the time was ripe to appoint sub-chiefs outside of their own localities, 'most of the talent at that time was to be found in Kumi . . . the exemplary county of the district.'[21]

Following the introduction of cotton and the establishment of a money economy, the advancement of a county chief could be measured by his transfer from Serere to Soroti and thence to Kumi, just as his fall from grace was evidenced by his 'banishment' to economically backward Usuku. Not all elements of the population were equally able to take advantage of the new economic opportunities. From the outset complaints of extortionate labour demands by chiefs filtered into District headquarters. Baganda Agents received labourers from sub-county chiefs for work on their own cotton and food gardens. Chiefs diverted corvée (*luwalo*) labour intended for public works to employment on their own lands; the manipulation of a labour force quickly became one of the most visible sources of power and prestige. An indication of the size of the labour force at the disposal of chiefs is given in Fig. 4. By 1926 concern was expressed at the extent to which Teso chiefs were hiring out labour to the Indians resident in their areas.[22] Marketing was solely in the hands of aliens and, when necessary, the Administration stepped in to keep prices high.[23] Although cash was paid to whoever brought in cotton, seed was distributed only to Agents and chiefs, whose office thus allowed them not only to divert labour and porterage to their own ends but also to gain control over the scarcer resource, cotton seed. As the counties developed economically so opportunities for chiefly aggrandisement increased; the career pattern of the civil service chief brought him at the end into direct confrontation with the opportunity chains of the developing economic structure. Promoted for honesty and responsiveness to bureaucratic requirements, many a man was ultimately overwhelmed by the relative magnitude of the informal power structure at the county level.

Economic opportunities brought abuse of power at all levels and the turnover of chiefs was extremely high. Further administrative development led to greater bureaucratic discrimination. The client chiefs whom the Baganda appointed and whose retention the British were beginning to question by 1920 were of two kinds. First, those Big Men of the indigenous system who had received recognition after their cooperation with the Baganda; secondly, lesser men who, by virtue of armed force, had been able to set themselves up as Big Men and clients of the conquerors. Yet, although those who benefitted most in these competitive years were men who had

FIG. 4 Distribution of Luwalo (compulsory, unpaid labour for local chiefs), 1935

	Total Luwalo *Labour*	*Paid Labour*	*Population Not in Labour Force*	*Total Population*
Kumi	13,426	3,047	3,258	19,731
Serere	3,733	4,928	339	9,000
Amuria	13,004	2,427	1,936	17,367
Soroti	7,657	3,378	2,020	13,055
Kasilo	3,452	2,812	118	6,382
Ngora	6,804	2,593	*	9,397
Usuku	9,266	961	1,508	11,735
Total	57,342	10,146	9,179	76,667

* Not known

acquired chieftainships under the Baganda and maintained them under the British, to perceive these alone as actors in the political arena, is to under-estimate the networks of patronage and power that had previously existed. A third category of leader, of whose presence the administration was not fully aware until 1934, was made up of those who had not succumbed to Baganda or been appointed to office, but whose local influence frequently underlay the success or failure of the government-appointed chief. In the populist era of Teso politics that follows these came to be known as 'clan elders'.

Shortly after 1912 many Baganda-instituted parishes and sub-counties were amalgamated upon the deaths of their chiefs. Many appointments to office had not resulted in efficient administration. Where the imposition of alien rule had been by the selective use of force, the power and authority of those who were not Big Men in their own right was liable to crumble when support was withdrawn. Many client chiefs selectively accepted patronage without accepting all the obligations that went with it. When such client chiefs were called upon to play more bureaucratic roles, some were able to make the transition, others were not. At this point the Administration began to appoint minor chiefs from Kumi and Bukedea, and school-leavers who had served as clerks in the District Office, as chiefs in the other counties. As early as 1913 there were transferred into Serere county, 'where there are no men of ability fit for selection as sub-county chiefs, able men from the advanced counties of Kumi and Bukedea who can hardly hope for the promotion they deserve in their own counties.'[24] The resentment caused by such appointments the Administration hoped to turn to advantage. 'The whole of the administration of Teso seems to pivot on Kumi,' the District Commissioner reported. 'The County Chief institution has already started the right sort of competition among counties, generally with a view to bettering Kumi.'[25]

Loss of office for Big Men in the 'inferior' counties did not necessarily mean loss of political prowess. Deposed client chiefs continued to operate behind the scenes for many years after they had been discharged and were to be found, serially incumbent as chief, parish councillor, 'clan elder', district councillor and political party patron, through the pages of Teso's political record. Much of their power derived from the personal networks of patronage established at the beginning of their political careers, and these they were able to operate regardless of shifts in administrative recognition. Finally in 1927 a regulation was introduced whereby dismissed chiefs had to move out of the areas of which they had been in charge 'to prevent the constant cases of intrigue in which dismissed chiefs endeavour to make the work and position of their successors as difficult as possible.'[26]

The Big Men who remained from Kakunguru's day were able to corner much of the African share of the new wealth of the district. They were also able to ensure its future control by their kinsmen and clients. Their early advantages in disposing of labour, acquiring land and educating those whom they chose to send to the mission schools, were articulated with, and often reinforced by, strategic marriage alliances with those recognised as members of their privileged cohort. By the mid-1920s, these chiefs comprised a formidable group whose political achievement could be measured both by the growing gulf between them and the peasantry and, in time, by the resentment that was beginning to be expressed by the 'northern' chiefs who were later in entering the administrative arena. The gap that existed may be suggested by a comparison of the cash incomes of chief and commoner and, further, by observing the sanctions that enabled a chief to exploit and widen this gap. A full series of statistics is not available but a fair approximation may be constructed.

FIG. 5 Salary Scales of Teso Chiefs, 1929

County Chiefs	Shillings Per Annum
Class 1	11,000–22,000
Class 2	9,600–19,400
Class 3	7,600–13,840
Class 4	6,000– 8,300
Class 5	4,160
Sub-county Chiefs	
Class 1	3,440
Class 9	560
Parish Chiefs	
Class 1	560
Class 5	240
Village Chiefs	
Class 1	320
Class 4	80

The salary scale of chiefs in 1929 ranged from Shs. 560/- a year for a newly appointed (Grade 9) sub-county chief to Shs. 22,000/- a year for the highest grade County Chief (Fig. 5).[27] It is with sub-county chiefs' remunerations that vast differences of wealth open up; those of lower chiefs were at the level of skilled peasant employees. At this time two sources of cash were available to most peasants: the sale of cotton and the sale of labour. The price of the former varied between Shs. 9/4 and Shs. 20/- per 100 lbs. between 1912 and 1927[28] so that from an average yearly production of 248 lbs. a grower would receive about Shs. 38/-. The highest wage for unskilled labour during these years was Shs. 5/- a month, without food.[29] If such work were available throughout the year (it rarely was), an unskilled labourer might expect a cash income of Shs. 60/- per annum, i.e. 25% lower than that of the lowest grade village chief.

In estimating relative costs for chiefs and commoners, it is useful to consider only school fees, taxes and fines, which accounted for most of the cash expenditure in the peasant economy. Education at Ngora High School cost a parent Shs. 60/- per annum, the total cash income of the unskilled labourer or 1/69th of the annual income of a Grade 5 County Chief.[30] Poll tax increased during this period from Shs. 6/- in 1907 to Shs. 21/-in 1927 (Fig. 6).[31] Many chiefs not only neglected to pay tax, but also received rebates of between 5–10% on tax collected so that, even in 1910, chiefs were already sharing among their number 39.8% of the district's total cash revenue.

How far chiefly sanctions reached down into the security of the peasants may be seen from the fines they were empowered to impose. For example, in 1927, a man might be fined Shs. 30/- for drunkenness—at the discretion of the chief; for bhang smoking a first offender was subject to a Shs. 20/- fine or twelve lashes; for moving

FIG. 6. Poll Tax and Cotton Revenue, 1910–1929

Year	*Poll Tax (in Rupees and Shillings)*		*Chiefs' Percentage*	*Cotton Production (in tons)*	*Average Price (in Shillings per 100 lbs)*
1910	R	62,949	6	500	
1911	R	138,189	6	1,100	
1912	R	163,086	6	2,800	9/4
1913	R	195,834	6	3,000	
1914	R	227,490	6	8,836	
1915	R	358,564	6	5,739	
1916	Shs	345,485	10	5,529	11/-
1917		350,560	10	6,658	
1918		351,200	10	2,340	13/4
1919		344,340	10	3,100	14/-
1920		502,332	15	5,813	20/-
1921	Shs			8,750	5/- to 8/-
1922		733,338	15	2,420	16/-
1923		872,637	15	11,357	18/-
1924		938,819	15	9,384	28/-
1925		985,384	15	14,000	20/-
1926	Shs	990,629	15	12,053	
1927		1,267,417	21	7,795	14/-
1928		1,410,306	21	8,719	18/-
1929		1,440,284	21	12,959	9/-

cattle without a chief's permission, penalties of Shs. 50/-, six months' imprisonment and twelve lashes could be imposed. Labour defaulters were fined Shs. 5/- for each day's absence and, of this, Shs. 3/- went to the chief. A peasant wishing to commute his compulsory labour obligation to chiefs had to pay Shs. 10/- for each 24 days he did not work.[32]

One might have expected the expansion of economic opportunities to have brought greater openness in the Teso chiefly oligarchy, but this does not appear to have been the case. The peasantry was not in a position to gain access to the administrative elite of these early years. Opportunities were certainly opened up to those who resided near missions, schools, markets and administrative centres but those in more remote areas barely entered the modern arena, since the physical mobility of the peasant was circumscribed by enforced *local* cultivation, labour and tax obligations. Although some individuals gained materially by working for chiefs, missionaries or Asian and European traders and officials, prestige could not be extended beyond kin and neighbours without converting material wealth into the currency of political office. This, however, could not be done, and acquired skills could not be transferred, while the chiefly class controlled access to the political arena. The initial burst of economic activity which built up external trade in cotton and established the district administration as a progressive contributor to the colonial economy thus served, within Teso itself, to sustain a conservative leadership determined to maintain the *status quo*.

Although the predominant cleavage in Teso society between 1907 and 1927 was that between chiefs and peasantry, a lesser cleavage developed among the chiefs themselves on the basis of differential economic opportunities—a cleavage between north and south. Penetration, consolidation and economic development had, as we have seen, been divisive between north, south and west. The political events that were set in motion in 1920 brought the centralising process to a new threshold at which, for the first time, Iteso chiefs were being given access to the outer corridors of power. It was perhaps inevitable that alignments took the form of the earlier competition between south and north, between the haves and have-nots of the earlier establishment.

There had clearly emerged in Teso a powerful, nominally Christian, salaried group of southern chiefs whose increasingly corporate interests brought into opposition those who had not been able to enter the political arena until later, when much of the southern power had been both consolidated and spread. Since the logistics of Protestant penetration into Teso had encouraged a working alliance between the administration and the Church Missionary Society at Ngora, northern chiefs seeking European patrons sought the support of the Roman Catholic fathers who had established schools in Usuku county as well as in the south. The Mill Hill Mission, having long chafed at the over-representation of Protestant converts among the chiefs, appears to have cooperated.[33] The specific event which provoked the mobilisation of the northerners and Catholics was the appointment of the first independent Iteso county chief in June 1920. For the British officers this was a 'most significant event in the History of Teso indicating that the local native is now considered to have reached the stage beyond the necessity of outside tuition and help in his internal affairs.'[34] They were dispensing at last with supervisory Baganda Agents. The Iteso chiefs, however, looked on this as an invitation to take a more active role in government, advancing the district along lines that would enhance their own autonomy, power and class interests. They began by confronting the district officers with a show of strength in the one area of strategic resources to which they had the closest access and over which they had the closest control: the sale of the peasants' cotton crop.

Prices for cotton (see Fig. 6) were extraordinarily low in the 1920/21 season and chiefs throughout the district persuaded the peasant growers to withhold their crop from the market. 'The chiefs were controlling the situation, the Bakopi (peasants) with few exceptions, were taking their lead from the chiefs.'[35] According to one report, in some places the persuasion took the form of intimidation but everywhere preparations were made to store cotton locally rather than sell it. The northern chiefs held out longer than those of Kumi and only the District Commissioner's exhortations to an assembly of all County and sub-county chiefs at Toroma in Usuku (following upon the intervention of the Assistant Superintendent of Police who threatened all present with criminal prosecution) settled the matter. He had been obliged to negotiate at lengthy late night sessions with the chiefs' spokesman, Epaku, County Chief of Soroti, and it was with him that an agreement was finally reached. Epaku issued a letter authorising the settlement, pledging that there would be no further delay in cotton reaching the market. This was communicated by the District Office to the ginners. It is not surprising that one historian, writing of resistance to alien rule in Teso, singles out the career of Enosi Epaku for special attention (Emwanu 1967).

By 1923 it would appear that a political machine was in the making. In its first appointment of county chiefs, the district office had hoped to form an administrative arm which, 'with these young chiefs to provide the initiative and necessary impetus and a percentage of elders to maintain the ballast,'[36] a steady course of political development could be pursued. Under-estimated were the corporate political interests of the New Men and, perhaps, the covert political interests of the missions, let alone the extent to which the skills of both could be brought to bear upon the stabilising 'ballast'. In 1926 Ecodu, the one remaining County Chief of the old school, asked to be moved from Serere where he could no longer 'get on with' his young, progressive chiefs. That he was transferred to Usuku and retired there shortly afterwards suggests the District Commissioner's inability to sustain the ballast and keep the political vessel on the slow but steady course envisaged for it. Ecodu's place was taken by Opit, 'young, clever and progressive but not altogether an ideal chief in the eyes of one administrator.[37] Shortly afterwards Opit put himself forward for appointment to Kumi and in March 1925 Onaba, Chief of Kumi, resigned, expressing his 'inability' to cope with the forces of change.[38]

The chiefs saw themselves as a privileged class. Their demands for a Chiefs' Ward at Soroti Hospital and for privileges at local dispensaries were acceded to by the District Office.[39] In 1924 native councils were introduced in Teso, largely so that elected representatives might offset the powers of the chiefs and a voice be given to peasant discontent. In 1926 the chiefs in the Teso Native Council openly challenged the authority of the Commissioner by voting a resolution to the effect that they disapproved of the Commissioner intervening in matters raised by subordinate councils without these matters having been brought to them. This may be seen both as a demonstration of the chiefs' political sensitivity to their strategic position controlling access to the peasantry, and as a reflection of their awareness that they were likely to be by-passed by the administration as it looked to councillors rather than chiefs as representatives of the Teso public.

The ultimate threat to the British administrators came from two directions—spearheaded again by Epaku and the Mill Hill Mission. It was averted by dismissals and deportations of both chiefs and priests. These affairs are politically controversial still, and the remaining records are obscure. It would appear that Epaku, seizing a moment of indeterminacy that accompanied the administrative shift towards popular representation even as that policy was being put into practice, again attempted to mobilise the peasantry to resist further economic exploitation. Ironically, his efforts at the grassroots level may be seen as an attempt to alleviate the same popular oppression that the district officers were trying to remove from above. It is not clear exactly what Epaku did to bring about his deportation. Perhaps his sole unpardonable crime was 'to argue about Protectorate policies.'[40] Lawrance is prepared to accept at face value the stated reason for Epaku's dismissal, namely corruption and inefficiency, noting: 'It was not always the gravity of the offence which dictated whether or not a dismissed chief was deported, but the degree of his standing and the effect which his continued presence would have on the maintenance of good order in the district. Epaku symbolised Teso 'nationalism' in opposition to rule by alien Baganda agents and was undoubtedly immensely popular. Given that he was to be dismissed, his deportation was perhaps inevitable.'[41] Emwanu (1967: 182) reports a battery of recollections from local informants: 'Epaku was so strongly opposed to forced labour that he became the champion of the underdog by openly speaking against it . . . the British administration wanted to introduce a system of land tenure that would allow individual freehold which Epaku opposed . . . Epaku had become so popular that the people wanted to make him "Kabaka" of Teso, a proposition which the administration would not allow.'

All these commentaries upon the Epaku affair tell us more about those who make them than about the event itself, let alone its political meaning. Perhaps the most we can safely say is that this would appear to be yet another occasion on which a political issue within the district arena was deflated by placing it within a larger context. Thus, in June 1927, the Provincial Commissioner addressed a large public baraza at Soroti and, after attacking the corruption and self-interest of chiefs in general, publicly dismissed the two County Chiefs, Epaku of Soroti and Opit of Serere.[42] He threatened others with dismissal, too, if they did not disengage from activities in certain unnamed political organisations. His allusion was probably to 'the League for obtaining for Roman Catholics of a greater share in the Administration of the country,' founded by Father Kiggen of the Mill Hill Mission. He reminded the assembled chiefs of their client status: 'It was the Government who introduced the position of County Chiefs into Teso where it had never existed before' yet 'the machinations of a few . . . had produced maladministration and unrest.' He spoke of individuals who had 'exploited the peasantry and made themselves rich by the sweat of *their* brow and at *their* expense.' He spoke further of excessive attention being paid to fashionable clothing and motor cars and, more pointedly, of nepotism, bribery and cliques in power. To prove the power of the patrons, Baganda Agents were reappointed to Teso[43] but the Provincial Commissioner was attacking a class in the making.

Two separate fighting issues are evident, one made explicit by the Commissioner—the exploitation of the peasantry—and the other, nowhere explicit, the challenge by indigenous leaders to the authority of the District Officers. The manipulation of a political machine had become increasingly apparent between 1920 and 1927, but the in-fighting was restricted to the elite—just as, later, factionalism between north and south in the District Council represented the ambitions of competing councillors for the patronage powers and spoils of certain offices. Neither had roots reaching to the local level. Although records are no longer in existence to judge the extent to which the Commissioner operated under a conspiracy theory in order to rationalise growing unrest at his own authoritarianism, the newly appointed County Chiefs had clearly been too ambitious in their political goals.

That these goals were to benefit the peasantry, rather than to profit the chiefly class, seems questionable.[44] Since the British administrator also claimed to be acting on behalf of the peasantry in protecting them from chiefly exploitation, it is perhaps in the condition of the peasantry that the case finally rests. Here we are more fortunate in the Teso records.

A continuity of experience rare in colonial administration led the Provincial Commissioner in 1929 to recall conditions when he was a District Officer in Teso and to assess the progress made in the intervening fifteen years. 'While there has been a great advance in material prosperity,' he remarked, 'and considerable superficial advance in Native Administration, the fundamental progress of the people themselves has been negligible.'[45] This assessment appears valid. Expressions of the relative deprivation of the population made themselves heard. When communication took place largely through a language not spoken by administrative officers and agents, the chiefs were strategically placed to control both the access of the District Office to the peasants and that of the peasants to their administrators. By the mid-1920s, however, streams of complaints, written in English as well as Ateso, began to flow into the District Office. There emerged a picture of oppression and injustice that could not be ignored, an impression confirmed when district officers began to tour more frequently. Visible evidence of peasant unrest lie in the records of arson, and even murder, of chiefs and their relatives that occurred during the late 1920s.

Conclusion

The exploitative nature of the chiefly class that grew up in Teso between 1896 and 1927 is a matter of record. Regardless of whether the chiefs were indeed a class in their own right, in the eyes of the peasantry they were certainly a class of oppressors against whom there was little appeal. This should not be a matter for surprise since, as we have seen, client chiefs were obliged to be responsible to the demands of office as defined by those above them. In their unrest at exploitation by their chiefs, the Teso peasants were expressing dissatisfaction with an oppressive system. However, it is also a matter of record that, perceiving the problem somewhat differently, the British administration began the third decade of the twentieth century as they had begun the first—searching for Iteso leaders who might be promoted to positions of authority as the 'true representatives' of the Teso people. The drama that was the political transformation of Teso District thereafter moved into its second act.

NOTES

[1] This is a revision of part of an essay prepared in 1970 for *Government and Rural Development in East Africa: Essays on Political Penetration*, Eds. L. Cliffe, J. Coleman and M. Doornbos (The Hague: Martinus Nijhoff), forthcoming. Research was financed by the Ministry of Overseas Development and carried out as a Fellow of the East African Institute of Social Research (1966–67) and by a Faculty Research Grant from Barnard College (1970). I would like to thank Barnard College for a grant towards publication.

[2] Fallers 1956: 197 distinguishes between traditional and civil-service chiefs. The Teso chiefly entrepreneurs of this essay resemble his 'client-chiefs'.

[3] See, for example, Arrighi and Saul 1973; Balandier 1951; Biebuyck and Douglas 1961; Fallers 1956; Vincent 1969.

[4] For accounts of the administrative set-up, which was similar throughout East Africa, see Fallers 1956; Richards 1960. Lawrance, a former District Commissioner of Teso, provides a useful account of political structure and development (1957) as does Burke 1964.

The substantive data in this section is drawn from Cohen 1972; Gray 1963; Kirkpatrick 1899; Kitching 1912; Roberts 1962; Roscoe 1915; Thomas 1939; Twaddle 1967; Webster et al. 1973.

[5] In 1966 the Teso District Council introduced a by-law whereby youths could be summoned for labour according to age-set principles. I was shown a copy of this in the field in January 1967 but, as far as I know, nothing came of the proposal.

[6] The type of political leadership to which the term Big Man is given in the ethnographic literature is commonly to be found in acephelous societies and peasant societies which are not feudal. See Worsley 1956; Barnes 1962; Strathern 1966. A developmental relationship exists between the Big Men of acephelous societies and the patrons and political brokers of the contemporary local scene.

[7] The implications of arming local leaders is discussed in Vincent 1971: 50–53.

[8] Emwanu (1967: 178) refers to 'Enoka Epaku who early in his career as a public servant led a spectacular expedition which marked the boundaries of the district, covering an area much wider than either his fellow chiefs or the British

administrators ever thought likely.' Emwanu notes, 'No written evidence of the boundary demarcation has come to light, but Nasanairi Okalebo of Ngora who was made a chief by Epaku, and took part in the expedition, was interviewed' (1967: 181). Not only Epaku's spectacular initiative but his patronage powers are evident.

[9] Teso District Archives (hereafter TDA) VADM/5 (1920). The decision to exclude Kabeŕamaido from Teso District defined out of existence 'the Kumam problem' which became critical at a later period. See Vincent, forthcoming.

[10] TDA 1911 District Census (Kumi).

[11] TDA 1913, XADM/6.14.

[12] *Ibid.*

[13] TDA 1913, XNAF/3.21.

[14] TDA 1913, XNAF/3.21/13.

[15] TDA 1916, XADM/5.98.

[16] TDA 1917, XADM/5.85.

[17] TDA 1917, XADM/5.127–9.

[18] E. Wolf's definition of a peasantry is most apt for our purposes since it focuses upon 'social relations which are not symmetrical, but are based, in some form, upon the exercise of power . . . Where someone exercises an effective superior power, or *domain*, over a cultivator, the cultivator must produce a fund of rent . . . It is this fund of rent which critically distinguishes the peasant from the cultivator' (1966: 9–10).

[19] TDA VADM/5.2; TDA, XADM/5.41.

[20] TDA XADM/5.41.

[21] TDA 1920 Annual Report.

[22] TDA 1926–27, XADM/2.106.

[23] TDA 1910, VADM/3/1.

[24] TDA 1913, XADM/6.14.

[25] TDA 1920, VADM/8/1.

[26] TDA 1927, VADM/5/2.

[27] TDA 1929, VADM/5/2.

[28] TDA XADM/5.41. These figures do not correspond with statistics derived from the Annual Reports and Blue Books of the Uganda Protectorate nor with the Cotton Commission Reports cited by Vail (1972). They are on-the-spot market figures recorded daily by the District Commissioner.

[29] TDA VADM/5.1.

[30] TDA VADM/5/2.

[31] TDA VADM/5.2; TDA XADM/5.41.

[32] TDA VADM/5/2.

[33] This statement is based on fragments appearing in miscellaneous files and correspondence between the DC Teso and the Provincial Commissioner. Letter books (TDA VADM/8/1.2) are sketchy, but correspondence between 1912 and 1922 suggests, in the form of address, tone etc., that the Administration's relations with the Catholic mission having at first been amicable and cooperative (cf. Postlethwaite 1947: 30), later became extremely tense, reaching a low point in 1927, when, 'Disloyalty was fostered by a Catholic Mission Priest who had to be deported from the District in June. It is still being fanned by a fanatical and anti-Government Sinn Fein lawyer who desires the Catholic Church to have temporal and spiritual power in Teso' (TDA 1927, XADM/9.15). I have not been able to look at the records of the Mill Hill Mission for this period and would not want to develop this argument without having done so.

[34] TDA 1920, XADM/6.11.

[35] TDA, VADM 8/1; TDA, XADM/7/4.21.

[36] TDA 1920, XADM/9.29.

[37] TDA 1923, XADM/6.4.3–5.

[38] TDA 1925, XADM/6.40.5.

[39] TDA 19, XADM/9.

[40] Ingrams 1960: 171, possibly expressing the view of J. Ogaino as suggested by the editors in a footnote to Emwanu 1967: 181.

[41] Lawrance's recollections appear to have been solicited by the editors of and as a footnote to Emwanu 1967: 181–2.

[42] TDA 1927, ADM/17.

[43] *Ibid.* The District Commissioner commented: 'This may appear paradoxical to our Western ideas of self-determination and democracy. In Teso, thank goodness, we are not yet troubled by either of these false premises. The peasantry has suffered so heavily from the contempt and exploitation by their black coated compatriots that they frankly welcome a protective shock-absorber above them' (TDA XADM/106.105).

[44] Emwanu 1967: 179 suggests that Epaku was discharged because of the 'immense popularity which he enjoyed among his own people . . . He was especially concerned with the welfare of the people of Teso as a whole.' A more penetrating analysis of the situation in which both colonial administrators and civil service chiefs claimed to be the defenders of the Teso peasantry might call for reference to Marx and Engels 19. Thus: '. . . each new class which (wishes to put) itself in the place of the one ruling before it is compelled, merely in order to carry through its aim, to represent its interest as the common interest of all the members of society . . . The class making a revolution appears from the very start, merely because it is opposed to a class, not as a *class* but as the representative of the whole society; it appears as the whole mass of society confronting the one ruling class. It can do this because, to start with, its interest really is more connected with the common interest of all other non-ruling classes, because under the pressure of conditions its interest has not yet been able to develop as the particular interest of a particular class.'

[45] TDA 1929, XADM/9.

REFERENCES

AJAYI, J. F. A. 1968 'The continuity of African institutions under colonialism', in T. Ranger (ed.) *Emerging Themes of African History*. London: Heinemann. pp. 197–200.

APTHORPE, R. (ed.) 1959 *From Tribal Rule to Modern Government*. Rhodes-Livingstone Institute, 13th. Conference Proceedings.

ARRIGHI, G. and SAUL, J. 1973 *Essays on the Political Economy of Africa*. New York: Monthly Review Press.

BALANDIER, G. 1951 'La situation coloniale: approche théorique', *Cahiers internationaux de sociologie* XI, 44–79.

BARNES, J. 1962 'African models in the New Guinea highlands,' *Man* 62, pp. 5–9.

BIEBUYCK, D. and DOUGLAS, M. 1961 *Congo Tribes and Parties*. London: International African Institute.

BURKE, F. G. 1964 *Local Government and Politics in Uganda*. Ithaca: Syracuse University Press.

COHEN, D. W. 1972 *The Historical Tradition of Busoga*. Oxford: Clarendon Press.

DYSON-HUDSON, N. 1967 *Karimojong Politics*. Oxford: Clarendon Press.

EMWANU, G. 1967 'The reception of alien rule in Teso, 1896–1927,' *Uganda Journal* 31, pp. 171–82.

FALLERS, L. A. 1956 *Bantu Bureaucracy*. Cambridge: Heffer.

GRAY, J. 1963 'Kakunguru in Bukedi,' *Uganda Journal* 27, 31–59.

INGRAMS, H. 1960 *Uganda, a Crisis of Nationhood*. London: HMSO.

KIRKPATRICK, R. T. 1899 'Lake Choga and the surrounding countryside,' *Geographical Journal* 13 (4), 453–64.

KITCHING, A. L. 1912 *On the Backwaters of the Nile*. London: Fisher-Unwin.

LAWRANCE, J. C. D. 1957 *The Iteso*. Oxford: Oxford University Press.

MARX, K. and ENGELS, F. 1963 *The German Ideology*. New York: International Publishers.

MEGGITT, M. R. 1967 'The pattern of leadership among the Mae-Enga of New Guinea,' *Anthropological Forum* 2 (1), 20–35.

POSTLETHWAITE, J. R. P. 1947 *I look back*. London: T. V. Boardman and Co.

RICHARDS, A. I. (ed.) 1960 *East African Chiefs*. London: Faber.

ROBERTS, A. D. 1962 'The sub-imperialism of the Baganda,' *Journal of African history* 3, 435–50.

—— 1963 'The evolution of the Uganda Protectorate,' *Uganda Journal* 27, 95–106.

ROSCOE, J. 1915. *The Northern Bantu*. Cambridge: Cambridge University Press.

SMITH, M. G. 1966 'A structural approach to comparative politics,' in D. Easton (ed.), *Varieties of Political History*. New Jersey: Prentice-Hall. pp. 113–128.

STRATHERN, A. 1966 'Despots and directors in the New Guinea highlands,' *Man* 62, 356–67.

THOMAS, H. B. 1939 'Capax Imperii—the story of Semei Kakunguru,' *Uganda Journal* 6, 125–36.

TOSH, J. 1973 'Colonial chiefs in a stateless society: a case study from northern Uganda,' *Journal of African History* XIV (3), 473–90.

TWADDLE, M. 1967 *Politics in Bukedi 1900–1939*. Unpublished Ph.D. Thesis, University of London.

VAIL, D. J. 1972 *A History of Agricultural Innovation and Development in Teso District, Uganda*. Ithaca: Syracuse University Press.

VINCENT, J. 1969 'Anthropology and political development,' in C. Leys (ed.) *Politics and Change in Developing Countries*. Cambridge: Cambridge University Press. pp. 35–63.

—— 1971 *African Elite: the big men of a small town*. New York: Columbia University Press.

—— forthcoming 'Teso in transformation: colonial penetration in Teso District, Eastern Uganda, and its contemporary significance,' in J. Coleman, L. Cliffe and M. Doornbos (eds.) *Government and Rural Development in East Africa: essays on political penetration*. The Hague: Martinus Nijhoff.

WEBSTER, J. B. et al. 1973 *The Iteso during the Asonya*. Nairobi: East African Publishing House.

WOLFE, E. 1966 *Peasants*. Englewood Cliffs: Prentice-Hall.

WORSLEY, P. 1956 'The kinship system of the Tallensi: a revaluation,' *Journal of the Royal Anthropological Association* 89, 37–75.

Résumé

CHEFS DE L'ÉPOQUE COLONIALE ET ÉMERGENCE DE CLASSES: UNE ÉTUDE DE CAS DE TESO

CETTE étude de cas du district de Teso dans l'est de l'Ouganda, au cours de la période d'administration coloniale qui va de 1896 à 1927, rapporte la mise sur pied d'un groupe de chefs qui avaient été nommés et le maintien de leur présence dans un milieu politique local où l'on n'avait pas reconnu jusque là l'existence d'une autorité traditionnelle ni le principe de passation héréditaire des pouvoirs. On passe ici en revue le développement de la bureaucratie et de la domination de cette forme d'autorité nouvellement créée ainsi que les changements qui ont marqué les rapports des chefs avec le régime colonial et le peuple qui leur était soumis. Peu à peu, leurs pouvoirs coercifs croissants et leur contrôle toujours plus fort des appuis entrainèrent l'apparition d'un intérêt de classe entre eux. Ceci se matérialisa vers le milieu des années 1920, lorsque dans leur ensemble ils maintinrent une attitude conservative au sein d'une administration coloniale tournée vers un besoin de changement.

Il s'effectua deux coupures importantes dans la société Teso: l'une sépara le chef du paysan, l'autre le sud et le nord du district. On comprend mieux l'évolution des évènements politiques de 1896 à 1927 à la lumière de ces deux oppositions; leur résolution est pour beaucoup dans l'orientation de la politique locale du Teso dans les années qui suivirent.

Dans les premiers temps, la création de l'arène politique se doubla de l'homogénisation culturelle du district par les administrateurs coloniaux, la continuité du pouvoir et de l'influence des personnages éminents indigènes et les problèmes d'administration de la population et du contrôle de la main d'oeuvre. Tandis que ce processus de consolidation progressait, certaines conditions locales entrainèrent une modification du travail administratif et de là on aboutit à l'apparition d'un déséquilibre économique. Les chefs du sud prirent le pas sur ceux du nord mais ils exerçaient tous une action coercive et développèrent leur puissance. D'énormes différences de revenus se firent jour entre chefs et paysans, ces derniers traduisant leur agitation par une action violente. On peut s'interroger sur le rôle des missions dans la politique des diverses factions. Un boycottage du coton en 1921 conduit par les chefs donna lieu à une confrontation ouverte entre le pouvoir colonial et les nouveaux hommes forts: les chefs furent vaincus et certains expulsés; quant au système, il fut revu dans son ensemble.

Colonialism in Angola: Kinyama's Experience*

David Birmingham

Kinyama was a thirty-six-year-old farmer who lived in a valley in southern Angola, on the northern slopes of the Benguela Highlands. By 1956 he was not rich for a man of his age, but he was comfortably off. He had three acres of hoe gardens. He also had fifteen acres of fallow land which he was able to use while worked-out land was resting. He had three cows, and this made him one of the more prosperous middle peasants in the valley. His farming, like all farming, was a risky business but not as risky as that of people who lived in the poorer and

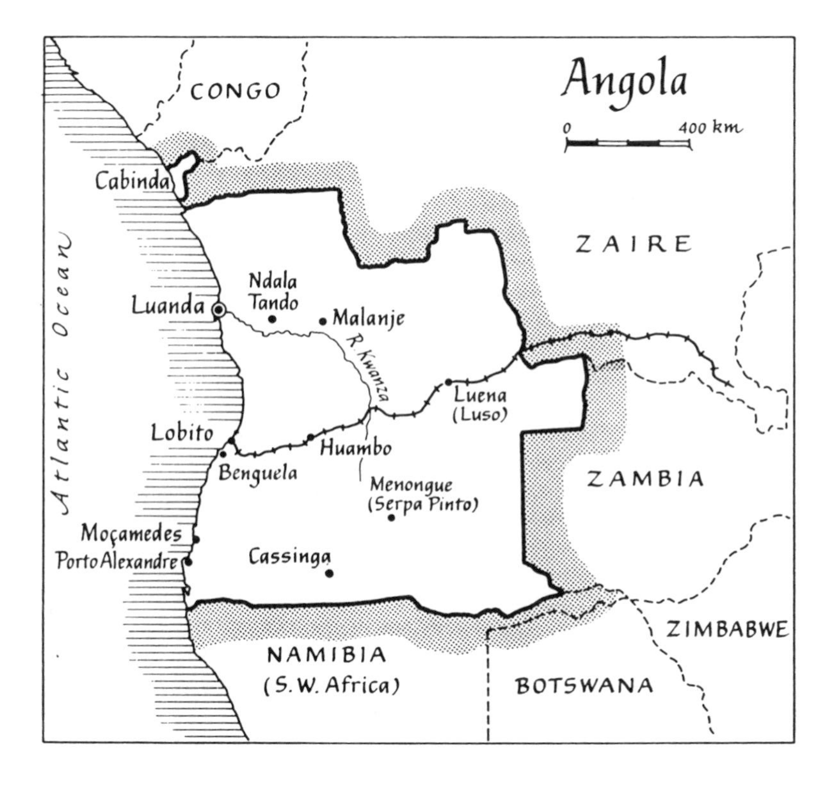

* This story is not history but it is based on historical circumstances. It was not intended for publication, but was given as a lecture at the University of Cape Town in an attempt to illuminate, for the benefit of South Africans, the colonial situation in which they had become involved.

drier and less fertile parts of Angola. Despite his comfortable farming circumstances, Kinyama nevertheless constantly felt that his prosperity was being threatened. Slowly, very slowly, the colonial system which the Portuguese were building in Angola had begun to encroach on the valley in new ways over the past five years.

The first way in which Kinyama had begun to feel the authority of the 'New State', which Salazar had founded twenty years earlier, was in the more systematic levying of taxes. Instead of using maize to feed his family Kinyama now had to sell it in order to pay tribute to a newly-appointed District Officer. Instead of being able to use his maize to buy consumer goods, Kinyama found that maize had become a sort of tax-crop to pay new or revived hut dues. Colonial taxes fell heavily upon a southern peasant growing three acres of maize.

When Kinyama tried to sell his maize he found only one trader in the valley to buy it. This was a Portuguese immigrant who had arrived in 1951 and had a monopoly. He could fix his own price for buying maize since there was no other trader nearby. Thus Kinyama had no bargaining power: he was a prisoner of a limited trading system. When he needed to pay taxes in cash he could only sell maize to the valley trader. The trader knew his plight and lowered the price.

In 1956 Kinyama's maize money was not enough to pay his taxes and he was declared a tax defaulter. The District Officer ordered that Kinyama, a respected farmer of the valley, should be beaten. He was taken into the closed courtyard behind the District Office where he was to receive twenty-five strokes. The beating was carried out with the *palmatória*, a wooden paddle drilled with holes. He was beaten on the palms of his hands.[1] Although Kinyama was a grown man, the beating was carried out by a young cousin of his own family who worked in the office. The resultant loss of family status and prestige was as painful as the colonial style of physical punishment.

A week after his ordeal Kinyama decided that the only way in which his family could recover from their financial difficulty was by sending his brother away to work on the coffee plantations of North Kwanza. The decision was a distressing one. The farm could not afford to lose the services of one of its best labourers. There seemed, however, no other way in which the colonial taxes could be raised. The trader offered Kinyama credit against the money his brother would earn if he signed a coffee worker's contract. With this credit he would be able to pay his taxes. The interest to be charged until his brother returned was to be 30 per cent.

The coffee industry in Angola had begun a hundred years earlier and many peasants from the valley had worked in it.[2] The town of Ndala Tando meant 'the place where the smoke rises', the name given to it by Bailundu coffee harvesters who arrived from the Southern plateau and had never seen a town before. When Kinyama's brother reached the coffee estates in 1956, he found problems in earning money there, for the estate owner would not pay his workers in cash but gave them tokens instead. These tokens could only be used in a store which the plantation owner ran himself, so although Kinyama's brother was able to buy some over-priced cloth for his work on the plantation, he was not able to raise money to take back to the valley.[3]

Gradually Kinyama succeeded in reorganising the work on his farm to compensate for having to send his brother to the North. A few months later, however, a new calamity struck the valley. A government labour recruiter came to the District Office and said that he required a levy of forty men immediately.[4] Forty men were rounded up and put on the back of a lorry. Kinyama was one of those who were caught. This represented a total disaster for his family and for his farm. At that point, however, Kinyama gained reprieve: he managed to speak to the African recruiting assistant and offered to find a substitute who would go on the lorry if he himself could be released. The assistant agreed, and Kinyama, with a heavy heart, offered his eldest son. Kinyama's son was only sixteen and did not know where he would be staying. Kinyama never did discover where his son was taken by the recruiter. In fact he went to the fisheries in the desert of Porto Alexandre in the far south of Angola. It was a remote and harsh country and the labour contracts were for two years. Living conditions in the low barracks of mud were crowded and very uncomfortable. Four months before he was due to return home, Kinyama's son caught pneumonia. He died a week before his eighteenth birthday.

Early in 1957 a policeman was appointed to serve in the valley. He brought with him the Portuguese tradition of hostility and antagonism between police and people. In Portugal a policeman was somebody to be feared.[5] The one who arrived in the valley came from a peasant family of seventeen children in the remote and depressed Tras-os-Montes district of Northern Portugal. He had been able to attend school for three years as a child and had rudimentary skills in literacy. In Africa everything he saw was new, incomprehensible and terrifying. He spent his time shouting at the frightening Black people around him. Soon after his arrival, the new policeman sent a message to Kinyama saying that his daughter was required to work in the policehouse laundry. Kinyama's daughter was fourteen. She did much of the hoeing on Kinyama's farm and the loss of even a child's labour was a serious blow. Kinyama only hoped that she would be able to earn a cash wage as the policeman's laundress.

Within months disaster struck Kinyama's family yet again. His daughter was violated by her new employer. The family were profoundly shocked to discover not only that their daughter was carrying a child, but that it was the child of a policeman. Even more shockingly it was the child of a White man. Kinyama was distraught, but there was no redress. The Portuguese prided themselves, regardless of the brutality involved, on the way in which their young soldiers and officials raped the Black women of their colonies. They hoped to create a mixed population which would entrench the culture and language of Lusitania in Africa.[6]

In June 1957 Kinyama's uncle arrived home in the valley from the port of Lobito. The uncle had been more successful than many inland migrants to the colonial towns. He had gained a training as a motor mechanic. After fifteen years, however, he suddenly found himself thrown out of his job. He was displaced by a new, White immigrant from Portugal. The immigrant was less well qualified and much less experienced. But in the towns of Angola by the 1950s the colour bar was gradually reaching downwards. Jobs for skilled and semi-skilled people were being taken away from Africans and given to the new Europeans and Cape Verdeans.[7] When Kinyama's uncle returned to the valley there were no mechanical jobs for him. He was unemployable as a wage-earner. Kinyama knew well that in the next season his uncle would be picked up by the sisal recruiter. He would become embittered as he moved from a relatively well-paid city job to cutting sisal, an unrewarding, prickly and unskilled drudgery. Like increasing numbers of Angolans he had been squeezed off even the narrow ladder of colonial opportunity which had existed before the 1950s.

In 1958 alarming rumours began to spread through the valley. The government in Lisbon proposed to settle White peasants from Portugal in Kinyama's valley. When they eventually arrived there were twenty-four families. The government built them brick houses, gave them free tools and seeds. Each new White peasant gained the shared use of a plough and the loan of an ox to draw it. These Portuguese farmers were free from all tax burdens. But most catastrophic of all, one of them was given Kinyama's maize farm. And another was given three of Kinyama's fallow acres which he had planned to use in the following seasons.[8]

The blow to Kinyama was severe in the extreme: his best land had been seized and he and his family had to move out of the valley and up onto the hillside. Overnight they were compelled to break new, stony ground. Instead of having a reasonably viable small maize farm, they were starting from scratch on the edge of the wilderness.

In 1959, shortly after the beginning of the rainy season, Kinyama's wife fell ill. There was no clinic in the valley; there was not even a shop which sold simple medicine. The nearest hospital to which Kinyama could send his wife was a Spanish hospital run by priests. This hospital was 250 miles away.[9] Kinyama assembled all his savings but still he could not raise the price of a bus ticket to the Spanish hospital. His wife got worse, so he decided to sell the fourth-hand bicycle he had bought only the year before. Despite her sickness his wife had to travel alone on the bus. She carried with her, Kinyama hoped, enough food to keep herself during her stay in hospital. It was five weeks before she was able to return home and three months before she was well enough once again to take her full part in running the farm.

Late in January 1961 rumours of fighting on the north side of the Kwanza began to reach Kinyama. The war in Angola did not begin in the highlands. At first it did not greatly affect the Ovimbundu farmers of Kinyama's valley. The war began further north in the lands of the Kimbundu. Among the Kimbundu the encroachment of the colonial economy had occurred earlier than in the south and its effects had been more severe. As far back as 1945 Kimbundu peasants had been protesting vigorously against a policy of compulsory cotton-growing. District Officers had written to Lisbon explaining that families were starving because people were required to use much of their time and much of their land growing cotton for the government. The government replied sternly that such famine only occurred in the imagination of an idle, Black colonial population. Compulsory cotton growing was to be pursued vigorously.[10] The consequence was a reluctant, and long delayed, but violent revolt of despair. Cotton

5.3. Angolan villagers in hiding in the forests, photographed in 1970

warehouses were burnt down in 1961 and cotton buyers were driven out. The colonial government reacted with speed and violence. An air force was brought to Angola to bomb the villages. Many Kimbundu fled to the new independent republic of Congo-Léopoldville (later renamed Zaïre) across the river border.[11]

Kinyama did not feel that the cotton war had anything to do with him. His farmer's caution led him to keep quiet. Although his life was precarious, and becoming more so, he had not yet suffered real famine in the family.

In February 1961, a few days after the cotton war began, news began to reach the valley of a second uprising in Angola. This took place in Luanda, the capital city. The frustrations of city people, experienced several years before by Kinyama's uncle, the mechanic in Lobito, were becoming less and less bearable. They rose in revolt and attacked the city gaol to free their imprisoned leaders. The White folk, many of them new to Africa, panicked. Young men bought guns and invaded the Black township, attacking anyone they thought might be responsible for the uprising. Many were killed, especially those who had been to school and who had begun to adopt European ways. None of Kinyama's family had ever gone as far as Luanda to seek jobs or schooling but others from the valley began to return as refugees. They sought ways of re-entering farming after the failure of opportunity in a capital increasingly dominated by White immigrants. To most of the peasants in the valley, however, events of the city seemed very remote and unreal.

In the middle of March 1961 a third phase of the Angolan revolution touched the people of the highlands more closely. The great coffee rebellion broke out in the north of Angola. In this rebellion it was not only White planters who were killed by Angolans who had lost their lands, but many of the Black plantation workers too. The latter were seen as collaborators—albeit forced ones—who enabled the planters to seize land from the former Black peasant coffee growers. Many of these Black conscripts had continued to come, as in former times, from the Ovimbundu Highlands, so an acute sense of fear seized the valley. But still no southern uprising occurred. It was not clear to the Ovimbundu how they should react to this third outbreak of war in Angola. Since several people from Kinyama's valley became victims of the nationalist uprising they found it difficult to identify with the aims of the rebels.

Kinyama took no part in the wars of 1961. In 1962, however, the war came to affect his family in a most personal and painful way. Back in 1958 a rare and unexpected ray of hope had come into the life of Kinyama. A Presbyterian catechist had passed through the valley and offered to find a place in school for his middle son, then aged twelve. The school was 200 miles away in Huambo, known as New Lisbon. Kinyama had not been able to afford thirty escudos for a bus fare to school and his son had to walk all the way. It took eleven days, and he never came home for holidays. Kinyama's son did well at school. It looked at last as though the fortunes of the family were to change. One person from the valley was gaining an education, and would be able to seek a job with a high income. This, however, was not to be. In 1961, when the fighting began, Kinyama's son was in the fourth form. A year later the PIDE police came to the school. They took away twenty-five children. One of them was Kinyama's son. Kinyama continued for several years to hope that he might return from some prison camp. But he was never heard of again.[12]

Although none of the highland peoples had become involved in the war, the colonial army was nevertheless occasionally in evidence. Late one afternoon towards the end of 1967 Kinyama was up on the hillside looking for one of his goats. A jeep drove into the valley and sped towards his house. In it there were three young White soldiers and one Black one. As they drove past the farm a soldier fired his gun at one of Kinyama's cows. The cow was killed instantly. In that moment Kinyama lost 30 per cent of all his wealth. The young lads drove away laughing at what they saw as an amusing incident. But for Kinyama it was a major disaster. There was no way in which he could even begin to seek justice or redress. In a few short years Kinyama's relatively comfortable peasant life had come to be threatened by the increasing encroachment of a colonial society. He was almost ready to leave the valley and become a freedom fighter. Almost but still not quite.

Very early in the war colonial authority in Angola had become afraid that war might become more widespread. Already it was more than Portugal could handle, despite large-scale help from Western allies in the North Atlantic Treaty Organisation. To forestall further uprisings the Portuguese, in the late 1960s, decided to follow a new policy in the as yet unaffected areas. One June day in 1968 a new army official arrived in Kinyama's valley. He called together Kinyama and the other heads of valley households and announced that from now on they would have to live in a government village. Each family would leave its farm and build a village house beside the road. Everyone in the village would be required to stay indoors at night. Farmers would be allowed to work their fields, but would walk to them each morning and return from them each night. A tarred road would be built to speed the military patrols.

The policy of forced villagisation, also adopted by Americans in Vietnam and by Rhodesians in Zimbabwe, greatly increased the difficulties of farming in the valley. Kinyama, his aunt, his wife and his two youngest children, had to walk for one and a half hours each morning to reach their fields. And at harvest time their bags of maize and beans had to be carried for one and a half hours back to the government village in which they were compelled to live. The government called it a security village but to Kinyama it sometimes felt almost like a concentration camp.

Two years after Kinyama had completed his huts in the security village, a great storm hit the valley. It swept through, destroying crops, tearing the roofs off houses and Kinyama lost nearly all his standing maize. He now had to find money for enough thatch to repair all four of his huts. He went to the trader, who said that he would be quite willing to sell Kinyama four sacks of maize on credit. He would also be willing to advance him 300 Escudos (£4) credit in cash to buy thatch. But in exchange Kinyama would have to sign a six-month labour contract to work on a new European ranch recently opened up in the highlands. Kinyama had no choice. He needed the maize and he needed the thatch. So he signed the contract and two weeks later went south to work for six months on a cattle ranch. But it meant leaving his farm with only women to work it. His wife, his aunt and his two small children managed to farm alone. Although compulsory recruitment of labour by the District Officer had officially come to a stop, the valley trader had become even more powerful than before as a recruiter of contract labour. The trader received a generous fee from White employers, sometimes exceeding the wage of the worker he recruited. In the new security villages the need for credit compelled even heads of households to become migrant labourers.

By 1971, when Kinyama returned from his contract, Angola had been at war for ten years. Kinyama had survived and was still farming on the edges of the valley. But he was now over fifty and ever since 1956 his condition of life had seemed to decline. He had been forced to sign a labour contract; he was still required to use a part of his crop to pay taxes; his eldest and second sons were now presumed dead; he could not return to his old farm on the flat, although it had long been abandoned by its White occupier who had gone to the city to become a taxi driver.[13] Kinyama finally overcame his farmer's caution. Carefully, furtively, he made contact with other members of the valley community who were ready to join the nationalist cause and take up arms against colonial oppression.

Kinyama was obviously too old to leave the valley and walk the many miles needed to join the freedom fighters. But as a well-known and respected community elder, he was ideally placed to recruit younger men who had decided to break with their colonial way of life. In 1971 young Angolans were being recruited into the colonial army in increasing numbers. Those who wanted to escape from fighting against their own people secretly visited Kinyama's house at night despite the curfew regulations. A local party cell was informally set up. The idea of freedom from colonial rule and the ways of achieving it were discussed. Local subversion was planned.

While Kinyama was beginning to organise and mobilise the people of the valley into novel political activity, the Portuguese army, on the other side of the war, was beginning to alter its tactics of dragooning and villagising the highland peasants. Senior military officers were becoming increasingly aware that they could not win a shooting war. They would have to try political methods of recovering initiative in the colony.

New ideas about how to create a satisfied and loyal colonial population had already been developed not in Angola, but in Guinea Bissau, then known as Portuguese Guinea. There General Spinola, the Portuguese Governor and Army Commander, changed his policy from one of direct military confrontation to one of political wooing. He argued theoretically that only by providing economic betterment could colonial subjects be persuaded to abandon national independence as their aim. In practice Spinola's policy seldom went much beyond verbal promises of a better Guinea (*Guiné melhor*), and failed to significantly undermine the nationalist movement. When such ideas and promises were introduced into Angola, however, they naturally met with much fierce White resistance. The traders objected most vehemently, for it was they who made the largest profit margins from buying peasant crops cheaply and selling them at town prices. Despite the anger of the traders, however, the army won its point. Early in the 1970s a policy of positive rural development was approved for Angola.

On the morning of 12 May 1972 Kinyama received a White visitor. It was the first time that a White man had ever come to his house. The White man was not a Portuguese but a German. He had been appointed as a rural development adviser. His interpreter explained to Kinyama that the government had decided to give back to him his three acres of flat valley land. It had also decided to allow him to grow a new cash crop on this land. The crop was to be the delicate *arabica* coffee of the highlands. Kinyama knew nothing about growing coffee, although his uncle had worked on the great lowland plantations of the coarser *robusta* coffee in the north. No-one in the highlands had ever tried growing his own coffee. The development officer assured Kinyama that rural education officers would teach him how to plant coffee trees, how to weed them, care for them, and prune them. In a few years' time he could expect to harvest a crop of coffee worth many times more than his old crop of maize.

For the next year fortune began to smile on Kinyama as it had never smiled before. He received government credit to improve his returned farm. The government brought transport to carry state-supplied fertilisers to his fields. The farmers of the valley were encouraged to set up a co-operative. Instead of selling produce to the one White monopolist trader, they would be allowed to sell it at better prices to wholesalers in the city. The co-operative would be allowed to buy a lorry instead of relying on White trucking firms. The whole colonial economy, which had increasingly oppressed Kinyama and the people of the valley, seemed to have been set in reverse motion. Kinyama's dreams and expectations had never been higher. The twin ideas of political freedom and economic betterment had both reached the valley.

Kinyama, like many people in different parts of Angola, was caught in a trap between two sets of expectation. The liberation movement offered visions of a new society in which the interests of a peasant would become those of the government. The development officer offered a counter-programme in which some peasants—Kinyama included—would escape from subsistence to become successful farmers, and even agricultural businessmen. In its search for survival the colonial government was creating confusion, despair and divisions within Angola. Kinyama, in his slow and careful way, was still keeping all his options open.

The prospect dangled before Kinyama of developing a prosperous family business in the highlands was actually a false one. The coffee experiment absorbed an unreasonable amount of finance from the government and could never be expected to return real profits. More seriously the Angolan highlands were becoming agriculturally exhausted by this time. The best maize lands had been worked out and the fallow periods were becoming too short. The cost of colonial government, the cost of transferring wealth from the African countryside to the European towns, and the cost of paying for the colonial war, were impoverishing the majority of Ovimbundu. The coffee scheme and the co-operative movement could only buy a little more time for the Portuguese and that at great expense. Time, however, was not on their side: suddenly, on 25 April 1974, the Portuguese Government in Lisbon was overthrown in a military *coup d'état*.[14]

5.4. New Angolans: primary school children greet Basil Davidson at Lobito in 1977

The collapse of the Portuguese Government was felt in Angola. Over the next seventeen months the political parties began to mobilise their supporters and the colonial army gradually withdrew its troops. Kinyama, meanwhile, kept on farming. He still had fifteen goats to pasture on the hillside. He kept his two surviving cows in the valley. He hid his corn seed in an old hut far from the village. He made charcoal in the woods on the hilltops. And he waited for independence. But independence was deferred in Angola. November 1975 did not bring peace and freedom but new invaders. In the South the invaders came from South Africa.[15] They entered Kinyama's valley in armoured cars early on the morning of 15 November, four days after the last Portuguese colonial flag had been lowered. One of the cars opened fire on the village. Kinyama's house was hit. His wife lost an arm. The children were terrified. Kinyama died instantly.

Angola had to go through a long and painful new war before independence was achieved. Many more innocent peasants died, like Kinyama, in the sorry aftermath of Portuguese colonialism.

1 For a description of the use of the *palmatoria* as an instrument of punishment amounting to torture see the account on p. 78.
2 For details of the early coffee plantations see David Birmingham, 'The Coffee Barons of Cazengo', *Journal of African History*, xix, 4, 1978.
3 The use of tokens to pay plantation workers in a way which restricted their economic freedom but increased the profits of their employers occurred in other parts of Africa as well as in Angola; special purpose wage tokens were also used in Europe in the past.
4 Officially government recruiters mainly enrolled conscript workers for government services such as road maintenance; in practice the government supplied forced labour to many private employers as well.
5 In 1957 the PIDE political police, which ruthlessly suppressed freedoms in Portugal, was introduced into Angola. Its methods of intimidation became world famous over the next seventeen years and the association of brutality with policemen spread in part to the other police services in Angola such as the fictional valley constable portrayed here.
6 John Marcum in *The Angolan Revolution*, vol. I, Cambridge, Mass., 1969, p. 19, cites the hope of an army officer in 1966 that each Portuguese White conscript soldier would father six illegitimate mulatto children before returning to Europe. The degree of violence, pain and trauma thereby officially sanctioned would be hard to exaggerate.
7 Elsewhere in Africa, even in South Africa, the late colonial period saw new and more skilled jobs becoming available to Africans. In Portuguese Africa these jobs were offered to migrants from Europe and the Atlantic islands of Madeira and Cape Verde whose education and skills were often little higher than those of rural Angolans.
8 Gerald J. Bender, *Angola under the Portuguese*, London, 1978, has a good account of White peasant colonies in the southern highlands.
9 The Spanish hospital was up country from Huambo, near the Benguela Railway on which patients were regularly to be met. As late as 1973, when

the colonial presence was at its height, sick Angolans, Black and White, often travelled several hundred miles to find a trustworthy doctor.

10 The 1945 rejection of all protests against compulsory cotton growing was signed by President Carmona, Prime Minister Salazar and Colonial Minister Caetano.

11 Details of the cotton war of January 1961 can be found in Marcum, *The Angolan Revolution*, vol. I.

12 Reports of genuine historical events of a similar nature taking place in the south were given to the author in New Lisbon (now Huambo) in August 1963.

13 The Cela White colony in the northern part of the Benguela highlands was planned in the 1950s for 8 400 families. In 1960 about 300 were there and 122 had already left 'either through their own volition or by being expelled for offenses ranging from alcoholism and refusal to work to theft or even rape'. Gerald J. Bender, 'Planned Rural Settlement in Angola 1900–1968', in F. W. Heimer, *Social Change in Angola*, Munich, 1973, p. 242.

14 Although this story is allegorical, this is of course the real date of the military *coup d'état* in Lisbon. This coup toppled the forty-year-old dictatorship of the Salazar-Caetano corporative government which, between the world wars, had created the Portuguese New State, somewhat along the lines of Mussolini's fascist state in Italy.

15 See Robin Hallett, 'The South African Intervention in Angola 1975–76', in *African Affairs*, vol. 77, July 1978. For a wider view of the War of intervention in Angola, see Ernest Harsch and Tony Thomas, *Angola: the hidden history of Washington's war*, New York, 1977.

Journal of African History, IX, I (1968), pp. 119–146
Printed in Great Britain

SOME ORIGINS OF NATIONALISM IN EAST AFRICA[1]

BY J. M. LONSDALE

HISTORIOGRAPHICAL contioversies surrounding revolutions and other periods of rapid political change are concerned in part with the interactions of the 'spontaneous element' of popular initiative and the 'conscious element' of direction and control by intellectual and political leadership.[2] Debate on the relative importance of these two elements is in most cases likely to prove sterile, for they are interdependent. Nevertheless there may well be such a debate with reference to African national revolutions, for emphasis on the one or the other element will derive from contrasting assumptions about the nature of African nationalism as a whole. Studies of the conscious element, the political *élite*, will tend to stress the extent to which a nationalist movement is a revolutionary exotic in its reaction to colonial rule, and its dependence on European ideas and organizational models. Analyses of popular spontaneity must on the other hand be concerned with the historical continuities of the specifically African contribution. This paper is a tentative attempt at probing both the sources of continuity—the patterns of precolonial society; resistance to the imposition of alien rule;[3] the problems in the inter-war period of settled administration and incipient development—and the spontaneous contribution to revolutionary change after the Second World War.

The framework of this paper is more assured than its content warrants. Its main concern is the role of ordinary Africans in the emergence of national movements. In the first section I try to outline the essential contribution of social change,[4] concentrating on the shifts in African leadership and communication which it involved. There are in any society

[1] Earlier versions of this paper were presented at the Cambridge University Commonwealth and Overseas History Seminar and at a postgraduate seminar of the School of African and Asian Studies, University of Sussex. While based on research experience, it owes much to the stimulus of my colleagues at the University College, Dar es Salaam, in particular Professor Terence Ranger and Dr John Iliffe. They and Professor J. D. Fage have also provided valuable textual criticism. The faults in argument and presentation are my own responsibility.

[2] Cf. V. I. Lenin, *What is to be done?* 3rd rev. ed. (Progress Publishers, Moscow, 1964), 28–51.

[3] This factor is discussed by Professor Ranger in two important and as yet unpublished papers: 'African reaction and resistance to the imposition of colonial rule in East and Central Africa', to be published in L. H. Gann and P. Duignan (eds.), *History and Politics of Modern Imperialism in Africa* (Stanford), and 'Connections between "primary resistance" movements and modern mass nationalism in East and Central Africa', University of East Africa Social Science Conference, Dec. 1966. A full discussion must await the publication of these papers.

[4] See Vincent Harlow and E. M. Chilver, assisted by Alison Smith (eds.), *History of East Africa*, II (Oxford, 1965), especially the chapters by Raum, Middleton, Pratt and Bates.

individuals who act as communicators of social needs within their locality and, if so activated, as communicators of political ideas between organizations wider than the locality and the people within it. It is tempting to suggest that there were definite stages whereby the old communicators within African society, the chiefs, became increasingly irrelevant not only socially, but also as political communicators with the colonial authority, so making way for a new type of communicating leadership. The background to this process seems to have been the slow metamorphosis from tribesman to peasant in some East African communities. But this did not necessarily entail a corresponding move from tribalism to nationalism, for social change was not the sole determinant of political change. The focus of action for the emerging political associations was also influenced by the nature of the administrative framework and the extent of government interference in methods of production and marketing. In the second section, then, I discuss the political preoccupations of the inter-war years. They seem to have been concerned mainly with the competition between the old and the new communicators for leadership within, and external representation of, the localities. I then go on to suggest that while the old communicators were becoming less suited to these tasks, the new men themselves did not make real contact with their potential mass following in these years, save perhaps in Kikuyuland. This contact was essential for the development of mass nationalism. I discuss finally how this contact was made after 1945. To an important extent the initiative in its making seems to have lain with the mass of ordinary Africans. The potential communicators of the inter-war years now became both social leaders within their localities and communicators outside, no longer points of contact with the colonial authority, but with the nationalist *élite*, with some of them winning that status for themselves.

I

The belief that African nationalism is the political expression of social change may be summarized quite simply. In general the colonial period saw within each territory the creation of a single, if deeply divided, political and economic system out of the multitude of pre-existing societies, tribes, peoples and kingdoms. For all but the most isolated of Africans there was a vast increase in social scale. With this there came the beginnings of proletarianization, especially in Kenya, and a growth of economic individualism through the introduction of marketable cash crops and outlets for food surpluses. On a lowly and obvious level, the social preconditions for a wider political consciousness—nationalism eventually—were provided. More importantly for this paper, the developing colonial situation was accompanied by a growing depersonalization of relations within African society.[5] This process, with exceptions and variations, seems to have been marked by three broad phases.

[5] Cf. Godfrey and Monica Wilson, *The Analysis of Social Change* (Cambridge, England, 1945, reprinted 1965), 40: 'Intensity [the total degree of dependence on others] in the

There was the initial period in which the administrations were establishing themselves, finding or creating political communicators, points of contact with the subject peoples.[6] In the ideal case the political communicator, king or chief, whether traditionally legitimate, traditionally recognizable as usurper, or jumped-up mercenary and buccaneer, remained also a social communicator, in close relationship with his tribesmen or peasants. His administrative duties, little more than tax collection and the maintenance of order, were not yet heavy enough to disrupt the known social pattern. Strains there were of course. But face-to-face relations were retained within the African societies, intrusion on the part of the British being confined to manipulation of the points of contact.

Then, with colonial authority firmly established, officials felt less dependent upon their African allies, being more preoccupied with administrative efficiency, development, and immigrant pressures. There was increasing economic and institutional change which tended to undercut the relationship between chief and people and between the people themselves. Government policy in Kenya and Uganda seems to have either ridden with or provoked this aspect of social change. In Tanganyika, governor Cameron tried to stem the tide with Indirect Rule. In evidence to the 1912 Native Labour Commission, the Kenya Secretary of Native Affairs, Claud Hollis, thought that 'One way to increase the labour supply would be to encourage the native to become more individualistic and less communistic, but one had to consider which was the better state for the native, to allow him to go his own way or to force the pace. His opinion was that the pace was being forced too much at present.'[7] Nevertheless, in deference to settler pressure, the pace continued to be forced. The government recognized that individualization or 'denationalization' would result from migrant labour;[8] its officials knew that their chosen communicators, the chiefs and headmen, if urged 'to use their power and influence to coerce their people in these [labour] matters...[ran] the risk of having their authority defied, ...thereby causing general mistrust and demoralization...'[9] The Kenya government continued to 'encourage' migrant labour until dissuaded by the Colonial Office. Its later responses to the political protest of the early 1920s betrayed the dilemmas facing any administration in a period of social change. The structure of communication remained founded upon the officially recognized chief in his tribal location. But in order to mollify the newly articulate educated men, administrators had

narrower circles of relations necessarily diminishes as intensity in the wider circles increases.'

[6] D. A. Low, 'Lion rampant', *J. Commonwealth Political Studies*, II, 3 (1964), 235–52.

[7] *Native Labour Commission, 1912–13: Evidence and Report* (Government Printer, Nairobi), 3.

[8] E. P. C. Girouard, *Memoranda for Provincial and District Commissioners* (Government Printer, Nairobi, 1910).

[9] Ainsworth to Chief Secretary, 30 Mar. 1914, Kenya National Archives (K.N.A.) PC/NZA.3/66/1.

'strained to the utmost the loyal support of the old chiefs, by demanding the inclusion of younger men' in tribal councils,[10] even before the institution of Local Native Councils (L.N.C.s) in 1925. Whatever their shortcomings, these L.N.C.s were crucial in that they enlarged the circle of recognized communicators between people and governmenment. Their membership comprised not only chiefs *ex officio*, but teachers, traders and the like. Executive orders were still transmitted downwards through the chief; communication upwards from the people did not always have to pass through the same narrow channel to secure official notice. The points of contact were multiplying, and with them the strains of chiefship.[11]

In Kenya such undermining of the official communicators' position was part of the government's response to pressure from the settlers and, later, from African political associations. In Uganda, similar treatment of the native authorities appears to have stemmed from a more positive approach to social engineering. Assured of the loyalty of the chiefs, the administration could afford to attend to the needs of the peasantry; it could pursue ends beyond its own maintenance.[12] This change in government priorities is well illustrated in a dispatch from Uganda's acting governor to the Secretary of State early in 1923.[13] Referring to the land situation in Toro and Ankole, the acting governor described the official decision to prevent further extensions of chiefs' estates as a 'concession to the peasantry'. Of no less concern to government were the chiefs' tributes in peasant labour and produce. In earlier years 'It would have been the gravest mistake for the British Government to have attempted to do away with these feudal duties. Firstly, it would have been an injustice to the Chiefs, and secondly the abolition of these time honoured dues would seriously have impaired the prestige and authority of the Chiefs, and would have led almost inevitably to a rapid breakdown in the existing social system, followed by tribal disintegration and decay'. Worried by the possibilities of abuse in this system, government had encouraged the commutation of part of these dues into a cash payment. Now it was proposed to go much further. Peasants were to make these payments not to individual chiefs, but to a common fund for chiefs' salaries and general local government expenses. 'The ultimate object of this policy,...is that the peasantry of all tribes should be brought in the course of years, by a process so gradual as to cause the minimum of social disturbance within the tribe, to a stage in which their entire obligations will be met by a payment of Poll Tax to the British Government and

[10] Revd. H. D. Hooper, Memo: 'Development of political self-consciousness in the Kikuyu native', Enclosure in Hooper to Oldham, 29 Mar. 1922. International Missionary Council Papers, file H.3, Edinburgh House, London.

[11] District and Provincial Annual Reports, K.N.A. I have been unable to find in Kenya any official discussion on the problems of chiefs in relation to L.N.C.s comparable in importance to the *Report of the Mangwende Reserve Commission of Inquiry* (Salisbury, mimeo, 1961), 68–77.

[12] For a full discussion, see R. C. Pratt in Harlow and Chilver, op. cit. 487–510.

[13] Jarvis to Duke of Devonshire, 31 Jan. 1923, Entebbe Secretariat Archives (E.S.A.), Secretariat Minute Paper (S.M.P.), R.18/1.

of a consolidated "Chiefs' Tribute" to their Native Government.'[14] In brief, government was pursuing a policy which could only result in attenuating the ties of dependence between chief and peasant.

In this second phase, then, governments were in some areas assisting in the social decline of the political communicators on whom their authority rested, a decline which was in any case likely with the widening influence of the market economy. To mark the third phase, in the 1930s a crucial new factor was added in each of the three mainland territories, namely increasing government intervention in the everyday business of life. There was a proliferation of marketing controls, stricter supervision of the educational system and, most important of all, the first attempts to change African methods of land usage. All this government activity had two significant and related results. The more enterprising Africans, traders, teachers, improving farmers, came in increasing individual contact with the machinery of central government. Secondly, African authorities were either by-passed by departmental experts or, if efficient, became faceless co-ordinators of improvement schemes, much like the new breed of desk-bound white officials themselves. The old communicators no longer occupied a sole focal point in local society.

The conclusion of this argument is vital. The combined effect of social change and the erosion of one form of African leadership was the emergence in some areas of groupings recognizable as peasantry. The term has been used already in this paper in contradistinction to tribesmen. There are difficulties in its application to the African situation,[15] but if it is accepted that the distinguishing condition of a peasantry is its semi-autonomy or partial self-sufficiency in political, economic and cultural spheres, it seems clear that the introduction of the colonial authority structure, agricultural production in excess of subsistence requirements, and the spread of Christian and Islamic literary cultures together produced such a condition, certainly in those areas most exposed to change.

A further difference between the tribe and the peasant community, and one not easy to define, seems to lie in the contrasting size of their constituent units. In tribal societies, an individual's social, economic and spiritual welfare is generally catered for within his lineage or clan. In peasant societies the same needs are met to a larger extent within the family household.[16] During the colonial period in East Africa the extended family has come to assume greater economic significance than the clan, especially in those areas where the value of land has increased, through its

[14] Ibid. There are many such statements of policy in the papers of the E.S.A.

[15] L. A. Fallers, 'Are african cultivators to be called "peasants"?', *Current Anthropology*, II, 2 (1961), 108–10; J. Iliffe, 'The organisation of the Maji-Maji rebellion', *J. Afr. Hist.* VIII, 3 (1967), 495–512. The discussion that follows is based also on the definitions offered by A. L. Kroeber, *Anthropology* (New York, 1948), 284 ; and Eric R. Wolf, *Peasants* (Englewood Cliffs, 1966).

[16] T. Shanin 'The peasantry as a political factor', *The Sociological Review*, N.S. XIV, 1 (1966), 7–9.

scarcity or economic potential. The point may be illustrated by examples from Kenya. Among the Kikuyu, the *githaka* system of corporate land-owning by the lineage was breaking down in the Kiambu district by the 1920s. In 1929 it was forecast that in another generation 'the Githaka would...have given place to the small-holding as the unit of land tenure'.[17] Similarly, outright sale of land between individuals of the southern Luyia tribes was on the increase a decade later.[18] In the same period, members of the Kipsigis tribe, notably mission adherents, were planting increasing acreages of maize; to resolve the boundary disputes attendant on this development, the community (*Kokwet*) courts had to resort to the permanent demarcation of individual plots.[19] In 1962 it was reported of the northern Luyia peoples that 'Clan names have little political or economic meaning to-day...Land ownership has been recognized and has been vested in the head of the extended family unit since the tribal dispersal [in the early years of this century] from the fortified villages to a scattered settlement pattern.' The extended family was 'the basic economic unit'.[20] All these examples predate the drive for individual land tenure which was such a marked feature of Kenya's agrarian policy after the Second World War.

An independent landowning peasantry was emerging. Chiefs, the old communicators, were irrelevant to many of the peasants' dealings with economic agencies or new social communities; for example, the churches. And, as members of a stable bureaucracy, their prestige and wealth was less dependent upon such involvement in local society. In Professor Low's phrase,[21] there was an atrophy of face-to-face relations, not only between the peasantry and their political leaders but, with the new incompetence of these leaders as social communicators, between the peasants themselves. In such a situation, with its openings for new leadership, Wolf sees the classic opportunity for effective political action on the part of the peasantry.[22] The way was clear for new communicators either to re-knit the old society in relevant terms, or to join the new interests in new associations, in order to regain effective popular contact with the colonial authority, if necessary through the medium of open conflict. The choice of unifying symbols, whether tribe or peasant class and nation, was determined by the pressures, from above and from below, which developed within the colonial situation.

[17] *Native Land Tenure in Kikuyu Province: Report of Committee, November 1929* (Nairobi, 1930), 11.

[18] S. H. Fazan, Memo: 'Native land tenure—Nyanza Province', 29 Dec. 1938. K.N.A. PC/NZA. 4/2/1.

[19] J. W. Pilgrim, 'Land ownership in the Kipsigis reserve', East African Institute of Social Research Conference Paper (1959), 7–9.

[20] G. M. Wilson *et al.*, *A.I.D. Survey, Elgon–Nyanza* (Nairobi, mimeo, 1962), 18–19.

[21] For an equivalent situation of great comparative importance, despite Buganda's peculiarities, see D. A. Low, 'The advent of populism in Buganda', *Comparative Studies in Society and History*, VI, 4 (1964), 424–44.

[22] Eric R. Wolf, op. cit. 108–9.

II

In the inter-war years the pressures from above, from the colonial authority, were still mediated almost exclusively through the official chiefs. The new opportunities for social mobility and status outside the chiefships were the most awkward signs of pressures from below. Together, they focused political attention on the possible alternatives for securing an effective African voice in the local councils of empire. The varied political focus employed by Africans was an index both of the changing nature of the colonial pressures and of the social confidence of their leaders. This focus was controlled by three factors: an estimate of the popular basis of support for a given action—an awareness of social change; an understanding of the enemy's most responsive and responsible point—a knowledge fostered by government action; and an appreciation of those features of the administrative and legal framework which could be turned to advantage. It defined political aims, tactics and organization.[23]

There is an obvious difference between the political focus of the Gusii when in 1908 they tried to kill their district commissioner because he 'was looked upon as their sole aggressor and conqueror',[24] and that of Bildad Kaggia, who in 1952 called for increased African representation in Kenya's Legislative Council in order to regain alienated land, on the ground that legislation rather than guns had been the means of alienation.[25] The Gusii action illustrates what I call *diffuse* political focus. Such was typical of the early colonial period, when the social groupings in each territory were many and disparate, and when understanding of the colonial authority was as yet very personal. Kaggia's programme on the other hand was *central* in focus. He was speaking at a mass meeting of 25,000 Africans drawn from many of Kenya's tribes; his and other speeches were translated into Kiswahili; he was demanding pressure on the colony's political centre. Between these two poles of awareness was a third, *local* political focus, which seems to have dominated much of the political activity of the Kenya Africans during the inter-war years and to have been a factor in Uganda for very much longer.

Until the end of the First World War, the African political focus in Kenya remained diffuse in the sense suggested above. The hardships of the war itself,[26] and immediately thereafter increased taxes, reduced wages,

[23] See also J. M. Lonsdale, 'The emergence of African nations', to be published in *African Affairs*.

[24] Assistant District Commissioner, Kisii (?Juxon Barton, 1916?), 'The Kisii', in *Native Tribes and their Customs*, IV (Central Government Library, Nairobi). Cf. R. Collins and R. Herzog, 'Early British administration in the Southern Sudan', *J. Afr. Hist.* II, 1 (1961), 124; referring to the same period: 'To the peoples of the Southern Sudan the local administrative official was the Government.'

[25] As reported in *Historical Survey of the Origins and Growth of Mau Mau* (the Corfield Report), Cmd. 1030 (1960), 308.

[26] For one aspect see Donald C. Savage and J. Forbes Munro, 'Carrier Corps recruitment in the British East Africa Protectorate, 1914–1918', *J. Afr. Hist.* VII, 2 (1966), 313–42.

an influx of fresh settlers, their rising demands for labour, and the renewed threat to African lands implicit in the change of status from East Africa Protectorate to Kenya Colony—all these factors presented Africans with a 'clearly defined enemy'.[27] In the protest associated with Harry Thuku there was then a nationalist understanding of the situation; but the new social bases for a sustained nationalist organization were lacking. The centrality of Thuku's focus was blurred. He applied pressure on the governor and settlers, in association with the African population of Nairobi and the Asian community, both in their different ways concerned with politics at the centre of the colony. The impact of his demands was lessened by the nature of his organized support, recruited from groups at the same time wider and narrower than Kenya's territorial bounds. The membership of his East African Association included Baganda and some individuals from Tanganyika, but the sense of 'Africanness' which this collaboration implies is not the same thing as nationalism.[28] More significant for the future was the response within Kenya's localities. Part of Thuku's appeal among his own tribe, the Kikuyu, seems to have been due to his demand for a paramount chief, a demand which later Kikuyu associations echoed.[29] Luo leaders similarly called for one of their own, educated and elected.[30] Such slender evidence as exists for Masai connexions with Thuku suggests that most interest was shown by the Kaputei clan, supporters of Seggi ole Lenana, who had recently been removed from his paramountcy.[31] The Kamba, perhaps because they lacked such potential focus for presenting their grievances, showed little enthusiasm.[32]

These demands for paramount chiefs were an integral part of the politics of local focus. The outburst of African protest in the early 1920s had been

[27] J. Middleton in Harlow and Chilver, op. cit. 354.

[28] The significance of the name 'East African Association' is debatable. Clyde Sanger and John Nottingham, 'The Kenya general election of 1963', *Mod. Afr. Studies*, II, 1 (1964), 1, seem to argue a pan-East African intention. Alternatively it could imply a desire to return to Protectorate status, an interpretation more in keeping with the paramount chief demands discussed below. Its supra-territorial membership was paralleled in Tanganyika. In 1926 the president and secretary of the Tanganyika Territory African Civil Service Association (founded in March 1922) were both Makua from Mozambique, one born in Zanzibar, the other in Mombasa. Of the seven members of its informal committee, only two were born in Tanganyika; minute, 11 June. 1926, in S.M.P. 3715, Tanzania National Archives (T.N.A.). Similarly many members of the Tanganyika Association, apparently founded in 1926 or 1927, were in 1930 not native to the Territory; Cameron to Secretary of State, 22 Aug. 1930, T.N.A. S.M.P. 19325/i.

[29] Thuku to Provincial Commissioner, Nyeri, 14 Dec. 1921 (Enclosure in Hooper to Oldham, 29 Mar. 1922, International Missionary Council Papers.); Kikuyu Central Association (K.C.A.) to Grigg, 31 Dec. 1921, K.N.A. PC/CP. 8/5/2; K.C.A. to Sir Samuel Wilson, 30 May 1929, K.N.A. PC/CP.8/5/3; 'Statement of various grievances' to Cunliffe Lister, Jan. 1934 by K.C.A. Kikuyu Loyal Patriots, Progressive Kikuyu Party, and Kikuyu Land Board Association, in Christian Council of Kenya Race Relations Committee papers, file 1/A.

[30] For the Luo and Luyia see J. M. Lonsdale, 'A Political History of Nyanza 1883–1945', University of Cambridge Ph.D. thesis, 1964, to be published in revised form by Clarendon Press as *A Political History of Western Kenya, 1883–1957*.

[31] Elliot to Lumley, 5 Oct. 1922, K.N.A. DC/KAJ.9/1/1/1.

[32] *Native Affairs Department Annual Report* (1923), 5.

met, in Nairobi at least, with bloody repression. Despite the subsequent declaration of the doctrine of 'native paramountcy', it was clear that the central government was more deferential to settler than to African opinion.[33] Appreciation of this settler strength at the centre was coupled for many Kenyans with a knowledge of the relative independence enjoyed by the Kingdom of Buganda.[34] If government could not be effectively challenged at the centre, perhaps it was possible to question the legitimacy of its authority in local concerns.

The institution of paramounts was seen also as a means of raising the status of chief from a mere executive agent to that of a genuine two-way political communicator with the colonial authority. As might be expected, the official chiefs were themselves prominent in the campaign. Luo chiefs resented the humiliations of labour recruiting, and asked for a chiefs' council independent of the district commissioner.[35] The chiefs who were the backbone of the Kikuyu Association, similarly demanded of the Hilton Young Commission a higher status for themselves.[36] In their requests for tribal home rule, the old African communicators were trying to disengage themselves from central government pressures and, in so doing, to strengthen their legitimacy in the eyes of their people. Among the Kikuyu, Luo and Luyia, the request was part of every political programme throughout the inter-war period; but it underwent a significant change in emphasis.

The demand for paramounts started as a non-controversial item of policy supported by all those articulate members of society who were anxious to erect defences against the central government. It promised greater local control over land and the allocation of resources for development. By the late 1930s the demand was related more to internal social concerns, with the popular election of a paramount chief seen as a means of overthrowing the official chiefs, who were government appointees. The struggle between the old communicators and their rivals was joined. The imperatives of political defence and social change were interdependent. If the district commisioner, as was argued by the Luo, was subject to settler pressure,[37] so too were the government chiefs. And if missions and government implemented their educational and other development programmes in alliance with the chiefs, so also the chiefs were often the first beneficiaries of change. If it was impossible for Africans to

[33] Cf. Norman Leys, *Kenya* (London, 1924), 318: 'To [Africans] the Government is not *their* government. In their view, everything it does, the tax, labour regulations and all else, is done for the benefit of Europeans.'

[34] Parmenas Mockerie, *An African Speaks for his People* (London, 1934), 11; and his story in M. Perham (ed.), *Ten Africans* (2nd ed., London, 1963), 163–4. The comparable situation in Central Africa is discussed in Terence Ranger, 'Traditional authorities and the rise of modern politics in Southern Rhodesia, 1898–1930'; in E. Stokes and R. Brown (eds.), *The Zambesian Past* (Manchester, 1966).

[35] Tate (Provincial Commissioner, Nyanza), circular letter to missionaries and officials, 8 Feb. 1922. Owen Papers, Church Missionary Society Archives.

[36] Kikuyu Association to Hilton Young Commission, Jan. 1928, K.N.A. PC/CP. 8/5/1.

[37] Minutes, Kavirondo [Luo] Taxpayers' Welfare Association (K.T.W.A), 25 Aug. 1936, K.N.A. DC/CN.8/2.

control their chiefs through a voice in the central government, the alternative could only be the introduction of popular control within the localities, both over the political communicators and over the incidence of social and economic benefits. The growth of new interest groups seeking political recognition of their educational and economic attainments;[38] disappointment in the official chiefs' performance as political communicators and demands for their popular accountability; these factors were concurrent and inseparable rather than a simple chain of cause and effect.

The politics of local focus could seem to be effective only if central government were prepared to concede a measure of local autonomy. This it appeared to do, as a complement to repression at the centre, by the institution of L.N.C.s. During preliminary discussions on the formation of these bodies, Kenya's acting chief native commissioner stated his aims clearly. They were 'to get some sort of assembly which will attract the younger and more vigorous brains among the natives and lead them to take an active part in their own administration, and thus to ensure that they are for the Government and not against it.'[39] The L.N.C.s were empowered to make bye-laws on matters of local concern, including land use, and to levy rates to support education and the development of local communications, agriculture and so on. Their membership was partly elected. On both external political and internal social grounds, therefore, they were welcomed by articulate Africans, as at least a step towards the implementation of the hopes implicit in the demands for paramount chief.

Failure on the political front accelerated the desire for internal social reform, with the aspirant new social communicators demanding political roles. The localities became cockpits of competition. On the one hand the official chiefs, by selection increasingly committed to material progress[40] and sometimes allied to senior mission adherents, tended to support government and mission programmes. Thanks to their official status they could hope, by their protests or their enthusiasms, to influence schemes for development; and in so doing they could manipulate the opportunities for patronage within the locality. On the other hand were those numerous individuals of enterprise who were excluded from the narrow executive structure, seeing official programmes not only as generally insufficient, but also as tending to favour the official communicators who helped to implement them. In the areas most subject to change, there were then two competing *élites*, the 'established *élite*', and that on 'the growing edge of social activity',[41] distinguishable in many cases only by their differential access to official goodwill. The manner in which this competition expressed itself and later influenced nationalist politics seems to have depended much

[38] Minutes, K.T.W.A., 14 Sept. 1935 and 25 Oct. 1936, ibid.

[39] Watkins to Archdeacon Owen, 7 Feb. 1921, Owen Papers.

[40] Many chiefs were of course 'backward' from both colonial and nationalist standpoints, but this is a factor too often exaggerated.

[41] A. W. Southall, 'The concept of elites and their formation in Uganda', in P. C. Lloyd (ed.), *The New Elites of Tropical Africa* (London, 1966), 342–66.

on the extent to which the colonial authority structure accommodated itself to indigenous social patterns.[42]

There seems to have been a significant contrast in this respect between the Kikuyu and the Luo, Kenya's major political peoples. The young men who led the K.C.A. in the 1920s, Jesse Kariuki, Joseph Kangethe and their associates, were by the late 1940s still engaged in overt political activity, now central in focus, after a period of detention during the Second World War. On the other hand Jonathan Okwiri, Paul Mboya[43] and other Luo politicians of similar vintage were by the 1940s senior chiefs. It was not that these Luo, and equivalent Luyia like Paul Agoi, had lost their fire, but that the general congruence between their peoples' lineage organization and the colonial framework, together with the administration's preference for 'progressive' chiefs, provided them with an avenue for advance in which official status could enhance political leadership. Kikuyu society was more decentralized; it was cut across by age grades within which leadership was achieved through individual merit.[44] Authority of such individual nature was clearly more fragile in the hands of an externally appointed chief, whether a man previously of influence in society or a chance ally of the first British,[45] than that conferred on official communicators by the indigenous chiefly institutions of western Kenya. Further, in their concern for stability, the British ignored the traditional handover of power between one Kikuyu generation and the next.[46] With this artificial closure of a previously open society, no politician who valued his indigenous social support could enter the colonial hierarchy even were it open to him. For all their hopeful participation in their L.N.C.s,[47] the leaders of the K.C.A. could not transfer the relative democracy of the channels of communication to the sphere of policy execution. They became aware of the inadequacies of the politics of local focus long before their Luo counterparts. As early as 1929 they demanded that 'ultimately the number of African representatives [in Legislative Council] should predominate altogether'.[48] The

[42] For a perceptive analysis of different aspects of the interrelation between traditional society and modern politics, see F. G. Burke, *Political Evolution in Kenya* (Syracuse University, Program of East African Studies, Occasional Paper no. 2, 1964).

[43] No relation to Mr Tom Mboya.

[44] J. Middleton and G. Kershaw, 'The Kikuyu and Kamba of Kenya', *Ethnographic Survey of Africa: East Central Africa*, v (1965), 23–53; D. L. Barnett and Karari Njama, *Mau Mau from within* (London, 1966), 42–51.

[45] D. A. Low in Harlow and Chilver, op. cit. 44–50.

[46] J. Middleton in ibid. 359.

[47] See the figures quoted by Kenya's governor, Sir Edward Grigg, in *Papers Relating to the Closer Union of Kenya, Uganda and the Tanganyika Territory*, Colonial, No. 57 (1931), 14, for the composition of the three Kikuyu L.N.C.s ('"Young Mission" means natives educated at missions, who have other organisations and are the main representatives, apart from the K.C.A., of progressive ideas'):

	Total membership	K.C.A.	Young Mission
Fort Hall	28	9	7
Kiambu	25	6	5
Nyeri	22	4	3

[48] K.C.A. to Wilson, 30 May 1929, K.N.A. PC/CP.8/5/3.

frustrations of a previously open and decentralized society, forced to bypass the closed local authority structure, crystallized in a renewed focus on the colony's political centre. This early contrast between Kikuyu and Luo was fundamental to the development of Kenya nationalism after the Second World War. In the Kenya African Union (K.A.U.), the Kikuyu activists were men with long experience and long-standing popular support. Leaders from western Kenya tended to be younger, with less flair for mobilizing local opinion for national ends.[49] In general they had gained prominence only after the politicians of the 1920s had become chiefs. The national movement was in consequence uneven in its composition, and this imbalance seems to have been no mean factor in the dynamics of Mau Mau.

A more dramatic contrast to Kikuyu is to be found in Buganda. These had been two open societies in their opportunities for individual advancement; both suffered a closure of their political system in the colonial period, Buganda through the consolidation of only one of its three chiefly patterns in the Uganda Agreement of 1900; both experienced the attenuation of mutual dependence and alienation of political affections between people and leaders during the inter-war period. Here the similarities end. Buganda's leaders had successfully resisted total domination by the British, while the Kikuyu had been conquered piecemeal; land alienation was not the impassioned issue in Buganda that it was in Kikuyu by the 1920s. These contrasts stemmed from the fact that Buganda was a centralized kingdom; it was able to threaten the whole existence of British rule in the early days, and in its chiefs it possessed economic innovators who, in their instigation of peasant-grown cotton, obviated the need for European settlers, the alternative revenue earners.[50] The K.C.A. had used Kikuyu's age set system as a symbol of modern protest. So in Buganda popular discontent used the symbols of the *bataka*, those clan heads eclipsed in the settlement of 1900. The competition of precolonial institutions was invoked to solve a modern problem, namely to bring the 'modernizing autocracy'[51] back to a sense of its social responsibilities by regaining for the people a stake in a political system once again open to the talents. But populist feeling within Buganda did not spill over into the rest of Uganda until some years after the Second World War, precisely because the chiefs' 'official nationalism',[52] the external aspect of the politics of local focus, was manifestly successful against the Protectorate administration. This success enhanced the remnants of popular legitimacy which the chiefs in any case enjoyed.

[49] B.A. Ogot, 'British administration in the Central Nyanza district of Kenya, 1900–60', *J. Afr. Hist.* IV, 2 (1963), 269–70.

[50] All the foregoing is grossly oversimplified. The sources for the discussion are chiefly D. A. Low and R. C. Pratt, *Buganda and British Overrule, 1900–1955* (London, 1960); D. A. Low, 'The advent of Populism', op. cit.; and C. Ehrlich, 'The Uganda economy, 1903–1945' in Harlow and Chilver, op. cit.

[51] D. E. Apter, *The Political Kingdom in Uganda* (Princeton and London, 1961), 25–8.

[52] Ibid. 114 ff.

A legitimate government in this sense may be reformed from within; an illegitimate one can only be bypassed or overthrown.

Kikuyu disillusion with local focus was one of the mainsprings behind the formation of the K.A.U. in 1944,[53] a development foreshadowed in the late 1930s by explicit Kikuyu links with the Kamba, Luo, Luyia and Teita peoples. In Uganda, the example of Buganda twice reinforced the search for local solutions: negatively in that Buganda's 'sub-imperialism' aroused alarm in the localities, and positively in that the kingdom's organization and special relationship with the British served as a model for effective local defence.[54] The influence of precolonial society on African politics in the colonial period seems to have produced in Tanganyika a third, quite different, pattern.

While in Tanganyika some African societies certainly seem to have engaged in the politics of local focus,[55] the territory's distinguishing feature was—and is—the existence of a Swahili Society[56] with a recognizable culture of its own.[57] Until the early nineteenth century, Swahili Society had been contained within the Islamic enclaves on the coast. By the early years of the twentieth century it had spread throughout the interior, thanks to the precolonial extension of the Zanzibar-based trade in slaves and ivory, the crisis of coastal resistance against the Germans in the late 1880s, and the later crisis of the Maji Maji rebellion of 1905–7. Swahili Society in this century may be characterized as based on the towns and trading centres, the vehicle of a literary culture predominantly but not necessarily Muslim, linked by a common language, and non-tribal in its social and political focus. Its relationship with the rural areas was equivocal. Economically the two spheres were interdependent. But culturally and socially Swahili Society stood apart, enjoying a much wider frame of reference. It could absorb both the poor and footloose, and also emergent educated groups who found the tribal frame too narrow for their energies. For within the society were many strata ranging from the conservative, collaborating Arab *élite*, to the radical 'Maniema' townsfolk, originally the social detritus of the slave-trade.

Perhaps the most remarkable aspect of this society, certainly for anyone more familiar with the modern history of Kenya, was its geographical mobility and its network of intercommunication. This was alarmingly demonstrated to the new British administration during and immediately

[53] Initially the K.A.U., and then, briefly, the Kenya African Study Union.

[54] A. D. Roberts, 'The sub-imperialism of the Baganda', *J. Afr. Hist.* III, 3 (1962), 435–50; for aspects of Buganda's impact on one area of Uganda, see M. Twaddle, '"Tribalism" in Eastern Uganda', to be published in P. H. Gulliver, *The Tribal Factor in East Africa*.

[55] M. Bates in Harlow and Chilver, op. cit. 636.

[56] This paragraph is based on J. Iliffe, 'The German Administration in Tanganyika 1906–1911: The Governorship of Freiherr von Rechenburg,' (University of Cambridge Ph.D. dissertation, 1965), ch. IX: my own researches on limited aspects of the British period, and discussions with Dr Iliffe, have done little more than confirm his thesis.

[57] J. S. Trimingham, *Islam in East Africa* (Oxford, 1964).

after the First World War in the activity of the *mbeni* dance societies.[58] These were brass bands, sporting expensive instruments, military titles and regalia, their members being mainly 'better class' Swahili government employees, clerks and police. These social clubs seem to have started, perhaps in Mombasa, just prior to the war, but their popularity increased vastly among the African members of the opposing armed forces and carrier corps during the East African campaign. There were several rival organizations, chief among them the Arinoti and Marine Bands, with branches throughout East Africa, in all the coastal towns from Kismayu in the north to Lindi in the south, and in the interior of Tanganyika, Mozambique and Nyasaland. These also seem to have had a loose central articulation. The Dar es Salaam branch of the Arinoti, for instance, closed down the Lindi branch for sixty days as penalty for a breach of the rules of hospitality. A band member could travel from Lindi to Nairobi with interbranch arrangements for his expenses. In his position as head of the *Königliches Marine Band Gesellschaft*, Saleh bin Mpangire, nephew of the late chief and resistance hero of the Hehe, Mkwava, could regulate promotions in the Kismayu branch, signing himself 'Seine Majestät König Friedrich August von Sachsen.' I have no information on these societies after 1922. Further research should be able to answer some of the fascinating questions which their activities raise. They provide striking evidence of the vitality and wide influence of Swahili society, its ability to adopt aspects of western culture for its own use. They seem also to have provided some sort of an organizational link between the coast and some of the interior tribes.[59] Perhaps too they provide a social bridge between

[58] This paragraph is based on correspondence in T.N.A. S.M.P. 075 (Confidential). Information on *mbeni* activity in Kenya may be found in K.N.A. files PC/Coast 54/1437 and PC/CP6/4/3.

[59] It was this aspect which most alarmed the British adminstrations. In October 1917, the following minute by the private secretary to the East Africa Protectorate's (Kenya) Acting Governor was circulated to the provincial administrations. (This minute was seen in the Kisumu district office in 1963; the relevant file, now numbered CN/51, has been transferred to the K.N.A., but the minute appears to be missing ;it is therefore quoted rather extensively.):

'The participation of natives in British East Africa in the campaign in German East Africa, whether as soldiers or as porters, has given them unprecedented opportunities of enlarging their ideas by contact with natives of other African dependencies. Certain of the men who return will have become acquainted with the pan-African ideal of the Ethiopian Church, with Native politics from Abyssinia, and, for the first time in the history of this Protectorate, a conception may have arisen in the native mind of the possibilities of a black Africa.

'It may be urged that the incoherence of the native tribes in Central and Eastern Africa, outside the littoral, renders any conflagration improbable, but such premises cannot be considered as a safe basis for argument in connection with native feeling after the war.

'It is in connection with a native conception of the idea "Africa for the Africans" that any conjunction of Islamic propaganda is to be regarded as a real danger. Islam would provide a cementing factor and the consequent fanaticism would enormously increase both the military and political difficulty in dealing with such a movement. Converts are notoriously fanatical.

'In Eastern Africa Islam has tended to consider itself a political as much as a spiritual force, and there has recently been noticeable a tendency on the part of the natives to call

ordinary townsfolk and those *élite* modernizers within Swahili society who staffed the African civil service of Tanganyika and gave to that territory its first articulate, centrally focused pressure groups.

The most important of these were the Tanganyika Territory African Civil Service Association (T.T.A.C.S.A.), and the Tanganyika African Association (T.A.A.).[60] In their territoriality they had no parallel during the inter-war years in either Kenya or Uganda, just as there was no equivalent to Swahili Society in these two countries. A full account of these associations' contribution to the early history of Tanganyikan nationalism must await further research. Meanwhile three characteristics may be indicated, of fundamental importance for an understanding of the later strengths of the Tanganyika African National Union (T.A.N.U.)[61] These are: a radical attitude to chiefly privilege, an apparent ability to communicate with tribal political organizations and, as already noted, an early centrality of political focus.

Martin Kayamba, head clerk in the Tanga district office, founded T.T.A.C.S.A. in March 1922. Its office-bearers were both Christian and Muslim, African and Arab.[62] If the association thus demonstrated the inclusive, absorptive character of modern Swahili Society, it seemed also to share that Society's sense of identity over against the tribal chiefs. For in its campaign for a regulated status for African civil servants, the association drew attention to the unfavourable status of Africans in central government service as compared to the tribal native authorities: 'Education and training should be rewarded.'[63] This was a claim for *élite* privileges; it revealed also a potentially radical attitude. The association seems to have

themselves members of the Mohammedan nation. After the war it may be expected that proselytising propaganda will be actively disseminated from Mecca, and, though such propaganda, it is almost sure to be of an anti-European character.

'German East Africa is common ground for Pan-Islam and Pan-Africa; many of the natives educated in the German secular schools have embraced Islam, and the German Administrators have confessed to a feeling of apprehension respecting an African Jehad, i.e. a conjunction of an African political Islam against Europeans. Such a Jehad is not an improbability, and, after the war, it might meet with enthusiasm.'

The minute went on to ask for views on the best means of implementing the suggestion that a 'definite policy of encouraging strong and isolated tribal nationalism may be one of the most effectual barriers against a Pan-African upheaval...'

While this apprehension was unfounded, it is a revealing commentary on the reactions of British administrators when confronted with Swahili Society, of which the *mbeni* groups formed a noisy part.

Professor Ranger's recent work on witch-eradication movements in Tanganyika in the 1920s and 1930s provides further evidence of the ability of Swahili culture to penetrate, at a popular level, the societies of the interior.

[60] For an earlier discussion of these and other associations see Ralph Austen, 'Notes on the pre-history of TANU', *Makerere Journal*, IX (1964), 1–6.

[61] Once again I am here merely elaborating a point first made by J. Iliffe, 'German Administration', cited above.

[62] H. M. T. Kayamba and Liwali Alkhidri bin Likhibri to the acting chief secretary, 5 April 1922, T.N.A. S.M.P. 3715; 'The story of Martin Kayamba Mdumi, M.B.E., of the Bondei Tribe', in M. Perham (ed.), op.cit., 198.

[63] B. E. H. Madalito and Edwin W. Brenn to Cameron, 1 June 1926, T.N.A. S.M.P. 11051/i.

faded out in the late 1920s; the T.A.A., in a sense its successor, but with a much wider membership, seems to have shared this attitude at an early stage. At its annual conference in May 1940, the T.A.A. called upon the Secretary for Native Affairs to interview the association whenever he went on tour up-country.[64] This demand clearly questioned the representative nature of the native authorities in the localities. In this connexion it seems pertinent to note that Thomas Marealle, shortly to be the anti-establishment candidate for the Chagga paramountcy, was at this time active both in the affairs of the radically minded newspaper *Kwetu* and in attempts to resuscitate T.T.A.C.S.A.[65] This evidence for a positive radicalism among the coastal *élite* is slender and inconclusive; and if this outlook did exist, it was perhaps to be expected from townsmen and government clerks, who were uncomfortably sandwiched between the higher status Asian trader and clerical class on the one hand, and the native authorities bolstered by indirect rule on the other. But a brief examination of the central associations' relations with the localities seems to strengthen the impression.

The geographical spread of T.A.A. branches was due initially to the government employee component in its membership. Muslim traders also aided its extension in the Bukoba area west of Lake Victoria, where in the 1930s the Bukoba African Association was active both against the native authorities and government's coffee improvement schemes.[66] The Dar es Salaam newspaper *Kwetu*, organ of the Tanganyika African Welfare and Commercial Association, was in 1939 nearly involved in a libel action after maligning Chagga chiefs.[67] Soon after the Second World War, such links between the coastal centres of political activity and interior discontents became more explicit and widespread.[68] While T.A.A. branches were growing more active, T.T.A.C.S.A., renamed Tanganyika African Government Servants' Association in 1943, both favoured closer collaboration with T.A.A.,[69] and attempted to represent not only central government but native authority employees.[70] The point is not that the central associations were stirring up radical discontent in the tribal areas. It is doubtful

[64] Resolutions passed by the 'East African Annual Conference of the African Association' 11–16, May 1940, T.N.A. S.M.P. 28944. At this time the T.A.A., based on Dar es Salaam, had, according to its letterhead, branches in Zanzibar, Pemba, Bagamoyo, Mpwapwa, Dodoma, Kondoa, Singida and Bukoba.

[65] R. R. K. Mziray to editor, *Tanganyika Standard*, 14 Oct. 1940; information from Erika Fiah, proprietor and editor of *Kwetu*, 1937–52, in interviews January 1965.

[66] Ralph Austen, op.cit.; Goran Hyden, 'Political penetration in a rural area', East African Institute of Social Research Conference Paper (1966).

[67] T.N.A. S.M.P.15938 contains the details of this episode.

[68] Provincial Commissioner Northern Province to Secretary for African Affairs, 15 Oct. 1948 and Provincial Commissioner Lake Province to Chief Secretary, 6 Oct. 1948, T.N.A. S.M.P.1928; G. Bennett, 'An outline history of Tanu', *Makerere Journal*, VII (1963), 16; J. Listowel, *The Making of Tanganyika* (London, 1965), 134.

[69] Intelligence and Security Bureau report on T.A.G.S.A. special meeting, 2 Feb. 1945, T.N.A. S.M.P.11051/ii. The T.A.A. itself was wary of civil servant influence at this stage; information from Hon. J. Kasella Bantu, M.P.

[70] M. B. E. Serunjogi (General secretary T.A.G.S.A.) to Chief Secretary, 4 Sept. 1945 (ibid). The demand does not seem to have been pressed in the face of government refusal.

whether there was sufficient articulation between headquarters and branches for this purpose even had it been desired. The significance is rather that at a time when in some localities discontent was mounting over the inadequacies of the politics of local focus, there were territorial bodies already in existence with which local leaders could associate. And this association was only the explicit aspect of the more generally pervasive interaction of Swahili Society and the tribes. Local frustrations could be linked to centrality of focus much earlier than in Kenya or Uganda. The existence of a non-tribal society made this practicable; government action helped too. The British continued the German practice of transferring African employees of the administration throughout the territory.[71] Consciousness of Tanganyika as one whole seems to have been further reinforced for many educated Africans by the changeover of the complete government machine as a result of the First World War. In its appeals for a regulated status for its members, T.T.A.C.S.A. could use the argument that African civil servants, most of them ex-enemy subjects, needed the reassurance that the new British regime was really better than the German.[72] But the social base for a central focus remains the most significant factor. The T.A.A.'s demand in 1940 that 'the African now be given [a] chance to speak on behalf of his country'[73] was clearly of a different order to any similar claim advanced by the Chagga or Haya—or Kikuyu.

By the end of the Second World War, the politics of local focus, entailing the reform of the colonial system, were in Kenya and Tanganyika proved to be a failure on the external front. Statutory L.N.C.s in Kenya could not even prevent the further excision of tribal land—as shown in the Kakamega Gold Rush of the 1930s. In 1951 the Meru of northern Tanganyika were powerless to prevent their own eviction to make way for white settlers.[74] And local pressure could do little to influence the central governments' allocation of resources for development. Internally also, L.N.C. elections in Kenya too often excluded those enterprising individuals who, travelling in trade or permanently employed outside their tribal reserves, lost touch with their lineage constituency. This lack of political adjustment to social change was officially admitted to be even more pronounced in Tanganyika's localities before the Second World War.[75] But the futility of these attempts to find local solutions to African problems does not mean that the inter-war period can be dismissed as of no account in the history of East African nationalism. The experience of failure was itself important. For in the long

[71] In Kenya and Uganda the same transferability seems to have applied only to Africans departmentally employed in public works, the post office, etc.

[72] Madalito and Brenn to Cameron, 1 June 1926, T.N.A. S.M.P.11051/i.

[73] Resolutions passed by the 'East African Annual Conference of the African Association', 11–16 May 1940, T.N.A. S.M.P. 28944.

[74] B. T. G. Chidzero, *Tanganyika and International Trusteeship* (London, 1961), 236–45; J. Listowel, op. cit. ch. 20.

[75] Chief secretary (Kenya), memo, 'Native political development and the representation of native opinion', 9 Sept. 1941, in which is quoted a discussion with a senior Tanganyika official, K.N.A. PC/Coast.2/286.

years before the local focus was discarded, emergent African groups became fully aware of the strength of officially entrenched privilege within their own societies. This awareness is a constituent part of the ideology of African socialism. And failure meant not only that many future nationalists would be radicals, but also that they would have a low estimate of the potential of local government as an instrument of change. The implementation of national goals would be the function of a greatly strengthened central government after independence.[76]

These generalizations point to similarities in the pre-nationalist inheritance of Kenya and Tanganyika. The experience of their first nationalist movements brings out the contrasts within that inheritance, contrasts that have here been explained in terms of the differing indigenous societies that were subject also to differing colonial situations. In its first three or four years, T.A.N.U. achieved a much stronger organization and wider network than did K.A.U. in the seven years of its legal existence. In other words, T.A.N.U. was much more successful in its encounter with the central paradox of any national movement. To be effective and credible, nationalist leaders must appeal for mass support; but such an appeal brings into central focus those rivalries of tribe, language and culture which have hithero been contained within their respective localities. In the inter-war years, the period of local focus, political argument had centred on the allocation of resources to the localities and the distribution of the ensuing benefits within them. The debates were conducted within fairly circumscribed groups of rival modernizers, African officials and those outside the mission or government hierarchies. These tended to present their conflicting claims to governments with but little attempt to mobilize popular followings. It is important to discuss why this was so—especially remarkable in Kenya by contrast with the mass meetings held by Harry Thuku and other leaders in the early 1920s. Fear of government repression or a tacit acquiescence in alien rule provide only a very partial answer.

III

A complex question has been asked. A brief and oversimplified answer will be attempted. It will be argued that the mass of Africans were in the inter-war years bereft of effective political communicators with the colonial authority. There were two main reasons for this. The first was the lack of heavy external burdens on the tribesmen or peasantry until the mid-1930s. The second was the existence of what may be conveniently called Christian Revolutions,[77] not only in the initial colonial period, as in

[76] S. N. Eisenstadt, in W. H. Lewis (ed.) *French-Speaking Africa, the Search for Identity* (New York 1965), 228–9 reaches the same conclusion from the different viewpoint that the central institutions were better equipped by the outgoing colonial power for the task of implementing change.

[77] D. A. Low, *Religion and Society in Buganda, 1875–1900* (East African Studies no. 8, Kampala n.d.) 9; C. C. Wrigley 'The Christian revolution in Buganda', *Comparative Studies in Society and History*, II (1959), 33-49.

some of the Uganda kingdoms, but inherent in the later development of missionary education elsewhere. This lack of effective political communication was a new development. In precolonial society each colonizing unit, based generally on the lineage, possessed its communicators over against similar and neighbouring units. In resistance to European occupation the mobilizers of mass action within the colonizing unit had been these traditional communicators, whether chiefs, warriors or religious leaders. If short-lived, military resistance took traditional forms; if drawn-out, new principles of organization might evolve. In post-pacification revolts, demanding a more conscious commitment than resistance, the task of communication within the rebellion seems to have been carried out more often by religious figures. Religious appeals, whether by priests of an established order or by revolutionary prophets, and in themselves implying a reorientation of society, permitted social mobilization on a wider scale than appeals by leaders of kin groups.[78] That African societies should commit themselves to the crisis of rebellion is striking evidence of the existence of leaders who could communicate effectively with their people. It was in the religious field that corporate action on a lowly social plane retained most vitality in the years that followed the collapse of armed African resistance and rebellion. Independent churches and indigenous sects were of many kinds, fulfilling as many social needs. Some sought relief for the oppressed poor in confused millennial dreams; some aimed at social sanity and order at a humble level on earth; others saw salvation in educational schemes as ambitious as any offered by the mission churches in which, as may tend to be forgotten, many political leaders continued to find 'a place to feel at home'. However much these churches differed in aims and recruitment (the above categories were not necessarily mutually exclusive), they all had one thing in common. They were able to enlist the continuing loyalties of many ordinary Africans, at however local a level, and however prone to further schism and segmentation. This was a quality more often lacking in explicitly political associations until the late 1930s.[79]

The two reasons advanced for this lack—the absence of heavy governmental burdens on ordinary Africans and the effects of the introduced Christian literary culture—were closely linked. Together, they both obviated the need for a continuing, committed presentation of mass problems before the colonial authority, and seemed initially to provide the individual and society with an assured, non-political means of attaining

[78] This argument is based on the papers, of seminal importance, by Professor Ranger, listed under footnote 3 above; also his 'The role of Ndebele and Shona religious authorities in the rebellions of 1896 and 1897', in Stokes and Brown, op. cit.; also J. Iliffe, 'German Administration' and 'The organization of the Maji-Maji rebellion', loc.cit.

[79] This brief discussion does not do justice to the role of independent churches in East Africa, but they are the subject of a growing and important literature, e.g. F. B. Welbourn, *East African Rebels* (London, 1961): F. B. Welbourn and B. A. Ogot,' *A Place to feel at Home* (London, 1966); T. O. Ranger, 'African attempts to control education in East and Central Africa 1900–1939', *Past and Present*, XXXII (1965), 57–85.

equality with the European rulers. When external pressure was felt by the mass of Kenya Africans immediately after the First World War, the reaction had been dramatic enough, not least because the officially appointed communicators felt their local positions to be threatened by popular discontent. Thereafter burdens on both chiefs and tribesmen were relaxed, partly through government policy, partly because of the growing African acceptance of the cash economy. Tax liabilities were increasingly easy to meet from employment or agriculture. Those Africans whose conditions were perhaps the hardest, the squatters on European farms, were also those most cut off from the potential communicators, whether chiefs or politicians.[80] Economic development in all three mainland territories before the late 1930s consisted almost entirely in providing better access, both institutional and physical, to the world market. Production methods and land tenure, even where the crops themselves were new, continued unaffected by direct external pressure, though there were, as already noted, changing attitudes to land, voluntarily and from within. In this atmosphere, there were rarely acute peasant complaints to articulate, and such as there were seemed to demand social rather than political remedy. On the other hand there was great scope for competition amongst the rival *élites* for access to the resources of modernization and to marketing outlets. This was the hallmark of the politics of local focus, political debate within the tribe. Certainly, part of that debate was over who would be the most effective communicators with the colonial power. But this was not an issue to generate a common front or mass meetings—rather the reverse. In such local concerns, lineage groups were still the rival interest groups. If the ground swell of social change had diminished the importance of the old communicators, it had not yet provided a mass constituency for the new.[81]

Christian education influenced this *élite* rivalry in two ways: both tended to keep the debate above the level of mass concern. Firstly, access to education was limited and it was worth competing for. In the colonial context it was obviously correlated with political power. The demand for better education, especially instruction in the English language, stimulated some of the first protest movements against both governments and missions. For traditional *élites*, education could mean the maintenance of old status by new means. For the newcomers it was equally the means to challenge old privilege. For both, it promised an amelioration of the rigours and indignities of the colonial situation. The realization that the Europeans' 'selective giving'[82] involved denial of social and political rewards, no matter what educational standards were attained, was slow in coming. Africans concentrated instead on perfecting what they imagined to be the

[80] Significantly, it was the independent African Orthodox Church which in the 1930s seems to have provided the first means of intercommunication for the 'squatter' families in the White Highlands (correspondence in K.N.A. PC/RVP2/27).

[81] As already suggested, and as will be seen again below, these remarks need modification in the case of the Kikuyu.

[82] B. Malinowski, *The Dynamics of Culture Change* (New Haven, 1945), 56–60.

means of acceptance. Again, this was a situation in which the presentation of competitive claims to missions and governments was more likely than talking and listening to the people. Indeed, recognition of the paucity of educational resources could mean that the educated *élite* sought 'to secure for themselves and their circle as large a share of the benefits as they can' at the expense of their less privileged fellows.[83]

Secondly, the acceptance of Christianity often involved an inner revolution for the individual convert. Examples abound in the literature.[84] In Ankole, Hima leaders destroyed their cult objects; Giriama converts would agree to pay their *Kaya* initiation fees but refused to join in the customary dances; in the Lukuledi valley of southern Tanganyika, converts had the courage to 'preach to the people and make them see, by the light of Christian Doctrine, the inherent evils in customs'; according to an admittedly partisan account, early Kikuyu converts took a more uncompromising stand than their missionaries over the female circumcision issue; Luo catechists established their own Christian villages, consciously apart from their lineages.[85] In all these examples the early Christians were in some measure standing outside and against their society. It was a time when a leading African could oppose European schemes to provide a more consciously African content to the school curriculum by declaring: 'People can say what they want, but to the African mind, to imitate Europeans is civilisation.'[86] Such views were held by many members of the first political and welfare associations. Desire for increased education and improvement stimulated rather than inhibited their opposition to government; it did not necessarily encourage identification with mass concerns. Further evidence for this view may be found in the relative lack of contact between the associations and the independent churches in the inter-war period, a situation best illustrated by its exceptions. For example, the Abamalaki sect was in the 1930s closely associated with the efforts of the Young Bagwere Association to achieve all kinds of local, including educational, improvements.[87] K.C.A. collaboration with the various Kikuyu independent churches was similarly a product of their mutual concern for the provision of better educational facilities. In Kikuyu, this African struggle for a

[83] Archdeacon W. E. Owen, 'Corban in Kenya, a criticism of state financing of African education' (1940). Copies of this memorandum were found in 1963 by the author in the attic of the Friends' Mission, Kaimosi, western Kenya. See T. O. Ranger, 'African attempts to control education', loc. cit. 54, for fuller quotation.

[84] J. Ngugi, *The River Between* (London, 1965), illustrates this more vividly than any amount of historical analysis.

[85] D. J. Stenning, 'Salvation in Ankole', in M. Fortes and G. Dieterlen (eds.), *African Systems of Thought* (London, 1965), 265–6; Kilifi subdistrict intelligence report, June 1925, in K.N.A. PC/Coast, 64/9/1923; A. M. Hokororo, *The Influence of the Church on Tribal Customs at Lukuledi* (Ndanda Mission, 1961), 14; *Memorandum Prepared by the Kikuyu Mission Council on Female Circumcision* (Kikuyu, 1931); and correspondence in K.N.A. PC/NZA.3/30/2, respectively.

[86] Samuel Chiponde (President of T.T.A.C.S.A. and High Court interpreter) at 1925 Education Conference, quoted by R. Austen, 'Notes on the pre-history of TANU', loc. cit.

[87] M. Twaddle, '"Tribalism" in Eastern Uganda', loc. cit.

greater share in, and control over modernization was given added edge by missionary opposition to female circumcision.[88] This European cultural pressure exposed the conflict of loyalties latent within the 'Christian revolutionary'; and at a time when, for reasons already discussed, the K.C.A. attached more importance to popular support than government approval. There was then contact between the independent churches and the associations, where the churches themselves stressed the value of education as part of a general tribal desire for improvement, or where the European-controlled agencies of development clashed most stridently with the structure and beliefs of indigenous society. Elsewhere that contact was less common. Most independent churches sought, at a lowly level, the reintegration of mass society in the new world. The associations were more preoccupied with the conditions of contact between that society and the colonial regime.

This dichotomy brings the argument back to the vital weakness in African politics before the Second World War: the lack of effective communication for mass concerns. There was certainly mass involvement in actions of resistance and rebellion and in the later membership of independent churches: but even if these entailed some reordering of society, they employed but diffuse political focus. In the politics of local focus there was little popular participation, the K.C.A. excepted. The T.A.A.'s implicitly central focus again had little popular support. Spontaneous initiative shown by the people or their aspirant *élites* was apparently not enough to generate a nationalist movement. For such a movement must combine central focus, mass participation and a desire to reorder society with that central focus in mind.[89] National movements answering this description did appear in East Africa, most markedly in Tanganyika, after the Second World War. The previous remarks notwithstanding, the spontaneous element provided much of their dynamism and direction.

IV

Effective national movements could not emerge until the aspirant new communicators had realized their potential role. This was a difficult task. In the 1920s, educated men had tended to ally with the traditional communicators. The known unit, the tribe, was seen as the focal point of the desired independent society. For some the focus was the wider ethnic community of which neighbouring tribes were but components. This

[88] F. B. Welbourn, *East African Rebels*, 113–61; for an account modifying Welbourn's in its emphasis on the educational, rather than cultural, factor see T. O. Ranger, 'African attempts to control education', loc. cit. 65–7.

[89] This definition by focus, narrower than others commonly used in accounts of African nationalism, is used also in 'The emergence of African nations', loc.cit. Analytically I find it more useful than the chronological 'awakening, incipient action and triumph' recently proposed by Robert. I. Rotberg, 'African nationalism: concept or confusion?', *Modern Afr. Stud.* IV, 1 (1966), 39.

wider scale of social endeavour was still more evident in the later phase of local political focus. The official nationalism of sectional chiefs was opposed by more radical movements demanding paramounts.[90] More recently young nationalist movements have used locally traditional communicators, but for national ends.[91] The focal point of the desired society was now the nation. The new men of the 1920s had made their alliances with the chiefs out of a sense of their own relative weakness. They recognized social facts. The nationalist politicians entered their alliances from a position of relative strength. They saw them as the prelude to social reform. But the politicians' freedom of action was not limitless. It depended rather on the continued exercise of diplomatic skill. And, in the words of one East African leader, the post-Independence strategy of development has still to use tradition in order to abolish tradition, to use the clan in order to create communities which are not clannish. Above all, nationalist parties were, and are, dependent on their local communicators whose political effectiveness depends on their social support.

Many accounts of African nationalism emphasize the role of the political party in creating this support, in rousing the people from the 'inertia of loyalty'[92] that attaches to any government in power, in this case the colonial regime. It seems possible to exaggerate this external morale-building function. For if in the inter-war period the mass of Africans were deprived of political communication by the lack of widely felt burdens and the minority attractions of western Christian culture, so from the late 1930s these conditions were reversed. As already suggested in the preliminary discussion of social change, purposive government action in economic, educational and agrarian spheres brought individual Africans, many of whom were now more peasants than tribesmen, into much closer and more irritating contact with the colonial regime. At the same time as many ordinary people were for this reason developing a more explicitly political interest, the potential new communicators, teachers, traders and clerks, were shedding their illusions. Improved education did not remove the colour bar, but it did help to remove a sense of cultural inferiority. The secondary school-leaver was better equipped than the barely literate to distinguish between the material and cultural aspects of the West. Concurrently, the new governmental pressures felt by the peasantry meant also the end of any hopes for effective local political focus. The expenditure of greater resources on economic development and social services brought with it more stringent central government control.

Such was the setting for the spontaneous contribution to nationalism. Of the many facets to this contribution, only four will be discussed here.

[90] As in the cases of the Chagga, Haya, Kikuyu, Luo and Luyia.

[91] J. Listowel, *The Making of Tanganyika*, 231–2; and the example of K.A.U.'s attempted use of paramount chief Mumia's family in Western Kenya—a fascinating parallel with the techniques of the earliest British officials in the area.

[92] I. Wallerstein, 'Voluntary associations', in J. S. Coleman and C. G. Rosberg (eds.), *Political Parties and National Integration in Tropical Africa* (Berkeley, 1964), 335.

Together they illustrate the shift in mass concerns from a political focus that was diffuse or local to one that was central. First, there is the question of agrarian change generally, which focused attention on central government as a sometimes incompetent agent of reform. Secondly, the social philosophy which inspired governments' land tenure policies, namely the creation of a stable rural middle class, provoked a clearly radical social response. Thirdly, the cavalier treatment of elected local authorities by governments in a hurry forced the new communicators, often members of these authorities, into open opposition on a popular issue. Lastly, and perhaps most importantly, the development of producers' co-operatives gave to the peasantry organizations that were both locally based and centrally concerned with governments' economic policies.

Soil erosion had been recognized as a threat by the East African governments long before the Second World War. Customary land usage was increasingly destructive of the soil with the growth of population and commercial pressure on the land. Both physical anti-erosion measures were needed and, in the long term, changed methods of African farming. Improved husbandry was required if African cash crops were to be assured of a continuing welcome on the world market. The wartime emphasis on increased production, together with a shortage of the necessary departmental staff, meant that the agrarian problem had reached crisis proportions by 1945.[93] More widely, the post-war era promised a new deal for the colonies from which both the dependent and metropolitan economies would benefit.[94] In both the metropolitan and local contexts, the governments were in a hurry. In Kenya, urgency was added by the hope that economic development would silence political unrest. The 1954 Swynnerton Plan for the intensified development of African agriculture was a direct response to Mau Mau. Government hoped to solve a political problem by economic means: it was this very economic solution which precipitated the wider rural revolt which hastened the end of colonial rule.

Results were sought in the enactment of a multitude of orders affecting communal anti-erosion work, crop and animal husbandry. In the long term these were extremely effective in raising peasant and national incomes.[95] But initially there were many failures. Insufficient time was allowed for experiment and demonstration. Risk-taking is anathema to subsistence farmers, and, in too many early improvement schemes, the risks, and the hard work they often involved, were clearly not worth taking. All over

[93] Sir Philip Mitchell, *The Agrarian Problem in Kenya* (Government Printer, Nairobi, 1948).

[94] See an article on the Groundnut Scheme by Obialidu in *WASU*, XII, 3, pertinently entitled 'Bigger plans, worse plight': 'now that Britain is a debtor country casting about for means of economic recovery, she suddenly discovers Africa as a long lost Aladdin's lamp, and she rubs her eyes in wonder'. As cited in P. Garigue, 'The West African Students' Union', *Africa*, XXIII (Jan. 1953), 66.

[95] H. Ruthenberg, *Agricultural Development in Tanganyika* and *African Agricultural Production Development Policy in Kenya 1952–1965* (Berlin, 1964, 1966).

rural East Africa there were instances of local resistance to the changes.[96] In these the peasants were committed against the officers of the central government, and their leadership combined tradional clan elders, intimately concerned with land usage, and the new men, traders and teachers. This was something new and portentous. Memories of earlier resistance to colonial occupation were revived as inspiration.[97] As disturbing as the changes themselves was the environment in which they were implemented. Development entailed a great increase in European technical personnel in the rural areas at a time when there was further European settlement. The forcible removal of some of the Meru of northern Tanganyika to make way for European farmers in 1951 aroused alarm not only throughout that territory—with the T.A.A. a ready vehicle for publicity—but in Kenya also.[98] It was unfortunate too that compulsory cattle culling appeared to be more immediately advantageous to European meat canners than to the African cattle owners.[99]

Government motives were suspect. The social implications were disturbing too. One of the features of precolonial African history had been the existence of free cultivators, unencumbered by landlords or indebtedness. But, in Kenya especially, it was accepted that development must be empowered by the individual profit motive. Land must be consolidated, not only to give the secure tenure necessary for capital improvement, but to enable African farmers to mortgage their land against development loans. Hitherto, government had not interfered with customary conditions of tenure, to limit the dangers of such indebtedness. In 1954 it was proposed that 'former Government policy [should] be reversed, and able, energetic or rich Africans will be able to acquire more land, and bad or poor farmers less, creating a landed and a landless class. This is a normal step in the evolution of a country.'[100] The proposals were accepted. They were implemented, like all other government programmes, through the official chiefs. These were in a position to reap disproportionate benefits in the land cases attendant on consolidation, and from the agricultural department's farm planning services. To the peasant, agrarian reform was not only change, but also another stage in the accretion of chiefly power and wealth, with individual land titles consolidating both. The danger was the greater where the peasantry were also migrant workers. On balance—it is a moot point—it seems that families whose heads were frequently away in European employment were less likely to change their farming methods.

[96] E. Huxley, *A New Earth* (London, 1960); L. Cliffe, 'Nationalism and the reaction to enforced agricultural improvement in Tanganyika during the colonial period', East African Institute of Social Research Conference Paper, 1965.

[97] Examples are given by Professor Ranger in the papers under footnote 3 above.

[98] Information from Mr A. Nelson, currently writing a book on the Meru Land Case.

[99] For Tanganyika examples, see L. Cliffe, op. cit; K.N.A. files DC/MKS. 10B/15/1 and DC/MKS. 14/3/1 for the Kamba destocking issue of 1938, also C. C. Wrigley in Harlow and Chilver, op. cit. 256.

[100] *A Plan to Intensify the Development of African Agriculture in Kenya* (the Swynnerton Plan), (Government Printer, Nairobi, 1954), 10.

The rural modernizers were rather the old welfare association leadership and the chiefs—some of whom were retired agricultural instructors. These were the 'able, energetic or rich Africans', long associated with government departments. When land consolidation was started, it seemed likely that those already dispossessed in the towns or on European farms would be permanently dispossessed in their home areas also. Urban and rural radicalism nurtured each other. In Kikuyuland this situation led to something approaching civil war.[101] More generally, this deepening alienation of the peasantry from their chiefs provided an open opportunity for a rural counter leadership.[102]

This alternative leadership was present already in the elected element of the District Councils that in Kenya superseded the L.N.C.s, and in Tanganyika supplanted the native authorities. In line with overall British colonial policy, these local government bodies were after the war given more democratic form, greater authority and increased financial responsibility. The irony was that these new features were being inculcated by the same governments which, in their haste to solve agrarian problems, were resorting increasingly to enforcement rather than consultation. This was a long-standing African complaint. In 1935 the 'loyalist' Kikuyu Provincial Association had asked agricultural officers to order their African subordinates, on going out 'to advise other natives, [to] give their advice in the form of advice and not as a compulsory order...Further they should explain the benefits of their advice.'[103] An African farmer's association near Dar es Salaam similarly complained of agricultural inspectors in 1948, that 'instead of teaching us how to produce more crops etc., they tell us to clean our coconut shambas at once and in the case of failing to do so,... heavy fines and imprisonment are imposed...'[104] This same sentiment was expressed in the District Councils. In 1947, Oginga Odinga, then a junior councillor, 'emphasized that if the soil was to be preserved, it was the duty of the community to do the work on their own land rather than waiting or depending on someone else to come and do the work for them'.[105] Resentment of outside direction was combined with desire for improvement under African control, for African benefit.[106] District Councils were quick to protest that their new powers were a sham. They had no say in the elaborate schemes of government departments. Early in 1959 the Luo

[101] This aspect of Mau Mau is touched on in D. L. Barnett and Karari Njama, *Mau Mau from Within;* see also M.P.K. Sorrenson, 'Counter revolution to Mau Mau land consolidation in Kikuyuland, 1952–1960', E.A.I. S.R. (n.d.).

[102] I discuss this more fully in my *Political History of Western Kenya.*

[103] Harry Thuku to Provincial Commissioner, Central Province, 14 Aug. 1935, K.N.A. PC/CP. 8/5/6.

[104] Saidi Salim to Chief Secretary, 16 Mar. 1948, T.N.A. S.M.P. 36781.

[105] Minutes, Central Nyanza African District Council, 10–12 June 1947, Council Offices, Kisumu.

[106] An attitude not peculiar to a colonial situation. See Trades Union Congress, *Trade Unionism* (London, 1966), 159: 'Unions are not against change as such, but they are extremely sceptical of the value and practicability of changes devised for and imposed upon them by outsiders.'

African District Council of Central Nyanza, acting under strong local pressure, voted itself into dissolution rather than accept government terms for the management of an afforestation scheme.[107] The government had to rely on nominated councils in Kikuyuland during the Mau Mau Emergency.[108] In Sukamuland, Tanganyika, there was the same story of council opposition to government instruction, even though the council was dominated by chiefs.[109] Two points here must be emphasized. Most of the stimulus to such council opposition came from within the localities. Peasants and councillors knew like frustrations. This first observation is reinforced by the second. Many of the elected councillors, greatly increased in number with the extension of local democracy after the war, were already closely associated with the people by virtue of their leading positions in trading companies or co-operatives.

These too had a long history. In the inter-war years independent traders had been a minority group. They were often involved in the more radical movements within local political focus, resentful of the marketing advantages enjoyed by the chiefs. The generally increased peasant participation in the cash economy during the war, and the business aspirations of demobilized servicemen thereafter[110] provided a much broader base for such commercial activity. African business careers were dogged by lack of capital and entrepreneurial experience, by Asian dominance in retail trade and produce marketing, by government marketing regulations and credit restriction.[111] Many failed.[112] Bitter experience taught the need for political assistance in the attack on economic privilege. Concurrently, there was a great expansion of producers' co-operatives, with which the majority of peasants in the more advanced areas had at least some connexion. They were concerned with the whole range of central governments' economic policies. Each co-operative society was also a miniature cockpit of tension between the initiative of their African organizer and officials, and the paternalism of government co-operative officers.[113] It is significant that co-operative or other commercial organizers were as prominent as the

[107] *Government Statement on the African District Council of Central Nyanza*, 22 Jan. 1959 (Council offices, Kisumu).

[108] *(Kenya) African Affairs Department Annual Report*, 1953.

[109] Information from Mr A. Maguire.

[110] For example, Sergeant Mwai wa Koigi, Kenya African Soldiers' Association (addressee and date indecipherable, but early 1945), referred to 'the problem which is the basis of all African questions—the use of Cooperative societies' (copy in T.N.A. S.M.P. 16490 (Confidential)); M. Koinange, *The People of Kenya Speak for Themselves* (Detroit, 1955), ch. 3.

[111] *East Africa Royal Commission 1953–1955 Report*, Cmd 9475 (1955), 64–76.

[112] D. E. Apter, *The Political Kingdom in Uganda*, 186; D. L. Barnett and Karari Njama, op. cit. 106.

[113] The relationship was most strained in Kikuyuland during the Emergency. Cf. M. Koinange, op.cit. 20–1: 'Most of these [African initiated co-operatives] have been liquidated by the Government during the Emergency. The Government encouraged instead the formation of co-operatives under the direction of Europeans. In this way the Government is always in control, knows the financial power of the co-operatives and controls their growth, instead of this remaining in the hands of their members.'

trade unionists in the national movements. Koinange, Odinga[114] and Muliro in Kenya; Musazi in Uganda; Bomani, Kahama and Kasambala in Tanganyika; all these and many more were genuine communicators in their relationship between their co-operative membership and central government. The national party had need of the same type of communicator with the localities.

The passion of peasant resistance to government dictate had moved the 'inertia of loyalty' to the colonial regimes. In many cases it had forced governments to admit failure, weakening colonial morale.[115] Rural radicalism had in many areas provoked open opposition to the old communicators, the chiefs. The opportunities for an effective opposition leadership were confirmed in government treatment of elected local authorities. Rural economic enterprise joined peasant and new communicator in the co-operative societies. A peasant revolt had thrown up its leaders—local men with central interests. As such the revolt was atypical. Peasant movements are historically anarchic. It was the function of the conscious element, the nationalist leaders, to maintain that centrality of focus. It remains their more exacting task after Independence.

SUMMARY

This paper attempts to provide a frame of reference for evaluating the role of ordinary rural Africans in national movements, in the belief that scholarly preoccupation with *élites* will only partially illumine the mainsprings of nationalism. Kenya has been taken as the main field of enquiry, with contrasts and comparisons drawn from Uganda and Tanganyika. The processes of social change are discussed with a view to establishing that by the end of the colonial period one can talk of peasants rather than tribesmen in some of the more progressive areas. This change entailed a decline in the leadership functions of tribal chiefs who were also the official agents of colonial rule, but did not necessarily mean the firm establishment of a new type of rural leadership. The central part of the paper is taken up with an account of the competition between these older and newer leaderships, for official recognition rather than a mass following. A popular following was one of the conditions for such recognition, but neither really achieved this prior to 1945 except in Kikuyuland, and there the newer leaders did not want official recognition. After 1945 the newer leadership, comprising especially traders and officials of marketing co-operatives, seems everywhere to have won a properly representative position, due mainly to the enforced agrarian changes which brought the peasant face to face with the central government, perhaps for the first time. This confrontation, together with the experience of failure in earlier and more local political activity, resulted in a national revolution coalescing from below, co-ordinated rather than instigated by the educated *élite*.

[114] Odinga's Luo Thrift and Trading Corporation, of which Achieng Oneko was for a time secretary, was organizationally the direct precursor of the Kenya African National Union among the rural Luo.

[115] Examples are given in L. Cliffe, 'Nationalism and the reaction to enforced agricultural improvement', loc. cit.

Journal of African History, XI, 4 (1970), pp. 591–603
Printed in Great Britain

THE ORIGINS OF NATIONALISM IN EAST AND CENTRAL AFRICA: THE ZAMBIAN CASE

BY IAN HENDERSON

THE literature on the origins of African nationalism in Zambia is still sparse, despite Robert Rotberg's pioneering work, published in 1966.[1] Compared with Malawi or Rhodesia, there is a lack of analytical material which tells us how the peculiar conditions of Northern Rhodesia affected the structure and character of the independence movement of the 1950s, and how and why Zambian nationalism resembled or differed from similar movements in other territories. This article will argue that the crucial years in the founding of nationalism in Zambia are 1930–50. In these years we see indications of both the unity and diversity of later mass nationalism. And lest we make the logical error of assuming that all anti-administration movements were necessarily also forerunners of mass nationalism, we have in Zambia the stark corrective of the Lenshinaist uprising of 1964 against an African government on the brink of independence. The discrete nature, therefore, of prenationalist movements must be taken seriously.

We shall examine first of all the framework of analysis for prenationalism which has so far been constructed for neighbouring territories, then in the light of this we shall attempt to point out the peculiarities of the Zambian movement, at the same time indicating possible directions for further investigation. Terence Ranger and John Lonsdale have made a masterly beginning to the analysis of nationalist origins in East and Central Africa.[2] Ranger emphasizes the important effect of African primary resistance on subsequent colonial policy. Resistance need not necessarily be futile in the long term: for example, the British Colonial Office refused to allow a major tax increase in Southern Rhodesia in 1903 because of fears of renewed rebellion by the Shona and Ndebele. Primary resistance was also important in that it provided memories on which later prophetic movements could build during colonial times, and it initiated a tradition of rural radicalism. In two articles in this *Journal*, Ranger elaborates on the connexions between primary resistance and later mass nationalist movements in East and Central Africa. He shows how memories of the Ndebele and Shona Rebellions, and of the Maji-Maji Rebellion, lingered

[1] Robert I. Rotberg, *The Rise of Nationalism in Central Africa* (Cambridge, Mass.: Harvard University Press, 1966).

[2] T. O. Ranger, 'Connexions between "Primary Resistance" movements and modern mass nationalism in East and Central Africa' (2 parts), *J. Afr. Hist.*, IX, 3 and 4 (1968); T. O. Ranger, 'African reaction and resistance to the imposition of colonial rule in East and Central Africa', in L. H. Gann and P. Duignan (general editors), *The History and Politics of Modern Imperialism, Vol I: Colonialism in Africa, 1870–1960* (Stanford, 1969); J. M. Lonsdale, 'Some origins of nationalism in East Africa', *J. Afr. Hist.*, IX, 1 (1968).

on among the people, to reappear and vitalize the mass nationalist movements of the 1950s. Although Ranger's discussion includes Zambia, we are struck forcibly by the fact that it does not fit readily into his analysis, since primary resistance there was on a very small scale: in a recent semi-official version of the Zambian independence struggle, little was made of the period of conquest, the greatest emphasis being laid on the politics of the colour bar during the colonial period.[3]

Lonsdale poses the problem of the historic relation between the popular element and the intellectual elite within the nationalist movement in East Africa. He notes the vital part played by the local 'communicators', and how social change brought about changes in the identity of the communicators. The elite did not occupy the position of the new communicators until after 1945, when modern mass nationalism with a central focus could be said to have begun. But peasant resistance to agrarian changes provided the raw material for nationalism: the anticolonial revolution was co-ordinated rather than instigated by the elite.

In Zambia, protest had no definitive starting point, since colonial rule was imposed gradually,[4] and there was no large-scale rising like Maji-Maji or the Ndebele and Shona Rebellions. It is true that Mpezeni's Ngoni and Kazembe's Lunda resisted the compulsory treaty-signing which was a feature of British rule north of the Zambezi. Some Bemba groups opposed the gradual invasion of their old raiding-grounds by the British South Africa Company. But the incidence of primary resistance in Zambia was patchy and small-scale. The Lozi and the Bemba, the most formidable state systems in the area, did not resist as articulate units, for reasons which have been examined by Gerald Caplan, Andrew Roberts and Eric Stokes.[5] We must, therefore, look to the period of colonial rule for the origins of Zambian nationalism. It is possible that future scholars will trace links between modern mass nationalism and Zambian society in the 1890s, but these links are unlikely to be as strong as the memories of the *chimurenga* in Southern Rhodesia. There is also the consideration that past tribal resistance might be linked with present-day tribal rivalries. Appeals to a glorious precolonial past can be made, for example, by Lozi or Lunda separatists as well as by the advocates of 'one Zambia, one nation'. The era of the colour bar and the independence struggle are far more central to the theme of national unity.[6]

[3] M. J. Chimba, M.P., 'The struggle for independence' in *Zambia News* (Lusaka), 20 October, 2 and 9 November 1969. Mr Chimba is Minister of National Guidance in the Zambian Government.

[4] I have made some of these points in my article 'Pre-nationalist resistance to colonial rule in Zambia', *African Social Research*, 9 (1970).

[5] Gerald L. Caplan, 'Barotseland's scramble for protection', *J. Afr. Hist.*, x, 2 (1969); Andrew Roberts, *A History of the Bemba to 1900* (Cambridge University Press, forthcoming. The title is provisional); E. Stokes and R. Brown, *The Zambesian Past* (Manchester: Manchester University Press, 1966), xxvii–xxxi; and chapter 12.

[6] Gerald L. Caplan, 'Barotseland: the secessionist challenge to Zambia'. *Journal of Modern African Studies*, 6, 3 (1968).

Although primary resistance is less important in Zambia than in neighbouring territories, the pattern of the subsequent first decades of colonial rule falls into line with the other East and Central African territories. The gradual imposition of tax and rising demands for labour, both for chiefs and for Europeans, led to tax revolts and to passive resistance to labour recruitment.[7] The most common institutional mode of resistance in this period was independency and millennarianism. African Christianity took many forms and was a response to many problems, as Ranger has pointed out for Tanzania.[8] The African Methodist Episcopal Church of Willie Mokalapa in Barotseland was, among other things, a means of protest by the new Lozi mission elite against the barriers to promotion imposed by the mission churches on Africans. It also offered to the elite the possibility of education, a facility substantially denied to them by the Company and by the Paris Evangelical Mission.[9] But by far the most widespread form of African Christianity after 1918 was Watch Tower, which reached Northern Rhodesia from Nyasaland towards the end of the First World War. Its fundamentalist teachings about the end of the world and the imminent damnation of all in authority made it a subversive and radical organization which was feared and closely watched by the Government. Separate villages of Watch Tower followers were set up, and ties between kin and between chiefs and their people were severed. Where normal life was disrupted, Watch Tower came into its own. Hanoc Shindano's preachings in the Abercorn District in the aftermath of the East African campaign of 1916–18 forced the Government to send troops to the area in 1919[10]; Fred Kabombo, the Watch Tower leader on the Copperbelt, never proselytized so successfully as after the violence and killings of the 1935 Copperbelt strike.[11]

Watch Tower's role as a radical means of protest against colonial rule is unquestionable. But its geographical and social scope have yet to be investigated, and we await a study of Watch Tower leadership and the ways in which it changed over the years. Sholto Cross's preliminary work shows a periodicity of Watch Tower activity: up to the mid-1930s its impact was a radical one; but after 1935 it began to adopt a more quietist role, partly as a result of closer control by the South African parent body

[7] Rotberg, 73–6; Henry S. Meebelo, 'African reaction to European rule in the Northern Province of Northern Rhodesia, 1895–1939: A study of the genesis and development of political awareness among a colonial people.' Unpublished Ph.D. thesis, University of London, 1969, 127–55.

[8] T. O. Ranger, *The African Churches of Tanzania* (Historical Association of Tanzania Paper, No. 5, Nairobi: East African Publishing House, n.d., ?1969).

[9] Rotberg, chapter vi; T. O. Ranger, 'The "Ethiopian" episode in Barotseland, 1900–1905', *Human Problems in British Central Africa*, 37 (1965).

[10] Rotberg, 136–9; Meebelo, 183–261. I follow Dr Meebelo's spelling of Shindano's name.

[11] *Evidence taken by the Commission [Russell] appointed to enquire into the disturbances in the Copperbelt, Northern Rhodesia, July–September 1935* (Lusaka: Government Printer, 1935 and Cmd. 5009 of 1935), 271, evidence of John Smith Moffat.

of official (European) Jehovah's Witnesses.[12] Many questions remain to be answered, the main one being why Watch Tower leaders fundamentally failed as 'communicators' in a modern political setting, whereas certain other African Christians, both in mission and independent churches, succeeded. Henry Meebelo suggests part of the answer when he recounts how, in the early 1920s, the young teachers and clerks who led Watch Tower in the Isoka District kept the officials of the Mwenzo Native Welfare Association at arm's length, and regarded the Association as being collaborationist.[13] Whether at this time Watch Tower represented an articulated popular radicalism as against the elite proto-leadership of the Welfare Associations is a question which will no doubt be answered as more work is done on religious movements of discontent.

When we turn to the study of Welfare Associations, we find a distinct lack of leadership and continuity until the late 1930s.[14] By the 1940s, a spate of leaders emerge: Kaunda, Nkumbula, Kapwepwe and many others. But this emergence is comparatively late, and is contemporaneous with the emergence of the leaders of the labour movement. Nyasaland, by contrast, although intrinsically the poorest of the British Central African territories, had a much higher proportion of educated Africans providing leadership, and indeed provided many of the early office-bearers of Welfare Associations in Northern Rhodesia. It is unlikely that further research into the Welfare Associations in the 1920s and 1930s will radically alter our picture of them. Like others throughout East and Central Africa, they were dominated by educated teachers, ministers and civil servants; though they claimed to speak for the African people as a whole, they restricted their membership to persons of 'good education and character', and made little or no contact with grass-roots rural discontent. But a study of the Welfare Associations in the 1940s may well provide us with vital evidence about how the elite began to make contact with the people under the threat of amalgamation and federation. More particularly we need a study of the process by which the educated men of the Federation of African Societies (formed in 1946, and the first territory-wide African political organization) made alliance with the labourers of the Copperbelt to form the volatile but effective mass nationalist movement of the 1950s, and how far they in fact captured the leadership of the labour movement from 'genuine' workers.[15]

This brings us to another peculiarity which distinguishes Zambia from

[12] Sholto Cross, 'The Watch Tower movement in Zambia: some historical questions', unpublished University of Zambia History Seminar Paper, 1969.

[13] Meebelo, 346–8.

[14] James R. Hooker, 'Welfare Associations and other instruments of accommodation in the Rhodesias between the World Wars', *Comparative Studies in Society and History*, IX, I (1966).

[15] In 'The Second World War and Northern Rhodesian Society' (Paper presented to the East African Social Science Council Conference, Nairobi, 1969), I briefly trace the formation of the African Mine Workers' Trade Union in 1948–49, and the role of non-mine Africans in it.

the other territories of East and Central Africa, and one which deserves further investigation: the presence of the vast copper-mining complex which, from 1925 onwards, transformed Northern Rhodesia's economy. The actual course of this economic transformation has been described by Lewis Gann, Kenneth Bradley and Robert Baldwin, and only a sketchy summary will be given here. But the social and political consequences have been assumed rather than investigated by historians. Nothing so comprehensive as Merle Davis's *Modern Industry and the African* has appeared since 1933, though the sociologists of the Rhodes–Livingstone Institute (now the Institute for Social Research of the University of Zambia) have provided a wealth of discussion on aspects of social change. The remainder of this article will attempt to suggest guidelines for a general historical approach to the immediate and more remote implications of the Copperbelt for our problem of nationalist origins.[16]

The romance of copper mining in Northern Rhodesia had achieved a happy and profitable consummation by the 1930s. Early difficulties had been amply rewarded in terms of company profits by 1940, and gross copper royalties paid to the British South Africa Company by 1964 totalled nearly £135 million.[17] By 1938 the Copperbelt was producing over 13 per cent of all the non-communist world's copper, and the number of Africans employed by the mines rose from 7,459 in 1933 to 26,203 in 1940.[18] The Second World War put the finishing touches to the transformation. The Allies needed copper for the war effort, and the British Government made a bulk agreement with the copper companies whereby their market was assured.[19] The copper industry also stimulated agriculture, with the result that during the Second World War the production of maize and wheat nearly doubled.[20]

By 1928 the control of copper mining was held by the South Africa-based Rhodesian Anglo-American Corporation and by the United States-based Rhodesian Selection Trust. They were roughly equal in size and

[16] L. H. Gann, 'The Northern Rhodesian copper industry and the world of copper, 1923–1952', *Human Problems in British Central Africa*, 18 (1955); Kenneth Bradley, *Copper Venture* (London: Mufulira Copper Mines Ltd., 1952); J. Merle Davis, *Modern Industry and the African* (London, Cass, 1967; first edition 1933). It is impossible to list all the publications of the Rhodes-Livingstone Institute touching on our theme. Three outstandingly influential publications have been: J. Clyde Mitchell, *The Kalela Dance* (Rhodes-Livingstone Paper No. 27, 1956); W. Watson, *Tribal Cohesion in a Money Economy* (Manchester University Press and the Rhodes-Livingstone Institute, 1958); and A. L. Epstein, *Politics in an Urban African Community* (Manchester University Press and the Rhodes-Livingstone Institute, 1958).

[17] *The British South Africa Company's claims to the mineral royalties in Northern Rhodesia* (Lusaka: Government Printer, 1964), p. 1. It is, of course, arguable that company profits in the late 1930s constituted only a modest return on a decade of heavy investment without return in the years 1925–35.

[18] *Report of the Commission appointed to enquire into the financial and economic position of Northern Rhodesia* (Colonial No. 145, 1938) (*The Pim and Milligan Report*), 19–20; Robert E. Baldwin, *Economic Development and Export Growth* (Berkeley and Los Angeles: University of California Press, 1966) 14–57.

[19] Gann, 9.

[20] Baldwin, 75–6.

divided the Copperbelt between them. Their arrival in what had been a remote backwater presents a picture of many-dimensional change. The copper companies were not only a new and powerful economic factor in the situation: they also introduced a discordant political note. The mines management was dominated by rough-hewn Americans and South Africans, who viewed the problems of African labour in a technocratic way, as part of the overall problem of mining copper. They were unwilling to brook government interference in their labour relations; they built their own compounds, which were patrolled by their own police, and the compound manager at each mine dealt out summary justice when he felt it necessary. Obviously the relations between the compound manager and the District Officer representing the government were delicate. John Smith Moffat (later Sir John Moffat), District Officer at Mufulira in 1935, came into conflict with Schaefer, the compound manager at Mufulira Mine, over the latter's brutal treatment of offenders, and a feud continued until Schaefer was dismissed in 1936.

In a broader sense, the mines and the government were rivals for the possession and distribution of wealth in the territory. The officers of the government were influenced by current trusteeship ideas, and assumed that these still applied in the territory, despite its growing white population. The administration wanted to lay down at least a minimum basis of tolerable working conditions, enough at least to avoid widespread discontent and consequent political unrest among Africans; the mining companies on the other hand resented the government's 'holier than thou' attitude, and were not loath to point out that the government paid their own African employees lower wages than the mines.[21]

Large-scale copper-mining, then, brought on the scene a serious political rival to the Northern Rhodesia Government. With their contacts in London, Johannesburg and New York, the groups could wield behind-the-scenes power outside the territory. Inside the territory, the government was a minor distributor of wealth compared with the copper companies: in 1937 the earnings of Rhokana Corporation alone were double the government's total expenditure for the year.[22]

But it is the social as much as the political dimensions of the changes after 1925 that concern us here. African migrant labourers travelled from all parts of the territory to work on the mines. Once they arrived there, they began to stay for longer and longer periods on the Copperbelt, bringing to the notice of the government and the mines the problem of 'the industrialized native'. It is important for us to specify what this social problem was, and what it was not. The expansion of the Copperbelt did not happen in a country which had had no experience of wage labour.

[21] SEC/LAB/79 items 77, 81, 83. This series of Northern Rhodesia secretariat files is in the National Archives, Lusaka.

[22] *Northern Rhodesia Approved Estimates of Revenue and Expenditure 1939* (Lusaka: Government Printer, 1939); Gann, 8.

The peoples of the Eastern and Southern Provinces had been working on the mines and farms of Southern Rhodesia since the turn of the century; from a slightly later date the peoples of the Northern Province had travelled to the Katanga mines, and by 1920 formed about half the labour force there.[23] The Lozi tradition of working in Southern Rhodesia and South Africa began as early as the 1890s, and ended only in 1967: Northern Rhodesia had been a labour reservoir for the white South since the beginning of the century.[24] Economic rather than physical compulsion was now the moving force, and it required a change in existing migration patterns rather than the tapping of new sources of labour to bring the required force to the Copperbelt. This was done with comparative ease. Some recruitment by the Mines Native Labour Bureau was necessary in the boom years 1929–32, but thereafter there was a permanent surplus of labourers who made their own way to the Copperbelt.[25]

The wages and conditions offered by the copper mines were poor by world standards, but were demonstrably better than those in Southern Rhodesia or Tanganyika.[26] This small differential was enough to persuade the Luapula peoples, the Bemba of Northern Province, the peoples of the Eastern Province and some Lozis to change their place of work. The most important of these groups were the Luapula peoples (who were Bemba-speaking) and the Bemba proper of Northern Province. From the beginning they together formed over 50 per cent of the total labour force on the mines and ensured that the *lingua franca* of the Copperbelt would be Bemba.[27]

Thus, wage labour was not a novelty to the labourers of the Copperbelt; nor were the copper companies massive employers of labour. Baldwin points out that 'the direct employment impact of the new industry was bound to be low in relation to its output in monetary terms'.[28] Up to the late 1940s more Zambians were employed in Southern Rhodesia alone than were employed on the Copperbelt mines. Though the mines were the largest single employer of labour, they employed only about one-quarter of the total wage-earners in the territory.[29] Thus, in terms of sheer numbers, the copper mines were not great consumers of labour in comparison with their need for capital, and they were able to obtain the labour they

[23] Merle Davis, 53.

[24] *Report of the Commission appointed to inquire into the disturbances in the Copperbelt, Northern Rhodesia* (Lusaka, Government Printer, n.d., but 1941) (*The Forster Report*), paras. 16–20.

[25] *The Pim and Milligan Report*, 29 ff; *The Forster Report*, paras. 27–30.

[26] *Report of the Commission appointed to enquire into the disturbances in the Copperbelt, Northern Rhodesia* (Lusaka, Government Printer, 1935 and Cmd. 5009 of 1935) (*The Russell Report*), para. 84.

[27] *The Pim and Milligan Report*, Appendix vi.

[28] Baldwin, 80.

[29] In 1940, for example, the average number of Africans employed on the copper mines was 28,034 out of a total of 121,939 wage earners within the territory. In the same year about 46,000 Northern Rhodesians were employed in Southern Rhodesia, and 7000 in South Africa. See my paper, 'The Second World War and Northern Rhodesian Society', Appendix, Table 2.

required without the conservationist restrictions which were from time to time imposed, for example, by the Nyasaland Government on behalf of its planters.[30]

It is, however, the concentration of mine labour into a comparatively small, urbanized area that constitutes the essential impact of copper mining on the social and political history of Zambia. As Sir Alison Russell put it in 1935:

> It is all very well putting a District Officer in the open in the middle of 100,000 natives and with half a dozen askaris to keep order.... But mining areas are a different matter. 6000 or so natives in a compound; more or less detribalised: without chiefs; unaccustomed to machinery; and with pathetic contentment rapidly giving way to divine discontent...might lead to a serious disaster... The whole position rests on bluff—the prestige of the white man—a good and effective bluff which must continue in this country—but not at the mines.[31]

Characteristically, the government regarded urbanization as primarily a problem of law and order, and gradually increased its police force on the Copperbelt.[32] But there was little serious attempt to intervene in the sphere of industrial relations, which were regarded, both in the 1930s and later, as a set of problems which the copper companies were responsible for solving, with only occasional participation by the government, in the form of commissions. Orde Browne urged the creation of a Labour Department in 1938, but the first Labour Officers were not appointed until after the 1940 Copperbelt strike.[33] Thus, a situation of sharp confrontation arose on the Copperbelt, with thousands of labourers living on the verge of absolute poverty facing the giant copper companies, whose welfare facilities were as yet rudimentary, with the government standing aside as an onlooker unaccustomed to such problems. 'Sudden mining activity', said Orde Browne, 'with a consequent rapid industrialization of a very primitive native population, has taken the existing government largely by surprise, with the result that experienced men and proper machinery to deal with such growth are lacking.'[34]

There was yet another sphere of conflict which brought Africans to a rapid and painful realization of their inferior position. This was the emergence of a well-organized and militant European labour force. This had two quite separate effects: on the one hand, white trade unionists tried from time to time to encourage militant action by the Africans, but on the other hand they strove to preserve the industrial colour bar. The encouragement is at first sight surprising, since many of the white mine-

[30] SEC/LAB/12: Minutes of a meeting of the Standing Committee [on the Salisbury Agreement] held at Salisbury, 25 October 1939; also Howe (Labour Commissioner) to Chief Secretary, 1 November 1939.

[31] C.O. 795/76/45083 item 100: Sir Alison Russell to Sir John Maffey, August 1935. The C.O. series is in the Public Record Office, London.

[32] *The Forster Report*, para. 17.

[33] G. St J. Orde Browne, *Labour Conditions in Northern Rhodesia* (Colonial No. 150, 1938), paras. 279–95.

[34] Ibid., para. 8.

workers were diehard Afrikaner nationalists and believers in European racial superiority. But there were on the Copperbelt some surviving remnants of the alliance between white communists and black workers which had been cemented by the South African Communist Party and Clements Kadalie's Industrial and Commercial Workers' Union in the 1920s.[35] Brian Goodwin, President of the (European) Northern Rhodesian Mine Workers' Union (MWU) in the 1940s, was a communist, who, for reasons which are too complex to enumerate here, attempted to form an African Mine Workers' Union in 1948.[36] White mineworkers were suspected by the government of having fomented the African strikes at Mufulira and Nkana in 1940.[37]

But the encouragement of black militancy did not mean that the white mineworkers were agitating for equality for Africans. Their ideal was a black union under white control, which would enhance the bargaining power of the whites and retain the industrial *status quo*, whereby Europeans enjoyed large monetary rewards as a result of their monopoly of skilled jobs. The MWU entrenched this monopoly through agreements with the companies in 1937 and 1945, with a 'closed shop' clause being added in 1941.[38] From its powerful position the Union insisted on the superficially liberal slogan of 'equal pay for equal work'. 'We do not wish the native to be exploited to the disadvantage of European labour', argued a MWU official in 1940. 'We have no objections to the native being a tradesman if he is paid tradesman's rates.'[39] Thus, on the Northern Rhodesian mines a situation was achieved comparable to that under the Southern Rhodesian Industrial Conciliation Act 1934, whereby Africans were not in practice employed in skilled jobs.

White trade unionism on the Copperbelt, therefore, encouraged Africans to act together as workers, but at the same time did all in its power to prevent Africans from achieving any improvement in their industrial status. It is hard to think of any situation more frustrating and instructive to the African labourers on the mines. It is not surprising that they formed their own union in due course; nor is it surprising that they did so under government, and not under MWU auspices, and that the first and principal aim of the Northern Rhodesian Afrcan Mine Workers' Trade Union (NRAMWU) under Lawrence Katilungu was the abolition of the colour bar on the mines.

[35] E. Roux, *Time Longer than Rope* (Madison: University of Wisconsin Press, 1964, 2nd ed.), chapter xvii.

[36] See my paper, note 29 above, for a more detailed account of this episode.

[37] SEC/LAB/78, I: note by the Chief Secretary, 1 April 1940; Provincial Commissioner, Ndola to Chief Secretary, 14 April 1940; SEC/LAB/70, II: Governor, Northern Rhodesia to Secretary of State, 9 April 1940.

[38] *Report of the Board of Inquiry appointed to inquire into the advancement of Africans in the copper mining industry in Northern Rhodesia* (Lusaka: Government Printer, 1954) (*The Forster Board Report*), paras. 16–21.

[39] *Evidence to the Commission [Forster] appointed to enquire into the disturbances in the Copperbelt, Northern Rhodesia* (typescript, 1940, ZP/12, Lusaka Archives), 708.

Enough has been said about the Copperbelt to indicate that it is there, and not elsewhere, that one must look for the origins of modern mass nationalism in Zambia. Zambians by 1940 starkly confronted both their own government and the white union in an urban situation where mediation by chiefs, mission elite, or independent churches was irrelevant. There was no ambiguity or blurring in this conflict between black workers and their white colonial masters. Nor were the black workers necessarily inexperienced in the work situation, as we have seen. The transformation from rural tribesmen to militant workers was rapid, all the more so because they were in their own territory and not on foreign soil.

It is from a central study of the Copperbelt that we can also indicate avenues of research for the future. There is, for example, the whole question of differential politicization in Zambia, and specifically the question of why the peoples of Northern, Luapula and Southern Provinces became early supporters of the nationalist movement of the 1950s. In other African territories this differentiation is clearly visible, and there are clearly defined reasons for it. In Ghana, the coastal peoples were active long before the peoples of the interior; in Nigeria the Northern Region came to politics late; in Kenya the Kikuyu were pioneers of the political movement. An explanation of these differences is not appropriate here, but it is striking that for Zambia there has been no attempt to explain why political mobilization was achieved at different paces in different parts of the territory. Caplan has pointed out that in Barotseland the traditional elite succeeded for long in preventing a rival source of power springing up, and this partly explains the late rise of UNIP in the area.[40] But we lack a general analysis for the whole territory.

This merely re-emphasizes the need which has been repeatedly stressed for more local studies of the African reaction during the colonial period, on which a general theory may be constructed.[41] The Northern and Western (formerly Barotse) Provinces of Zambia are receiving perhaps most attention from research workers in the field, but the Eastern Province is in need of a study at a local level to ascertain the impact of migrant labour and land alienation on local forms of protest. Peter Harries-Jones points out that this province had a higher rate of labour migration (measured by Harries-Jones's 'masculinity ratio') than any other province in the 1950s.[42] We usually think of the Northern Province as the classic case of agricultural distress due to a high rate of labour migration. Audrey Richards and Godfrey Wilson have perhaps focused our eyes too closely on the Bemba.[43] A closer study of the Nyanja-speaking people of the Eastern

[40] D. Mulford, *Zambia, The Politics of Independence* (London: Oxford University Press, 1967), 228.

[41] For example, in T. O. Ranger (ed.), *Emerging Themes of African History* (London: Heinemann, 1968). See also D. H. Jones's review of this book in *J. Afr. Hist.*, x, 4 (1969).

[42] Peter Harries-Jones, 'The tribes in the towns' in W. V. Brelsford, *The Tribes of Zambia* (Lusaka: Government Printer, n.d., ?1965).

[43] Audrey Richards, *Land, Labour and Diet in Northern Rhodesia* (London: International

Province (grouped as 'Ngoni' by employers) would provide comparative material. The effects of the North Charterland Concession and the links with neighbouring Nyasaland would also be fruitful topics for research on the Eastern Province. The road from Fort Jameson to Feira and Southern Rhodesia via the Luangwa Valley was an important labour route for Nyasas throughout the twentieth century, and the consequences of this constant two-way flow also merit study.

The African National Congress had its first stronghold in the Southern Province, and the reasons for this have not been made clear. There was white settlement there on a scale approaching that of the plateau of Southern Rhodesia. The Tonga farmers of the Southern Province seized the opportunity presented by the proximity of the line of rail to produce maize and cattle for the market. Like the Shona of Southern Rhodesia, the Tonga farmers were hindered from competing with Europeans by being moved out of commercially viable land, and by a system of differential prices for their produce. It would be interesting to ascertain how far the liberal professions of the government survived where white settlers could exert pressure. It would also be useful to analyse what part the Tonga commercial farmers played in the rise of Congress, and whether their local grievances became transformed into national ones.[44] The fact that the politicization of the Tonga was not directly connected with the rise of the Copperbelt (only a very small number migrated there for work; most went to neighbouring Southern Rhodesia) may also account for the later split between the followers of Nkumbula (whose home is at Namwala, Southern Province) and those of Kaunda and Kapwepwe in 1958, when the Zambia African National Congress (ZANC) was formed, later to become the United National Independence Party (UNIP). Nkumbula was never able to build up a power base on the Copperbelt, except in Mufulira, and from 1958 ANC became a local Southern Province party, though still retaining pretensions to a nationwide organization, and capable in 1968 of gaining seats in a disaffected Barotse Province. UNIP's strength lay in an alliance between the rural Luapula and Northern Provinces and the workers of the Copperbelt. Thus the role of the Copperbelt in African politics is once again emphasized.

A final problem of present-day nationalism, which may be explicable by a study of prenationalist resistance, is that of the political role of the Bemba, and of the Bemba-speaking Luapula peoples. This is, of course, a living issue. The temporary resignation of Vice-President Simon Kapwepwe in 1969 was due to the 'mud-slinging' which he had had to

African Institute and Oxford University Press, 1939); Godfrey Wilson, *An Essay on the Economics of detribalisation in Northern Rhodesia* (Lusaka: Rhodes-Livingstone Institute Papers No. 5 and 6, 1941 and 1942).

[44] Robert Rotberg, *The Rise of Nationalism*, 126, quotes Chief Musokotwane of the Tonga as complaining in 1930 that the Europeans were 'chasing us from our lands where our forefathers died to lands which are strange to us where we are not allowed to cut down trees'. The chief was attending a meeting of the Livingstone Native Welfare Association.

endure as a result of his position as unofficial leader of the Bemba.[45] 'Tribal wranglings', evidently between the Bemba speakers and the others, were the reason given for President Kenneth Kaunda's equally temporary resignation in 1968.[46] In 1958, Governor Benson considered the Bemba 'our problem children': 'They have an intense national or tribal consciousness...they are not neutral or nondescript people. They can either be a tremendous cause of trouble in the territory or a valuable asset.'[47] John Smith Moffat in 1935 thought that 'a wholly industrialized Wemba is, I should think, a very unpleasant person indeed, and it will come when this generation grows up here. He will require very strong discipline...I think he will be a very difficult man indeed to manage, and his son will be worse.'[48]

There is no need for us to subscribe to tribal stereotypes to acknowledge that there is need for an explanation for the 'troublesomeness', or advanced political consciousness, of the Bemba, which meant that they spearheaded the political movement of the 1950s. Part of the explanation may be that they had their economic and political base in Zambia. Few emigrated to other territories after about 1932, except to Tanganyika, whereas many people from the Eastern and Barotse Provinces found work in the south. The poverty of Lubemba, it has been suggested, made the Bemba a radical people. This radicalism did not need to take the form of support for nationalism, for Lenshinaism was as much a product of the Northern Province as UNIP. In 1961 Rotberg argued that Lenshina's Lumpa Church was basically 'sympathetic to the mainstream of African nationalism', but might confine itself to giving the movement moral encouragement only,[49] but the Church's rising against an African government on the verge of independence must cause us to revise this view.[50]

The argument of this article has been that the key to the understanding of the peculiarities of the early nationalist movement in Zambia is the Copperbelt. The towns of the Copperbelt contained a fissile mixture of poverty-stricken, underprivileged Africans, and a rich white elite operating a blatant colour bar. In the background, a mildly liberal government merely provided a convenient fuse for the inevitable political explosion. The first explosion took place when Africans on the Copperbelt

[45] See my essay on Zambia in *The Annual Register: World Events in 1969* (London: Longmans, 1970); also Robert I. Rotberg, 'Tribalism and politics in Zambia', *Africa Report*, XII, no. 9, December 1967.

[46] Richard Hall, *The High Price of Principles* (London: Hodder and Stoughton, 1969), 194.

[47] A. Wina, 'The future of local government in Zambia' (Lusaka: Government Printer, Zambia Information Services Press Release, No. 1229, 1968), quoted in B. Magubane, 'Pluralism and conflict situations in Africa: a new look', *African Social Research*, 7 (1969).

[48] Evidence to the Russell Commission, 1935, 282.

[49] Robert I. Rotberg, 'The Lenshinaist movement of Northern Rhodesia', *Human Problems in British Central Africa*, 29, (1961).

[50] See Andrew Roberts's essay on the Lumpa Church in Robert I. Rotberg and Ali Mazrui (eds.), *Protest and Power in Black Africa* (New York: Oxford University Press, 1970).

went on strike in 1935 and 1940. It is in these vital episodes that we may find indications of how African workers adapted or discarded traditional institutions, and manipulated their environment so as to articulate their grievances effectively. A common pan-tribal front, the uncompromising presentation of complaints, and the organization of thousands of men for a period of weeks—all these were achieved during the Copperbelt strikes. Yet we know very little about their organization and leadership, as opposed to the grievances which brought them about. It is with these questions, vital in explaining the genesis of the nationalist movement in Zambia, that I hope to deal in a subsequent article.

SUMMARY

This article draws attention to the comparative lack of material on the origins of African nationalism in Zambia, and suggests a framework of analysis and possible future areas of research on the subject. In contrast with some other East and Central African territories, Zambia offered little or no primary resistance to the imposition of colonial rule, but in other respects the country resembled neighbouring territories in the first three decades of colonial rule. There is a need for further study of Watch Tower and the Welfare Associations, the former in the inter-war years, the latter in the 1940s. The Copperbelt from 1930 to 1950, with its problems of urbanization and the colour bar, is a vital factor setting Zambia apart from other tropical dependencies. Here, Africans were confronted with the determination of Europeans to retain political and economic power, whatever the policy declarations of the government. The politicization of the territory can be traced from here, and the role of the Bemba-speaking peoples as the spearhead of protest had its origin in their powerful position on the Copperbelt.

THE SOURCES OF COLLECTIVE REBELLION

Nationalism in Buganda and Kikuyuland

Meddi Mugyenyi, Department of Government, University of Nairobi

How can we *explain* nationalist rebellions in Africa? The question is still worthwhile although massive literature exists on nationalism in Africa. Impressive work has been done on the tricky subject of why men rebel,[1] but few claims can yet be confidently laid to having the subject under control. The sources and dynamics of human rebellion are continuing subjects of intellectual debate. Among the factors likely to contribute to the longevity of the debate is the relative inaccessibility of insights into the subject because such insights are often shrouded by the disciplinary obscurantism of psychology and psychiatry.[2] It is probable that the esoteric goings-on of these disciplines, the disciplinary compartmentalization which has bedevilled contemporary studies of man in society, and the differential sophistication of research methodologies will continue to deny the humbly-educated an opportunity to understand the nature of human rebellion.

Notwithstanding the wealth of valuable explanations advanced by the study of African nationalism and the politics of decolonization, there are still some irritating gaps in our understanding of African nationalism as a form of collective rebellion against external intrusions. The gaps are ultimately reducible to theoretical inadequacies in the comprehension of human rebellion in general. Once nationalism is relieved of its political trappings and its cultivated emotive paraphernalia, it remains only one of the forms of collective human behaviour whose elucidation might justifiably borrow from a wide range of social theory. The comments ahead take off from this presumption to propose a mode of explanation.

But first, some guiding questions. Once the frame of reference is limited to Africa a number of issues become immediately critical. Why did some African societies rebel against colonial intrusions while others more or less acquiesced? Why, for example, did the Kikuyu rebel against British colonial intrusion while the Baganda did not rebel nearly as dramatically against the same intruders? Was it because the two African societies were culturally different in the sense that one was culturally conditioned to rebel while the other was not? Can it be safely propounded that the propensity to rebel is intrinsic in certain cultures but not so in others? Or can an argument of method be advanced to the effect that the nature of British intrusion in Buganda and Kikuyuland was different, and that the difference of method accounts for acquiescent reactions on the part of the Baganda and rebellious reactions on the part of the Kikuyu?[3] One possible approach to providing explanatory answers to the questions will be outlined with the benefit of liberal borrowing from social theory.

This paper contends that *the tendency to rebel, at least in the case of nationalist rebellions against colonial intrusions, is often a response to the violation of cultural cores by the intruding actors.* Cultural cores are those central values, traits, symbols, procedures and commodities which form the cultural nerve-centre of a society. This definition opens a pandora's box of the stratification of cultural elements. The position taken here is that such a stratification is legitimate and potentially demonstrable by empirical procedures. Thus it is a basic premise of the present contention that not all the cultural paraphernalia of a society are equally important both subjectively and objectively. Cultural cores are the more important while cultural peripherals are the less important elements of a society's culture.

The premise of differential importance in the elements of culture is vital though certainly not entirely beyond debate. The principle contention is predicated on that differential. To elaborate the contention, issues of collective response behaviour might be formulated in terms of intrusion into cores and intrusion into peripherals. The violation of some peripheral cultural paraphernalia by an intruding external actor does not always excite spontaneous uproar and rebellion on the part of the society intruded upon. But the violation of cultural cores by intruding external actors is likely to excite rebellion against the intruders. In other words, the probability of a cultural group's rebellion is higher when its cultural cores are violated by external intruders than when only its cultural peripherals are violated.

But of course the formulation above is not insensitive to the mediation of intervening variables. A supplementary proposition is called for. Quite briefly, it is expected that the manner of violating a society's cultural elements has some mediating impact on the reactions of the violated society. The methodology of colonial intrusions into African societies helped to shape the various African responses to colonialism. The literature on African nationalism involves attempts to demonstrate systematic differences in the styles of colonial intrusion.[4] From the tactical point of view, some of the styles can be said to have been subtle and tactful while others were aggressive and tactless. It is then possible to argue that tactful intrusions preempted or neutralised rebellious responses while tactless intrusions performed the contrary. The style of intrusion is likely to remain significantly mediating even when the zones of intrusion are sensitive elements in the cores of a culture.

Intrusion and the Probability of Rebellion

External Actors	Zone of culture violation	Probability of rebellion
Intrusion	Cores	High*
Intrusion	Peripherals	Low*

*subject to the style of intrusion

Rebellion is a phenomenon of *contact*. And some interesting propositions exist in contemporary social science literature about *conflict*.[5] Quite clearly, there is no conflict without contact. In understanding nationalist rebellions the aligned concepts of contact and conflict can be usefully employed. One possible interpretation is that nationalist rebellions are phenomena of contact between cultures and societies, but they are of the conflictual form of active disapproval of the ramifications and consequences of particular contact. Nationalist rebellions involve the perception of contact as being culturally and politically asymmetrical, with the perceiving society or group persuaded of its disadvantaged position in the total situation of contact. This characteristic is somewhat close to the perception of relative deprivation.[6] Subject to the conceptual distinction between cultural cores and peripherals, relative deprivation will probably be a rebellion-promotive factor when the targets of deprivation fall within the cultural cores of a society. Deprivation in cultural peripherals might be assumed to have inferior potential for generating rebellious responses.

A slightly different, albeit compatible, conceptual avenue can be explored to reinforce the propositions so far outlined. Take stimulus. There is no response without some kind of direct, indirect, or incorporated stimulus. It is not entirely clear whether the intensity of social response depends on the depth of stimulus penetration into the social fabric of society. But if colonial intrusion is viewed as a stimulus and rebellion there against or acquiescence therein as the response, the present thesis can be reinforced by postulating that the deeper colonial stimulus penetrates into the cultural cores of a society the greater the likelihood that the penetrated society will consider itself violated and, consequently, the greater the probability that rebellion against colonial intrusion will arise. The stimulus-response interpretation must of course be cognisant of the problems of deciding on the critical depths of penetration, the modes of penetration, and the response behaviour of the penetrated actors.[7] Counter-models for explaining the response of the Baganda and the Kikuyu to British colonialism might pick up some of their theoretical gear from this area of problems.

Now, when the principal contention and the propositions of the style of intrusion are merged the theoretical position taken here becomes clearer. The propensity to rebel is not culturally intrinsic to some societies and absent from others. Rather rebellion will arise when tactless and agressive external intrusions into the cultural cores of a society are encountered. It is not accidental that societies without a history of deep external intrusions are also without exciting data for the students of rebellions.

There are good reasons for considering the Baganda in Uganda and the Kikuyu in Kenya comparable in several regards. Numerically, they are both the most dominant ethnic groups each numbering over two million people. Geographically, they are both situated in the centre of their respective countries where the national capitals have evolved. Developmentally, they remain the most advanced compared to their other compatriots in terms of social services, educational attainment and economic wealth. Historically, they have both experienced greater interactions with the British and other foreigners than any of their other compatriots have. Politically, they have both played central roles in mediating the evolution of their nations all the way from the period of colonial contact.

There were, however, important differences between the two people's traditional social organization, culture, and encounter with British colonialism. The Baganda had a hierarchical social organization built around a centralized monarchical structure that effectively controlled a large traditional kingdom.[8] But the Kikuyu had a non-monarchical system of social organization which was comparatively decentralized in its overall operation. And in post-independence politics the Kikuyu turned out to control power in Kenya while the Baganda did not in Uganda.

For all their intervention into the traditional society of the Baganda the British left virtually intact the central cultural institution of the Baganda. That institution was the monarchy as a political symbol and an administrative structure. It is true that the British had some occasional clashes with the monarchy; they were tempted to undercut its control on the Baganda and to coerce it into a useful colonial servant. But the one thing they never seriously tried to do was to dismantle the monarchy altogether. Ironically, they seemed to have been concerned to ensure its survival in spite of the general expansionist ambitions of colonial adventurism.

One of the most basic sources of conflict between colonialists and indigenous societies was the clash of European and African cultures as well as the sheer determination of the colonialists to dismantle

African cultures. But there was also a chance that the colonialists could have avoided some of the conflicts by not intruding too contemptuously on the cultural sensibilities of the natives. In their entry into Buganda the British appear to have been aware of that chance. By allowing the monarchy to continue essentially undisturbed the British facilitated the continuity of the central interger of Ganda cultural identification. The Baganda were not deprived of their symbolic and institutional point of unity, and their sense of cultural pride was given a chance to persist.

Discussing the continuity of the Buganda monarchy brings to fore the practice of Indirect Rule which was Lord Lugard's historic contribution to the administrative economy of colonization.[9] The British needed the monarchy, and as long as they succeeded in securing its cooperation in running colonial business in Buganda and extending the imperial flag beyond Buganda, the monarchy was not unduly harrassed. But what is additionally important for the present argument is that Indirect Rule was also an important instrument for sparing the British more encounters with rebellious natives. By leaving the natives' central institutions intact and working through them rather than overtly against them, the British were able to keep the responses of the natives well below the point of serious rebellion. Indirect Rule as an aspect of staying clear of the cultural cores of the Baganda was instrumental in neutralising Ganda rebellion against the British.

For emphasis by contrast, an examination of the degree to which the mere policy of allowing the monarchy to continue helped to allay the Baganda through most of the colonial period must extend to the post-colonial period. By the time Uganda finally became independent in 1962 the Buganda monarchy was still a formidable political institution which was bound to impinge on the future of the country as a whole. Apolo Milton Obote who led Uganda to independence was aware of the special political stature of the Buganda monarchy in the politics of developmental nation-building. So he skilfully courted the monarchy by contriving an alliance between his Uganda People's Congress and the Kabaka Yekka party which was expressly committed to the political preservation of the monarchy within the politics of independence. In the early 1960s Obote exploited the strategic value of collaborating with rather than fighting the monarchy at that particular time. By the mid—1960's Obote was ready to abandon collaboration with the monarchy and to move more resolutely in the direction of republicanization. When in 1967 Obote dismantled the monarchical apparatus throughout Uganda, sent the Kabaka of Buganda fleeing to Britain, and established a republic which rudely terminated the special role which the monarchy had played in the history of the country, the Baganda were especially angry at Obote. The man who had been the darling of the Baganda in 1962 when he had arranged for the Kabaka of Buganda to become the first President of independent Uganda, suddenly became perhaps the most hated leader among most of the Baganda once he had moved against the monarchy. Among the various forms of opposition which Obote had to encounter in running the Uganda republic was the special dimension of Buganda's unextinguished disaffection several years after the monarchy had been discontinued. Some of the alleged subversive activities in Obote's republic hinted at the complicity of the Baganda.

The explanation of nationalist rebellions should ideally aim at wide generalizability developed on the basis of exploring many cases of rebellion and non-rebellion. Short of that it should be possible to cite cases in history which shed light on the proposed explanation. The Masai of Eastern Africa serve as a further example which will remain semi-hypothetical. If the British had moved directly against the central cultural value of the Masai, namely cattle, they would probably have incurred bitter rebellion from the Masai people. In fact during the first decade of the 20th century there was some Masai resistance when the British interfered with some of the former's grazing grounds and when there was an attempt to fight rinderpest in the area. The Masai have not been left totally unassaulted by the advance of Western culture through British imperialism; they are presently under independent states in some of whose affairs they participate actively. But their cattle-centric culture has not been dismantled entirely. While the policy-makers are unlikely to discuss the problems of such a move in the terms suggested by this paper, it is clear that few politicians would be prepared to move recklessly against the cultural cores of the Masai. The point is hardly that the Masai in Kenya or Tanzania have a special capacity to pose a real threat on the battlefield with the military arm of the state. Rather, it is that because of the centrality of cattle to Masai culture, a serious move to dismantle cattlekeeping and its allied cultural paraphernalia would excite deep resentment among the Masai thereby risking rebellion. Whenever it can be helped politicians avoid exciting rebelliousness by intruding on those cultural elements which a people hold dear as the very essence of their identity.

The politics of development deal in the management of cultural change such that the perceived forces of development are reinforced and facilitated. The ministries of culture which exist in the developing countries testify to the need to harmonize the cultural persistence of the past with the developmental needs of the future. In that harmonisation new and broader indentities have to be created. Striking a balance in the formation of new identities without creating the psychological problem of cultural anomie is a challenge to nation-builders. The challenge involves the delicate task of penetrating cultures in order to shape new cultures, but the penetration must be calculated to ensure that the penetrated people do not view it as a declaration of war on their cultural being. It involves penetration calculated to induce co-operation rather than rebellion.

This assessment is most compelling when the total historical experience of Anglo-Baganda encounter is viewed as a cummulative thrust of cultural penetration. Besides leaving intact the monarchy the British engaged in a number of remarkable strategies of colonial penetration designed to improve co-operation from the Baganda. They played on the security of Buganda by involving themselves in beating off some of Buganda's traditional enemies; they were ready to protect Buganda if Buganda helped them in turn. Turning to land the British secured some of Buganda's land through a series of measures and ordinances[10] which appear to have been designed not to deprive the monarchy too suddenly of its material base. Interestingly, the British took some of Buganda's land while on the other hand they rewarded Buganda with a chunk of Bunyoro's territory in recognition of Buganda's military role in helping the British to defeat the Kingdom of Bunyoro.

Although Indirect Rule stands out as a vital innovation in the political economy of colonial style, there is another remarkable element in the way in which the British went about securing land previously owned by Buganda. The term *gradual deprivation* is proposed to refer to their style of agrarian acquisition. The style involved acquiring land in such a way as not to provoke large-scale Ganda objections at a time.[11] Thus, the land was taken gradually piece after piece over the years through a series of measures and ordinances. In the end Buganda lost large chunks of land but the spread duration of her loss dispersed her reactions over historical time. Dispersion can amount to neutralization. In colonial days thinly spread native reactions were what you needed to keep the natives busy but not actively rebellious. The gradual deprivation of land from the Baganda fitted into this calculation. In its inconspicuous nature gradual deprivation is unlikely to be dramatically provocative.

In a sharp contrast with the story of Buganda, the encounter of the Kikuyu and the British produced the Mau Mau rebellion. The rebellion arose out of the decision by the British to do in Kikuyuland what they would not do in Buganda. Plainly speaking, the British assaulted directly the cultural cores of the Kikuyu and thereby provoked a Kikuyu rebellion. The rebellion arose from the psychological and material depth of colonial violation of Kikuyu society. The territory where the Kikuyu made their home became especially attractive to the British who appropriated it to themselves regardless of Kikuyu interests. There was a certain aggressiveness and an arrogant finality in the manner in which the British snatched what once belonged to the Kikuyu. But there was also a rebellion, one of the most dramatic of nationalist rebellions in Africa.

In Buganda British colonialism spared much of the traditional social organization, important institutions and relations were allowed to continue. But in Kikuyuland traditional social organization was assaulted in the course of re-locating masses of people from their traditional homes to make way for colonial farms. People were simply moved out of their territorial homes and herded into locations on the fringes of extensive colonial farms on which they were to provide slave labour. The lands which formed the nerve centre of an agricultural society were crudely deprived of the Kikuyu. The British went so far as to interfere with Kikuyu identity by challenging practices like the circumcision of females. Circumcision of both males and females had always been fundamental to the rites of initiation in this African society. In fact the British themselves were not entirely unfamiliar with the circumcision of males if only for alleged hygenic reasons. But what they could not accept was the circumcision of females among the

Kikuyu. They developed passionate arguments to the effect that the practice was inhuman, immoral, and uncivilized; as a part of their evangelized humanitarian duties they exhorted the natives against female circumcision. In the absence of a clear medical warning that the ritual clipping off of the tiny piece from the tip of the clitoris constituted a health hazard, or that the sexual efficiency of the female in the realms of intercourse and procreation was likely to be undermined, colonial evangelists nevertheless sought to discourage the clipping of the clitoris. In so doing they intruded on sensitive areas of self-identity and cultural respectability among the Kikuyu.

But the Kikuyu rebellion does not testify to a unique cultural endowment of rebelliousness. The Mau Mau together with the earlier protest movements like the Kikuyu Association which was formed in 1920 is not conclusive proof that the Kikuyu are intrinsically more rebellious than their neighbours. In fact this position can be extended into the realms of consciousness and the propensity to participate in politics. The point is that in many ways the Kikuyu were more deeply violated as a society, more offended as a culture, more coerced into interaction with foreign cultures, and more intensively oppressed by settler colonialism than their neighbours. Their cummulative reactions turned out to be more dramatic in method and ambition in response to their more ruthless colonial predicament. Their reactions had to do with the degree to which they had been penetrated and the roles to which they had been subjected. *No amount of propaganda could establish in favour of the Kikuyu that the Mau Mau rebellion would have arisen all the same if the British had chosen to establish their farms, cities, settlements, and railway routes in central Tanganyika rather than in the highlands of Kenya.* The Kikuyu would not have been in contact with the British had the latter chosen to settle elsewhere. Had the stimulus of colonial penetration been applied elsewhere in a comparable manner the stories of rebellious heroism would be focusing elsewhere. Needless to say, these comments reinforce the denial of cultural determinism in explaining nationalist rebellions. Care must always be taken not to equate historical accidents with the functions of cultural uniqueness.

Presumptions about cultural uniqueness and their related temptation to explain events in terms of cultural determination often lead to paradoxes and inexplicable events in collective history. In a conference paper on Kikuyu and Masai responses to the establishment of British administration G.H. Mungeam belaboured the paradox that while the Masai as a militarist pastoral people were expected to provide more resistance to the British, it was instead the agricultural Kikuyu who resited the British most dramatically.[12] Mungeam found the historical paradox to be worthy of scholarly attention. But the alleged paradox appears to have existed only because of superficial cultural expectations. Moreover the paradox was not an important theoretical discovery. Strictly speaking it existed analytically because factual evidence simply flew in the face of cultural prediction which is the weakest point of cultural determinism. Someone had told the British that the Masai were warriors so the former expected military resistance from the Masai. From the settled agricultural Kikuyu the British expected less resistance. But when the Kikuyu turned out to rebel more seriously than the Masai the so-called paradox emerged. Well, there was no paradox of theoretical interest, and Mungeam ought not to have wondered. The story was straightforward. The British found that they needed more from the Kikuyu than they did from the Masai, and they went ahead and got it. But what they got deprived the Kikuyu more extensively and violated them more deeply as a culture than was the case with the Masai. The Kikuyu lost practically all their usable land which was culturally vital to them, they were physically and culturally disrupted; but the Masai kept most of their grazing territory and continued keeping their vital cattle, their cattlecentric culture remained much less disrupted. The Kikuyu did not like it so they rebelled against the British and demanded their land back, among other things.

The concept of gradual deprivation and its limited capacity for provocation was introduced in regard to British agrarian acquisitions in Buganda. In their acquisitions in Kikuyuland the British preferred to be less inhibited and certainly more overt. Gradual deprivation was not applied. Rather the British simply moved in bluntly and grabbed all the attractive land there was to have; they established farms and forced the Kikuyu to provide labour on the farms. The comparative suddenness, aggressiveness, and large scale of the land involved, compounded with the misfortunes that befell the Kikuyu as a result of forcible land transfer made deprivation just too conspicuous. Conspicuous deprivation of that nature, especially when it fell within the cultural cores of the Kikuyu, had to be provocative. It is interesting to note how agrarian greed forced a method of acquisition which was so unimaginative as to provoke a major rebellion against the general interests of colonial settlers as well as the grander ambitions of Imperial control.

To sum up then; the prospect of Baganda rebelling actively against British colonial intrusion was neutralized because the British stayed clear of assaulting too rudely the institution of the monarchy around which the rest of the cultural fabric of Buganda was woven. Through Indirect Rule which recognized the effectiveness of traditional social organization and political systems the monarchy was allowed to continue. That continuance provided the Baganda with a durable focus of cultural identity. Having allowed the monarchy to continue providing the basis of cultural continuity, British colonialists were able to secure the co-operation of Buganda most of the time. We say most of the time because the story of co-operation was not perfectly smooth from start to end; there were occasions when disagreements led to exile for the Kabaka of Buganda. The evolution of colonialism also meant undermining the monarchy in some regards, the environment in which the monarchy had to survive was gradually weakened. But the monarchy was never dismantled. It survived into postcolonial days to be terminated by the republicanization of Uganda under President Obote in 1967.

But the story of Kikuyu encounter with the British was a sharp contrast. The Kikuyu rebelled against the British in the Mau Mau partly because the British had deprived the Kikuyu of land which was culturally central to their being. Not only had the land been deprived, culture, identity, and social organization had been disrupted as the people were physically re-located and herded into locations. Deprivation had been too conspicuous while culture had been too ruthlessly assaulted by foreigners.

In analyses which adopt historical perspectives there is always the problem of how to link particular events to particular stimuli in the past. Restrospective causal linkages across time are often hazardous. An objection could be raised that colonialism entered Kikuyuland in the last quarter of 1800 but the Mau Mau rebellion materialised in the 1950s; how then can the Mau Mau be considered a response to those many years of encounter? Could we not explain the Mau Mau in terms of more recent social stimulation? Well, the Mau Mau should perhaps be considered a delayed response which needed time for enough psychological accummulation to occur as a prerequisite for its final eruption. There have of course been some spontaneous or anomic collective rebellions in political history, but most collective responses take time to emerge from the combination and multiplication of individual dispositions. Emotional accummulation takes time to get collectivized. It took years of encounter and emotional accummulation on the part of the Kikuyu for the final explosion to force its presence on the political horizon of colonial Kenya. During the interim period other factors certainly came into play to mediate the ultimate rebellion. Most of the variables associated with modernization may be viewed as having mediated the materialization of the Mau Mau. But even then, when the rebellion finally exploded, it manifested an agrarian emphasis of politicized grievances; it revolved around that central cultural element of the Kikuyu – the land – which the British had grabbed with consuming greed.

Finally, cross-cultural research and theory contruction concern themselves with explanations which are culturally transcendental. The extent of generalization across cultures and societies is a central interest. Even Karl Marx shared with contemporary theory-builders the ambition to generalise. And implicit in that ambition is a refusal to accept cultural determinism as its acceptance would undermine much of what scientific social theory is about. If Marx had allowed for cultural determinism in respect of revolution and radicalism, he would have thereby foregone the opportunity to claim that all people are capable of executing revolution in given conditions. He would have had to excuse some people on account of their cultures not being of the kind that facilitate revolutions. His explanatory instrument would have had to be selective and therefore diminished in its universality. The present proposition that nationalist rebellions are a function of the depth and style of external penetration into a people's cultural cores also rejects the premises of cultural determinism. It leaves open the possibility that any culture could be pushed into a position of rebellion against intruders. Theoretically, monarchies just as well as nomadic cultures are equally capable of rebellion if they are aggressively penetrated into their cores by rude foreigners. The business of conferring honours for heroic actions in nationalist history should never overlook the experiential differences of encounter in assessing the comparative ignition and dampening of rebellion. Heroism is too human to be subject to cultural monopoly.

Notes and References

1. Ted Robert Gurr, *Why Men Rebel* (Princeton: Princeton University Press, 1970).
2. Unfortunately there is a paradoxical limitation. On the one hand interdisciplinary approaches are desirable, but on the other hand they are increasingly complicated rather than simplified by growing sophistication in the different disciplines.
3. James C. Davies (ed) *When Men Revolt and Why: A Reader in Political Violence and Revolution* (London: Free Press, 1971).
4. Thomas Hodgkin, *Nationalism in Colonial Africa* (1956); see for example the section on policies of the powers' pp. 29 — 59.
5. Lois Kriesberg, *The Sociology of Social Conflicts* (Englewood Cliffs, New Jersey Hall, Inc., 1973).
6. Ted Robert Gurr, *Why Men Rebel* (1970).
7. At the highest level of theoretical rigour these matters would have to be resolved empirically.
8. Consult the works of Lloyd Fallers especially his *The King's Men* (London: Oxford University Press, 1964); and *Inequality: Special Stratification Reconsidered* (Chicago: University of Chicago Press, 1973).
9. Lord Lugard, *The Dual Mandate in Tropical Africa* (London: Frank Cass and co. 1965).
10. For a listing of some of these consult T.B. Kabwegyere, "Land and the Growth of Social Stratification in Uganda: A Sociological Interpretation" in Bethwell A. Ogot (ed) *Hadith 6: History and Social Change in East Africa* (Nairobi: East African Publishing House, 1976) p. 124..
11. The concept is developed to capture a pattern in colonial actions over time regardless of whether the actions were collectively calculated over the entire colonial period or whether they were individually expedient from time to time. Some policy analyses proceed this way too by deriving patterns from seemingly chaotic governmental actions.
12. G.H. Mungeam, "Kikuyu and Masai Responses to the Establishment of British Administration in the East Africa Protectorate," *University of East Africa Social Science Conference Proceedings*, Nairobi, December, 1966, Volume 4, Number 438.

MISSIONARIES, COLONIAL GOVERNMENT AND SECRET SOCIETIES IN SOUTH-EASTERN IGBOLAND, 1920–1950

OGBU U. KALU
Department of Religion
University of Nigeria, Nsukka

In our recent historiography a critical and nationalist approach has replaced the hagiographical celebration of the triumph of christianity by missionary writers. They wrote propagandist accounts to boost morale and materials. But now the ideology which propped the missionary enterprise is questioned, and missionaries are being characterized as agents of imperialist colonial governments.

This nationalist perspective has been most clearly purveyed by E. A. Ayandele whose stimulating writings constitute an important niche in modern Nigerian historiography. Put succinctly, Ayandele argued that the intrusion of the white man into Nigeria has wrongly been studied "in the light of the administrator and trader, the missionary receiving no more than a casual observation". In fact, missionaries were the *path-finders* of British influence; their *propaganda* not only prepared the way for the government and exploiters but ensured the smooth and peaceful occupation of colonialist forces. Ayandele posited three reasons why the missionaries easily provided such a link: the political environment, patriotic instincts and the logical outcome of their activity which willy nilly made them emissaries of both the government and chiefs. He used the examples of the christianization of Yorubaland and the Niger Delta communities to illustrate the politically pernicious influence of missionaries who ostensibly bore the Gospel but covertly ensured the subjugation of black peoples.[1] This fact explains the importance he attached to the nationalists who fought against the politics of the new religion.

This paper does not intend to debate whether the missionary was a covert agent of imperialism or not. Evidence abounds of collaboration between missions, colonial government and mercantile powers. Rather, it is argued that the relationship between these three powers was far more complex than it is often portrayed. The clash over the role of secret societies is a classic illustration of the complexity. For specific case study, the focus is on South-Eastern Igboland* from 1920 to 1950 when the conflict between secret societies and missionaries assumed serious proportions and occupied the attention of the colonial government officers.

*We refer to Ngwa, Aba, Umuahia, Bende as far as Arochukwu as South-Eastern Igboland.

[1] E. A. Ayandele, *The Missioanry Impact on Modern Nigeria, 1842–1914* (London: Longmans, 1966), chapt. 2.

As mentioned earlier, there is no doubt that missionaries collaborated with traders and the colonial government. Their racial identity and common image of africans bred an underlying ideological homogeneity. The quests for Gold and Glory were sanctified with spreading the Word of God. The traders ensured transport and supplies for missionaries while the colonial government provided grants-in-aid and security. Missionaries, who appear to be the weaker of the trio, domesticated European culture and supplied intelligence data on the communities whose souls they sought to capture. District Officers, in their Annual Reports, often measured the spread of Pax Britannica by the yardstick of the spread of missionary influence.[2]

But the inner relationship of the trio was not as harmonious. They differed on fundamental points. Mongo Beti's novel, *The Poor Christ of Bomba*[3] captures vividly the element of tension or dissonance. For one, the missionaries were often scandalized by the loose morality and rapacity of the traders. The merchants seem to be exploding the myth that every white man in England was a christian. The traders, on their part, took every occasion to betray the hypocrisy and failings of missionaries. For instance, when Captain Burton wrote the report of his *Mission to Gelele King of Dahomey*. the Wesleyan Methodist Mission at Whydah was put on the defensive while Sierra-Leonian Anglicans were bristling against his earlier exposee.[4] The fact that most missionaries were ill-trained and came from artisan classes did not help their image; they could not expect the type of respect accorded a rector in England from merchants.

The more interesting relationship was that which existed between missions and the colonial government. Initially, the Roman Catholic Mission was French and so, they were on the defensive in a British colony. They bent double to please. For instance, their educational policy was deliberately attuned to government's man-power needs. The Protestant missionaries, on the other hand, easily assumed that as co-agents of British influence, colonial officials were obliged to assist them and to heed their informed and godly advice. So, missionaries were often loudly critical of colonial officials and their policies. Mary Slessor once tried to bully a young District Officer at Arochukwu to set aside his previous punishment of people of Akpap who had refused to build a road. The road ran through a piece of land which they alleged to be sacred. The D.O. informed the Resident at Calabar that the grove was not traditionally sacred because

2 See, National Archives, enugu (NAE), C/277/18 CALPROF 5/8/228.

3 Mongo Beti, *The Poor Christ of Bomba* (London: Heinemann, 1971).

4 Captain Burton, *A Mission to Gelele King of Dahomey* 2 vols. (London, 1864); W. Rainy, *The Censor Censured* (London, 1865); Paul Ellingworth, "Beginnings of Methodism in Ouidah", *Bulletin of the Soc. for African Church Hist.*, 1/2 (Dec. 1963), 35–40.

the secret society which had just made it sacred was a new one. The land could not, under the circumstances, be regarded as a communal sacred grove. Mary Slessor caustically told the D.O. that she lived with the people and knew that the land was sacred and that it was impertinent of the officer to ignore her advice. The Resident excused her intemperance on account of her age, and cautioned the officer that the lady was now a legendary figure who must be handled with care; that, in the future, her correspondences should be forwarded to the Resident to treat.[5] Mary Slessor's claim was shared by most missionaries and since there could not be two captains steering a ship to different shores, altercations arose.

Beyond this structural conflict there was disagreement over specific issues like educational policy, ranging from goal, curriculum, personnel to funding. The missions used schools as an aspect of denominational rivalry and evangelism while the government wanted clerks to man the new administrative machinery. However, the long debates on personnel and funding are beyond the scope of this paper. Suffice it to say that the government would have preferred fewer and better-equipped schools and wished that opening of schools should not be an aspect of missionary rivalry for spheres.[6]

But it does appear that the most sensitive area of disagreement was over the attitude to indigenous cultures. The nature of this disagreement could best be understood within the context of South-Eastern Igboland during the period of the first contact with British influence.

British influence in the Igbo heartland was established in the first decade of the 1900's and it took about five more years to actually register an overall presence. Just then, the First World War broke out. The political goals of the Colonial Office were to quell opposition and build a new economic order and a new administrative organ through the Residents, District Commissioners with their Assistants and the Native Courts. The aim was to do these while maintaining core indigenous political and cultural structures. As G. I. Jones put it,

> "What the colonial government did and subsequent governments have always done was to leave the internal government of these communities alone but to provide a superstructure which brought them together into larger units and so tied them into the wider administrative organisation which it constructed for the country"[7]

[5] RHODES HOUSE LIB., OXFORD, MSS. AFR. S. 1037(1)–(6).

[6] NAE. OW 20/1920A RIVPROF 8/8/18.

[7] G. I. Jones, "From Direct to Indirect Rule in Eastern Nigeria", *Odu* (University of Ife Journal of African Studies), 2, 2 (Jan. 1966), 74.

Thus, the officials attempted to select warrnat chiefs who also had viable authority within the indigenous political structure. Traditional cultures would be left intact as long as they neither constituted opposition to British rule nor impeded the new administrative structure. Limited human and material resources engendered the policy of limited involvement.

Within this perspective, the government moved against identifiable cultural norms – human sacrifices, killing of twins, oracles which competed against native courts and slavery. Children rescued from slavery and twin murder were fostered out to missionaries, educational institutions and prominent local chieftains. The government paid upkeep charges ranging from five to nine pounds per child. District Officers were ordered to visit the children regularly and to make yearly returns of children-in-care within thei districts.[8]

The government was paranoid about oracles. After the elaborate expedition to wipe out the Aro Ibin Ukpabi (Long Juju), officials kept a close watch on its possible revival. In 1912 a second expedition was sent against the revivalists but the tradition persisted as was noted in various District Officers' reports in 1916, 1917, 1921 and 1922. In 1916, seven men were convicted in Arochukwu District for taking part in rituals of Ibin Ukpabi. But the more revealing case occurred in Ogoja Province in 1922. The people of Akpanwudele in Ikwo-Abakaliki area had suffered a series of disasters, drought, high infant mortality, epidemics and poor farm yields. The chiefs appealed to a certain Aro man, Ugoji, who lived in nearby Amaka. Ugoji left for a month, made preparations and led a delegation of Akpanwudele people to Asaga (Aro) near Atani. He was paid a fee of $3.10s. while a ram and cock were provided for the juju. At the grove, Ugoji called out to the Juju, "Perripi, Ndewo!" The juju answered back. He, then, introduced his clinets and their predicament. According to the deposition in a court trial,

> "We heard a voice say that Ongele and Alowa are witches. They are the cause of all this trouble. You must kill them".

But realizing the consequences of such judgement under the new dispensation, the Juju added rather cautiously

> "but do it quietly otherwise there will be trouble".

In fact, there was trouble when the chiefs accepted the verdict and commissioned two age grades to execute the alleged offenders.[9] The Resident, Calabar, noted that there were so many ravines in Arochukwu that the persistence of *Ibin Ukpabi* cult could not be wiped out.

[8] NAE. C. Conf 682/14 CALPROF 5/4/365, 5/4/366; C.681/1915 CALPROF 5/5/428.

[9] NAE. C/£0/21 CALPROF 4/10/31; C.145/7 CALPROF 5/7/97.

More important is the fact that the new judiciary system had not grown deep roots in the 1920's and the new order provided neither solutions to deeply felt needs nor viable means to control space-time events. On the contrary, the emergent forms caused confusion and bred opposition, however weak. The new interest in Ogbunorie Juju based at Ezimoha (Owerri) in the 1920's was alleged by British officials to be a form of revival of the Long Juju. It not only divined the culprits in cases of theft but sanctified opposition to the new order. For instance, a community would visit Ezimoha to perform rituals and swear that

> "If any of the people in our town attend the Whiteman's court or do what he tells us for the space of one year, Ogbunorie must kill him".

The clients would touch their throats with a stick provided by the priest. Invoking the "Unlawful Societies Ordinance" section 3, the Political Officer in the Escort covering Okigwi and Owerri Districts ordered the destruction of the grove and the arrest of twe /e priests.[10]

This act must have pleased the missionaries who came at the heels of the Escort. As long as the government used military clout to destroy customs which the missionaries considered to be harbarous, the two agents were in full agreement. But the missionaries wanted the government to go the whole hog in the destruction of Igbo cultures. The missionaries realized that Igbo "heathenish and pagan" religions were intricably woven into other cultural ingredients; therefore, all were to be destroyed before a new christian religion could be radicated. Their analysis was accurate. They plumbed deeper tc capture the souls of their hosts and realized that selective destruction or official policy of limited involvement will not achieve their goal. Right up to the 1940's one could hardly find a missionary whose perception of Igbo cultures was as deep and empathetic enough as G.I. Jones's, a District Officer, who in 1943 wrote on "The Development of Nigerian Arts and Crafts". Jones bemoaned the dangerous loss of indigenous arts and crafts industry as foreign artifacts became the fashion. A. E. Afigbo has shown the antecedent, in 1938, of Jones's report in an analysis of Murray, Hunt-Cooke and J. O. Field's contribution to the founding of museums in Nigeria.[11]

A crucial aspect of missionary attitude to traditional cultures was that in spite of the biblical doctrine of creation, "the missionaries' image of the non-Europeans blended with the existing cultural arrogance and with the pseudo-scientific argument for racial superio-

[10] NAE. PC 10/1911 UJPROF 6/1/2

[11] NAE. OW 5050E UMDIV.3/1/565 f. 27-30; A. .E. Afigbo, "The Museum and Rural Society in Nigeria" Paper Presented at Silver Jubilee of Jos Museum, Aparil, 1977.

rity"[12] which characterized the 19th Century. The missionaries contributed the raw materials for the racialist theories of the age. Missionaries collected cultural curiosities and wrote detailed, embellished reports about their hosts. These propagandist reports were published in gentlemen's magazines like *Blackwell's Magazine* and provided raw date for arm-chair theorists. Simon Fraser of *The Golden Bough* built his evolutionary theory of the origin of primitive religion on such data. Even more infectious, such paternalistic and racist ideology pervaded recruitment and fund-raising campaigns. New missionaries and children imbibed and perpetuated it.[13] Besides this dose of superiority were bound to clash with African world-view and the sense of dignity which characterized religious and social cultures.

Armed with such an ideology, missionary strategy in those early days was to literally skim off and foster a band of converts. To be a christian meant rejection of one's societal customs especially those connected with marriage, burial customs and social clubs. An Owerri Provincial Resident in 1919 pin-pointed the goal of missionary enterprise in this period:

> The influence of the Churches is increasing to such an extent that parish cohesion and organization is fast becoming at least as strong as indigenous cohesion under Native Chiefs.[14]

However, this note of optimism could not be fully maintained in the 1920's especially in Ngwa, Umuahia and Bende areas. Traditional forces which were thrown into disarray at the first contact with Europeans attempted to reorganize. The conflict with traditionalists ranged over a wide front but the opposition of the secret societies became the most serious and at some point subsumed the other issues.

To appreciate the seriousness of the conflict, one has to understand the role of secret societies in South-Eastern Igboland. The predominance of secret societies is a cultural peculiarity of these border communities of Igboland. The societies range from young people's *Obon* to more serious affaris like *Akang* and *Ekpe/Okonko*. All are borrowed from the non-Igbo peoples, especially the Ekoi of the right bank of the Cross River. Other cultural groups like the Efik and Aro assisted the Ekoi in the spread of the secret societies.

In the social order of these areas, "the secret societies and the age groupings in particular symbolize the village as a cohesive whole,

[12] P. D. Curtin, "Scientific Racism and the British Theory of Empire", *Journ. of the Hist. Soc. of Nigeria, 2/1 (Dec. 1960), 48.*

[13] Ogbu Kalu, "Children in the Missionary Enterprise of the 19th Century" forthcoming in *The Calabar Historical Journal, 2, 1 (1977).*

[14] NAE. File 42/19 OWDIST 9/5/6.

pulling men from the domestic routine to meet with nonrelations in a wider social world, with its own sense of history, ceremony and ritual".[15] Sex and wealth differentiations, the power and wonder of the spirit world, the mystic of secrecy and in some cases, political power attracted people to join seceret societies.

Obon paid no political dividends but parents ensured that their young male children (from the age of ten) joined it. If a father or uncle failed to pay for a child's initiation, the mother would provide the fee (money and food) to any male surrogate to act as a guardian. When *Obon* is being played, the guardian or sponsor would take the frightened child by the hand and walk to the precinct of the cloth-house and announce his intentions. After the necessary fees and negotiation, the child would be led in and shown the mysteries while members give him knocks on the head for having been a fearful weakling, *Ikpo.* An oath of utmost secrecy with threats of dire consequences would be administered. The salient features of the initiation ceremony contain the social importance: a child is weaned from his family (nuclear and extended) into a wider social goup where he begins to know his age-group or peers. He becomes distinguished from females and is socialized into male roles and group activities like bird hunting, fishing, farming and so on. He acquires the skills and knowledge of customs necessary for survival in his environment. It was considered embarrassing and a social stigma to be told to stay indoors with females when *Obon* was playing. Other children felt free to molest such a boy because he had neither *protectors* nor rights. Some went to the extent of never calling him by his name but by the nick-name "Little Ignoramus" (nwa ikpo). *Obon* provided a great source of entertainment: the rich rhythm and theexerting dance style suit the energetic young people. Moreover, the temptation to betray the secret is so great that secret societies offer a very impressive schooling in the moral solidarity among these young boys.

As the child grew to be a young adult, he could decide to join *Akang.* The fee for this society was much higher. The initiation ritual put the candidate through an obstruction or endurance course as a test of his manliness. The location for the ritual is usually in the bush behind the village compound. The leaders would be blindfolded the candidate in such a way that he could see very hazily. His task was to take a specified route through the bush to the *Obu* (compound hall) where *Akang* was being played. Members hid along the route to beat him, make frightening noises or placed logs of wood on the candidate's course. The candidate dared not touch the blindfold or take a

[15] Simon Ottenberg, *Leadership and Authority in an African Society* (University of Washington Press, 1971), 154.

different course. Some unlucky candidates weakened from the blows an ran back to the village – such failures incurred worse taunts. Those who suffered through it all were initiated.

In the days when inter-village warfares were rampant or when Ohafia, Abam and Uwana communities were head-hunters, joining Akang was like a test of one's abilities to work with a group and suvive the long, tedious head-hunting campaigns. When a raiding band was organized, no consideration could be given to a young man who had not joined *akang*. This meant that he will never parade a head. Peers would tease him as an *ujo* (coward). Girls would avoid accepting his hands in marriage. In the village people would refer to him as merely a pair of scrotum but not a man.

In certain parts of South-Eastern Igboland such as Ututu, Ihe and Ibeku, Akang was regarded as the premier social club. Entry fees were therefore, high enough to reflect the social prestige. In most others, however, the most important social club was the *Ekpe* or *Okonko*. It had seven grades and it cost about 800 manillas (in 1920 currency) to join the lowest grade.[16] In the pre-colonial period, virtually every village in this part of Igboland possessed a club house and the paraphernalia of the masquerade for outings. Social status and wealth could be measured by membership in the society. Meanwhile, pressure was put on those who did not join and various forms of discount arrangements were made to encourage fathers who wished to enroll their children or for wealthy freed slaves. The situation was such that every one of local prominence joined. In 1933, Chiefs Kamanu and Nnadede of Chambele informed the D.O., Aba, that "any one who called himself chief or Eze ala should (be) able (to) join Okonko in our Town. It is same at Azumini and Ohanku; any one who fail to join Okonko Club in their town should not be called Eze ala or chief. It is our old custom".[17] Once a member in one village, participation in Ekpe activities in other villages was allowed. Besides the financial earning when new men joined, the club collected all palm wine tapped on certain days and drank it in their club house. Like all club houses, the Ekpe ones provided resting, gossiping, drinking places for members only. But the financial consideration was much: membership was regarded as a form of investment of money that would yield dividends as new members joined.

[16] NAE. CSE 3661/14. The MSS ordered in 1920 and produced in 1922. Note confusion of Okonko with Akang. They are quite different. In some places, Okonko is used for the masquerade and Ekpe for the club. This may indicate that both Okonko and Ekpe came from different cultural influences.

[17] NAE. OW 529/20 ABADIST 1/26/278 f.9. (17 b) NAE. OW54/20, ABADIST 1/12/54.

This tendency to regard Okonko as a mutual aid society was best exhibited by certain people from Amuozu Ihie (Ngwa) who begged the D.O., in June 1920, to permit the formation of a club called *Amuozu Ihie Okonko Society* whose motto shall be, "Bear ye one another's burden". The aims were to foster unity, relieve one another in times of troubles, distress and death and encourage interest in their country. Perhaps, they wished to christianize Okonko but the D.O. was not interested.

A crucial aspect of the Ekpe society is that in certain areas typified by Ohuhu and Ngwa Igbo "government was shared by the kinship system and the secret societies. Decisions reached in the lineage councils were enforced largely by the Ekpe, Akang and Okonko".[18] Adult secret societies served as upholders of morality. They welded the instruments of social control.

In others, the secret societies were purely social clubs and were not a part of decision-making process. They provided entertainment and also a member could look forward to a decent burial ceremony by the club. The D.O. at Bende vividly described the gaiety and social significance of an Okonko ceremony. He had watched an Okonko outing in Uzuakoli:

> Every man in the village was out in his best clothes. There were children but no women to be seen. Palm wine was flowing freely. Each quarter of the village had its own object or shrine, which was paraded through the village. Several were gaily bedecked pyramids about 10' tall, hollow frames covered by clothes and others adornments. One was a kind of stage elephant with men inside it. From within these came a continual grunting noise. When the object moved about, it was preceded by a herald shouting the single word, *Ekpe* at the top of his voice and closely followed by a throng who I assumed were members of that particular club. As the procession advanced, everyone on its path had to retire or stand aside under the eaves of the houses linking the village street. This would appear to be a demonstraton of the society's former power.[19]

In the precolonial days, secret societies were so powerful that the outing of a secret society sent uninitiates scurrying. This created a subtle pressure on male non-members.

The structure of the secret societies meant that in any given village in this part of Igboland, they were regarded as steps in social and economic advancement. The very successful individuals not only showed their status by marrying many wives, they tenaciously climbed the various ranks of Okonko society. It was a prideful cultural form which engendered dignity. In certain places, Okonko was virtually regarded as the Government. Since the ruling kingroup were also members, the two bases of authority merged. Even in areas,

[18] A. E. Afigbo, "The Indigenous Political Systems of the Igbo", *Tarikh*, 4, 2 (1972), 13–23.

[19] NAE. OW 8358 UMPROF 5/1/138.

like Ohafia, where the society was a private club, totally unconnected with government, the status of her members, including the rulers, gave her considerable influence. As the sociologist, Georg Simmel observed, the sociological significance of the secret is that it determines the reciprocal relations among those who share it in common: reciprocal confidence among members, protection, and strength.[20] Beyond these, secret societies contributed to the development of literature in traditional society. They propagated *nsididi* (secret language) which perhaps originated from neighbouring non-Igbo groups. Some years ago, M. M. Green collected 108 sayings or proverbs which she alleged to have been recited during Okonko outings at Ohuhu; thus, Okonko contributed to the preservation and propagation of communal wisdom and values. It is most unlikely that all these sayings were recited in connection with Okonko only.[21]

Given the nature and importance of the secret societies in South-Eastern Igboland, the conflict with the new christian change-agents was inevitable. With varying degrees of intensity, the conflict has persisted to the present day as the recent clash between Agbala Society and the Presbyterian Mission in Edda shows. The conflict, however, appeears to have been most intense in the first decade of British colonization until the visit of the Lt. Governor in 1922. As Bishops Howell and Lasbery noted, persecution of christians by the secret societies became less blatant after the visit for about three years. Matters flared up briefly in 1925 and 1933. By 1951, however, the D.O. Bende, commented that the Okonko society was strongest in Ibeku, Olokoro, Ubakala clans around Umuahia and in the Ala Ala Clan near the Aba boundary. He insinuated that the power of the society was generally on the wane. A major conflict in that year confounded the assessment but there is little doubt that both the colonial government and the missions had made enough impact in the 1950's to curtail the real power of the secret societies.[22]

The problem, however, is to explain why the conflict was so intense between 1920 and 1922. Perhaps the influenza of 1918/19 caused anxious searching and fingers pointed to the new order. A. E. Afigbo has laid the roots of the so-called Nwaobiala or Dancing Women Movement of 1925 to this.[23] More certain is the fact that

[20] Kurt H. Wolff (ed), *The Sociology of Georg Simmel* (Toronto: Collier-Macmillan Co., 1950), 345.

[21] M. M. Green, "The Sayings of the Okonkọ Society of the Igbo-Speaking People", *Bull. SOAS*, 21 (1958), 157–173; "The Unwritten Literature of the Igbo-Speaking People of South-Eastern Nigeria", *Bull. SOAS*, 12 (1948), 838–843.

[22] NAE. OW 557/20 RIVPROF 8/8/433;OW 8358 UMPROF 5/1/138.

[23] A. E. Afigbo, "Revolution and Reaction in Eastern Nigeria, 1900–1929". *JHSN*, 3, 3 (1966), 539–558.

the full implications of missionary enterprise became palpable and the indigenous authorities fought back. Women petitioners from Ngwa latched their plea against monogamy, sexual habits of teachers and increased incidences of exogamy to the fact that Okonko secret society which bred moral discipline and order was under attack from christians. Umuahia women remonstrated that they "asked the Niger Pastorate to come here and train up our children but not to interfere with any Society".[24] The scales have not fallen off their eyes as their guests became bent on turning the society topsy-turvy. Secondly, the Colonial Government was about to formulate a policy on native customs. Communities took the opportunity to defend their customs against the invectives of missionaries and to influence the proposed official policy. In September 1920, the Lieuter nt Governor of Southern Provinces ordered that a book should be compiled on the customs and superstitions of the tribes of the Colony and Southern Provinces. He added that the book

> "will not only contain valuable information for the instruction of junior officers of the Administrative Service and for the study and reference by all officers but will also serve to notice both customs which should be discouraged by the Administraion and customs which tend towards progress and may therefore receive encouragement."[25]

District Officers invited the Native Court clerks and missionaries in their relevant districts to submit reports. The efforts of E. M. Falk, D. O. at Aba and one of the most enterprising District Officers in the period are fully documented. Thirdly, the Lt. Governor was due to visit the following year and each party loudly peritioned against the other.

Fourthly, new Native Court system had recently taken off and it became quite obvious that the Warrant Chiefs used the court to defend attacks, real or alleged, on the secret societies, especially on Okonko/Ekpe. The chiefs did not see this as misuse of the judiciary. At Aba, members of the Okonko told the D.O. that

> "If any member says that Okonko is nothing, we have to issue summons and claim £4".[26]

Those at Oloko put the matter just as bluntly

> "We have decided to inform your honour that anyone who is a member of the Okonko club who refuses to carry the orders according to our native customs we will bring him before the court for a fine of ten pounds or six months imprisonment but the fine should go to the Government Revenue".[27]

[24] NAE. OW 557/20 RIVPROF 8/8/433 f.48A.

[25] NAE. OW 54/20 ABADIST 1/12/54 Circular dated 3/9/20.

[26] *Ibid.*

[27] NAE. OW 557/20 RIVPROF 8/8/433.

Since they defined "member" to include current as well as those who resigned on becoming christians, conflict was bound to arise. Both christians and Okonko members attempted to force the government's hand in favour of one party or the other. Rev. Ockiya, the most enterprising native agent of the NDP warned the Chiefs of Oloko Court that christians

> "are prepared to resist if you really mean to carry out threats. In fact they are decided not to be ruled by you so long as you choose to remain heathen Chiefs of the Court under such oppressions as you generally practice under the strength of your judicial warrant".[28]

Finally, the conflict which had been simmering since the missions conjoined the spread of the gospel with the destruction of traditional culture surfaced because the NDP forced the issue. At a Provisional Council meeting in March 1920, they decided to issue a clear directive to all their members "that no church member or adherent can be a member of the Okonko Club".[29] Those who had sat on the fence were forced to get down on either side. The church now became a *Riber Between* which divided communities, as Ngugi's novel puts it. Armed with this directive, priests attempted to enforce a clear distinction of christians from non-christians. Membership in secret societies became a yardstick. Zealous and evangelical youngmen were now given the imprimatur to assault the most prestigious social club in their communities.

The Okonko members reacted swiftly. They realized that the new directives would mean loss of current and prospective memberships and this meant financial ruin to investors. More dire consequences were that the new converts would in misguided zeal reveal the secrets of Okonko and the whole social order which Okonko underpropped would collapse. Some communities alleged that the attacks on Okonko and Akang were already creating moral chaos; that indiscipline had set in, christianity was shattering the bulwarks of the traditional order. It would have been irresponsible of the chiefs to sit and watch their world fall apart. So, the Okonko members refused to permit the converts to disengage from the club. Affirming that Okonko rules applied to christians and non-christians alike, they applied traditional sanctions on christian dissidents: they insisted on proper Okonko burial rites even if the ex-member died a christian, they insisted on second burials, they prevented a dissident from using his palm wine as he liked and from gathering nuts, brushing farms and cutting sticks for building houses. This was a policy of deliberate ostracism.

[28] *Ibid.*, f.26.

[29] *Ibid.*, f.33.

Next, the Okonko moved to cut off the propagators of dissident ideas, namely, school teachers. From Amavo, Akpa and Umuocha (Ngwa), christians appealed to Bishops Howells and Tugwell in 1920 and 1921 to intervene over the removal of teachers by the chiefs. It was alleged that chiefs

> "stated openly in Court that their main reasons for asking them [teachers] to quit is that they [teachers] would not allow the youngmen of their Towns who are christians to play Okonko, perform Second Burial of the dead and other country customs".

Chief Ugoala opposed the sacking of the teachers and was fined £6 while his chair was hurled out of the court house. Other sympathisers were brutally fined £5 each.[30] As a corollary to this tactic, the chiefs started withdrawing children from school by sending them on errands. In some cases, they failed to contribute enough money for the teacher's upkeep. In other cases, they exploited missionary rivalry by supplanting the offending mission with an opponent.

Still fuming against the missions, the chiefs utilized their clout in the Native Courts not just to prosecute offenders against Okonko and Akang but to harass and penalize any christian who appeared in court. Bishop Lasbery informed L. T. Chubb, D.O. Bende, in 1925 that

> "Chief Agunuo openly stated in the court that christians were to be punished whether guilty or not or words to that effect".[31]

He had two converted chiefs, Maduemere and Njoku, to testify to the veracity of the allegation. But Maduemere was a controversial figure. As a former Vice-President of the Native Court, it was alleged that he once sentenced seventeen christians to six months' imprisonment for maligning Okonko. Then, he converted to christianity and became a turn-coat agent of the Bishop. Petitioners from Umuahia, Ubakala, Ibeku and Olokoro informed the Lieutenant-Governor that Maduemere confessed that when the Bishop gave him a red-carpet treatment at Aba, he reciprocated by saying that Okonko was fetish.

F. W. Dodds, the Methodist missionary based at Uzuakoli, accused the Akang Society at Iyi Eyi, Ibeku, of a worse strategy – deliberately trumping up an excuse to molest christians and sack schools. They accused a christian of having slashed an Akang drum. Dodds was

[30] NAE. File 22/1921 ABADIST 1/13/19; OW 54/20 ABADIST 1/12/54. See, my article, "Waves from the Rivers: The Spread of Garrick Briade Movement in Igboland, 1914–34", *Journ. of Niger Delta Studies* (forthcoming) for more examples. At Amavo, Rev. Ockiya feared that the teacher might be poisoned; he withdrew him but the council of the church forced him to send the teacher back to the war front.

[31] NAE. OW 557/20 RIVPROF 8/8/433. Lasbery to Chubbs, 9/11/25, Nwogu to Lt. Governor 11/8/21.

certain that the Akang people forged the incident and proceeded to beat christians. "In a number of towns in Ibeku", he wrote,

> "the Chiefs have informed the people that the Resident had made a law that all teachers were to be ejected from the towns, church property damaged and worship in the christian manner stopped".

It sounds incredible but the rampage ensured on 14 January 1920 and spread to Abo-Ibeku, Ajata Isieke, Umu Elegh-Ibeku, Umu Abo-Ibeku, Umu Eze, Ameki and Amafo Isingwu. Lanterns, books, doors, bells, stools and mats disappeared as teachers took to their heels. Christians fled to Uzuakoli or huddled together in a patron's house too fearful to stir abroad.[32]

At Lodu, Uzuakoli, the Okonko people had a genuine excuse when a zealous teacher in December 1920, asked church school children, male and female, whether anyone would join Okonko. One lifted his hand. The teacher informed him that there was nothing of consequence in Okonko and proceeded to reveal the symbols. The females laughed with gusto. As Okonko was then playing, the teacher ordered the church bell to be rung. The chiefs moved swiftly, summoned him to the village square, later refused to parley wth the white missionary from Uzuakoli and fined seventeen christians three to five pounds each and six months' jail with Hard Labour. Nine in fear paid while the missionary appealed to A. L. Weir, A.D.O., to review the case.[33]

Revealing Okonko secrets was the most provocative action of the missions which occurred in December 1950. A leader of True Faith Tabernacle Gospel (TFTG), Bailey Epelle, claimed that Christ revealed to him that the secrets of Okonko should be exposed. His adherents, ex-members of Okonko, proceeded to fulfill the revelation at Ohokobe Afara. They also burnt Okonko shrines at Ohokobe, Ohobo, Itaja Olokoro, Mgbaja Osa and Ezuama Osa. They removed secret objects to be displayed in the market and obviously women took good looks at the tabooed objects. In spiritual frenzy, the TFTGers promised more exposees. The news spread like bush fire throughout Umuahia, Ngwa to Bende and Arochukwu on the east and Mbawsi on the west. A massive revenge was spontaneously started by the Okonko societies. At Umueze, Umuosu, Umuala and Mbawsi (proper) churches were burnt and looted. In one week, 22nd to 29th December, 1950 the Okonko society destroyed church properties valued at £4,759:15s at Ovodum, Ipupe, Ohokobe Afara, Old Umuahia, Uzuakoli, Umuagu and Umu-nwa-nwa. The Society at Aro affirmed their solidarity. In their rage, there was no distinction between The Faith Tabernacle and the TFTG which seceded when

[32] *Ibid.*, Dodds to D.O. Bende, 1/2/21.

[33] *Ibid.*, 31/1/21; OW 529/1920 ABADiST 1/26/278.

Pastor E. T. Epelle was expelled for wrong doctrine in 1947. Pastor Epelle apparently had swallowed hook, line and sinker his brother's claim to be Jesus' alter ego. It took the D.O.s for Bende, Aba and the ASP, Aba several weeks of negotiations to calm these areas and bound over nearly seventy people.[34]

Finally, the secret societies followed up with massive petitioning between 1920–1921 when the Lt. General visited. They even used women in the agitation believing that "white man pay more respect to women than to men".[35]

In the face of the opposition of the secret societies to missionary presence and ideology, the churches adopted the pose of a persecuted cell-group which must nonetheless stand fast. It was hardly a pose of passive resistance; rather, the church now turned to the government demanding protection for themselves and destruction of their enemies. Compromise was ruled out. Archdeacon Crowther and Bishop A. W. Howells told Okonko Chiefs of Umuahia on February 27th, 1922 that compromise was "positively an impossibility".[36]

It was then that the complexity in their relationship became stark. Wherever there was violence, the law enforcement agency moved in. The government made it clear that lawlessness will not be tolerated. But instead of using heavy force, they used the police, parleyed with chiefs and communities, patiently explained and sternly warned them against social disorder.

Beyond this, the government produced a different analysis of the situation. J. Watt, Resident, Owerri, observed that Okonko was an ancient, secret club, the bulwark of political and social order and the organizer of government labour at the grass-root.[37] Therefore, it has as much legality, right and freedom as any other religion. He blamed the conflict of the 1920's on the divisive and provocative March edict of the NDP. He argued that church agents most unwisely gave excessive prominence to this announcement in the outlying district, and that the withdrawal by those who knew the secrets bred the fear and possibility of exposure. The Lieutenant Governor added that such exposure of Okonko signs "should be dealt with as an offence likely to case a breach of the peace."[38] He sympathized with chiefs who felt that the church was using the red herring of membership

[34] NAE. OW 8358 UMPROF 5/1/138.

[35] NAE. OW 557/20 RIVPROF 8/8/433.

[36] NAE. OW 557/20 RIVPROF 8/8/433. Howells to Resident, Owerri, 27/2/22.

[37] NAE. OW 54/20 ABADIST 1/12/54. Resident Owerri to D.O., ABa.

[38] NAE. OW 557/20 RIVPROF 8/8/433 f. 42.

in Okonko Club to exclude them from church. The government was least concerned with the allegation that Okonko had fetish rituals. Rather, the government argued that the zeal of young boys and incautious agents, fear of financial loss by chiefs, the lack of government schools sans religious indoctrination and the syncretism among converts exercabated the conflict. Chubb infomed Basden in 1932 that it was precisely the converts' dalliance with both secret societies and the church which made it difficult to confirm allegations of harassment.[39]

The Government officials, therefore, informed the missions that the Native Courts were within their competence in trying cases involving Okonko laws under sect 11(2) of Chapt. 5 and that chiefs could remove teachers. When Okonko played, no other dance group should compete because it is the native law and "in no country would two bands be allowed to compete against each other". This ruling killed off "asiko" which the church was introducing as a substitute for Okonko dance.[40]

The Lt. Governor enjoined both sides to show tolerance: Okonko should not force people to join or retain membership, the missions should curb their agents, eschew exposing Okonko secrets and co-operate with D.O.s and Residents. In some cases, the D.O. reduced the fines imposed by the Ntive Courts. The only exception was at Ututu in 1949. The Ekpe Society had provocatively danced into the churchyard during a funeral ceremony. When one of the church elders (Presbyterian Church) went into the Ekpe cloth-house to warn them off the church grounds, they had him prosecuted for transgression. The A.D.O. inexplicably sustained the fine of £5 against the church officials. After petitions and tedious court appearances, the Resident, Calabar, set aside the Native Court decision and fined the Ekpe Society instead with costs.[41]

When the missionaries failed to root out secret societies with the clout of their allies, the colonial government, they swallowed the bitter pill and bent down to achieve their end through education.

39 *Ibid.*, Chubb to Basden, Mbawsi, 14/6/32.

40 *Ibid.*, Resident, Owerri 8/12/1925; D.O. Bende, 28/11/25.

41 NAE. AD 495/B/49 ARODIST 1/1/7.

Acknowledgments

Kiwanuka, M. Semakula. "Colonial Policies and Administrations in Africa: The Myths of the Contrasts." *African Historical Studies* 3 (1970): 295–315. Reprinted with the permission of the African Studies Center. Courtesy of Yale University Sterling Memorial Library.

Graham, James D. "Indirect Rule: The Establishment of "Chiefs" and "Tribes" in Cameron's Tanganyika." *Tanzania Notes and Records* 77 (1976): 1–9. Reprinted with the permission of the Tanzania Society. Courtesy of Yale University Sterling Memorial Library.

Samuel-Mbaekwe, Iheanyi J. "Colonialism and Social Structure." *Transafrican Journal of History* 15 (1986): 81–95. Courtesy of Yale University Sterling Memorial Library.

Esedebe, P. Olisanwuche. "The Growth of the Pan-African Movement, 1893–1927." *Tarikh* 6 (1980): 18–34. Courtesy of Yale University Sterling Memorial Library.

Newman, Richard. "Archbishop Daniel William Alexander and the African Orthodox Church." *International Journal of African Historical Studies* 16 (1983): 615–30. Reprinted with the permission of the African Studies Center. Courtesy of Gregory Maddox.

Rich, Paul. "Race, Science, and the Legitimization of White Supremacy in South Africa, 1902–1940." *International Journal of African Historical Studies* 23 (1990): 665–86. Reprinted with the permission of the African Studies Center. Courtesy of Gregory Maddox.

Cooper, Frederick. "Peasants, Capitalists and Historians: A Review Article." *Journal of Southern African Studies* 7 (1981): 284–314. Reprinted with the permission of Oxford University Press. Courtesy of Gregory Maddox.

Bundy, Colin. "The Emergence and Decline of a South African Peasantry." *African Affairs* 71 (1972): 369–88. Reprinted with the permission of African Affairs, The Royal African Society. Courtesy of Yale University Sterling Memorial Library.

Comaroff, John L. and Jean Comaroff. "The Madman and the Migrant: Work and Labor in the Historical Consciousness of a South African People." *American Ethnologist* 14 (1987): 191–209. Reprinted with the permission of the American Anthropological Association. Courtesy of Yale University Sterling Memorial Library.

Maddox, Gregory H. "*Mtunya*: Famine in Central Tanzania, 1917–20." *Journal of African History* 31 (1990): 181–97. Reprinted with the permission of Cambridge University Press. Courtesy of Gregory Maddox.

Van Zwanenberg, Paul. "Kenya's Primitive Colonial Capitalism: The Economic Weakness of Kenya's Settlers Up to 1940." *Canadian Journal of African Studies* 9 (1975): 277–92. Reprinted with the permission of the Center for Urban and Community Studies. Courtesy of Gregory Maddox.

Anderson, David. "Depression, Dust Bowl, Demography, and Drought: The Colonial State and Soil Conservation in East Africa During the 1930s." *African Affairs* 83 (1984): 321–43. Reprinted with the permission of African Affairs, The Royal African Society. Courtesy of Yale University Sterling Memorial Library.

Dobkin, Marlene. "Colonialism and the Legal Status of Women in Francophonic Africa." *Cahiers D'Etudes Africaines* 8 (1968): 390–405. Reprinted with the permission of Editions de l'Ecole des Hautes Etudes et Sciences Sociales. Courtesy of Yale University Sterling Memorial Library.

Isaacman, Allen, Michael Stephen, Yussuf Adam, Maria João Homen, Eugenio Macamo, Augustinho Pililão. " 'Cotton Is the Mother of Poverty': Peasant Resistance to Forced Cotton Production in Mozambique, 1938–1961." *International Journal of African Historical Studies* 13 (1980): 581–615. Reprinted with the permission of the African Studies Center. Courtesy of Yale University Sterling Memorial Library.

Vincent, Joan. "Colonial Chiefs and the Making of Class: A Case Study from Teso, Eastern Uganda." *Africa* 47 (1977): 140–59. Reprinted with the permission of the International African Institute. Courtesy of Yale University Sterling Memorial Library.

Birmingham, David. "Colonialism in Angola: Kinyama's Experience." *Tarikh* 6 (1980): 65–75. Courtesy of Yale University Sterling Memorial Library.

Lonsdale, J.M. "Some Origins of Nationalism in East Africa." *Journal of African History* 9 (1968): 119–46. Reprinted with the permission of Cambridge University Press. Courtesy of Yale University Sterling Memorial Library.

Henderson, Ian. "The Origins of Nationalism in East and Central Africa: The Zambian Case." *Journal of African History* 11 (1970): 591–603. Reprinted with the permission of Cambridge University Press. Courtesy of Yale University Sterling Memorial Library.

Mugyenyi, Meddi. "The Sources of Collective Rebellion: Nationalism in Buganda and Kikuyuland." *Transafrican Journal of History* 8 (1979): 94–104. Courtesy of Yale University Sterling Memorial Library.

Kalu, Ogbu U. "Missionaries, Colonial Government and Secret Societies in South-Eastern Igboland, 1920–1950." *Journal of the Historical Society of Nigeria* 9 (1977): 75–90. Courtesy of Yale University Sterling Memorial Library.